T0139257

BEST PRACTICES SERIES

Internet Management

THE AUERBACH
BEST PRACTICES SERIES

Broadband Networking, James Trulove, Editor,
ISBN: 0-8493-9821-5

Electronic Messaging, Nancy Cox, Editor,
ISBN: 0-8493-9825-8

Financial Services Information Systems, Jessica Keyes, Editor,
ISBN: 0-8493-9834-7

Healthcare Information Systems, Phillip L. Davidson, Editor,
ISBN: 0-8493-9963-7

Internet Management, Jessica Keyes, Editor,
ISBN: 0-8493-9987-4

Multi-Operating System Networking: Living with UNIX, NetWare, and NT, Raj Rajagopal, Editor,
ISBN: 0-8493-9831-2

Network Manager's Handbook, John Lusa, Editor,
ISBN: 0-8493-9841-X

Project Management, Paul C. Tinnirello, Editor,
ISBN: 0-8493-9998-X

Server Management, Gilbert Held, Editor,
ISBN: 0-8493-9823-1

Enterprise Systems Integration, John Wyzalek, Editor,
ISBN: 0-8493-9837-1

Technology Management, Christian Kirkpatrick, Editor,
ISBN: 0-8493-9827-4

AUERBACH PUBLICATIONS

www.auerbach-publications.com
TO Order: Call: 1-800-272-7737 • Fax: 1-800-374-3401
E-mail: orders@crcpress.com

BEST PRACTICES SERIES

Internet Management

Editor

JESSICA KEYES

AUERBACH

Boca Raton   London   New York   Washington, D.C.

Library of Congress Cataloging-in-Publication Data

Internet management / Jessica Keyes, editor. - 2000 ed.
     p. cm.
     Includes bibliographical references and index.
     ISBN 0-8493-9987-4 (alk. paper)
     1. Business enterprises - Computer networks - Management.
     2. Internet (Computer network)   I. Keyes, Jessica, 1950-.
HD30.37.I56   1999
658'.054678—dc21   99-20395
                                                                      CIP

This book contains information obtained from authentic and highly regarded sources. Reprinted material is quoted with permission, and sources are indicated. A wide variety of references are listed. Reasonable efforts have been made to publish reliable data and information, but the author and the publisher cannot assume responsibility for the validity of all materials or for the consequences of their use.

Neither this book nor any part may be reproduced or transmitted in any form or by any means, electronic or mechanical, including photocopying, microfilming, and recording, or by any information storage or retrieval system, without prior permission in writing from the publisher.

All rights reserved. Authorization to photocopy items for internal or personal use, or the personal or internal use of specific clients, may be granted by CRC Press LLC, provided that $.50 per page photocopied is paid directly to Copyright Clearance Center, 222 Rosewood Drive, Danvers, MA 01923 USA. The fee code for users of the Transactional Reporting Service is ISBN 0-8493-9987-4/00/$0.00+$.50. The fee is subject to change without notice. For organizations that have been granted a photocopy license by the CCC, a separate system of payment has been arranged.

The consent of CRC Press LLC does not extend to copying for general distribution, for promotion, for creating new works, or for resale. Specific permission must be obtained in writing from CRC Press LLC for such copying.

Direct all inquiries to CRC Press LLC, 2000 N.W. Corporate Blvd., Boca Raton, Florida 33431, or visit our Web site at www.crcpress.com

Trademark Notice: Product or corporate names may be trademarks or registered trademarks, and are used only for identification and explanation, without intent to infringe.

© 2000 by CRC Press LLC
Auerbach is an imprint of CRC Press LLC

No claim to original U.S. Government works
International Standard Book Number 0-8493-9987-4
Library of Congress Card Number 99-20395
Printed in the United States of America   4 5 6 7 8 9 0
Printed on acid-free paper

Contributors

CHRIS AMMEN, *Vice President of Advanced Technologies, Television Associates, Mountain View, CA*

ANNE ANDERSON-LEMIEUX, *Electronic Publications Specialist, Speedware Corporation, Montreal, Quebec, Canada*

MARC BEAULIEU, *Cofounder and Managing Principal, Ariel Technologies, Inc., Boston, MA*

NORMAN BEAULIEU, *Cofounder and Managing Principal, Ariel Technologies, Inc., Boston, MA*

MICHAEL BLANK, *Senior Engineer, WebMethods, Inc., Fairfax, VA*

JULIANNE CHATELAIN, *Head of Usability Program, Trellix, Waltham, MA*

DAVE CHISTE, *Senior Systems Analyst, Cadeon Strategic Technologies Inc., Alberta, Canada*

MADISON CLOUTIER, *Vice President, Marketing, Tower Technology Corporation, Austin, TX*

RICHARD K. CRONE, *Vice President and General Manager, CyberCash, Inc., Reston, VA*

ANDREW CSINGER, *Founder, Xcert Software Inc., Vancouver, British Columbia, Canada*

STEVE DOLHA, *President, Cadeon Strategic Technologies Inc., Alberta, Canada*

DEBORAH GALEA, *Marketing Manager, GFI FAX & VOICE, Webster, NY*

MICHAEL D. GANTT, *Senior Vice President and Chief Technology Officer, Policy Management Systems Corporation, Blythewood, SC*

IAN GOLDSMITH, *Manager, Directory Technology and Products, ISOCOR, Santa Monica, CA*

SHIMON GRUPER, *Founder, eSafe Technologies Inc., Seattle, WA*

WILLIAM R. HACKLER, *Director of Development, Hamilton Technologies, Inc., Cambridge, MA*

MARGARET HAMILTON, *Founder and Chief Executive Officer, Hamilton Technologies, Inc., Cambridge, MA*

JIM HEWITT, *Principal Consultant, Brainstorm Technology, Cambridge, MA*

JEFF HILL, *Director of Marketing, Voxware, Princeton, NJ*

MICHAEL HUANG, *Chief Technical Officer, Ariel Technologies, Inc., Boston, MA*

KIM HUMPHREYS, *Vice President, nFront, Inc., Bogart, GA*

Contributors

MICHAEL KENNEDY, *Enterprise Vendor and Service Provider, Strategic Networks, Sunnyvale, CA*

JESSICA KEYES, *President, New Art Technologies, Inc., New York, NY*

RICHARD LAMB, *Cofounder and Chief Executive Officer, Nevod Incorporated, Weston, MA*

PAUL LAMBERT, *Product Strategy Development and Implementation, Certicom, San Mateo, CA*

DENNIS LAUGHREN, *Webmaster, Quarterdeck Corporation, Marina del Rey, CA*

CHARLES MAPPIN, *Technical Writer and Associate Webmaster, Speedware Corporation, Montreal, Quebec, Canada*

MICHAEL MCCLURE, *Vice President, Marketing, Marketwave Corporation, Seattle, WA*

RON MORITZ, *Director, Technology Office, Finjan Software, San Jose, CA*

TONY MULQUEEN, *Technical Writer, ISOCOR, Santa Monica, CA*

BOB PACKER, *Independent Consultant, Cupertino, CA*

STEWART PADVEEN, *Founder, Chairman, and Chief Executive Officer, HotOffice Technologies, Inc., Boca Raton, FL*

KAY PALKHIVALA, *Director of Technical Documentation and Education, Speedware Corporation, Montreal, Quebec, Canada*

RICHARD PETERSEN, *Manager, Customer Marketing Group, Interwoven, Inc., Sunnyvale, CA*

JOY PINSKY, *Vice President of Marketing, FreeGate Corporation, Sunnyvale, CA*

STEPHEN PURDHAM, *President, surfCONTROL Division, JSB, Scotts Valley, CA*

STUART ROSOVE, *Founder and Vice Chairman, Sequel Technology Corporation, Bellevue, WA*

LIZ SARA, *Cofounder and Marketing Manager, SpaceWorks, Rockville, MD*

DAVE SCHNEIDER, *Chief Technology Officer, Internet Dynamics, Inc., Westlake Village, CA*

JOHN SEASHOLTZ, *Director of Business Consulting, Free Range Media, Seattle, WA*

STEVEN SEMELSBERGER, *Strategic Alliances and Market Development Manager, Acuity Corporation, Austin, TX*

JEET SINGH, *Cofounder, Art Technology Group, Boston, MA*

VALERIE TAYLOR, *Research and Development, Web-Based Learning Technologies, Palo Alto, CA*

WILLIE TEJADA, *Vice President of Marketing, Aeneid Corporation, San Francisco, CA*

PAT THOMAS, *Technical Communication Manager, Packeteer, Inc., Cupertino, CA*

HOLLIS TIBBETTS, *Director of Marketing, OnDisplay, Inc., San Ramon, CA*

DEBORAH TYROLER, *Director, Webstream & Interactive Services, International Communications, Inc., Framingham, MA*

PETE WELTER, *Senior Software Engineer, Freshwater Software, Inc., Boulder, CO*

FREDERIC M. WILF, *Special Counsel and Chair, Technology Group, Saul, Ewing, Remick, & Saul LLP, Berwyn, PA*
ELANA YELLIN, *Website Producer, International Communications, Inc., Framingham, MA*
MOLLY OLDFIELD YEN, *Online User Assistance, Trellix, Waltham, MA*

Contents

Contents

Preface

IT MANAGEMENT HAS CHANGED FOREVER. The culprit? The Internet. Where we were once secure in the fact that in spite of increasing technological complexity we could keep pace with the latest advances and even incorporate some of them into our systems, today's Internet is a bird of a different color.

The keyword here is convergence. The Internet is a single-delivery vehicle which uses a multitude of seemingly incompatible technologies: databases, text, graphics, animation, audio, video, chat, telephony, and real-time transaction processing. The Internet, as if by magic, makes all these disparate technologies converge, to present to the end user a single interface to noncentrally located information.

When the Internet was still in diapers (some three or four short years ago), the heady issues and problems of gluing all of this together were in the domain of those slick companies which cropped up both in the Silicon Valley as well as in the newly (and unfortunately) named Silicon Alley in New York.

Since the early commercial adopters of Internet technologies were corporate marketing departments, IT departments were rarely involved. That's where the Alley and the Valley came in. It was not uncommon, in those heady days, for sites to have a price tag in the millions.

Then a funny thing happened. Some will call it a fallout to the proliferation of Web design shops out there. Others will call it a natural reaction to the high prices that the Alley–Valley guys were charging. I like to attribute it to my nephew, Andrew. You see, developing a standard Web page was not as difficult as those Alley–Valley guys said it was. My nephew, Andrew, and many other nephews around the country proved this by building Web sites for the price of a beer and a pizza.

Companies across America, and the world, began to realize that Web development was something that really could be handled in-house. Not that the Alley–Valley guys were put out of business (actually, there's much consolidation going on today among these Web development companies because most companies have already built their Websites and there's much less opportunity for new business), but the vast majority of CEOs yielded to bottom-line pressures and the pure sensibility of bringing the task back home.

It should come as no surprise that the newly designated "keeper of the corporate Net" would be the IT department. It just made a lot of sense. As Net technology matured, with the introduction of intranet/extranet, broadcasting, and E-commerce capabilities, the technology surrounding the Net became much more complex, too. Gone were the days of simple HTML and GIF or JPEG graphics. In were the days of three-tier architectures and E-commerce solutions. The Web was here to stay.

If you're reading this book you are probably an IT manager who has had the responsibility of Web development placed squarely on your shoulders. Maybe you have other responsibilities or maybe your company has just designated you Webmaster and your purview is solely the Web. Whatever the case you are now responsible for your company's image on the Web.

This means it is also your responsibility to keep up with the latest and greatest of technologies, understanding not only the technological ramifications of these new technologies but the management ramifications as well.

That's what this book is all about.

It's one-stop shopping for the IT manager in all things Internet — 45 chapters and over 130 exhibits. And a multitude of experts giving you the advice you need to run a smooth operation.

Many industry experts contributed to this book. Reading their bios will give you some insight into the depth of expertise that has been provided for you all in one place (i.e., an encyclopedia of Internet knowledge). The book was not meant to be read from cover to cover. Instead, skip around and read those chapters germane to the project you are undertaking now.

To make this easier for you, I've divided the book into six sections. In Section I we discuss trends in the new media. Here we cover such topics as building Internet and facilitating competitive intelligence in the twenty-first century.

In Section II we discuss strategic issues in Internet Management, covering such topics as measuring return on investment (ROI) in Internet development, using the Internet to improve competitive position and reduce costs, and how to strategically manage Internet resources. This is also the section to find out about the legal ramifications of Internet site development.

In Section III we provide a manager's perspective on Internet security and networking management and in Section IV we delve into E-commerce management, touching base on such issues as relationship commerce, the E-commerce market impact, and XML-based E-commerce.

In Sections V and VI we cover the nitty-gritty issues surrounding Web development and advanced Web development. Here you'll find out how to connect your LAN to the Internet, the value of Web traffic analysis, things you should know before you start developing multilingual Websites, managing e-mail, and lots more.

Interestingly, the more complex the Web becomes the more it becomes necessary to use traditional client/server- and object-oriented development methodologies. In other words, the techniques you've been using to develop standard applications are usable in the development of Internet applications. But more so. A set of four chapters (Chapters 30 to 33) has been included in this book that will open your eyes to a whole new way of development. Equally applicable to traditional development, but especially applicable to complex Internet development, the "Development Before the Fact" methodology is a radical shift in perspective that I don't ever get tired of proselytizing.

Last but not least, I've provided, a product guide in the Appendix which will help you get started in choosing the right tools for your job.

All of these chapters have been written from the technical manager's perspective so they're all equally balanced between enabling you to understand the technology as well as the issues surrounding the technology.

I'd like to take the opportunity to thank all of those who contributed their time and expertise to this book. I'd also like to thank you, the reader, for reading this book.

You're in for a wild ride.

Jessica Keyes

Section I
Trends in the New Media

TODAY WE STAND ON THE THRESHOLD OF A MAJOR REVOLUTION in the way we think and feel about computers and the information they process. Where information processing was once a closed-end process evidenced by internal networks and proprietary systems, today's IT manager must embrace the global technologies of the Internet.

Recently, Cisco has been advertising heavily on television. In case you don't know who Cisco is, they're the people that make the routers that make the Internet possible. Their commercials essentially forecast not just the death of paper (of course we've heard this before) but the death of the telephone as well. While I don't expect this to happen in my lifetime, Cisco's marketers notwithstanding, there are some technology trends worth discussing.

In this section we will discuss the ramifications of traveling on the information superhighway and learn how this "new media" affects you as an IT manager. Perhaps more importantly, we'll discuss how the use of the Internet empowers business and facilitates competitive intelligence.

Chapter 1

Building the Twenty-First Century Internet

Joy Pinsky

THE INTERNET COULD CHANGE THE WAY WE BUY AND SELL, the way we learn and teach, the way we communicate with friends or entertain our children. It could — but will it?

To most, the Internet is a vast global network, and that's a part of the truth. In fact, the Internet is a vast global information resource wrapped in a network that connects information seekers to information providers, and also connects both types of users to each other. Information is the key to the Internet, and information providers on the Internet are the key to its information.

Today, less than one Internet user in a thousand is a true contributor of information. The great majority of users of the Internet, even business users, have two crippling shortcomings in their relationship with this new information community:

- *Transient connection.* To be an information provider on the Internet, you must first be "on the Internet" in a permanent sense. The World Wide Web is the commercial heart of the Internet, yet most businesses in the world today have no Web presence.
- *A technically complex set of Internet publishing alternatives.* Just getting connected to the Internet isn't enough. A company has to have its information properly presented and maintained, and its activity monitored for market research.

There are many options for creating an Internet presence, and most users find them all bewilderingly complex, and frighteningly costly. If the Internet is to be all that it can be, we must all be able to participate in it fully, both as consumers of information and providers of information. We have to populate the Internet.

0-8493-9987-4/00/$0.00+$.50
© 2000 by CRC Press LLC

SMALLER ORGANIZATIONS NEED TO CREATE A PERMANENT INTERNET PRESENCE

The Internet is a community, but to date it is a very select one. While there are more than 25 million households on the Internet, and more than 7 million business purchasers browse its product and service information each week, only about a million businesses are actually publishing product and service information on the Internet, and the number actually supporting electronic commerce on the Net is so small as to be insignificant.

The group most likely to be absent from the Internet is the very group most likely to benefit from its scope — the more than 11 million small and midsize businesses worldwide. These 5 to 200-employee companies could expand their markets and profits by becoming accessible to the collection of buyers (growing daily) who browse the Internet for information. Today, fewer than 1 in 20 has an Internet presence.

The lack of participation of these businesses as information providers on the Internet impacts more than their bottom lines, however. The Internet is a rich source of information today, but imagine how much richer it would be if the number of publishers of information increased by 1000 percent.

It doesn't stop there. Commerce on the Internet today must proceed with fewer than one seller in ten and one buyer in a thousand being permanently connected. With such a small participating community, it's no wonder that many companies question the value of electronic commerce.

With sellers on the Internet, two things happen. First, buyers are attracted there, which increases the total Internet population and makes it even more attractive to have a presence there. Second, revenues from electronic commerce begin to flow, swelling the budgets of Internet Service Providers (ISPs) and allowing them to expand their infrastructure, supporting new services such as multimedia.

Internet presence in a permanent sense is more important than access speed per se. While a business would surely want its access connection to the Internet to be fast enough to serve its prospects, customers, suppliers, or other partners, the first goal must be to be accessible to these partners full time.

OPTIONS FOR INTERNET PUBLISHING

How do you get on the Internet in a publishing sense? In the broadest sense, businesses have two choices: self-hosting and ISP hosting.

Self-hosting means acquiring your own Internet access connection from an ISP, and then building an Internet node that provides the full range of services you'd like to project to partners. That would include a Web server to support browser access, an e-mail server, a file transfer protocol (ftp) server if partners are to pick up and drop off files at your site, and possibly a news server to support your own newsgroups. In addition to this, you'd need Internet technical components like a Domain Name Server (DNS).

The costs of the components required to self-host typically add up to more than $15,000. In addition to the one-time cost, expect to pay a recurring hardware and software maintenance charge (15 to 18 percent of the purchase price), charges to house the facility and staff it, and the other costs usually associated with running a small computer center.

The administrative tasks associated with self-hosting are both expensive and complex. Many Internet servers are based on the UNIX operating system. While popular with university and technical organizations, UNIX has a reputation among business users of being complex in both its command structures and documentation. Complexity in administering the platform itself only increases the difficulties in controlling the functionality of the Internet node. Many Internet servers accept only terse, terminal-oriented command access to set up mailboxes, passwords, directories, etc. Many provide no user-friendly authoring software to build Web pages.

Not surprisingly, most smaller organizations have found all of this too difficult and costly. In fact, nine out of ten cannot even identify the components needed to build a self-hosted Internet node, much less describe how to set up and control one. Some ISPs are offering a variation on self-hosting that lets you install hardware at the ISP location. This can reduce communications connection charges and facility costs, but the cost of the basic equipment and software must still be paid, and administrative tasks may still be the user's responsibility. This option is only somewhat interesting to most small and midsize businesses.

Full ISP hosting is the option most commonly used by smaller businesses that have a direct Internet presence. With full ISP hosting, sometimes called "shared-host" access, your business is given part of a shared set of Internet servers. Your cost is lower because other companies are sharing the total cost of the configuration, but you must also share the resources of the Internet server with those other companies. This poses three problems: performance, flexibility, and ease of use.

The performance issue is a thorny one. ISPs who offer shared-host services cannot really make performance commitments to their users because the servers are shared among a number of companies, each of which may have its own patterns of activity. If you happen to be sharing a host service with a company that receives thousands of hits a day on its Website, it's clear that the resources available to your "virtual site" will be curtailed.

A more serious problem is that of flexibility. The price of sharing a computer resource (which is what an Internet site really is) among multiple companies without adverse interaction is the restrictions it imposes. Some

Internet features (like anonymous ftp, the ability to support partner pick-up and drop-off of files without password control) are often not available in ISP shared-host systems. If your business needs one of these facilities, you'd have to either seek another ISP or self-host. You may not have access to all the statistical information you'd like about people who access your site, or the number of e-mail mailboxes you need, or support for Java applications.

In addition, ISP-hosted Websites often tend to be static — Web pages are not updated regularly because changes can't easily be made. Dynamic publishing, in which you can change Web pages on the fly, requires computations that ISP-hosted sites cannot do easily, and requires a tight integration between your Web server and a back-end database. For electronic commerce, this close interaction between your Web server and inventory database is critical.

Ease of use may be the most difficult issue with ISP hosting. While it is true that the ISP absorbs the routine systems administration tasks, users must still control their mailboxes, author their Web pages, upload changes to files, monitor usage, and more. Many users report significant problems with administering their ISP-hosted sites, and some studies show that more than three quarters of such users must pay to have some or all of these tasks performed by outside specialists. Considering the fact that ease of use was one driver for moving to ISP hosting, the difficulty users have with the concept is troubling.

Ease of use issues may be particularly significant if it becomes necessary to change ISPs. Companies who use the Internet report an average of three ISP relationships over the course of their Internet commitment. If each ISP-hosted service has its own rules and restrictions, how easy will it be to move your Internet presence from one to another? A business-owned Internet node is portable from one ISP to another in a very literal sense — unplug one ISP connection and plug in the second, if the business owns its own IP addresses. It's not that easy if the ISP provides the facilities, and the new ISP may not offer all of the services of the previous one, or offer them in exactly the same way.

So far, our attention has been focused on the issues of becoming an information provider, but information providers also use the Internet for their own research. Most businesses who adopt ISP hosting do so to avoid the cost of a permanent access connection to the Internet. These organizations must dial in to the ISP modem pool, often sharing the pool with recreational, nonbusiness users of the Internet. The lower analog modem speeds and frequently reported difficulties in connecting may interfere with attempts to use the Internet for research, or even to access your ISP-hosted site for administration.

For users unhappy with this set of choices, there is hope. The cost of dedicated access to the Internet is declining. Most ISPs offer the option of a dedicated modem connection at a very affordable price. Most also offer ISDN access in dedicated mode, and this affordable attachment strategy provides a company with more than 100 kbps of access bandwidth. Other options, including frame relay, are often available at surprisingly affordable prices, and new local access technology based on Digital Subscriber Loop (DSL) service is available in some areas already, and is expected to be available nationally by 1999.

With access prices falling, it's time to address the other cost problem associated with self-hosting — the cost of the Internet node and its administration. With the use of e-mail for electronic commerce on the rise, and with companies becoming ever more dependent on the Internet to reach their customers and suppliers, it's clear that another option for Internet attachment is needed. This option should provide users the benefits of self-hosting — flexibility of features, dedicated resources for predictable performance, and a faster access connection to support the company's own browsing of the Internet. It should also provide the benefits of ISP hosting — lower cost and simpler administration.

ALL-IN-ONE INTERNET ACCESS

Present and future business applications for the Internet require that four basic services be provided: Web publishing, electronic mail, Internet access, and support for collaborative applications like NetMeeting. This range of services will accommodate today's business uses of the Internet — promotion of the goods or services a business sells, and support of e-mail inquiries for prospect- and customer-building. They will also support the extension of these early applications into the realm of electronic commerce.

New all-in-one Internet devices called Internet edge servers (or sometimes, thin servers) provide all these services and the communications and directory services needed to attach them to the Internet, in a single easy-to-use solution. These systems provide routing, firewall security, Internet access, and domain name services, but are more than a router. They provide e-mail, Web publishing, and file transfer, but are more than an applications server. And they provide simple tools to facilitate Web page development, but are not just an authoring system. They can even simplify Internet administration, whether you're a user, a VAR, or a service provider, but they are not just another Internet or network management system. They are truly a new class of product — one of the most complete answers to businesses looking to create a strong Internet presence.

There are two aspects to the use of any product or product set designed to create an Internet presence: the setup and administration, and the daily use. Because businesses don't buy products to administer them, but to use them to improve profitability, we'll start with that aspect.

An Internet edge server will typically look to internal and external users like a full-service Internet node. The system can provide connection to the Internet using a variety of leased-line technologies, including xDSL technologies, and speeds from analog modem levels to full T1 are often available to match the range of access technologies. Some systems can even be stacked to provide additional computing and disk storage resources.

In connecting to the Internet, the Internet edge server will appear as a router/firewall. As a router, it needs to support the popular router topology protocols used with TCP/IP, both outward into the ISP network and inward toward the desktop. This will allow standard desktop clients to access the system from inside the company, and partner companies or individuals can access your site from the Internet. To protect internal information assets from security breach, it should provide a full security firewall to protect sensitive internal data, even when stored on the system.

Storage of internal data on the system can allow you to link your Internet applications with those of an internal intranet. Attaching the system to a LAN can create a complete internal TCP/IP network, with domain name services, DHCP address assignment, and disk storage for Web pages or storage of files. Just adding the system makes any small business TCP/IP LAN more flexible, and integrates Internet access for internal users as well.

As interesting as the internal use of these systems may be, it is their value as an Internet business resource that makes them truly unique. As we noted earlier, most small and midsize businesses don't publish on the Internet today, and those who do have a very static and simple Web presence. They're not equipped for the evolving electronic marketplace the Internet is already becoming.

The first step an Internet edge server can take when building an Internet presence is structuring the task of building a set of Web pages. Any HTML, Java, or ActiveX authoring system should be used with the system, so you can build page content on any platform you find convenient. Popular software from Corel, IBM, and Microsoft can let you use standard presentation or word processing tools to create pages. Tools provided with the system can help you to organize your pages and test them internally prior to being made visible on the Internet.

When you've created pages that meet your needs, the system's tools should be able to publish them on the Internet, making them part of the public portion of the system's disk. This allows the system to be used in conjunction with ISP multiclient hosting services, where it takes the guesswork out of building your own Website on the ISP's server. You can try your pages out on your own system, and that means you eliminate the risk that the page will contain embarrassing errors your prospects (or competitors) will detect.

E-mail is an important feature for companies doing business on the Internet. Over 99 percent of business Websites solicit inquiries or even orders via e-mail, and many companies don't manage these important leads properly. With the system's built-in mail server, a permanently attached Internet user has as many mailboxes as is needed. You can also route a copy of the inquiry to a sales followup file to close the loop.

The combination of the permanent Internet connection provided by the system, the built-in "mail-to" facilities of Web pages, and the powerful capability offered in the system's mail server combine to create a very responsive e-mail lead management system. Prospects who browse a Web page can invoke a mail-in inquiry via their browser. The e-mail that is generated can be received by the system as soon as the mail transfer is completed, because the connection to the Internet is permanent. Incoming mail can be directed to the right mailbox and routed to a desktop for response within seconds of reception. This fast response to e-mail inquiries is critical to the success of Web-based commerce.

An easy-to-use browser-based setup and parameterization can actually make the system easier to set up than most PC clients. For end users installing their own system, this simple setup can provide all the administrative support needed. But many businesses will build their Internet presence with the help of an ISP or VAR specializing in the Internet. These organizations will often provide the system, and for these providers remote management and support features will be a key to a successful and profitable relationship with their clients.

When an Internet edge server is sold, the reseller should have the option to initialize the system locally using the user interface, or remotely by entering the initial configuration in a secure server. In this case, the reseller can then provide the customer a setup key that permits the customer to call an 800 number through an integral modem, access the configuration information on a server, and download the correct software and tables. This process can save significant time and prevent many mistakes for the reseller.

Once the initial configuration is loaded, the system should be able to be accessed via the Internet using a secure browser interface. Through this interface, the reselling organization can run diagnostics, upgrade software, etc. This remote management system provides users many of the benefits of on-site specialists, but without the cost, and reduces the startup and sustaining support efforts of resellers.

BUILDING YOUR INTERNET PRESENCE

There are three basic areas of Internet interaction you'll want to review to optimize the business benefits of the Internet: Internet, e-mail setup, and Web publishing.

You may want to use the Internet edge server to limit access to the Internet based on a number of screening criteria. A simple setup screen should let you define how clients who are permitted to access the Internet can be identified.

If the system is the only router on the site, which will usually be the case, client systems would be set up to use it as the default system. Instructions on parameterizing the client systems will often be provided in the system's help system, and all of the address values should be available from easy-to-access screens. If other routers are present for internal routing, the system will often advertise its Internet access routes to them, and thus make itself available as an Internet edge server through current routers to the desktop clients. Note that if the system is not directly connected to the Internet, but rather connected through another router which could send data to other areas, the system's firewall may not "see" all traffic, and thus will protect only the network area it controls.

E-mail setup will require client systems setup as well. The system's help file and information screens should provide the parameter values to be used to set up mail connections. It should also allow users to filter incoming and outgoing mail to provide features like automatic reply, automatic multiple routing, and enforcement of a maximum size. The setup for these functions is based on user-friendly browser screens, with extensive help file support.

For businesses creating an e-mail-based electronic commerce prospecting and lead-building system, the system's mailbox system can allow incoming information requests to be forwarded to a number of clients for response. If the mail clients of the associated workers are configured to alert the user to incoming mail, these inquiries can receive almost real-time responses.

Web publishing is another key area for these systems. The task of a Web site setup should be clearly explained in help files, using step-by-step procedures:

- Build a site map. This means organizing a simple picture of how the Web pages will link among themselves. Each page may be given a name and temporary description to "hold its place" until the real content is developed.
- Define directories and pages that require security authentication, and select the secure protocol or protocols to be used.

- Fill in content. Using HTML authoring tools, Java, or ActiveX development facilities, or scripting languages, fill in the content of each page with text, pictures, etc.
- Add "mail-to" links in the HTML to permit prospects to request additional information or request a sales contact. The subject line of the e-mail message may be prefilled with a code phrase to permit script-based routing.

All of the initial pages may be built in the internal portion of the system's database. These pages can be changed, tested, and even used internally until the content and flow is optimized. When the task is complete, the system may provide a simple "publish" command to move the pages to the public Internet side of the database, where it becomes available to others.

A very interesting and important set of these Internet edge server features for supporting businesses on the Internet should be an extensive set of statistics on usage. These statistics can tell how many people are accessing your site, and with support for Web server scripts they can even help you decide who's visiting, whether you have repeat visitors, and what pages are being accessed most often. Using these statistics and the Web publishing facilities of the system, you can then change your site to optimize access.

With the system, it should be easy to change your site weekly, or even daily, to generate new content and attract visitors. Changes can be made to the internal version of the pages, tested and reviewed by your own users, and then moved to the public side of the database for others to see. There's never a risk that the content of your public pages will create unexpected effects or problems, because those pages are never staged to public view until they've been certified internally.

EXTENDING YOUR INTERNET PRESENCE WITH VPN

Many businesses are looking to the Internet and Virtual Private Networking (VPN) services to extend their Internet presence and access to branch offices, telecommuters, and customers. By establishing secure transparent links across public and private networks, VPNs make these divergent users feel like they're "right next door" and provide significant cost savings on telecommuter dial-ins and leased lines to branch offices, as well as establishing effective extranet communication with customers and suppliers.

But in practical terms, the benefits of VPNs have been off limits to smaller businesses because of the technical complexity of setting up and administering multiple sites and servers, synchronizing software upgrades, replicating Web servers, and enforcing management policies. To be useful for a smaller organization, VPNs must be more than just a secure transport — the network "plumbing."

The Internet edge server with virtual services management (VSM) software can provide this common administrative framework, making VPNs realistically deployable not only in large enterprises but also in small and midsize companies without a technical staff.

It provides a single, simplified point of administration from which common services — e-mail, name directories, Web access, firewalls, file sharing and access control — are delivered across multiple locations and networks as if on a single local network.

For example, you can assign a user a common directory and e-mail service and give him or her ordinary or privileged access to files. One-touch administration propagates the user's information across the entire network, and the VSM software provides synchronization for all Internet edge servers on the network regardless of the ISP with which they are associated. Data security across the VPN is implemented through the industry-standard IP Security (IPsec) protocol, which provides DES encryption, authentication, as well as remote access via PPTP and/or L2TP.

THE FUTURE OF INTERNET BUSINESS

About a half-million small businesses and a half-million larger ones solicit customers or provide services on the Internet today. Most are high-tech companies with enough internal skills to integrate the complex hardware and software components that combine to create an Internet presence.

Plummeting prices for Internet access and increased competitive pressure to be "on the Net" will change rapidly over the next 5 years. Carriers are already reducing frame relay prices, and the monthly cost of frame relay access to the Internet at 56 kbps could fall to below $100 by the year 2000. DSL technology could push prices even lower. Considering all of these factors, the number of businesses that can afford a full-time connection and publishing on the Internet will quadruple in the next 5 years, and most of these gains will come via small businesses or branch office sites.

As these changes in access technology and pricing make an Internet business presence more affordable, other changes will be making the task of maintaining that presence more complex. The growth in interest in secure transaction handling and the transfer of confidential information has already been noted. Major banks and credit card companies will certainly provide many tools for completing credit card payment or a form of prepaid voucher payment for goods and services. These changes will be reflected in all-in-one Internet edge server products.

The Internet is also a likely forum for the exchange of commercial transactions like purchase orders, shipping notices, etc. Electronic Data Interchange (EDI) standards like X.12 in the U.S. and EDIFACT worldwide are

12

already being used by some firms for Internet commerce, simply by transporting the EDI formats within an e-mail message, but most EDI today is carried over specialized networks at a cost far higher than the Internet would impose. It is certain that more and more EDI will be transported on the Internet, and that permanent Internet connection for EDI handling alone will be a requirement for many firms, just as EDI itself is required today in many industries. EDI features should be added to the Internet edge server as the specific requirements for integration of EDI with e-mail and with local business applications are established and standardized.

The Internet itself will be changed by all of this. As companies move to the Internet, the current system of assigning addresses to new sites will come under more pressure, and it is likely that the Internet will migrate to a new standard (called IPv6) that provides ample capacity to assign addresses to the vast number of new sites coming in the next ten years. The Internet edge server should provide features to support the conversion to the new Internet numbering system as part of its router/firewall feature set, so users will not have to change their client and server software to accommodate the new protocols and address forms.

Today no technology is more important to business than the Internet, and few pose a greater threat of change in the next decade. Technology is the business of the Internet, but not the business of most firms who want to use it. Coping with the changes the future will bring demands a new approach to building an Internet presence — an approach that the new Internet edge server products will provide.

Author's Bio

Joy Pinsky *is vice president of marketing at FreeGate Corporation, a leading provider of all-in-one Internet solutions, combining Internet server, firewall, remote access/VPN, router, and network management functionality for smaller organizations and sites that can't afford a complex assembly of devices and huge technical staff.*

Pinsky joined FreeGate from Lucent Technologies, where she was General Manager for mixed media applications. At Lucent, she was responsible for creating a business, marketing, and development team for a new business focusing on merging telephone communications with IP networking. Previously, she had spent 3 years with Network Equipment Technologies, where her most recent title was director of business development. In addition to running an independent consulting practice, she has held senior marketing management positions with Wyse Technology, Sytek and Rolm, and spent 2 years as a member of Bell Laboratories' technical staff.

Pinsky holds an M.S. degree in electrical engineering and an M.B.A., both from Stanford University, and a B.S. in electrical engineering from the University of California at Davis.

Note

Market statistics provided in this article are from CIMI Corporation, Voorhees, NJ, 1997.

Chapter 2

Web-Based Networking Empowers and Links Businesses

Stewart Padveen

INTERNET AND INTRANETS, EXTRANETS, WANs and LANs. E-mail, E-commerce, E-trade and more. It's a wired, wired world. And for some companies, it has been more wired than for others. Until now.

From major corporations deep with information technology staffs and the budgets to empower them, to a burgeoning army of small offices that handle information technology as needed, the Internet has made it possible to link businesses of all kinds, making communications and transactions immediate, transparent and commonplace.

While LANs, WANs, and intranets traditionally have been the tool that have linked large businesses' operations on a local, regional, national, or even international scale, smaller companies typically have had fewer resources — in both finances and manpower — to accomplish the same task. This has left some companies too weak to compete against larger rivals.

But, increasingly, it is the Internet, the World Wide Web, and an emerging host of private, subscriber-based services and networks that have become the connective tissue for and between enterprises large and small. Like the arrival of powerful, inexpensive personal computers and the Internet itself, this "leveling of the playing field" will serve to bring smaller businesses closer to equality with their larger corporate counterparts.

Further, many of the tools being created and provided over Web-based services are rivaling those traditionally available only to well-financed or leading corporations. Web-based networking is being heralded as the next generation of networking. Currently, there are services on the market tar-

0-8493-9987-4/00/$0.00+$.50
© 2000 by CRC Press LLC

geted to businesses of any size that provide an instant Web-based network of business applications traditionally only found in large companies' intranets. Applications such as e-mail, document management, search capabilities, bulletin board systems, online chat rooms, Internet telephony, and more are now accessible to organizations of any size, without the management and maintenance that had been required from technical staff in the past. Some services even go a step further to include E-commerce and E-business services such as company profiles, credit checks, manufacturer searches, travel services, business matchmaking services, and more.

This aggregation of Web-based business services is a very powerful tool for companies of any size. Even for large companies with full intranets or extranets already in use, these services can help provide more information, content, and data to either a displaced or in-house workforce. As a tangential but functional and empowering adjunct to emerging Web-based network services, these programs work to further unify the Internet with intranets and extranets. This brings to life the vision of the totally interconnected world, interlinking customer with company with supplier. Efficiencies are increased, streamlined, waits on information are shortened, and service is improved.

For large organizations with overburdened Information Technology (IT) staffs and those small companies otherwise unable to afford expensive intranet hardware, software, and IT personnel costs, the concept of Web-based networking has turned a once disparate and disconnected business world into a real solution of connectivity and interactivity. It has even opened the once-whimsical but often practical concept of telecommuting — scattering the workforce to their homes at least 1 day a week.

With its low cost, high functionality, reliability, and ease of use that's as simple as any Website, arguments for Web-based networking solutions are growing as quickly as the applications they're being used in. For the executive of a small or large company looking to empower his or her workforce, the solutions are strong.

The information technology community's positioning strength has been built on the importance of the technicians who design, construct, and maintain such applications. Still, the arrival of Web-based network solutions should not be seen as a threat to job security and importance in the corporate community. It instead should be viewed as a tool to empower their client community with simple, easy to use applications, while freeing up the IT staff to handle more pressing and technically challenging tasks. This realization will not be lost on management who, in seeing the benefits of virtual, off-site networking, likely will steer appropriate funds toward empowering management teams to partake in emerging Web-based network solutions.

A HOST OF BENEFITS

Web-based networking offers a host of benefits in today's highly diverse and increasingly connected and global workplace. There's little to no up-front costs associated with implementation, because there is no need to purchase or set up servers, software, or hard wiring and there's no application development necessary. And because the services are hosted and maintained off site, the applications eliminate the increasing personnel costs associated with hiring, training, and retaining today's information technology department.

In a very real sense, companies of all sizes empowered with a PC and Internet connection can log on to any one of a host of low-cost Internet-based services. Today's tools include internal and external networking, instant messaging and electronic mail, paging, long-distance communications, video conferencing, calendaring, presentation creation, online sales and "storefronts," and other services that can empower their operations and help bring parity between them and their larger corporate counterparts. The list of tools available is growing quickly, encompassing many of the software products today's workforce has come to expect and rely upon in daily business.

The applications' functionality goes further in many instances. For example, some services include document publishing performed by a desktop button, encrypted file transport between network subscribers, private chat rooms for subscriber clients, and even the ability to integrate with audio and video conferencing, assuming the bandwidth exists to provide for quality transmissions.

In many instances, Web-based solutions rival or outperform traditional intranets. Consider those systems that have powerful internal messaging capabilities, but no means to message customers, clients, or even remote workers or executives beyond the corporate offices. Instant officing applications provide real answers to immediate, worldwide connectivity.

Minimum system requirements are typically a 486 PC with 32 MB of RAM and Windows 95 or 98 operating software, an Internet connection via a traditional modem, and a Java-enabled Web browser. With even more titles planned for future implementation, the strategy of using the PC to enhance the Web's networking experience is truly brought to life for all business segments, from a small business to a remote business unit of a large corporation.

That said, with prices dropping quickly across the landscape of personal computing, many companies would find increased performance and power with Pentium-equipped hardware. Most services work well with traditional dial-up accounts ranging from 28.8 to 56 kbps. Considering the arrival of cable modems, the abundance of T1 lines, and even ADSL and ISDN lines into home offices nationwide, remote workers will find service and access often rivaling that of their corporate offices.

What does all this mean? Simplicity is an embedded benefit in many of these applications. Most importantly, neither the rank and file client nor the existing IT workforce is required to perform any technical setup, maintenance, or even upgrades. Many services host applications and provide immediate access to programs and applications. When new versions are issued, the entire user community has access to the feature, unless otherwise restricted. Some advanced services allow system operators to assign feature access rights to individual users. With certain product offerings, access is as simple as a button embedded on the desktop — a button that enables the full functionality of a powerful office, all within one, low, monthly subscription fee.

The freedom involved with these applications means management, employees, and the IT workers are free to handle more important tasks. This has two benefits for non-IT-related companies. First, a company involved in shipping, manufacturing, or publishing, for example, can use these services without needing to hire additional IT personnel or otherwise stray from the company's core competency or business focus. Second, where once a main function of the IT community was to watch over the corporate server, because all the technology is housed off site, server maintenance is the now the host's responsibility.

COST NO LONGER A FACTOR

When weighing whether to build a corporate intranet, the scales of business empowerment often have tipped in favor of those companies financially capable of handling the costs associated with the task. The result for smaller companies without the requisite finances to handle such implementation is a communications burden for its workforce. Traveling executives are unable to retrieve important data without calling on compatriots on-site to gather and either fax or e-mail the data to a personal account. They're essentially laid bare and unarmed in an increasingly competitive business battlefield.

Web-based networking solutions provide a viable, working alternative to the traditional high cost of implementation and maintenance of advanced electronic networking communications. Typically priced on a per-user basis, system subscriptions can cost far less than traditional networking solutions. Prices range from $10 to $15 per user per month, yielding inexpensive access to a powerful virtual intranet. Typically, these arrangements are made on a month-to-month basis, providing corporate executives or the client community the ability and agility to grow or shrink their subscription base depending on current demand. And as access often is immediate and subscriptions conducted real-time online, decisions can be made "on the fly," without lengthy discussions. For a group of corporate executives, teleworkers, or displaced sales team members in need of a network to facilitate communications for either an immediate project or long-term correspondence, the network's price point is low enough that the expense likely wouldn't require approval by management.

Web-based network solutions also are an ideal application for professional organizations and associations that have membership over a wide geographic area. Designed to accommodate hundreds of users, once disjointed and disconnected populations will have an immediate and cost-effective community link drawing them together. For those accustomed to building an extranet to service this type of user community, these solutions not only mimic that function but also actually create an extranet at a fraction of the cost.

Consultants and resellers also will find Web-based solutions to be a low-cost solution for their clients' networking needs. Resellers can offer these solutions as an alternative to setting up expensive and technically challenging systems. All the client would need is an industry-standard PC, a dial-up connection to the Internet, and a Java-enabled Internet browser. For a consultant or reseller hired to design or recommend a networking solution, the application provides nearly immediate answers for clients often demanding solutions "yesterday." Both communities will find they can sell these services to larger organizations with workgroup environments as well as small businesses — a growing and fertile market that formerly would have been unreachable because solution costs were too high. What's more, because of their service-based model, resellers can often generate residual income on a monthly basis — something that no other networking solution can provide.

WEB OFFICING OPENS TELECOMMUTING

The benefits of Web-based networking extend beyond the brick and mortar walls of the corporate workplace, into the virtual world of computing. Companies that turn to the Internet as the foundation for their traditional, office-based connection toolkit can now utilize telecommuting, remote officing, and other forms of virtual work styles to increase productivity and decrease the hard and recurring costs associated with real estate space, communications, and telephony service. They can even cut those costs devoted to an anchored and permanent staff. Once it was considered a technical nightmare to link disparate workers into the company's network. Now instant Web-based networks provide reliable, immediate, and thorough connectivity to a company's system with a graphical, Web-based interface that helps to dramatically shorten the learning curve.

The applications also allow a company to set up a virtual network for a displaced community. Imagine a company with a 10-person sales team scattered across the country. By using a Web-based network solution, that client community will have access to not only corporate records as needed, but more direct connections to each other. This type of connectivity shortens the time involved in tracking down information or sales lead notes, for example.

IT WORKERS REMAIN A NEEDED POPULATION

This technology truly is at the intersection of Internet- and Web-based and low-end intranet creation. How company managers take advantage of these offerings can determine how much a company pays or how successful its networking can be. How these applications affect current and future IT workers remains to be seen.

To be sure, IT workers play an increasingly important role in the current connected landscape. In fact, demand for a skilled IT workforce has never been greater. New hires and competitive "bidding" for seasoned workers are at all-time highs, with those workers commanding richer salary and benefits packages from employers who realize their lifeblood flows along lines of connectivity — lines that are laid, programmed, maintained, and upgraded by the IT community they hire.

The IT community may view Web-based networking as a threat to its existence. This is similar to the threat that was perceived by many people when personal computers were introduced. Most people thought PCs would replace many jobs. This has proven to be inaccurate. The doomsday scenario professed by some early naysayers never happened. Instead, it allowed people to let PCs do the mundane work so they can focus on more important work, accomplishing more in less time. There has also been a fundamental shift in the economy from the industrial age to the digital age. While many jobs have been replaced by PCs, many new ones have been created as the computer and high-tech industry prospers. Similarly, Web-based networking will free up IT time and allow IT'ers to focus on more important tasks rather than the tedious requirement of maintaining a server-based network.

Second, the client community in the Web-based network environment likely would not have turned to an intranet application as an alternative. Traditionally, fears of cost, maintenance, a perceived steep learning curve, and even a lack of functionality for a smaller company have made proprietors of small businesses seek other alternatives to virtual officing and connectivity. What's more, for an otherwise astute business executive, hiring a new and often expensive employee to handle something that's as foreign to the executive as the guts of his or her PC is a frightening experience.

"Hands-on control" loses all meaning for many executives when it comes to computing.

What does this mean for the IT community? It means that a workforce educated to handle pressing information systems tasks is freed from the minutia of detail involved with setting up less-than-systemwide networks or mininetworks, or responding to client queries about system confusion. Information technology experts once hired to handle the intranet, either as staff or outsource, will continue to oversee network service and provide service to the client population. Web-based network solutions actually free up IT specialists who otherwise would find themselves handling requests from subsets within a larger corporation.

The Web-based nature of this form of networking solution means ease of use will lead to the IT community being removed from most educational responsibilities as well. Very simple, with a short learning curve, the applications are self-explanatory; meaning information technology workers will not be burdened or inundated with questions from befuddled workers. This is frequently called the "PalmPilot" theory of networking and computing. Accessible and friendly functionality is essential to the service's usability and acceptance by its target community. Web-based network solutions deliver only the required services and important business applications, making them simple to use. The applications will replace complicated or confusing remote dial-up networking and access to the company intranet.

The IT community should view Web-based networking as an alternative to the labor-intensive process of setting up smaller, department-specific applications. For example, imagine a 10-person marketing department wants its own network or intranet. Certainly, creating this independent application is not the best use of time or talent for the internal IT department. Instead of the burden falling on the IT department to build that network, they can subscribe to Web-based solutions. It's also ideal for displaced teleworkers who must maintain contact and share information with other similarly displaced workers through an intranet-type application.

What's more, the Internet-based nature of the applications means the "mobile" workforce can be global, accessing the services remotely from any Internet-enabled PC at any location worldwide. And again, since the system is run over an Internet Web browser, which many workers today are familiar and comfortable with, IT staffers — especially those on after-hours call for larger corporations — will not find themselves fielding calls at odd hours from executives in remote locations having trouble logging onto the corporate network.

Many IT managers view the arrival of Web-based solutions as real and tangible supplements to their abilities to offer powerful connectivity for their client populations. They also realize that their staffers couldn't provide similar service at the current price point at which executives are costing instant Web officing alternatives. Concerns about job security are misplaced, they're learning, as companies still will require permanent and traditional intranet applications — and the skilled specialists to install, maintain, service, and answer questions about those intranets.

Non-IT executives in larger corporations that currently lack IT staffs also will realize the merit in these applications. While many of the Web-based solutions have been designed with small offices in mind because of limited solutions designed to mimic the corporate intranet, a trend has arisen among larger companies to go with these services to expand upon basic needs provided by intranets. These services provide many of the functions that companies use daily, but at a fraction of the cost and with a much easier learning curve. After all, in today's Web environment, many people who may not know how to work the corporate intranet know how to surf the Web.

The emergence of Internet and Web-based network solutions will open up a plethora of benefits to the modern, agile corporation, both large and small. And the ubiquity of Internet access, the cost of ownership, and the ease of use will become primary factors that will drive this technology to small businesses.

In an increasingly competitive workplace and business environment, every edge must be gained and every advantage needs to be capitalized upon to ensure success for those companies positioning themselves as truly globally empowered enterprises.

Author's Bio

Stewart Padveen is founder, chairman, and CEO of HotOffice Technologies, Inc., developers of the award-winning HotOffice Service. Padveen has dedicated his professional career to providing products and services that level the playing field for companies of all sizes to compete in the emerging economy. He frequently speaks on the topics of Internet/intranet and extranet development and Web-site marketing and promotion.

Prior to founding HotOffice in 1995, Padveen was the founder and president of American Financial Directories, a national software and book publishing company. During this period, he built AFD's product line, developed its distribution channels, and expanded sales nationally. AFD was acquired in 1995. Padveen began his technology career in 1985 as a programmer and cofounder of Boca Business Systems, a developer of inventory management and accounting systems. He holds a degree in economics from McGill University.

The HotOffice™ Service is the first product to be awarded both "Premiere Product" at Demo 97 and "Debut Company" at PC Forum, two of the industry's most prestigious events. Among its many accolades, HotOffice has received the PC Magazine Editor's Choice Award, a "Four Star Award" by PC Computing Magazine, and is listed as the Best Small Office Internet Solution in the Gadget Guru's Guide to the Best (syndicated *columnist and NBC Today Show correspondent). HotOffice Technologies, Inc. is based in Boca Raton, FL and is funded in part by Intel Corporation and TBG Information Investors, a partnership of Blumenstein/Thorne Information Partners and GS Capital Partners II, an affiliate of Goldman Sachs Group.*

Chapter 3
The New Media

Jessica Keyes

WELCOME TO THE WIRED GENERATION. We're tuned in and turned on. We use it for school, to shop, and to conduct our financial transactions. And the more prurient among us use it as a "low-res" *Playboy* substitute.

There are anywhere from 50 to 75 million hardy souls, depending on the flavor of statistics you're quoting, webcrawling on any given day. Although the initial mix of crawlers was decidedly academic and governmental, the advent of graphical browsers, such as Netscape, opened the doors for the rest of us to crawl right in and log on.

The new webcrawler can be anyone. From the business person who needs to look something up to his son who uses it for homework. A doctor in a remote area may use the Internet to get assistance from a teaching hospital in the city. And her patients may use it to purchase that special something that just can't be found in town. What all these webcrawlers have in common is opportunity. An opportunity to expand one's horizons beyond the geographic and physical borders we now operate within.

It's a vast opportunity for business as well. Yahoo, one of the original Web directories, lists over 10,000 corporate sites in their directory. But that's only the tip of the iceberg. Look at the statistics that have made headlines during the last year or so:

- ActivMedia measured the first-year growth rate of Web business marketers at an astounding 1800 percent.
- Hambrecht & Quist forecasts Internet-related sales soaring to $14.5 billion in the year 2000.
- A Nielsen Media study finds an astonishing 68 percent of Net surfers are business related.
- The Internet Society announced that the number of hosts on the Internet has passed the 320 million mark.
- Lycos has indexed over 1.53 million Web pages, with possibly thousands being added daily.
- Hambrecht & Quist forecasts that Internet equipment sales will grow to $2.5 billion in 2000; network services to $5 billion; software to $4 billion; consulting/integration services will increase to close to $3 billion.

0-8493-9987-4/00/$0.00+$.50
© 2000 by CRC Press LLC

Which came first the chicken or the egg? This is actually quite a meaningful question if you replace chicken with technology and egg with need. So which did come first? The technology or the need for the technology?

Well, both actually. There have been many cases when technology was introduced into the marketplace where there was apparently no real need for it — until it was introduced, that is, and then suddenly everyone began using it. These are the "market shapers." Visicalc, the first automated spreadsheet, was a market shaper nobody asked for, but when it was introduced it jumped into the marketplace like gangbusters — and ultimately changed the way we think about computers. Essentially, a market shaper is a piece of software or hardware that is pivotal in changing the face of business.

On the other hand, the introduction of the word processor was not a pivotal event in the history of business computing. For years before the introduction of the first word processor the typewriter industry had been successfully making and selling millions of souped-up typewriters. These typewriters were electronic, contained some memory, and had built-in functionality such as spell checks. The PC-oriented word processor was the next logical step in the technological advancement of typing. It wasn't dramatic. It didn't shape the industry. It was just a nice, easy progression from mechanical typewriter to electronic word processor to PC word processor. So, as you can see, technology creeps through the door in two ways. One as an egg and the other as a chicken.

The most dramatic difference between today's PC and yesterday's is not in the hardware but in ways the hardware is utilized. Networks now enable instantaneous access to global information. Innovative "groupware" software packages are now commonly used to ease collaboration and the pooling of knowledge. The PC has all but replaced the telephone as a purveyor of messages, essentially turning the PC into a mini post office. In the not too distant future, our e-mail facilities will be even more intelligent by providing the capabilities of organizing voice mail, faxes, and e-mail, including messages sweetened with video clips.

The past couple of years has seen the rise, with the introduction of Lotus Notes (IBM), of the groupware paradigm. Webcasting falls under this rubric. Groupware enables people in different locales to work together in real time. Groupware is actually a generic category under which several disciplines fall, the common denominator being providing the "ability to collaborate," The technologies of chat, conferencing, audio streaming, and video streaming all fall under this umbrella. Webcasting is nothing more and nothing less than the art and science of "putting all of these technologies together."

THE WEBCASTED WORLD

The PC as broadcast medium is an apt description. We've grown accustomed to watching TV news where an anchor interviews one or more guests, perhaps thousands of miles apart. This is done with a camera crew at each location, some TV monitors, and some satellite equipment for transmission of the actual broadcast. The same is being done on the PC.

Cuba Memorial Hospital, a typically small-town health facility in a typically western New York small town, has seen the technological future — and seized it. It's a choice that will enable them to save even more lives in their bucolic community. Already being utilized as a tool to connect its patients with some of the top specialists in the country, Cuba is now expanding telemedicine to its emergency room. Healthcare professionals will now be able to turn on a video camera and computer; dial another hospital miles away, and seconds later a trauma specialist will appear on the screen. The off-site physician will then, with continuous use of the camera and other high-tech tools, be able to observe and diagnose treatment for the emergency admittee, and later, via video conferencing, be available for consultations.

The virtual hospital has arrived! Without leaving their own community patients can now consult some of the country's top specialists. Relying on a multitude of high-tech communications devices such as video cameras that can zoom in on things as minute as skin melanomas; electronic stethoscopes that magnify a heartbeat and transmit it hundreds or even thousands of miles away through phone or cable lines; virtually instantaneous computer access to a patient's medical charts and large-screen TVs that permit doctors to see and chat with patients and other medical professionals, the small-town hospital has dramatically increased its value to its patients.

Dr. Francis Tedesco, president of the Medical College of Georgia, a pioneer in this growing communications network, passionately champions telemedicine, stating that doctors can look into the eyes, hear a heartbeat, and listen to the lungs.

According to Dr. Jane Preston, president of the American Telemedicine Association in Austin, TX, the ER is definitely going to be where this technology shines. And James Toler, codirector of the bioengineering center at Georgia Institute of Technology, adds that the ability to administer treatment to patients during that first golden hour saves lives and results in less serious medical complications. Heart attack or stroke victims, natural disaster or vehicular accident victims — telemedicine will enable all to receive the quickest help possible.

Aside from a treatment tool, telemedicine has also produced benefits in terms of education. Many states have already approved programs allowing doctors to obtain continuing education credits working with a specialist on telemedicine systems.

Military uses are also conceivable in the near future. A backpack system for the military that would use two lipstick-size cameras inserted in a helmet has been designed. It will enable a medic to transmit information in real time from the battlefield. Doctors at military bases could then examine the wounded soldier, advise treatment, and prepare for arrival at the hospital.

Dr. Jay Sanders of Massachusetts General Hospital, an early booster and user of this technology (in the early 1970s he set up one of the first telemedicine systems between his hospital and Boston's Logan Airport), would like to see it employed in schools as a teaching tool, and in peoples' homes to enable doctors to make house calls whatever the time of day! A true believer, he sees telemedicine as one of the factors that will radically change healthcare.

Other industries are making use of network broadcasting too. New York's Citibank is typical of those banks looking to cash in on the virtual business. Citibank recently made a giant leap toward virtual banking by making stock quotes and securities transactions available at its 1800 proprietary automated teller machines (ATMs) nationwide This service was inaugurated during the Fall of 1994 in New York, Chicago, Miami, San Francisco, and Washington.

Citibank's ATM users are able to see up to 10 stock quotations, buy and sell stocks, or invest in money market funds simply by following the instructions on the screen. This is just the first of many virtual banking programs under development at Citibank. The bank is also improving its phone option with sophisticated screen phones, and is expanding its PC banking through software giveaways on the Internet.

In addition to the convenience offered their customers, there's the cost-saving benefits of this new technology. According to Mark Hardie, an analyst with the Tower Group, a bank technology consultancy in Wellesley, MA, electronic transactions are more economical than those processed by personnel. And the high operational costs of branch offices can definitely be reduced.

IBM video conferencing kiosks are offering the $150-billion Royal Bank of Canada in Toronto the chance to centralize its intelligence and services. According to Dennis Graham, manager of advanced concept networks for Royal Bank, these kiosks will definitely make more sense than having licensed, experienced salespeople stranded in seldom-visited branch offices.

Allowing the bank to situate their experts in one central location, lessening these employees' downtime and increasing their availability to a wider range of customers via the video conferencing kiosks, this new technology has definitely improved their customer service and management of personnel.

Another financial institution that has forayed into the world of virtual business is Huntington Bancshares, Inc. of Columbus, OH. This $16.5-billion institution is currently converting its branch offices to accommodate these new customer-intensive technologies — allowing the bank to expand without building or leasing new office space — thus pleasing the bank's financial managers as well.

To make automated check-cashing services possible, Huntington has hooked up with AT&T Global Information Solutions to add imaging technology to its teller machines. More detailed transactions, such as opening deposit accounts, are handled separately through interactive video conferencing terminals or telebanking. The reason, according to Jan Tyler, research and development manager at Huntington, is the desire to keep ATM lines and transactions short. The key driver behind the virtual business is video conferencing, which allows groups, over long geographic distances, not only to share a common PC blackboard, but to see and hear each other.

The Danvers, MA-based PictureTel is one enterprising organization that is marketing such a technology. LIVE Share operates using affordable dial-up digital lines. A small video camera is mounted to the top of the PC which transmits the individual's image while audio is transmitted through a PictureTel telephone. Software enables users on both ends of the connection to share a PC session. So I can be in New York and a staff member can be in San Diego, and both of us can pour over a spreadsheet in real time, talking with and seeing each other the entire time. TV or a PC, the future, it seems, is really here.

THE VIDEO CONNECTION

You need only peruse the trades, by using your intelligent agent software, of course, to find numerous articles on the coming boom in video.

A video camera that connects to mobile computers via a PCMCIA card was released in November, 1994 by the Scottish company, VLSI Vision Ltd. The company sees as their target market such on-the-go professionals as real estate agents, site inspectors, and graphic designers.

Named PC Card Camera by VSLI Vision, the device consists of a hand-held camera and mounting apparatus, PCMCIA Type II interface card with cable, and documentation. Camera exposure can be set either automatically or manually and optional lenses are available. Vision sees the PC Card Camera being utilized in presentations, document imaging, real estate applications, and conferencing.

Though business applications for video are still in the very beginning stages, some companies are already using this new technology. For example, NBC News is using the Oracle Media Serve to log video clips.

This is the side road, but the main path chosen by many companies for video servers is training. As vast libraries of interactive courseware continue to be accrued by corporations, they are beginning to stress the existing standard LANs. Bruce Yon, multimedia analyst at Dataquest of San Jose, CA, states that the ever-increasing amount of software being installed within organizations is surpassing the ability of businesses to absorb servers or CD-ROM jukeboxes. Intranet-based video servers enable employees to train themselves at their PCs as their time allows, instead of completing a whole course or jamming the network.

Video Servers have definitely found a home in manufacturing. Defense contractor Nordon Systems Inc., is using the technology to help educate their workers to perform certain manufacturing processes, feeding the video instruction live to their terminal for convenient review. Video servers are a hot topic in the electronic commerce arena as well.

To succeed in the era of the information superhighway, some believe we will need to create megacompanies that embrace — and control — as many of the converging technologies as possible. Others say that the small, high-tech venture companies, particularly software firms, will lead us into the convergence era.

While most experts agree that consolidation is inevitable in the communications industry, no one large company can create the intense focus and agility needed to compete successfully across the breadth of the information superhighway. And no small firm will be able to generate the intellectual and financial capital necessary to control a segment of the highway in the same way that Microsoft and Intel did in their respective industries. An alternative way to achieve the benefits of both large-company scale and small-company flexibility is by creating joint ventures with partners who have complementary technologies.

NBC is giving it that old cheerleader try, however. In 1991 it spent $150 million to buy the Financial News Network as part of its launch of CNBC. And the 1996 launch of MSNBC, the all-news cable-online hybrid, is the progeny of its long-term alliance with Microsoft Corp. (see Exhibit 3.1).

In spite of technical problems and criticism from the press and the public, MSNBC makes an excellent example of what Webcasting really is. It's not a rehash of news and video from its cable counterpart and it's not just

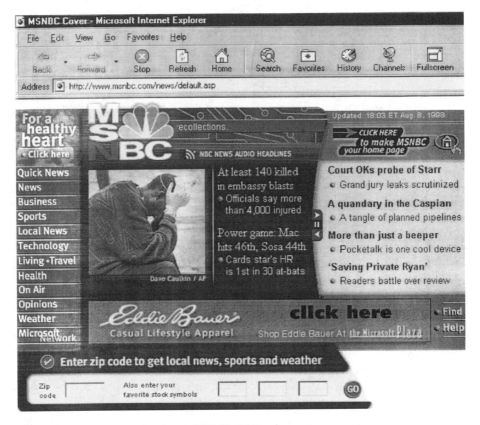

Exhibit 3.1. MSNBC's Webcast environment.

a marketing and promotional Website for NBC and Microsoft. Rather, it is a unique amalgam of the best of both the broadcasting and Internet arenas. It is a full-fledged news effort, staffed with both journalists and technologists, who work as a team to exploit the best features of the Webcasting environment.

NBC often collects more material (audio, video, and images) than it can use in its half-hour nightly newscast or weekly hour-long news magazines such as "Dateline" and "Meet the Press." This excess broadcast material, much of it background and analysis, is customarily excised from the broadcast due to network time constraints. What better venue than to use it on MSNBC, thought the producers.

This they did, with background information on the topic at hand. For example, the embassy bombings in Africa that includes history, geography, as well as the biographies of the major players. The producers are of the opinion that, "when you have gone through the site and absorbed what's in it, you can better understand what you see night after night on the news."

But MSNBC isn't all serious news. They've also created complementary content such as an online honesty quiz that accompanied a week-long series called, "Lie, Cheat, and Steal."

While MSNBC does typify the very high end of webcasting, which is something that many readers of this chapter may aspire to but never reach, nonetheless its introduction does provide some insight into what makes a webcast successful.

MSNBC is no mere digital extension of its cable counterpart. Journalists and technologists work as a team to exploit what is unique about the medium rather than repurposing broadcast content and/or using the site as a marketing medium. The producers insisted that the effort be a journalistic effort and not a marketing enterprise, therefore, MSNBC Online has been staffed with a combination of journalistically savvy technologists and technologically savvy journalists. In other words, everyone concerned understands both sides of the business. Interestingly, one of the job requirements is that everyone, even content providers, must learn HTML.

Online honesty quizzes and backgrounders on a geographic "hotspot" are the kinds of capabilities that are the "core" or the Microsoft/NBC alliance. Says the president of NBC Interactive Media, "We are not playing this game for what it is today. We are playing this game for what we believe it will become: a video-oriented, mass-market information vehicle."

While MSNBC may be the flagship of NBC's online empire, it's not the only ship in the Internet fleet. NBC.com (Exhibit 3.2) and SuperNet, a Microsoft Network (go word = nbc) product, figure in the equation as well. Where NBC.com is essentially a TV guide for the network, SuperNet utilizes a more sophisticated level of technology.

But there's a lot more up NBC's sleeve. For several years, Desktop Video has been delivering coverage of corporate announcements, congressional testimony, and CEO interviews to the desktop. Customers will be able to retrieve that same information from a Website directly from NBC or from one of the Internet service providers it will license the product to. So, if a CEO from Bankers Trust sees an interesting broadcast from, say Citibank, he or she can copy the video clip to the corporate intranet for companywide viewing.

NBC also plans to license this software to its affiliates who can put up their 6:00 o'clock newscast on their Websites so people who missed it can get in at 9:00 or 10:00 o'clock to pull up the big story.

NBC's ultimate goal is intercast, a technology that embeds data into video signals. Intercast would allow the network to send HTML pages along

Exhibit 2. NBC.com acts as a TV guide for the network.

with its regular programming. Both the television show and the associated HTML- encoded information travel the same route as a normal television signal. So if an anchor is discussing events in Washington in the main TV window, the viewer can scroll through information in a small "window-in-window" (which, of course, can be enlarged for easier viewing).

Ultimately all the networks want to play the Web game for what it ultimately will become — a video-oriented, mass-market information vehicle.

WEBCASTING IN A NUTSHELL

To view most multimedia or webcasted content using a network, the files must first be completely downloaded to a local hard drive and then displayed or played. The network's role is to retrieve the file, so that all the information resides locally. The user's online experience is a combination of click, wait, and view. Most people connected to the Internet have extremely slow connections at the rate of about 5.5 kbps (i.e., 56 kb modems).

If the multimedia file that is being downloaded is l00 kb in size, users have to wait at least 18 seconds before they are able to see anything (100 kb divided by 5.5 kb/s). Most multimedia content files are much larger than l00 kb and, therefore, the wait is usually much longer.

Streaming works differently. Streaming transfers the beginning of a file, then starts playing it while continuously transmitting more data. In effect, streaming allows a viewer to watch and listen to the beginning of the multimedia content, while the middle is being sent. While playing back the middle section the end is transmitted, and then the end plays. Of course, the data isn't really broken up into sections, it just continues to be downloaded as it is played back. Streaming technology enables developers to reduce the waiting and create an online experience of click and view, with little or no wait.

Depending on the content, streaming can significantly improve the user's experience. Multimedia content that might have taken minutes to download in its entirety can now begin playback within just a few seconds and play for several minutes while later pieces of the content are being streamed.

Much has been said about how slow the Internet is and about how long users have to wait before they are able to view their favorite Websites. There are several reasons for this, but the most common is lack of bandwidth. Bandwidth refers to the capacity of a connection between two machines or devices connected to the network to transfer data. Different types of connections have different bandwidths (capacities) or speeds associated with them. The Internet is made up of many different connections, but it is important to remember that the smallest connection in the path through which data flow sets the maximum rate at which data can be transferred.

A 14.4 modem that can transfer data at approximately 1 kbps per second is considered to be very, very slow, while a Tl line that can achieve average rates as high as 70 to 80 kbps is considered very fast. However, it is important to realize that a single-speed CD-ROM can transfer data at 150 kbps. So, even a fast Internet connection is still slower than the slowest of CD-ROM drives. This assumes that the data being transferred have not been compressed using a data compression scheme.

Data compression is a technique by which the actual size of a data object is reduced. Using a mathematical algorithm, the original data are transformed into a new format that represents the same data but that uses fewer bytes. There are several different schemes for reducing the amount of data, but they all fall into two distinct categories: lossless and lossy. Lossless data compression means that although the data size is reduced, it is possible to create an identical version of the original data. Lossy compression means that it is impossible to ever restore an identical version to the original data.

Compressing data that are going to be transferred over a network makes it possible to effectively increase the bandwidth available at a given connection speed. For example, if it were possible to compress all data with an algorithm that yielded a 10:1 compression ratio (10 bytes of data are compressed into 1 byte), then it would be possible to effectively increase throughput by a multiple of 10. So, a 28.8 modem that could receive 2 kbps of uncompressed data could receive a theoretical 20 kbps of data. Of course, only 2 kbps of data is actually transmitted, but the recipient could then decompress the data and get a reasonable representation of the original data. Actual bandwidth has not changed, but the effective rate at which data are transferred has increased.

Compression helps reduce the amount of data that actually needs to be transferred. However, when creating content for online delivery with a "streaming" system, the most important factor is the rate at which data is used by the content. Streaming algorithms, then, are the real secret behind webcasting.

PUSH COMES TO SHOVE

Webcasting, when first invented, became the dream technology of those wishing to "push" information to targeted consumers. It wasn't good enough that millions of folks were browsing the Net because, for the most part, those Net-eyeballs only lingered for mere seconds on a site — hardly long enough to get a marketing message across. Thus were born the Wall Street darlings, Marimba and Pointcast.

"Push" technology is a client-side form of webcasting where a permanent receiver sits on a PC with the user either instructing it to automatically or manually call the sending Website. The goal? To gather tailored-to-the-user news and other information such as stock quotes. The marketing message usually comes along for the ride.The problem is bandwidth. Push is a hog. A very large one. So much so that network administrators all over the world began banning push from company intranets and corporate Internet connections. Companies like Marimba had to quickly reinvent themselves. As of this writing, Marimba and friends are still in business, but the luster is definitely off the term "push."

CONCLUSION

What all this means to the MIS manager is that he or she needs to be open to new, and perhaps unfamiliar, technologies. The technology has most definitely matured since Webcasting first premiered in the mid-1990s. The tools and techniques are there to be able to (almost easily) merge audio, video, imagery, and text into an information-rich delivery medium. Welcome to the Webcasted world.

Author's Bio

Jessica Keyes is president of New Art Technologies, Inc., a high-technology software development firm. Keyes has given seminars for such prestigious universities as Carnegie Mellon, Boston University, University of Illinois, James Madison University, and San Francisco State University. She is a frequent keynote speaker on the topics of competitive strategy using information technology and marketing on the information superhighway. She is an advisor for DataPro, McGraw-Hill's computer research arm, as well as a member of the Sprint Business Council. Keyes also is a founding Board of Director member of the New York Software Industry Association. She has recently completed a 2-year term on the Mayor of New York City's Small Business Advisory Council.

Prior to founding her company, Keyes was managing director of R&D for the New York Stock Exchange and has been an officer with Swiss Bank Co. and Banker's Trust, both in New York City. She holds a Master's from New York University, where she did her research in the area of artificial intelligence.

A noted columnist and correspondent, with over 150 articles published, Keyes is the author of 23 books.

Chapter 4

Facilitating Competitive Intelligence: The Next Step in Internet-Based Research

Willie Tejada

USING THE INTERNET TO GATHER STRATEGIC COMPETITIVE INTELLIGENCE is becoming a reality — a mission-critical process that professional organizations can no longer ignore. Until recently, competitive intelligence was confined to monitoring information such as how much they were spending on advertising, what they were doing in research and development, and who they were hiring. Today, however, the vast amount of information readily available through the Internet has the potential to greatly expand the scope of competitive intelligence and catapult it to new levels of importance embracing market changes, customer expectations, and developing global trends.

Internet-based research for competitive intelligence holds the potential to discern important forces like adoption of technology, buying habits, and other behaviors often buried in seemingly unrelated, unstructured information sources — articles, press releases, financial statements, etc. Many tools currently exist to make it easier to spot trends in structured information such as profits, revenues, or sale figures, but there are no tools to aid in analyzing unstructured information over time. As a result, Internet-based research remains a mostly manual, ad hoc process that demands too

0-8493-9987-4/00/$0.00+$.50
© 2000 by CRC Press LLC

Exhibit 4.1. Companies that Failed to Monitor CI Trend.

Company:	Wang
Driver:	Technology
Mistake:	Failure to understand technology trends in product development
Company:	IBM PC Division
Driver:	Business
Mistake:	Failure to predict commoditization of industry
Company:	Apple Computing
Driver:	Marketing
Mistake:	Failure to market superior technology and product
Company:	Pan Am
Driver:	Societal
Mistake:	Failure to understand societal trends contained in financial analysis

much time and costs too much money to yield truly useful results and become an intrinsic part of business life.

To stay competitive in the information age, executives know that they must improve methods to acquire and manage unstructured information from the Internet, and convert it to useful, pertinent knowledge to share with others. Research firm Dataquest Inc. estimates that by 1999 corporations will spend $4.5 billion to better leverage their knowledge resources. Of the top applications of knowledge management identified by the Gartner Group, competitive intelligence is the only one that requires the collection of external information, with the Internet emerging as the primary source.

Knowledge derived from information in the vast ocean of the Internet, at best, is random and elusive. Until now, using the Internet required extensive manual searching, ad hoc analysis, and cumbersome sharing. In most cases, the process has proven to be so time-consuming and so costly that it winds up being performed poorly or not at all. Yet the failure to track competitive intelligence from organized research can be disastrous. Business history is rife with examples of firms that missed important trends, as shown in Exhibit 4.1.

Without new technologies designed from the ground up to implement the revolutionary changes in the way research is collected, analyzed, and shared, organizations have little chance of improving competitive intelligence through Internet-based research.

The broad field of knowledge management is still emerging as a way to facilitate the process of locating, organizing, transferring, and more efficiently using the information and expertise within an organization. Although substantial funds are being expended on information and knowledge management solutions, until now there has been an absence of efficient Internet-based research systems that specifically target the day-to-day needs of those involved in competitive intelligence.

This chapter explores the extent and limitations of today's technologies and offers a new way of implementing an effective Internet-based research system.

INTERNET-BASED RESEARCH

The Internet makes information that can be used for competitive intelligence more readily available. Today, public information or publishable business information, from patent filings to bankruptcy notices, is available on the Internet.

When asked if they do Internet research, almost anyone in a modern corporation would probably answer "Yes, I use a search engine." But searching for information is merely the first step in a much more extensive process. In general Internet-based research follows a process with three distinct steps:

1. Information collecting and sourcing.
2. Information discovery and analysis.
3. Knowledge sharing and transfer.

This core process is consistent across many industries and jobs, specifically high technology, market research, financial services and biotechnology. While the content, the sources of information, and in some cases the methodology, will change from instance to instance, the core process — collecting and sourcing, discovery and analysis, and sharing and transferring — remains the same.

MORE THAN A SEARCH ENGINE

Business people performing research start with an objective; something they are looking to prove or learn, such as a market statistic or information on a technology. They then begin collecting information, an essentially manual process. Assuming they know where to look, they use a search engine, or more likely several searching facilities, type in keywords and phrases to search for, sort out the useful results, and gather a collection of research materials. If the search and retrieval has to be interrupted and continued at a later time, it cannot simply be picked up at the same point. Search engines don't work that way. The same keywords and phrases have to be reentered and the search started all over again. Useful information is later stored and organized in a way that makes it accessible when needed, perhaps as separate documents or cut and pasted into a master document. Before the Internet, this phase of the process was called "building a research set," and was accomplished by collecting a pile of clippings, papers, and reports.

The second phase, analysis and discovery, begins after the information has been collected and saved. The collected materials are explored by opening documents and reading them to find out what's been discovered. Knowledge is gained by making connections between the discrete items of information, mentally linking the pieces of information that will speak to a conclusion. Typically, this is an iterative process of discovering and analyzing, and potentially, stepping back to add new information to the research set.

After searching, collecting, discovering, and analyzing all the information, conclusions are shared with others in some form of research summary. Typically, some very exact impacting statements, key statistics, and charts and graphs are extracted from the source materials and placed into the report. The report contains not only facts and figures, or explicit knowledge, but also the methodology and thought processes employed to reach the conclusion. This tacit knowledge is the value the individual brings to the research process.

This last phase of the process can be quite tedious and time consuming, because much of the background information needed to support statements and conclusions exists in a format that cannot simply be imported into the report. These nuggets of information have been extracted from a variety of sources and must be recreated into a form suitable for inclusion in the final report.

THE PROBLEM WITH POINT SOLUTIONS

A number of technologies are being used today to aid people performing Internet-based research. From search engines and push technology, to market research sites, information aggregators, and desktop software, many point solutions are available to address specific, individual parts of the research process.

These technologies were never designed to work together as a system to facilitate the entire Internet-based research process. None of them enable information to be stored and viewed over time or collected as sets. Even if it were possible to combine these existing point solutions, they would not provide a way to capture the methodologies — the thought process that determines what information to look for and how to use it.

Search engines are a valuable technology, providing access to vast amounts of information. But search engines cast too broad a net, often returning excessive information in no particular order. Users must waste time rejecting junk in order to organize data. What's more, the quality of the information returned is often disappointing because the searches cannot be tailored to the more focused and narrow, but much deeper, needs of researchers in specific industries.

Today's search engines are similar to the Yellow Pages. They cover a broad spectrum of information on a wide variety of topics, but lack the precision and depth required for specific information. Auto parts dealers, for example, do not use the Yellow Pages to locate parts for customers. Instead, they use a special, vertical directory of auto parts manufacturers.

Push technologies try to deal with the limitations of search engines by profiling a user's information needs, watching for that information, and then delivering it to the user automatically. But as attractive as push technology was when first introduced, it is no better than passively watching television for conducting research.

While search and push technologies bring information to people, market research sites and information aggregator sites collect huge databases of information and act as clearinghouses. They provide useful indexes and some organization of the information, but they are essentially large databases, with no automated collection and fairly static information.

A needle and thread may be useful for sewing on a single button or mending one hole. But a professional tailor requires the speed and accuracy of a sewing machine to make enough suits every day to support a business. Similarly, search engines and other technologies may do a good job for the masses, but they require too much time and are too cumbersome to be useful for performing mission-critical Internet-based research on a daily basis.

THE SYSTEMS APPROACH TO INTERNET RESEARCH

Professional researchers — those who approach Internet research with clear objectives, who collect information, analyze it, and communicate it to others — require an integrated, systems-based approach to research that facilitates the entire research process. They need a system that automates many of the repetitive and time-consuming tasks while providing a framework to help organize, manage, and communicate the collected information. To be truly useful, such a research system should be targeted to the special needs of the individual practitioner working within a particular vertical industry.

While many point technologies play a role in aiding the research process, current implementations outside the context of a system are not sufficient for the next-generation Internet research product. A database is a highly useful technology, but it is not an accounting system. Similarly, a search engine is a highly useful technology, but it is not an Internet research system. Only a systems approach is able to address all phases of the research process within the context of the overriding objectives, the practitioner who is setting the objectives, and the industry within which the practitioner works. Such a system should provide:

- An industry/practitioner-specific information map or catalog to guide searching and collecting information
- An object store to manage information and let it be viewed over time
- Conversion capabilities for extracting and publishing information
- A containment model for capturing and articulating methodologies

The sheer volume of information that makes the Internet so attractive also hampers research because there exists no map or catalog of this information to help guide people in their search. Therefore, the next-generation Internet research system must provide a highly qualified catalog of sources for collecting information that is relevant to the research objectives. The best catalogs must be narrow in scope yet deep in detail, focusing on thorough classification of specific industries. To be truly useful, a catalog should include technology for both classifying and collecting the information. The catalog should consider not only the industry (high-tech, finance, biotech, etc.), but also the genre of practitioner doing the research (marketing researcher, financial broker, public relations account exec.) because two people within the same industry can have different information needs depending on their roles.

By displaying information sources that are highly relevant and qualified for this domain, the catalog streamlines the collection process by letting the researcher only zero in on useful information. The way in which the catalog sources are organized is also important, because this can greatly enhance the ability to discover new information while browsing the catalog. The system can then automate the actual collection process, allowing the researcher to skip this tedious task.

To help quickly determine which items of the collected information might be useful during the discovery and analysis phase, an Internet research system should provide the facility to store information about the information, or metadata. Metadata describe various aspects of the content and allows a detailed structured analysis to be performed. Like electronic Post-It notes, the metadata makes it easier to catalog and retrieve the unstructured information. Using metadata, reports can be created to determine, for example, how many documents in a collection were written by a particular author or what events occurred on a particular date.

Some Internet sites already add metadata to the information they publish, including, for example, the type of article (such as a product review) as well as identifiers for the product, the company, and the author. Even this minimal level of metadata provides very useful information.

Both the catalog and metadata should be able to be customized by the user to reflect individual needs. This makes it possible for a user to organize the catalog information in such a way that others using the catalog can achieve the same insight. The metadata also makes possible another byproduct — information appreciation. Just as data mining can provide insight for structured information, knowledge mining can provide insight for unstructured information enhanced with metadata. Over time, as users collect information that is highly relevant to their business and save it in the system's object store, the ability to mine this information to gain additional insights will be a tremendous information asset.

As yet, no point solution exists for performing this kind of trend analysis on unstructured information. Today's point solutions use information once and then discard it. They provide no means for storing information over time, thus precluding useful trend analysis.

In order to make the extracted information usable for analysis and to facilitate sharing and communication, format conversions are required to move the information from its published state to one compatible with whatever output application is being employed (i.e., a word processor). This is essentially a manual process that mostly entails re-creating the information in another application.

Finally, the ability to customize a system and make it work the way the individual wants it to is extremely important. A research system needs a way to tune the constituent technologies to solve very specific problems. It is not possible simply to take a search engine, a database, a word processor, format converters, and other utilities and integrate them through APIs and such, and have a useful research system. Business logic for each specific industry and practitioner must drive the operation of the entire system. Business logic is what turns a general purpose, horizontal tool into a precision instrument designed for a specific research domain. It converts the generic research process into one especially designed to collect, discover, and share information for a specific vertical niche.

Internet-based research is now being performed frequently enough to consider competitive analysis a mission-critical business process, one that will be extremely important for achieving a competitive advantage in the next millennium. The time and money spent on Internet-based research can be greatly reduced by automation accomplished through a systems approach that supports all phases of the research process — from knowledge acquisition and discovery to sharing both explicit and tacit knowledge — and one which provides the ability to discern trends before it's too late.

Author's Bio

Willie Tejada is the vice president of marketing for Aeneid Corporation. Tejada has an extensive background in networking and collaboration, bringing to Aeneid his ex-

perience in the roots of knowledge management. In management positions at Novell, he contributed to the explosive growth of the local area networking (LAN) market, the precursor to today's Internet. He then brought his understanding and experience of LANs to Novell's groupware efforts, where he served as vice president of marketing for the groupware division. Prior to cofounding Aeneid, Tejada held the position of vice president of product marketing for NetManage.

Chapter 5
Traveling on the Information Superhighway

Jessica Keyes

BEFORE THE "INFORMATION HIGHWAY" BECAME SYNONYMOUS with the brave new world of video-on-demand, high-powered multimedia, and 24-hour home shopping, it was a road well traveled by those needing an efficient and productive way to keep on top of their business.

For corporate employees and their organizations, the information highway, or information services as it was known pre-Al Gore, offers a wealth of information that will help you do your job faster, better, and smarter. And in spite of all the hubbub about it, it has been easily accessible for more than a decade.

The difference is that today it's no secret anymore. While not everyone knows how to get to it, everyone at least knows it's out there. Most organizations are quickly realizing that they simply don't have a choice any longer. Not hitching a ride on the information highway (IH) is becoming a distinct competitive disadvantage.

The IH is really a misnomer (at least for now). Look at a map of the U.S. and you'll see what I mean. While there are some major arteries crisscrossing the country, the map is really a spider's web of roads all connected together to enable you to go from any one point in the U.S. to any other point in the U.S. It's the same with the IH. Really a collection of interconnected networks, understanding how to navigate it enables you to get from any one point in the IH to any other point in the IH.

While the IH probably has more information nuggets tucked into its collective servers than the New York Public Library, for some strange reason it's e-mail that seems to have captured everyone's attention. The ability to communicate with millions of people across thousands of computers across seven continents is no mean feat. It's also a productivity booster.

0-8493-9987-4/00/$0.00+$.50
© 2000 by CRC Press LLC

Of course, the IH is far more than e-mail. It's also a series of databases and bulletin boards. Both provide sources of information that are worth looking into. Bulletin boards are exactly what they sound like, places to post information. Public forums are open to anyone who has a urge to take a look-see. For example, many of the software companies have bulletin boards that enable users to file trouble reports and/or download "fixes" for those troubles.

The most interesting of bulletin boards are those that are maintained by the various special interest groups that have sprung up on the IH. Sometimes referred to as forums, these are veritable goldmines of camaraderie and information. For example, CompuServe has a legal forum where I've been able to get assistance that would have cost me thousands of dollars if I had spoken to a nondigitized attorney.

CompuServe's finance forums are similarly well endowed. The Investors Forum's libraries, for example, include such esoteric items of interest as stocks/bonds, fixed income, option trading, futures, commodities, newsletters, theories, charting, and technical analysis.

There's also all that shareware. CompuServers are a "sharing" lot so there's quite a bit of "free" software. Shareware is, for all intents and purposes, free, however, you are often asked to make a donation of a rather nominal sum for the care and feeding of the developer of the program you are using. Payment is optional, but always appreciated. If you were to access the charting and technical analysis library of the aforementioned Investors Forum, you could download QCharter 1.3, which is a shareware program for historical quote charting. Similarly, you could download useful ratios, macros, and text files such as an index of the SEC's EDGAR database.

While shareware software and databases dominate the forums, the database research services of the IH are the real prize here. Knowledge-Index (KI), the night-owl version of Dialog's very expensive professional research database service, is a veritable goldmine of financial information. For a paltry $16/hour (after 6 p.m. and all weekend), you get access to dozens of databases including: *Books in Print, Business Dateline, BusinessWire, Pr NewsWire, Harvard Business Review,* practically all of the computer news and business publications (including *Pravda*), as well as *Standard & Poor's Daily News* and *Corporate Descriptions*.

If you recall our earlier discussion comparing the IH to a network of interconnected roads, you'll begin to understand how it works in relation to the services on CompuServe. When you sign on to CompuServe you log on to CompuServe's computers, but when you request access to KI, CompuServe actually passes your request across a bridge to Dialog's own computer — hence the accurate analogy of a series of connecting roadways.

CompuServe offers numerous other financially oriented services (i.e., bridges). Basic Quotes provides delayed quotes for items such as stocks, options, indexes, exchange rates and mutual funds. Citibank's Global Report, which happens to be the primary information resource for many large corporations, integrates and organizes news and financial data including real-time foreign exchange rates, spot commodity prices, and industry news. Commodity Markets and Pricing offers exactly what its title says it offers.

Company Analyzer provides public company information including income statement, balance sheet, and ownership information from Disclosure (which is also available) and an S&P estimate on future earnings. All you need is the company name, ticker symbol, or CUSIP number.

It wouldn't be feasible to describe the myriad other services offered on CompuServe. They run the gamut from D&B's Business Directory to FundWatch Online to Thomas Register Online to TRW Business Profiles to Investext, which is a full-text online version of all the research reports done in the last 2 years.

America Online, which bought CompuServe not so long ago, as well as some of the smaller networks, offer commensurate services. Most organizations will benefit from enabling their employees to use these services for research purposes. But the organizations will also benefit from using CompuServe and America Online for their marketing endeavors as well. Companies such as D&B and Thomas Register Online are profiting handsomely by making their information available (sometimes for a fee) to the millions of subscribers to these proprietary services.

For the most part, systems development in this venue is surprisingly easy and affordable. For example, CompuServe provides free access to an online area where the organization can develop its service as well as access documentation for software with which to build the service. The developing organization is merely responsible for the time and labor necessary for creating, maintaining, and promoting its database, including transmitting and reformatting the product during the developmental stages.

CompuServe and other proprietary service providers (e.g., America Online) approaches all information provider relationships as a partnership. They provide sufficient training, documentation, connect time, and disk storage for product development at no cost. They also provide the full support of their marketing and technical staff to assist in the development of the organization's product to its full potential.

Be forewarned, however. America Online is beginning to view the partnership in a more profit-making way. Where they once paid companies to "display their wares" on the service, America Online is now looking to charge hefty fees for the "privilege" of their captive audience. (Well, no one said that marketing came cheap!)

Interestingly, programming knowledge is not necessary, though it is helpful to be familiar with videotext services and menu-driven formats. The actual format for the product will depend upon the nature of the information. For example, CompuServe makes available, at their cost, several programs to facilitate the service's delivery:

- *Menu-Driven Display:* This program can be likened to an electronic magazine, whereby menus serve as the "table of contents" and lead the user to articles of information. This works well for concise factual information.
- *Keyword Search:* This program enables the developer to assign keywords to each entry and allows the user to enter the word(s) he or she wants to find. It is particularly appropriate for dictionaries, access to information by state, date, or special interest, and other reference material.
- *Gateway Arrangement:* This is where information resides on the organization's host computer and the user is "transferred" to the host computer to access the information. This is particularly appropriate for information that requires immediate responses or minute-to-minute updating, such as stock prices.
- *Wire Service:* This CompuServe program gathers a continuous stream of information and makes the information available to users as soon as it is received. Information is dynamically added to menus in reverse chronological order. This continuous updating is typically used for news wires which require timely processing of large amounts of data.

Developers can transmit information to CompuServe by various means. With a terminal and a modem they can dial CompuServe's network and directly type the information into a CompuServe database using a CompuServe word processing program. Other means available are uploading and submission of diskettes and tapes to CompuServe's computer center.

A host of savvy organizations have been using these information superhighway service providers for years for definite competitive advantage. But with the thousands of articles and growing interest in the Web, most of these organizations have begun to port their wares to the Internet as well. But what they're finding is that the Internet is as different from the proprietary service providers as night is from day, from a development perspective.

Where CompuServe and its competitors work as partners to help the organization deploy its service — going as far as providing access time and disk space — development on the Internet means going it alone. As you'll see in the rest of this chapter, there are many choices as well as issues that need to be grappled with if the organization is to use the Internet success-fully.

USING THE INTERNET

A commonly asked question is "What is the Internet?". The reason such a question gets asked so often is because there's no agreed-upon answer that neatly sums up the Internet. The Internet can be thought about in re-lation to its common protocols, as a physical collection of routers and cir-cuits, as a set of shared resources, or even as an attitude about interconnecting and intercommunication. Some common definitions given in the past include:

- A network of networks based on the TCP/IP protocols
- A community of people who use and develop those networks
- A collection of resources that can be reached from those networks

Today's Internet is a global resource connecting millions of users that began as an experiment over 20 years ago by the U.S. Department of De-fense. While the networks that make up the Internet are based on a stan-dard set of protocols (a mutually agreed upon method of communication between parties), the Internet also has gateways to networks and services that are based on other protocols.

In many ways the Internet is like a church: it has its council of elders, every member has an opinion about how things should work, and you can either take part or not. It's your choice. The Internet has no presi-dent, chief operating officer, or pope. The constituent networks may have presidents and CEOs, but that's a different issue; there's no single authority figure for the Internet as a whole.

The ultimate authority for where the Internet is going rests with the In-ternet Society, or ISOC. ISOC is a voluntary membership organization whose purpose is to promote global information exchange through Inter-net technology.

The council of elders is a group of invited volunteers called the Internet Architecture Board, or the IAB. The IAB meets regularly to "bless" stan-dards and allocate resources, like addresses. The Internet works because there are standard ways for computers and software applications to talk to each other. This allows computers from different vendors to communicate without problems. It's not an IBM-only or Sun-only or Macintosh-only net-work. The IAB is responsible for these standards; it decides when a stan-dard is necessary and what the standard should be. When a standard is required, it considers the problem, adopts a standard, and announces it via the network.

No one pays for the Internet. Instead, everyone pays for their part. The National Science Foundation pays for NSFNET. NASA pays for the NASA Science Internet. Networks get together and decide how to connect themselves together and fund these interconnections. A college or corporation pays for their connection to some regional network, which in turn pays a national provider for its access. What makes the Internet even more tenuous is that originally the government, in the form of NSFNET, had at least some supervisory authority since the Internet was really created at their behest. This is no longer true since during 1998 NSFNET withdrew from its customary administrative role, leaving all of us to sink or swim on our own.

Interestingly, many large corporations have been on the Internet for years. Until now, their participation has been limited to their research and engineering departments. Businesses are just now discovering that the Internet can provide many advantages to their bottom line:

- Providing information to end users is less expensive than with the proprietary networks such as CompuServe, which normally charge a royalty on profits made.
- There are many more users of the Internet than on all the proprietary networks combined. At last count there were between 20 million and 50 million users of the Internet (depending on who's doing the counting) compared to less than 10 million on proprietary networks.
- Advances in technology have provided the ability to build visual storefronts which include liberal use of images and even video and sound. This is made possible through deployment of the Netscape and Internet Explorer graphical user interfaces and use of the Hypertext Markup Language (HTML) which has quickly become an Internet standard.

Perusing the Glossary at the end of this chapter demonstrates the great variety of capabilities that the Internet provides organizations looking to it to provide information. Although interfaces currently dominate the press, the readers should be aware that the Internet was successfully disseminating information long before HTML was ever developed.

Essentially the Internet is being used by organizations in five venues:

1. *E-mail*: Organizations are making good use of e-mail to correspond to clients and staff members. Updates and notices can be inexpensively and quickly routed to all four corners of the world.
2. *FTP:* One of the oldest of the Internet technologies, File Transfer Protocol enables organizations to provide databases of files (i.e., text files or programs) that others may download to their personal computers.
3. *Gopher.* A distributed information service that makes available hierarchical collections of information across the Internet. It uses a simple protocol that allows a single Gopher client to access information

from any accessible Gopher server, providing the user with a single "Gopher space" of information. Public domain versions of the client and server are available.

4. *Telnet*: This technology enables those outside of the organization to remotely log into a host computer as a guest to access information that resides on that host.

5. *World Wide Web*: The newest of Internet technologies; when used in conjunction with the Netscape Navigator or Internet Explorer graphical interfaces, it provides the ability to store hypertext and images for use by current and future customers.

Organizations are using all of these technologies to take advantage of what is, for now at least, a practically free worldwide network.

USING FTP AND E-MAIL FOR SUPPORT

Network Software Associates (NSA) is a consulting firm that supports the government and industry. With offices on the West and East Coasts, NSA needed to find a way to better support their customer base. For NSA, the solution turned out to be the Internet.

NSA found that a large percentage of customer support traffic comes from the user requesting help in locating information or help in performing a certain function. The other important task in customer support was in providing timely software updates and fixes. If the request is not time-critical, the user can be trained to e-mail a request for help to the customer service group or, alternatively, to other users. This second option is a form of e-mail known as Usenet.

Both the IS organization and the user community can greatly benefit from setting up Usenet discussion groups. In essence, Usenet is Internet e-mail with a twist: it is a mailing list to which users subscribe where a message is sent not to one individual, but to the entire mailing list of individuals.

Starting a Usenet

NSA is one of many who have opted to start its own Usenet group on the Internet. Although an organization doesn't require permission to start a discussion group, it does require some special intelligence and some computer resources.

In the tradition of the Internet, the software to manage the Usenet mailing list is provided on the Internet itself. The software, known as Listserv, can be downloaded free of charge using the Internet's File Transmission Protocol (FTP).

Usenet enables NSA customers to solve some of their own problems. Responding to questions and problems from the user community is only half of NSA's customer support problem, the other is providing fixes, patches, and software updates. NSA feels there is no reason to use sneakernet anymore when you can distribute software to users through the network. (Sneakernet is the network created by physically walking from location to location to deliver software to users.)

Using FTP

To accomplish this, NSA decided to implement an FTP (File Transfer Protocol) server. The support of NSA users is handled using FTP for file transfers. NSA places the files in a common access location and then sends users an e-mail to inform them of the latest release, thereby giving them the option to obtain it or not.

According to NSA, becoming an FTP server is not as straightforward as it would be if one were dealing with a centralized organization complete with tech support personnel. Connecting to the net is no easy task and requires developing a careful plan (see below). NSA didn't, and as a result suffered from it. For example, NSA did not accurately predict the high level of customer usage of its Internet-based services. As a result, they had to increase capacity by installing a higher-speed line.

That this was so difficult a task is the result of the Internet relying on physical numerical addresses called IP addresses. IP, or Internet Protocol, is the network layer for the TCP/IP Protocol Suite. It is a connectionless, best-effort packet-switching protocol. For example, a server that we know as ns.uu.net has a physical address of 137.39.1.3. Since getting a higher-speed line also requires a new address, there is a big conversion effort that must be undertaken to change the mapping between logical and physical addresses.

FTP IMPLEMENTATION ISSUES

There are a plethora of implementation issues that the NSA had to consider when opting to create an FTP server.

Hardware

The first decision was to consider the type of hardware to be used as the FTP server. Most organizations opt for high-powered, UNIX-based workstations since they understand that the higher the number of users the more powerful the machine must be.

NSA opted for a Sparcstation and the UNIX operating system since the number of users was large. However, most companies starting out can get by with a 486-based IBM PC-compatible.

Software

UNIX is the operating system of choice for most servers since most of the software running on the net (i.e., FTP itself) is UNIX based. In addition, of all the server-based operating systems, UNIX is the most robust in the client/server arena.

In addition to the operating system, the organization must also ensure that Telnet and FTP software is available on that server. While Telnet is your basic remote telecommunications software readily available from a variety of sources, FTP comes in a couple of flavors. The traditional flavor of FTP is simply a series of UNIX commands. This can be confusing to non-UNIX users. Vendors have recently come out with a more graphical form of FTP, but there is a high financial cost associated with it. So instead, NSA decided that, although difficult to use, a bit of training and support would go a long way towards alleviating the problem of dealing with the UNIX shell.

Phone Line

The organization must order, install, and test the circuit or phone line that is connected to the server. Before this can be accomplished, however, a model of the expected usage of the Internet must be developed to accurately determine line capacity. Model variables include number of users, number and type of services being used, and amount of data being uploaded and downloaded.

NSA uses a dedicated connection to hook its FTP server to the Internet. This requires a dedicated point-to-point telecommunications circuit and an IP router, which is a dedicated networking device, linking the organization to the Internet. Line speeds usually range from 9.6 kb to 45 Mb, with the most common connection speeds being 56 kb and 1.54 Mb. NSA ultimately required a 65-kb line to assure good response time for its users.

An alternative is to use a dial-up connection. This method uses a regular phone line and a workstation. When a network connection is needed, the workstation is used to establish a connection over the modem and phone line. At the end of use, the connection is broken. Line speeds range from 9.6 to 56 kb, with lower speeds being the most common. Obviously slower than a dedicated connection, this solution is used by organizations with fewer users dialing into the network. The trade-off here is increased response time vs. lower costs.

Costs

Depending upon the number of users and the hardware configuration, the cost of implementing an FTP server ranges from $1000 to $5000 per month, with a one-time hardware and phone line installation cost averaging $13,000.

What you will wind up paying is really dependent upon the number of servers you use, the number of customers you have, what they're doing, the amount of time they spend on the net, the type of software you're running, and the speed of your line.

INTERNET SECURITY CONSIDERATIONS

Ten of the largest securities firms — including Scudder, Salomon, and Goldman Sachs & Co. — have joined together to establish the Financial Information Exchange or FIX for short. FIX is a common protocol for sending and receiving equity trading information including orders, execution details, fill reports, and account allocations.

With the goal of eliminating the proliferation of proprietary order routing systems, one standard industry protocol means that brokers will be able to reach multiple clients while buy-side traders can reach multiple brokers.

The most intriguing aspect of FIX is that the protocol, to enable open communication between firms, has been written to allow messages — including equity trade orders — to be sent over the Internet. Wary of Internet hackers, those participating in FIX over the Internet have deployed stringent security measures including data encryption as well as strong firewalls.

The Internet poses a particularly high level of security risk. Few need to be reminded of the case of Cornell University graduate student Robert Morris, Jr., who programmed an Internet worm that single-handedly brought down 6000 machines. In November 1991, the U.S. General Accounting Office reported that computer hackers from the Netherlands broke into military computers. More recently, a group of students known by the name The Posse have been taking down systems just for the thrill of it.

Setting security policies and procedures really means developing a plan for dealing with computer security. A procedure for creating a security plan includes the following steps:

- Look at what you are trying to protect
- Look at what you need to protect it from
- Determine how likely the threats are
- Implement measures which will protect your assets in a cost-effective manner
- Review the process continuously, and improve things every time a weakness is found

Most organizations utilize several methods to ensure security.

Passwords

Many organizations are lax in enforcing password assignment and maintenance for users of their mainframes and other in-house servers. Shadow passwords, which means that no public password files are available for the casual browser, is the preferred method.

Of course, all of this is worth nothing if security isn't an intrinsic part of the corporate mindset. Security begins with the individual. There has been more than one instance of employees giving out Internet IDs and passwords to friends — incidents usually immediately followed by a few break-in attempts.

Data Encryption

Encryption is perhaps the most popular method of security for financial firms using the Internet. But it comes with its own set of problems.

Other than a lack of standards in the industry, there remains the problem that people need to have some way of decrypting the message. If the messaging is done internally (i.e., over the organization's own network), or between two or more cooperating organizations (e.g., securities firms transmitting buy and sell information between each others' computers), then a private encryption key can be used. But if you're messaging on the Internet and a customer needs to transmit private financial information, a public key needs to be sent along with the message. The problem is that this public key needs to be decrypted at the receiving end of the message.

Firewalls

The hardware and software that sits between the computer operation and the Internet is colloquially known as a firewall. Its specific mission is to examine Internet traffic and allow only approved data to pass through.

One type of firewall is a software-driven filter in the network connection. An organization may have 60 machines handling Internet e-mail, however the use of a software filter makes it appear to the outside world that they only have one. It is also a good idea to strip the organization's host address. In this way it is possible to lock out those who would attempt to get into a system through e-mail.

A second approach to building a firewall is to use computers as routers or gateways. The main thrust of this solution is to route all Internet traffic through what is sometimes referred to as a bastion (bastion meaning a wall, as in a wall between the main computer and the Internet) host. Essentially, this technique is simple. The bastion host is a server which is connected both to the Internet and the organization's main computer installation. Only users and/or information with the proper security clearance is routed through the bastion host to the organization's computers.

CONCLUSION

The information superhighway is an amalgam of services including e-mail, proprietary networks such as America Online, file transfer protocols, and, of course, the Web itself.

Savvy organizations are taking a long hard look at all of these services and determining which are the most profitable for them.

Author's Bio

Jessica Keyes is president of New Art Technologies, Inc., a high-technology software development firm. Keyes has given seminars for such prestigious universities as Carnegie Mellon, Boston University, University of Illinois, James Madison University, and San Francisco State University. She is a frequent keynote speaker on the topics of competitive strategy using information technology and marketing on the information superhighway. She is an advisor for DataPro, McGraw-Hill's computer research arm, as well as a member of the Sprint Business Council. Keyes is also a founding Board of Director member of the New York Software Industry Association. She has recently completed a 2-year term on the Mayor of New York City's Small Business Advisory Council.

Prior to founding her company, Keyes was managing director of R&D for the New York Stock Exchange and has been an officer with Swiss Bank Co. and Banker's Trust, both in New York City. She holds a Master's from New York University, where she did her research in the area of artificial intelligence.

A noted columnist and correspondent, with over 150 articles published, Keyes is the author of 12 books.

INTERNET USERS' GLOSSARY

address — There are three types of addresses in common use within the Internet: e-mail address; IP, intranet, or Internet address; and hardware or MAC address.

anonymous FTP — Anonymous FTP allows a user to retrieve documents, files, programs, and other archived data from anywhere in the Internet without having to establish a user ID and password. By using the special user ID of "anonymous" the network user will bypass local security checks and will have access to publicly accessible files on the remote system.

archie — A system to automatically gather, index, and serve information on the Internet. The initial implementation of archie provided an indexed directory of filenames from all anonymous FTP archives on the Internet.

archive site — A machine that provides access to a collection of files across the Internet. An "anonymous FTP archive site," for example, provides access to this material via the FTP protocol.

Cyberspace — A term coined by William Gibson in his fantasy novel *Neuromancer* to describe the "world" of computers, and the society that gathers around them.

Dial-up — A temporary, as opposed to dedicated, connection between machines established over a standard phone line.

Electronic Mail (e-mail) — A system whereby a computer user can exchange messages with other computer users (or groups of users) via a communications network.

e-mail address — The domain-based or UUCP address that is used to send electronic mail to a specified destination.

encryption — The manipulation of a packet's data in order to prevent any but the intended recipient from reading that data. There are many types of data encryption and they are the basis of network security.

File Transfer Protocol (FTP) — A protocol that allows a user on one host to access and transfer files to and from another host over a network. Also, FTP is usually the name of the program the user invokes to execute the protocol.

Gopher — A distributed information service that makes available hierarchical collections of information across the Internet. Gopher uses a simple protocol that allows a single Gopher client to access information from any accessible Gopher server, providing the user with a single "Gopher space" of information.

57

internet — While an internet is a network, the term "internet" is usually used to refer to a collection of networks interconnected with routers.

Internet — (note the capital "I") The Internet is the largest internet in the world. Is a three-level hierarchy composed of backbone networks (e.g., NSFNET, MILNET), mid-level networks, and stub networks. The Internet is a multiprotocol internet.

Internet Relay Chat (IRC) — A worldwide "party line" protocol that allows one to converse with others in real time.

Internet Society (ISOC) — The Internet Society is a nonprofit, professional membership organization which facilitates and supports the technical evolution of the Internet; stimulates interest in and educates the scientific and academic communities, industry, and the public about the technology, uses, and applications of the Internet; and promotes the development of new applications for the system. The Society provides a forum for discussion and collaboration in the operation and use of the global Internet infrastructure. The Internet Society publishes a quarterly newsletter, the *Internet Society News,* and holds an annual conference, INET.

Point-to-Point Protocol (PPP) — The Point-to-Point Protocol provides a method for transmitting packets over serial point-to-point links.

Serial Line IP (SLIP) — A protocol used to run IP over serial lines, such as telephone circuits or RS-232 cables, interconnecting two systems.

Telnet — Telnet is the Internet standard protocol for remote terminal connection service.

Wide Area Information Servers (WAIS) — A distributed information service which offers simple natural language input, indexed searching for fast retrieval, and a "relevance feedback" mechanism which allows the results of initial searches to influence future searches.

World Wide Web (WWW or W3) — A hypertext-based, distributed information system created by researchers at CERN in Switzerland. Users may create, edit, or browse hypertext documents.

Section II
Strategic Issues in Internet Management

THE INTERNET IS MOST DEFINITELY A STRATEGIC RESOURCE. But it's a strategic resource that we, as traditional IT managers, have to learn how to leverage. There are probably very few substantial organizations in the world who are not on the Internet. Whether it's used for e-mail, information gathering, marketing, or E-commerce, the Web is today's premier corporate strategy.

But the Internet is a chameleon. And if you're don't use it strategically, its benefits will be all but invisible. This section provides some critical insight into how to use the Internet strategically: from ensuring that Internet access actually means business access, to using the Internet to improve competitive position and costs. From the politics of content, to how to develop an architecture that facilitates the sharing of knowledge, to how to do this all legally, this section adds some grist to the sometimes abstract nature of the Net.

Chapter 6

Return on Internet Investment: Measuring the Success of Online Business Solutions

John Seasholtz

CORPORATIONS BUILDING ONLINE BUSINESS SOLUTIONS are beginning to recognize the value of measuring Return on Internet Investment (ROI2)[1] early. Determining methods to measure ROI2 needs to be one of the first major steps in the up-front planning process, and continually evaluated and applied throughout the entire project life cycle. ROI2 provides a foundation for corporations to determine the success of their online business solution and develop future plans to bring the project to the next level.

This chapter examines return on investment and how it has traditionally been applied to measure business initiatives. It will explain how ROI2 applies to every online business solution or Web project (Internet, intranet, and/or extranet sites). In general, this chapter will

- Bring greater clarity to ROI2
- Help companies define their goals so they can anticipate ROI2 for their Websites
- Present ideas and concepts about how to measure ROI2, with a special emphasis on measuring indirect returns

By considering these issues at the very onset of the project, companies will have a greater understanding of how their online business solution has met their objectives. Plans to measure ROI2 will be different for every corporation, and companies should include only the measures that make

0-8493-9987-4/00/$0.00+$.50
© 2000 by CRC Press LLC

sense. This chapter proposes a framework that companies can use to help determine what to expect from their investment in a Web site.

TRADITIONAL RETURN ON INVESTMENT

No matter what the situation, individuals and businesses alike ask a series of questions to help them figure out what return on investment to expect. At its simplest level, use these four questions as a framework for thinking about rate of return:

- What is my goal?
- What situations or events will I use to know that I've met my goal?
- How many of these situations or events will show me I've met my goal?
- How will I measure/count these situations or events?

Obviously, there isn't just one set of answers to these questions. Each goal might have more than one kind of situation or event that can assess how well the goal has been met.

Return on Internet Investment (ROI2) should be considered in the same manner. Some returns a company may look for are direct; some are indirect. A direct return, for example, might be the dollars a company makes as a result of selling products via their Website. An indirect return might be retaining customers because they find it easier to order products from the Website than to try to reach the company's sales people by phone. The recipe for determining ROI2 is different for every company.

RETURN IN INTERNET INVESTMENT (ROI2)

There is no cookie-cutter formula for ROI2 and it is different for every company. It should be stressed that ROI2 is the end result of an effective Web strategy. The Web strategy should support corporate objectives and should have a clear plan for measuring its effectiveness. Identifying planned benefits and a means to measure them is a critical first step to measuring ROI2.

ROI2 should be seen as a compilation of both direct and indirect returns. Direct returns can be measured and linked to a Web solution. Indirect returns are "softer" and are realized over a longer period of time.

Direct Returns

In its purest form, direct ROI2 can be expressed as the incremental dollar benefits resulting from a Web solution divided by the Web investment. Optimally, the return is greater than the company's cost of borrowing and/or greater than returns that could be earned on other business opportunities.

$$ROI2 = (\text{Incremental Dollar Benefits/Web Investment}) - 1$$

Incremental dollar benefits can be split into revenue enhancement benefits and expense and capital reduction benefits.

$$\text{Incremental Dollar Benefits} = \text{Incremental Increases in Revenue} + \text{Reduction in Expenses}$$

Direct Revenue Benefits. Businesses can develop an online store or catalogue where customers can actually browse products and product literature, download demos, as well as purchase items without having to pick up the phone or go to a store. Selling via the Web reduces overall cost, turnaround time, and the ability to update. Selling over the Web is often referred to as E-eommerce.

E-commerce Web solutions usually provide the most obvious revenue benefits. These solutions build marketing and selling capabilities into a Website. Incremental revenues are those sales that would not normally have taken place if the Web solution had not been implemented.

E-commerce allows online marketers to personalize Websites to individual customers. This practice is often referred to as one-to-one marketing and it helps facilitate a sense of community for surfers. These Websites may pull information from other sites that is of particular interest to a customer. Chat rooms are another means of building a community as surfers can chat online with others that share similar interests.

As surfers register to obtain membership for Websites, request a demo download, or when they purchase a product, information is gathered. This information can be used by online marketers to further refine their target markets and thus implement more effective online or offline marketing campaigns.

Other revenue benefits can result from more efficient sales lead processing, increased purchase frequency, and average order size. The Web makes purchasing easier and more repeatable. Therefore, purchase frequency may rise as a result of Web selling.

For example, 1-800-FLOWERS allows visitors to their Website to view and choose a flower arrangement online, add the item to a shopping cart that stores all of the items chosen, fill out a form online for billing and shipping information, and process the request. So, if a visitor buys a flower arrangement for $29.95, a direct ROI2 is the $29.95 minus the costs of arranging and delivering the flowers. Traditionally, 1-800-FLOWERS would have had the extra costs of paying a customer services representative to take the call and process all of the information manually. Additionally, 1-800-FLOWERS also saved costs in that they did not have to pay for printing and shipping a catalog — the visitor was able to view the flower arrangements online.

Expense Reduction Benefits. Another way to measure a direct ROI2 is to calculate how the Web site has reduced corporate expenses. For instance, the costs for paper, printing, postage, software distribution, mailing, order processing, documentation, corporate licensing, etc. will all be significantly less if information and documentation can be accessed online.

Business processes that utilize large quantities of paper and time, such as procurement or the order and delivery process for supplies, can be made more efficient and cost effective. Traditional procurement systems entail having an employee search for and find the supply they need, fill out the paperwork for a supply, send the paperwork through an approval process, wait for a check to be cut and sent, and then wait for the supply to be shipped and delivered.

Purchasing over the Web also enables companies to streamline the fulfillment process by implementing electronic catalogs that provide pricing, availability, shipping, configuration, and detailed product information online. This reduces the time from order to delivery, making the process more efficient, and reducing administrative costs.

Using the Web, companies can also open new lines of distribution for ordering products, checking order status, receiving advice, and obtaining shipping and/or billing information by developing an extranet for their distributors and partners. Doing these activities via the Web reduces the need for printed manuals, lessens the overhead costs needed to maintain a customer service representative answering phone calls, and makes information that is in the corporate database immediately accessible online as opposed to having a representative search for it.

For example, Sun Microsystems was able to measure a direct ROI2 by calculating the amount of money they saved by publishing online their 700-page catalog of books on Sun and Sun-related technologies. The cost of the Website at $5000 was much less expensive than the printing and distribution of a 700-page paper catalog. In addition, the number of accesses of the Web book catalog increased by threefold during its first year.[2]

Overhead expenses for maintaining personnel dedicated to customer service, technical support, reception, administration, etc. can all be saved as a result of bringing business to the Web. Companies can also save money by downloading tools and products off the Internet, and sharing and reusing tools internally. For example, Swedish Medical Center, the largest and most comprehensive medical center in the Pacific Northwest, saves more than $6 in staff cost for each online referral to a physician, compared to a telephone referral. Online referrals are also bringing in more than $40,000 in new revenue each month. Calculating the overhead expenses saved, a direct monetary return allowed Swedish to measure their Return on Internet Investment (ROI2).

Online business solutions provide a wealth of information for customers, employees, and business partners. For example, the Web makes the distribution of marketing materials much more effective, saving both time and money. Leads are most often worked manually — a call comes in, the inside sales rep takes down the information, then enters it into the customer management database and sends a note to the field representative. The field representative then puts an information packet together, mails it, and follows up. Using the Web, the customer can obtain the exact information they require anytime of the day and from anywhere in the world. This not only satisfies the customer but saves the company printing and distribution costs.

Making processes easier and faster to execute saves everything from paper and printing costs to the overhead expenses for having a full-time staff member executing the process. For example, an inevitable part of running an effective business is making the delivery process for supplies more efficient. Traditional procurement systems entail having an employee search for and find the supply they need, fill out the paperwork for a supply, send the paperwork through an approval process, wait for a check to be cut and sent, and then wait for the supply to be shipped and delivered.

Reduced Capital Benefits. It is quite feasible that Web solutions will allow companies to significantly reduce capital expenditures in the future. Capital expenditures typically include plant and building equipment that are carried on a company's balance sheet.

Let's say that a company implements a global sales and marketing extranet from which customers can gather product information, negotiate prices, and receive training and customer service. Previously, this company may have used field offices to coordinate the selling process. These offices can now be significantly reduced or even eliminated, generating significant benefits through reduction in capital expenditures for buildings, land, vehicles, and computer equipment.

Elements of the Web Investment. Before direct ROI2 can be measured, the dollar value of the Web investment must be calculated. According to Forrester Research Inc., companies will spend approximately $300,000 for a purely promotional site and $3.4 million for a transactional site. Salaries for Webmasters and other dedicated personnel add to ongoing expenses. There are also costs associated with design and gathering content, which often take time from existing employees unless the company decides to outsource to consultants. Content collection can become expensive, especially on global sites where translation is necessary.

Measuring Direct Returns. A direct return is a return on investment that produces or saves dollars as a result of the investment. Direct sales and

Exhibit 6.1. Metrics and Goals

Web Benefit	Metric(s)	Goal
More efficient customer service	Cost per customer response	Reduce from $10 to $5 per response
Reduced time for sales cycle	Cost per customer acquisition	Reduce from $500 to $400 per customer acquisition
Increased sales	Website revenues	$500 Incremental sales per week
Employee empowerment of benefits management	Time required to access benefits data and cost per employee contact	Reduce time from 5 hours to 2 hours per month and costs of contact from $12 to $6 per employee contact

money saved in corporate costs and expenses can all be direct measurements of an online business solution. If a company pays $100,000 to build a Website and saves $20,000 per month in overhead for customer service representatives by having customer service and support online, the ROI2 for their site is approximately 140 percent for the year.

Businesses must identify the process metrics before the Website is implemented. A baseline must be established before the efficiency of the site can be measured. Some examples of metrics and goals are shown in Exhibit 6.1.

Indirect Returns

Many companies view Web investments as "costs of doing business" much like having an ad in the Yellow Pages or an 800 number to gather customer feedback. Some companies have adopted "balanced scorecards," as shown in Exhibit 6.2, that outline "softer" goals that will help them achieve their strategy. Financial measures only make up a portion of these goals, whereas the others are more indirect and harder to place dollar values on.

Typical indirect goals include customer loyalty, employee satisfaction, supplier relations, learning, and innovation. Shareholder value is measured using direct ROI2, although indirect benefits also affect shareholder value. It is beneficial for companies to put weights on these metrics and evaluate each Web solution to see where it will benefit. We have elaborated on customer retention and employee satisfaction below.

Customer Retention. Marketing initiatives can be tailored and personalized on the Web. Rather than treating all customers the same, online marketing enables companies to use the Web for one-to-one more personalized marketing. Each visitor is treated as a unique individual and will only view the information they care about vs. getting advertisements, brochures, products, and other materials that are created for the general public. Elec-

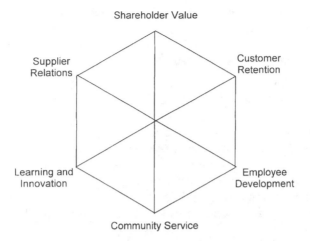

Exhibit 6.2. A hypothetical balanced scorecard.

tronic marketing enables companies to provide unique and tailored information at an efficient price.

Greater customer service is almost always a number one business priority, and the best example of an indirect return. Traditional measures taken to improve customer service include providing an 800 number for toll-free customer service calls, more customer service representatives to take telephone calls, and automated answering machines to help customers direct their own questions, complaints, and suggestions to the correct departments.

Online customer service has continued this progression of customer self service. By using the Web for customer service, companies empower customers to serve themselves at their own convenience. Not only can customers access general information online, but also online support centers, enabling the end user to log complaints, search for status on a problem, or look up solutions. This creates community by enabling customers to not only use, but also add to a shared knowledge base, facilitating exchange of information. The company benefits by limiting the number of customer support representatives needed and reducing the costs of training and documentation.

Employee Satisfaction. One important aspect of every business is effective internal communication and sharing of knowledge. Information on medical benefits, 401k plans, vacation, holidays, sick days, emergency contacts, etc. should be made readily available to every employee. Traditionally, this information is usually stored in pamphlet or brochure form with the human resources department. The pamphlets are often just general information. In order to find confidential information (for example, information on company stock options or specific medical coverage), it is often necessary for employees to ask a human resources representative to locate the material and then explain how it can apply to them.

Intranets offer employees quick and confidential access to the information they need. In addition to posting the general brochure information, companies can also post more company-specific information. An intranet allows businesses to gain more control over internal processes by providing faster, more accurate updates to contact information, detailed statements, and summaries, and is an efficient method for posting key corporate communications messages. It also streamlines project management efforts and sharing of resources. Web solutions can improve the quality, frequency, and clarity of communication throughout the company.

Training and recruitment are other areas where the Web offers benefits. National training programs can be rolled out simultaneously and feedback can be given through e-mail and chat rooms. Job openings are posted on Websites, which increases the reach of the company and makes the job search easier for prospective employees.

Another indirect benefit is improved learning and innovation. It is also one area where Web solutions can offer the greatest benefits. Collaborative working environments have become the norm and productivity increases as a result. Files can be sent and stored on Web applications, which enables employees to work together no matter the time or location. Enhanced communication that results from the ease of Web-based applications improves employee skills, develops new relationships, and provides a platform for solving complex problems.

Measuring Indirect Returns. It is much more difficult to obtain benchmarks to measure indirect benefits. For example, how will a company measure whether or not a new intranet is improving employee morale? There are metrics such as monitoring employee turnover that can track its effectiveness, as shown in Exhibit 6.3. However, an employee satisfaction survey may be the best way to track its impact. It is important that such a survey is instituted before the site goes live, so that employee reaction can be tracked after it is up and running. Employee feedback should be used to further refine and improve the intranet.

Web solutions also often enhance communication. Besides direct benefits such as reduced communications expenses, improved communication enhances planning and morale. For example, improved communication between suppliers and buyers through an extranet allows for the sharing of sales projections and allows for more efficient planning and scheduling.

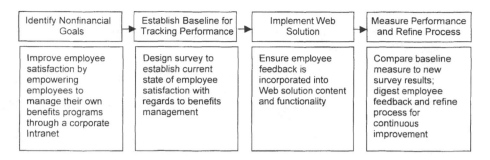

Identify Nonfinancial Goals	Establish Baseline for Tracking Performance	Implement Web Solution	Measure Performance and Refine Process
Improve employee satisfaction by empowering employees to manage their own benefits programs through a corporate Intranet	Design survey to establish current state of employee satisfaction with regards to benefits management	Ensure employee feedback is incorporated into Web solution content and functionality	Compare baseline measure to new survey results; digest employee feedback and refine process for continuous improvement

Exhibit 6.3. Measuring indirect benefits.

Like direct benefits, metrics should be identified for each set of indirect goals before a Web solution is implemented. Examples of some indirect goals and potential metrics are shown in Exhibit 6.4.

Surveys, focus groups, and interviews are some of the tools that will allow managers to establish baselines and measure changes going forward. Questions regarding customer or employee attitudes and behaviors, learning, and innovation are common baseline measures for tracking the effectiveness of a Web solution.

CASE STUDY: SWEDISH MEDICAL CENTER

Swedish Medical Center is the largest, most comprehensive medical center in the Pacific Northwest. Home to companies like Microsoft, Boeing, Amazon.com, and Teledesic, the Pacific Northwest has a work force that is well educated and computer literate, and Seattle is the fifth most-wired city in the country. Swedish decided that an Internet solution was critical to strengthening their business position in a rapidly expanding and technically sophisticated economy. After the launch of their site in July 1997, Swedish immediately received a Return on Internet Investment (ROI2).

Exhibit 6.4. Indirect Goals and Potential Metrics

Goals	Metric(s)
Customer retention	• Average time per customer relationship
	• Customer attitudes toward company
Employee development	• Performance appraisal ratings
	• Employee loyalty
Learning and innovation	• Decisions made and problems solved
	• Successful projects completed
Community service	• Community attitudes toward company

Strategic Planning

Swedish Medical Center crafted a strategic plan for an online business solution with clear, measurable objectives.

- Reach a premium, technically sophisticated audience and generate incremental revenues through online referrals
- Provide the same information and ease of use as the toll-free 1-800-SWEDISH telephone service
- Enhance the well-being of patients and build ongoing relationships with clients by providing a superior Web experience
- Maintain consistency with existing marketing campaigns in print and other media

Through a collaborative and interactive process, Swedish was able to focus their Internet strategy.

Building the Solution

Swedish's solution was developed using Microsoft technologies including Windows NT, Microsoft SQL Server, and Active Server Pages (ASP). These technologies enabled a solution that was scalable, flexible, and interactive. Using ASP to generate custom Web pages from criteria submitted by users, visitors to the Swedish site are able to search and select various titles or links to books from Swedish's "Book Store," services from their "Guide to Services," and physicians from Swedish's "Physician Referral" program.

Measuring ROI2

The Swedish Website went live in July 1997, on time and on budget. The Web solution rendered a ROI2 above and beyond Swedish's expectations.

Direct Benefits

- Incremental Revenues. Online referrals are bringing in more than $40,000 in new revenue each month.
- Reduction in Expenses. Each online referral to a physician saves more than $6 in staff cost, compared to a telephone referral.

Indirect Benefits

- Improved Target Marketing. In February 1998, there were 1500 Website visits from Microsoft employees alone. Total visitors numbered nearly 8000 and the volume is growing at 30 percent per month.
- Improving the customer's experience. Online referrals offer the same information as 1-800-SWEDISH. As a result, the number of online referrals is now greater than the number of telephone referrals. Prospective clients can now get referrals directly from the Web, and Web

referrals are more private than telephone referral since there is no need to confide any medical details to an operator.

- Better information on promotional effectiveness. When a visitor links to the Swedish Website, Swedish can see what company they are linking from. This helps Swedish track which marketing campaigns — and which communications channels — are most effective. The site is carefully organized so users can self-navigate through a large amount of material. Content is served dynamically according to the requests of each visitor. This engages visitors and at the same time captures demographic information that helps Swedish understand its customer base.
- More effective human resources management. Swedish is planning additional cost-saving initiatives as a result of the site's success. The Human Resources department, which has already seen a reduction in their paperwork costs and staff time as an effect of the successful site, will now be able to focus more directly on the core tasks of selecting, hiring, and training the best people.
- Enhanced community service. The Volunteer Services department has also benefited with online volunteer recruitment. Without any promotion whatsoever, they have been able to recruit several high-quality volunteers each week through the Website.

Next Steps

In late 1998 and early 1999, Web-site development will split into two distinct paths: marketing and patient care. The marketing path will continue and expand the success of the current initiatives and strategies. The patient care path will focus on improving services for current and potential patients, even enhancing the quality of care in some areas.

"Building long-term success on the Web is not done by just momentarily grabbing people's attention," said Douglas D. Waite, Chief Financial Officer of Swedish Medical Center. "A successful site should not only provide immediate results, but should be built on a foundation that allows for future growth and development."

SUMMARY

Measuring return on investment has traditionally been difficult to define because it is different for every situation. People calculate their return on investment for situations in their lives everyday — from choosing which brand of paper towels to buy in the supermarket, to deciding how their business would profit with the installation of new technology. Return on Internet Investment (ROI2) needs to be weighed in a similar manner — taking into consideration both direct and indirect returns. When a company is determining whether it would be profitable to invest in an Internet, intranet, or extranet business solution, it needs to factor in everything from direct sales and cost savings, to better customer experience and more effective internal communication. Internet, intranet, and extranet sites benefit customers, employees, and partners, respectively — ROI2 entails both tangible and intangible benefits and costs. Companies need to figure out which balance would best fit their online business objectives.

Author's Bio

John Seasholtz, Director of Business Consulting for Free Range Media, joined Free Range Media in June 1998 as Director of Business Consulting. Seasholtz specializes in Return on Internet Investment (ROI2) planning and measurement, providing Free Range Media's clients the strategy necessary to measure their Website's success. Prior to joining Free Range Media, Seasholtz worked as a strategy formulation manager with Andersen Consulting Strategic Services, where he developed and implemented strategic plans for clients in the consumer products, retail, and utilities industries. While at Andersen Consulting, Seasholtz participated in the award-winning Consumer Direct Consortium, which identified emerging online business models in the grocery industry. He has also held marketing and finance positions with Ford Motor Company and EDS in both the U.S. and Europe. Seasholtz earned a master's degree in business administration from the University of Michigan, and a bachelor's degree in finance from Miami University (Ohio).

Notes

1. Return on Internet Investment (ROI2) is a trademark of Free Range Media, Inc. All product and company names should be considered trademarks of their respective companies.
2. See other examples of how Sun Microsystems saves money using Internet technologies at http://www.sun.com:80/960101/feature1/index.html.

Chapter 7
Ensuring Internet Access Means Business Access

Stephen Purdham

ANOTHER MONDAY MORNING AND THE OFFICE MANAGER SMILES as he surveys his department and sees everyone focusing hard on their computer screens. Satisfied, he closes his door and settles down to produce that report that should have been finished last week.

What he doesn't realize is that Sally from Sales has just arrived (for the fourth time this month) at that Caribbean island of her dreams — should she book her vacation there or settle for the romanticism of Venice, a city she only visited less than an hour ago; Mark in production is reliving the sport results from the weekend, play by play; Steve in Administration inwardly congratulates himself as his investment portfolio shows a $1000 increase. Meanwhile, Mary from Finance has just received that e-mail she has been waiting for from her long-lost sister in Australia, the sister she hasn't heard from since last Thursday; Dave from production loads his newly acquired pump action shotgun and is slowly stalking Andrew from Marketing, it will be an easy victory ... as long as the guys from the IS department don't get that hi-powered laser again!

It is irrelevant whether this is a real scenario or just another scare story, but it sets the scene. What it effectively illustrates is that as businesses connect to the Internet there is a significant new management issue which needs to be understood so that it can be efficiently handled. The problem is easily stated: how do you ensure within the workplace that Internet access is business access.

As Internet usage becomes more widely accepted within the corporate space, several concerns surface regarding such usage within a business environment. Once the emotional rhetoric is removed, these concerns can be distilled into four main areas:

0-8493-9987-4/00/$0.00+$.50
© 2000 by CRC Press LLC

- Impact on productivity
- Impact on network infrastructure
- Legal and reputation exposure
- Security

In addressing these issues, solutions can take many forms: from the simple, but draconian, measures of not allowing corporate connection to the Internet at all, through to total open Internet access to all information, at all times, by all people. In a real business environment, neither of these extremes are adequate so we must strive to understand the needs and then propose a practical solution.

The core of any solution will be the Internet Acceptable Use Policy for the organization. Simply, *who can do what, when, and how* with the new Internet resource so as to maximize the business benefit. This will create an environment which on the one hand delivers all the benefits to the corporation, yet on the other reduces the risks of nonbusiness usage to an acceptable level. Any individual implementation of an Acceptable Use Policy must recognize that it cannot create unrealistic administrative loads or create a myopic view of the Internet such that the business value is diminished.

This chapter will provide an overview to the areas of concern, i.e., productivity, network impact, legal and reputation, and security. Once a basic understanding of the management issues have been covered we will then explore the tools and technologies available today and then conclude with a look into where the world of business Internet management is likely to go.

PRODUCTIVITY

In a European survey of key decision makers, 59 percent stated that they found surfing for personal use totally unacceptable during core business time. Yet a U.S. survey found that more than 60 percent of employees are accessing inappropriate sites during work hours. Most managers fear the impact on productivity of nonbusiness browsing and the much publicized access of pornographic sites has increased this factor.

But it is not the pornographic issue that is the main culprit in the workplace. The ICSA (formerly the NCSA, the National Computer Security Association) published the fact that the financial sites have taken over from the pornographic sites for frequency of access from within the workplace.

The nature of information being accessed within the workplace is irrelevant whether it is pornographic, financial, or sport, the main management issue is — is it business or nonbusiness. Intelligent agents and filters are being designed to automatically surf, extract, analyze, collate, and notify users of information based upon a series of "personal profiles." This can be great news for the executive/engineer/marketing professional looking to fulfill a specific business need. The result, unfortunately, is a dynamic personal magazine delivered direct to an individual's desktop which may, or may not, have any business relevance. Additionally, the power of the Internet means that this information can be passed quickly and effortlessly to other individuals with similar interests and beliefs.

It is fair to say that most people using Internet technology don't intentionally "time waste," but this easy access to high-value personal information can be seductive, especially to task-orientated workers who often have boring, repetitive jobs. It is also clear that this type of casual surfing could mean a severe loss of productivity to a business.

Intentional or casual surfing to nonbusiness sites assumes that the user will utilize the resources of the Internet to fulfill personal desires and creates a general management issue to solve. But there is another phenomenon that can also impact productivity known as involuntary surfing.

Involuntary surfing is the browsing of business-based sites where the information is presented in such a way that people are easily distracted from their primary goal and their attention is diverted into other areas. To guide people to other material, after all, is a feature of the Web, even of internal sites, and part of the job for any good Webmaster.

In a personal example of this, once while looking for some financial information about a company, I was presented with the information shown in Exhibit 7.1.

How many "mouse operators" faced with this wouldn't be tempted to take a quick look? (If they have fun then they tell their colleagues and the spiral starts.) The temptations are there in volume and the result of both involuntary surfing and casual surfing means a loss of both productivity and focus for the workforce.

There is a case to be argued here that a well-informed individual can be more effective. But, as always, it is a balance, and organizations need to be conscious that even business-only browsing can have a downside. But in looking for a balance it is also found that the needs of the creative workers need to be separated from the needs of the task-orientated worker.

NETWORK IMPACT

The Network is the freeway of the company and as with any freeway if you increase the traffic beyond a specific point all traffic slows down and eventually stops. So the impact of nonbusiness Internet use is obvious — it consumes essential bandwidth and slows down business operation.

Nonbusiness usage of the Internet is like allowing thousands of VW Beetles with surfboards hanging out of the windows to block the access of the trucks as they go about there business. The solutions are to increase the

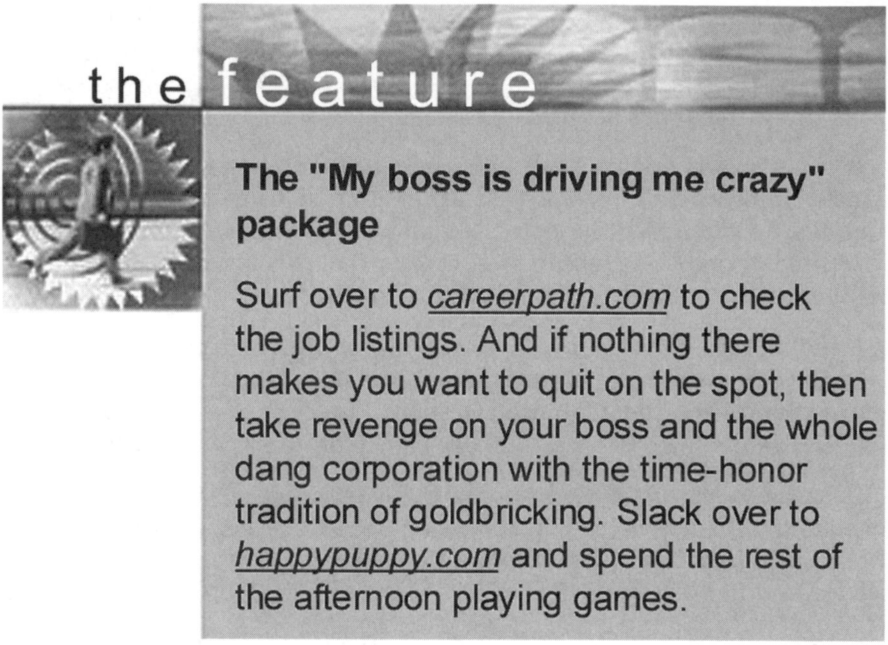

The "My boss is driving me crazy" package

Surf over to _careerpath.com_ to check the job listings. And if nothing there makes you want to quit on the spot, then take revenge on your boss and the whole dang corporation with the time-honor tradition of goldbricking. Slack over to _happypuppy.com_ and spend the rest of the afternoon playing games.

Exhibit 7.1. Web as temptress.

Network size, usually at an unacceptable cost, or manage the traffic to relevant times of day, e.g., nonbusiness traffic is allowed at off-peak times, say.

It can be quite amusing that many organization feel these types of things never affect them, especially when they install a firewall, but the fact is only a small number of companies connected to the Internet use firewall (less than 100,000 units at the end of 1997). Also many firewalls are also very badly configured, resulting in many things getting through.

Here are two examples for illustration which were both "protected" by a firewall, to no avail. Firstly, a site had their production department listening to the radio all day. No management problem there, except the radio was being audio-streamed from the Internet to all the PCs in the department. Impact on the organization — significant; solution — give the production manager $50 to buy a radio.

Secondly, a VW enthusiast got permission to build a personal Web server on his office machine out of hours. No management problem there — until the external search engines found the site and suddenly thousands of external hits a day were crippling the internal network.

Bandwidth is precious and will continue to be so for years to come. Good Internet management protects this resource.

LEGAL AND REPUTATION

This headline in a news article sums up this area superbly:

"What's worse than Sex, Drugs, and Violence?
Sex, Drugs, and Violence on COMPANY TIME."

Although very few companies are willing to discuss this openly, various independent studies have unearthed some disturbing trends in this area. A Nielsen Media Research audit of the Penthouse site showed heavy traffic from blue-chip U.S. organizations. This growing trend of corporate resources being used to access X-rated material parallels the fear and concern about home access to X-rated material and the need to protect children from unintentional access to these sites.

The legal points and definition of undesirable content is being heavily debated as is who is responsible. The case in Germany of suspended jail sentences being served on former CompuServe employees for allowing pornographic material to be delivered via the ISP continues to raise issues.

Employees have a right to protection from certain materials and the corporation has to clearly define the rules so people understand where the line is. Many company executives still don't realize that when an individual visits an undesirable site, it is the company domain that gets recorded. This record is also now public.

SECURITY

The significant rise in Internet technology has also seen an almost paranoid, parallel rise in the fear of being breached from a security perspective. This is due to Internet technologies being built upon TCP/IP, open addressing, UNIX, and the fact that most transferred information is text based. The common knowledge of these products, along with several other factors, provides a basis for abuse should people desire to do so. Unfortunately people do. The press is increasingly playing its part in fueling this paranoia with a constant stream of scare stories.

It is known, for example, that with mobile code (Java , Java Script, Active/X, etc.) that it's possible to visit multiple sites, each downloading dormant code which when brought together can become hostile.

Employees of the National Computer Security Association reported that as much as 75 percent of information-related losses came from trusted employees and that outside intervention represented less than 20 percent of the actual threat. This fact was also supported by the Yankee Group, whose survey found that only 14 percent of breaches were by external users. By definition, firewalls usually do nothing to prevent such in-house crimes.

Security isn't a single problem and as such doesn't have a single solution. Take building access security — most organizations have security personnel to prevent unauthorized access into a building. Depending upon the situation, this can vary from a gray-haired, uniformed senior citizen at the reception desk, to armed guards with dogs and perimeter security fences. However, inside the building a different level of security is in place that is designed to ensure the protection of internal information from employees, for example, personnel records locked in a filing cabinet. Again, depending upon the need, the security ranges from simple door locks to sophisticated access control card entry systems.

In the same way, the Internet security problem cannot always be solved by a single piece of technology, such as the firewall. While a firewall is a barrier to protect companies from external invasion it does not necessarily protect them from internal security breaches.

Managing Internet access to business-orientated sites statistically reduces the security threats. It is equivalent to defining the boundaries of what is considered to be a "good neighborhood."

INTERNET ACCEPTABLE USE POLICY

The ability to manage the issue ensuring Internet access in business starts with the definition of an Internet Acceptable Use Policy. Any Internet Acceptable Use Policy should start from the premise that Internet technology will be widely available across an organization, allowing the full benefits of effective communications. With this in mind, the issue becomes one of who, what, when, and how.

An Internet Acceptable Use Policy resides at the cultural core of an organization and it is essential that you first understand why you need an Internet Acceptable Use Policy and what are the real driving forces behind the policy. Companies can take a conservative or a liberal approach to Internet access, or fit somewhere in between. Each approach is valid and should be considered equally, as shown in Exhibit 7.2.

Conservative   **Liberal**

Exhibit 7.2. Conservative and liberal approaches to providing Internet access.

The criteria to the driving force behind Internet Access Control Policy are

- Protection of employees from objectionable material
- Protection of productivity from casual surfing — sport, news, leisure, etc.
- Ensuring Internet access has a business focus
- Internal security access
- External security access

With these criteria in mind how do the approaches differ?

The Conservative Approach — *No One Can Access Anything at Anytime*

This approach values the benefits of Internet access but means that access is only granted on an *as and when* basis as the need becomes understood and defined. For this approach, access control technology which can allow access to specific business-related sites, is paramount.

The Liberal Approach — *Anyone Can Do Anything at Anytime*

In this case monitoring and reporting will be essential so that any abuse of this privilege can be properly managed and access can be systematically restricted for any offenders.

The Common Sense Approach — *Some People Can Do Some Things Some Times*

This approach takes a balanced view for individuals, groups, and departments, controlling and/or monitoring as they see relevant. This approach is more likely to lock out general access to Internet/intranet resources during prime business time, but takes a more liberal view of employees who wish to browse outside of the core business time. This recognizes that Internet access can be an employee benefit if offered by the corporation outside of business time.

Having defined its Internet Access Control Policy, the company should then decide upon the technology to implement the policy. This will probably be a mixture of technologies, some of which are already available, and some of which are still evolving.

Many products provide an element of access control, e.g., routers, gateways, firewalls, but their levels of refinement and central manageability are restricted. That is to say that although you can stop 193.193.109.20 going to the www.playboy.com site, the granularity is not fine enough to allow you to easily define that *"Bill cannot have Web access to adult sites during 9:00 a.m. to 6:00 p.m. Monday to Friday, but the rest of the time it is up to Bill."* The choice of technology should not be used to define the Internet Acceptable Use Policy but rather be used to refine the policy.

Finally and most importantly, once the policy is defined it needs to be shared with the rest of the organization to ensure that everyone is educated as to the Internet Acceptable Use Policy.

MONITORING OR FILTERING — THE MECHANISMS FOR MANAGING CORPORATE INTERNET ACCESS

At a macro level, the mechanisms that are available to provide the tools to manage Internet access are monitoring or filtering technologies.

Monitoring

As the name suggests, monitoring records who is doing what and when, and then produces management reports as required. Monitoring can introduce a self-regulation phenomenon that reduces the impact of nonbusiness browsing and increases management comfort and acceptance of Internet usage.

This phenomenon results from the fact that most people are responsible. By openly publishing reports such as the Top 10 site hits by department, or business vs. nonbusiness usage charts, then the impact is that employees self-regulate their Internet access to business use within business hours.

The issue can now become a "management by exception" issue, with the corporation using its Internet Acceptable Use Policy to communicate acceptable levels of nonbusiness usage.

Legal issues apart, it is key and fundamentally ethically correct that if any monitoring is to be installed that it be common knowledge. It is only by making the fact known that monitoring is in place does the self-regulation effect takes place.

Filtering Technologies

Filtering technologies extend the monitoring aspects and provide the ability to control access based upon defined criteria such as time, sites, or user.

These mechanisms provide means of implementing rules which reflect the company's Internet Acceptable Use Policy. The level of sophistication of the rules vary between products in the marketplace. Access rules are normally controllable via a range of criteria:

- Who: Workstation; IP Address; MAC Address; Username; Groups
- What: Protocols, i.e., http, Telnet, IRC, SMTP, FTP, etc.
- Where: URLs, Addresses, Domains, IP Addresses, Control Lists
- When: Time of day, days of week

It is worthwhile spending a few moments understanding how you define the "where" component. In a business context defining where people can go via the Internet becomes one of the significant challenges to management.

From the parental control market has grown the concept of negative control lists, i.e., places you cannot visit. These control lists have become more sophisticated over time with the addition of different categories and also with the addition of many ten of thousands of inappropriate sites. The problems with negative lists is they are constantly growing by the day.

Many people are moving to positive control lists, i.e., business places you can go to. But at the moment this is still in its infancy and requires some internal works to decide what are business and what are nonbusiness sites.

Also in this arena is a promising technology from the W3C called PICS — Platform for Internet Content Selection, which can allow sites to be rated so a decision can be made as to their appropriateness. Child protection rating systems such as RSACi and SafeSurf use PICS as the mean to control access. The difficulty for business is that current implementations require Websites to self-rate, and RSACi is only rated on about 75,000 sites. However, PICS usage will become more important in the future as business-specific rating mechanisms become the order of the day.

It is the automation of "what" is considered a business site which is under major review by most suppliers.

Internet Monitoring Architectures

Understanding the difference between monitor architectures is essential in evaluating specific monitor products. Monitor architectures split into two types:

- Pass-Thru Technologies
- Pass-By Technologies

Pass-Thru Technologies. Pass-thru technologies, as shown in Exhibit 7.3, require all Internet communications to be redirected to a third-party server. As the information packets "pass-thru" the server it is possible to monitor, understand, and control the outcome of the traffic. Basically information is analyzed at defined "bottle-necks."

Examples of this technology are gateway servers (i.e., protocol gateways), proxy servers (e.g., Microsoft proxy server, routers, and "router style" servers. At these bottlenecks it is possible to integrate control and decision products, however, by their nature this could increase the load and impact network performance if great care is not taken.

Pass-By Technology. This passive architecture utilizes "packet sniffer" technology where all TCP/IP packets passing the server are detected and

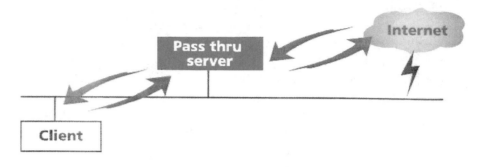

Exhibit 7.3. Pass-Thru architectures.

---

can be recorded and controlled as shown in Exhibit 7.4. The advantage of this style of technology is it does not create bottlenecks.

Monitoring and control can be achieved effectively, but placement of these solution is paramount as they can only monitor and control what they can "see." That is, they have to be on the network segment where the traffic to be monitored or controlled is traveling. This type of passive technology is increasing in the market as it does not interfere with the general flow of data traffic.

THE WAY AHEAD

One thing is certain, technology in the Internet management space will continue to evolve — in particular, the move towards positive control lists defined specifically for business and the ability to automatically profile what are classed as suitable business sites for a particular business. (Don't forget, www.playboy.com is a business competitor to Penthouse and for them these are business sites.)

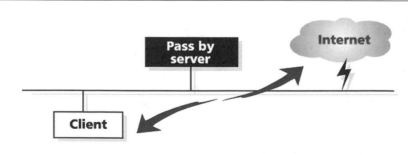

Exhibit 7.4. Pass-By architectures.

The language of the Web HTML is already under significant review with the W3C proposals for XML (extended Markup Language). This is leading to the increased potential use and definition of metadata — the ability to tag attributes to data so that the data themselves can be described in areas such as content, quality, target audience, etc. New initiatives in this area include PICS Rules and its likely successor, RDF (Resource Description Framework).

What will all these new initiatives mean to most people? Quite simply, they will provide the mechanisms and standard for the evolution of new generations of products which remove some of the restriction that are around today. For example, in the near future business agents will exist which understand your business profile and will deliver facilities such as "powersearches" which automatically filter out sites which do not match both your individual and business profile.

So to conclude, when you connect your business to the Internet be prepared but do not be afraid. It is the correct way forward for the business. Just do the right things, which are

1. Decide upon your own Internet Acceptable Use Policy (don't let the technologies define your policy).
2. Communicate the policy clearly to all Internet users.
3. Implement monitoring technologies to identify potential problem areas. Use monitoring as an "exception" management tool.
4. Use filtering and control technologies to reduce the chance of the management issue becoming a problem or to control problem areas if they exist. (Try not to confuse Internet management and external security issues.)

The Internet is a source of rich business information and access to it will continue to benefit business in ways people have yet to define. So rather than be fearful of the challenges embracing the Internet for business use, just be confident that this issue can be managed and, therefore, using one of the world's best sales messages — JUST DO IT!

Author's Bio

Stephen Purdham *is president of JSB's surfCONTROL Division. His initial experience was as a technical strategist for a major European computer OEM, with specific focus on the financial sector. During the early 1980s, he was intimately involved with the emergence of the Open Systems market. Since 1995 he has worked with major worldwide software organizations to understand, analyze, and define the exploding Intranet marketplace. His white paper "The INTRAnet, a corporate revolution," has been widely acclaimed and used by many organizations worldwide. Purdham is a recognized and well-known figure in the industry, specifically in the U.K. and Europe, and his often controversial views and presentation style has resulted in a significant number of presentation on industry matters at a wide array of forums over the past 5 years.*

Chapter 8
Using the Internet to Improve Competitive Position and Reduce Costs

Hollis Tibbetts

BY THE YEAR 2000, THE MARKET FOR ELECTRONIC COMMERCE TRANSAC-
TIONS — for both business and consumer applications — will exceed \$300
billion. The Internet, with its promise of universal low-cost connectivity,
will revolutionize many industry segments over the next several years.

Today, the Internet can be used by companies who wish to differentiate
themselves in the marketplace. These companies will achieve a competitive advantage by improving customer service, offering better products,
and making better use of working capital, while simultaneously reducing
costs.

The Internet facilitates this by providing a universally available backbone for sharing information between customers, distributors, manufacturers, and suppliers — the so-called "supply chain." All businesses
leverage a variety of information to deliver products, plan for resource
needs, and to manage the overall business. This information can take many
forms — the content which businesses leverage to achieve competitive advantage has traditionally included structured, nondynamic data like databases and delimited or fixed-field data files. Increasingly, organizations
need to further leverage the nonstructured information served up by
things such as ERP-packaged solutions, legacy operational systems, e-mail
systems, business reporting systems, and middleware frameworks. With
the advent of the Internet, this has grown to include dynamic, nonstructured information such as Web information (HTML, XML), content-management systems and Web-enabled applications (such as catalogs). Those
companies which are able to share timely information across the entire

0-8493-9987-4/00/\$0.00+\$.50
© 2000 by CRC Press LLC

supply chain will become the new leaders in their industries or will widen their lead on their less nimble competitors. In some industries, laggards risk being driven out of business completely, as some industries will be so transformed by the Internet as to make its adoption as a core business platform a requirement for doing business.

This chapter discusses the market dynamics which are shaping business Internet usage, how this information sharing involves linking various disparate applications and data sources across enterprises, the various different types of software packages and information sources which are linked, and the emerging technologies and standards which are involved in the process.

MARKET DYNAMICS

There are a number of market forces which are the impetus behind the adoption of Internet technologies for integrating customers and their suppliers.

Consumer Demand

Increased demands from customers, both individuals as well as businesses, for product delivery that is faster, cheaper, and better is creating a need to improve corporate agility and efficiency.

Improved Inventory Management. Several industries, most notably high-technology and automotive, are aggressively seeking to decrease inventory. The impetus in high-tech is the rapid obsolescence of inventory. In the automotive industry the motivation is for suppliers to provide JIT services to the major manufacturers. In both instances, the "carrying costs" of inventory are a significant factor as well.

Limitations of Traditional Technology. In the past, traditional technologies such as EDI defined electronic commerce. However, its batch personality, lack of message flow control, complex and expensive implementation issues, and fixed message formats have limited its utility.

EDI has fallen short for large hubs needing to get smaller trading partners on board due to the costs and complexity of implementation. For a large company, only about 20 percent of its trading partners typically participate in traditional EDI.

Increased Outsourcing

Companies are increasingly outsourcing noncore functions such as manufacturing, warehousing, and logistics. This new business model will realize its full potential, both in terms of efficiency and profitability, when it is based upon tightly integrated electronic business partner systems.

Because of these dynamics, the need to integrate operational systems such as electronic catalogs, purchasing applications, financial systems, supply chain planning (SCP) systems, and ERP (enterprise resource planning) systems between organizations is rapidly growing. By linking these systems, organizations achieve competitive advantage through automated, collaborative processes and shared information. Internet technologies, which offer vast potential for open information exchange, further enable the evolving concept of supply chain integration.

Internet "Ground Zero" Industries

Some industries, more than others, will be at the forefront of the Internet commerce movement. These are industries which are undergoing fundamental shifts, either because of market conditions, regulatory conditions, or technological innovation. These industries are characterized by short product life cycles, changing consumer demand, and rapid technology innovation — factors that break down corporate inertia and reward the adaptation and agility that collaboration brings.

Media and Publishing

Media and publishing are truly at the forefront of the Internet (and information) revolution — precisely because media and publishing are information. Organizations in this area will be driven by competitive pressures to leverage the Internet to gather, host, and re-purpose information from a variety of sources. The range of companies involved here ranges from newspapers, classified ad companies, entertainment, travel-related organizations, and business information providers like consulting firms.

Distributors

Companies in this category have a pressing need to exchange data with many business partners, both upstream and downstream. These frequent interactions make a real-time communication infrastructure cost effective. By sharing real-time information with trading partners, entrepreneurial manufacturers and distributors can improve their efficiency to gain a competitive advantage. For example, a manufacturer or distributor can closely track inventory levels, so when inventories dip, the system will trigger automatic replenishment from an online supplier. Collaborative information exchange with business partners can also help streamline business processes and improve customer satisfaction. For instance, by sharing sales forecasts with preferred suppliers, manufacturers can strive for JIT manufacturing.

High-Tech Manufacturing

Adoption of outsourcing is common in the high-technology industry, which is defined by cutthroat competition, short selling cycles, and rapid technological churn. High-tech companies are also aggressive technologically, looking to reduce inventory, and increase speed-to-market. This stems from the need to minimize inventory depreciation costs by better inventory and manufacturing management, particularly in the PC and semiconductor segments. Companies can no longer afford to carry inventory that may within days become obsolete.

Commodity Goods

Vendors of commodity goods will be driven to the electronic commerce space by falling profit margins, which will be brought on by increased competition and increased ability by consumers and businesses to "comparison shop" using the Internet. Faced with declining margins and the inability to compete based on product differentiation (almost by definition), manufacturers of commodity goods will seek differentiation through brand awareness (advertising and marketing) and through providing added-value goods and services over the Internet. Examples of this might be an office supply vendor using the Internet to "manage" a client company's stocks of office supplies, or a commodity product vendor building a "super site" by providing their products, as well as products from other vendors, in a an effort to capture mindshare from their customers.

Configurable or Customizable Goods

Due to the nature of their business, manufacturers of customizable or configurable products — for example, the telecommunications, PC, electronics, and office furniture markets are typically constrained by the availability of components rather than by their ability to assemble or manufacture the final goods. By sharing information between the manufacturer, the end customer, and the suppliers to the manufacturer, the assembly and manufacturing cycle time for products can be greatly reduced.

TACTICAL VS. STRATEGIC COMPETITIVE ADVANTAGE

The Internet can be employed for both tactical as well as for strategic advantage. The tactical approach is taken to either reduce costs or achieve incremental increases in revenue without impacting the core business processes or primary business relationships of the company. This path is typically taken based on a Return On Investment (ROI) approach, and as such, represents the majority of Internet projects undertaken in the business world at this time.

Achieving long-term strategic advantage, i.e., to dominate new markets, change the way products are created from conception to final customer delivery, fundamentally change the relationship between the customer and the vendor, or even recast the nature of an entire market typically require a substantial overhaul in the way a company thinks, is organized, and does business. This path is typically taken by either upstart visionaries (like Amazon.com) who succeed in shaking up an entire industry, or by companies in industries which are in the midst of tremendous upheaval — because of competitive, technological, sociological, or regulatory forces. These are visionary undertakings, with the possibility (but certainly not the guarantee) of tremendous ROI. From this perspective, companies that embark on this route are the ones with everything to gain, or conversely, everything to lose.

Attention must also be paid to the electronic commerce undertakings of the competition. From this perspective, it's important to understand to what degree the proposed E-commerce initiatives are simply catching up to the industry leaders, or even to the industry "norm" (i.e., maintain market share), and to what extent they are designed to increase market share (i.e., become an innovator). In the end, those solutions which integrate best with the organization's operational systems (financial, customer service, order entry, etc.), require the fewest changes in organizational structure and process, and those with the lowest acquisition and total ownership costs are the most appropriate ones for implementation, as shown in Exhibit 8.1.

ACHIEVING STRATEGIC COMPETITIVE ADVANTAGE

The extended enterprise concept has been advocated by industry analysts as the model organization of the future, and the Internet is by far the most likely candidate for being the "glue" that holds the components of this model together. The extended enterprise represents a shift away from the traditional vertical integration business model and toward a model where each organization focuses on its core competencies, and forges strong partnerships to "complete" the enterprise.

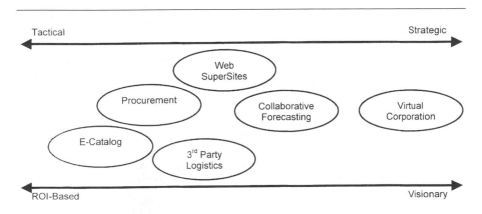

Exhibit 8.1. Tactical vs. strategic implementations.

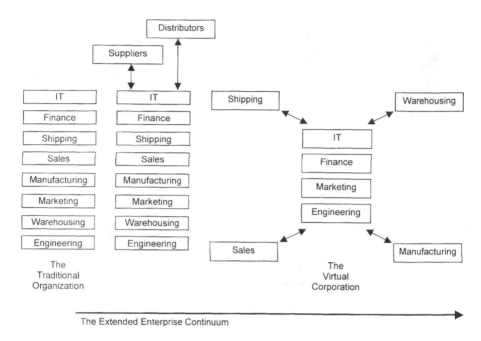

Exhibit 8.2. The extended enterprise continuum.

The extended enterprise, illustrated in Exhibit 8.2, is really a continuum. There are different degrees of "extendedness," depending on the level an organization is willing to commit to. The vertically integrated company maintains arms-length relations with its trading partners, whereas the virtual enterprise sticks to its core competency and outsources many functions. Virtual companies act as relationship managers and brand marketers — they manufacture little or nothing. To adapt to changes in demand, they need to have excellent, real-time visibility into their trading partners' capabilities and current activities.

"High Tech" companies like Monorail Computer Corp. are examples of virtual enterprises. Monorail Computer Corp. was founded in 1995 by a number of computer industry executives to provide high-quality products and services for practical computing needs. Monorail Computer Corp. focuses on management, design, and vision (their core competencies) and outsources functions such as manufacturing, support, and logistics.

The model leverages key partnerships with industry leaders that offer world-class expertise in logistics, service, and support and manufacturing. These partnerships deliver extremely efficient operations, maintain a flexible, variable cost model, and continually deliver outstanding products and services to the customer, all the while maintaining lower overhead costs. The result is high-quality, world-class-managed PC products at industry-leading prices.

Monorail's variable cost growth model ties almost all of its corporate expenses directly to sales volume and eliminates the large overhead carried by its competitors. Monorail has accomplished this by working with world-class firms who *can accomplish certain tasks with more efficiency and effectiveness* than Monorail.

FedEx, the acknowledged leader in overnight delivery services and logistics, provides a variety of services related to order entry, shipping, and delivery. Through FedEx's Logistics, Electronic Commerce & Catalog (LEC&C) Division, *Monorail's channel partners can reduce inventory stocking levels from 8 weeks to as little as 8 days*, greatly increasing inventory turns, significantly reducing the costs associated with obsolescence, and substantially *improving cost competitiveness*.

SCI, based in Huntsville, Alabama, is Monorail's desktop and minitower manufacturing partner. SCI is a global leader in computer component and system assembly. This relationship allows Monorail *to leverage SCI's vast experience and scale in ordering, warehousing, and assembly* of the units. The result is *world-class quality and timely delivery*.

SunTrust Bank, Inc. is a premier financial services company based in Atlanta. The Factoring Division of SunTrust acts as Monorail's credit department, collections department, and accounts receivable department. Through factoring its accounts, *Monorail has instant access to cash and can fund very high growth rates* with little additional financing.

These unique relationships have enabled Monorail to create a business model whereby most of Monorail's costs are tied to sales volume. Additionally, by *avoiding the investment associated with high cost, low value-add activities, Monorail can scale its business to very high volumes in a very short period of time*. The result is unparalleled responsiveness and efficiency, all of which allows Monorail to deliver the best products at the best prices.

In summary, benefits realized from the extended enterprise model include improved time to market for products, shortened manufacturing cycles, more efficient inventory management, reduced waste, better use of working capital, more accurate forecasting, and improved customer satisfaction.

The Internet is clearly the technology platform of choice for realizing the full potential of this business model.

ACHIEVING TACTICAL COMPETITIVE ADVANTAGE

Tactical advantage is achieved by automating and integrating systems, and for the most part require no significant changes to corporate processes, structure, or mind set. The areas which offer the fastest payback are usually purchasing (often starting with office supplies) and online selling (via an online catalog). The growing trend for products in these areas is demonstrated by the June 1998 announcement of the Online Retail Store and Business-to-Business Procurement products by the software Titan SAP.

Although the "tactical" word often has a negative connotation, using the Internet for tactical advantage should not be viewed in a negative light — companies can impact the bottom line significantly by employing so-called "tactical" techniques. For example, Global 2000 companies typically spend about a third of their revenues on nonstrategic/nonproduction goods and services — things like communications and capital equipment, computer hardware and software, industrial and office supplies, and MRO (maintenance, repair, and operating) supplies. Typically, these purchasing processes are loosely managed and monitored and labor intensive, which result in high costs and little opportunity for optimization.

Case studies have consistently shown that companies can realize savings in the 15 percent range by automating, coordinating, and monitoring these purchasing activities. The Internet provides a natural mechanism for automating these processes. These savings are then passed directly on to the bottom line in the form of increased profitability. Tactical? Yes. Insignificant? Hardly. Industry analysts have generally predicted that nearly all "Global 2000" organizations, as well as a fairly large number of small and midsize businesses will have implemented some level of automated purchasing using the Internet within the next 4 years, with the rapid ROI providing the justification for these projects.

Automating Purchasing

For many companies, automating purchasing represents the first logical step in internet-enabled electronic commerce. The key to the success of this kind of project is to provide enough flexibility and ease of use so that it can be used by the majority of corporate employees, and so that the "masses" don't subvert its effectiveness by going outside the system. ROI is achieved by having an automated system which typically aggregates purchases (reducing accounting and administrative overhead) and then places these orders with the lowest-cost vendor (typically, comparison shopping over the internet). ROI is also significantly enhanced by having a full reporting system which allows for spending trends to be viewed, allowing better "preferred customer" prices to be negotiated.

The costs associated from automating purchasing in this fashion can be expensive — large companies can easily face project costs in the millions of dollars, regardless of whether this automation is achieved by purchasing a package or whether a solution is custom developed; however these costs are typically recovered in 12 to 18 months.

Setting up Shop Online

The logical complement to automating purchasing using the Internet is selling via the Internet. These "sell-side" solutions were the first to appear in the electronic commerce space. Many of these sites will grow to become "Supersites," where the catalog content will consist not only of products from the company, but also from other companies. An example of this would be an office supply company who wishes to sell computers, office furniture, and business books online as a method of offering additional value to its customers. The company would create a Supersite where all of these product information from the various vendors would be aggregated, and all purchases could be executed through the single site.

Selling online typically involves engaging either a catalog hosting service, or purchasing catalog software. The price range spans from a few thousands of dollars to hundreds of thousands of dollars, depending upon need. Because of the potential expenditure, and a number of publicized "failures," where returns were not as high as expected, decisions to implement these sell-side solutions typically need to be justified on an ROI basis. Before investing in any of these technologies, organizations must evaluate the appropriateness of sell-side electronic commerce technologies to their sales and marketing strategies, customer needs, and customer management agendas. Businesses must evaluate their customers' (or potential customers') needs and profiles, and craft a value proposition that reflects true business needs. Efforts targeted at customers who are unlikely to interact online, or offering no additional value through ease of transaction or incremental benefits such as price discounts or extra/additional products, should not be undertaken as they are almost certain to disappoint.

The benefits of a sell-side E-commerce implementation will fall into the two categories: cost savings and revenue enhancements. Cost savings are primarily driven by reduced costs of doing business — for example, orders can be taken and tracked without "human" intervention. Revenue enhancements come from the potential to increase the customer base and market share by creating an E-commerce site which makes it easy for customers to interact with, and offers compelling business value. Aside from these somewhat measurable benefits, there is also the reality that without such an E-commerce presence, many organizations will find it difficult to compete in their markets. An example of this is in the office supplies market, where it is rapidly becoming a "ticket to entry." Those companies who are looking to make the electronic commerce sales channel as a more strategic investment, will be the ones who view this decision in light of factors such as business cycle acceleration, preservation of existing client base, and on market (and new market) penetration.

ISSUES AND CHALLENGES

For electronic commerce to thrive, there are a number of technical and cultural issues which must be addressed.

Information Sharing

Electronic commerce requires that we link applications and share information with upstream and downstream supply chain partners, regardless of computing and information storage environments. For instance, information once reserved for internal company use, such as inventory or product availability, now needs to be shared with supply chain partners in the context of an electronic commerce system.

Corporations must also be able to integrate their business systems with the business systems of their partners and suppliers without requiring modifications to a partner's applications. Some of the barriers to implementing these cross-organizational processes are beginning to fade, with the Internet providing a low-cost, ubiquitous network connecting business partners. An ongoing challenge, however, is that all supply chain partners need a far simpler approach to data integration and information sharing. The limiting factor is that supply chain partners have had to develop and maintain additional APIs or object interfaces significantly increasing the cost of electronic cooperation between companies, because these applications were never designed to work with one another.

The bottom line is that information developed by all supply chain partners for inventory management, forecasting, and sales force automation needs to be shared and updated. Prepackaged solutions currently do not exist for this kind of implementation, so market leaders will need to look at the emerging category of Internet-focused software solutions which allow data from multiple unstructured data sources of all types. This need fits into the category of "Content Integration," which is the ability to leverage all of the data and information which a company uses by integrating it with existing operational systems, such as ERP and E-commerce applications (Exhibit 8.3).

The content which businesses leverage to achieve competitive advantage has traditionally included structured, nondynamic data like databases and delimited or fixed-field data files. Increasingly, organizations need to further leverage the nonstructured information served up by things such as ERP packaged solutions, legacy operational systems, e-mail systems, business reporting systems, and middleware frameworks. With the advent of the Internet, this has grown to include dynamic, nonstructured information such as Web information (HTML, XML), content management systems, and Web-enabled applications, such as catalogs.

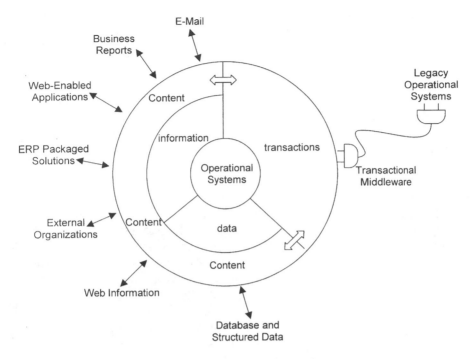

Exhibit 8.3. Content integration.

Leveraging this content, to date, has been a process which has been largely manual, involving a hodge-podge of different tools and custom-written programs, some of which support structured nondynamic data, some of which support interfaces into operational systems, and some of which support Web information. None of these tools support the challenges of data inconsistency, changing schemas, or varying data formats — issues which are typically resolved manually or by writing complex custom applications.

Electronic Catalog Implementation

Catalogs are key repositories of information in E-commerce. In the case of the sell-side implementation, the e-catalog must be populated with product information, and that information must be kept current on a regular basis with regards to pricing, features, and inventory status. This implies interfaces with systems as far ranging as Quark (where the paper equivalent of the electronic catalog may have been created) to SAP (where the inventory information may be stored) to Vantive (where the customer service information is kept). In the case of the buy-side implementation, an electronic catalog is usually kept locally. Information on products must be loaded into that catalog, either by having that information presented in one of the several evolving "standard" formats such as CIF, or by other fashions. Emerging products in the content integration space can provide a valuable bridge between these different worlds.

"Operational Systems" Integration

Electronic commerce requires integration with the applications which traditionally "run the business." These "operational systems" are made up of both "back office" systems, i.e., finance, human resources, and purchasing, as well as "front office" systems like customer service. Depending on the sophistication of the E-commerce system, information such as inventory status, prices, payments, purchase orders, and customer and supplier information must be integrated. For procurement systems, information from HR systems is valuable, to help determine who is allowed to purchase and who is allowed to approve purchases. This integration can be done manually (through custom-developed scripts, and usually a "batch-loading" methodology), by using products from "processware "vendors who focus on automating the integration of certain processes between certain software vendors packages — for example automating the ability of a customer-service package to deal with a customer return, and send the appropriate information to the financial package for a credit, and to the inventory management system to update inventory. This is also an area where content integration software can be helpful, as none of the "processware" packages can support all combinations of processes and packages to interface.

Structural Issues

Scalability and reliability are key "structural" requirements for any serious electronic commerce application. Many commerce applications have failed because they became victims of their own success, i.e., the application or Website became significantly more popular than originally anticipated. This unanticipated load results in crashed servers, and unacceptable response times. Generally, the flaws which result in lack of scalability and reliability are structural in nature — and generally cannot be resolved by adding more hardware or making quick "fixes" to the software. By the time the issues are addressed in the application, the initiative has typically been declared a failure. It is important "up front" to have a clear picture of how many tens, hundreds, thousands, or millions of hits this application will need to cope with, both initially and down the road, and have a clear understanding of how well the application can scale to handle the anticipated transaction levels.

Similarly, interoperability and manageability are structural issues which are important to address during the design phase of a project. Electronic commerce systems never operate in a vacuum — they must (one way or another) interface with systems both internal and external to the enterprise — for example, financial applications, inventory systems, customer care applications, human resource packages, and EDI implementations. These interfaces may be built into the electronic commerce package, which is occasionally the case, or left up to the end customer to either manually move information from one to the other (for example, manually rekey product orders which come in via EDI or manually extract the employee list from the HR system and load it into a procurement application), write custom software to do this automation, or leverage information integration types of software for more rapid implementations. Manageability is core to any enterprise-class software implementation. Issues which come to hand are the ability to diagnose problems, make and manage changes to the applications functionality, "tune" the application for optimal performance online, etc.

Cultural and Organizational Issues

The largest impediments to the success of electronic commerce are cultural and organizational in nature. These impediments vary, but include:

- The mistrust of suppliers, reluctance to cede "control" to outsourcers, and other insular behaviors
- The view that the Internet is not strategic to the business
- Lack of understanding of the customer or market needs
- Overreliance (or underreliance) on cost justification for Internet projects
- Attempts to implement electronic commerce "on the cheap," without examining the ramifications of a poorly planned and poorly executed system
- Lack of holistic planning — where Internet-related projects aren't coordinated across different business units and departments, are at cross-purposes with each other, and end up lacking important support from departments within the enterprise

SUMMARY

Clearly, the Internet is reshaping the way that business is done. We are at the beginning of a transformation which will possibly prove as significant as the industrial revolution. The Internet "revolution," like the industrial revolution, is about the automation of processes. They both create tremendous gains in wealth by providing for tremendous efficiencies in the economy. Almost every entity, from entrepreneurs to government to major corporations are having, or will experience major paradigm shifts because of this.

This global revolution is creating a single-market world. This pace of change continues to accelerate as the information float collapses further, bringing the sender and receiver instantly together. With the collapse of the information float, the financial float has also collapsed (i.e., the time it takes to move money around the world). Money, like information, is now only data.

As an interesting measure of the potential impact of this social, economic, and political phenomenon, examine John Rockefeller. In 1913, at the height of his power and the wealthiest man in North America, John Rockefeller was worth over $900 million. This equates to nearly $20 billion in 1998 dollars — less than one third of Bill Gates' $60 billion fortune. One can also look at the 40,000+ millionaires who have been created in Silicon Valley in the past few years alone to get an idea of how powerful this transformation will be.

Eventually, every organization will harness the power of these new technologies. We're just at the starting point of this metamorphosis — the technology is young, the markets are nascent, and the risks are high. In the end, every business will need to analyze the risks and rewards as they position themselves as leaders or followers in the race for competitive advantage.

Author's Bio

Hollis Tibbetts is the Director of Marketing for OnDisplay, Inc., the leading provider of software solutions for Extraprise Integration, and has held a number of marketing, sales, product management, and technical positions at software companies over the past 12 years. Prior to OnDisplay, Hollis has held positions at KIVA Software (since acquired by Netscape), was employed by Sybase for nearly 6 years, holding a variety of positions including Group Product Manager for Distributed Products (Data Replication and Message Queuing products), and Midwest District Technical Manager, and has held technical positions at a number of other RDBMS and 4GL software companies.

Chapter 9
The Politics of Content: Ownership, Relevance, and Access

Julianne Chatelain
Molly Oldfield Yen

WHY A CHAPTER ABOUT CONTENT? Because *the presence or absence of good content* is another key factor that, along with the others mentioned in this book, critically influences the quality, effectiveness, and popularity of an online Website. You may have heard friends or colleagues say, either seriously or jokingly, "On the Net, *content* is the next frontier." We agree.

Unfortunately, unless you work for a company that already produces high-quality content, which can simply be revised for online presentation and made available, you may also come to agree with another cliche we've heard recently, "Content is hard." This chapter discusses basic issues involved in producing and deploying high-quality content.

WHAT IS CONTENT?

The philosophers ask, "What is truth?" And the answers are complex. However, a practical, useful definition of *content* is well within our grasp. There are two kinds of content:

- Facts
- Expressions of a point of view (also called *opinions*)

We believe that all good online content consists of one or both of these elements, either separately or in combination, as the following examples show.

0-8493-9987-4/00/$0.00+$.50
© 2000 by CRC Press LLC

99

FACTORS THAT AFFECT THE QUALITY OF BOTH FACTS AND OPINIONS

When you present content to readers, some aspects of its quality are intrinsic, inherent in the content no matter who reads it, and others are dependent on the readers' interests. As you evaluate the content you are planning to present, keep the following issues in mind:

- Use all your techniques and skills to ensure that your content actually reaches the readers who are interested in it. In the second half of this chapter we'll discuss techniques for clearly explaining *what* content you are presenting, and *where* it is. Content is useless unless readers can find it *and* scan through it based on their individual interests.
- Facts must be as accurate as you can make them, potentially useful to others, and well presented.
- Opinions should be honest, specific, compelling, and well written.
- In the case of both facts and opinions, an explanation of how they were produced can add great value, as shown in the examples below.
- Ideally, content should be original. If it cannot be original, its organization and presentation, added by you, should provide specific benefits over the organization and presentation of the content in its original form, and the original producers should be credited. (We'll return to these points in more detail.)
- The general trustworthiness of your name, or your company's, affects how your content is perceived. If you are working on behalf of a well-established, well-respected brand, this can reflect positively on your content. (And of course, your content reflects on your brand, an excellent reason to carefully consider the issues raised here.)

Examples of Good (and Bad) Content

You may still be disagreeing with the assertion that all good content can be divided into facts, expressions of point of view, and combinations of these two. Examples will help explain our assertion. Obviously, media and research companies have access to both facts and opinions on a grand scale, but we'll use examples from the simplest possible cases, personal Websites. From these it is easy to generalize to larger sites and intranet systems.

Facts Can Be Formally or Informally Presented

Facts informally presented: *My garden's soil is sandy and mildly alkaline (pH 8-9). Through trial and error, I've found several varieties of annuals that thrive here ...*[1]

All other things being equal, the more work it took to produce or discover a fact, the more interesting it will be, because it will be more rare and valuable. In other words, it's more interesting to read a report from a man who has been gardening in sandy soil for 30 years, than from one who just threw in some plants for the first time this year. To this extent the cliche, "Content is hard," is true. However, content producers should take this not as discouragement, but as incentive to capitalize on whatever hard work they have already done. Many people have done more content-producing work than they are aware of.

Facts based on experience: *A wedding is an experience some families experience only once ... others only a few times. In contrast, our company has managed over 250 weddings since our founding in 1992! By far, the most common problem we've seen is that the bridal party leaves too many tasks to the last minute. Here is a checklist of issues and tasks that can easily be addressed a week or more ahead of the wedding, that otherwise tend to distract the bridal party by surfacing unexpectedly on the wedding day itself ...*

Also note that the preceding examples of facts include or imply some information about how they were produced. On Nets of all kinds, such details let readers further evaluate whether the facts will be useful to them. Always include them, to the extent you can. An example of a fact that is poorly supported will drive home this point.

Facts should include details of their production so readers can evaluate their usefulness: *Every member of our seven-person Board of Supervisors is a cold-blooded assassin. At the recent public forum on Waste Management, I looked deeply into their eyes and knew that it was true. My repeated appeals to the Sheriff's Department have produced neither inquiries nor arrests.*

In this example, the writer's information on how the fact was produced — by looking into the supervisors' eyes — allows the reader to use common sense to determine that, in the absence of proof via due process of law, her fact is likely to be wrong.

Note also that the presentation of facts can help aid or hinder their usefulness. Elsewhere in this volume you can find guidelines that will help you present facts clearly and summarize data visually in ways that aid your readers' understanding.

Expressions of Point of View Can Be More or Less Honest, Specific, Compelling, and Well Written

Each of us has an unique point of view, part of our birthright as humans, close to our very existence. Wealth, health, mobility, youth, and maturity come and go without affecting our ability to think and express our thoughts. (Physical challenges that *do* affect our ability to think and communicate are more tragic for that reason.) Our brains also have the ability to temporarily share, or enter into, the points of view of other humans, whether by reading their writing or viewing their works of art. Most humans find this mental "travel" enjoyable, depending on the destinations reached. An opportunity to share one's own opinions — tell one's own travel stories — can add further pleasure to the experience.

Personal expressions of point of view have, in common with facts, that they are more interesting based on the amount of work their authors have put in. This work may be the same type of work used to produce the facts, or it may be the "work" done by simply living in a particular place, in a particular body.

However, even more than facts, expressions of points of view, including both opinions and emotions, depend for their usefulness on the way they are expressed. And that too takes work, whether the work is the struggle to be honest enough with oneself to express a viewpoint fully, or the effort to create works and pictures that fully express that viewpoint. The following examples show "points of view" on which less and more work has been done, respectively.

An opinion that doesn't seem to have taken much work to express. *I love the Spice Girls!!!! Geri, how could you quit!!!!*

An opinion expressed with some effort: *I've been trying to figure out why I am so obsessed with the Spice Girls. As a productive senior bond trader, happily approaching mid-career, I'm embarrassed to be following music preferred by 8-to-10-year-olds, ducking into Tower Records and slipping out with a new Spice Power tee-shirt or Sporty Spice doll in my power briefcase. In some ways the Girls are like the dolls I never had time for as a child (I went right to paper routes, and mowing my neighbors' lawns, and invested every penny). I also take pleasure in the way the Girls deliberately set up, and then play with, different stereotypes, showing that there's no one way to be female, even in pop culture, but many different options, as many options as there are women. I can survive the defection of Ginger Spice: first of all, per Girl Power, Geri has the right of self-determination, and second of all, her character never really came into focus for me ...*

Even with these seemingly trivial examples, the benefit of taking some effort with an expression of point of view is obvious.

Complex Combinations of Fact and Opinion Are Not Only Possible, but Useful

When you combine facts and opinions, make sure readers can tell the difference between the two. In most cases, the transitions are smooth and easy to manage in a variety of ways.

Fact plus opinion, with both clearly labeled (two examples): *Our club network has conducted a regional bird census annually since 1971. The data over time are summarized in this chart; our expanded notes can be found be-*

low … . We believe that these data show that native finches are unable to compete with the invading sparrows …

In the past 2 years the Spice Girls have had three different managers, and now they're trying to manage themselves. Every time I hear about turmoil, I worry …

A Variety of Sources Adds Value

Another way to provide good content is to let many people help you compile it. In some content areas, you can produce a fascinating site simply by letting visitors post their own facts and opinions. You may have to do some judicious editing to remove junk postings, but the added richness your readers will find, from being able to skim a variety of facts and opinions, will materially increase your site's usefulness.

Be sure to provide some good initial postings to show visitors the kind of content you expect, and provide clear instructions for posting (and revising, if applicable). In most cases, subcategories will help both contributors and readers find the content that is of most interest to them.

The following example postings are from a site (fictional, as are all of the examples in this section) where the owners of home bagel machines are invited to add content. One is almost completely factual, one is pure opinion, and the third is a mix of the two.

Content provided by readers: *My wife and I bought the two-bagel machine from Acme the first year it came out (1995). Since then we've made two bagels every morning, five times a week in winter, twice a week in summer, with no maintenance problems. The ceramic bagel chamber snaps on and off, and we put it through the dishwasher once a week.*

I got the Universal bagel-maker as a gift, but I ended up passing it on to a rummage sale. Don't give me a bread machine either! Bagels and bread are easy to make if you know how, and letting a machine do all the work takes the fun out of it. When I knead dough, I feel a strong connection to the way my ancestors cooked and ate: setting a timer to get a half-dozen bagels may be convenient, but I don't feel the same way about the "product," which is what matters to me.

We've got the Acme half-dozen, and are very happy with the way it makes plain, onion, and whole wheat bagels. However, we haven't had much luck with the vegetable-bagel recipes in Acme's book: most types of vegetables just stick to the ceramic, leaving ugly holes in the bagel crust. And then Acme says, "Try your own!" Well, I love broccoli, and I've tried and tried to make a decent broccoli bagel, but the florets just go limp and soggy. Not even the dog will eat my experiments! I'd love to hear if others have a recipe that works.

Subcategories would help the bagel machine stories: they could be organized by experience with specific models, recipes wanted or offered, and so on.

Annotations Can Be Content, Too

The final major way to add content is through annotation, usually annotation of links. We've been asked whether "lists of links" fit our definition of content, and the answer is, "It depends." An unsorted list of links, with no annotations, does not qualify as original content. However, the minute you group links according to any sort of scheme, you begin to add value. And a carefully annotated list of links can provide a great deal of value. Again, the annotations must be original, and must have required effort, to be worth reading.

Content in the Form of Annotations. *Recommended ABI Web Sites:*

Another British Import is the official site for the popular television satire, which has been syndicated in the U.S. and Canada since 1997.
Where To Buy ABI provides an international list of dealers (online and in person) who carry Another British Import merchandise and videos.
ABI: Threat or Menace? is a U.K. fan site that summarizes the debate in the British press as to whether or not ABI contributes to delinquency and decadence; includes links to the complete articles on newspaper sites (registration required).
ABI in the Classroom, created and hosted by Eastern Southwest University, provides an excellent ABI-focused teachers' guide and study materials targeted at middle school (junior high) classes.
ABIFANS is an international English-language fan club, with a list of links to fan fiction and art sites (of varying quality); links to X-rated sites are clearly segregated and marked.

If the World Wide Web is cluttered with mediocre sites devoted to ABI, that this author is providing valuable content, probably the fruits of countless hours of surfing and reviewing. Good annotations include not only content summaries that help readers decide whether each link is of interest, but also advice about whether registration is required, what languages are supported, and how sexually explicit material is handled.

From these brief examples, you can see that many types of content-rich information can be created from simple facts and opinions. The suggestions in the rest of this chapter can be applied to all of these kinds of content.

GUIDELINES FOR WORKING EFFECTIVELY WITH CONTENT

Some of the following guidelines are uniquely content-related, and others apply to all aspects of online Websites. We have developed our opinions partly during usability tests of content-rich online documents.

Explain Your Sources and Perspectives

As described above, it's vital to explain the sources of the facts and opinions you place online. Source and perspective information lets readers feel more confident about what you provide, and evaluate its quality for themselves. The more honest and organized the content is, the more readers will tend to trust it.

Keep Content Current

As Darrell Myers once said, "A Web site is like a garden, it requires constant maintenance." We'd extend that to any online content. Depending on its subject, it may ripen and become obsolete at a different rate, but we recommend that you periodically revisit even existing content to check for dead links and material that needs refreshing. There is no better way to convince readers that your site is useless than to display prominent content that is outdated or obviously wrong.

Providing archives of previous postings, or previous material, is an excellent solution; however, such material should be clearly marked as historical.

Date Each Chunk

Place an absolute date with each chunk of content, so readers can see when it was last updated. Avoid vague temporal references like, "Last month." Tim Berners-Lee recommended dating each page in his very first Web styleguide, but it's still not practiced widely enough.

Dates help readers understand when they are looking at archival content, as noted above. The date can be in an unobtrusive (and ideally, standard) location on each page.

Solicit Feedback

Provide an easy way for readers to give you feedback and advise you of errors of fact. If you are posting opinions, you may not welcome feedback, but even a site that doesn't allow regular visitor posting might gain interest from posting a few exceptional communications its author has received. Edits made as a result of feedback should be marked with a date change and, if appropriate, a note of acknowledgment.

Include Appropriate Copyright Notices, Give Appropriate Credit to Others

These guidelines go hand in hand. The first amounts to properly signing and marking your work. The second is almost too simple: don't steal. Just as original content reflects well on your site, theft reflects badly. Whether or not one admits a moral principle here, theft is boring and unoriginal, and inefficient (resulting in multiple copies of material that could be well maintained, just once, in a central location).

Use "credits" to acknowledge everyone who helped you prepare and present your own content. Get permission before using content from others: provide attribution, including a direct link if possible. If permission is not granted, provide just a direct link with annotation. Request the same courtesy from others, and protect your own copyrighted material as vigorously as local laws permit.

Kory Hellmer's was the first Web styleguide that we saw explicitly mentioning ethical issues, and many guides still do not mention them. In general, credit and copyright matters should be handled far more carefully than they are currently being handled.

- Strive to present relevant content
- Group related content together
- Within a site or a group, provide cues that let your readers determine relevance

This chapter has discussed all measures of the quality of content except relevance. On a large scale, as described in other chapters, you determine the audience for your online material, and then create content that you believe will be relevant to your audience. (In some cases, you also have the challenge of attracting the audience to your site.) However, once you have your readers' attention, you must provide sufficient cues for them to determine whether they have reached a useful site, and then to find the content that is of most interest to them.

Within a site, we recommend that you group content so that like items are together. A reader who finds content that she likes will be near other content that has a good chance of being interesting to her. Graphical cues (colors and icons) can emphasize the larger divisions within your content, but should not (due to hardware limitations) be the only way content is distinguished.

At an even lower level of detail, at the level of individual chunks of content, the best way to cue readers is to write extremely descriptive titles and summaries, to facilitate skimming. The next section describes these techniques in detail.

WORK TO MAKE ACCESS EASY

The quicker your readers can access your content, the happier they will be. There are many ways to improve access to content, depending on your project's technical parameters. Here are a few.

- Set up a page-naming scheme that can be useful over time. Too often, key content is given a page name like "update.html." When the next update is written, all the other sites that linked to this update will be sadly disappointed. If possible, make "update.html" an alias that always leads to the current update, and use a page-naming scheme with absolute dates, for example, "update_990211.html," so that other sites' links will remain intact. (Or the other sites can link to plain "update" to always get the latest.) With some thought, you can organize a naming scheme that allows minimal renaming.

- Let readers bookmark pages within your site, not just the main page. Even when you use frames, it's possible to support free use of bookmarks. Dan Bricklin discusses how to make frames bookmarkable as part of a larger discussion about when to use frames on his Website, www.gooddocuments.com.

- Provide a text-only version of your site for readers with slow connections or text-only browsers. Since many readers surf with pictures off, provide ALT tags that recapitulate (or explain) the content of all included graphics.

- Consider whether sophisticated features, such as registration or the use of cookies, are truly necessary for your application, since they discourage access by some readers. If you decide to use these features, clearly explain to readers the benefits they provide. Our own company's site provides a "cookie warning" that explains what our site's cookies are used for: to help us provide a better experience by knowing whether you've already visited other parts of a site. Similarly, a page that invites readers to register should clearly explain the benefits of doing so, and how the collected information will be used.

- If you provide a search engine, make sure its scope is clear and its output is useful. Too often engines search only part of a site or take readers outside a site altogether, without providing cues that this is what is happening. User Interface Engineering has published results of several studies that suggest how to make search engines more effective.

- Provide multiple language versions of your content, as appropriate. Yes, there are "instant translation" facilities online, but vital content still needs to be explicitly translated so that all its target readers can apprehend it.

KEYS TO POWERFUL CONTENT

Now that you understand what you want to say and who you are saying it to, here are some simple rules to follow to make it easy for your readers to find exactly what they want.

Write Links that Tell Enough of the Story

Readers are thinking about something just before they click to follow a link. It's critical to provide enough information as part of the link itself so that they understand what they'll see when they arrive at the link's destination. By creating descriptive titles and providing summaries as part of the link text, readers know why they're clicking and where they'll end up.

Leverage the Technology

Use color and graphics to enliven your content — but not overwhelm — and to give readers the cues they need to find what they are looking for. Make sure that the fonts that you use are highly legible online and that the page designs that you use are for the screen and not paper designs that you've modified. Use different layouts for different page types.

Be Concise but Add Enough Detail

Understand that a reader may arrive at any page from anywhere. Is the content of the page sufficient for them to get what they need and move on? Clear, concise writing is the key.

Authors' Bios

Julianne Chatelain has been working with online, interactive, information since 1979. In the 1980s she was the "first user" and founder of the courseware department at Primarius, makers of a Z80-based multimedia hypertext system. Since then, she has been prototyping, creating, and testing online information, and speaking on topics such as "object-oriented documentation" and "effective online writing." Recent employers included Index Technology/INTERSOLV and Lotus/OneSource. In 1996 she became Trellix's "first user" and is currently head of Trellix's usability program (for both software and content).

Molly Oldfield Yen has worked in training and documentation since 1981. After completing her Ed M at HGSE, she spent several years as a partner in MicroWorkshop of Cambridge, writing hands-on books and presenting training. She left MicroWorkshop for Lotus where she managed documentation efforts for both print and online material. She has worked for Lotus full-time, at Caliper, Inc., The MESA Group, and Dragon Systems as a contractor since 1984. In 1997, she joined Trellix to help produce cutting-edge, online user assistance, including online Help, a guided Quick Tour, Web-based training, samples, and templates as the Director of User Assistance.

Notes

1. "Songbirds of the Mississippi Delta," originally published in *Ornithology Review,* 35:2 and 35:3, 1982. Copyright authors.

Chapter 10
Using Net-Based Interactive Technology for Online Marketing, Sales, and Support

Steven Semelsberger

THE IMPORTANCE OF IMPLEMENTING SOFTWARE SOLUTIONS to improve customer service and provide operational efficiency has been well documented. Most likely, you've already experienced several waves of euphoria as vendors have promised significant returns on investment from the latest in software gadgetry. From the mainframe boom of the 1970s through the UNIX and client/server explosion of the late 1980s to the "thin client is in," multitiered approach to computing in the 1990s, solutions have come and gone as application writers and software manufacturers have pushed each other to develop robust, easy to implement, highly scalable solutions for critical business functions.

While various front- and back-office applications have become automated and computerized, most leading corporations have yet to move beyond the physical store, field agent, or the telephone to actually interact with their customers. The Internet is now changing the playing field. Most companies today have established a marketing presence on the Web, utilizing the easy access of the Net to hawk products and services. Others, spurned into action by Web-centric innovators, have invested in the infrastructure needed to sell goods and services online.

Still, actual Web-based customer interaction for sales and service support has been limited to a few basic frequently asked question (FAQ) sections and an occasional "e-mail for more information" link. Only a few

0-8493-9987-4/00/$0.00+$.50
© 2000 by CRC Press LLC

visionaries have truly embraced the Internet's potential for a complete array of interactive services.

When one examines the typical customer life-cycle model, it becomes evident that the rise of the Web offers companies an unprecedented opportunity for efficient, effective, and personalized interactive service through marketing, information gathering, selling, supporting, and cross-selling/up-selling. The Internet provides a significant advantage for four key functions:

1. *Community building.* The interactive nature of the Web enables companies to give their customers a global forum to express ideas, concerns, thoughts, and demands, both with each other and with company representatives. While the idea of these "many-to-many" forums can be daunting for some, as Hagel and Armstrong noted in their 1996 manifesto on virtual communities, *NetGain,* interactivity is the most proven means to develop a sense of allegiance to an on-line destination or brand. Ongoing threaded discussions and interactive chats are two proven methods to bring customers together around a concept, product, or service. Each will be discussed in detail below.

2. *Marketing events.* The Web also creates new opportunities for organizations to hold interactive events in a "one-to-many" manner. Individual customers, spread across boundless geographies, can now have access to high-ranking company officials who may have never been reachable through traditional communication channels. Video/audio streaming in conjunction with moderated chats has given rise to a new era in communication and will be explored below.

3. *E-commerce.* With Forrester's prediction for Internet commerce to rise to $327 billion by 2001, most organizations are scrambling to unlock how they can utilize the Web to efficiently and effectively increase top line revenue. While E-commerce payment and tracking systems are discussed elsewhere in this book, this chapter will focus on how interactive communication mechanisms can be utilized to increase purchase conversion rates through cross-selling and up-selling. Specifically, live interaction, offered as a main component of a corporation's Website, (through interactive text conferencing, screen synchronization, telephony callback, and even voice and video over IP), provides the human touch that is often needed to encourage a purchase decision.

4. *Customer support.* Once an individual has become a customer, it is critical that he or she receives an appropriate level of service and support. The Internet offers a multitude of new, efficient, interactive support channels, ranging from self-service options all the way through an array of live communication channels. The

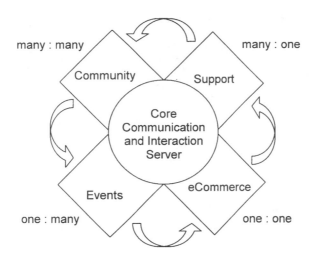

Exhibit 10.1. The four pillars of Web-based customer interation.

Internet-enabled customer support process will be explained in an upcoming section.

The four pillars of Web-based customer interaction can be summed up in Exhibit 10.1.

This chapter will focus on describing interactive applications that enable organizations to effectively build Internet communities, market to their customers, communicate with prospects to sell products and services online, and finally, provide efficient customer service and support. It will also set basic expectations for technical and human resource requirements to implement and maintain customer centric, Net-based service systems.

BUILDING INTERNET COMMUNITY: MANY-TO-MANY DISCUSSIONS

At this point, many Websites are vast arrays of "brochureware," or jumbled pages of marketing materials. However, analysts and executives alike have realized the need to improve both information and interaction if they are to fully realize the potential of the Internet. John McCarthy, an analyst at Forrester, says that corporations need to be thinking about how to provide a compelling experience for their customers. "Static Web pages that you have to go and fetch just aren't going to make it," says McCarthy.

McCarthy stresses that the next wave of Websites will focus on "intelligent interactivity." These effective applications will draw customers in with engaging content, collect information, and use the information to direct clients to products and services of targeted interest.

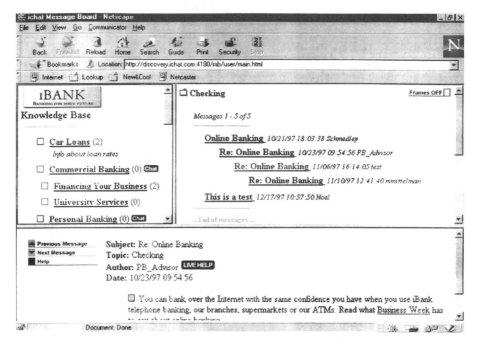

Exhibit 10.2. A threaded discussion group.

A major component of these intelligent sites will be the use of interactive, threaded discussions and live chat. Both offer compelling advantages and can be used as standalone solutions or as an integrated system.

Threaded Discussion Servers

Users of Usenet servers are quite familiar with the concept of threaded, topical discussions. The idea is simple: a customer, community member, or corporate representative initiates a thread with a question or statement posted in an online bulletin board accessible by other forum members. Individuals who visit the thread can then post follow-up statements and replies, or initiate new conversation threads.

An example of a threaded discussion (also frequently called message board) environment is shown in Exhibit 10.2.

In this instance, iBank, a fictional Internet financial services corporation, has set up a threaded discussion environment to provide user forums where individuals can search for information, browse, and post questions about various topics of interest such as car loans and online banking. Threaded discussion servers have several key benefits:

- Information posted is accessible by all future users, increasing knowledge transfer.
- Website visitors can view information in a self-service mode, decreasing their reliance on live bank representatives for information.
- Threaded discussions can be viewed from within the browser, allowing easy integration into existing Websites or corporate intranets.
- A sense of community can be quickly established without having the constant site traffic that chat requires. (See below for information on text-based chat.)
- Users can visit and post messages and replies at their convenience, without having to meet at predetermined times.

Threaded Discussion Requirements

Generally, threaded discussion servers are fairly quick and easy to set up. The majority of the effort can be in maintaining and monitoring threaded discussion topics. Depending on the level of human filtering, threads and posts can be monitored by a single individual on a daily basis, or could become a multiperson full-time task.

Most message boards applications work with major Web servers (Microsoft IIS, Apache, and Netscape Enterprise Server), post information in straight HTML (meaning that firewalls shouldn't pose a problem), and support numerous databases, including SQL, LDAP, and ODBC compliant storage applications. Windows NT 4.0 and Sun Solaris 2.x are by far the most popular operating system versions available.

While vendors have a variety of requirements for system memory, 32 Mb should get you started. Plan on setting aside plenty of disc space (100 Mb just to get off the ground) as growth in message posts can quickly fill up a hard drive.

Chat Servers

Long a key "late night" component of proprietary online offerings such as CompuServe and America Online, chat exploded onto the Web in early 1996. Since then, chat has become a must-have for major Internet destination and portal sites. Initially, text-based chat was seen as a gimmick to draw traffic to a Website and allow users to banter about frivolous topics of discussion.

However, the rise of several prominent discussion areas on the Web quickly ended any preconceived notions about the application of chat to major corporations. For example, Yahoo!'s financial forums (Exhibit 10.3) have drawn substantial attention, serious, worthwhile discussions, and even advertisers' dollars.

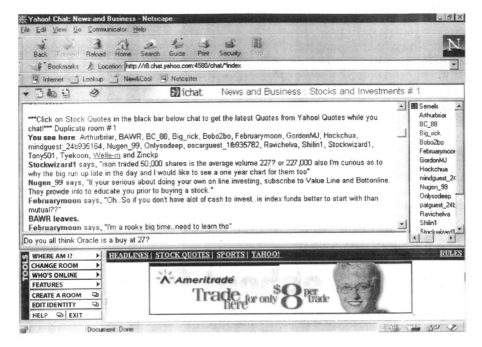

Exhibit 10.3. Sample financial forum on the Web.

As the Yahoo! screen shot exemplifies, text-based chat is a simple, flowing process that entails users entering into conversations in an open forum. Conversations are often dynamic and spontaneous, and regular users are quite often outspoken and critical. Yet no other application has demonstrated to have as effective a draw for Web users: *Business Week* estimates that chatters stay on Websites for up to 3 times the 10-minute average and chat-enabled Websites report up to 50 percent increases in traffic.

Additionally, for today's geographically distributed companies, open chat rooms can also be utilized as ad hoc meeting areas, enabling teams to collaborate on problems, discuss market trends, and work on projects—all in real time.

The major benefits of adding chat capabilities to your Website or corporate intranet include:

- Increased user loyalty—users who develop a community perspective around your Website have a significant probability of returning.
- Immediate information exchange—sites have the ability to use chat rooms for real-time market research, discovering issues of importance and major customer concerns immediately.

- Logging user feedback — information exchanged in chats can be stored for future reference.
- Captured eyeballs for advertising — chat rooms, with their long average visit times, provide an excellent forum for advertisers.

Chat Server Requirements

Most chat servers handle both administrative functions and user sessions from within a standard browser environment. Setup and configuration time is generally minimal, but can become quite lengthy, requiring up to a few days if user loads are anticipated to go above 1000 concurrent chatters, the company has an extensive firewall setup, or the site desires significant user interface customization.

Most chat servers work with major Web servers (Microsoft IIS, Apache, and Netscape Enterprise Server). Firewalls can be tricky, since the chat information is often passed through a port other than the standard :80 port open for HTTP transfer. To counteract these concerns, major chat vendors have developed firewall proxy servers to encapsulate chat text and browser synchronization commands in straight HTTP.

Various chat servers come with proprietary user information databases or support standard apps, including SQL, LDAP, and ODBC compliant storage databases. As with threaded discussion servers, Windows NT 4.0 and Sun Solaris 2.x are by far the most popular operating systems available.

While vendors have a variety of requirements for system memory, 32 Mb should get you going. Storage requirements are not as great as message boards, since (unless you leave logging options on) information transmitted is not stored. Plan on a minimum of 20 Mb to get started.

Case Study: Citicorp (www.citibank.com)

Citicorp firmly believes in offering user forums to build a sense of community around its products and services. The bank has added both threaded discussion and real-time chat capabilities to provide customers with an interactive resource to learn about investment options and bank services from both company representatives and other users. Additionally, the Website utilizes guides who host financial subject areas such as mortgages, credit cards, and pension plans. At each customer information section, the guides answer questions, steer users to information, write columns, and moderate chats.

The bank's embrace of real-time, interactive communication software represents a paradigm shift in the corporate approach to the Web, says Forrester analyst Emily Green. "Service companies are starting to grasp the intimacy aspects of the Web," she says. "With the size of the investments that they make online, [banks] need to make sure people stick around."

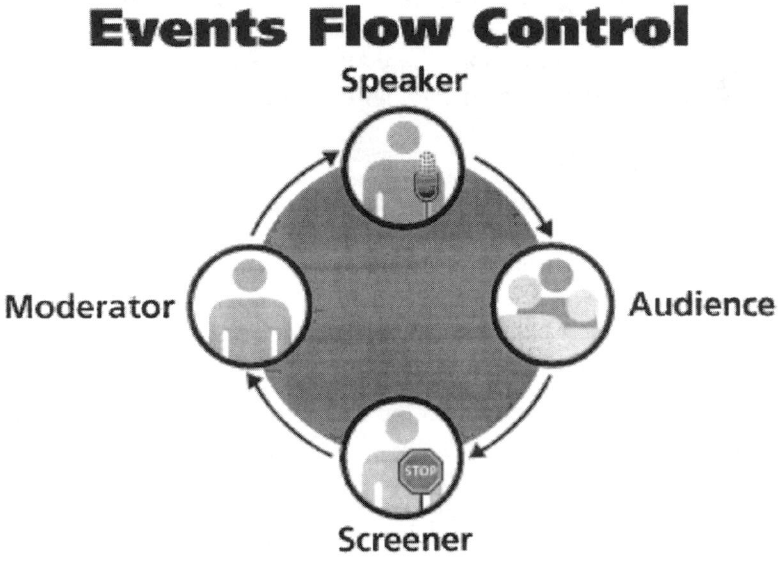

Events Flow Control

Exhibit 10.4. The normal flow of an Internet event.

ONLINE EVENTS: ONE-TO-MANY DISCUSSIONS

While threaded discussion boards and open chat rooms create community forums that draw allegiance to a company's brand, moderated online events are an excellent means to bring targeted customers together to exchange information in a controlled manner.

Internet events are the "Larry King Shows" of the Web — users have an opportunity to submit questions directly to the individuals running the event. Usually, a group of screeners will filter and edit incoming questions. Appropriate and interesting inquiries are then presented to the speaker and to the audience as a whole — to be answered in real time. Exhibit 10.4 demonstrates the normal flow of an Internet event.

While Internet events are typically run using special moderation add-ins to leading text chat software packages, many organizations have turned to a blended multimedia offering for their online discussions. For example, using video-streaming technology, an investment bank could bring one of their sector analysts online to present his or her conclusions about a specific investment vehicle or market trend.

During the course of the presentation, the analyst could also present slides, graphics, and charts to the audience. Since the entire event is pushed out to the users' browser (generally by breaking the browser into frames for text content, video, and presentation graphics), the attendee

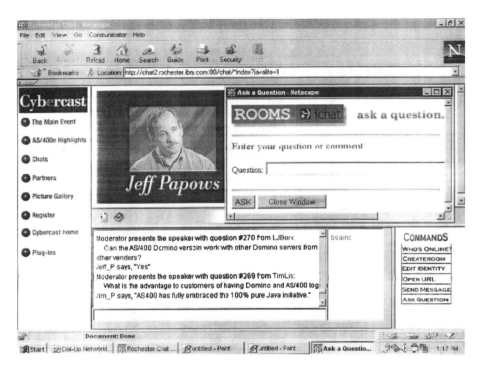

Exhibit 10.5. The IBM Web event.

won't need any additional software or hardware (such as microphones, Internet phones, or video cameras) to receive a multi media-rich experience. Exhibit 10.5 demonstrates an online event that was held by Jeff Papows, president and CEO of Lotus, to introduce the new IBM AS400e server.

One of the major challenges of running online events is actually communicating to the targeted audience the location, time, and content of the event in a manner that draws significant attention and ensures participation by audience members. Instant messages, generally text-based announcements that pop up in the forefront of open windows on users' computers, are a great way to invite targeted participants to online forums.

Using instant messaging technology, clients can be notified the second that critical new investment information is available. They can then join a real-time, interactive discussion in a moderated chat environment. For instance, as Federal Reserve Chairman Alan Greenspan is testifying, a broker can send instant messages to her clients, inviting them into a closed session with leading analysts and company economists who offer insight and advice into appropriate market plays. An example of an instant message is shown in Exhibit 10.6.

117

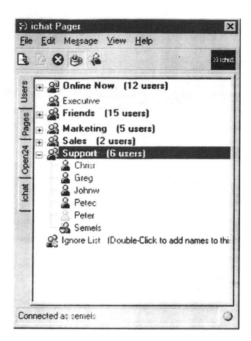

Exhibit 10.6. Instant messaging.

Online Events Requirements

Hosting online events requires more human intervention and thought than merely providing an open chat forum. Still, most event moderation tools are quite simple to use and can be installed and running in a few hours. Systems and technical requirements are comparable to the chat server section discussed above.

Case Study: Merrill Lynch

With nearly $1 trillion under management, Merrill realizes the importance of providing exceptional services that will enable it to continue to strengthen its customer relationships. For example, it was one of the first major financial services organizations to utilize e-mail for more efficient client interaction.

During the fall of 1996, Merrill Lynch began to look for a software solution that would allow it to hold moderated events where its technical and financial experts could conduct online seminars. After reviewing various products and considering proprietary online service companies, it chose an open, Internet solution. Joe Corriero, director of interactive technology, summed it up this way: "After we experimented with events on America Online, we realized that we would never reach our targeted customer base through AOL's closed community business model. We clearly saw the Web as the future for our customer interaction needs."

Online events represent a logical progression of the use of Internet technology and mark an exciting new opportunity for Merrill customers to interact directly with leading company minds. Merrill actually holds three types of online events:

- Public events — industry luminaries present their predictions on market trends and technological innovations.
- Private events — financial consultants interface with their key clients over the Web to discuss investment strategies and appropriate market moves.
- Financial consultant-only events — financial consultants gather together for training and focused discussions.

E-COMMERCE: ONE-TO-ONE DISCUSSIONS

The Internet is an exciting new communication channel for E-commerce-motivated interaction. Where companies and customers were once locked to the phone or face-to-face meetings to communicate, the Internet enables customers to go beyond the telephony and brick and mortar world to sample, research, and purchase goods.

With Web-based transactions expected to grow to more than US$220 billion by 2000 (source: International Data Corp), the returns for investments in technology that provide the means for customers to gather information and make informed purchases will be enormous.

What's been missing, until recently, has been a means to actually communicate with a company representative online for advice during the course of a purchase. Many would-be buyers have left Websites in disgust after they've been unable to find the answer to a key question. Forrester reports indicate that only 2.7 out of every 100 browsers that enter a commerce-centric Website actually buy. And 67 percent of consumers who make it through the purchase process to the order page still give up before completing the transaction. According to Yankelovich Partners, 63 percent won't buy over the net until there's more human interaction.

To make sure that prospects receive information and have the purchase assurance offered through live human contact without having to logout and make a phone call or wait for an e-mail response, several new solutions are being offered.

Text-Based Conferencing, Screen Synchronization, and Web ACDs

Chat solutions, either in open forums or in specific one-to-one channeled environments, create the capacity for instant correspondence. Upon

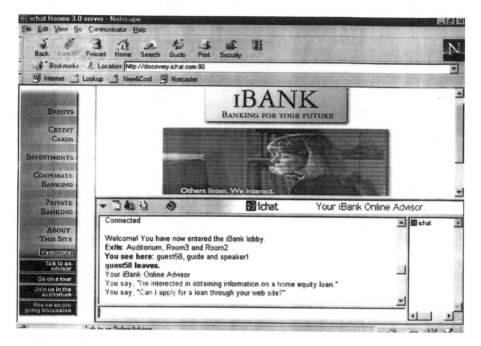

Exhibit 10.7. An example of text-based conferencing.

clicking on a "live help" button, a prospect can be given the opportunity to enter into a text dialogue with a sales rep who can then push information such as charts, diagrams and product/service descriptions (through browser screen synchronization) directly to the customer. Exhibit 10.7 represents one potential application for text-based conferencing.

While several standalone chat applications can function for basic live support, the integration of a Web-based automated call distributor (ACD) to route requests for help to appropriate agents, based on customer attributes, work flow rules, and agent availability, will be needed to handle heavily trafficked call centers that wish to complement their telephony commerce efforts with Internet-based sales assistance.

CTI CallBack

Offering a callback mechanism for customers is another option for live correspondence. While a button that allows a customer to submit a request for a phone call brings one close to true Internet interactivity, the delays inherent in actually routing a call to the appropriate agent in conjunction with the limits for customers with a single phone line (such as an individual dialing in from a hotel room) make CTI callback a secondary option at this point.

Voice and Video Conferencing

H.323-based voice and video transmissions have been heralded as major new breakthroughs in Internet communication. However, the bandwidth, processing power, and hardware requirements to actually run a video transmission, and the limited quality still inherent in live, packet-switched communications, make this option one to consider on a limited basis. Within 2 years, IP telephony apps based on the H.323 protocol family will become much more prevalent.

Benefits of Live Interaction

Live interaction, through singular applications of the technology described above, or through a multi-option, multichannel communication center, offers several benefits to E-commerce efforts, including:

- Higher closure rates
- Higher average sales prices due to agent cross-selling and up-selling activity
- Improved customer satisfaction due to live human availability

Live Interaction Requirements

Each of the applications described above requires a variety of hardware and software depending on the scope of the project and the integration into telephony support processes. In most cases, it is recommended to work with the vendor and a leading E-commerce and/or call center system integrator to develop the optimum solution for your efforts.

Once launched, live Internet interaction can be run as a standalone environment, or be integrated into telephone-based sales efforts. Human requirements can range from a single, part-time agent to monitor activities all the way through, to a multihundred rep call center to handle thousands of concurrent transactions. An additional benefit to consider with text-based conferencing is the multitasking capabilities and voice breaks that text correspondence enables agents to experience.

Case Study: Roxy Systems

Roxy.com is a major E-commerce merchandising partner for Web-based enterprises including ABC NEWS/ESPN Internet Ventures, The Microsoft Plaza, CBS Sportsline, and Excite!, and is a leading reseller of Direct TV and other consumer electronics products. In order to convert more browsers to buyers, Roxy has turned to offering live customer sales reps through its Website.

"Live, Web-based support is an outstanding solution for relaying information to customers in real time during their purchase process," said Patrick Hudgin, VP of operations at Roxy Systems. "Our online sales have increased significantly this year using live reps across the Internet. We are confident that our online purchase conversion rates and average sales prices will continue to rise as live customer/agent interaction capabilities speed the sales process and make our customers more comfortable with net-based transactions."

On the Roxy Systems Website (www.roxy.com) and on customized commerce sites that Roxy is creating for ABC and ESPN, sales prospects are given the option to receive live help during the research and purchase process.

When the customer requests live help, the system's dynamic queuing mechanism routes the individual to the appropriate sales agent based on customer profile, question urgency, and agent availability. At that point, the agent and customer have multiple options for live interaction, including text-based conferencing and synchronized browser screens.

Roxy has found that by presenting information directly to the individual in real time, the prospect is able to quickly return to self-help mode and complete the online transaction. Following the live session, question resolution and session data can be automatically stored in Roxy's customer management system, posted in the online knowledge base for future self-service sessions, and, when requested, e-mailed directly to the customer.

Moving forward, Roxy plans to integrate other communication channels such as automated e-mail routing, phone callback, and voice/video conferencing. Additionally, Roxy expects to utilize additional automated knowledge base and FAQ self-help capabilities.

CUSTOMER SUPPORT

As discussed thus far, Internet-based interactive technology can be used to bring a prospect to a company's Website to participate in ongoing discussions and debates over various issues. It can also be used to hold major online events, further closing the gap between an individual's transition from prospect to customer. Live interaction then can be the critical element in E-commerce initiatives, as customers seek to buy everything from consumer commodities to complicated electronics systems online, and often need assistance before actually completing a transaction.

The final piece of the customer life cycle arises from the support side of the equation. Customer service is at the forefront of most organizations' concerns. With U.S. companies losing half of their customers every 5 years and 67 percent of clients leaving because of inadequate customer care, organizations are turning to the Internet to serve as a new channel for efficient customer service.

Through both online self-service and live help, companies also hope to reduce their share of the $60 billion that Brean Murray Institutional Research estimates is spent on support labor costs. According to Forrester Research, increased self-service, better distribution of information, and more efficient agent utilization can enable organizations to experience a 43 percent decrease in labor cost per customer contact through deployment of Web-based customer interaction solutions.

Internet-Based Customer Support in Action

One easy method to envision Web-based customer interaction is through a description of a customer's experience on a major Website.

Research indicates that over 80 percent of customer call center inquiries are routine questions, so the support process starts by giving customers easy self-help options, allowing valuable support agents to focus on more complicated inquiries, premium customers, and sales opportunities. Browsable and searchable self-help options, including dynamic frequently asked question (FAQ) and knowledge-based searching capabilities, ensure that customers can easily find answers to investment questions, account status, or portfolio position.

If they are unable to locate the support information required, customers can then have the option to send an e-mail inquiry or enter into a live help mode. Automated e-mail routing and response capabilities ensure a timely response in conjunction with escalation to a live agent if the question is unrecognized.

Should the customer request live help, dynamic queuing mechanisms route the request to the appropriate agent or group based on customizable business rules and attributes such as customer profile, question urgency, and agent availability. Ideally, the agent and customer will have multiple options for live interaction, including text-based conferencing, synchronized browser screens, phone callback, and voice and video conferencing (see the E-commerce section above for descriptions of each). Exhibit 10.8 and Exhibit 10.9 demonstrate a text-based interaction session from both a customer and agent perspective.

Following the live help session, customer and session data can be automatically stored in a third-party customer management system, posted in the organization's knowledge base for future self-service sessions, and when requested, e-mailed directly to the customer.

With the live help option, customers can be guaranteed a response in real time, without having to logoff a company's Website to pick up the telephone.

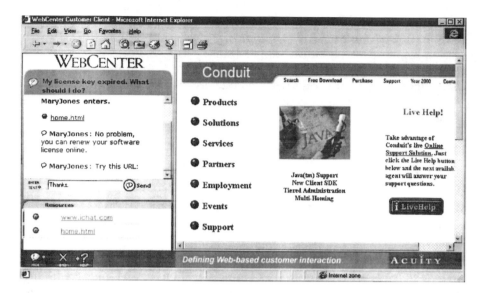

Exhibit 10.8. Text-based customer interaction.

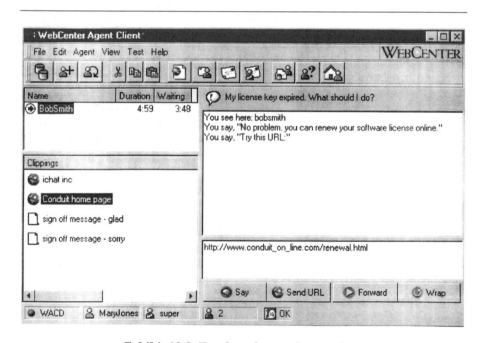

Exhibit 10.9. Text-based agent interaction.

Customer Support Requirements

As with major E-commerce undertakings, each of the applications described above requires a variety of hardware and software depending on the scope of the project and the integration into telephony support processes. In most cases, it is recommended to work with the software vendor and a leading customer support and/or call center system integrator to develop the optimum solution for your efforts.

Case Study: Charles Schwab & Co.

Schwab's help desk group, responsible for supporting 700 distributed financial executives, uses Web-based interactive technology for self-service and live help. At Schwab, employees are given the option to search and browse various online FAQs and knowledge bases to discover new investment vehicles, analyst recommendations, and HR information. They also have the ability to receive technical support online in a self-service mode. If the employee wishes to click into a live help session, Schwab's interactive, net-based system enables text conferencing and browser screen synchronization. "Web-based customer interaction is the foundation of Schwab's leadership position," says Rick Washburn, VP Customer Technology, Charles Schwab & Co. "Our vision for delivering an outstanding client experience through efficient self-service, online delivery and personalized, real-time, interactive support, has created an excellent environment for efficient, effective service."

CONCLUSIONS

As described in the opening section, Web-based interactive software enables organizations to effectively build communities, hold online events, assist their customers during the purchase decision process, and provide personalized support options, ranging from self-service through to live assistance.

With Forrester's reports that the deployment of Web-based customer interaction software can lead to a 43 percent decrease in labor cost per customer contact, and studies demonstrating that live help on a Website can increase sales margins by 15 to 25 percent through up-selling, cross-selling, and efficient content distribution, the return on investment (ROI) for interactive initiatives can be substantial. Forrester envisions that a $650 million company will save approximately $1 million in the first year alone through the integrated use of interactive customer support software.

With these types of figures and a new array of outstanding products from a multitude of vendors, now is the time to turn your static Website into a major interactive marketing, sales, and support system.

Author's Bio

Steven Semelsberger *is the Strategic Alliances and Market Development Manager for Acuity Corporation, the leading provider of Web-based customer interaction solutions. With over 2000 customers, including top Fortune 500 organizations such as Merrill Lynch, IBM, Oracle, Western Digital, and Charles Schwab & Co., Acuity has gathered extensive expertise in developing Net-based enterprise applications for marketing, E-commerce, customer service, and support. Semelsberger has extensive experience with major software and consulting services organizations through a variety of sales and marketing roles. He holds an MBA in high-technology marketing and finance from Duke University's Fuqua School of Business and a B.S. in management from Binghamton University.*

Chapter 11
Strategically Managing Internet Resources

Stuart Rosove

MORE SO THAN ANY OTHER TECHNOLOGY, the Internet and its related technologies have infiltrated Corporate America's technology infrastructure, rather than being proactively integrated into that infrastructure. This infiltration remains unparalleled in the Information Age, and presents issues that in many cases transcend technology. In effect, the infiltration of the Internet and its proliferating technologies pose an interesting challenge to both technical and executive management: how do you manage a dynamic, prolific, and oftentimes elusive technology from a strategic perspective?

On the surface, this challenge may seem daunting, especially since the issues are not immediately evident. However, once the real, potential, and *relevant* impact of the Internet's infiltration on an enterprise infrastructure is understood, it becomes easier to create a short-term plan to regain control and a long-term strategy to align the Internet, and ultimately manage it from a strategic perspective.

INFILTRATION NOT INTEGRATION

Many companies believe that they have taken more than sufficient measures to analyze the potential impact of the Internet on both their networks and businesses. In fact, as the Internet became more prevalent, it was not uncommon for IT shops of large enterprises to form task forces to produce integration and adoption recommendations for this new technology medium.

Take, for example, the highly publicized methodology upon which the large drug maker Eli Lilly & Co. used back in 1995 in order to develop its Internet adoption strategy. According to a feature in an early 1995 issue of *Computerworld*, this early adopter left no stone unturned in order to establish its strategy. In fact, the company's task force included representation from five different departments to ensure that it covered issues ranging

0-8493-9987-4/00/$0.00+$.50
© 2000 by CRC Press LLC

Exhibit 11.1. Eli Lilly & Co.'s Task Force

Department	Roles/Issues
Human Resources	Global cultural issues, people issues
Legal	Content, security, liability
Regulatory (Operations)	FDA issues, security, content
Marketing	Content issues
Information Systems and Support	Technical expertise, training issues, support, finance, and budgetary considerations, checks and balances

from training, support, and finance all the way through to the FDA and global/cultural issues (see Exhibit 11.1).

Many other Fortune 500s heeded this methodology as a common-sensical way in which to cover off all bases and took similar, if not identical approaches. However, the sheer dynamic and prolific nature of the Internet and its technologies has blind-sided many corporations as they execute against these task-force-driven integration and adoption recommendations.

E.I. du Pont is a strong case in point. At the 1998 Crossroads Conference in Palm Springs, CA, John H. Taylor, a du Pont Fellow/Information Technology Group, outlined his company's extensive Internet, intranet, and extranet implementation — an implementation against which it had taken the company 18 months to execute. According to Taylor, his department had consulted with divisions, departments, business units, and external consultants in order to develop their plan. He also noted that as their Internet integration and roll out called for noticeable capital expenditures he had to personally present the plan to reams of management throughout this 70,000+ person organization in order to gain buy-in.

With budgets fully approved, Taylor and his team started deploying distributed Web servers throughout du Pont, connecting this array through various internal lines, and ran multiple lines to the outside world to Internet Service Providers. As part of the company's plan, in 1997 his team had to identify and secure all connections to the outside world. Due to the complexity of the du Pont infrastructure and the distributed nature of their business units, this did not prove to be a simple task. However, according to Taylor, once the exercise was complete, he and his team felt fully satisfied that they had indeed secured the outer perimeter from any potential threat.

At the conference he stated that since his budgets were now exhausted on security products in order to ensure the highest level of protection from the outside world, a new concern had arisen — a concern that no one on his team had identified or even speculated about during the early formation of the company's adoption and integration plan. Specifically, he expressed concern with the fact that, through du Pont's intranet, he had just given his employees and business partners unfettered access to a host of distributed servers. More to the point, he added that recent findings clearly demonstrated that most attacks on data do not come from outside the enterprise, but rather from within!

This is just one example of the types of issues that have arisen through the execution of an Internet integration plan and strategy. Taylor cited additional issues that he felt had to be addressed which related directly to his new concern. One issue was the responsibility for extranet partner employee's activity inside the du Pont firewall. To him, this represented both a significant issue and a challenge, because it raised technological, legal, and business issues that had never been accounted for in the initial du Pont Internet strategy planning or budget process.

And du Pont is not alone. The anecdotes from midsize to large corporations and government agencies that have experienced significant issues during and after integration of the Internet are mounting. Within the du Pont, and these other corporations' experiences, lie invaluable lessons that should be studied by any corporation intending to truly manage their Internet resources from a strategic perspective.

LESSONS LEARNED

The lessons are varied, but share a common theme: unplanned "incidents" and/or issues translated into major productivity, legal, and other operational/cost implications. For example, a large government organization that is focused on research believed that the Internet's enormous amount of academic and interactive content would be an invaluable tool for their staff scientists. As a result, this agency, which supports over 100,000 users on their network segment, invested in a sizable pipe and large servers in order to provide responsive Internet access to the staff. Several months after providing service, the IT group wanted to ensure that the noted increase in network traffic directly correlated to Internet access. So, the IT group used an IP filter designed specifically to analyze protocol usage. To the group's surprise, neither HTTP (Web), FTP (file transfer), SMTP (outgoing mail), nor POP3 (incoming mail) was the top protocol. In fact, the protocol discovered was a Network-based gambling/gaming protocol! The resultant issue was how to technologically shut down certain protocols and enforce compliance to the agency's Usage Policy. More importantly, how to identify *new* protocols as they emerged, analyze their relevance to the business at hand, and then manage their usage.

Another unplanned or unforeseen issue that is common was recently experienced by a Fortune 500 company that took the tack of centralizing Internet access and essentially acting as service provider. In order to accommodate remote business units and users, this company provided

129

dial-up access via their 800 number. Shortly after implementation of this scheme, the company's monthly cost shot up in excess of $100,000. Here, the IT staff discovered that costs were being driven by users who remained online for extraordinarily long periods of time. The new issue became one of login management with time restrictions in order to manage cost and educate remote users on acceptable usage policy.

This company's experience also led to investigation of ways in which to effectively implement a charge-back model. In fact, a Wall Street brokerage found that their ongoing cost for maintaining service on a given pipe was much higher than anticipated, and realized that they did not have the corporately sponsored budget to maintain quality of service, especially as they extended the service provision to extranet partners. In this instance, the solution they sought "after-the-fact" had to provide an "equitable" charge-back model based upon usage rather than a flat fee being charged across the entire organization.

Another common occurrence that has been experienced by a number of midsize to large corporations is unnecessary Internet traffic being propagated onto corporate WANs. The issue then becomes one of unforeseen costs relating to upgrading the links that provide connectivity to these companies' headquarters.

UNDERSTANDING IP CREEP

A subtle yet, important underlying theme in many of the previous examples is the fact that when each corporate entity set out to study, recommend, and then implement an Internet strategy, they did not account for the fact that Internet protocols are proliferating at quite a clip. And, because these companies did not account for this, they could not foresee any related "after-the-fact" issues. At time of study and recommendation, most of these corporations depicted the Internet as being comprised solely of four protocols: HTTP (Web), FTP (file transfer), and SMTP/POP3. What they did not appreciate though, is that the Internet is an application deployment medium and that the protocols themselves are, in many cases, representative of applications.

And, as the Internet is a deployment and distribution medium, many new protocols managed to find their way into the IT infrastructure, and then proliferate onto numerous desktops. Take, for example, push or streaming technology such as PointCast or RealAudio. In both cases these products are based on their own protocols, and their propagation inside the Enterprise was not foreseen. In these cases, new traffic levels managed to literally bring networks to their knees, crippling the responsiveness and availability of the more mission-critical Internet protocols (or applications) such as access to a search engine (HTTP) or sending time-sensitive e-mail (SMTP).

Today one can easily make a case that the Internet/intranets host in excess of 300 different protocols. The not-for-profit organization, Internet Assigned Numbers Authority, hosts a site that specifies (www.iana.org) everything from unique port assignments to registration of character sets. According to information found on this site, one can count over 174 discrete assigned packet types, each which delineates a packet of a specific protocol. At the IP level, one discovers approximately 163 assigned protocols. So, even before you consider strategy, remember that Network Operating Systems and Network management products including Netware, Vines, and LanManger, each have their own protocols.

RECOGNIZING ALL INTERNET RESOURCES

The point behind enumerating the various protocols, understanding their functionality and appreciating the proliferation of new protocols is an important step toward managing Internet resources strategically. Simply put, one cannot manage what one cannot see or understand.

Armed with this understanding, it becomes apparent that a critical step toward effective management of the Internet is to be able to somehow identify *all* protocols being introduced into an environment and to understand their impact on that environment on an ongoing basis. However, if we heed the lessons learned previously in this chapter, intuitively we know that protocol discovery and analysis alone cannot paint the entire picture. Instead, we need to identify *all* Internet resources — both variable and fixed — that may have some unforeseen implications after initial integration of the Internet into the corporate computing environment, and somehow be able to manage them.

To achieve this end, the definition of "Internet Resource" which has been presented at a variety of industry conferences by a number of industry luminaries seems most practical: "An Internet Resource is *any* resource regardless of its tangibility, that is used to build on or derive value from the medium commonly known as the Internet in order to support a business objective." With this definition, there are at least four types of potential Internet resources to consider: hardware, such as servers, routers and switches; software, such as firewalls and Web-enabled applications; protocols such as HTTP (Web), FTP (file transfer), and RTSP (real-time streaming protocol); and end users.

GAINING CONTROL: CLASSIFYING RESOURCES

A first step toward gaining control over an Internet implementation gone awry, or for those just starting the implementation process, is understanding the nature of each resource type. Once understood, then the task of ultimately juxtaposing resources *against* a set of business objectives/actions can be achieved. The result of this exercise is that both the short-term "control gaining" tactics and forward management of Internet resources becomes readily apparent.

Hardware is the easiest to classify. It is the one fixed asset that is tied to a capital expenditure budget that has been established against a top or bottom line. And, in most cases, the most desirable strategy is to find ways in which these expenditures can be managed year after year. The classification then becomes a static one of: "Plan For and Manage To."

Software, although more of an intangible asset, also falls in this category. In fact, almost all corporately sanctioned software has, for the most part, also been tied to a capital expenditure budget. Here the exceptions become "new innovations" and "vendor throw-ins" such as a proxy server. However, these costs are oftentimes minute and not terribly upsetting to any budget line. The classification, again, for this category, is also the static: "Plan For and Manage To."

Protocols, because they are not static and are easily accessible by the user population (i.e., anyone with a browser can download an audio or video streaming product and almost immediately tax a pipe) must be classified as "Plan For, Monitor, Assess, and Dynamically Manage."

Users, because they are the most erratic and unpredictable resource, must also be classified as "Plan For, Monitor, Assess, and Dynamically Manage."

BUSINESS OBJECTIVES DICTATE ACTION PRIORITY

Clearly, it is impractical to attempt to enumerate all potential business objectives as they relate to Internet access and connectivity. However, there is a core principal against which all apply:

> Establish your fixed budgets to the best of your ability according to objective (i.e., enterprise-wide access vs. specific departmental/business unit access) and then monitor ALL the variable, nonstatic resources on an ongoing basis to ensure adherence to the stated business objectives.

Here, the following case studies are offered as examples.

Case 1. Business Objective: Provide Internet Access for Productivity Gains by Department

In this case, the business objective clearly dictates Enterprise-wide access, which enables IT to plan budgets for all hardware and software related to Internet service provision. The action also suggests the formation of a Best Use Policy, with some technological means to monitor by department. In addition, the full satisfaction of the objective requires some way in which to measure productive use of the Internet by department. This, in turn, suggests that departmental monitoring of usage by time, by protocol, and even by site, may be appropriate. The technological investment, therefore, is to identify cost-effective ways in which to extract the information and ultimately effect some form of policy enforcement. Here, the range of solutions are broad, including proxy server log files, firewall event log files, and specialized Internet access filtering products.

Case 2. Business Objective: Decentralize Costs for Internet Connectivity by Functional Department

In this case, the business objective clearly dictates enterprise-wide access, with a notion that IT needs to be a service provider to business units and departments. As such, it needs a way in which to monitor usage from a time, protocol, department, and site perspective. It also suggests that as the organization is going to charge back for usage in some meaningful fashion, that on-the-fly drill-down capabilities are going to be required on an ad hoc basis. Here the technological investment is to identify a solution, or set of solutions that enable continual monitoring and integration with a charge-back/financial package.

CONTROL TO MANAGE

In this chapter we have tried to illustrate the issues that companies face in "after-the-fact" implementation of Internet connectivity and then offered some suggestions for regaining control and moving forward. As the focus here has been on problem identification and technological solution, it only represents a foundation upon which to base short-term decisions such as monitoring usage. Certainly there are a variety of technology solutions that can monitor usage based on a variety of criteria. The right solution, however, is dependent on each organization's ultimate business objective. For some, proxy logs will be the answer, for others a fully integrated Internet access solution will be more appropriate. Hopefully, this chapter has prepared you to understand your criteria and to be better equipped to make your technology decisions.

Author's Bio

Stuart Rosove *is the founder of Sequel Technology Corporation, the leading provider of Internet Resource Management Solutions. Prior to stepping to the Board of Directors at Sequel as President and CEO, he was accredited with leading his 3-year-old start-up to hold the position of 43rd among Software Leaders, according to* Washington CEO Magazine *(1997).*

Prior to founding Sequel, Rosove was a principle of Rosove & Associates, a high-tech marketing consultation practice based in Seattle, WA. And before heading up his own marketing practice, Rosove was the corporate and marketing communications director for Delrina Corporation (1993). Other positions held by Rosove include manager, mar-

keting and public relations for QNX Software (1991), and founding partner of a Toronto-based advertising and public relations agency (1988).

Today, Rosove is the founder and Vice Chairman of Sequel Technology and sits on a variety of boards of advisors including ValGen Software and Design Intelligence. He also provides consultation to a handful of start-ups in the application management and proprietary network (services) markets.

Chapter 12
Law (or the Lack of It) on the Web: A Primer for Financial Services Technology Managers

Frederic M. Wilf

THE INTERNET APPEARS TO BE LIKE THE "WILD WEST" — ABOVE OR UN-CONNECTED TO THE LAW. The reality is that the Internet is pretty wild, but the law of each and every country, state, province, county, municipality, town and borough applies to the Internet, and its most famous aspect, the World Wide Web ("Web"). Website developers, programmers, users, and others (this chapter uses the term "Webmaster" for convenience) all need to be aware of the mechanisms of the law to get the maximum amount of protection for their work, while making sure that they do not trip over someone else's rights by mistake.

WHY THE WEB IS DIFFERENT: A LEGAL PERSPECTIVE

The law responds to each new technological challenge by first studying it, and then, if appropriate, doing something about it. For example, the Copyright Office started accepting copyright registrations for computer programs as early as 1964, but it was not until 1980 that Congress amended the U.S. Copyright Act to explicitly protect computer programs. Moreover, when the law initially confronts an issue, it usually does so in fits and starts.

The law tends to pigeon-hole issues. The Internet breaks all of the pigeon holes as it is a different form of communication that, in itself, can carry virtually all prior forms of communication. Distinctions that make sense

0-8493-9987-4/00/$0.00+$.50
© 2000 by CRC Press LLC

in hard copy or on television may be irrelevant on the Internet, while the technology of the Internet creates new distinctions that do not apply to any other media. A single Website may contain text, photographs, artwork (two-dimensional and three-dimensional), music and sound recordings, video, software, scripts, databases, and so on, all of which have been altered and arranged to form a single integrated work.

The law deals with Internet legal issues by analyzing each element that goes into a Website as if the element were by itself. An element by element analysis may take a little more time to complete, but as you will see, you do not need a lawyer to conduct this analysis. Much of this you can do yourself.

WHAT THIS CHAPTER COVERS

This chapter discusses legal issues that Webmasters should be aware of under U.S. law. For example, if a Webmaster would like to copy and use a photograph from another Website, and there is no copyright notice, can the Webmaster do this legally?

Suppose a Webmaster has completed a Website that consists of text, video, and sound, as well as searching software. How can the Webmaster protect the work, or at least have the right to sue anyone who pirates the work?

There are fairly simple techniques to protect what the Webmaster has created, as well as methods to enforce that protection. The other side of the coin is that the Webmaster does not want to unwittingly infringe on the rights of others, so a basic understanding of common legal problems can be helpful.

This chapter briefly discusses copyright, privacy, and contract law as they apply to Websites.

WHAT THIS CHAPTER DOES NOT COVER

This chapter discusses a number of legal issues that Webmasters face, but it does not cover every legal issue. Nor does it say everything that needs to be said for each issue that it does cover.

This chapter discusses the law in the U.S. Except for a few brief references, it does not discuss the law in any other country. More importantly, many issues in U.S. law (such as contract law) are a subject of state law, which means that the law will be different from one state to the next.

This chapter does not provide the "final word" on the state of the law. The law continues to change. One example is the U.S. Copyright Act, which was completely rewritten in 1976. However, Congress has seen fit to amend the Copyright Act several times each year since then. All of the areas of law discussed in this chapter are also subject to constant change.

Finally, this chapter does not provide legal, accounting, or other professional advice. If legal advice or other expert assistance is required, the services of a competent professional should be retained.

DO'S AND DON'TS

Normally, a list of do's and don'ts would be placed at the end of a chapter. We place it at the beginning, so that you have the answers while you read the details.

Do:

- Consider patents.
- Use "SM" (service mark) and "TM" (trademark) for your marks for services and goods; consider filing trademark applications with the state, federal, or foreign governments; place copyright notices; file copyright applications for your Websites.
- When multiple companies or parties work on a Website agree beforehand in a written document who will own the copyright and other rights; review contracts with your attorney before signing them and use an attorney to develop written agreements with your customers; investigate the law of every country in which your Website is used to provide services or sell goods.

Don't:

- Mail HTML or software files, or other works, to yourself to secure rights (it's an urban myth); wait until after signing an agreement to call your attorney; assume the law doesn't apply to you because you're on the Internet; assume the First Amendment protects you throughout the world (as one pundit likes to say, the U.S. Constitution is a local ordinance in Cyberspace); assume that the law in other countries is like that of the U.S.

COPYRIGHT LAW

Copyright law is the primary means to protect Websites. Copyright law is designed to protect "expressions" of ideas, while making available to others the underlying ideas, facts, and information. Copyright law defines what is and is not protected, as well the methods by which protection is enforced.

Owning a Copyright as Opposed to Owning an Object

When a person buys a book or a record, that person then owns the physical object — the book or record. Owning the book or record does not give the purchaser the right to copy the book or record, or make new versions of the book or record.

137

So, if you purchase a videotape of a 10-year-old movie, you can watch that movie and show it to your friends. However, you cannot copy scenes from the movie into your Website that is your guide to cinema without the permission of the person or company that owns the copyright to the movie.

As for the videotape, you can also sell it to another person (so long as you don't keep any copies for yourself). In copyright law, this is called the "first sale doctrine." Once the physical copy embodying the copyrighted work is sold, the purchaser can use or dispose of that copy any way she likes, so long as she does not make copies of the work (or portions of it).

Source of Law

The United States Copyright Act is the sole copyright statute in the U.S. This has been so since Congress preempted the field with the Copyright Act of 1976, which became effective on January 1, 1978.

No state is allowed to legislate in the area of copyright law, so there is no state copyright law. Nor is there a "common law" (judge-made) copyright law, so that judges cannot create new rights or responsibilities as they can in other areas of the law. Judges may interpret the U.S. Copyright Act, which means that a judge can create explanations and structures for resolving disputes where the Copyright Act is ambiguous, unclear, or incomplete.

For those who have access to federal statutes, the Copyright Act may be found in Title 17 of the United States Code. When this chapter refers to a section number, it will be to a section number of Title 17. For example, the definitions of copyright terms are found at Section 101 of the Copyright Act.

Definitions of Key Copyright Terms

Copyright law is whatever Congress says it is. Key to an understanding of copyright law is the terms that Congress uses in the Copyright Act. The definitions are important because a particular term will have one meaning in copyright law and a different meaning in a different area of the law. For example, the term *publication* in copyright law means dissemination to the general public; while *publication* in libel law means any dissemination of libelous matter to any other person, in public or private.

The following are key terms defined in Section 101 of the Copyright Act.

Work: A *work* in the copyright lingo is any embodiment that contains expression that may be protected under the copyright law. Works include building designs, drawings, books or any kind of text, two-dimensional and three-dimensional art, computer programs, movies, etc. All of the things protected by copyright law and discussed in this chapter are called *works*.

Audiovisual Works: An audiovisual work is a series of related images and any accompanying sounds that are intended to be shown by the use of machines, such as projectors or electronic equipment, including computers and televisions. It does not matter whether the audiovisual work is embodied in tape, on film, on floppy or CD-ROM, or in an MPEG file.

Derivative Work: A derivative work is a work that is based upon one or more preexisting works, regardless of the type of preexisting work. The derivative work can be in any form in which a work may be recast, transformed, or adapted. Digitizing a photograph creates a derivative work (the digital version) of a preexisting work (the film-based or analog photograph). A derivative work can constitute an original work of authorship that is separate and distinct from the preexisting work. As noted above, however, the copyright owner can control whether a person is allowed to make derivative works of the copyright owner's work.

One key issue involving derivative works is the point at which a derivative work is no longer considered derivative. For example, if you digitize a photograph, that creates a derivative work that can be recognized as a copy of the original. If you then alter the digitized version to the point where it is no longer recognizable in any way as a derivative of the original, then you have created a new work.

Think of it as melting down a bronze statue. If you melt it down partially and part of the original is still recognizable (even a small part), then you have a derivative work. However, if the bronze is melted completely into a liquid and then poured into a new mold, an original work is created that no longer owes anything to the prior work, except for the raw material.

Thus, if you take a photograph on print film of the White House, that is an original work. If you digitize the print, you have created a derivative work. If you then use the digital version (the first derivative work) of the White House photograph to create new images, such as a Blue House, a Pink House, a Green House, or a Fuchsia House, each of these variations would be a separate derivative work, owing to the original print-based work. However, if you so changed the digital version of the photograph that none of the original work is recognizable, then the newest version is no longer a derivative work of the original work.

Fixed in a Tangible Medium of Expression: The Copyright Act automatically protects all works — including Websites — as soon as they are written on paper, stored on a disk, or saved in some other medium. As an example, if one person talks to another person face-to-face, no copyrighted work is created. However, if one person records the conversation on audiotape or videotape, or in an MPEG or WAV file, then a copyrighted work is created.

Copyright Exclusive Rights: The Copyright Act grants five exclusive rights to a copyright owner, who may: (1) copy or reproduce the work, (2) prepare derivative works, (3) distribute copies, (4) perform the work, and (5) display the work. Thus, the owner of the copyright can control who copies the work, who can make new versions of the work, who can distribute copies of the work by hard copy mail or e-mail, who can perform the work on stage or screen, and who can display the work on the walls or monitors of an art gallery.

Author and *Owner:* The *author* is the person who creates a work. The creator of the work is called an *author* even though the creator may be creating a photograph, a videotape, a sound recording, or a Website.

The *owner* is the owner of the copyright at any given time. Initially, the author and the owner are the same person, because the author is the initial owner of the copyright. Then, the author may transfer the copyright to another person, who becomes the owner. Often, the terms *copyright owner* and *copyright holder* are used interchangeably.

License: A *license* is a contract by which the copyright owner allows another person to exercise any one or more of the five exclusive rights. An *exclusive license* means that only the licensee can exercise the licensed rights. A *nonexclusive license* means that the owner is free to allow people other than the licensee to exercise the licensed rights.

Assignment: This is a document by which the copyright owner transfers all of the exclusive rights to another person, who then becomes the copyright owner.

Publication: This is the distribution of a work by sale, rent, or lending copies of the work. Generally speaking, any distribution of a copyrighted work to the general public is deemed a publication of the work, regardless of whether copies of the work are sold by mail order, door-to-door, or while standing on a street corner. As soon as a Website is publicly available on the Web, it is *published* for the purpose of copyright law.

WHEN COPYRIGHT ATTACHES

Copyright law automatically protects any copyrightable work that is "fixed in a tangible medium of expression" (see above). Another way to think of it is that copyright law protects any work that has some physical embodiment, even if it is only a series of magnetic blips on a tape or disk.

You do not have to register your copyright, although registration is recommended for most works that can be copied and which are worth more than the few dollars it costs to register the copyright with the Copyright Office. (See Copyright Registration, below.)

WHAT COPYRIGHT PROTECTS

At its most basic form, a copyright is a right to copy. The owner of the copyright can control who can have a copy and what can be done with it.

The copyright owner can allow one person to have five copies, another person to have three copies, and refuse to allow a third person to have any copies.

The copyright owner of a photograph can allow one person to make a copy of the photograph and incorporate it into a Website, allow another person to use the same photograph for advertising purposes only, while licensing a third person for the sole purpose of distributing e-mail copies of the photograph to Internet addresses that begin with the letter "q."

The Idea/Expression Dichotomy

Copyright law does not protect ideas, but only expressions of ideas. If there are many ways to express an idea, then copyright law will protect one expression from being copied or incorporated into another expression without the permission of the copyright owner. In copyright lingo, this separation of ideas and expressions is called the "idea/expression dichotomy."

If there is only one way or just a handful of ways to express an idea, then the Copyright Act may not be used to protect that idea, and other people may use any expression of that idea.

The problem with drawing a line between ideas and expressions is that the line is drawn at a different place for each work. Thus, for one computer program, the line may be drawn in one place, while in another computer program the line is drawn in a different place. Moreover, since most copyrightable works contain many elements and pieces, each element is separately evaluated for the purpose of drawing the line between idea and expression.

So, if a brochure contains photographs, text, and drawings, then each photograph, each paragraph of text, and each drawing constitute a separate element that must be evaluated to determine where the line is drawn between idea and expression. Is one photograph an unadorned picture of a man in a business suit? If so, then anyone can use the idea of photographing a man in a business suit, but this particular photograph cannot be copied or reproduced without the permission of the copyright owner.

WHO IS THE COPYRIGHT OWNER

Under Section 201 of the Copyright Act, ownership of the copyright goes to the person or persons who created the work (the "authors" of the work). Thereafter, the copyright owner may transfer ownership to another person, partnership, corporation, or other entity that can own property.

141

The exception to this general rule is "work for hire," which has two distinct and different definitions found in Section 101 of the Copyright Act.

Work for Hire in Employment Relationships

Under the first definition of "works made for hire," an employer is deemed to be the "author" of all works created by an employee within the scope of his or her employment.

It does not matter whether the work was created at the office or at the employee's home, and it does not matter whether the work was created when the employee was being paid, or was on a lunch break. As long as the type of work created falls within the broad boundaries of the tasks the employee performs, then the employer automatically owns the copyright to that work. No written documents are necessary.

As an example, if a person who works as an accountant as an employee of a large accounting firm creates a rock video Website at night, then that accountant would personally own the copyright to the Website. Creating Websites is not within the "scope of employment" of the accountant.

By contrast, if a person is employed to create Websites of all types by day, then her employer may own the copyright to any rock video Website she creates at night.

Work for Hire in Independent Contractor Relationships

The first definition of "works made for hire" is limited to employment relationships. By contrast, the second definition of "works made for hire" is completely different in that it applies to independent contractors who create certain types of copyrightable works, and requires that each contributor sign a written document.

The second definition of "works made for hire" states that the copyright in specially ordered or commissioned works will be owned by one party where all the parties expressly agree in a written document or documents signed by all of them that the work to be created is a work for hire.

This definition is limited to (1) contributions to collective works, (2) parts of a motion picture or audiovisual work, (3) translations, (4) supplementary works, (5) compilations, (6) instructional texts, (7) tests, (8) answers to tests, and (9) atlases. These nine classes of works may be thought of as "commissioned work for hire." This definition of work for hire does not apply to any other type of work. A Website can be a "work made for hire" under this legal definition if the Website is instructional, and if the contributors agree in writing beforehand that the Website is a work for hire.

Where Work for Hire Does Not Attach

Work for hire does not apply to self-employed individuals who are creating copyrightable works by themselves. A person working alone (and not as an employee of anybody else or of any partnership or corporation) will own the copyright and will be called the "author" of the work.

Work for hire does not apply to independent contractors creating works that are not commissioned works for hire (see above). So, a photographer who takes photographs of a product for an advertising campaign does not come under either definition of work for hire, and the photographer will own the copyright for each photograph. Photographs are not one of the nine types of commissioned work for hire discussed in the Copyright Act, even though the photographer was commissioned by someone else.

Work for hire does not apply to independent contractors creating commissioned works for hire where there is no written agreement. If ten people agree to contribute to the making of a film, but there is no written document signed by them, then the film is not a work for hire. Instead, all ten people who contribute will be joint owners of the copyright in the film.

How to Ensure that Only One Person or Company Owns the Copyright

The Copyright Act defines who will own the copyright by default. However, the default may be changed at any time by use of a written document signed by the parties.

Regardless of whether either definition of "work for hire" applies to a type of work, you can always write and sign an agreement among those who contribute to a work that one person or company owns the copyright. Thus, an independent Website developer can assign her copyright to her client in writing. An employee and an employer can even agree in writing that the employee will own the copyright to everything she creates, regardless of whether it is within the scope of her employment.

COPYRIGHT NOTICE

Section 401 states that copyright notices are optional, but if you are going to use them then the notice should consist of three parts: (1) "Copyright," "Copr." or "(c)"; (2) if the work is "published" (see above), then include the year of first publication; and (3) the name of the copyright owner. Copyright notices are still strongly recommended, but are no longer required.

Under the Copyright Act, if the author places a copyright notice on a work, and then later sues an infringer, the infringer cannot claim in court that she did not know the work was protected by the author's copyright.

Prior to 1989, any work published without a copyright notice ran the risk of losing its copyright protection. This approach allowed readers and users to assume that any published work that did not bear a copyright notice was in the public domain, and thus available for reuse by everyone else. Now that the law has been changed, you must assume that all works are protected under copyright law, regardless of whether or not the work bears a copyright notice. The good news is that it is tougher to lose a copyright, but the bad news is that you must assume that everything is protected by copyright law, unless you are told otherwise.

COPYRIGHT REGISTRATION

The first thing that you should know about copyright registration is that it is optional, but recommended for many works. Section 408 will tell you that. The second thing that you should know about copyright registration is that you do not need a lawyer to do it for you. The Copyright Act does not say that, so I will. Registering a copyright is a fairly simple and painless process.

Congress uses a "carrot and stick" approach to copyright registration. The "carrot" is that if you file the copyright application early enough, you get additional rights should you need to go to court and sue an infringer. The "stick" is that you cannot file a copyright infringement lawsuit unless you have received the certificate of registration, or at least have filed the copyright application.

Why You Should Register Your Copyright Early and Often

Copyright registration is recommended for any work worth more than the filing fee (presently $20), and for any work that may be stolen or otherwise infringed. If the work is worth less than the filing fee, why bother? If the work cannot be stolen or infringed (which is not the case for most works), then there is no need to bother.

There are several reasons why early registration of copyrights is recommended. First, under Section 411, you need to have a certificate that shows the copyright is registered before you can sue anyone for infringement (although Congress has been debating removing this requirement). Since it normally takes several months to receive the certificate of registration, you would have to wait several months before suing an infringer, or you would have to pay an additional fee to get the certificate of registration back in a week. By filing early, you will already have the certificate of registration in hand in case you have to sue someone.

Second, in a copyright infringement suit, under Section 412, the copyright owner may get attorney's fees and additional types of damages if the copyright application was filed prior to the start of the infringement, or shortly after publication (i.e., within 3 months of the date of first publication). If the copyright is registered after the infringement begins, then the copyright owner cannot ask for attorney's fees or additional types of damages called "statutory damages" (see Damages and Remedies, below). Congress has been debating removing the filing of a copyright application as a prerequisite for attorney's fees and statutory damages, but Congress had not passed a bill changing this part of the law as this book went to press.

How to Get and File an Application for Copyright Registration

You should not need a lawyer to file a copyright registration. Unlike federal trademark and patent applications, the process is simple.

Call the Copyright Office at 202/707-3000 for free copyright application forms and instructions, or download them in Adobe Acrobat (.pdf) format from <http://lcWeb.loc.gov/copyright>. The telephone number currently is an extensive voice mail system that will allow you to leave your name and address, and the Copyright Office will mail you forms and instructions on how to fill them out. It usually takes 4 to 6 weeks to receive the forms. Once you have the forms, you can always make more forms for yourself by photocopying the hard-copy forms onto a good-quality white bond paper. This will make the Copyright Office happy because they don't want to mail out any more forms than they have to. Of course, if you download the forms and instructions, you will not need to wait 4 to 6 weeks to receive them and you can print an unlimited number of copies without having to photocopy them.

To register a copyright, you need to send the completed application (two sides of one piece of paper), a check for the filing fee (presently $20), and a copy or other specimen of the work. Different forms are used for different types of works, and the specimen will also be different from one type of work to another. For most Websites, the specimen of the work is one copy of the site printed on paper, plus up to 50 pages of code or scripts used on the site.

Once you file the application, it often takes 3 to 8 months to receive the certificate of copyright registration. Neatness counts on the application because the Copyright Office will make a few marks on the application, and then photocopy the application onto a nicer piece of paper to create the certificate of copyright registration. If you can't easily read the application, neither will anyone else, least of all a judge who is trying to enforce the registration as shown on the certificate. If you later lose or misplace the certificate that you receive, you can always get another from the Copyright Office for a small fee.

TRANSFER OF COPYRIGHT

A copyright owner may transfer all or part of a copyright by a written document, or by bequeathing the copyright in a will like any other family heirloom. A copyright may not be transferred by an oral agreement, although the parties can make an oral agreement effective by following it up with a written document.

If the copyright is transferred by a written document, the person transferring the copyright needs to sign the document. The person receiving the copyright may sign the document, but it is not effective unless the person transferring the copyright signs the document.

A copyright is "divisible" which means that the owner of all five exclusive rights can transfer one of the five rights to one person, another of the rights to a second person, and the rest of the rights to a third person. This often makes it difficult to track down who owns which rights when the copyright has been parceled out among several owners.

COPYRIGHT TERM

Knowing the copyright term is useful, since it allows you to plan how long you will have rights to your own work, as well as help you determine whether another person's copyright has expired.

Works Created Since 1978

Under Section 302, for all works created by individuals since 1978, the copyright is good for the life of the author, plus 50 years. If two or more individuals are the creators of a work, then the copyright expires 50 years after the last author dies. Thus, if a particular work is created by a Webmaster in 1999, and the Webmaster dies in the year 2030, the copyright will be good until the year 2080.

For all anonymous works, pseudonymous works, and works made for hire, the copyright is good for 75 years from the date of first publication, or 100 years from the creation of the work, whichever occurs first.

Thus, for a Website where all the contributors signed "work for hire" agreements, the copyright will last for 100 years from the date that it is created, or 75 years from the date that it is first made available to the public, whichever term is shorter. Another example is where an employee creates an Intranet Website for her employer in 1999, and if the work is not made available outside the company the copyright will be good until the year 2099.

This assumes that the Copyright Act is not changed again in the interim; however, the Copyright Act will likely be changed on this issue. As this book went to press, it seemed likely that Congress would change the length of copyright protection for individuals from life-plus-50-years to life-plus-70-years. The term for anonymous works, pseudonymous works, and works made for hire would be extended to 95 years from the date of first publication, or 120 years from the creation of the work, whichever occurs first.

Works Created Before 1978

During the period 1909 through 1977, the copyright on a published work was good for 28 years, and then had to be renewed (by filing a paper with the Copyright Office) for another 28 years. Unpublished works received unlimited protection. Just to complicate things, Congress wrote in Section 304 that the copyright in any work published prior to 1978, but still protected as of 1978, would be protected for up to 75 years. As you might expect, this led to confusion and has made a lot of work for copyright attorneys.

Unpublished works under prior law were protected so long as they were not published. Thus, a personal diary written in the 1860s would be protected from copying forever under prior law, so long as the diary remained unpublished. However, under Section 303, all works not published by 1978 remain protected under the Copyright Act, but that protection would terminate no later than 2002 if the work remains unpublished, or no later than 2027 if the work is published between 1978 and 2002.

As a rule of thumb, you should assume that any work published before about 1922 is in the public domain (which means that anyone can use it), and that any work created (published or not) in or after 1922 is protected by the Copyright Act, unless proven otherwise.

THE REAL MEANING OF "PUBLIC DOMAIN"

In the copyright context, the term "public domain" means that nobody owns or has a claim to a particular copyrightable work. Thus, anyone can use, copy, or make derivative works of a public domain work. Some people confuse the "public domain" with "published work" or "publication." A work that is publicly available or published via the Web or otherwise is not necessarily in the public domain.

When a copyrightable work enters the public domain, it never leaves the public domain. However, anyone can take a public domain work, add new expression to it, and claim a copyright in the new work. However, the copyright in that circumstance covers only the new expression (the aspects that were added), so the original work will continue to be in the public domain for anyone else to use.

As an example, the stories of the Brothers Grimm are now in the public domain because they were published well before 1922. Anyone can copy the original stories, translate them into English, edit them, add new art

147

work and video, and publish the result on a Website. Copyright law will protect the new art work, the video, the new translation (translations of human languages are considered derivative works), as well as the editing if the editing is more than trivial. If anyone does copy the Website or protected elements of the Website, then that person can be sued for copyright infringement. However, copyright law will not prevent anyone else from going back to the original stories, making their own translation, and publishing them with other art work on their own Website.

INFRINGEMENT OF COPYRIGHTS

Once you have a copyright, you may need to sue a pirate. On the other hand, you may need to know what you face if someone accuses you of being a copyright pirate.

Filing a Copyright Infringement Action

As noted above, U.S. citizens cannot file a copyright infringement action unless they have received a certificate of copyright registration from the Copyright Office. Although Congress has debated removing this requirement, it was still in effect when this book went to press.

By contrast, a French citizen who created a Website in Germany for a Japanese company that hosts is Website in Sri Lanka can file a copyright infringement suit in Peoria, IL, without first obtaining a U.S. copyright registration.

You should always have an experienced attorney represent you in court. Like the television commercials that show professional race car drivers on race tracks, you should not try litigating a copyright infringement case by yourself.

Damages and Remedies that a Court May Award

Under Section 504 of the Copyright Act, the copyright owner asks the judge to award either "actual damages" or "statutory damages."

Actual damages is measured by taking the money lost by the copyright owner and adding to that the amount of money made by the infringer as a result of the infringement.

Statutory damages means that the judge picks a number in a range (presently $500 to $20,000) per work infringed and awards that amount as damages. Moreover, if the judge finds that the infringement was committed "willfully," then judge picks a number from a larger range (presently $500 to $100,000) per work infringed. Statutory damages are usually chosen when the infringer has not lost much money as a result of the infringement, yet needs to teach the infringer a lesson by making the damage award much higher. Unfortunately, statutory damages are available to copyright owners only when the copyright is registered prior to the beginning of the infringement, or shortly after the work is first published.

The judge can always assess court costs and order the seizure and destruction of all infringing copies. The judge can also issue injunctions. Under Section 505, if the copyright was registered prior to the infringement, the judge has the option of making the infringer pay the attorney's fees and expenses of the copyright owner, which can total tens or hundreds of thousands of dollars.

FAIR USE OF COPYRIGHTED WORKS

Certain uses of a copyrighted work may not be prosecuted. One set of uses is called "fair use," which is defined in Section 107 of the Copyright Act. Fair use is not a magic formula that instantly turns copying into a permitted use. Rather, it is a set of guidelines that balance the rights of the copyright owner with other rights and needs, including First Amendment concerns and the need to give students and teachers additional leeway for educational purposes.

Fair use is limited to a handful of certain types of uses, mostly related to teaching, comment and criticism. Four factors are weighed to determine whether a particular circumstance is a fair use or an infringement.

In one case, several publishers sued a nationwide chain of copy shops located on college campuses. College professors assembled copies of articles from magazines and journals into a sort of text book, and left the copies at the copy shop. The professors then told their students to go to the copy shop and pay for one copy of the hand-made textbook. When the publishers sued the copy shop, the copy shop claimed that it is allowed to make copies as a fair use because the professors wanted the copies for teaching purposes. The courts sided with the publishers because the professors did not bother to ask permission from the copyright owners before copying the articles, and because the handmade text books competed with text books sold by the publishers. Similarly, if the professors had posted the same text on a Website for reading by their students, the outcome would likely have been the same.

Types of Uses Recognized as Fair Uses

The making of copies without permission is excused as a fair use only when the purpose of the use is criticism, comment, news reporting, teaching (including multiple copies for classroom use), scholarship, or research.

The purposes are fairly narrowly constrained. So, teachers can invoke fair use when they make copies for their classroom, but publishers of classroom books cannot claim fair use, because the book publishers are not directly teaching students.

First Factor: Purpose and Character of the Use. The first factor weighed is the purpose and character of the use, including whether such use is of a commercial nature or is for nonprofit educational purposes. Thus, if the person making the copies is doing so for a profit, that weighs against fair use. However, if the person is making copies for teaching at church, this factor will weigh in favor of fair use.

Second Factor: Nature of the Copyrighted Work. If the copyrighted work is one that generates large amounts of money, such as advertisement-funded Websites that receive a great deal of traffic, popular books, records, or movies, then any copying will be closely scrutinized. If the copyrighted work is not a moneymaker, then fair use is easier to prove.

Third Factor: Amount Used. It is an axiom of copyright law that an infringement occurs when even a small part of a work is copied, especially if the portion copied is of high quality or is important to the rest of the work. The third fair use factor recognizes that by weighing the amount and substantiality of the portion copied in relation to the copyrighted work as a whole. If one paragraph is copied from the text of a large Website, then the portion is not substantial. However, if 20 seconds are sampled from a 2-minute song, that is substantial, especially if the 20 seconds segment contains the chorus of the song.

Fourth Factor: Effect on the Market. One of the primary purposes of the Copyright Act is to ensure that authors of copyrighted works are compensated. So it is not surprising that the fourth factor of fair use is the effect of the copying on the potential market or value of the original, copyrighted work. If each copy made without permission replaces a copy that would have been sold, then that weighs against fair use. If the copies made do not affect the sales of the original, then this factor weighs in favor of fair use.

Application of Fair Use

Initially, the use of the copy should fit into one of the categories (criticism, comment, etc.) stated above. Then, all four of the factors are weighed together. Some factors can be more important than others. There is no mechanical application of "three-out-of-four factors wins."

For example, what happens when a publisher creates a Website containing the copyrighted works of a living playwright without the playwright's permission? The Website contains all of the text of all of the playwright's plays, plus full-motion video of one play that the publisher captured off a television rebroadcasting an old movie version. The Website is intended for students who pay $2 each time they access the Website. Is this a fair use?

First, you must consider the type of work. Teaching, scholarship, and research are all included as fair use purposes, so the Website should be weighed under the four factors. The first factor cuts against a fair use. The publisher is making money in this venture, even though the purchasers may be nonprofit educational users. Second, the nature of the copyrighted work consists of highly profitable works (plays and movies, which are subject to video rental income and broadcast royalties), even though the sales of texts of plays probably do not generate large amounts of income for playwrights or other copyright owners (since the producer of the movie may own the copyright to that production).

The third factor also cuts against fair use because the Website contains an entire movie and the entire text of each play. Finally, the fourth factor also cuts against fair use since each access to the Website potentially replaces one copy of each play manuscript that could have been sold, as well as one copy of the movie that could have been sold. So, this is not a fair use, and the publisher should seek licenses from the playwright and the owner of the copyright in the movie.

INTERNATIONAL COPYRIGHT LAW

The U.S. has signed a number of treaties over the years that grants protection of U.S. copyrights in other countries, while protecting in the U.S. copyrighted works created in other countries. At this time, the number of countries that are not a party to a copyright treaty to which the U.S. also belongs is fairly small. Accordingly, you must assume that works created outside the U.S. are as well protected as works created inside the U.S. Similarly, works that are created in the U.S. are protected outside the U.S.

Most of the better-known copyright treaties use "national" treatment, which means that Websites created in Germany are protected in the U.S. as if they had been created in the U.S. by U.S. citizens, while U.S. Websites are treated in Germany as if they had been created by German citizens in Germany. The details of the laws do change from one country to another, so caution is urged before marketing your products in any country that does not have a tradition of protecting copyrighted works.

COPYRIGHT COLLECTIVES, STOCK HOUSES, AND AGENCIES

You should consider what permissions, if any, you need for a Website long before you begin development. You may find that a piece of music or a video clip is either unavailable for licensing, or is so expensive that it may as well be unavailable. License fees are negotiated based on the type of use, the market that you are selling to, and the number of years you expect to use it.

You can license the use of copyrighted works from others by using stock houses, copyright collectives and other agencies. Each agency has the right to license the use of copyrighted works to others on the basis of a set scale of fees, or they have the power to negotiate fees with you on behalf of the copyright owner.

The agencies provide a large selection of works to choose from, which makes it easier to conduct one-stop shopping for licenses to use copyrighted works in your Website presentations. If your work needs only one or two permissions, for example, to use the music and lyrics of a few popular songs which you are personally performing for inclusion on your Website, then you should contact the copyright owner or collective agency yourself and negotiate the transaction. By contrast, if you need permissions to use dozens of works, and you intend to sell your work commercially around the world, then you should consider hiring a permissions company to track down the permissions and negotiate on your behalf.

There are hundreds of agencies from which to choose. Several agencies have offices around the country. The names and principal addresses of several of the better-known agencies follow.

PERMISSIONS AGENTS

Websites are at their best when different types of elements are juxtaposed. However, using preexisting elements requires that you seek and obtain all necessary permissions. A permissions agent or company can do the work for you, and probably be more efficient, which helps your budget. One of the better known permissions companies is

BZ/Rights & Permissions, Inc.
125 West 72nd Street
New York, NY 10023
(212) 580-0615

TEXT

Most text can be licensed directly from the author or the publisher. Terms are generally negotiable, although the license fees vary widely.

The Copyright Clearance Center was formed to help collect royalties on a variety of journals and other hard-copy publications, and more recently has started licensing online rights. The Center may be reached as follows:

Copyright Clearance Center, Inc.
222 Rosewood Drive
Danvers, MA 01923
978/750-8400
http://www.copyright.com

Licensing of Original Music Compositions

The licensing of music is broken down into several categories based on the type of music-related work, and the type of license sought.

Website works may need (1) an original composition license if the final product includes covers of original compositions not previously recorded, (2) a mechanical license to cover a previously recorded song, and (3) a synchronization license where music is combined with video.

Original compositions are the sheet music and lyrics written by composers and lyricists. Anyone who wants to record or perform an original composition should contact the appropriate rights organization for this purpose. Two of the best known are

American Society of Composers, Authors, and Publishers (ASCAP)
One Lincoln Plaza
New York, NY 10023
212/621-6000
http://www.ascap.com

Broadcast Music, Inc. (BMI)
320 West 57th Street
New York, NY 10019
800/366-4264
212/586-2000
http://www.bmi.com

Mechanical and Synchronization Rights

Once a music record or CD is made available to the public for private home use, any song (original composition) on that record or CD can be recorded by another Webmaster or group. This is required pursuant to Section 115 of the U.S. Copyright Act. The type of license is called a "mechanical license" (because records used to be considered "mechanical" reproductions) or a "compulsory license" (because the Copyright Act makes it difficult for the copyright owner to refuse permission). Mechanical licenses do not apply to music used for movies, television, or other visual images.

"Synchronization licenses" are licenses to use music in combination with visual images in movies, television, or home video. Synchronization licenses are negotiated on a case-by-case basis, and are not subject to compulsory license rates.

The agency best known for mechanical, synchronization and related licenses is

The Harry Fox Agency, Inc.
National Music Publishers' Association, Inc.
711 Third Avenue
New York, NY 10017
212/370-5330
http://www.harryfox.com

PHOTOGRAPHY

Photography is often licensed through stock photography agencies, one of which can be found in virtually every city and many large towns (check the phone book).

Almost all of the stock agencies are aware of digital uses, and many offer images in digital form in popular binary formats. License rates depend on the type of use and how many people are likely to see the photo or other image.

One agency on the cutting edge of digital uses of images is listed below:

Media Photographers Copyright Agency (http://www.mpca.com)
American Society of Media Photographers, Inc. (http://www.asmp.org)
Washington Park, Suite 502
14 Washington Road
Princeton Junction, NJ 08550-1033
609/799-8300

MOVIES AND VIDEO

Several stock houses that handle still photography also license video stock. Movies and television video can be licensed directly from the copyright owners (usually the production firms) or their distributors.

You have to be careful about using movies and television, because like other audio-visual work, they incorporate the copyrighted works of others, including music and still photographs. The copyright owners of the movies may not have the right to license to you the background music or other preexisting works incorporated into the movies. In those cases, ask the copyright owners for their licensing information so that you can get all of the permission that you need in writing.

TRADEMARK LAW

A trademark is anything that designates the source of goods or services, including words or terms, drawings, graphics, sounds, and even colors in some cases. Certainly, domain names can serve as trademarks. In creating your Website, you must be careful not to infringe on someone else's trademark by associating your Website with the other person's trademark.

Trademark law is a matter of commerce. Trademark law is not concerned so much with originality as with the commercial impression created by the trademark owner. If you place on your home page a roaring lion above the phrase, *Ars Gratia Artis,* then MGM's present owner may sue for infringement of their trademarks, which includes both the roaring lion and the Latin phrase.

SOURCES OF TRADEMARK LAW

Unlike copyright law, there are several levels of trademark law in the U.S. A "common law" trademark is one that accrues rights merely through use. If you adopt a distinctive term for your business and promote it, then you gain common law trademark rights on a "use it or lose it" basis. Your rights do not begin until you start using it, and are limited to the goods you sell or services you provide in the geographic area in which you provide them, and last only so long as you continue to provide them. The price is reasonable, however, since there is no application and no filing fee.

Each of the states has adopted a trademark law. Any trademark registered with a state agency receives additional rights within that state, but those rights do not extend outside the state of registration. State trademark registrations are useful for marks used within only one state, and which are not worth the additional cost of filing a federal application for registration. Most states use simple application forms, and the filing fees tend to be between $50 and $150.

The third source of trademark law is Congress, which in 1988 substantially revised the federal Trademark Law (also known as the "Lanham Act" after Rep. Walter Lanham). A federal trademark registration provides the trademark owner with the right to sue any infringer in federal courts throughout the U.S., and provides substantial remedies in favor of the trademark owner against infringers.

Unlike common law trademarks, where rights do not accrue without use, an application for a federal trademark registration can be filed without any use of the mark. Called an "intent to use" or "ITU" application, the ITU application allows the trademark owner to gain a reservation on the trademark long before the goods are ready for market, but the registration does not issue unless and until the applicant files another document stating that the applicant has begun use of the mark on goods or in connection with services in some form of commerce that Congress can regulate, usually by selling goods from one state to another. Applications can also be filed on an "actual use" basis, which means that the goods or services have been sold across state lines, or between the U.S. and another country.

Federal trademark applications are more extensive than state applications, and the filing fee is, as this book went to press, $245 per class of goods and services. Websites are in one class, while packaged software is in another class. Unlike copyright applications, trademark applications are difficult enough that you should consider retaining an attorney to file and prosecute the application.

STRENGTH OF A TRADEMARK

The more distinctive a trademark, the "stronger" it is. Trademarks are characterized by their strength. Stronger marks provide better protection and can be enforced against a wider range of other marks for different goods or services. Weaker marks can only be enforced against virtually the same mark for virtually the same goods or services. The spectrum of trademark strength follows.

Generic Terms

A generic term or design is one that is used for a category of goods or services. A generic term cannot be protected as a trademark, because it is needed for the purpose of classification. The term "Website" is generic.

Descriptive Terms

A descriptive term or design is one that describes the goods or services but is not generic for the goods or services. A descriptive term cannot be used as a trademark unless it gains a "secondary meaning," which means that when people hear the term they think of a particular source or set of goods, rather than all goods with that characteristic. The term "WINDOWS" is descriptive of all software that uses windowing technology, but the term "WINDOWS" has gained a secondary meaning, that of Microsoft's operating environment, "Microsoft Windows."

Suggestive Marks

A suggestive term or design suggests what the goods or services may be, but is not descriptive of them. The term "MICROSOFT" suggests microcomputer software, but the term does not describes the products of Microsoft Corporation. Suggestive trademarks are protectable and make for good trademarks.

Arbitrary Marks

An arbitrary term or design has a real meaning to most people, but the meaning is different from the goods or services it is associated with. The term "APPLE" by Apple Computer Corp. is a good example of an arbitrary mark because most computers are not made of apples. Arbitrary terms and designs make for excellent trademarks.

Coined Marks

A coined term is one that has no meaning except that it is associated with the goods or services. The term "BORLAND" is a good example of a coined term as the term has no meaning outside of the fact that Borland International uses the term on its software. Coined marks are on the opposite side of the spectrum from generic terms.

TRADEMARK NOTICES

Any goods you sell or service you provide can bear a notice in the form of "TM" (trademark) or "SM" (service mark). It doesn't cost anything, but it puts the world on notice that you claim your trademark rights.

The circle-R character ("®") is reserved for owners of current federal trademark registrations. It cannot be used by owners of state registrations (unless they also have a current federal registration). Similarly, filing a federal application is not sufficient to use the "®" symbol; a federal certificate of trademark registration must first issue.

Each of your works may also contain a notice that "[your trademark] is a trademark of [name of your company]." If you have a current federal registration, you can state that "[your trademark] is a registered trademark of [name of your company]."

If you are properly using the trademarks of another, then you should include a trademark notice. For example, if you prepare a training CD-ROM called "How to Use Microsoft Windows," then you should include the trademark notice that "'MICROSOFT' and 'WINDOWS' are registered trademarks of Microsoft Corporation." You can use the approach for each trademark of which you are aware. Many works also bear a catch-all trademark notice; "[your trademark] is a [registered] trademark of [name of your company]. All other trademarks are trademarks or registered trademarks of their respective owners."

LIKELIHOOD OF CONFUSION

Trademark infringement is generally a matter of determining whether the consumers of the trademark owner are "likely to be confused" by a trademark used by another. In determining "likelihood of confusion," a court will consider how close the marks are in sound (since trademarks are often passed from person to person by word of mouth), how close the goods or services are, and whether the goods or services are provided in the same way or in the same "channels of commerce."

For example, the trademark "EXCEL" is a good one for both Hyundai and Microsoft. However, there is no likelihood of confusion, because consumers will not mistake a Hyundai Excel car with a Microsoft Excel spreadsheet.

TRADE DRESS

In addition to the protection trademark laws provide to names and logos, the law also protects the distinctive nonfunctional packaging of a product. The totality of a distinctive product's packaging is known as trade dress.

This total package includes the look of the product, the packaging, and can even include the design and shape of the product and its packaging. Trade dress can be protected by two different methods: (1) if distinct enough it can be registered on the Principal Register of the U.S. Patent and Trademark Office, and (2) if it has achieved a secondary meaning in the marketplace, it can be protected under the guise of unfair competition.

CHARACTERS

Trademark law will protect the use of two-dimensional and three-dimensional characters, and terms associated with the characters, so long as they are associated with goods (such as videos, T-shirts and other clothing, lunch boxes) and services (e.g., cable services).

A well-designed character such as Mickey Mouse can be protected under trademark law indefinitely, so long as the character continues to be used on goods and associated with services. With the power of Web technology, it is tempting to copy well-known characters from cartoons, animation, and toys. However, almost all such characters are trademarks of their owners, and their use without permission from their owners is to invite a trademark infringement suit. The Walt Disney Co. and the rights owners of children's cartoons have been especially active in policing their marks against infringement.

TRADEMARKS ON WEB PAGES

Trademarks are part and parcel of a company's marketing and advertising efforts. The World Wide Web has proven to be one of the most effective communication mediums since the invention of television. So it's no surprise that many companies are using the World Wide Web to advertise their wares and display their trademarks.

There is little doubt that the use of a trademark on a Web Page connected to the Internet is used in interstate commerce for the purpose of advertising services to generate goodwill. As noted above, use of a mark in connection with a service generally means that the mark is placed on advertising or marketing materials, or other materials that may be associated with the provision of services, such as letterhead and invoices. Use of a service mark on a Web page will also qualify as a service mark for use in interstate commerce so long as the Website is associated with the provision of services. Even the simplest of "brochureware" Websites that contain service marks will be deemed to be a good use of the service mark in interstate commerce.

Use of a mark for goods on a Website is generally unlikely to be deemed use of that mark in interstate or other commerce. Marks for goods (unlike marks for services) must be placed on the goods or packaging for the goods. Even in the case of packaged software (which is considered a goods, not a service) sold via Website by downloads to users, the placement of a mark on the Website will not be a good use in commerce. Instead, the mark should be in the software itself (e.g., on a boot-up or "splash" screen) since software downloaded from a Website will not have any hard-copy packaging.

TRADEMARKS UNDER WEB PAGES

Search engines on the Web, such as Yahoo!, AltaVista, Lycos, Webcrawler, and HotBot, do not actually search the Web each time that a user enters a query. Instead, each search engines create an index of Websites by reviewing each Website that it finds or is told about, and then building an index of terms that it deems relevant. Most search engines look at keyword meta tags to help create the index, because keyword meta tags indicate what the author of the Web page considers important.

Of course, some Web page authors fill the keyword meta tags with terms that they consider important to attract the type of users they would like, as well as repeating certain key words dozens of times in the hope that the search engines will rank their page as more "relevant" than those of their competitors. And then there are the Web pages in which the keywords in a Web page will include terms and trademarks of the author's competitors in the hopes of attracting users away from the competitors' Web pages. This has led to several law suits.

There have been several cases in which the author or owner of a Web page placed trademarks belonging to others in the keyword meta tags of the page in the hopes of attracting users who are interested in the trademarks. In each of the cases so far (as of this printing), some or all of the defendants consented to removing the plaintiff's trademarks and notifying the search engines to reindex the defendant's Website, so as to remove the plaintiff's trademarks from each search engine's index of the defendant's Website.

TRADEMARKS ON SOMEONE ELSE'S WEB PAGES: LINKING AND FRAMING

In several cases, the owner of one Website has sued the owner of another Website because the first Website includes links to the second Website. Generally, the allegation is that the link on the first Website associates the contents of the second Website with the goods or services offered by the first Website, especially when the link is not clearly marked to show that the user will be obtaining a document from a different Website.

For example, one newspaper in the Shetland Islands sued and obtained a preliminary injunction against another newspaper in the Shetland Islands on the allegation that the defendant's Website misled users into thinking that the defendant was the source of the some of the articles accessed from the defendant's Website when, in fact, the defendant was linking to discrete articles on the plaintiff's Website. Although initially couched in terms of copyright law, the claim sounds better in trademark law as a claim that the defendant was passing off plaintiff's information reportage as its own. The parties subsequently settled.

In another case filed and subsequently settled, the Washington Post and several other large news organizations sued a small Website owned by a company called Total News with numerous allegations of trademark infringement and unfair competition. A user who surfed on over to the site would receive a frame that contained the first site's own content and advertising in several windows, plus buttons that served as links to the Washington Post Website, CNN Website, Fox News Website, and so on. A user who clicked one of the buttons would receive the content of the Washington Post or other Website in one large window of the frame on the user's screen, but the first site's buttons and advertising would remain in the other windows of the frame. Unfortunately, the Total News site had never asked for permission from any of the news organizations because it believed that it did not need permission. After all, all that the first site did — so it argued — was to establish the frame and the buttons, and it was the user who downloaded the content of the other Websites by clicking on a button. The parties settled, and the Total News site as of this writing is still linking to some news organizations, presumably with their express permission.

DOMAIN NAMES AS TRADEMARKS

A domain name can serve as a trademark for the goods or services provided or advertised by a company on the Internet at its domain name, so long as the domain name is used as more than just the computer address for a Web or other Internet site.

A domain name can be registered as a trademark so long as it is used as more than "just" an Internet address or URL. Since each domain name (usually a combination of top-level domain and second-level domain) must be unique for the domain naming system to work, domain names are generally issued on a first-come, first-served basis. The result is a number of lawsuits filed by plaintiffs who claim that they should have the sole right to use a domain name registered by the defendant.

To illustrate the connection between domain names and trademarks, a writer by the name of Josh Quittner registered the domain name "mcdonalds.com" and established an email address for himself as "ronald@mcdonalds.com." His article, Billions Registered (*Wired*, Oct. 1994, page 50) sounded the charge for others to register trademarks they did not own as their domain names in the hope that the trademark owner would then ransom the domain name. Quittner's own demands were relatively modest; McDonald's complied with Quittner's demand that it pay to have one public school in New York City connected to the Internet.

Many who followed Quittner's lead did so by registering large numbers of domain names incorporating the trade names and trademarks of well-known companies. Unlike Quittner, they did not offer to turn over the domain name in response to an act of charity, but sought payments of large sums of money. Called "domain name arbitrage," "cybersquatting," "domain piracy," "domain grabbing" and any number of other terms, the practice has led to many suits against domain name owners by trademark owners claiming that the domain name infringes on or dilutes a trademark. Several of these cases have alleged dilution of famous trademarks under the federal and state dilution statutes.

In cases where the domain owner does not compete in any way with the trademark owner, the dilution claims have been more successful, although the courts have strived mightily to find that a plaintiff's trademark is "well-known" to fulfill the condition precedent of the dilution statutes. In what appears to be a self-fulfilling prophecy, if not a matter of circular logic, the courts note that the domain name owner had hoped to sell the domain name to the trademark owner, thus suggesting that the mark must be sufficiently "well known" to attract this unwanted attention.

The use of a domain name can also lead to a tarnishment claim. Thus, the use of a domain can reduce the value of the trademark owner's right in its trademark. In one case, the owners of the TOYS 'R' US trademark sued the owners of the "adultsrus.com" domain name on the grounds that the domain name was associated with the advertising and sale of sex-related products on a World Wide Website at <http://www.adultsrus.com>. The court expressly held that defendants' use of the second-level domain name "adultsrus" for sex-related products tarnished the rights of plaintiffs in the 'R' US family of marks for children's toys and clothing.

PRIVACY AND PUBLICITY LAW

The rights of privacy and publicity are two sides of the same coin. The rights of privacy and publicity apply even if you photograph or record (video, audio, or both) a person out-of-doors in a public location, such as a park, town square, or walking down the street. The law deems that a person has the right to control how/her image is used.

This is a growing area of law that is more closely related to trademark law. California and New York have passed statutes that protect privacy, and other states are likely to follow.

Don't Make Private People "Public" Without Their Permission

If the person is a private person, then she may prohibit the use of her image for your profit or gain. A private person has the right to remain private.

Celebrities Have the Right to Control Their Publicity

If the person is a public person or celebrity, she may be able to prohibit your use of her image without proper compensation, primarily because she is deemed to have a property interest in her image. In other words, she can make money from her status as a celebrity, so you cannot use her status to help sell your product without her permission.

One good example of the right of publicity is the Bette Midler case. A car manufacturer wanted to run a series of commercials that featured Ms. Midler's singing. Ms. Midler decided not to participate, so the car manufacturer hired someone else who sang just like Bette Midler. Ms. Midler sued and won about $400,000 because people who listened to the commercials thought that she was singing in the commercial. Even though no image of Ms. Midler was used, her vocal style was sufficiently distinctive to serve as her trademark. Since everyone agreed that Ms. Midler's vocal style helped sell cars, Ms. Midler was held by the court to have the right to control when her voice and vocal style could be used to help sell cars.

RELEASES

There is no better way to ensure that you have all the rights that you need to use a person's image or other distinctive features than to get a release. Professional photographers use releases all of the time. You may need to consult an attorney to ensure that the release you would like to use is enforceable under the law of the states in which you will use the release, and to make sure that the release covers every type of use that you contemplate.

WHEN YOU CAN USE THE WORKS OF ANOTHER PERSON

There are several ways in which you can use and incorporate the works of others into your Websites. Ask yourself a few questions.

First, is the work in the public domain? As discussed above, public domain means that nobody owns the copyright or other rights to the work. If you have access to an original Leonardo da Vinci painting or manuscript of a Mozart concerto, then make your own copies without fear of copyright violation.

Second, if the work is not in the public domain, can you get a license to use or copy the work? The saying goes that "it is easier to beg forgiveness afterwards than to ask for permission beforehand." However, for copyrighted works, permission is often easy to get and costs very little, while forgiveness is very expensive. At the very least, forgiveness (including legal fees, court costs, and damages) costs a great deal more than permission.

Third, will any original work that you copy be recognizable as a derivative work? As noted above, a derivative work remains a derivative work only so long as any part of it is still recognizable as originating with its predecessor.

Fourth, does the work affect anyone else's privacy or publicity rights? If a person can be recognized by her looks, voice, or other distinctive attributes, that person can request compensation. So long as you have appropriate releases from each individual, or the person that you have licensed the work has the appropriate releases, then this will not be an issue.

Author's Bio

Frederic M. Wilf is special counsel with the law firm of Saul, Ewing, Remick & Saul LLP, where he chairs the firm's Technology Group. Wilf is resident in the firm's Berwyn office where he practices technology and intellectual property law, with an emphasis on the Internet, telecommunications, and computer industries. Wilf's clients include Internet service providers, Website and software developers, vendors and consultants, as well as companies of all sizes that use technology. He may be reached via the Internet at fwilf@saul.com or fwilf@compuserve.com, and at the following address: Saul, Ewing, Remick & Saul LLP, 1055 Westlakes Drive, Suite 150, Berwyn, PA 19312. Saul Ewing's home page on the World Wide Web is at <http://www.saul.com> and Wilf's listing appears at <http://www.saul.com/lawyers/5082.html>.

Chapter 13
Using Internet Architecture to Share Knowledge

Michael D. Gantt

THIS CHAPTER EXPLAINS HOW A MANAGER CAN TAKE ADVANTAGE OF IN-
TERNET ARCHITECTURE to share knowledge that significantly increases
corporate productivity. As some have said about the 400,000-person strong
German electronics giant Siemens: "If Siemens only knew what Siemens
knows, it would be a rich company." Even the current state of technology
offers the potential of dramatic increases in productivity in any company
where departments are willing to share knowledge with each other.

UNDERSTANDING THE POWER OF INTERNET ARCHITECTURE

The architecture of the Internet is a powerful force for information technology developers. It provides a way of organizing computers and the information that they handle. It also provides a way of sharing that
information between those computers. Fundamentally, the Internet is a
network of networks. In fact, it is the network of networks, establishing a
way for all developers to potentially connect all computers. Harnessing the
power of all the world's computers — that's powerful!

Distinguishing the Internet from its Architecture

To better appreciate the power of the Internet's architecture, let's distinguish the physical Internet from its architectural design.

The Physical Vs. the Logical. Having its origins in Cold War defense thinking, the Internet began its life as a packet-switching network of existing
computers. The fundamental design principle was to keep the network running even if a given computer was taken out, whether by malfunction or enemy attack. Thus, a message could be routed through any sequence of
network nodes in order to reach its final destination.

0-8493-9987-4/00/$0.00+$.50
© 2000 by CRC Press LLC

Over time, the number of connected computers increased. Simultaneously, a variety of protocols arose to deal with the ever-increasing activity of the network. One protocol, or standard, was used to transport a file. Another would be used for e-mail. And yet another for reading text. And so on. As new uses were envisioned, new protocols were established to support that activity on the Internet.

Once people saw the potential for the commercial use of the Internet, the types of activities it could support began to grow even more rapidly. The World Wide Web has been the most notable example of this growth. It began as a means of providing a graphical, as opposed to mere textual, presentation to users of the Internet. A whole new protocol was developed to establish this dimension of the Internet. Hence, we find places on the Web by first typing http://www ... . That represents HyperText Transfer Protocol for the World Wide Web.

Note that the protocols or standards enabled the Internet, but their use could not be restricted to the Internet. There was nothing to keep someone from copying all the Internet standards and building an entirely separate microcosm of the Internet. A company, say, could connect all of its computers with the same protocol and standards (read "architecture") without being physically connected to the actual Internet. Hence, there is the distinction between the physical network we call the Internet and the logical structure, or architecture, that supports it.

Internet, Intranet, Extranet. There is only one Internet. That is, there is only one physical Internet. But there can be, and are, many intranets and many extranets. This is because intranets and extranets mimic Internet architecture but only physically connect with it in controlled ways.

An intranet is a "private Internet" built by a company along the lines described above. The organization's computers are connected by means of the same architecture (standards and protocols) that connect the Internet itself. But it is a separate physical network. Note the appropriate naming: intra- implies connections *within* an entity (commercial, government, or nonprofit organization); inter- implies connection *between* entities.

When a company wants to make its data accessible by people outside of itself, it connects its data with the Internet. The resulting phenomenon is called an extranet. The "extra-" in this case refers to connections *from outside* the entity. The best example of an extranet is a shipping company allowing its customers with access to the Internet to also have access to its private company data.

Connecting the Nets

The amazing power of Internet architecture is most obvious in the combination of networks, or Nets. The more computers that are connected, the more computing power that is amassed. And Internet architecture allows the Nets to be connected in a disciplined way. It is not fire run rampant; it is fire contained to a furnace, from which can come warmth and power. We can call the overarching architecture that provides this discipline a "knowledge management architecture."

Inside and Outside the Firewall. Organizations use a combination of software and hardware to keep its own computers segregated from other computers. This combination is called a firewall. As a firewall in a building exists to protect the inner rooms from fire that might come from outside the building, so a computer firewall exists to protect an organization's computers from hackers and viruses that lurk outside.

Exhibit 13.1 depicts the logical location of the firewall. Above the firewall sits the data accessible by those outside the organization. Anyone on the Internet can reach the data in Level 1. This is where general information about the company resides and is usually accessed through a browser by typing something like http://www.acmeconsulting.com.

Just beneath this uppermost level lies information that is accessible only by specifically authorized users. Normally this would be customers or clients. And they would be provided a user ID and password to allow their access. Thus, we have an extranet for clients.

Below, or inside, the firewall we have the company's data which exist solely for its own departments. But we can categorize it into two layers: data for all employees and data for management only. As was the case above, access to the management data can be controlled by issuance of a user ID and password to authorized managers.

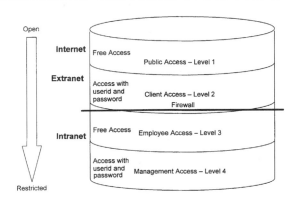

Exhibit 13.1. The logical location of a firewall.

As noted by the arrow on the left, there is a progression in the security of the data. Access to the public data is most open; access to management data is most restricted. And there are degrees of security in between. This "knowledge management architecture" provides a conceptual construct for information sharing. This architecture also possesses a power, which we are now going to explore.

Correlating Existing Databases. The most important aspect of this knowledge management architecture (we call it KM architecture for short) is that you don't have to build new databases to take advantage of it. You can use the architecture to link existing databases. That is, in the same way that Internet architecture allowed us to connect preexisting computers and networks, so this KM architecture allows us to connect existing databases.

Take a look at Exhibit 13.2. Note the depiction of databases on the right. Most companies have an existing Website. This could be called a marketing database. And many companies host support activities, such as a help desk, on their extranet.

Consider also the Human Resource database that exists inside a company. Financial system databases, too, are available to access. All that is necessary to make these databases as accessible as the marketing and help desk databases is to Web-enable them. That is, make their data accessible through a browser. There are many tools coming on the market that will help with the process of Web-enabling or browser-interfacing existing databases.

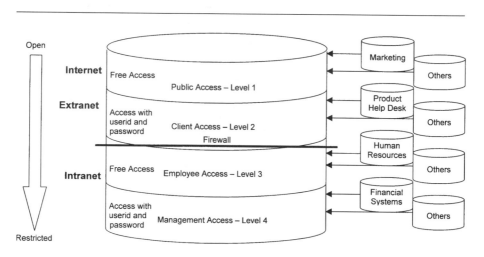

Exhibit 13.2. Knowledge management architecture.

The Web browser becomes the common interface, therefore, to a host of databases. Through that common interface information and knowledge can be shared both inside and outside the organization. Thus, the four-level database depicted in Exhibits 13.1 and 13.2 is not a physical database but a virtual one — for the underlying databases can be quite disparate in nature, as long as all data are accessible through a browser.

Accessing the Data

With a virtual super database of databases, we can now begin to take advantage of the power of a KM architecture.

Stop Mailing So Much Data! Imagine this: the end of a quarter is approaching and the financial department e-mails a spreadsheet to all business units showing the current outlook. All around the company managers dutifully receive the e-mail, detach the attached spreadsheet, launch its application, and view the contents. Then he or she stores that spreadsheet somewhere on his or her personal computer. With a constant barrage of this sort of e-mail, however, only God knows whether it can ever be found again — much less found quickly!

But with a KM architecture, finance just sends an e-mail with the URL (uniform resource locator — that http://... address) and a manager can look at the spreadsheet through a browser. And no more worrying about where to file it because it can only be in one place. And from that one place, anyone in the company can access it.

Ease of Update. Not only does a KM architecture simplify access of data, it simplifies update as well. As the quarter's end comes closer, finance may want to update the spreadsheet with fresher numbers. With a KM architecture, that one spreadsheet is updated and a simple notice can be e-mailed to all appropriate managers. No attaching a new spreadsheet to send and no worries about different versions floating around. No one can have an old version because only the up-to-date version can be found at the appropriate URL.

Speed of Access. The limited bandwidth of most business networks is taxed when spreadsheets, presentations, and other documents are e-mailed around the company in multiple copies. With a KM architecture, the network simply handles the browser inquiries to one file — the least demand, greatest supply scenario. In fact, the preparer of our fictional spreadsheet had better send out the e-mail notice of updates right away because once the change is made, every browser hitting on that page will see the updated numbers. The speed of the access is virtually as fast as the speed of update. Compare that to the speed of the typical request to another department for information.

SHARING THE KNOWLEDGE

The power of knowledge management is the power of shared knowledge. Our architecture provides a highway for information to travel from department to department. Just as blood energizes the human body as it flows throughout, so information nourishes the company as it flows throughout.

Departmental Knowledge

A company is comprised of component parts, called departments, divisions, or business units. Using the term departments as a representative one, let's consider how knowledge in the company can be built up through the accessibility of information that resides in its various departments.

Departments Know Things. The finance department knows about the financial condition of the company. It possesses the financial information. Likewise, the marketing department knows about products or services of the company. It possesses marketing information. Each department possesses information relevant to its respective purpose in organizational life.

Corporate Knowledge Is the Sum of Department Knowledge. One could say that a corporation knows the total of what its constituent departments know. A company, by definition, cannot know anything unless one of its departments knows it. The purpose of calling attention to this obvious reality is that knowledge management gets to its goal quicker if it begins by focusing on existing departmental knowledge rather than focusing on building a grandiose corporate database from scratch.

Much of the knowledge that resides in departments is already digitized. The finance department has its spreadsheets, the sales department has its customer lists, the operations department has its production schedules. As information technology has evolved and computers of all sizes have proliferated, more and more departmental information has taken digital form. And for our purposes, any one of these digitized forms constitutes a database — whether it be as simple as a file of word processing documents or as sophisticated as a 10-Gb relational database.

Until the advent of Internet architecture, there was no compelling framework around which to organize all these disparate databases. The data were hidden away in them, isolated by proprietary systems and protocols. But with Internet architecture and our focus on knowledge management through it, we have a way to connect all that departmental knowledge into a corporate whole that can, in fact, be worth more than the sum of its parts.

Departments Need to Know More

Departments need to know more. And often what one department needs to know is stored away in some other department. The marketing department needs to know more about the product delivery schedule being maintained by the production department. The production department needs to know more about the costs to date on the project which is being managed by the finance department. The finance department needs to know more about the expected revenues which are being estimated by the marketing department.

Gaining Knowledge. There is a mutual dependency upon data between departments. And to the degree that departments provide their information to other departments, the productivity of the entire organization is increased. Our KM architecture gives each department reasons to share its knowledge. Some of those reasons were seen in the speed of access and the ease of update. But the greater reasons lie in the power of shared knowledge throughout the organization.

The promise of *receiving* information, therefore, motivates individuals and departments to *share* information. The very fact that the KM architecture addresses both the giving and receiving of information by departments supports this mindset. It's not a case of one department demanding information from another. That scene plays out, often with unpleasant consequences, every day in corporate life. With our KM architecture we are establishing the environment of department equality — which departmental sharing implies.

Granting Knowledge. The hope of gaining needed knowledge prompts departments to Web-enable their existing databases. Where security is an issue, user ID and a password can limit access. And there can be different user IDs and passwords for different databases. A manager who has access, say, to the HR bios on all employees might not necessarily be given access to the database containing all bonus plan details.

As stated earlier, there are an increasing number of tools which help to enable Web access to existing databases. It is even possible to have Web access to a spreadsheet that sits on the hard drive of an administrative person's personal computer. Even so, individual departments will need help from a centralized IT Web team in order to achieve the promise of a KM architecture. That team, however, does not have to be large. It does have to provide common guidance to all departments so that information sharing through browsers is achieved.

Note that the Web team is not focused on building databases — the place that some knowledge management efforts start ... and stall. Rather they are focused on establishing the *links* that connect databases that departments have created. This keeps data maintenance distributed in the departments where it belongs. The central IT team focuses solely on linking those with a need for data to the data they need.

ACHIEVING THE POSSIBLE

The longer someone has worked at a company, the more they know about the company and its business. And — all other things being equal — the more valuable such an individual is to a company. But what if it didn't take 10 years to get 10-year's-worth of knowledge? Isn't there sometimes a resistance in a company to sharing knowledge? Don't people sometimes hoard information as its scarcity made it more valuable? What if you could get people to see that knowledge was like a seed ... and the more you planted, the more you received back?

Paint the Vision

Implementing a knowledge management architecture implies a belief through the organization that knowledge hoarded loses value while knowledge shared increases in value. The vision must be painted; it must be championed. This starts with one or a few individuals inspiring others, who in turn inspire still others.

The vision is supported by the infrastructure depicted in Exhibit 13.2. But it is ultimately a vision of a company where you can learn in 2 years what used to take 10. It is a vision of a company where employees are increasingly knowledgeable and, therefore, valuable both to the company and its customers.

Obtain Department Buy-In

The first step toward the vision is to find a department that has something immediate to gain by pursuing this architecture. In the case of our company, it was the marketing department. They publish a glossy print catalog of our products three times a year. The same data are accessible on our company's home page. Their problem was that, over time, the data on the Internet were not updated while the print version was kept up to date. Thus, the two versions were out of sync.

The person who kept the catalog used a word processor. He was a writer, not a programmer. He had provided the same soft copy to the printing department and to the department that kept up the Website. The printer kept up, but the other department fell behind, being swamped with other work.

The solution? We made the word processor document accessible through a browser and linked it to the Website. Therefore, whenever there was an update to the word processor document, it was immediately viewable by those browsing the Website. The printer could still be provided a soft copy whenever it was time to produce a print catalog. The marketing department now had its Website and print catalog automatically synchronized without any additional ongoing effort.

Experience the Results

There is effort in the Web-enabling phase of such efforts, so you have to give time for the benefits to be experienced. Fortunately, it doesn't take much time for those benefits to manifest themselves. And for departments to feel empowered.

From our initial project, we then moved to allowing the production department to input detail data about products into their own database, which was then linked to the marketing department's catalog database. This would be a new database, one that captured data that previously resided in dispersed notebooks, file drawer cabinets, and people's heads. The production department wanted such a database for its own needs so that it could track the development of redundant product components.

There came then, more importantly, the synergistic benefit to all other departments of the combined databases. The two databases were linked by the central Web team in such a way as to appear as one seamless database, with both general and detail information about all products. Two departments, each maintaining its own database for its own needs, but now to the benefit of all departments.

The next logical step, of course, is to link the financial records of each product which lie in the finance department databases so that comparative profitability can be tracked according to specific product details.

And once that phase is completed, yet more new uses will be seen for the integrated information. Therein lies the greatest proof that knowledge shared is more valuable than knowledge hoarded.

SUMMARY

We can all substitute the name of our own company into the line "If _____ only knew what _____ knows it would be a rich company." But this is not a cause for grief. On the contrary, Internet architecture viewed from a knowledge management perspective can link the ever-increasing amounts of digital data that reside in company departments. Your company can "know what it knows." Your employees can experience the reality of sharing information in such a way that it results in an ever-increasing flow of information in return. It begins with a vision — and a manager who will champion it.

Author's Bio

Michael D. Gantt is Senior Vice President and Chief Technology Officer of Policy Management Systems Corporation. Gantt joined PMSC in 1972 and was instrumental in its early success. He left the company in 1978 and spent 15 years in the Christian ministry. His sabbatical over in 1995, he returned to PMSC. He holds bachelors, masters, and doctorate degrees. In addition, Gantt holds numerous professional designations, some with special honors, and also has authored a number of articles and books. One of these books, Computers in Insurance, *has been used as a test for individuals pursuing their CPCU designation.*

Chapter 14

Internet Banking: Leveling the Playing Field for Community Banks through Internet Banking

Kim Humphreys

THE IMPACT OF NONBANK COMPETITORS ENTERING THE FINANCIAL SER-VICES INDUSTRY over the past several years has been significant. As a result, the banking industry has had to reevaluate its role in the payment system and redefine goals in order to retain and grow its customer base. With the objective being to retain current customers and attract new ones, banks are looking to provide improved customer service and convenience. Internet banking offers a viable delivery channel, allowing banks to meet these goals, without increasing operating costs. The Internet also presents the opportunity to level the playing field for banks of all sizes, an increasingly significant benefit in view of the reemerging trend toward megamergers taking place in the banking industry today.

By the year 2000, home banking and online brokerage will more than double current usage to exceed 5 million households, predicts Meridien Research of Needham, MA. Every day more than a 1000 companies of all types, including financial institutions, go online. What is happening is a revolution in the way individuals and companies do business. And unlike other technological advancements within the marketplace, the Internet revolution is being driven by the consumer.

It took nearly 30 years for technology like ATMs to be widely accepted by the public, and screen phone technology never really took off. Even the

0-8493-9987-4/00/$0.00+$.50
© 2000 by CRC Press LLC

first attempts at direct-dial PC home banking by some of the larger banks in the middle 1980s met with little success. Internet banking is different — this is the first time customers have led the technology and encouraged banks to move forward, rather than the banks pushing the technology on the customer. Consumers want Internet banking because they have the necessary technology — a computer and Internet access — and they are already using it to conduct electronic transactions.

WHY BANKS SHOULD CONSIDER INTERNET BANKING

Developing an Internet branch demonstrates that the financial institution is responsive to consumer demands. Internet banking also provides community banks with the tools necessary to offer complete customer service and around-the-clock convenience, while streamlining operations and ultimately reducing customer service and operating expenses. In fact, many institutions have found that through the successful implementation and marketing of their Internet branches, they have already recouped development costs and are realizing profits through this new delivery channel.

One case in point is First National Bank & Trust of Pipestone, a $147-million institution in rural Minnesota that began offering Internet banking in December 1996. FNB&T Pipestone was able to substantially grow the asset size of the bank without incurring the high cost of building brick and mortar branches. In just over a year, FNB&T Pipestone reported an increase in deposits of more than $5 million through its Website, with deposits averaging approximately $24,000. The bank's Website, www.fnbpipe.com, averages between 2000 and 3000 hits per day, and online product applications and "hot product" pages, used to selectively market the products the bank wishes to promote at any given time, account for the most heavily trafficked areas. Nearly $2 million of FNB&T Pipestone's online deposits were generated near the end of 1997, indicating growing consumer acceptance of the new retail delivery channel.

As previously noted, the Internet offers a real income opportunity and is a long-term strategic necessity for financial institutions. An Internet branch offers financial institutions the ability to grow inside their traditional markets as well as to expand into nearby geographic locations at a much lower cost than building traditional brick and mortar branches.

There is a distinct population of profitable customers who will terminate their current banking relationships and move their money to banks in their areas offering Internet banking as an alternative delivery channel. They want the convenience of doing their banking online, around their hectic schedules, not just during bankers' hours. These Internet savvy customers are typically better educated, wealthier, and have more need for value-added products and services than the population as a whole.

And although today's users are considered "early adopters," the mass market is quickly following suit. Financial institutions waiting to offer Internet banking should get online soon or they will have missed their best opportunity to offer a service customers are demanding today — meaning lost market share opportunities and an eroding customer base. And this applies at least as much to community banks and credit unions as to large institutions.

Using the Internet as a new delivery channel to market to a highly targeted and profitable segment of consumers, FNB&T Pipestone increased market share outside its traditional market without increasing its marketing budget or staff. And because Internet banking transactions cost far less than those conducted through traditional channels, FNB&T Pipestone was able to lower its operating expenses, while providing customers with personalized service and the ability to bank on their own terms.

INTERNET BANKING RETAINS CUSTOMERS AND BUILDS VALUABLE HISTORY

According to the International Customer Service Association, it costs five times more to acquire a customer than to retain an existing one. The Internet branch plays a valuable role in reducing attrition by providing customers with improved service and convenience and detailed account information collected over the life of the customer relationship. The more transactions customers conduct, the more their account histories grow — account histories that are retrievable online. The older these account histories, the less likely the consumer will go through the trouble of moving to another financial institution, thus losing all of those data. This phenomenon is another reason why it is so crucial for banks to build an Internet branch today. The competitive edge of offering Internet banking capabilities is eroding rapidly. With several more financial institutions offering Web-based banking every week, it will be only a short time before financial institutions without Web banking will be the exception rather than the rule. "If we don't offer this, the customer will find someone else who does," explains Todd Morgan, president of FNB&T Pipestone.

According to a recent Grant Thornton study, more than 90 percent of community banks cited "employing technology" as the most important factor in their success, with promoting their identity as a community bank a close second. Superior customer service and a more personalized approach to banking being the community bank's appeal, it is imperative that these institutions combine their emphasis on personal attention with their use of technology.

The One-Hour Rule of Internet Marketing

There are no distance limitations on Internet banking. Customers can bank from Boston or Birmingham — or Birmingham, England. Indeed, early marketing efforts yielded customers from all over. This happened primarily when there were only a handful of financial institutions on the Internet, often without a local presence, so the consumer had to go to Wells Fargo or Bank of America or another financial institution to do their banking online.

But this trend is largely ending as more and more community institutions begin offering products and services online. While most consumers want to conduct the majority of their financial business online, at their convenience, they still take comfort in working with a local institution. The real strength of the Internet branch in expanding the bank's reach is to attract out-of-market customers within an hour's drive of the home community. As a result, an institution can capture a new market without the brick and mortar expense of a physical branch, while still being considered a "local" financial institution.

For example, a financial institution within an hour's drive of a college can capture this Internet-savvy market, as students and faculty alike are using the Internet in their daily lives for research, to sign up for courses, to transmit grades, and more. FNB&T Pipestone followed this philosophy when establishing its Internet branch to attract customers from nearby Sioux Falls, SD and Worthington and Marshall, MN, all of which are within a 50-mile radius of Pipestone. Shortly after launching the Internet branch in December 1996, FNB&T Pipestone began to draw customers from these previously untapped markets. To date, the bank has acquired more than $6 million in new deposits — three times its initial goal and more than enough to cover start-up, development, and maintenance costs. Additional profits from the Internet branch will further add to the bank's bottom line.

Internet Banking Can Lower Overhead

The Internet is arguably the least expensive retail delivery channel available today, with Internet transactions costing less than one cent apiece. Compare that to $0.27 per ATM transaction, $0.54 and $0.73 per telephone and U.S. mail transactions, respectively, and as much as $1.50 or more for "live" transactions conducted at a brick and mortar branch. Furthermore, an Internet branch can be developed for about the cost of adding one to two tellers, but without the added expenses associated with payroll — health benefits, FICA, Social Security, disability, unemployment, etc. And, an Internet branch doesn't get sick, nor does it take vacation.

Additionally, savings are realized by the bank when customers use an Internet branch to access account information and to open new accounts, minimizing reliance upon personal bankers and customer service representatives for the most basic transactions. This savings on overhead allows the bank to offer Internet customers preferential rates, helping the bank attract "price shoppers" to add to its market share. Customers know that it costs the bank less to operate an Internet branch than traditional brick and mortar branches, so they want to share in the financial benefit. Therefore, many companies offer customers financial incentives to conduct their banking over the Internet. Both the customer and the bank see this as a win-win situation.

Sometimes Even Break-Even Services Can Be Profitable

The obvious reason for offering Internet banking is to make a profit, and this usually means offering profitable services. For example, bill payment might be a "for profit" service, as customers have shown they are willing to pay for the convenience of electronic bill payment. The exact amount an institution can charge depends largely on market conditions and what competitors offer.

To gain market share, however, a savvy marketing initiative may be to provide bill payment services free of charge for a limited period of time. Even when bill payment is priced at a break-even level, it gives the financial institution another relationship with the customer. Industry studies show that the more relationships an institution has with a customer, the less likely that customer is to go to a competitor. So bill payment can become a tool to build share of market.

Cross-Selling with Internet Banking

As Internet transactions become widely available commodities, banks will have to find new ways to differentiate themselves. Meridien Research suggests the evolution of online services will lead to customized financial advice. Using a "fat server" solution, the bank can learn a great deal about a customer's finances and spending habits from the abundance of data collected online. Mining these data through the system's customer-specific reporting and Internet branch-reporting features, the bank can begin targeting select customers for cross-selling opportunities. For example, at its most basic level, the bank may choose to query the database in order to compose a list of all its checking account customers with an average balance of more than $5000. The bank could then alert these customers to attractive CD rates, or money market and savings accounts, by using automatic e-mail notification system, through statement stuffers, or with telephone solicitations. According to Meridien, only 2 percent of the world's largest financial institutions currently utilize such programs, giving community banks a possible time-to-market advantage.

The Internet branch also serves as a valuable sales and marketing tool in promoting services offered through the brick and mortar branch. Even though they aren't performed over the Internet today, FNB&T Pipestone prominentiy advertises its trust services on its Website. It is important to include this type of information to make customers aware of the availability of these services at the community bank with which they have existing relationships. As a result, they will not feel compelled to take their business to a larger competitor.

HOW TO SPEED PROFITABILITY OF INTERNET BANKING

While there is little question that Internet banking makes sense for the bottom line, one question does remain. When can a bank expect to see a return on its virtual branch investment? As with the construction of a new physical location or the implementation of other types of banking technologies, the costs of building an Internet branch are not justified overnight, but instead are amortized over several years. In the case of an Internet branch, however, the payback will be realized in a much shorter period of time. The financial institution that takes full advantage of this unique delivery channel with effective marketing and cross-selling can make an Internet "branch" profitable in a relatively short amount of time.

To achieve that shorter payback, there are certain strategies the bank should follow:

- Treat the Internet branch as a true branch. "Build it and they will come" might work in *The Field of Dreams*, but it doesn't work with Internet banking. The financial institution that supports the Internet branch just as it would a brick and mortar branch — with advertising, customer service, and other support — will realize profitability sooner.
- Make customer retention and market share growth the goal, then offer special rates to customers using this less expensive delivery channel, and even give away services to profitable customers. Once customers begin using Internet banking services, they quickly recognize the time and money savings and are willing to pay for the convenience.
- Actively involve bank personnel in the new Internet branch. Employees that use the service and understand first-hand its benefits and ease of use will be better able and more inclined to promote it to existing and potential customers.

WHY IT IS IMPORTANT TO ACT NOW

Consumer use of the Internet is growing faster than that of any technology before it — including radio, telephone, and TV. With a mere 3 million people online in 1994, that number had jumped to more than 100 million by the end of 1997. And more and more people are logging on every day. Industry experts suggest that as many as 16 million households, as shown in Exhibit 14.1, will be banking online by the turn of the century. And as some 1000 companies of all types, including financial services firms, jump on the Internet each day, the bank without an Internet branch will soon become the equivalent of a bank without an ATM.

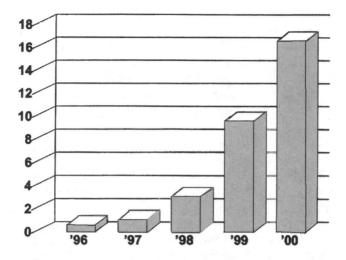

Exhibit 14.1. Internet banking households 1996–2000.

As long as a bank recognizes the need to offer Internet banking to compete, the most prudent course of action is to be first in the market. This gives the institution the opportunity to build long-term relationships with online customers today, rather than trying to win back those customers after they've gone to a competitor that offers Internet banking. Internet banking has leveled the playing field for community banks and positioned FNB&T Pipestone to compete nationally, regionally, and locally against financial institutions of all sizes.

TEN QUESTIONS TO ASK WHEN EVALUATING AN INTERNET BANKING SOLUTION

1. *Does this solution allow me to collect and store important customer data that can be mined for targeted marketing and cross-selling promotions?* The best solution is a "fat server" solution, meaning it is constructed on top of a database that allows the bank to collect and store important customer data, such as spending and saving habits. The bank can then mine these data to segment its customer base and direct specific marketing promotions toward a highly targeted group. For example, the bank can elect to target all customers with checking account balances of more than $5000 to alert them to its savings or money market account offerings.

2. *Can my Internet branch administrator instantly update rate and product information, or must they submit requests and wait for a service bureau to make the changes?* The administration interface must allow the Internet branch administrator to update rate and product infor-

mation at any time from anywhere, and does not rely on a third party to make these important and timely changes. In addition, the changes are written to audit tables in the database that can be used for specific audit procedures in the future.

3. *Can prospective customers submit account applications online or must they print and mail them to my bank?* The bank must be able to customize account applications and allow prospective customers to submit applications immediately online.

4. *If the solution offers electronic account submissions, are they secure?* Applications should be written directly to a secure database. An e-mail notification is then sent to the designated bank official who opens the application through a secure administration site.

5. *Does this solution provide error checking, or will my customer service staff be required to manually review all incorrect or incomplete applications?* The software must automatically check all applications for appropriate and complete information. Applicants should be prompted to correct any errors and complete submissions before they are sent to the bank, thus expediting the process and saving valuable customer service time.

6. *Will my customers be able to pay all of their bills through this solution's electronic bill payment service?* A user-friendly interface allows the bank's Internet branch customers to create and edit their own payee menus. Therefore, customers can elect to use electronic bill payment services to pay any business or individual, regardless of their ability to accept electronic payments.

7. *Can my customers access the Internet branch using any Internet access device, such as PCs and televisions?* The solution of choice must be designed to not only allow a bank's customers to access the Internet branch from anywhere in the world, but also through any secure, Internet-enabled device such as WebTV™.

8. *Can my customers download active statements into personal financial management (PFM) programs such as Microsoft Money™?* Most Internet banking solutions allow customers to download account information into their PFMs. The best solution should go a step farther by downloading active statements to eliminate redundancies. For example, if a customer enters transaction information into their PFM that is then downloaded from their Internet account, the active statement alerts them to the redundancy. Therefore, a customer will not record the same deposit twice.

9. *Is this solution scalable, and what effect will customer growth have on its performance?* The chosen solution must be capable of accommodating any size customer base, and providing peak downloading performance regardless of a consumer's hardware and software limitations.

10. *How will this solution allow me to track the success of my Internet branch?* Perhaps the most valuable tool an Internet banking solution can provide, the reporting feature, allows the bank to accurately gauge the success of its Internet branch and determine what modifications can be made to increase that success.

Author's Bio

Kim Humphreys *is vice president with nFront, Inc., a leading provider of full-service Internet banking for community banks and winner of Microsoft Corporation's Best Internet Banking Solution Award. With more than 8 years of marketing and public relations experience, Humphreys was instrumental in introducing the world's first Internet bank, Security First Network Bank, in 1995, and for generating public awareness of the ensuing Internet banking industry. In her current role with nFront, and in her previous position as director of public relations for Security First Network Bank and Security First Technologies, Humphreys has contributed to more than 100 publications worldwide on the subject of electronic commerce and Internet banking. She also is a contributing author for* Banking and Finance on the Internet, *Van Nostrand Reinhold, New York, 1997.*

Section III
Internet Security and Networking Management

Before the Internet, information resources were mostly clois-
tered and, therefore, secure from attack. But today's Internet-driven network is severely at risk from predators from around the country and
around the globe. One has only to pick up the newspaper to read about various attacks, most of them benign, but not all. And we've all probably had
a virus or two encroach on our systems by way of e-mail attachments.

Tomorrow's attacks will make today's cyberviruses and break-ins look
like kid stuff. Though we don't delve into it in this book, the government
and its consultants have coined the term cyber-terrorism or cyber-war to
describe the potential for breaking into national security computers or
those banking and securities systems that hold up the framework of our industrial society.

In addition, the Internet is quickly becoming part and parcel of our internal networks. This adds a layer of complexity that is unparalleled in the an-
nals of computer development.

In this section, we will address the issues of security management in
terms of how to keep vandals and hackers out of your Website and enabling
safer deployment of mobile code technologies. We will also talk about using the Internet as a Virtual Private Network, or VPN, as they are now commonly called.

Chapter 15
Making Your Website Hacker Safe: Internet Security

Jim Hewitt

THE INTERNET SHOULD BE A BOON TO YOUR BUSINESS. Your customers and competitors are all there. It provides cheap, 24-hour global access, and makes it easy to link up with your partners and prospects.

But most users believe the Internet is unsafe and fear it for this reason. This lack of confidence is one of the greatest obstacles slowing the profitability of most Internet commerce. If you do business on the Internet, you are obliged to make sure your assets are adequately protected. If you participate as a user or a customer you should know what the risks are and how to manage them.

Opening your business to the Internet exposes it to a vast number of unseen potential attackers. Attackers are more numerous than ever and several trends favor them:

- The Internet has grown far ahead of the technical people and tools available to protect its users
- Much of the technology is new and immature, with the unpredictability that entails
- The business processes are new, too, without the safeguards of fully developed practices

The problem is not software. The problem is people. With few exceptions, hackers exploit human errors, not core technical vulnerabilities.

You may be charged with convincing you company's management that risk to company assets is properly mitigated. The way to do that is by creating and implementing a security policy.

When data is sent from one computer to another on the Internet it makes dozens of "hops" from one intermediate machine to another. Every

0-8493-9987-4/00/$0.00+$.50
© 2000 by CRC Press LLC

computer inbetween presents an opportunity for prying eyes to see what is being sent. This poses an obvious security problem. There are several solutions:

Prevention — Keep problems from occurring in the first place.

Vigilance — Keep on top of events at your site; don't assume that "all quiet" means you are safe.

Remediation — When problems come up, fix them immediately.

STEPS TO MAKING YOUR SITE SAFE

- Know what your assets are
- Know what your risks are and how to mitigate each one
- Educate your users
- Lock down the superuser/administrative user IDs
- Make sure your system is physically secure
- Take "trust" out of your organization
- Create a comprehensive security plan
- Hire, train, and manage the best system administrator you can find
- Minimize your system's exposure to the Internet
- Find and fix all known security holes
- Stay current on news about new ones
- Create an ongoing defense plan
- As you do more on the Internet, expand your security work to keep pace

Computer Security Basics

A computer system is called "secure" when the following conditions are established:

- Integrity
- Access control
- Authentication
- Availability
- Confidentiality
- Nonrepudiation

There are two sources of vulnerability:

- Outsiders — Barbarians at the Gate: "If you build it, they will come"
- Insiders — The Enemy within the Walls

Your site may be used as a base for attacks on other sites.

Some hackers are criminals. Most are a mere nuisance, like vandals. Given the choice between the thief who steals your car and the vandal who scratches the paint, most car owners will choose to avoid them both. This chapter explains how to do that without keeping your wheels locked in the garage. It is for nontechnical people who need a practical approach to computer security.

DEFINITIONS

This chapter uses the term "hacker" to mean anyone who tries to get in where you, the system owner, do not want him or her to go. The following characteristics are not relevant:

- *Motivation*. It does not matter whether the hacker has illegal or malicious intentions, or is just curious
- *Success*. An attempt at illicit entry is not innocent just because it is unsuccessful
- *Stranger or insider*. Anyone who goes where he or she is not welcome

In computer industry terms, a "hacker" is anyone who delves into the inner workings of computer hardware or software, and a "cracker" is someone who uses this arcane knowledge in a malicious way. For the purpose of this chapter, a hacker is anyone who wants to get in where you do not want him or her to go.

GOALS FOR INTERNET SECURITY

No Internet site is perfectly safe. The best approach for a business-oriented Internet site owner is the following:

- Assess and understand what your risks are
- Take a series of measured preventive steps to comprehensively manage this risk
- Make site security an ongoing part of your organization's daily work

Since "perfect safety" is not the goal, what is? The goals in securing your site is to:

- Raise the cost to potential attackers
- Make sure site manager can detect a violation and react to it quickly
- Contain and minimize potential damage
- Make recovery as easy as possible
- Install strong security measures that enable you to present your site as "certified secure;" use this as a selling point privately with your customers; do not advertise it too loudly

COMPUTER SECURITY FUNDAMENTALS

- Sooner or later someone will attack your site
- An attack is defined as any attempt to get access to more system resources than the system owner intends the user to have
- An unsuccessful attack is still an attack, and the attacker should be identified and held accountable for it

- Your system has hundreds of features you don't know about, and will probably never care about. Many of these features make it vulnerable to attack
- Most operating systems are insecure in their default configurations; they come out of the box with widely known default passwords and most of their security features turned off
- Find out what the security features of your system are; turn them all on
- Get all available patches for your operating system and applications, and install them; many of these patches close security holes, whether published or not

Tips

- Most logging facilities are turned off by default. Turn them back on. Historically, logging was turned off because it consumes lots of disk space. In the late 1990s disk space became cheap, and dropping by 50 percent per year, so you can afford it.
- Backup your files thoroughly and often. It is an excellent low-cost way to limit the damage from a virus or malicious attacker.
- Do not store credit card numbers on any machine that is connected to the Internet. That goes for any other data that absolutely must not be accessed by unauthorized users.
- Most e-mail traffic is extremely insecure. Do not put anything in an e-mail message you would not want to be made public. If your e-mail must be kept confidential, use e-mail encryption.
- Limit the questions your staff put on Usenet, especially with regard to security and system configuration.

RISK

What are your risks?

- Your firm's reputation, and the trust and confidence of your customers.
- Destruction of data and equipment crucial to the operation of your business.
- Loss of the investment in time spent on your Website.
- Expense of the cleanup.
- Loss of business due to your site's downtime.

Assessing risk

If your data are extremely sensitive, such that theft, loss, or tampering would cause loss of life or imperil the future of the company, it should not be on any machine that is directly or indirectly connected to the Internet. Store it on a machine that is accessible from your internal network only.

Identify your assets. Inventory all hardware components and software including third-party products, utilities, home-grown applications, driver programs, and operating systems. Identify all data — online, archives, backups, and even users.

If your Website is a "brochure" site, with static pages of sales material, consider the cost of developing it and the expected sales benefits that would be lost if it were tampered with.

Assume there will always be holes and vulnerabilities you do not know about. This is all the more reason to close every single hole that *is* documented. No hole is too small

In the 1970s, security holes were allowed to remain open in the belief that they were accessible only to a tiny number of "experts." Today, the information is easy to find, and well-engineered "burglar's tools" obviate the need for a high level of technical talent.

Cost-Effective Risk Management

- Limit the assets you expose to the Internet
- According to CERT (see *References*), the majority of breaches come from weak passwords. Weak passwords are 100 percent preventable (see *Password Guidelines*)

Types of Attack

Typical attackers' objectives include:

- Deleting files from your site
- Changing passwords so authorized users cannot log in
- Stealing online assets, such as competitive information
- Stealing files that can be used for commercial gain, such as credit card numbers

Hackers search for one weak point or pinhole in your site's security. Attacks are typically carried out by making a small, crucial changes to your system. For example, some remote login utilities may be secure in themselves, but are a little too verbose in that they tell outsiders what operating system and version you are using. Once a hacker knows that, he can research the security bugs in that OS, and he is off and running.

A good example is the German hacker detected and finally caught by Cliff Stoll in *The Cuckoo's Egg*. The hacker exploited an obscure bug in an e-mail program that allowed him to substitute his own version of a system executable file on the victim's system. This one change allowed him to make several other changes, each one small, and eventually run rampant through the victim's system. Stoll first detected the miscreant only by careful reading of system audit logs. He tracked the hacker's activity across many other systems. Virtually all of the other system managers were unaware of the hacker. Some of the systems were owned by the U.S. Department of Defense and thought to be impregnable. The hacker was competent and persistent, but no guru. Yet he was enormously successful in breaking into dozens of systems, and took part in a worldwide scheme to steal U.S. government secrets and sell them to the (then) Soviet Union. The e-mail bug that gave him a foothold was widely known and quickly fixed by the program's author.

Intrusion consists of either an unknown person gaining access to your system's resources or a known person accessing resources not intended for him or her. Results of intrusion are modification and/or loss of data, breach of confidentiality, denial and/or disruption of service.

Note that many intrusions are carried out for the purpose of making your system the base for attacks on other systems.

THE SYSTEM ADMINISTRATOR: CARE AND FEEDING

To protect your site, you must manage, train, and motivate your system administrator (sysad). The sysad is charged with keeping hostile elements from damaging your system. The sysad's job objectives are

- Establish confidence in the integrity of the system
- Minimize risk to the company's system assets

The above objectives are accomplished by planning, designing, and implementing technical measures and organizational programs within the enterprise. If this sounds more demanding than setting up PCs and backing up files, it is.

- Invest in training to keep your sysad's skills up to date
- If your sysad does not have time to pay adequate attention to security issues, restructure his or her duties
- Establish a career path for system administrators; after 2 or 3 years a good sysad should be kicked upstairs; this works wonders as a motivational and recruiting tool

There will always be new bugs and holes to take advantage of. Despite this, the hacker's best path into your system is by social engineering. This means getting to know the sysad, calling up posing as a user with a forgotten password, and watching the Usenet newsgroups for questions or problems that indicate vulnerabilities. An attacker may be able to get into your system, despite all its safeguards, by finding a "helpful" employee who gives away more than he or she should.

Vendors' notification of security fixes is usually limited. Announcements typically go to security-related newsgroups and mailing lists only. It is the sysad's job to monitor these actively and keep the system current.

Recruiting Your System Administrator

Hire the best sysad you can find. Get one with real experience in security, not only in system management.

When interviewing candidates, ask the following:

- If his or her previous sites have had explicit incident response procedures
- If he or she has handled a break-in, or break-in attempt, or other incident of unauthorized resource access, malicious or not
- Which system services are typically turned off for Web servers

Here is a list of preventive measures from Farmer and Venema (see *Notes*). Your sysad candidate should be familiar with them:

- The *finger* service can reveal things about your system's OS and users that no one needs to know; disable it or replace the program it with a less "generous" version
- Export read-write file systems only to specific, trusted clients
- Alternatively, export read-only file systems only
- Restrict the *ftp* service, and disable *tftp*
- Disable NIS
- Get a list of machines that have "trust" relationships (see *Definitions*) with your own machines; a "trust" relationship means the machines mutually allow cross-logins without password verification; this means that the security of your machine is out of your control, never a good thing
- Consider eliminating trust entirely

The sysad weekly status reports should include the following:

- Any relevant security advisories received and implemented. There are typically several new CERT advisories (see *References*) every month
- System monitoring and auditing work done
- Maintenance work done to keep the site secure
- Software patches made available by vendors
- Software patches applied
- All user accounts added, deleted, or modified, with all privileges listed

Design your site to play to your sysad's strengths. If your staff does not have UNIX experience, get a Microsoft Windows NT box.

Ironically, hackers see the sysad as their primary pathway into the system. A common tactic is for a hacker to target a site after he makes a study of the sysad's habits, skills, and weaknesses. Your sysad must be mature and capable enough not to be vulnerable to these tactics.

MANAGEMENT STRATEGIES

If you engage an ISP, you are dependent on them for security. As a rule of thumb, the more things you run on your machine, the more security holes there likely will be, so your Internet server should run only the required minimum of services. Ask your Internet Service Provider if the same machine on which your data resides is running mail, POP3, NNTP, print serving, FTP, or login authentication. With each extra service, the likelihood of a security hole greatly increases.

SYSTEM AUDITING

A system audit lists all accounts and their privileges for every server and workstation, and all trust relationships.

In general, you should adopt several overlapping strategies and combine them at low cost.

1. Explicitly deny all services, file access, etc. except those specifically allowed
2. Restrict, monitor, and audit access

Establish your enterprise's acceptable risk level. If you can't tolerate any risk, you shouldn't be on the Internet at all.

Connect only the required minimum of your network to the Internet, and assume it will come under attack by hackers. Put everything else behind the firewall.

SOURCES OF INTERNET MALFEASANCE

Your system is at much greater risk from your own employees than from hackers or computer criminals. Data security professionals at large companies typically spend 90 percent of their time making sure the internal staff are able to see and do only what their duties entail, and nothing else, and that they handle this responsibility professionally. They spend only small fraction of their time worrying about intruders, and so should you. In almost all cases, more valuable information walks out on floppy disks then will ever be taken by hackers.

Internal breaches are made by company staff who are supposed to have some access to the system, but contrive to get more. They may want to look in personnel files, pirate software, read the boss's mail, or just grab some extra disk space. Many fall into the "disgruntled employee" category.

An insider can see passwords taped to the front of terminals. Most company staff place assets at risk through carelessness and ignorance. As a manager, your time and budget will be very well spent working on these.

Internal staff who try to break into system resources they should not use have a variety of motivations: mischief, ego, boredom, or personal conflicts with other staff members. Some will say, "I have to break through system security to do my job." If this is true, then your business process is broken, not your Website. Fix the process and close the hole your staffer used to hack it.

All of these indicate that the business process and your security policy are defective. Fixing these will do much more for your business than worrying about hackers.

More than 50 percent of vulnerabilities come from sheer carelessness. To test your own site's security, try this social engineering test: pretend to be a sales rep, and phone in from the field with an emergency system access problem. Tell the system administrator you just need a favor to get out of a jam — having a password reset to a known value, or access to a dial-in number.

Next, pretend to be a system administrator. Phone a field sales rep and say you need his or her password to "fix a system problem." If either of these scams succeed, you have a problem.

The bane of the system administrator's existence is the employee who asks for a favor in violation of the Security Policy and says the sysad had better accede to his or her request or the boss will get ticked off. If you are the boss, make it clear ahead of time that you will support the sysad in refusing requests of this kind.

In large organizations, a basic assumption is that most internal theft will occur in small amounts over long periods of time. For this reason, an employee who is found misappropriating even a tiny amount is immediately subject to firing and prosecution.

HACKERS

Most hackers are like vandals — a costly and damaging social nuisance; only a minority are in it for profit.

The most dangerous person is not the unknown outside attacker but the malicious insider with sanctioned business on your system. Much more valuable information leaves victims' sites by floppy disk and voice phone calls than by outside intruders.

A common tactic among hackers is to watch newsgroup messages and bulletin boards for messages signed, for example, "Richard Roe, System Administrator, XYZ Corporation." Let's say the newsgroup is devoted to baseball, and Mr. Roe says he is a Boston Red Sox fan. The hacker goes to the site and attempts to break in with passwords like "RedSox," "pennant," and so on.

A related tactic is to send Richard Roe e-mail, claiming to be another Red Sox fan, and begin a long exchange of e-mail messages. In the course of online dialogue, the hacker learns Mr. Roe admires former Red Sox star

Ted Williams. He goes to the site, tries "TedWilliams" or "400hitter" and bingo! Without using any technical skill the hacker comes in through the front door.

Never put anything important in an e-mail message. This especially applies to passwords and credit card numbers. The first thing most miscreants do is scan the mail directory for the words "password" and "Visa."

The scheme should be fail safe. If the system fails it should fail harmlessly. Just as the way a car's steering wheel lock makes the car more difficult to steal, the best approach is to deter hackers and make them move on to easier targets.

When Protection Is Not Protection

Several security schemes purport to protect your data, but in fact provide little or no protection. These may keep the honest people honest, but do not rely on them to provide any real security.

Security by Obscurity. Hackers' tools exist that will scan an entire site and show its complete directory structure. It will not work to put valuable files in an out-of-the-way directory and assume no one would bother to look there.

MS-Office and Zip File Password Protection. The encryption algorithms for both are known to be weak, and methods of defeating them have been widely circulated. If you must encrypt a file, use real encryption software such as PGP and F-Control.

SECURITY POLICY (INTERNAL)

There are two approaches to this, a "zero-based" approach and an "everything but" approach.

- Zero-based policy: the minimal, additive approach. Each user gets only what his or her day's work requires. Each system service is enabled with only the minimum required functionality. Explicitly deny all services not absolutely required and justified. The firewall stops everything except those few permitted services, such as e-mail.
- Everything-but policy: the services known to be vulnerable or dangerous are turned off, but most other services are left on. System security manages, monitors, and audits access more than restricting it.

To implement:

- Determine the resources needed for each business process and for each person involved in it.
- Based on this, decide which files and programs to make available
- Lock down all other system facilities

- Consider removing the restricted resources from the network entirely

The key is not to take a reactive stance or wait for a problem to develop and try to play catch-up.

User Education

Make sure each user is clear on the following:

- Each person is responsible for his or her own password and anything that is done while using it
- Each person is responsible for the equipment, software, and login account resources entrusted to him or her
- Each person is obligated to report untoward system behavior that may indicate an attack

Computer misuse is just like any other type of crime, and the consequences are the same. Plug the holes in the dike. This approach entails creating a list of known security weaknesses, and takes steps to close each one.

Clearly, your site should use both approaches. You should take the zero-based approach first. Then start the "plug the holes" stage, which will be much smaller and simpler because of the first steps. Most sites start and finish with a "plug the holes" approach, or do nothing at all.

The job of the system administrator and the manager responsible for security is to find creative ways to reduce privileges to a minimum without creating undue complexity, hurting productivity, and making the users unhappy.

Finally, you should reassess your security policy at regular intervals, and whenever a major change occurs.

Incident Response Procedures

Formulate a series of steps to be taken:

- When a breach is discovered in progress
- When evidence of a past violation is discovered
- When a virus is suspected or positively determined to be present

Example: all security warnings/failure reports will be recorded and investigated, with their causes and actions taken forwarded to management. It is the employee's responsibility to:

- Report possible security breaches
- Know protocol for handling attacks

The CERT site is a gold mine of information on this topic. Go to http://www.cert.org/nav/securityimprovement.html.

System Configuration Standards

Keep in mind that most of the areas in which your system is vulnerable are caused by incorrect configuration settings.

Pay special attention to home-grown software. It is rarely built with security in mind. Connect only a limited segment of your network to the Internet. Expect that these machines will come under attack and that some attacks will succeed.

Consider making the file systems on the exposed machines read-only, thus by definition resistant to tampering.

SECURITY POLICY (EXTERNAL)

Your primary external defense is your firewall. A firewall is a group of system components whose job it is to enforce your system's security policy. Firewalls allow in some traffic and restrict everything else. The critical issue is that you must know what you want your firewall to do, what to allow, what to restrict. This is your security policy. Some firewalls are built using software alone, some use separate hardware components.

To keep out hackers, you need a comprehensive security program. The security policy should explicitly state rules for accessing the system via all available means. If there are dial-in modems attached, specify who is allowed to get in and what they may do. Management decides what will be visible from the Internet. Only those resources are made available and everything else is locked down.

Creating an Internet site means you want your system to be partially accessible to authorized users. "Partially" means that users get to the level of access you specify. If you have a static brochure site, readers may read some of your files, but only the ones you authorize, and they may not modify or destroy them. If your site is interactive, users can enter data where permitted, but cannot wreck or steal the resources the site presents.

PASSWORD GUIDELINES

CERT estimates that 80 percent of problems result from weak passwords. Educate staff on their obligation to maintain secure and unguessable passwords, and ensure they comply. Your site will become much more secure overnight. A "guessable" password is

- Anything you can find in a dictionary — a word, name, place name, abbreviation, etc.
- The company name and the person's own name are used so often that intruders routinely guess them and frequently succeed.

Hackers often attempt to break into to users' accounts by guessing passwords. This approach is very simple and staggeringly successful.

Common passwords are used so much that this approach is often successful. According to a popular anecdote within the computer security industry, the second most common password is "love." The most common is a four-letter synonym for "love." *Hint*: If your site is dedicated to the study of orchids, the root password should not be "orchids."

One recommended guideline is that passwords contain a combination of numbers and uppercase and lowercase letters. A popular method is to take a phrase that is easy for the user to remember, such as a movie title, create a mixed-case acronym from it, and use that as a password. For example, "Titanic starring Leonardo Dicaprio and a big boat" would contract to "TsLDa2b2." This seems like a complex string to type, but it will become automatic within a day or two.

Password rules should be enforced by an automated utility. There are many of these on the market for every operating system. Typical password enforcement functions are

- Require a reasonable minimum password length, usually eight characters
- Automatic password expiration parameters to force password changes quarterly; users generally find monthly password changes to be onerous
- Check for and disallow use of already-used passwords
- Disallow obviously weak passwords, such as the company name, or the user's name

A widely available hacker's tool wages a "dictionary attack" which repetitiously attempts automated logins using words in a large dictionary file. If a password is a word in the English dictionary, the program will discover it and so will the hacker.

An especially bad choice is the name of any family member. Working in data security for a large financial services firm, I would routinely see an employee's desk with a child's picture and perform the following:

- Ask the name of the child
- With the employee looking on, log in as him and enter the child's name as the password

This works in an astonishing number of cases. Add the child's birth date to the name and the success rate climbs even higher. (Stranger still, I could visit the employee again a few weeks later, and log in again with the same unchanged password.)

Use a different password for each system you log in to. If you subscribe to an online Website specializing in orchids, use a different password there from the one that protects your e-mail account or your Website. Many hackers set up sham "promotion" sites, under the pretext of providing free software or special interest forums, for the purpose of collecting passwords.

I met a system administrator who uses the same password for the root accounts (see Glossary) on dozens of different machines. That password is an easily guessable word in English. I would like to borrow his ATM card!

PHYSICAL SECURITY

Anyone who can physically touch a machine can break into it. If you cannot restrict physical access to a machine that houses your system, it is not safe.

PROFESSIONAL HELP

Penetration-testing companies will attack your site to help your determine how vulnerable you are. These attacks simulate a real attack.

Consultants from penetration-testing companies provide the following services:

- Check your system for technical compliance with security standards
- Train your staff on how to find and fix holes
- Provide ongoing strategic and technical advice to keep your site safe

These are consulting companies that field a penetration assessment team. Their methods are the same as those used by hackers. Their job is to identify your site's vulnerabilities, and train your IT staff on how to find and fix them.

Recommendations:

- Don't engage a penetration service company that only operates remotely. To do the job they will have to gauge social engineering and physical access vulnerabilities. This cannot be done effectively away from your site.
- The assessment team should be knowledgeable about security and about your business, not only about technical issues and security products.
- Many companies are concerned about penetration service companies learning too much and using the information against them. Select your vendor carefully, and talk with the customer references they supply.
- Costs are typically near the top of high-end IT consultancies.

Keep in mind that the best value is the knowledge retained by your own staff.

Author's Bio

Jim Hewitt has worked in data security, system administration, and software engineering for more than 10 years. He has held engineering and management positions in several well-known financial services, manufacturing software and healthcare systems companies in the U.S. and Asia. He is a principal consultant at Brainstorm Technology of Cambridge, MA.

Notes

The U.S. General Accounting Office conducted a test break-in of the U.S. State Department's automated information system and found it prone to attack. The problems they found are present in many, if not most, companies' systems.
Most of the best information sources are academic or other noncommercial organizations, and are publicly available. Take advantage of this fact.
To get some insights on how hackers work and think, look into these two usergroups:
   Alt.2600
   Alt.2600.hackerz
"2600" refers to the frequency of a whistle used by a legendary phone system hacker to fool Ma Bell into providing free phone service.

Other good sources:

* Stoll, Clifford, *The Cuckoo's Egg,* Pocket Books, 1995, ISBN: 0671726889.
* Farmer, D. and Wietse, V., Improving Your Site by Breaking Into It, at www.best.com/~mld/unix/papers/improve_by_breakin.html. This is an excellent white paper, focused on UNIX but widely applicable.
* The mother lode of online security references: www.cs.purdue.edu/homes/spaf/hot-lists/csec-top.html.

GLOSSARY

Trust — A relationship among two or more computers, whereby users who are permitted to access one are automatically permitted on the others.
Firewall — A hardware or software component that restricts outside access to your system.
Service — A function performed by a computer. An example is a print service.
Hole — A defect in a computer program or operating system that allows a breach of security.
Social engineering — Nontechnical break-in methods that use information accidentally divulged by sanctioned system users. Typically this means tricking the victim into revealing a password, or providing clues that allow the hacker to guess it.
Hacker — A technical person who explores the inner workings of computer systems, usually without illegal intentions.

Cracker — A hacker who uses his or her technical skills to illegally break into other systems. "Crack" originally referred to the process of decoding passwords, something like cracking a code.

Root — The "superuser" login account that allows full access to every file and resource on the system, and can create other user accounts. The root password is the keys to the kingdom. Only the systems administration should know the root password.

Chapter 16
Vandals: The New Internet Threat

Shimon Gruper

TODAY'S ANTIVIRUS SOFTWARE PRODUCTS ARE ABLE TO COPE with all existing viruses and virus technologies. The penetration and success of the Internet and its innovative technologies such as Java and ActiveX, have created a new type of Internet-specific threat, collectively called vandals. Unfortunately, existing antivirus software products are not able to deal with these new threats. As opposed to viruses, vandals are auto-executable applications that "hit-and-run"; they do not linger in the users' computers in order to replicate themselves. Since vandals are usually unknown, standard methods of scanning for known virus patterns do not work. As I write this, the majority of corporations that have connected their networks to the Internet do not allow in Active Content (Java and ActiveX), choosing for security reasons to block them all at the gateway level. In order to open these networks — without risk — to all of the positive functionality that Active Content can bring, a new antivandal technology must be used. This chapter will investigate ways to deal with vandals in order to provide an adequate solution to this problem.

VIRUSES

A computer virus is a program that can infect other computer programs by modifying them in such a way as to include a (possibly evolved) copy of itself. Computer viruses are not necessarily designed to cause damage, but often do. They are transmitted from computer to computer when the user runs infected programs, or when infected documents are opened.

Types of Viruses

Viruses have several things in common: they require a "host" program that has executable content, they replicate, and they can be detected by signature scanning.

Viruses can be separated into several categories:

0-8493-9987-4/00/$0.00+$.50
© 2000 by CRC Press LLC

1. File infectors that attach themselves to ordinary program files. They usually infect .COM and/or .EXE programs, although some can infect any program containing executable code, such as .SYS, .OVL, .DLL and .PRG files. The majority of file infectors hide themselves somewhere in memory the first time an infected program is executed and infect any program that is subsequently launched. Some file infectors are polymorphic viruses, which produce varied yet fully operational copies of themselves, usually through self-encryption with a variable key. This is done in the hopes that virus scanners will not be able to detect the new variant.

2. File system viruses are those that modify directory table entries so that the virus is loaded and executed before the desired program. The program itself is not modified, only the directory entry.

3. Macro viruses infect Microsoft Office documents (such as Word or Excel). They are generally written in a scripting language, except in Office 97 where they are written in Visual Basic for added power. These viruses are responsible for the majority of virus infections, mostly due to the sharing of documents via e-mail. Macro viruses can switch words around in documents, change colors on the screen, format the hard drive, send documents by e-mail without notifying the user, etc.

4. System/boot record infectors infect executable code found in certain system areas on a disk, which are not ordinary files. Some are boot-sector viruses, which infect only the DOS boot sector. Others are MBR viruses, which infect the Master Boot Record on fixed disks and the DOS boot sector on diskettes. Some viruses modify CMOS settings as well. However, CMOS memory is not in the normal CPU address space and cannot be executed. A virus may corrupt or modify CMOS information, but cannot hide there. Multi-partite viruses infect both files and boot records.

INTERNET VANDALS

In contrast to viruses (which require a user to execute a program in order to cause damage) vandals are *auto-executable* applications. They are likely to be made with malicious intent by programmers, but can also be normally harmless programs that are misused in order to steal or damage data.

Early in 1997, the world heard about a serious threat involving a free plug-in advertised as a multimedia viewer that played Web movies. The free plug-in silently redirected the computer's modem from the Internet access line to a 900 number which cost users thousands of dollars in phone bills. Within a few months of this attack, a hacker organization used an ActiveX control to steal data from Quicken files located on the local drives of people viewing their Web page.

Vandals can be written into the code of Java Applets, ActiveX controls, JavaScript, or any number of new programming languages designed to enhance Web pages. They can also be hidden in pushed content, e-mail attachments, or harmful plug-ins for Web browsers.

Where Vandals Hide

E-mail. E-mail is the most common application used on the Internet today. In addition to message text, e-mail can also include attachments of all kinds, as well as boobytrapped shortcuts and vandal applets. E-mail attachments can carry vandals, Trojan Horses, or viruses. Anybody can send and receive e-mail containing hostile content or attachments without knowing that they have been attacked or have unwittingly attacked another. In an unprotected corporate environment, the hostile attachment will have access to any file on the network.

Web Content. Web surfing is the second most popular Internet activity, and it is the least secure. The newest Internet technologies, especially Java and ActiveX, are used to create dynamic, content-driven Websites. Unfortunately, these compelling new technologies also pose the highest risk. Java applets and ActiveX controls are downloaded and executed automatically by simply viewing a Web page. In this manner, you are essentially allowing an unknown person to copy an unknown program to your network and run it. Instructing Web browsers not to download any Java or ActiveX content is possible but increasingly less practical, as many Websites require these technologies to provide full functionality.

In addition, just because you are viewing a so-called "trusted" Website does not mean that its content could not have been altered to include vandal programs. For example, in August 1996, the CIA Website was altered — an earlier victim was the Department of Justice. And on December 4, 1997 the Yahoo! Website was penetrated. In fact, hackers often target traditional bastions of security because of the challenge. If someone can change the wording or graphics on a site, he can also add a vandal program that may damage or steal your data.

File Downloads. Although transferring files is common on the Internet, and carries many of the risks noted previously, it poses less of a threat because it is an activity usually undertaken by experienced users. However, by trusting a product's description to be factual, a user can inadvertently download a program that does something unexpected upon execution.

Netcasting Content. Netcasting enables news and other content providers to automatically supply subscribers with information by downloading content to the user's desktop. This technology also often provides the means by which nonsecurity-conscious software companies automatically supply their users with updates. Netcasting technology is activated when a user installs a small program onto the PC called a "push-client," which constantly polls the provider's server and transports the latest news, stock quotes, sports scores, etc. Just as software developers (such as Microsoft) have inadvertently provided CD-ROMs to customers that included viruses, it is very likely that vandal programs and viruses will be inadvertently supplied along with the expected pushed content. To make matters worse, the nature of vandals makes them ideal tools for people trying to target a particular network or company. Someone can easily send the vandal as an e-mail attachment or place it on a Website visited by the company's employees.

EXISTING SOLUTIONS

Authentication

Up to this point, the only proposed solution to deal with vandals is authentication, which applies a digital signature to every application. Both Microsoft (with their ActiveX technology) and Sun (for the Java language) are champions of authentication, and argue that digitally signed auto-executable applications cannot be vandals and thus can be "trusted." Digitally signed applications have a unique key, given by the Certification Authority (CA). This CA is also responsible for identifying and authenticating the applicant who is the supposed author of the signed application.

This entire authentication process lacks some security basics. Even if the CA does its job in identifying the applicant, this does not mean that the applicant actually wrote the application or that this application does not contain any vandal code. We all know that providing a passport to an individual does not mean that that individual is not carrying a bomb in his suitcase. All it means is that *after* the bomb explodes and the damage is caused we might know who was responsible.

The existing Certification Authority today, Verisign, merely checks that the applicant's Social Security number is valid and that he has records in the Credit Bureau. There have already been instances in which individuals were illegally trying to sell issued, active authentication keys.

When an authenticated auto-executable application is downloaded into a user's machine, a browser option allows the user to see the application's certification and decide if it will allow it to be executed. Since, in truth, one cannot rely on the CA and because the authentication of auto-executable applications does not provide us with any real sense of security, there is no way the average Internet user can make the right decision as to whether or not to allow its execution.

Scanning

Several antivirus vendors claim that existing virus scanning technology can be used to find and eliminate vandals as well. We have already established the fact that viruses replicate and thus tend to stay in the host system for as long as possible. This is not true of vandals, which are known to be "hit-and-run." Once a vandal application is downloaded and auto-executed on the client computer, its discovery will, by definition, be too late to do anything about it. Indeed, usually the victim is completely unaware of a vandal attack, making it virtually impossible to even recognize an assault let alone attempt to prevent one. Unlike viruses, the full vandal payload has already been delivered by the time the actual vandal program is identified. Virus-scanning technology looks for known patterns and will not successfully identify the unknown nature of vandals. In light of these facts, any protection against vandals needs to be proactive and needs to cope with new, unknown vandals.

THE ANTIVANDAL SAND BOX

We have seen that, unlike viruses, vandals are designed to deliver their payload immediately. Therefore, application servers and file servers cannot be a target for vandals because browsing and the auto-execution of Active Content is being carried out on client computers only (PCs connected to the network). It is clear that vandals target the information inside client computers, because this is the place where Internet "happens."

Preventing Vandal Behavior

Because vandals do not attempt hostile activity on servers and they are generally unknown, there is no practical way to identify hostile vandals at the gateway or server level. The only practical way to minimize vandal damage is by utilizing security or access control measures and by monitoring auto-executable applications in real time.

Access Control Lists are used in every up-to-date security system to control users' access to various system resources. We are all used to having a very limited guest-user profile, which is used when temporary or nontrusted users need to work in our systems. Since vandals are nontrusted guests in our systems, the same concept should also be applied to them.

Vandals are actually small applications that are executed (automatically) as a process in the operating system or as an internal process of the browser. The solution is to use a security system that verifies access of those applications to system resources against a predefined limited Access Control List.

For the purpose of clarity we will call this security system with the predefined limited Access Control List a *Sandbox*, as shown in Exhibit 16.1. Vandals in the Sandbox are like children playing safely within limits — they cannot touch or damage anything outside the Sandbox (the term Sandbox was originally used to describe the limited security system built into the Java language).

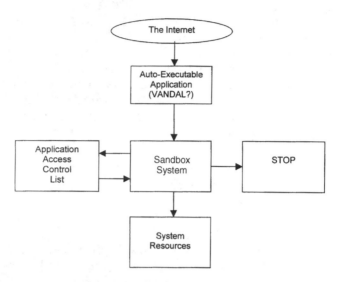

Exhibit 16.1. Security Sandbox.

Implementation

The majority of Internet users today are working in Microsoft's Windows 95 environment. Unfortunately, the Windows 95 operating system does not provide any Access Control means either for users or for running applications and processes.

This Sandbox implementation provides a security layer on top of Windows 95 or a similar operating system that will monitor each and every running process and application. A special system driver (VXD in Windows 95) that will verify the use of system resources (system calls and other resources) against a predefined list of allowed activities can accomplish this.

An example of a predefined Sandbox for Netscape Navigator would be as follows: Netscape Navigator will be allowed to write only to cache and temporary directories, and will be allowed to read only from the Windows system directory. All other activities — read, write, execute, create, or delete — in any directory other than those mentioned above, will be disallowed. Therefore, when Netscape Navigator (or a process within Navigator, like Java or a plug-in) tries to read from the My Documents directory, this will be designated as a vandal activity and access will be denied.

Another example of the Sandbox implementation can be limiting a new process invoked by an e-mail client to establish a TCP/IP connection and send information out. This would prevent e-mail-attached vandals to steal information from the hard disk or system memory (Windows 95 keeps network passwords in memory) and send it to somebody across the Internet.

CONCLUSION

Today's antivirus software products are able to detect, disinfect, and protect against nearly all existing computer viruses. However, current antivirus technology is not designed to detect auto-executable content in e-mail, file attachments, or the World Wide Web. Internet vandals, which take advantage of Active Content languages such as Java or Active X, are the newest Internet-borne threat, which must be dealt with using a new Sandbox quarantine method.

Because vandals are virtually unknown and require no action on the part of the user to execute their code, traditional antivirus scanning practices will not detect the vandal before it performs its given mission. Similarly, traditional security methods such as Authentication and Certificate Authorities only verify the identity of the sender, they do not guarantee the integrity of the content.

The Sandbox implementation provides a security layer on top of the operating system, which monitors every running process and application, isolating potential vandals before they strike. Using this risk-free method, corporations may safely access all of the positive functionality that Active Content provides.

Author's Bio

Shimon Gruper is the founder of eSafe Technologies Inc., an EliaShim company, specializing in antivirus, security, and antivandal software. Gruper founded EliaShim immediately after finishing his compulsory service in the Israeli Military in 1984. In 1987, he developed one of the first antivirus software programs when the first computer virus appeared. Since then he has been published in numerous scientific and trade journals on the topics of Internet Security, PC/LAN security, and antivirus software. His expertise includes viruses, client and network security, as well as the emerging issue of Internet vandals (Internet-borne Active Content threats).

Chapter 17

Enabling Safer Deployment of Internet Mobile Code Technologies

Ron Moritz

HIGHLY FUNCTIONAL APPLICATIONS — isn't this the Holy Grail that information systems managers have been searching for since the 1960s? Historically we move back more than a decade to the client-server platform whose technologies included third- and fourth-generation development tools and, later, Visual Basic and C++, and whose infrastructure included relational database servers in a distributed UNIX environment communicating over TCP/IP. More recent history is built around the Web platform where we find development technologies that include HTML and multimedia authoring tools, Java for developing program objects, and a variety of scripting languages used to glue various systems together.

New network computing initiatives require technologies that push both data and code between remote servers and local clients. Since mid-1996, mobile code technology, also referred to as active or downloadable content, has received considerable attention. Mobile code changes the model of client-server computing. Mobile code allows us to deliver both data and program code to the desktop without user intervention. By removing user participation in the download, installation, and execution of software, mobile code helps advance the reality of network computing.

Mobile code is contributing to the maturing infrastructure of Web servers and browsers and is being assimilated with existing technologies and information system investments, often termed as legacy applications and systems. The next generation of client-server services is emerging using the Web architecture to develop and deploy application servers.

0-8493-9987-4/00/$0.00+$.50
© 2000 by CRC Press LLC

Application servers have enhanced the performance and scalability of Web-based applications. Connecting such servers to the Internet, an open network connected to hundreds and thousands of other networks, results in new threats. Despite the growing threats, most organizations have done little to protect themselves against mobile code moving between Web servers and browsers. Security has taken a back seat.

Corporate security policies that block mobile code adversely affect the evolution of the Internet, intranet, and extranet. The benefits of distributed subprograms and routines are lost if Java applets, ActiveX controls, scripts, and other mobile code are diverted or prevented from reaching the browser. While no security implementation is absolute, functionality is not achieved by disconnecting users from the network and preventing access to programs.

In this chapter we will

- Explore the problems associated with and alternatives available for allowing untrusted code to execute on the corporate network
- Examine both the current and historical security issues associated with mobile code
- Outline the risks of executable content within the context of new client-server computing
- Describe Java security and author and capability signing models
- Provide guidance for using mobile code on the corporate network
- Provide a roadmap for mobile code deployment
- Review mobile code security solutions available today

HIGHLY MOBILE CODE

Imagine no longer having to jump into the car and drive to the local computer superstore to buy software. Imagine not having to wait for your favorite mail-order house to ship software to your home or office. Imagine not having space-consuming software boxes lining your shelves. Imagine not having to spend hours installing software. Imagine loading software only when you need it.

Mobile code technologies allow Web users to automatically download and run platform-independent code from all over the world on their own machines without technical skills. This "breakthrough" is actually not a new theory; several languages have been introduced with this same goal. What is important today is that we recognize that the underlying computer communications infrastructure has provided the vehicle for a legitimate paradigm shift in computing: real programs that make the Web dynamic by delivering animation, computation, user interaction, and other functions to the desktop.

The emergence of mobile code as a Web-based client-server tool has been made possible through the

- Positioning of Sun Microsystem's Java™ as a platform-independent language and standard
- Acceptance of Microsoft's Internet Explorer™ browser supporting ActiveX™ controls
- Ability to plug-in or add services to Netscape Communication's Communicator™ browser

The desire to create applications that install without the user's participation in the download, setup, and execution processes is logically equivalent to the concept of just-in-time inventory management systems deployed in the manufacturing sector. This is the premise on which the next generation of computing has been planned: Locally run programs, dynamically loaded over the network, taking advantage of distributed computing horsepower, allowing "fresh" software to be distributed "as needed."

Java and ActiveX are being used today to create new business applications. Scripting languages, such as JavaScript™ and Visual Basic Script™, are used to create interfaces between new Web services and older, back-end data servers. In large enterprises you will find even the most lightweight application developer deploying programs on department servers. Such code follows no formal software development methodology, seldom undergoes a third-party quality assurance process, and frequently lacks the support services normally available with applications developed by the information services group. The desire for just-in-time software along with the infrastructure that facilities the transport and delivery of the code has resulted in a large and growing base of uncontrolled software.

JAVA

"The Java programming language and platform is a tsunami that will sweep through the economy. In the face of this tide of change, Microsoft and Apple are both forces from the past."[1] Ironically, this statement was issued on the same day that Microsoft infused Apple with $150 million. Nevertheless, it is important to understand the impact Java has had on the Internet and specifically with respect to next generation, client-server computing.

A 1997 research study of 279 corporations that had deployed or were planning to deploy Java-lended support to the Java story.[2] The report claimed that a major shift had taken place in the way corporations viewed the Internet, intranet, and extranet: 52 percent of the companies surveyed were already using Java applications, the balance were in the testing or planning phase. The report predicted that 92 percent of the corporations surveyed would be using Java as an enterprise-wide solution for mission-critical applications by 1999.

Mobile code technology is a critical part of any online business model. For information publishers mobile code provides ways to customize information delivery and consumer interactivity. For users, it translates into more productive use of the network. In organizations surveyed, Java is being used for serious computing applications such as information sharing, resource scheduling, and project and workgroup management.

Simultaneously, there are emerging dangers associated with the deployment of Java. These threats, while not yet materialized, could potentially threaten system integrity at least as extensively as viruses do today. Fundamental shifts in the uses of the Java programming language may weaken the overall security of Java. A new wave of more powerful Java attacks are expected to appear in coming years.

Java attacks consist of Java code which contains malicious instructions, embedded in Web pages and e-mail with HTML attachments. In the past, these Java attacks have had rather minor effects, such as freezing the browser or consuming desktop resources, and at worst required a reboot of the workstation. The current threat has escalated dramatically. New Java applications could open the computer to attacks on the hardware itself. Such attacks could affect data on the hard drive, interfere with CPU operations, or corrupt other hardware-based services.

Java Technology

Unlike other languages, the Java compiler does not translate from the program language written by programmers directly to machine code. This may be obvious in that machine code is processed, hence, machine dependent while Java is marketed as machine independent. Java code is compiled into "bytecodes" (called applets) that are interpreted by the Java run-time system on the target computer. This run-time system is called the Java Virtual Machine, or JVM, and an operating system-dependent version of this interpreter is required.

How Applets Execute Locally Without User Participation

HyperText Markup Language (HTML) pages can contain pointers or references to graphic images, tables, Java applets, and other "objects." Like the image, the applet bytecode is contained in another file on the Web server. When the Java-enabled browser encounters an applet "tag," it sends a request to the remote server to fetch the file containing the applet bytecode; the file is passed to the browser's JVM where it begins to execute. The JVM is multithreaded, which means that several applets can run simultaneously.

Browser vendors Java-enable their applications by integrating the JVM into the browser. The specification for the JVM is available from JavaSoft, the Sun Microsystems subsidiary. Vendors are free to determine the level of security in their implementations.

SCRIPTING LANGUAGES

"Scripting languages get to the point of a problem more concisely than do C++ or Java [object-oriented programming languages]. Programmers can create [some] solutions quickly and succinctly [using scripting languages]."[3] A script is a much higher language that allows the programmer or, as in most cases, a nonprogrammer to focus on the business problem and not the language. The downside is that the computer is forced to do more work during execution of the script and, consequently, system performance limitations are reached more quickly.

Scripts are best applied when applications must be set up and deployed quickly, require frequent changes, or are used to glue together existing components such as Web access to legacy systems and services. Scripts are not used for performance-intensive applications.

Scripts tend to be safer than object-oriented programming languages because most scripting languages, having recognized that programmers who understand how to allocate and use memory correctly are rare, minimize errors by automating memory management and related functions. Of course, Java is supposed to do that but we know better.

JavaScript is a light programming language created by Netscape Communications that is used to develop code that is embedded in HTML documents and executed in the browser. Text between the JavaScript tags in the HTML file is passed to the JavaScript interpreter; browsers that do not support JavaScript simply ignore the JavaScript tags and code. JavaScript does not run in the Java Virtual Machine and is, therefore, not sandboxed by the same security models developed for securing Java applets.[4]

JavaScript is used in a variety of applications. Most commonly it can be found opening windows for user input in order to verify that input parameters, such as date fields, are correct or fall within a prescribed range. Prior to the introduction of mobile code, this level of data validation of form input was performed through CGI scripts on the host Web server or on programs developed for back-office servers. JavaScript enables programs to take advantage of the local processor and computing services to perform such checks.

JavaScript also introduces security problems. Most JavaScript security violations require only minor user interaction, such as a mouse click, to activate the malicious code. By simply creating a pop-up window that asks the user to click "OK" to continue, JavaScript attack code can be executed.

Based on the risks associated with known JavaScript security violations, many have advocated turning JavaScript off.

Today, blocking JavaScript is less common. One reason is that corporate users find it necessary to run JavaScript to enable required services. Consider an application that enables browsers to be used as clients of legacy systems through custom Web pages that link to various host applications. To improve services to users the application relies on JavaScript to automate tasks such as login sequences and menu navigation. In the travel industry, several sites have emerged that deliver services only when JavaScript is enabled. There is little doubt that blocking JavaScript or other scripting languages will not be an option for long.

PLUG-IN SERVICES

Today's browser technology supports the ability to automatically download and install plug-in applications that support user interaction with multimedia data. Although independent software vendors are traditionally responsible sources of such plug-in products, it is possible for well-known plug-ins to be maliciously modified. Since the browser gives users a window to collect plug-in applications, the result is an environment in which uncontrolled software is freely distributed and used, often in contradiction with an established computer security policy.

ActiveX

An example of ActiveX is the embedding of a Microsoft Excel spreadsheet (object) into a Microsoft Word document. The object contains information that tells the document how the object should behave, what operations it can perform, how it looks, and so forth. The document is the Object Linking & Embedding (oh-lay) container and the spreadsheet is the OLE control. OLE is the interface through which they communicate.

In the Web world, a browser that supports ActiveX acts as an ActiveX container by allowing ActiveX controls to run inside of it. When you open an HTML page, the browser runs out and downloads the graphics then displays them. With an ActiveX browser, the browser can also download ActiveX objects (including viruses) and run them in the same way that Word runs the Excel spreadsheet. ActiveX is the interface through which the browser communicates with the downloaded program or control. That is, an ActiveX control is a program that implements an ActiveX interface.

ActiveX controls are native programs and have the capabilities of native programs including access to the hard disk, system memory, and other local system and network resources. They differ from Java applets in three significant ways: they are much less secure, they are not cross-platform in that they require the Windows 32-bit operating system, and they are very large. ActiveX controls were birthed from the OLE technology and OLE was never intended to be used across bandwidth-constrained networks. The OLE object or ActiveX control must contain a lot of extra information to let the container, either the Word document or Web browser, know how it works. In contrast, Java applets were designed from the start to be used across wide-area, limited-bandwidth networks.

There is nothing native to the ActiveX environment that protects the user. An ActiveX control can perform any action on the desktop, making it the perfect vehicle for the delivery of a Trojan Horse. For example, an ActiveX game could, on the side, scan your hard drive for documents and send them to an attacker's Web server using a series of encrypted HTTP commands. It is so dangerous that Wired Magazine wrote:

> Microsoft's ActiveX technology is the single greatest technological threat to the future of the World Wide Web. Microsoft's ActiveX promoters are either so blinded by their own rhetoric that they don't see the danger of this new technology, or else they are so cynical that they would destroy the very essence of the Internet rather than compromise their market dominance.[5]

BUGGY CODE

Programs, by their nature, are inherently buggy and untrustworthy. Mobile code technology enables these buggy and untrustworthy programs to move to and execute on user workstations. The Web acts to increase the mobility of code without differentiating between program quality, integrity, or reliability. Consider multimedia documents such as Web pages. Such files, regularly created and distributed by nontechnical employees, are containers for textual content, graphic images, sound files, and programs. Using available tools, it is quite simple to "drag and drop" code into documents which are subsequently placed on Web servers and made available to employees throughout the organization or individuals across the Internet. If this code is maliciously designed, poorly programmed, or improperly tested, it can cause great distress. Although the effect of running such code cannot be anticipated, its delivery and execution is the default.

In the new world of network computing, employees have more access to create and deploy serious threats with fewer skills. How can managers be sure that programs delivered over the network through interaction with remote application servers is bug-free, crash-free, virus-free code? Are we certain that the code is noninvasive? Can we guarantee the proper operation of code?

MOBILE CODE AND SECURITY

We frequently hear that the only way to ensure 100 percent security for your computer assets is to "disconnect them from the Net, turn them off, and lock them away in a safe." While worthy of an academic thesis, business realities do not afford managers such luxuries. The ability to gain control over mobile code that reaches into and executes on the workstation connected to the corporate network is a business requirement.

Security is evolutionary. Four security concepts that can be applied to mobile code today can be summarized as follows:

- Java is reasonably secure and is becoming more so all the time
- The Java language provides features that assist in the development of secure applications
- The Java Virtual Machine deploys a "sandbox" concept designed to control access to local resources and to reduce the probability of introducing programs with undesirable effects
- Security extensions, such as Java Archive (JAR) signing and Microsoft's Authenticode™, provide for encryption keys and digital certificates used by software publishers to sign code

Sun Microsystems, Java's creator, knew that it would be essential that Java provide both software developers and users a secure development and run-time environment. To a large extent, they were successful: Java has made and continues to make a significant impact on the world of computing. But is it riskless? Clearly, the answer is no. The idea that untrusted executable content in the form of data is distributed across the network and is automatically executed on a local host wherever it goes means serious security concerns.

Additional strategies, optimized for mobile code security, are required to realize the full potential of the new client-server code exchange. These are accomplished through a powerful, cooperative set of technologies. A security infrastructure optimized for the mobile code is one that provides both client and server facilities that do not exist in the Web browsing environment. For example, a signing system to address the issue of how software publishers provide downstream assurance vis-à-vis their mobile code enables an entire class of applications that are not practical on the Web today due to the untrusted nature of software.

There are basic differences between the Java and ActiveX approach to security:

1. Java provides users with a security manager. The security manager acts according to his design to enforce preprogrammed security policies. Error recovery enables high-risk functions to be stopped while allowing the code to continue running.
2. Microsoft's Authenticode is simply a technology designed to identify the publisher of the code. One of the true values of code signing is its ability to assure end users that the code has not been tampered with or altered before or during the download process.

3. When Java applets are found to create insecurities, it is usually a bug in the specification of the JVM or its implementation. Since Java applets (by language specification) are designed to be safe, an insecure applet is exploiting a previously undiscovered weakness in the security scheme Java uses.
4. ActiveX controls do not contain security bugs since ActiveX technology was not designed with security in mind. ActiveX controls have total and complete control of your system.

Let's examine the two security models in more detail.

Digital Certificates

Authenticode is Microsoft's code signing strategy in conjunction with digital certificate vendor Verisign. Signed code contains the author's digitally encrypted signature so recipients of the code can, based upon the publisher, determine whether the program is permitted to go outside the secure partition where it would normally run. Applets whose authors are trusted are granted full access to network and file resources.

From the attacker's perspective, Microsoft's Authenticode or code signing strategy is equivalent to asking mail bombers to include a return address on bombs sent through postal mail. As a recipient of a package, aware of the threat from letter bombs, am I more concerned with knowing whom a letter is from or what is inside? Clearly, given the choice, knowing what the contents are is more critical to security than knowing who sent the letter. Besides, how often do you reject packages simply because they have no return receipt? So it is with code coming from the network, regardless of whether that network is internal or external, regardless of the source, trusted or untrusted.

Even within the enterprise we are at risk. Between 60 and 80 percent of attacks, hacks, and computer crime come from within the corporation. What makes us so confident that we can trust our own software and application developers? Do applets and controls pass through a quality assurance process that instills upon us confidence that the code is free of bugs or malicious behavior?

Users are already weary of the "possible threat" warning box every time they download a non-HTML object. These warnings are simply not understood, ignored, or disabled. Given that it is straightforward to write an ActiveX control that scans the hard drive, sends all your files to a remote server, writes a virus to your boot sector, shouts obscenities at you, and formats your hard drive, it is reasonable for managers to be alarmed. It should be clear that a certificate attached to the code will not, in and of itself, keep you out of harm's way. By digitally signing the code using a stolen digital signature, or one registered under a false name, the unsuspecting accidental tourist to whom the control was pushed is lulled into a false sense of security: "It's signed; therefore it is safe." Besides, whom would you prosecute when it is found that the digital certificate owner does not exist, or lives in a country that is not concerned with computer crime, or with whom your country does not maintain criminal reciprocity?

We conclude that Authenticode, based on who and not what, does not deliver authorization and does not provide control over the execution of the signed mobile code. More important, code signing, whether applied to applets or controls, does not ensure bug-free, virus-free, noninvasive, or safe code. On the other hand, code signing does provide assurance that the code was not altered when moving from point A to point B; if it was malicious at A, it will be malicious at B.

THE JAVA SANDBOX

JavaSoft's security theory, often referred to as the "sandbox model," is based upon a protected area in the computer memory where Java applications are allowed to "play" without risking damage to the system that hosts them. This security model, built into the Java Virtual Machine or applet run-time environment, was designed to restrict or control malicious applet behavior. There are a number of documented examples that show that the model, in its current form, is susceptible to attack. For example, applets with hostile intent could access system files or extract data without the user's knowledge or interaction.

Some of the Java security we hear about is inherent in the Java language itself. For example, Java attempts to provide only one way to program a particular task. But the real security advantages can be found in the Java run-time environment. The Java run-time performs several safety checks before a downloaded applet can execute. The model is based on three components that work together like legs of a three-legged chair to create a fence around each applet. The model works as follows.[6]

- Byte code downloaded from a Web page undergoes format and static-type checking courtesy of the **byte code verifier.** The verifier is the system component that inspects untrusted, foreign, and potentially malicious code performing dataflow analysis to determine if the code adheres to the virtual machine's safety constraints. The verifier checks code for typesafety, the key security property on which Java depends.[7] Any failure of the verifier to reject code that does not conform to the Java bytecode specification is a flaw as it can result in a circumvention of typesafety and can lead to security violations.
- The **class loader** instantiates the applet and the classes referenced in namespace. It also determines when and how an applet can add classes to a running Java environment. For example, the class loader pre-

vents applets from installing code that could replace components of the Java run-time.

- When an applet executes in the Java virtual machine there may be many active class loaders or applets, each with its own namespace. If the applet attempts a dangerous method or function, the **security manager** is consulted before the method runs. It is the Security Manager that implements browser level security policies, as specified by the browser software vendor, by performing run-time checks on certain methods.

The Java security manager implemented in today's popular Web browsers provides only an initial layer of protection and is available only at the Java Virtual Machine level. The "sandbox" idea is problematic if you want to do something useful with applets. Another issue is that all applets that run on the browser get the same privileges, no matter where they come from. This doesn't make sense for real applications.

In an effort to make new applications based on Java more powerful, browser developers enabled code that arrived with a publisher signature or digital certificate to operate beyond the confines of the sandbox. Such efforts to enhance Java by getting the code "out of the sandbox" and deeper into the local system weaken the security model built into the Java run-time. Newer initiatives, including JavaSoft's Java Development Kit (JDK) 1.2, provide access beyond the sandbox based on capabilities requested by developers. For example, a developer with a need to write data to a temporary directory may announce his intention and allow the user to decide whether this request is legitimate. Problems with such initiatives are grounded by the inherent lack of confidence we have in our end users. Leaving an access or capability request decision to the user is functionally equivalent to eliminating all security controls. We cannot expect the user to answer "no" when presented with a grant request by an enticing site.

SECURITY SOLUTIONS FOR MOBILE CODE

Remember computer security 101? The most important penetrations of computer systems have not exploited bugs; rather, they used some feature that had been carefully designed into the system in a way that the designer did not anticipate. Dr. Bill Wulf, a leading security researcher from the University of Virginia, suggests that the Java sandbox model suffers from the same problems as the Maginot Line, a strong line of defense that prevented the Germans from invading France directly.[8] The Maginot Line had engendered a false sense of security in France and Wulf claims that however strong a sandbox model may be to a frontal attack, "once it is breached the battle is lost completely and irrevocably."[9] As the Germans demonstrated, the way to defeat the Java sandbox is to use an attack other than the ones anticipated. Wulf concludes that as long as a sandbox or single line of defense is the dominant model of computer security, there will be no security against a determined attacker.

Current solutions include disabling mobile code at the browser or at a gateway server. But disabling Java at the browser is like giving your teenager the car without any wheels. Distributing preconfigured Java-disabled browsers does not prevent users from downloading functionally equivalent software without such restrictions. Even blocking mobile code at the firewall does not prevent users from pulling applets on board through other protocols such as FTP or SMTP (e-mail).

The original code signing solution was binary. The code was either blocked or allowed through and granted full system access. An alternative to signing is to grant specific permissions to each Java program. For example, applet "alpha" may request and be granted permission to read from the TEMP directory and access the FTP service in order to send a specific file to a remote server. Applet "beta" may request the same access and be granted only the read operation.

This approach, called capability signing, was introduced by Sun's Java-Soft but implemented uniquely by Microsoft and Netscape. It is still not well defined nor effectively implemented by any vendor. Specifically, asking each Java application to ask for the specific privileges it needs when it starts up or during execution would require a rewriting of the Java Security Manager to examine each request and decide whether to grant or deny it based on the user's security policy.

An alternative is to consider solutions that deploy heuristics. Heuristics is a method of analyzing outcome through comparison to previously recognized patterns. Using heuristics, it is possible to inspect and profile applets and controls to determine the program's intentions. After all, we are more interested in what a program will do than who wrote it. This approach, sometimes referred to as content inspection, offers a way to add another layer of security around the sandbox.

MOBILE CODE SECURITY ARCHITECTURE OVERVIEW

There are several approaches to the design of mobile code security solutions. As with any security strategy, maximum protection and risk reduction is achieved through a layered solution approach. The philosophy is rather straightforward: use different technologies deployed at several levels in order to push the risk away from the resources you are trying to protect.

The first, and simplest, approach is a client-only solution where the security is built into the client Web browser. This approach can be classified as "internal protection" since the technology that enables mobile code to be pulled from the Web and executed automatically on the client machine is also charged with protecting the desktop. Examples of this type of solution include the security manager or sandbox built into the Java virtual machine and the identification of the code publisher as the criteria for allowing code to execute.

The second approach is also client-based, but involves installation of a security service outside the Web browser. In this solution both the Web browser and the operating system on which the browser application operates are protected. The approach at this level is analogous to creating a demilitarized zone or DMZ between the Web browser and the operating system; the mobile code is executed inside or through this DMZ. In this way, operations requested by mobile code delivered by the Web browser can be monitored, in real time, and risk level evaluated. Moreover, the user is able to set access control policy to suit his security needs. Operations that fall outside acceptable tolerance levels can be automatically rejected. There is no theoretical limit to the number of different policies that can be configured. However, like all reasonable security solutions, implementation of a DMZ requires isolation of a finite set of policies that can be clearly and rapidly understood by the desktop user.

The third approach is the next generation of the second approach. This solution still places the security service — real-time monitoring — at the desktop where applets can be watched as they execute and shut down before doing damage. But it moves policy management, logging services, and a data repository to a central location for administration, control, and enterprise-wide information sharing.

The fourth approach is server based: dedicated content inspection servers check incoming code. In this approach a gateway machine is used to intercept mobile code moving from a Web server (host) to a Web browser (client). Risk level and delivery decisions are assessed through the static evaluation of that code. The resultant applet security profile is used as a basis for policy application to control and manage which applets are allowed into the corporate network.

The fifth approach is a derivative of the third and fourth approaches. This solution combines the effectiveness of real-time monitoring (dynamic code testing) with security policy management services (static code testing) available through a gateway server. Moreover, since client traffic must pass through the gateway server, policies can be established that require clients to have the desktop mobile code security software installed and operational prior to being allowed access to a Web server or mobile code host.

The sixth approach is the identification of mobile code features and characteristics even before the code is placed and made public on a Web server. This solution requires the attachment of a nonmodifiable digital profile to the code. The profile can later be read and evaluated by downstream gateways, servers, and clients. Go and no-go decisions can be issued on the fly, with high confidence level and little or no performance overhead.

CONCLUSION

Java is an interesting programming language that has been designed to support the safe execution of applets on Web pages. But execution of remotely loaded code is a new phenomenon and "Java and ActiveX pose serious security risks" to firms that are doing little to protect themselves from malicious code.[10]

Using advanced Java programming techniques, computer security research teams have developed stronger, more damaging Java code that could be easily modified for use in a major Java attack. Applets that allow the security of the Java Virtual Machine or run-time environment to be compromised have been created to demonstrate service denial, show the ease with which passwords can be stolen and cracked, and simulate theft of corporate data. Reports of attacks resulting in stolen digital certificates have been verified — all of them able to take advantage of reduced security services available when Java runs "outside the sandbox." It is only a matter of time until more serious Java attacks are widely reported.[11] Although vendors have done a good job responding to the findings and research, it is believed that additional flaws will continue to be found. A new Java vulnerability was announced even as this chapter was being finalized.[12]

What is known is that when the theoretical possibility of threats are discussed among academicians, theory usually turns into practice as irresponsible members of the technical community try their hand at the new game. As Java moves into its new phase, threats from downloaded Web pages will continue to pose a serious threat. Given the explosive growth of the Internet, such threats could become far more dangerous than any posed by viruses.

Attacks using Java code may become more severe as incoming Java code is allowed to interact more with computer hardware. Because of the limited nature of Java attacks in the past — crashing a user's browser, playing unwanted sound files on the user's computer, and so forth — Java security has been largely dismissed as a minor issue by the technical community. Today's defenses of blocking Java and ActiveX at the firewall are analogous to holding a finger in the breach of the dam: the floodgates are opening as corporations begin to rely of services provided by mobile code. With major applications written in Java being deployed, Java security should return to the focus of Internet security practitioners.

We are entering a window of opportunity for malicious Java code writers. New, advanced Java code is now being developed in laboratories. This means that it could emerge in malicious form unexpectedly. With viruses, little if anything was done to preempt an attack and action was seldom taken until an infection was noticed. Inaction against the dangers posed by applets is not an option. Fortunately, despite their surreptitious movement onto the user desktop, there are solutions to the mobile code threat. Several computer software companies have developed Java security solutions that work to capture and eliminate bad Java applets before they can affect a computer. Expect other solutions to emerge. It is important to be on the lookout for Java security solutions as they mature and to plan to use these defensive systems as faithfully as antivirus and firewall software.

Author's Bio

Ron Moritz *is director of the Technology Office at Finjan Software where he serves as primary technology visionary. As a key member of the senior management team interfacing between sales, marketing, product management, and product development, Moritz helps establish and maintain the company's technological standards and preserve the company's leadership role as a developer of advanced Internet security solutions. He was instrumental in the organization of Finjan's Java Security Alliance and established and chairs Finjan's Technical Advisory Board. He is one of a select group of Certified Information Systems Security Professionals, and earned his M.S.E., M.B.A., and B.A. from Case Western Reserve University in Cleveland, OH.*

Moritz has served in various capacities, including president, with both the North Coast chapter of the Information Systems Security Association and the Northeast Ohio chapter of the Information Systems Audit and Control Association. He has lectured on Web security, mobile code security, computer ethics, intellectual property rights, and business continuity and resumption planning. Over the past year, his presentation on mobile code security has been well received at the European Security Forum (London), the FBI's InfraGuard Conference (Cleveland), CSI's NetSec (San Antonio), MISTI's Web-Sec Europe (London), and RSA Data Security (San Francisco).

Notes

1. George Gilder, *The Wall Street Journal*, August 8, 1997, p. A12.
2. Zona Research Industry Report, "The Java Enterprise," July, 1997.
3. "Get a Grip on Scripts," Cameron Laird and Kathryn Soraiz, *Byte*, June 1998, pp. 88-96.
4. See section titled "The Java Sandbox" for a discussion of the Java security model.
5. "Will ActiveX Threaten National Security?" Simson Garfinkel, *Wired News*, November 20, 1996, <http://www.wired.com/news/story/451.html?/news/96/47/4/top_stories4a.html>.
6. *Java Security: Hostile Applets, Holes & Antidotes*, Gary McGraw and Edward Felten, Eds., John Wiley & Sons, New York, 1996.
7. A language is type-safe if the only operations that can be performed on the data in the language are those sanctioned by the type of the data, *Java is not Type-Safe*, Vijay Saraswat, AT&T Research, 8/15/97, <http://www.research.att.com/~vj/bug.html>.
8. Germany ultimately succeeded in invading France through the back door — Belgium. For more information refer to <http://www.grolier.com/docs/wwii/wwii_4.html>.
9. JavaSoft Forum 1.1, <http://java.sun.com/forum/securityForum.html>.
10. "Securing Java and ActiveX," Ted Julian, et al., Forrester Research, Vol. 12, No. 7, June 1998, <http://www.forrester.com/cgibin/cgi.pl?displayOP&URL=/network/1998/reports/jun98nsr.htm#focus>.
11. Some analyst reports suggest that these applets will be in widespread use within 2 years.

12. Another Java security flaw was announced on July 15, 1998. The vulnerability allows a malicious applet to disable all security controls in Netscape Navigator 4.0x browser. After disabling the security controls, the applet can do whatever it likes on the victim's machine, including arbitrarily reading, modifying, or deleting files. A demonstration applet that deletes a file was developed by the Princeton University Security Internet Programming Team, <http://www.cs.princeton.edu/sip/History.html>.

GLOSSARY AND WEBSITE SECURITY LINKS

Definitions

Mobile Code — Any code that is implicitly delivered and automatically executed on a desktop host during network access. Users may not be aware of mobile code activity. Mobile code is typically driven by HTML (Web) documents. It may be delivered by various tools and protocols.

Applet — In this chapter it is used as a generic name for a mobile code unit. May refer to Java applets, ActiveX controls, JavaScript scripts, Visual-Basic scripts, plug-in modules, and so forth. Applets may also be referred to as *Downloadables* or *Executable Content.*

User — An individual browser client user. A user is typically identified by his user name, domain or group name, and the IP address of his computer.

Security Policy — The operations that are allowed to be performed on the resources of desktop computers.

"Sandbox" Policy — The default security policy that is assigned by the Java Security Manager to applets. The sandbox denies any access to the file system, allows network access only to the local host computer and to the applet's server, and allows very limited access to properties of the local host and of the local JVM.

Administrator — The person charged with defining and implementing the enterprise security policy.

Websites

Java Security at Corporations

- Applet Security Frequently Asked Questions:
  http://java.sun.com/sfaq/
- JavaSoft Security Site: http://www.javasoft.com/security
- JDK 1.1 Security Tutorial:
  http://java.sun.com/docs/books/tutorial/security1.1/index.html
- Microsoft Java Security Page: http://microsoft.com/java/security
- Finjan Java Security Resource Page:
  http://www.finjan.com/resources.cfm
- Java Security Hotlist: http://www.rstcorp.com/javasecurity/links.html

Java Security at Universities

- Java Security Frequently Asked Questions:
  http://www.cs.princeton.edu/sip/java-faq.html
- Links to Java Security Sites: http://pantheon.yale.edu/~dff/java.html
- Guidelines for Java Security:
  http://daffy.cs.yale.edu/java/java_sec/java_sec.html
- Yale Java Security Papers:
  http://pantheon.yale.edu/help/programming/jdk1.1.1/docs/api
- UC Davis Security Lab:
  http://seclab.cs.ucdavis.edu/~samorodi/java/javasec.html
- Gene Spafford: http://www.cs.purdue.edu/homes/spaf/hotlists/
  csec-body.html#java00
- UW Security Flaws in Java: http://kimera.cs.washington.edu
- UA's Research on Mobile Code: http://www.cs.arizona.edu/sumatra
- Java Applets With Safety:
  http://cs.anu.edu.au/people/Tony.Dekker/JAWS.HTML

ActiveX Security

- Java vs. ActiveX: http://www.sun.com/sunworldonline/swol-09-
  1996/swol-09-activex.html
- Deadly Controls: http://www.hotwired.com/packet/
  packet/garfinkel/96/47/index2a.html
- ActiveX Exploits:
  http://www.thur.de/home/steffen/activex/index_e.html

Mobile Code Security Solutions

- Advanced Computer Research: http://www.secure4u.com
- Digitivity: http://www.digitivity.com
- e-Safe: http://www.esafe.com
- Finjan Software: http://www.finjan.com
- Network Associates: http://www.nai.com
- Security-7: http://www.security7.com
- Trend Microsystems: http://www.antivirus.com

Chapter 18
Security Management

Dave Schneider

Now that we've mastered the art of developing and deploying Internet applications, we need to ask how can we assure that:

- The intended audience will be able to access the applications
- All others will be unable to access the applications
- The applications are safe from modification by hackers
- The applications can be safely maintained and updated

These questions bring to light a basic conflict: encouraging proper access and use of our Internet applications, while discouraging inappropriate use and modification. The aim of security management is to make safe usage and maintenance possible, but to prevent modification and improper use.

THE HACKER THREAT

In order to understand the solutions available, first we need to discuss the mechanism by which Web applications are used and maintained. Exhibit 18.1 shows the salient parts of a computer that is used to support one or more Web applications.

The computer runs an operating system; the Web server — an application — runs under that operating system. One possible configuration would be an Intel Pentium-based system running Microsoft Windows NT operating system using the Microsoft's Internet Information Server (IIS) Web server.

Web applications usually consist of two types of files:

- Data files that contain text formatted according to the HTML specification.
- Support programs — executable code components — that conform to the CGI-BIN convention. These support programs may be written in a variety of programming languages, including Perl, C++, Basic, or Java.

0-8493-9987-4/00/$0.00+$.50
© 2000 by CRC Press LLC

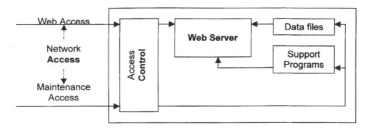

Exhibit 18.1. Components supporting a Web server.

Users access the Web applications via network connections, which go through the operating system's access control component. Similarly, company personnel who use network connections in order to update the data files and support programs go through the same operating system access control component. This component must allow a large user audience to access the Web applications, but a much restricted audience to perform application maintenance.

The root of the hacker problem is in the execution of support programs. If our application were only composed of data files that presented static information, it would not be vulnerable to hacking. The problem arises from the fact that the support programs are executable code that can, in principle, do anything to the files on the computer. The support programs can affect other running applications; and they can read, write, or transmit data from the disk.[1] Even if these programs are not intentionally malicious, they can do unintended damage.

For example, a popular attack is called *buffer overflow*: a very long string of characters is given to an application that is only expecting a short string. If the application does not check for this condition, the extra characters may be stored in memory and overwrite other data, most often resulting in the program's outright failure. However, a clever hacker may use the string as executable code! The famous *Internet worm* used this kind of attack. The code could cause unintentional data transmission or compromise the operating system's access control component, allowing the hacker to perform the same activities as legitimate maintenance personnel. The hacker could then damage, replace, or delete any of the application's data, support, or other disk files. The hacker could capture and export any data — including passwords.

Any interesting Web applications require the use of support programs. However, there is no way to absolutely guarantee that these support programs are not vulnerable to security compromise. You can take steps, however, to minimize this risk by performing these steps on a regular basis:

- Ensure that the operating system's access control component is configured to allow only the appropriate personnel to perform Web application maintenance. Do not provide more access to users than they need. For example, an application that provides users with access to their account information does not need to provide write access to the database itself — only read access.
- Review all support applications for proper operation. In particular, perform a separate review centering on security alone. Be paranoid!
- Review logs and audits. Both the operating system and the Web server keep logs of their operation. Review these logs for suspicious activity. A number of tools are available to analyze these logs, which are often voluminous. Don't be afraid to query users about any unusual accesses that the logs show.

WEB SERVERS

Web Server Placement — Use of ISPs

Now that we have paid attention to configuring, logging, and monitoring access, we should consider where within our networks we should attach the Web server computer. One answer is to make it someone else's problem! An Internet Service Provider (ISP) or other value-added network provider is willing to host your Website at their facilities and using their equipment for a nominal charge. Such providers generally have thought through the issues of security, and they have personnel available 24 hours a day, 7 days a week to deal with security issues.

The feasibility of having an ISP host your Website depends on the nature of the data that users will access by means of your Web server. If primarily users from the Internet access your Web application and the data are not dynamic, that is, it can be copied to the ISP on an occasional basis, then this type of hosting may work well. ISPs generally have much faster Internet connections than you do, making for a happier user. If, however, the data change dynamically and are located at your site, having an ISP host your Website may be inappropriate. You and your ISP should discuss such feasibility issues.

If contracting with an ISP to host your Web applications seems like the appropriate course of action to you, please don't stop reading! The remainder of this chapter acquaints you with the questions concerning the security of your Website that you need to consider regardless of whether you contract with an ISP or host your own Website.

Web Server Placement — In-House

If having an ISP host the Website is not feasible, you need to consider the location of the computer running the Web server with respect to other

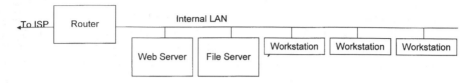

Exhibit 18.2. Simple direct LAN configuration.

computers on your LAN. One possible solution is to attach the server directly to the LAN. Exhibit 18.2 is a possible LAN configuration.

One side of the router[2] connects to your local phone company and hence to your ISP. The other side of the router is connected to your internal LAN, which connects employees' workstations, company file servers, and the Web server. This appears to provide everything needed — external and internal access to the Web server and local access to the Internet.

This is not a good configuration, however. Anyone, including users on the Internet, may try to access the internal file servers or workstations. Such access often succeeds due to a lack of knowledge or care on the part of your user community.

The most common solution to the problems exposed by this solution is the use of a *firewall*. Exhibit 18.3 shows the same configuration with the addition of a firewall.

A firewall is situated between the internal network (your LAN) and the external network (the Internet). The firewall allows network traffic to proceed only if the firewall is configured to allow it. You can configure a firewall to prohibit external users access to all internal resources except your Web server,[3] while allowing internal users to access resources on the Internet. This solves the main problem of attaching the LAN directly to the ISP: it prohibits outsiders from accessing internal resources other than those public resources managed by the Web server. However, hacking of the Web server may still open an indirect channel to other computers on your network. In addition, any internal workstation user may attempt to modify the

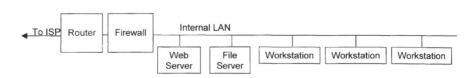

Exhibit 18.3. Firewall network placement.

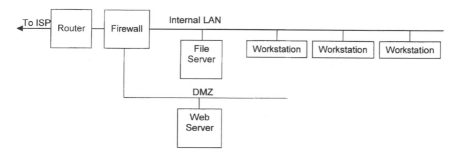

Exhibit 18.4. Use of a firewall with two internal networks.

Web application[4] where the operating system's access control component is the only line of defense.

Exhibit 18.4 shows another popular firewall configuration. This configuration features *two* internal networks.

The firewall in Exhibit 4 controls a separate LAN segment, often referred to as the *DMZ* — for demilitarized zone, to which the Web server is connected. Here you configure the firewall to control three major flows of traffic so that:

- No external traffic is allowed to reach the internal LAN
- Only external Web traffic is allowed to reach the Web server on the DMZ
- Web and maintenance[5] traffic is allowed from the LAN to the Web server on the DMZ
- No traffic is allowed from the DMZ to the LAN

If a hacker breaks into the operating system on the Web server computer, the firewall isolates the hacker from the internal LAN.

Web Server Placement — It's Not Always Simple

Things can get more complex than we've pictured here. Firewalls themselves are vulnerable. A hacker may break into the firewall's operating system and change the firewall's configuration. Doing so allows potential access to any DMZ or LAN server. Some companies employ two or more firewalls to minimize this risk. I should hasten to add that the vendors of firewall systems take this threat very seriously and provide very secure solutions, but *your* staff must install these solutions on *your* computers. Make sure to read and follow all of the vendor's instructions to ensure the safest possible installation.

In addition, the Web server often needs to access information contained in databases on other computers. You must consider these other computers with respect to normal and maintenance access as well. For these complex situations, it's best to engage a professional security consultant.

WEB APPLICATIONS DESIGNED FOR THE INTRANET/EXTRANET

The foregoing solutions work well for Web applications accessed primarily from the Internet. But what about Web applications designed to provide information to *selected* internal intranet users or to *selected* outsiders in an extranet?

Exhibits 3 and 4 show how a firewall can be used to protect Web applications that are intended to be accessed only from within the intranet, by prohibiting access from the Internet. This configuration limits the scope of such Web applications to those appropriate for access by everyone on the intranet — for example, company HR policies.

To achieve the best value out of our intranets, internal Web applications can and should provide more valuable, timely, confidential business information. To do so we must provide tools that can identify users and control their access to Web data more precisely. The most difficult problem is the identification of users who access the Web server. Web servers use either one of two techniques to identify users and control access to Web applications:

- Simple authentication. The user provides a name and password to the Web server. The Web server checks the information against a list that is maintained by your security staff. The list specifies which applications are available to which users.
- Digital certificates. In order to use this feature, each user installs a digital certificate on their own Web browser. This certificate contains the user's name and other validated information. When the user accesses the Web server, the Web server uses the information to allow access to a specific list of applications — again using information that your security staff maintains.

A number of vendors not associated with the primary Web browser and server developers — Microsoft and Netscape — offer software components for browsers and servers that augment the common identification and access controls included in the Web servers.

Alternatively, you can configure a firewall as shown in Exhibit 4 to identify intranet users and provide controlled access to Web applications. Most modern firewalls include a variety of identification techniques:

- IP address or computer name. This technique equates the user to the computer. This is not always appropriate; users may work on several different computers during the course of their normal work week. This is also a relatively insecure means of identification because users can configure their own workstation with the same IP address as another workstation.

- Authentication tokens. These handheld devices look like small calculators and uniquely identify the holder.
- Network IDs. Where LAN users log into their network, such as in Microsoft Windows NT, the firewall can identify users by their network ID.
- Digital certificates. A digital certificate is issued by a certificate authority and contains information that identifies the user. A digital certificate and a passport are analogous: they both identify you. An authority that validates those data issues both.

Using one or more of these techniques, the firewall can identify each user and control access by that user to Web applications and other network resources. Typically, firewalls can limit a user's access at a number of levels:

- To the server. The user is allowed, or denied, access to all information on the server.
- To the directory. The user is allowed access to a particular directory on the Web server and to all subdirectories.
- To the file. The user is allowed access to a particular file.

Although we've been talking about intranets, most of the identification techniques and all of the access control techniques are applicable to extranets as well.

THE PROBLEMS OF SCALE

Scaling any solution brings with it its own problem. All but the smallest organizations now have multiple locations that are connected through public or private networks. In addition, most have homeworkers or traveling employees that desire the same access to network resources as they have at the office. The growing size of an organization and the deployment of network connections can require a substantial amount of administrative effort.

If valuable information is to be shared among multiple company locations, it is essential that the locations communicate in a secure and private manner. Historically, this was accomplished with leased lines or frame relay connections. Today, in most cases, this can be accomplished by using the Internet as a communications backbone, and by using encryption to maintain privacy of the transmitted data. Such a configuration is called a *virtual private network (VPN)* because all of your LANs appear as a single network using common facilities.

Since anyone can author information for sharing on the intranet, information can originate from servers located anywhere in the VPN. Likewise, the information consumers are located throughout the VPN and include

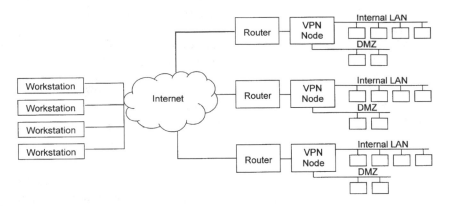

Exhibit 18.5. Virtual private network (VPN) configuration.

home and remote users. Exhibit 18.5 shows a network configuration that makes sense in this context.

In Exhibit 5, the firewall from Exhibit 4 is replaced by a more sophisticated hardware/software device — a *VPN node*, whose responsibilities includes:

- All firewall functionality.
- Encryption and authentication of communications with other VPN nodes. The encryption enforces the privacy of communications between the nodes; it is the "P" in VPN. Authentication assures that encrypted communications is indeed coming from another node in the *same* VPN.
- Encryption and authentication of communications with home and remote users. This ensures privacy for users not housed within the various sites of the VPN.
- Access control. Enforcement of rules governing *who* is allowed to access *what* information.

With these capabilities and by virtue of the placement of the VPN nodes between information sources and information consumers, you can support enterprise-wide sharing of information. Indeed, this is the very same structure that allows you to create an extranet to allow partners to access selected information resources.

When choosing such a VPN node product, be sure to consider its scalability — its ability to accommodate the growth in size and complexity of your intranet and extranet. Specifically:

- Make sure that the tools used to construct the VPN are all integrated into a central management interface. VPNs constructed out of a number of different products, each with its own administrative interface, can suffer increasing maintenance burdens and can hinder rather than facilitate expansion.

- Make sure that the product is of enterprise scope. That is, it must provide for information that originates anywhere and can be delivered to individuals anywhere — to intranet, Internet, and extranet partners.
- Make sure that the product has a way of safely distributing and delegating administrative responsibility. A product that must be administered centrally by one person will eventually limit growth. Multiple people must be able to perform administrative tasks simultaneously. Finally, it is wiser to use a system in which each administrator is delegated a specific sphere of authority rather than a system in which all administrators are allowed full and equal authority.
- Make sure that the product uses role-based user identification. Avoid products that require each and every user to be entered into a database. Doing so is an unnecessary administrative burden and can lead to security holes. Use a product that uses existing *role* information from network IDs, and plan to migrate toward the use of digital certificates in the future.

A product chosen using this set of rules will be capable of handling your current needs and future needs as well.

CONCLUSION

Let's summarize the recommendations made here:

- Carefully check all Web application support programs for accuracy and security.
- For Web applications that do not require constant access to database information, consider using an ISP to host your Website.
- For Internet access to Web applications at a single site, install a reputable firewall system and utilize a DMZ to hold your Web server.
- For small intranets and extranets, look into user authentication and access control solutions based on the Web server itself or on third-party products that you can install with Web browsers and servers alike.
- For larger intranets and extranets, or for future growth, look into enterprise-scale VPN solutions that encompass firewall, VPN, and remote access capabilities.

Author's Bio

Dave Schneider, *Chief Technology Officer of Internet Dynamics, Inc. (IDI); received MS, EE, and CS from MIT (1973). He worked in the fields of ATE (automated test equipment), compiler and operating system development, office automation, desktop publishing, and massively parallel database architectures before founding IDI. IDI develops Conclave, a highly scalable, integrated Internet security system that is de-*

signed to enable high-value intranets and extranets through the use of policy-based, high-resolution access control, encryption, and delegated administration.

Notes

1. Java programs operate in a restricted environment that makes them somewhat safer. Recently, however, bugs in Java language implementations have made them susceptible to abuse.
2. A box called a CSU/DSU often accompanies the router, but is not shown in the exhibit.
3. You can configure most routers to make these kinds of distinctions. Routers, however, lack the sophistication to operate in a strictly secure manner.
4. It has been well documented that most security break-ins are attributed to employees working from the inside. This problem should not be minimized. In Microsoft networking terms, this would be accomplished through file sharing.
5. Although this chapter has concentrated on the issues surrounding Web application development and deployment, other applications play an important part in the Internet — FTP and News to name two. The VPN node product must include provisions for handling all Internet protocols.

Chapter 19

Public Key Infrastructure: Using the Internet as a Virtual Private Network

Andrew Csinger

WHEN PEOPLE LOOK BACK ON THE BEGINNINGS OF THE INFORMATION AGE, they will remember not the networks, the affordances, the hype and gimmickry, and the technological window dressing that was all the talk of the times, but with the benefit of hindsight, they will talk about what made it possible for human activity to migrate into and then flourish in the new electronic medium.

They will remember the development that took the Internet from the realm of mere entertainment and curiosity — albeit on a mass scale — to a true virtual world. A world in which people meet people, and businesses do business. They will recall a development, now only poorly understood, quietly being evolved and enhanced in a few private labs around the world.

What is this technology? What are these developments of such import? What is the crucial development that enables people and businesses finally to project themselves out into the global network, to recognize each other there, and to engage each other in new ways as well as old?

Public Key Infrastructure (PKI) is what everyone will remember. Until you're part of the Global PKI (GPKI), you're not empowered, you're not a citizen of the global electronic community. You're not a citizen of your country unless you can prove your nationality. Likewise, you're not an

0-8493-9987-4/00/$0.00+$.50
© 2000 by CRC Press LLC

agent to be reckoned with on the Internet unless you can prove who you are on it. This is what it means to be part of the GPKI.

VIRTUAL PRIVATE NETWORKS: ELECTRONIC COMMUNITIES

The GPKI is composed of Virtual Private Networks (VPNs). VPNs are like countries, or like country clubs. You're either a member or you're not. Members of a VPN are identified by their certificates — their passports, if you like, or their membership cards. Unlike countries, VPNs know no geopolitical boundaries. In fact, VPNs know no fixed boundaries at all. VPNs, being virtual, can be erected on a whim, and can disappear just as easily. On the other hand, the virtuality of a VPN is no hindrance to its vitality; it is a first-class legal entity and, as in the "real" world, membership can have its privileges. The fluid boundaries of a VPN can adapt quickly to change, respond to threats, and take advantage of new potentials much more effectively than the fossilized geopolitical entities we are leaving behind.

Examples of VPNs are easy to find. Consider your favorite magazine. The subscribership of the publication is a VPN. When this magazine makes the leap to the Internet, as many already have, and makes its editorial material available to its membership — and only to its membership — it becomes a true VPN. A library is a kind of virtual community, defined in large measure by the common interests of the readers who frequent it. A traditional library is limited by the geographical and political landscape it occupies: people from one side of the tracks may not be allowed to borrow books from a library on the other side of the tracks. Strange, but it happens all the time. A digital repository on the Internet, on the other hand, can "lend" material to a membership defined entirely independently of these geographical inconveniences, and need take no account of ancient conventionalizations. The butterfly collectors of the world, united by their common interest, can finally find each other and find strength in each other and speak to the world with a common voice. You get the picture.

The means it uses to identify its members and, hence, the means by which it controls access to its information, determines the extent to which a VPN participates in the GPKI.

INTERACTING VPNs: THE GLOBAL PKI

It's not enough for the VPN to just offer its information to whomever finds it interesting. This was the basis for the inception of the Internet in the first place. A common misperception today is that the Internet is ill conceived because its computer protocols are insecure; although accurate in its assessment for current use, this diagnosis misses the historical mark. The Internet did not anticipate the need for security simply because it was initially designed not for global electronic commerce in the large, but for the communications purpose of a single VPN. The global, virtual community of researchers needed a vehicle to improve their communications, and a means by which to share information in a collegial forum. The Internet, far from being insecure, was a tightly controlled environment — a private network where membership was determined by a lofty technical wizardry requirement and affiliation with distinguished research and development organizations. As soon as the Internet became popularized, the issue of security arose because of the need to establish boundaries between different VPNs with different interests, divergent philosophies, and widely ranging membership criteria. In effect, the growth of the Internet was an unwelcome incursion by other VPNs into the territory of the original, founding VPN of researchers.

It's also not enough for a VPN to restrict access to its information by locking it behind what's known today as a firewall. This metaphor is the death knell of the VPN, and anathema to global communications. Blinded by their security fixation, some information systems managers have run amuck and tried to strangle their information behind monolithic, vise-grip firewalls that make it more difficult for legitimate users to get the information they need, when they need it. No one is really sure whether these exaggerated efforts actually keep out determined hackers with lots of time on their hands. The metaphor is wrong: if information is the lifeblood of the organization, it needs to flow, to circulate, to be available to the right people at the right time, conveniently, easily. Rather than locking it up behind a barrier, we need the metaphor of a door, readily opened to those with the right key, solidly closed and bolted to those without.

Other systems in use today involve issuing "users" with passwords. Besides requiring people to remember a different password for each information service they use, the worst thing about this approach is that the ad hoc, usually locally implemented access control system does not make it possible for the individual or the organization to participate in the global network as a first-class citizen or first-class entity. Passwords do not really define a true VPN.

Giving someone a password is a little like giving them the key to the executive washroom. Giving someone a public key certificate is like giving them the keys to the kingdom.

PUBLIC KEY CERTIFICATES: THE KEYS TO THE VPN

A public key certificate is a digital document signifying membership of an individual in a VPN. A PKC is created by a certification authority (CA). A CA is a service run by or on behalf of a VPN that decides who should have membership privileges in the VPN. The PKC uniquely identifies the individual as a member of a VPN. It can be used by the individual as part of a pro-

241

cess to sign digital documents in a legally binding manner, and it can be used to encrypt information to guarantee its communication only to intended parties. Most of all, a PKC gets the bearer access to the GPKI.

Of course, not all certificates are alike. Some VPNs are more important than others, in certain respects. For instance, although a certificate issued by the International Brotherhood of Butterfly Collectors is entirely meaningful to the Brothers, and may have well-understood consequences when presented as proof of membership at the IBBC's Website, it's not at all clear what value such a certificate has at the Expensive French Wine Internet Shop. Different certs for different folk? No doubt. But one side of the tracks on the Internet is just as clean and safe as the other.

Cross-Certification: PKCs from Unknown VPNs

However, life in the GPKI is not lived entirely behind VPN boundaries. One VPN can make ad hoc decisions about its relationships with other VPNs. Just like in the "real" world, where a business makes a business decision to transact with another business, a VPN can decide to honor the PKCs issued by the CA of another VPN. It can honor these other certs in any way it chooses, from complete equivalence with its own certs, to restricted, specialized access to a subset of its information space. It's entirely up to the VPN and its CA. Even if the VPN has never seen this user before, it can decide to grant access on the basis of the signature on the certificate presented by the user. The VPN is saying: "I don't know you, but I know and trust your CA. On the basis of that trust, I'm willing to trust *you* enough to give you access to this information." These CAs have agreed to *cross-certify* (Exhibit 19.1) each other's certificates. (The term is used loosely here.)

What happens when someone with a certificate from a heretofore unknown CA approaches the boundary of a VPN? The local VPN has several choices. It can simply deny access, saying, in effect: "Go away. I don't

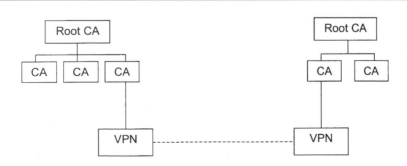

Exhibit 19.1. Cross-certification between disjoint hierarchies.

know you or the guy who signed your certificate. You're not part of the club." This is unfriendly, but makes perfect sense for some kinds of organizational VPNs.

Alternatively, the VPN's defenses can try to *authenticate* the user. Since it doesn't recognize the CA in question, it can try to find out more about the CA in order to decide whether to permit access or not. One way to do this is to search the GPKI for this CA, to see how it stands in relation to other CAs, which may be known to the VPN. If this unknown CA is subsidiary, for instance, to another CA that *is* known to the VPN, then the VPN has some basis for deciding to trust the certificate being presented. The specific means of achieving this objective are not important here. Suffice it to say that, in order to be able to search for an arbitrary signer with any reasonable chance of finding what we're looking for, there needs to be a fairly sophisticated and widespread directory service in place. Another way of addressing this issue is to have an implicit hierarchy of CAs (Exhibit 19.2), implied by the order of multiple signatures on the certificates of users. When presented at the gates of a VPN, the certificate's signatures can be checked one by one, in order, until the VPN finds a signature from a CA that it already knows.

The general goal of identifying the owner of the certificate that is presented *is* important, and is often referred to as *cross-authentication* between different domains, or realms. Note that in all cases, trust comes only *after* identification. Keeping this important detail in mind helps to avoid all kinds of confusion.

CERTIFICATE REVOCATION LISTS: THE VPN'S ELECTRONIC BLACKLIST

What happens when someone breaks a membership rule? Membership in a VPN, like in "real" organizations, is conditional and can be revoked. The CA of a VPN maintains a *Certificate Revocation List* (CRL). This is the list of revoked certificates, and is checked whenever someone tries to use

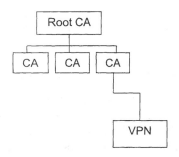

Exhibit 19.2. Hierarchy with a common root.

a certificate issued by that CA. In other words, it is not enough that some-one's certificate be signed by a CA that is recognized by a VPN; the VPN will try not only to authenticate the user on the basis of the certificate present-ed, but will also try to *validate* the user by making sure that the certificate is not on the CA's CRL. To minimize delays and bandwidth usage, cooper-ating CAs can arrange to cache local copies of each other's CRLs, or more sophisticated cross-authentication protocols can be used to validate cer-tificates on the fly.

APPLYING FOR MEMBERSHIP: THE VETTING PROCESS

How do you acquire a certificate? You apply for membership in a VPN. The people and processes at the VPN decide whether you should be in or out, and either approve or deny your request for a certificate. They put you through a *vetting* process.

CERTIFICATE POLICY STATEMENTS: THE VALUE OF MEMBERSHIP

What does the signature of a CA really mean? Good question. As we've already seen, not all certificates are alike, and there are many reasons for this. In addition to its certificate repository and its CRL, a CA should, by convention, maintain and offer for inspection to its peers a *Certification Pol-icy Statement* (CPS). This is, as implied, a statement about the certification policies of the CA. It describes the vetting process in conventionalized terms, so that other VPNs can decide whether or not to accept certificates issued by this CA.

ONE CA OR MANY? BIG BROTHER VS. LITTLE SISTER

Most of the thinking about the GPKI until today has envisioned a strict hierarchy of CAs, where the root CA is the ultimate authority, and is the uni-versally trusted third party to which all other CAs defer, and from where all trust relationships are derived. This model, on further analysis, simply does not appear realistic. Several unexamined assumptions underlie this vision of the future GPKI.

The first one is that everyone will trust, or even want to consider trust-ing, a single third party. This is fantasy. People can't agree on what to have for breakfast or on what constitutes a good book, let alone matters of trust in global hierarchies that will branch into all areas of commerce.

Second, although there may be a secure place for a Big Brother hierar-chy in credit card clearance and other impersonal one-to-many transac-tions, and though this is indeed and will continue to be Big Business for Big Brother, it completely ignores the needs of business-to-business transac-tions. This, problem is *much* more interesting, and much more difficult to solve than the first. Or rather, the problem is very different.

In the Big Brother model of GPKI, the central issue appears to be *trust*, in the sense that there is a transitive commodity that somehow issues from an anointed source — the trusted third party Root CA. Big Brother wants to act as a *trust broker*.

In the Little Sister model, trust is outside the scope of the GPKI, and it is mere *identity* which is directly encoded by the relations between peer VPNs and their CAs. Two VPNs decide to do business with each other and reflect this agreement (tacitly or otherwise) in the access control rules with which they define the boundaries of their respective VPNs.

Of course, as in most things, there is a lot of middle ground between a rigid Big Brother hierarchy and the almost anarchic Little Sister philosophy. On the original Big Brother view, *all* certificates in the GPKI would be issued by a single CA. This perspective has softened, ostensibly in recognition of growing competition for the role of central CA, and in reaction to new and very flexible PKI technology being developed by companies who want to give every network device on the Internet its own unique certificate ID.

The picture of the GPKI as a strict hierarchy emerges from the Big Brother model: the Root CA certifies certificates issued by subsidiary CAs, or certifies the subsidiary CAs themselves (or certifies their CPSs ...). If your CA isn't part of The Hierarchy, your VPN is not part of the GPKI, and you're not *in*. This is bad. Your alternative is to beg (and pay) for certification by the Root CA. Or you can start your own PKI.

I strongly suspect that there is enough motivation in the business world for many organizations to seek to become VPNs under their own authority. The resulting volume of anarchic grass-roots certification activity will seek to resolve itself via ad hoc cross-certification techniques of the sort that have already been described, leading to nonhierarchical constellations of VPNs. The topology of the GPKI doesn't *have* to be hierarchical, though it's difficult to conceive of a truly global alternative.

Big Brother can have a significant role to play, even in a democratic, distributed GPKI with lots of CAs cross-authenticating business-to-business relationships between disjoint VPNs. For instance, as part of an extended audit, Big Brother could study the practices of a VPN and certify the CPS of its CA. This way, cross-authenticating VPNs would have the word of one or more third parties as to whether or not the certificates are to be honored.

There are other intermediate positions. For instance, a large bank may wish to issue certificates for all of its employees, management, and each and every one of the banking customers of each of its many service branches. In the interests of name brand recognition, it insists that the signatures on all of the certificates be the same: that of the central office. However, even if the central office could generate the millions of signatures required, and perform the attendant logistics, it could never keep up: customers close accounts, overdraw, and die in alarming numbers. The branches themselves are in the best position to undertake the vetting processes, since they actually *know* their customers, can stare them in the face, and study their handwritten signatures. In this case, the branches can each run what is known as a *registration authority* (RA).

The function of an RA is to vet certificate requests and forward them to a CA for signing. The CA *knows* its RAs, of which there can be many, and rubber-stamps the requests with its signature, thereby generating a certificate, and returns this electronic document to the respective RA, who forwards it, in turn, to the customer, the end user of the certificate. Alternatively, the CA can send the certificate directly to the customer.

The GPKI will probably end up as a syncretic combination of a few Big Brother hierarchies and many subtly interconnected constellations of VPNs.

CERTIFICATES REVISITED

Certificates are just specially formatted electronic documents, with a specific intended interpretation (CA-*xyz* states that *Fred* is the bearer of this certificate). They are generally intended to be public documents; the security of the PKI is in no way compromised by publication of the certificate. In fact, most of the purpose of the PKI is to expedite widespread knowledge and availability of all certificates.

How does it work? The whole notion of a PKI is built from public key cryptography. A PKI is nothing more than an elaborate set of commonly accepted policies and procedures governing the application of public key cryptography. Luckily, you don't have to be a cryptographer to understand PKI. Here are the basics.

Public Key Cryptography: The Basics

Public key cryptography involves the use of two encryption keys called the *public key* and the *private key*. These keys are mathematically related in such a way that, in conjunction with certain cryptographic algorithms, a message encrypted with one key can be decrypted only with the other. Another important attribute of the keys is that it is extremely difficult, if not impossible, to determine the value of one key from the other. By convention, one of the keys (always the same one) is used to encrypt messages, and the other to decrypt.

The keys of the pair are named aptly. The public key is the encryption key. To send a message to Bob, so that only Bob can read it, I would use Bob's public key to encrypt it. Bob would use his private key to decrypt it. Were Bob to send me a reply, he would use my public key to encrypt the message, and I would use my private key to decrypt it. In this way, public key cryptography ensures the *privacy* of communications.

Senders can *sign* their messages as well. First, they create a unique fingerprint, or *digest,* of their message using a mathematical *hash function*. The result of encrypting this message digest *with their private key* is called a signature. The signature is sent along with the message. The receiver can decrypt the message and recreate the digest using the same hash function. Decrypting the signature with the sender's public key produces the original digest. If the digests match, the receiver can be certain that the message was actually sent by the signer, and is further certain that the message has not been tampered with in transit since the time it was signed. In this way, public key cryptography ensures the authenticity and the integrity of communications. Since the sender can not later deny having sent the message, nonrepudiability is also ensured.

That's all we need to know about cryptography in order to understand PKI. The remaining issues surround the mechanisms by which public keys are made public, and by which private keys remain private. This is the raison d'être of PKI. Out of so little is built so much. The entire GPKI emerges from the application of simple, well-understood, and commonly accepted policies and procedures to the key pairs of individual end users and organizations.

Joining the PKI: Getting a Certificate

To become part of a PKI, a user needs first to generate a public/private key pair (henceforth *key pair*). A VPN can perform this function on behalf of the user; for instance, a bank may create the key pair for a user, lodging the private key in a semiconductor device, perhaps a smart card, to thwart unauthorized use and increase security. The Butterfly Collector's club may let the user generate the key pair and might not care where the user stores the private component at all.

The user then needs to acquire a certificate from a VPN, as discussed. Technically, this involves sending the VPN's CA the user's public key, along with some relevant personal information, like the user's name, e-mail address, and so on. The CA vets the applicant as discussed, and then, if approved, signs the message consisting of the user's public key and associated information, producing a signed document called a certificate. The CA then publishes the certificate in its certificate repository, for all to see. How much *confidence* VPNs can place in the certificates issued by other CAs depends upon the level of *assurance* afforded by the vetting processes of these CAs.

CAs also have key pairs of their own, which they use for signing and other functions. The privacy of the CA's private key can be a serious security concern, since compromise of the CA's private key can mean compromise of all of the certificates it has signed. Serious issues lurk just beneath the surface here, and we will tread lightly indeed, so as not to disturb them in our shallow overview of the subject. Suffice it to say that considerable care and attention has gone into specification and review of CA management policy and practice, and that specialized tamperproof hardware can be deployed for secure storage of CA private keys.

Author's Bio

Andrew Csinger received his Ph.D. and M.Sc. degrees in Computer Science from the University of British Columbia and a Bachelor's degree in Electrical Engineering from McGill University. His work on artificial intelligence techniques has been published in journals and conferences around the world. Csinger was a Natural Sciences and Engineering Research Council (NSERC) Post-Doctoral Fellow and his research continues in the area of user-modeling in intelligent multimedia interfaces.

He founded Xcert Software Inc. in 1996, a technology leader in the emerging business of Public Key Infrastructure (PKI). As President of Interspect since 1992, Csinger has successfully implemented many Internet projects for medium to large corporations including the Canadian Bankers Association. He also offers 5 years experience as a software engineer, as a consultant in electromagnetic design to Fortune 500 companies, and prior experience in software sales and technology niche marketing.

Csinger is regularly invited to speak at conferences and events on technology and its effects on society and business.

Notes

"Legislating Market Winners: Digital Signature Laws and the Electronic Commerce Marketplace," by C. Bradford Biddle (http://www.acusd.edu/~biddle/LMW.htm).

Chapter 20
Putting VPNs to Work for Small Businesses and Offices

Joy Pinsky
Michael Kennedy

MODERN BUSINESS PROCESSES DEMAND TIGHT LINKS between mobile users, customers, and third parties on both a temporary basis (project-based) and permanent basis. Virtual Private Networks (VPNs) can provide significant business benefits by overcoming the barriers to achieving widely available and secure communication. VPNs provide the appearance of a single network connecting corporate offices, telecommuters, customers, and even competitors, while using separate public and private networks. A company retains control of user access and the privacy and integrity of its data even though the data travel on the public Internet. VPNs can provide as much as 60 percent cost savings over private leased lines and significantly reduce telecommuter dial-up charges.

VPNs and their many benefits, however, have traditionally been the domain of larger organizations. These huge companies enjoy access to the capital and scale necessary to build VPNs and have the technical staff to maintain them. They are able to use VPNs to enhance and sustain their competitive advantage over their smaller and less technically sophisticated competitors. In practical terms, the benefits of VPNs have been off limits to small- and medium-size businesses. And, even larger organizations have had difficulty deploying VPNs in branch offices because they are often too small to justify on-site IT staff.

The barriers to creating and maintaining a VPN include the need to construct and maintain a secure physical infrastructure and administer a wide range of data communications services. The infrastructure challenges include setting up access equipment, firewalls, servers, telecommunications services, and maintaining connections to multiple Internet Service Providers (ISPs) at hundreds or even thousands of enterprise locations. Adminis-

0-8493-9987-4/00/$0.00+$.50
© 2000 by CRC Press LLC

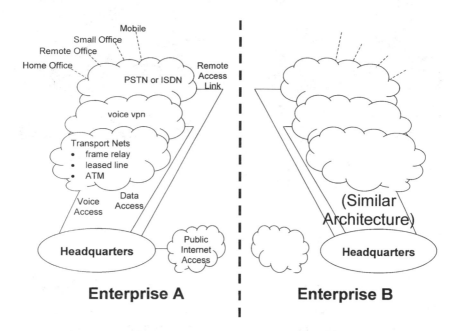

Exhibit 20.1. Today's enterprise networks.

trative challenges include maintenance of servers, synchronization of software upgrades, replication of Web servers, and sophisticated policy management spanning the whole network. Services that must be supported include e-mail, directory, internal and external Web, firewall, ftp, and access control.

Virtual Services Management (VSM) technology and secure VPN transports are making VPNs realistically deployable for smaller organizations and branch offices. VSM solves the service-related headaches of multiple points of administration required when setting up multiple sites, users, devices, and Internet Service Providers (ISPs). Through use of low-cost, easily managed, and secure VPNs, the benefits of improved business management practices can be realized by even medium and small companies.

EMERGENCE OF THE VIRTUAL PRIVATE NETWORK

Today's private networks resemble the network in Exhibit 20.1. Basic connectivity is provided to a wide variety of locations, but the overhead costs are severe. The functionality includes the following services.

Remote Access

Remote access has matured from a "nice-to-have" option to a business-critical requirement to support a mobile work force and telecommuters.

For example, utility companies are increasing the productivity of their field service workers and eliminating the cost of maintaining distribution centers by applying remote access technologies. Line crews take their vehicles home with them and receive their day's work orders through either telephone or wireless dispatching systems. This setup eliminates the time it takes to report to the service center, pick up the service vehicle, and drive to the first job site. Remote access creates a win-win-win situation for the company, worker, and customer. The utility company realizes increased worker productivity, reduced transportation costs, and reduced building and land costs. The worker eliminates commuting time and expense, while customers obtain faster, more responsive service, and lower rates.

Sales and marketing organizations are especially reliant on remote access capabilities. The use of remote access capabilities and laptop computers enables sales people to complete contracts and obtain real-time technical sales support while being face-to-face with customers — meeting customer needs and resolving buyer objections through a single sales call and resulting in more successful sales and shorter sales cycles.

Intracorporate Core Connectivity

Business process reengineering programs and application of Enterprise Resource Planning (ERP), such as SAP, succeed by eliminating barriers to communications across departmental boundaries and by replacing slow paperwork procedures with shared electronic databases. These management practices and the associated computer software require reliable, high-speed, and secure communications among all employees. The same high level of communications connectivity is required at all of the enterprise's establishments. This setup typically requires that small offices and branch offices be upgraded to the higher standards more commonplace at large headquarters locations. The payoff for successful ERP implementation is an order of magnitude reduction in cycle times, increased flexibility and responsiveness, and sharp reductions in IT overhead costs.

Closed User Groups with Partners, Customers, and Suppliers

Some of the most dramatic improvements in business processes are obtained by eliminating certain subprocesses entirely. The supply chain is one business process where big improvements are being realized. For example, Boeing suppliers are required to participate in its supply network. This enables Boeing to eliminate stores and parts costs entirely by moving those functions back into the supplier's operation. Similar successes have been achieved in sales and marketing. In another example, Saturn customers can step through the entire sales process online. Saturn reduces selling costs and provides prospective customers with full and accurate examination of options and features, independent of high-pressure sales people.

251

Saturn also offers prospective buyers direct access to engineers and product experts at its headquarters.

Highly technical sales organizations can create lock-in relationships with their customers through creation of closed user groups. For example, semiconductor manufacturers provide online engineering design tools so that circuit designers can incorporate the manufacturer's chips directly into finished designs. Closed user groups not only assure product loyalty, they also provide value to circuit designers by reducing cycle times.

Public Internet Access

Essentially all functional areas can benefit from public Internet access. Accounting organizations retrieve forms and advice from federal, state, and local revenue offices. Human resources organizations use the Monster Board for recruiting. Mechanical designers can peruse online parts catalogs and download CAD/CAM drawings directly into their blue prints. Energy marketers buy and sell natural gas through Internet-based trading systems and retrieve weather data from government and private sources. Pension fund managers follow the financial markets and retrieve stockholder information from company Web pages. IT professionals stay ahead of industry developments and product releases by studying computer and software vendors' online product literature. The business benefit of most of this activity is faster and better-informed decision making.

Internet-Based Customer Interaction

Retail sales and service companies operate on thin operating margins. Their success depends on executing transactions rapidly and at low cost while giving the customer the appearance of custom-tailored service — this is sometimes referred to as mass customization. Industries such as airlines, utilities, banks, brokerage, insurance, and mail-order retailers know that market segmentation, customer loyalty, and low transaction costs are the keys to their success (or survival). Of course, the more time customer service representatives spend with customers and the more they can learn about customers, the better the market segmentation and the customer relationship. Unfortunately, this tender loving care costs money and drives up transaction costs.

Well-designed Internet-based customer interaction systems resolve this dilemma by eliminating customer service staffing costs and simultaneously providing customers with many custom choices. Information provided by the customer during these online sessions flows directly to the enterprise's data warehouse and is used by data-mining tools to further refine the market segmentation models. Brokerage and financial services firms are especially effective at using the Internet to drive down small-lot trading fees and eliminate the cost of account representatives. For example, a trade of 100 shares that once cost several hundred dollars can be done on the Internet for $10. As another example, airlines, including United Airlines, provide Web pages where customers can shop for the best price and schedule, and book their travel over the Internet.

Web Presence

The public Internet is rapidly replacing mass media including television, radio, and print as the vehicle for certain product and institutional advertising. While practically all businesses feel compelled to have a Web page, it is essential in many industry segments. Use of Web pages is firmly entrenched in the IT industry itself, financial services, education, and government services. The key item these enterprises share in common is a need for dissemination of large quantities of time-sensitive information to millions of people.

While these enterprises gain high value from rapid and cheap dissemination of information through Internet Web pages, they also face large risks. Incorrect or false information could destroy the public trust that was built up over decades. Slow information access or unreliable access could create an image of ineptitude or unresponsiveness, damaging institutional loyalty and trust. Failure to safeguard customer data and protect privacy could, at best, destroy trust and, at worst, cause financial ruin. Thus, a Web presence can be effective in reaching the mass market, but security and reliability must be assured.

GETTING REAL BUSINESS VALUE FROM VIRTUAL PRIVATE NETWORKS

The preceding section describes six ways data communications can be used to produce business value. However, today's data communications networks are failing to deliver the value, because they are too complex and costly. VPNs provide more efficient and secure data communications at a fraction of the cost of today's network architectures. In particular, VPNs reduce the administrative effort and costs of building and operating private networks. This is particularly true as customers, suppliers, and third parties are added to the network. Exhibit 20.2 shows the emerging VPN architecture.

One difference between the VPN architecture and today's private network architecture is that the VPN architecture is seamless. Users in each enterprise, regardless of whether their location is at headquarters or on a wireless link, obtain the same access and logical view of services, despite being served by a number of ISPs and through different physical media. Another difference between the private data communications network and the VPN is that business users never see the network complexity, and network administrators are freed from complex network engineering tasks.

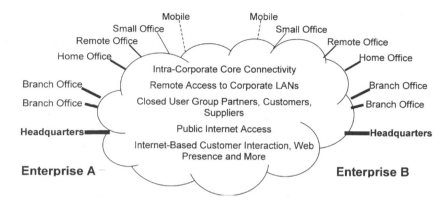

Exhibit 20.2. Emerging VPN architecture.

VIRTUAL SERVICE MANAGEMENT

Many of today's VPNs have focused only on providing a secure transport, the network "plumbing." But in practical terms, the benefits of VPN have been off limits to smaller businesses and organizations with limited IT staff and resources, because of the technical complexity of setting up and administering a VPN. Virtual Services Management (VSM) is critical to making a VPN easy to administer and manage across multiple locations and services.

The administrative challenge of creating and maintaining a VPN is formidable. A single enterprise often must accommodate headquarters, campuses, branch offices to home offices, and users who want to use a range of applications and services, and have specific accessing privileges and options. In addition, modern management practice requires many additional links to suppliers, customers, and third parties, as well as access to the public Internet with its 100 million computers.

Through a single point of administration anywhere on the network (local or remote), VSM technology simplifies the administrative burden of setting up multiple branch office e-mail, Web, firewall, and other user services; multiple domain and user names; and coordination among multiple ISPs. It also simplifies the administrative burden through automatic synchronization of software upgrades, replication of Web servers, and sophisticated policy management. VSM overcomes the barrier to private network implementation and VPN that could previously be addressed by only a handful of the largest, more technically sophisticated enterprises.

VSM can help resellers by making it easy for them to add services without raising the level of technical support they will need to provide. This can by done with service providers or as a stand-alone value-added feature. Similarly, service providers can take advantage of VSM and VPNs to provide a value-added network feature to their customers. VPN services are typically provided on a monthly fee basis and often require customers to perform the network configuration and route determination for their VPN. Where the customer is doing much of the work already, customers often acquire the lines and build a VPN network using CPE products such as an all-in-one Internet system (described below). Many enterprises are finding if they partner with their service provider to produce a VPN solution, it can be a very effective way to take development costs out of the equation.

SECURE AND RELIABLE NETWORKING TRANSPORT

To provide secure and reliable transport across the network, three main issues must be resolved:

- Overall network security
- Wide-area network tunneling
- Class of service and quality of service

Products and standards are in place to provide overall network security while emerging standards will soon resolve the other two issues.

Four functions are key to overall network security:

1. Authentication — verify the identity of the user
2. Authorization — verify which services the user is allowed to access
3. Accounting — create an audit trail of the user's network activity
4. Encryption — protect data privacy

These four functions are typically provided by access control lists in routers that restrict access to data packets and network segments in both directions. Firewalls provide more sophisticated control of incoming and outgoing packets at the network's edge. Authentication and authorization is provided by services such as PAP or CHAP and by security servers. Proxy application servers and the network operating system provide additional network security. These necessary services and products are now widely deployed in ISPs and private networks.

Wide-area network tunneling is a technique that establishes a secure network connection across the public Internet. Trade press articles sometimes equate VPNs to tunneling. Our view is that tunneling, while an essential ingredient of the VPN solution, is but one element of the VPN and that administrative and reliability issues are at least as important to successful VPN adoption. Major networking vendors have advanced proposed tunneling standards such as Point-to-Point Tunneling Protocol and L2F. Much marketplace confusion has resulted from these competing standards. Happily, it appears that a compromise approach called L2TP will resolve the differences between these competing standards and will soon emerge from the IETF standards-setting process.

IMPLEMENTING THE VPN

The key to deploying a VPN is to give the appearance of a seamless network with identical user services at all locations — headquarters, branch offices, home offices, and those of partners, suppliers, and customers. One approach to VPN implementation for small- and medium-size organizations is to deploy all-in-one Internet systems, sometimes called "Internet edge servers," at the network edge between each enterprise site and the local ISP. The all-in-one Internet system integrates Internet server, firewall, and networking functionality for organizations that want to take greater advantage of the Internet without adding a complex and costly assembly of boxes and IT staff.

VSM capabilities supported by the system can then provide single-point administration of VPN services. Exhibit 20.3 shows how the three versions of VSM technology — in-branch, remote, and extranet applications — can be used.

A multibranch VPN can be used to connect a company's remotely located, LAN-attached offices. An all-in-one Internet system will be required at each office, in this case. Class of Service policies, such as access privileges and priorities, can be applied as if the branch users were physically located at headquarters. Security can be implemented through the emerging industry-standard IP Security (IPsec) protocol, which will provide DES encryption, authentication, and key management.

A remote VPN can enable mobile workers and telecommuters to dial into a local ISP to access corporate information and service, making it appear as if they were sitting at their desks in the main office. An all-in-one Internet system will be required at headquarters and Microsoft's Point-to-Point Protocol (PPTP), available with MS Windows clients, will be required on the remote user's desktop or laptop system. A Point-to-Point Protocol server in the system can authenticate the remote user, then open an encrypted path through which traffic flows as if through the LAN.

An extranet VPN opens a corporate network selectively to suppliers, customers, strategic business partners, and users having access to a limited set of information behind the corporate firewall. An extranet VPN implementation differs from branch and remote VPN implementations in that its use is likely to involve temporary virtual networks which may be set up for specific projects and dismantled as the project's end.

It is important that all necessary service management, security, and Quality of Service functions are combined in the system so that multiple

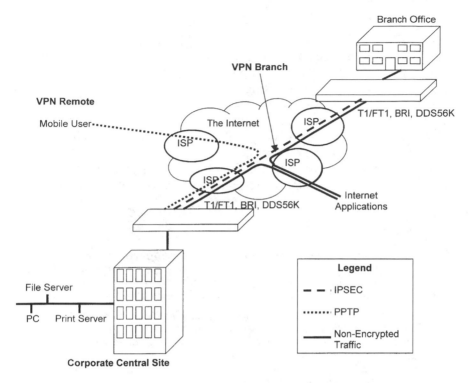

Exhibit 20.3. The three versions of VSM technology.

systems can be administered as though they are on a single local network. The supported services should include all of the administrative, security, and reliability requirements of the VPN:

- IP router
- Web server
- Firewall
- E-mail
- File transfer (FTP)
- Domain Name Service (DNS)
- Dynamic Host Configuration Protocol (DHCP)
- Remote management

Hardware costs can also be minimized because all the necessary administrative, security, and reliable transport functionalities are combined in a single unit. Administrative and operating expenses can be controlled through VSM, which permits management of all sites from a single point — minimizing the need for costly data communications experts.

CONCLUSION

The VPN supports the business needs of a company by eliminating the technical and administrative obstacles to rapid electronic information flows within a company and with partners, customers, and suppliers. The VPN delivers the same networking services to all parties, whether at large or small sites, and across multiple ISP networks. Virtual Services Management makes it economical for small- and medium-size enterprises to build VPNs and permits delivery of corporate networking services out to even the most remote corporate outpost. The VPN's low cost and uniform networking environment supports the implementation of business strategies necessary to achieving and maintaining a sustainable competitive advantage.

Authors' Bios

Joy Pinsky is vice president of marketing at FreeGate Corporation, a leading provider of all-in-one Internet solutions, combining Internet server, firewall, remote access/VPN, router, and network management functionality for smaller organizations and sites that can't afford a complex assembly of devices and huge technical staff.

Pinsky joined FreeGate from Lucent Technologies, where she was general manager for mixed media applications. At Lucent, she was responsible for creating a business, marketing, and development team for a new business focusing on merging telephone communications with IP networking. Previously, she had spent 3 years with Network Equipment Technologies, where her most recent title was director of business development. In addition to running an independent consulting practice, she has held senior marketing management positions with Wyse Technology, Sytek and Rolm, and spent 2 years as a member of Bell Laboratories' technical staff.

Pinsky holds an M.S. degree in electrical engineering and an M.B.A., both from Stanford University, and a B.S. in electrical engineering from the University of California at Davis.

Michael Kennedy, Ph.D., leads engagements for enterprise, vendor, and service provider clients. He works with end users to develop network architectures, strategies, and designs that meet corporate business goals. He has also helped utilities, aerospace companies, and others develop market entry strategies in the emerging local communications markets.

Kennedy has 30 years experience in the networking industry. He is a widely quoted authority on the dynamics of the communications industry, and has more than 100 articles, speeches, and major conference presentations to his credit. Kennedy's Telecommunications magazine column focuses on the business applications of networking technology.

Prior to joining Strategic Networks, Kennedy was a management consultant for Arthur D. Little, Inc., Cambridge, MA; led Stamford, CT-based Gartner Group's telecommunications strategy advisory service; provided equity research for Soundview Financial Corp., Stamford, CT; and held planning and engineering positions at AT&T, Bell Laboratories, and IBM. He also served as a part-time faculty member of the Graduate School of Business Administration at Fairleigh Dickinson University, Madison, NJ, where he lectured in economic statistics. Kennedy holds a Ph.D. in engineering from New York University, where he wrote a thesis on the application of statistical commu-

nication theory to telephone demand forecasting. He also holds a Master's in electrical engineering from the Massachusetts Institute of Technology, Cambridge, MA, and a Bachelor of Science in electrical engineering from the University of Akron in Ohio.

Chapter 21

Elliptic Curve Cryptography: Delivering High-Performance Security for E-Commerce and Communications

Paul Lambert

ELLIPTIC CURVE CRYPTOGRAPHY (ECC) PROVIDES THE HIGHEST STRENGTH per key bit of any known public-key security technology. The relative strength advantage of ECC means that it can offer the same level of cryptographic security as other algorithms using a much smaller key. ECC's shorter key lengths result in smaller system parameters, smaller public-key certificates and, when implemented properly, faster performance with lower power requirements and smaller hardware processors. As a result, ECC is able to meet the security and performance demands of virtually any application.

With the increased amount of sensitive information being transmitted wirelessly and over the Internet, information security has become a critical component to many applications. Cryptography in turn has become a fundamental part of the solution for secure applications and devices. Across a variety of platforms, cryptographic technology provides security to a

0-8493-9987-4/00/$0.00+$.50
© 2000 by CRC Press LLC

wide range of applications such as electronic commerce, access control, and secure wireless communications. The ongoing challenge for manufacturers, systems integrators, and service providers is to incorporate efficient, cost-effective security into the mobile, high-performance devices and applications that the market demands. While other cryptographic algorithms cannot effectively meet this challenge, ECC's strength and performance advantages make it an ideal solution to secure Internet commerce, smart card, and wireless applications, as will be demonstrated further on in this chapter.

UNDERSTANDING ECC'S STRONG, COMPACT SECURITY

All public-key cryptosystems are based on a hard one-way mathematical problem. ECC is able to deliver strong security at smaller key sizes than other public-key cryptographic systems because of the difficulty of the hard problem upon which it is based. ECC is one of three different types of cryptographic systems that are considered to provide adequate security, defined in standards, and deployed in today's applications. Rather than explaining the complete mathematical operation of each of these three systems, this chapter will serve to introduce and compare each system.

First, what is meant by a hard or difficult mathematical problem? A mathematical problem is *difficult* if the fastest known algorithm to solve the problem takes a long time relative to the input size. To analyze how long an algorithm takes, computer scientists introduced the notion of *polynomial time* algorithms and *exponential time* algorithms. Roughly speaking, a polynomial time algorithm runs quickly relative to the size of its input, and an exponential time algorithm runs slowly relative to the size of its input. Therefore, easy problems have polynomial time algorithms, and difficult problems have exponential time algorithms.

The phrase *relative to the input size* is fundamental in the definition of polynomial and exponential time algorithms. All problems are straightforward to solve if the input size is very small, but cryptographers are interested in how much harder a problem gets as the size of the input grows. Thus, when looking for a mathematical problem on which to base a public-key cryptographic system, cryptographers seek one that cannot be solved in less than exponential time because the fastest known algorithm takes exponential time. Generally, the longer it takes to compute the best algorithm for a problem, the more secure is a public-key cryptosystem based on that problem.

What follows are the three different types of cryptographic systems along with an explanation of the hard mathematical problems on which they are based.

RSA and the Integer Factorization Problem

The best-known cryptosystem based on the integer factorization problem, *RSA*, is named after its inventors, Ron Rivest, Adi Shamir, and Len Adleman. Another example is the Rabin-Williams system.

The core concept of the integer factorization problem is that an integer p (a whole number) is a *prime number* if it is divisible only by 1 and p itself. When an integer n is the product of two large primes, to determine what these two factors are we need to find the prime numbers p and q such that: $p \times q = n$. The integer factorization problem, then, is to determine the prime factors of a large number.

DSA and the Discrete Logarithm Problem

The Diffie-Hellman key agreement scheme, the grandfather of all public-key cryptography schemes, is based on the discrete log problem. Taher Elgamal first proposed the first public-key cryptographic system that included digital signatures based on this problem. Elgamal proposed two distinct systems: one for encryption and one for digital signatures. In 1991, Claus Schnorr developed a more efficient variant of Elgamal's digital signature system. The U.S. Government's Digital Signature Algorithm (DSA), the best-known of a large number of systems with security based on the discrete logarithm problem, is based on Elgamal's work.

The *discrete logarithm problem* modulo prime p is defined in terms of modular arithmetic. This problem starts with a prime number p. Then, given an integer g (between 0 and $p-1$), and a multiplicand y (the result of exponentiating g), the following relationship exists between g and y for some x: $y = g^x \pmod{p}$. The discrete logarithm problem is to determine the integer x for a given pair g and y: find x so that $g^x = y \pmod{p}$. Like the integer factorization problem, no efficient algorithm is known to solve the discrete logarithm problem.

ECC and the Elliptic Curve Discrete Logarithm Problem

The security of ECC rests on the difficulty of the elliptic curve discrete logarithm problem. As with the integer factorization problem and the discrete logarithm problem, no efficient algorithm is known to solve the elliptic curve discrete logarithm problem. In fact one of the advantages of ECC is that the elliptic curve discrete logarithm problem is believed to be more difficult than either the integer factorization problem or the generalized discrete logarithm problem. For this reason, ECC is the strongest public-key cryptographic system known today.

In 1985, mathematicians Neil Koblitz and Victor Miller independently proposed the *elliptic curve cryptosystem* (ECC), with security resting on the discrete logarithm problem *over the points on an elliptic curve.* Before explaining the hard problem, a brief introduction to elliptic curves is needed.

An *elliptic curve* defined modulo a prime p, is the set of solutions (x,y) to the equation: $y^2 = x^3 + ax + b$ (mod p) for the two numbers a and b. This means that y^2 has the remainder $x^3 + ax + b$ when divided by p. If (x,y) satisfies the above equation, then $p = (x,y)$ is a *point* on the elliptic curve.

An elliptic curve can also be defined over the finite field consisting of 2^m (even numbers) elements. This field, referred to as $F_2{}^m$, increases the efficiency of ECC operation in some environments. One can define the addition of two points on the elliptic curve. If P and Q are both points on the curve, then $P + Q$ is always another point on the curve. The elliptic curve discrete logarithm problem starts with selecting a field (a set of elements) and an elliptic curve. (Selecting an elliptic curve consists of selecting values for a and b in the equation $y^2 = x^3 + ax + b$.) Then xP represents the point P added to itself x times.

Suppose Q is a multiple of P, so that $Q = xP$ for some x. The elliptic curve discrete logarithm problem is to determine x with any given P and Q.

A COMPARISON OF CRYPTOGRAPHIC SYSTEMS

Of the three problems, the integer factorization problem and the discrete logarithm problem both can be solved by general algorithms that run in *subexponential time,* meaning that the problem is still considered hard, but not as hard as those problems that admit only fully exponential time algorithms.

On the other hand, the best general algorithm for the elliptic curve discrete logarithm problem is fully exponential time. This means that the elliptic curve discrete logarithm problem is currently considered more difficult than either the integer factorization problem or the discrete logarithm problem.

In Exhibit 21.1, the graph compares the time required to break ECC with the time required to break RSA or DSA for various key sizes using the best-known algorithm. The values are computed in *MIPS years.* A MIPS year represents the computing time of 1 year on a machine capable of performing one million instructions per second. As a benchmark, it is generally accepted that 10^{12} MIPS years represents reasonable security at this time, since this would require most of the computing power on the planet to work for a considerable amount of time.

To achieve reasonable security, RSA and DSA need to use a 1024-bit key, while a 160-bit key is sufficient for ECC. The graph in Exhibit 21.1 shows that the gap between the systems grows as the key size increases. For ex-

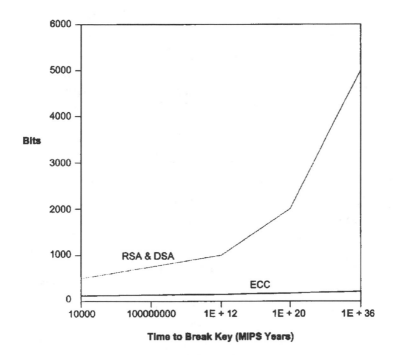

Exhibit 21.1. Comparison of security levels.

ample, note how the ratio increases with the 300-bit ECC key compared with the 2000-bit RSA and DSA keys.

With this background in ECC's high security relative to small key size, we can explore how ECC benefits today's leading-edge applications.

SECURING ELECTRONIC TRANSACTIONS ON THE INTERNET

One prominent application that requires strong security is electronic payment on the Internet. When making Internet-based credit card purchases, users want to know that their credit card information is protected, while the merchant wants assurance that the person making the purchase cannot later refute the transaction. Combined with these authentication needs, a secure electronic payment system needs to operate fast enough to handle consumers' needs conveniently. It must be capable of handling a high volume of transactions reliably and, simultaneously, be accessible from multiple locations, and be easy to use.

ECC can meet all these needs. For example, consider the role ECC plays in securing a recently launched experimental pilot for Internet commerce. The pilot is based on the Secure Electronic Transaction (SET) specification developed to address the requirements of the participants in these Internet transactions.

The SET specification is administered by an organization known as Secure Electronic Transaction LLC (SETCo) formed by Visa and MasterCard. The initial specification provided a complex security protocol using RSA for the public-key components.

Since the release of the SET 1.0 specification, implementations of the protocol have been increasing worldwide along with the growing consumer confidence in electronic commerce. Vendors and financial institutions have proposed a number of enhancements to the protocol to further its appeal.

In an ongoing effort to explore ways to improve the SET specification, an experimental pilot program was launched in July 1998 that ran until September 1998. A consortium of players joined together to implement some exciting leading-edge technologies for use with the SET protocol including ECC, chip cards, and PCI cryptographic hardware.

During the pilot, up to 200 selected participants received a smart card, which was a Zions Bank MasterCard with an embedded microprocessor, along with a SET software wallet, and a Litronic card reader. These participants shopped at the U.S. Department of Treasury's Bureau of Engraving and Printing Website and were assured that their transactions were protected.

Pilot Operation

1. Cardholder certificate request and receipt.
2. Visit Website at www.bep.treas.gov. Select goods and initiate payment.
3. Exchange certificates and digital certificates.
4. Purchase order and digital signatures sent via the Internet to the MasterCard payment gateway. Both parties are authenticated, data are decrypted and reformatted.
5. The data are sent via leased lines to Global Payment Systems in Atlanta.
6. GPS send reformed credit card information and purchase data over MasterCard's private BankNet leased line network to Zions Bank.
7. Zions debits cardholder account and issues payment to the Bureau's account via its acquiring bank, Mellon Bank.

As represented by Exhibit 21.2, upon receiving the card and reader, the cardholder applies online for a digital certificate with the ECC smart card-enabled GlobeSet Wallet through Digital Signature Trust Company (DST). DST issues certificates on behalf of Zions Bank using GlobeSet's ECC-enabled CA. The public key is securely sent to DST where a certificate is created and sent back to the cardholder via the Internet. The certificate is stored on the smart card for future use.

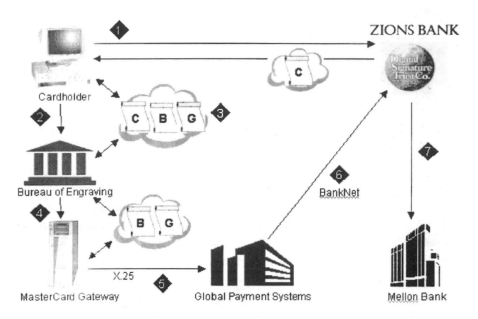

Exhibit 21.2. Experimental SET™ pilot.

Procedure. The shopper visits the Bureau's Website at www.bep.treas.gov and selects an item to purchase with his or her Zions Bank MasterCard. The ECC-enabled GlobeSet POS (point of sale) submits a SET wake-up message to the wallet and the cardholder initiates a transaction by inserting his or her card into the Litronics reader. All sensitive communication between the two parties is encrypted for privacy and the data are digitally signed for integrity and nonrepudiation according to the SET specification. The purchase order and accompanying information are sent via the Internet through the merchant to the ECC-enabled GlobeSet payment gateway at MasterCard, also employing certificates, signatures, and encryption. The gateway decrypts the data, authenticates both parties, and reformats the data. The data are sent over MasterCard's private BankNet leased-line network to receive payment authorization from Zions Bank, which debits the cardholder's MasterCard account and issues payment to the Bureau through its acquiring bank, Mellon Bank. Cardholders receive their merchandise via the U.S. Postal Service in the usual manner.

Implemented end-to-end within an algorithm coexistent system, ECC is an enabling technology adding performance and cost advantages to SET as demonstrated in this pilot.

Improving Performance. A comprehensive benchmarking process comparing the performance of ECC and RSA was completed at GlobeSet and audited by a team from SETCo. Improved performance is especially desirable for banks and vendors because cryptographic processing is frequently a bottleneck that can be cleared only with increased hardware costs. In preliminary software-only benchmark tests, ECC demonstrated a positive and significant performance advantage, with overall cryptographic processing overhead reduced by 73 percent. ECC is around 40 times faster than RSA on the payment gateway, which is the SET component most prone to bottlenecks. Signing alone is more than 100 times faster with ECC on this component.

Increasing Cardholder Security. Smart cards offer a higher level of security than software-only-based digital wallets because a user's private key and certificate can be stored on the card. As a cryptographic hardware token, smart cards provide stronger user authentication and nonrepudiation than software. Their use translates into lower risk and less fraud for banks, merchants, and consumers.

Reducing the Cost of Smart Card Deployment. Smart cards (Exhibit 21.3) are small, portable, tamper-resistant devices providing users with convenient storage and processing capability. As a result, smart cards have been proposed for use in a wide variety of applications such as electronic commerce, identification, and healthcare. For many of these proposed applications, cryptographic security is essential. This requirement is complicated by the fact that smart cards need to be inexpensive in order to be practical for widespread use. The problem is not how to implement cryptography on a smart card but how to do so efficiently and cost-effectively.

The smart card is amenable to cryptographic implementations for several reasons. The card contains many security features that enable the pro-

Exhibit 21.3. The smart card.

tection of sensitive cryptographic data, providing a secure environment for processing. The protection of the private key is critical; to provide cryptographic services, this key must never be revealed. The smart card protects the private key and many consider the smart card to be an ideal cryptographic token.

However, implementing public-key cryptography in a smart card application poses numerous challenges. Smart cards present a combination of implementation constraints that other platforms do not: constrained memory and limited computing power are two of them. The majority of the smart cards on the market today have between 128 and 1024 bytes of RAM, 1 and 16 kb of EEPROM, and 6 and 16 kb of ROM with the traditional 8-bit CPU typically clocked at a mere 3.57 MHz. Any addition to memory or processing capacity increases the cost of each card because both are extremely cost sensitive.

Smart cards are also slow transmitters, so to achieve acceptable application speeds, data elements must be small (to limit the amount of data passed between the card and the terminal). While cryptographic services that are efficient in memory usage and processing power are needed to contain costs, reductions in transmission times are also needed to enhance usability.

Use of EEC in Smart Cards

ECC is ideally suited for implementations in smart cards for a number of reasons:

Less Memory and Shorter Transmission Times. The strength (difficulty) of the ECDLP algorithm means that strong security is achievable with proportionately smaller key and certificate sizes. The smaller key size in turn means that less memory is required to store keys and certificates and that less data need to be passed between the card and the application, so that transmission times are shorter.

Scalability. As smart card applications require stronger and stronger security (with longer keys), ECC can continue to provide the security with proportionately fewer additional system resources. This means that with ECC smart cards are capable of providing higher levels of security without increasing their cost.

No Coprocessor. ECC's reduced processing times also make it ideal for the smart card platform. Other public-key systems involve so much computation that a dedicated hardware device, known as a *crypto coprocessor*, is required. The crypto coprocessors not only take up precious space on the card, they increase the cost of the chip by about 20 to 30 percent, which translates to an increase of about $3 to $5 on the cost of each card.

With ECC, the algorithm can be implemented in available ROM, so no additional hardware is required to perform strong, fast security functions.

On-Card Key Generation. As mentioned earlier, the private key in a public-key pair must be kept secret. To truly prevent a transaction from being refuted, the private key must be completely inaccessible to all parties except the entity to which it belongs. In applications using the other types of public key systems currently in use, cards are personalized (keys are loaded or injected into the cards) in a secure environment to meet this requirement. Because of the complexity of the computation required, generating keys on the card is inefficient and typically impractical.

With ECC, the time needed to generate a key pair is so short that even a device with the very limited computing power of a smart card can generate the key pair, provided a good random number generator is available. This means that the card personalization process can be streamlined for applications in which nonrepudiation is important.

EXTENDING THE DESKTOP TO WIRELESS DEVICES

Wireless consumers want access to many applications that previously have only been available from the desktop or wired world. In response to the growing demand for new wireless data services, Version 1.0 of the Wireless Application Protocol (WAP) provides secure Internet access and other advanced services to digital cellular phones and a variety of other digital wireless devices. The new specification enables manufacturers, network operators, content providers, and application developers to offer compatible products and secure services that work across different types of digital devices and networks.

Wireless devices are not unlike smart cards in that they also introduce many security implementation challenges. The devices themselves must be small enough to have the portability that users demand. More importantly, the bandwidth must be substantially reduced. The WAP Forum, the organization that developed the WAP specification, has responded to these market and technology challenges by incorporating ECC into the WAP security layer (Wireless Transport Layer Security, WTLS) specification. With ECC, the same type of sensitive Web-based electronic commerce applications (such as banking and stock trades) that are currently confined to the fixed, wired world can run securely on resource-constrained wireless devices. Strong and efficient security that requires minimal bandwidth, power consumption, and code space is uniquely achievable with ECC. ECC meets the stringent security requirements of the market by incorporating elliptic curve-based Diffie-Hellman key management and the Elliptic Curve Digital Signature Algorithm (ECDSA) into a complete public-based security system.

Exhibit 21.4. Signature Size for a 2000-Bit Message

System Type	Signature Size (bits)	Key Size (bits)
RSA	1024	1024
DSA	320	1024
ECDSA	320	160

Exhibits 21.4 and 21.5 compare the signature size and encrypted message size for each of the three cryptosystems discussed earlier. The reduced digital signature and encrypted message sizes result in huge savings of bandwidth, a critical resource in the wireless environment.

CONCLUSIONS

Three types of public-key cryptographic systems are available to developers and implementers today: integer factorization systems, discrete logarithm systems, and elliptic curve discrete logarithm systems. Each of these systems can provide confidentiality, authentication, data integrity, and nonrepudiation. Of the three public-key systems, ECC offers significant advantages that are all derived (directly or indirectly) from to its superior strength per bit. These efficiencies are especially advantageous in thin-client applications in which computational power, bandwidth, or storage space is limited.

ECC's advantages and resulting benefits to a wide range of applications are well recognized by many in the industry. ECC is being incorporated by a growing number of international standards organizations into general cryptographic standards such as IEEE and ANSI, and is being considered for integration into vertical market standards for telecommunications, electronic commerce, and the Internet.

Meanwhile, an increasing number of computing and communications manufacturers are building ECC technology into their products to secure a variety of applications for corporate enterprise, the financial community, government agencies, and end users alike. ECC technology has earned its reputation as a truly enabling technology by making many of these products and applications possible by providing viable security.

Exhibit 21.5. Size of Encrypted 100-Bit Message

System Type	Encrypted Message (bits)	Key Size (bits)
RSA	1024	1024
ElGamal	2048	1024
ECES	321	160

271

Author's Bio

Paul Lambert *is responsible for the development and implementation of Certicom's product strategy to meet and exceed current market demands, trends, and forecasts for cryptographic security technologies. He is currently a government appointee to a technical advisory committee for federal information processing and an active contributor to technical standards for such security technololgies as digital signatures and network, e-mail, and LAN security.*

Lambert was previously at Motorola, where he served as a top security architect, designing the security architecture for a family of products to protect Internet communications. Prior to Motorola, he was director of security products at Oracle, where he was responsible for the development and product management of core security technololgies for all Oracle products.

Lambert has published numerous papers on key management and communication security and is the founder and co-chair of the IP security working group in the Internet Engineering Task Force (IETF). He holds Bachelor of Science Degrees in both Electrical Engineering and Computer Science from the University of Colorado, Boulder.

Section IV
E-Commerce Management

ACCORDING TO RECENT INDUSTRY ESTIMATES, electronic commerce will be a $6 billion business by the year 2000. To put it mildly, this is one hot topic!

E-commerce is really one of those win-win concepts. Most companies are involved in sales of some nature. Whether it be consulting or widgets — we've all got something to sell. But selling has some very high costs as any marketing, public relations, or sales department staffer will attest. Even the printing of a catalog can run into the tens of thousands of dollars. And the cost of postage is ever rising. The first class stamp just rose from 32 to 33 cents. While a one penny difference might not mean much to most of us, multiply that by 10,000 or even 100,000, which is the size of a mid-sized mailing, and those pennies add up fast.

E-commerce is a vehicle made in heaven. It permits you to create an on-line catalog (saving all those thousands of dollars) and use e-mail to get to your customers (saving all those pennies). My own company could not sell the software it does without using E-commerce. It permits us to compete on an equal footing with the likes of Computer Associates.

In this section, we'll discuss the ramifications of E-commerce, including the use of XML, and the next great thing — relationship commerce.

Chapter 22
The Electronic Commerce Market Impact

Liz Sara

THE IMPACT OF THE INTERNET ON BUSINESS will be no less total than the impact of the personal computer on business, and it will happen much, much faster. Forrester Research projects that the value of business-to-business Internet commerce will grow from $8 billion to $327 billion by 2002, a 40-fold increase. As a result, every organization must now embrace a strategy for Internet-based electronic commerce or risk facing a tremendous competitive disadvantage. A huge potential exists for offering new products and services, for establishing new markets, and for redesigning business processes for improved efficiency, quality, and scope — and likely at far reduced costs compared to traditional phone and paper-based processes. Today, Internet-based buying and selling represents an opportunity for competitive advantage. It will become tomorrow's standard operating environment.

Organizations should move quickly, but thoughtfully and pragmatically, into this new domain. Despite the burgeoning interest and intense vendor activity, this is a young industry segment still making its imprint. There is a dizzying, ever-changing array of technologies, solutions, services, and approaches available that makes it quite daunting for even the most entrepreneurial business leaders to know how and where to get started.

This chapter attempts to cut through the confusion to help guide organizations to a pragmatic, successful electronic commerce (EC) Internet presence. We explore in depth two key issues:

1. The potential for EC solutions. What benefits accrue to an organization by embracing electronic commerce solutions in its business practices? Is there a business case with positive return on investment and long-term strategic benefit to justify the investment?

0-8493-9987-4/00/$0.00+$.50
© 2000 by CRC Press LLC

2. The age-old and always difficult question of whether to develop in-house or utilize third-party products and/or services.

We then conclude with some guidelines that can be useful in evaluating third-party offerings, and we include a detailed checklist of product, technology, and vendor criteria which comprise the critical success factors of an EC strategy.

A BUSINESS-TO-BUSINESS FOCUS

While commercial retail Websites get a majority of the popular media attention, business-to-business (B2B) electronic commerce dominates the discussions in corporate executive offices. IDC (International Data Corporation) projects that through 2001 at least 80 percent of Internet commerce will be business-to-business in nature. Business-to-business EC can reshape the bonds between trading partners across the supply chain, fostering long-term revenue growth and improving the quality and lowering the cost of business transactions and communications.

Just Get Started!

Every business should be earnest in pursuing Web-based buying and selling. It is clear that a growing dollar volume and proportion of business-to-business commerce transactions will be conducted electronically over the Internet. Within the next few years, the Internet will rival other channels in its top-line contribution, and will service a growing percentage of the total revenue stream, with substantial bottom-line impact.

Organizations that do not participate in this phenomenon will, at best, be missing out on opportunities for growing their business. Forrester Research[1] positions the Internet as the Fourth Channel, complementing person-to-person, written, and telephone communications for transacting business and providing customer service. In fact, it is already becoming the preferred and will emerge as the dominant channel for many classes of business transactions. Two unique characteristics of this channel will drive this:

1. Its ability to support the self-service paradigm. A gradual and ultimately substantial shift toward more "pull" and less "push" in the channel will result.
2. Its ability to support the automation of complex, inter-enterprise transactions that span the supply chain.

This shift to the self-service paradigm and the lowering of barriers to process restructuring will drive a continuous and cumulatively dramatic reshaping of business relationships as we move into the next millennium.

JUSTIFYING A B2B EC

What is the potential value of an Internet order processing and management presence? While very attractive benefits can be projected, there are also significant costs — direct dollar investments, opportunity costs, and structural and operational impact. An electronic commerce investment should be founded on a solid understanding of the potential benefits and confidence that qualitative and quantitative goals will be achieved.

Sell- and Buy-Model Solutions

More than 90 percent of Fortune 1000 sites have established an Internet presence with marketing-oriented home pages. Almost universally, organizations have a strong sense that these have provided improved industry visibility and communication, extending real value to employees, customers, suppliers, and investors.

The logical next step is to evolve the marketing site into an Internet sales and service presence. Often referred to as sell-model sites, they offer the potential for top- and bottom-line financial contribution and improved customer service and retention. Wholesalers, distributors, and manufacturers implement sell-model sites to establish an active electronic channel with their authorized community of trading partners (buyers) that lowers costs, extends market reach and enhances the buyer experience. These sites also can extend back into the supply chain, facilitating optimization over the entire product life cycle.

Another compelling but more specifically focused solution is a procurement system, implemented by large manufacturing and service firms with massive purchasing expenditures and operations. Also known as a buy-model site, a Web-based procurement capability can automate purchasing transactions, improve control over purchasing functions, and better leverage strategic supplier relationships from a single "buying" enterprise to multiple "sellers."

Most organizations start with one or the other, or possibly both in disjoint initiatives. A multiplier effect can come into play with an integrated buy-sell presence — servicing customers from the front and leveraging an automated supply chain out the back. Enterprises should look for an adaptable approach that lets it move in this direction when ready.

Benefits of an Internet-Based Sales Presence

An effective Internet commerce presence has the potential for far-reaching impact on the bottom line, customer satisfaction and revenue generation. The Aberdeen Group says the benefits are "… extraordinarily compelling." A company that implements a Web-based sales presence can expect to experience a significant reduction in order processing costs, with notable customer service enhancements and an expanded market for increased revenue.

Reduced Costs

Automation of Order Processing. Requisitions, purchase orders, invoices, and payments can be generated and processed electronically, eliminating rote manual tasks. No longer does a customer, trading partner, or inside marketing representative need to pick up the phone or send a fax to conduct business. Errors are reduced with significant time-savings — resulting in a total reduction of 75 percent or more in order processing costs.

Integration with Manufacturing, Distribution and Logistics. The electronic capture of order information based on accurate, customer-maintained records forms a solid foundation for optimization of back-end manufacturing, distribution, and logistics operations. It paves the way to implementing just-in-time or build-to-order manufacturing techniques. Internal optimization of warehousing and distribution operations is facilitated, and outsourcing these functions altogether becomes a legitimate option.

Reduced Channel Service Marketing Costs. Electronic catalogs can replace paper-bound catalogs, price lists, fliers, and all their associated distribution costs. The Web-based EC system links directly to product information in "real time" allowing the user to "see" immediately what is in stock, what isn't, and where to find companion goods.

Increased Support and Service Productivity. Up to 75 percent or more of routine customer service and support inquiries such as those relating to inventory availability of a particular product, or the status of an order previously placed, can be handled without support personnel intervention. Thus, such staff are freed up for customer relationship building and value-added services. Hewlett-Packard, for example, handles more than 80 percent of its customer support inquiries over the Web.

Reduced Returns. Electronic orders, which are created once and electronically submitted to multiple back-end systems for processing, are inherently more accurate than those manually keyed and rekeyed by central order desk staff. Fewer clerical errors mean fewer returns, and ultimately lower costs, and the ability to provide more complete and descriptive information on products reduces returns resulting from the misunderstanding of product specifications.

Enhanced Quality of Customer Experience

Nurturing and retaining good customers should be a strong driving force behind EC initiatives, for the only group harder to sell to than prospects are ex-customers. Internet commerce sites powerfully support this goal in a number of ways.

Self-Service Paradigm. Users are empowered to a much greater degree than with any other medium. We all get frustrated at having to deal with separate groups and individuals in an organization in order to buy something, to check an order status, to get a service question answered, etc. Multiple phone calls, extended waits, and the need to repeat account information all add up to a very unsatisfying experience over time. A single sales and service Web presence for obtaining company and product information, for product browsing and buying, for help desk services, for business communication, and for order tracking completely eliminates those objections. The bottom line: all relevant information required by the customer is available whenever needed — not merely when convenient to the seller.

Consistent, Quality, Multimedia Presentation. Economic realities force most organizations to use entry-level staff for rote customer interactions. Limited training and poor people skills often result in unsatisfying customer experiences. Shifting these interactions to a well-designed, expressive Web-based system will ensure quality communications to customers and prospects alike. Furthermore, as bandwidth increases and the deployment of multimedia add-ons becomes ever more prevalent, future options will increase geometrically — allowing for the most savvy Web-based presentation available.

Accurate, Up-to-Date Product and Price Information. Problems stemming from outdated, paper-bound product descriptions, prices, and marketing materials are dramatically eliminated as electronic updates instantly replace outdated information and become the documents of record.

Faster Delivery of Products and Services. Speed of order fulfillment is an increasingly important consideration in vendor selection in this age of a "just-in-time" mentality. With real-time inventory searches and order allocation, an Internet-based order capture and purchase order can knock days or weeks off product delivery cycles.

Customized Support for Buyer Communities. Each customer has individual needs including varying buying habits, shipping preferences, credit terms, etc. Advanced solutions can support specific business relationships so that a customer's Web experience accurately and transparently reflects the negotiated pricing and business terms that apply to them, while intuitively providing information that particularly interests that client.

Improved Market Intelligence. A wealth of data can be generated every time a user accesses the E-commerce solution. Powerful tools are available for collecting and analyzing this "data exhaust" to better understand customer buying and site usage patterns and preferences. For example, ABC Company may only have purchased printers and ink cartridges in the past, but suddenly, very recently, has begun buying photocopiers and toners. This new information can be used to help reshape and redefine a corporation's market and customer knowledge base and uncover new opportunities in the process.

Expanded Market Coverage for Increased Revenue

Provide Global, 24×7 Customer Access. An EC Website eliminates geographic and temporal barriers to products and services. Internet access is already available at the desktop of most corporate decision makers and buyers, and it soon will be virtually universal. Business professionals are rapidly becoming more and more facile with Internet usage and are proactively adapting their work habits to utilize the Web more actively. With a 24×7, "real-time" user interface, the market is significantly expanded.

Lift Revenue. Revenues are increased by automated, context-sensitive upgrades and add-on promotions as buyers make electronic catalog product selections. An electronic storefront can track and correlate product selections and offer alternatives and options specific to the buyer's immediate needs. For example, XYZ Company may be purchasing several monitors. A sophisticated Web-based buying and selling site can "suggest" companion products including everything from multimedia speakers to desktop printers, ultimately leading to a larger volume of ordering.

Shift Revenue. Buyers naturally will migrate to Internet buying when it's faster, easier, and less expensive, and to encourage online migration companies may offer special introductory incentives. One large computer distributor, for example, offered free freight on Web-based orders to encourage customers to utilize its new Internet channel. Changing customer buying habits from phone- and paper-based ordering to online purchasing increases seller margins by transferring revenues to a lower-cost, highly automated channel.

Service Marginal Market Segments. New, previously uneconomical market segments easily are made ripe for harvesting. Once an EC Website has been designed to encourage existing customers to shift certain buying to the Web, it is easily extended to offer additional products and services that were not viable before. It also can support walk-up buying needs of new customers.

Maintain and Improve Market Access and Share. A quality Web presence creates market pull. There is an increasing trend for professional buyers to use the Web for sourcing — to find and qualify potential suppliers — and many other aspects of their jobs, including the direct purchase of goods.

The results of a recent *Purchasing Online* magazine survey indicate a strong shift toward Web-based procurement. Organizations without a strong Web presence cannot help but lose market share.

Benefits of Internet-Based Procurement. Procurement EC systems focus on improving the overall effectiveness of purchasing goods and services through cost reduction, optimization of the value of strategic supplier relationships, and process improvement. MRO (maintenance, repair, and operations) spending in the U.S. is estimated at between $250 billion and $400 billion and up to 60 percent of a company's expenditures. It also is a notoriously paperbound activity with typically dozens of interface points between manual and computerized accounting, order processing, invoicing, etc. subsystems of participating trading partners. Medium to large organizations can benefit greatly from Internet-based procurement.

Lower Transaction Costs. Typical MRO purchasing transaction costs are often estimated at $100 or more, and often exceed the actual cost of goods on a purchase order. Organizations with large purchase transaction volumes of off-the-shelf goods that can be offered through an electronic catalog, requisitioned, ordered, and even paid for electronically can incur substantial savings. RDQs, POs, change orders, bills of lading, shipping/receiving instructions, invoices, and functional acknowledgments constitute 80 to 90 percent of all formal communications associated with commercial transactions — all candidates for eradication with an integrated procurement system.

Reduced Number of Suppliers and Strengthened Supplier Relationships. Providing broad access to supplier products through an electronic catalog redirects buying to preferred vendors. Increased volume provides the leverage to negotiate better prices and other terms and conditions. The increased importance and dependency of the relationship fosters improved communication and focus on new value-added business practices that benefit buyer and seller alike.

Self-Service Procurement. The ability to decentralize the front-end aspects of goods purchasing — product selection, requisitioning, and even order placement — to authorized end users has real value. With paper-based systems, decentralization is a recipe for disaster. An Internet procurement system can safely distribute responsibility while maintaining central control over who can purchase what, from whom, to what dollar limit, etc. Users have the satisfaction of being able to initiate orders and track their status. An organization's professional buyers can focus on vendor relationships and other strategic purchasing functions.

Reduction of Rogue Buying. Even in organizations with highly centralized purchasing functions, rogue buying (purchases of unauthorized goods and use of unauthorized suppliers) is a chronic problem: 30 percent or more of most companies' spending is rogue. A quality electronic buying experience can help reshape corporate culture and minimize this problem.

Process Reengineering. In its research, the Aberdeen Group sees the ultimate benefit of electronic commerce as its ability to force organizations to think "out of the box" and drive toward a state of Infinite Resource Planning (IRP), a term that Aberdeen has coined. IRP should be viewed as a broad, multidimensional extension of ERP. It extends ERP to span the entire supply chain — raw materials suppliers, component manufactures, integrators, distribution, and fulfillment. It also extends it with new business models, new roles in the supply chain, and new economics of doing business. All of this will result from the unique new characteristics of the Internet and the network computing model, where the hard-to-breach walls between enterprise information systems are rapidly being torn down.

Today it is already possible to achieve many of these benefits. Advanced procurement Websites leverage the integration of buyer, seller, distributor, and financial service provider systems to strip costs and dead time out of complex, cross-enterprise business processes.

An Analysis of Paybacks

Before-the-fact return on investment (ROI) analyses of planned EC initiatives are difficult. Gartner Group, in January 1998 research,[2] cites the rapid evolution of Internet technologies, the limited role models upon which to base comparisons, and difficulties in costing complex business processes, among others, as inhibitors to quantitative comparisons of extranet applications. A Gartner survey indicates that, of organizations embarking on their first EC initiative, less than 50 percent expect a positive ROI or have any idea whatsoever of when to expect a return.

Gartner Group's conclusion, however, is not to avoid these investments, even though returns can only poorly be quantified. In fact the overall tenor speaks clearly to the point that an aggressive EC strategy is an imperative for most organizations. This parallels the conclusions of almost every other authoritative analysis of the business impact of the Internet. The question is "how," not "if" or "when."

Fortunately, empirical evidence supports this "damn-the-torpedoes" mentality of establishing an Internet EC presence. Well-fashioned, well-executed strategic electronic commerce initiatives can pay for themselves quickly, often in 6 months. The hands-on experience gained also accelerates the enterprise's achievement of greater strategic long-term returns.

Gartner Group published the following analysis of Website development and operational costs (Exhibit 22.1), including payback period estimates based on independent analysis and customer interviews. What is interest-

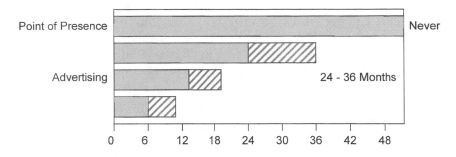

Exhibit 22.1. Range of payback periods by site objective.

ing is the inverse relation between scope and payback. The more strategic the initiative, the shorter the payback. This points to the worth of a complete solution, one that provides comprehensive value-add to all users — internal, supplier, and customer. A true multiplier effect comes into play.

Emphasize Risk/Reward Assessment

Gartner implies, however, that these estimates are pretty subjective. Proven analytical techniques won't be established for a number of years. In the near term, they recommend what is called an "ROI risk assessment" approach. This involves identifying and documenting on the one hand the benefits of an EC initiative, and on the other the costs and risks. All substantive tangible (measurable) and intangible examples of each should be tallied and used to hone the goals for the initiative, bound its scope for periodic assessment of successes and failures, and to refine the strategy over time.

Build or Buy?

Many factors need to be considered when an organization embarks on its EC implementation strategy. One of the biggest dilemmas a company faces is the decision of whether to build or buy. Of obvious concern are the direct costs, including hardware and software and initial development and ongoing operational and maintenance costs. The availability of internal resources and how well their current skills map to very different technology and business frontiers also is key.

Time to market also is a critical consideration in a fast-moving environment where delays translate directly to lost opportunities and competitive disadvantage. And the pace of change will only accelerate, requiring a constant reinvention of an enterprise's EC presence. Every organization will be hard-pressed to keep up.

All these factors point strongly to acquiring one or more proven, adaptable solutions from established products and service providers as an implementation strategy cornerstone. Building an application from the ground up is, in most cases, undesirable — leading to serious implementation delays which in turn result in a deterioration of a company's competitive advantage. It is estimated that an in-house build can take as long as 1 year; packaged applications can be implemented in as little as 2 months.

In addition, the cost of building a solution can be astronomical — with figures approaching $1 million or more. Buying saves a company, on average, 75 percent. In the end, an EC packaged solution reduces costs, helps a company establish a Web-based buying and selling presence much more quickly, and complements internal resources with technology and business experts committed to the market over the long term.

The Costs of Implementing Web-Based EC

Establishing a quality Internet-based buying and selling site requires substantial financial and executive commitment. The costs are highly dependent on the goals and expectations for the site but, as was discussed earlier, so are the returns. Costs are also a function of specific individual implementation strategies, which can vary dramatically.

A Gartner Group Research Note breaks down a site's implementation costs into five broad categories: Hardware, Software, Content, Soft Costs, and Maintenance. These costs must be evaluated individually and collectively for each of the alternative implementation strategies under consideration. And, there is substantial interplay between the cost components. For example, the purchase of a packaged solution can substantially drive down initial development and future maintenance costs.

The Gartner Group identifies four broad objectives for marketing and commerce on the Web — point of presence, advertising, sales/marketing, and distribution. The sales/marketing and distribution "objectives" are representative of medium to high-end business-to-business EC configurations. Gartner Group estimates that the total costs of developing and operating these sites can range from $400,000 to more than $3,000,000. The incremental cost of adding EC capabilities to an existing site can be substantially less. In any case, these figures include a very high component of difficult-to-manage Soft Costs (typically more than 50 percent), and organizations must minimize their exposure to cost overruns. Gartner Group cites one example of an enterprise that incurred an overrun of $400,000 on a budgeted expenditure of $150,000.

Packaged EC applications can significantly lower these costs and bound them — to minimize the risk of cost escalation while maintaining assurance that the expectations of customers and suppliers are met.

The Advantages of Buying

There are many proven benefits to buying commercial software solutions — benefits that have been achieved by thousands of organizations worldwide since the birth of the software industry in the late 1960s. A thriving software market has serviced the full gamut of solution requirements — enterprise to personal desktop and systems software to applications. The most important advantages of packaged solutions include:

Reduced, More-Controllable Costs. The cost of packaged solutions is amortized over the many organizations that purchase it, reducing the net cost to each individual user. The cost of packaged solutions can be as low as 10 percent of the cost of in-house-developed solutions of comparable functionality.

Faster Time-to-Market. By definition, packaged solutions provide built-in functions specific to the problem domain. The completeness of the solutions will vary depending on the type and sophistication of the package, but in any case substantial development work is eliminated, shortening delivery cycles accordingly.

Proven Solution. Market-accepted packaged solutions enjoy the exposure of use in a number of installations, often with highly varying computing environments and usage demands. This results in improved quality and lower risk of failure.

Value of Partnership. Acquiring a packaged solution should mean much more than just licensing a piece of software. There is the opportunity for developing a strategic partnering relationship with the vendor. Vendors have the opportunity to cross-pollinate in their many customer experiences. A quality vendor will reflect this in its products and in the consulting and support services provided.

Insurance Against Change. The pace of change driving all aspects of Internet technologies and markets, and the change it's effecting on business processes, customer, and supplier relationships and almost every facet of a business is mind numbing. Few organizations have either the capacity or skills necessary for developing and maintaining complete home-built solutions that can adapt rapidly and cost-effectively to stay apace.

Focus on Core Competencies. Whatever the approach, the design, development, deployment, operation, and maintenance of a full-function electronic commerce Website is demanding and stretches the capabilities of any organization. Use of a packaged solution lets the enterprise focus on the business models, marketing, and packaging issues that truly differentiate it in the market.

Afterthoughts on Build Vs. Buy

Utilizing a third-party packaged solution does not guarantee success. The quality, focus, and strength of the solution must be assured through a thorough due-diligence process. Each enterprise also must ensure that it acquires a class of solutions that most effectively complement its in-house capabilities. However, there are many qualified options from which to pick and choose to ensure a good fit.

"Differentiation" is often championed as the driver behind the ground-up "build" of a strategic business system like an EC Web presence. Companies find themselves asking, "How can one create a truly personalized presence that provides unique benefits to the enterprise with a packaged solution?"

Many of today's solutions totally neutralize this objection. Today's packages provide complete out-of-the-box experiences and the ability to customize the UI, extend and adapt the application functionality, and integrate it with legacy environments, rapidly and at low cost. The more strategic a Web presence, the more important are these characteristics.

In addition, putting off an EC Web strategy can be detrimental to a company's competitive stance. The products are available today to get the job done right. They provide the necessary flexibility to grow and change with a company, crossing all business boundaries — and inherently shorter product payback periods.

A Role for Service Providers?

In addition to packaged solutions, some enterprises also should consider third-party service providers to operate certain aspects or their entire EC Website. The arguments that justify packaged solutions can, taken to the next level, also justify a hosting or commerce service provider partner. Special skills, e.g., catalog content management, and substantial capital investments are required, and hosting services that amortize these costs across many subscribers may be able to provide higher-quality service at lower cost.

Also, in high-end solutions that support the automated processing of purchasing transactions across the supply chain, logical business transactions are multi-enterprise in scope. This presents real challenges in managing issues like transaction ownership, service levels, recovery-restart, etc. Similar issues existed in the batch EDI world, and value-added networks (VANs) were born. The role of intermediary commerce server providers and electronic marketplace operators can be just as important.

PICKING AN EC APPLICATION

Having made what we think is the pretty clear-cut argument for using packaged solutions, there is still more work to do. The range of choices is broad, deep, and the differentiators not nearly as clear-cut. As pointed out earlier, the EC software products market is still relatively nascent. While there have been products in this space for a number of years, the rapid evolution underlying Internet technologies, user requirements, and expectations, and the products themselves, present us with a large number of overlapping, sometimes conflicting solutions that continue to evolve at a rapid pace. It is highly likely that this will persist for years to come.

Some Views of the Market

Life would be far simpler for everyone if electronic commerce solution choices could be neatly classified. Vendors would have an easier time describing their offerings and targeting their marketing efforts. Buyers could more rapidly short-list products and make their purchases more quickly and with more confidence. But no clear taxonomy exists. All major IT analyst firms with EC practices have published research describing how they group products and, in some cases, services. While each individually has value, the conflicting views can be confusing. Here are a few examples.

Gartner Group[3] identifies five groups of EC applications: EC frameworks, financial transaction management, requisition/procurement, catalogs and shopping, and general-purpose EC systems. Aside from the vast differences in the constitution of the groups, huge price ranges in each category (e.g., catalogs and shopping price points range from $1500 to $600,000) clump totally different classes of products together.

The GIGA Information Group[4] takes a different tack, identifying three incremental strata of solutions with the implication that a total solution will include components from each of the layers. The layers are infrastructure, middle-tier services, and front-end tools and applications.

Finally, the Aberdeen Group[5] identifies seven classifications with an emphasis on the ultimate class of solution (e.g., distribution & logistics), and one broad class for middleware and development tools.

The wide variety of views is not a reflection on the quality of the research, but rather the hectic pace of change and constant restructuring of the market. However, the market research does help identify available products and services and their general characteristics, which establishes a good starting point. But then there is no easy formula to apply. Every enterprise will have to carefully match its EC requirements against the specific features and overall strength of widely divergent products.

Guidelines for Evaluating Solutions

We have had the opportunity to work with a number of prospects and customers as they grapple with the muddle in the market. Our experience lets us offer the following guidelines to assist in evaluating the suitability of specific products for an electronic commerce initiative.

The solution and supporting services should mesh well with and complement in-house skills and the resource portfolio. Large, well-funded IT organizations that have already invested substantially in developing Internet capabilities have a broader range of choices than those that are more resource-constrained. In any case, most organizations should opt for a more complete solution and services offerings. High-quality, commercially viable packaged solutions will have a breadth and depth of functionality that would be difficult if not impossible for any IT organization, however capable, to match.

The solution should support "out of the box" as many near-term Internet commerce system requirements as possible. Extensive, low-level customization and development dramatically extends time to market.

The solution must be able to integrate easily with the back-end legacy or modern ERP operational systems that are part of the EC offering. It should provide value-add functionality, extending operational systems into the electronic commerce domain. Replacing or replicating functions in legacy systems should be avoided whenever possible.

Ensure that the solution can adapt to future anticipated and unanticipated requirements. Inspect the architecture, kick the tires, and talk to the developers. Does the architecture scale and is it easily adaptable to future standards that will facilitate migration to integrated supply chain process automation? The developers should have a strong vision, based on an educated sense of what the next few years will bring.

Most importantly, assess the vendor's capabilities, commitment, and focus.

A Checklist of Criteria

Below we provide a checklist of specific items that organizations evaluating packaged solutions should consider. The are arranged in three groups — EC Application Functionality, Technical Foundation of the solution, and Vendor Strengths. This checklist isn't exhaustive; the range of requirements is very broad. But it does include the most important features and attributes that should be at the top of everyone's list.

EC Application Functionality. First ensure that the solution can meet functional requirements. For most organizations, time to market is a key consideration. Select an application that is a complete solution (as shown in Exhibit 22.2), not one that provides only basic tools with which developers must handcraft solutions. Business-to-business EC sites have a minimum baseline of important features that must be there to meet user expectations and provide the anticipated return on investment.

Technical Foundation. The requirements placed on a successful EC Website will not be static. Plan on success. Assume growth in users, user com-

Exhibit 22.2. E-Commerce Solutions

Comprehensive electronic catalog	• Powerful multiparametric and free-text search engines • Multimedia product data management and presentation • Compare competing products • Data-driven sell-up and add-on promotion support • Ability to support normalized, multivendor catalog data • Two-tier capable for optimizing performance and access to real-time stock levels, etc. • Partner-specific pricing • Price and terms negotiation • Simplified content management
Life cycle order management	• Comprehensive support for requisitioning, purchase order generation, and order submission. • Ability to save and retrieve orders for amendment and deferred submission • Workflow engine for single and multitier approval routing • Support for popular payment and fulfillment systems • Order acknowledgment, confirmation, and tracking • Flexible integration with internal, supplier, and customer back-end systems for invoicing, inventory control
Creation and administration of user communities	• Support of multiple customer and supplier organizations in a single implementation with personalized pricing, approval, and payments algorithms • Creation and management of user profiles • User validation and authorizations
Configuration, management and security	• Fully customizable GUI • Definition and maintenance of channel partner security groups • Customized reporting covering all aspects of system usage • Performance monitoring and troubleshooting tools • User authentication and access control • Data encryption and integrity validation • Security groups for controlled access rights and privileges

munities, trading partners, transaction volumes, and functional scope. Assume that new technology standards and third-party service offerings for processing payments, automating fulfillment, and enhanced security will emerge that require support. Evaluate candidates that pass through the functionality filter according to their ability to accommodate change and support growth. The quality of the underlying technology is key. Look for a solution that was developed from the ground up as an Internet solution, as shown in Exhibit 22.3.

Exhibit 22.3. Solutions Developed from the Ground Up

Scalable, robust architecture	• Linear scalable design • Heterogeneous UNIX and Windows NT server support • Efficient process sharing, state management, and session caching • Automated load balancing and fail-over support • RDBMS foundation • 24×7 Online availability
Systems integration	• Open, adaptable object architecture that isolates EC application functions from back-end interfaces • Common interfaces for internal, supplier, and customer transactional and ERP systems • Component model, messaging, and ERP API support • EDI support
Extensible application framework	• Ability to modify and extend built-in application objects • Ability to add custom application objects • Multiple language support • Isolation of business rules and presentation • On-the-fly application and system component updates
Open standards support	• Internet-based • Industry-standard browser clients • Interfaces to popular payments and fulfillment service providers
Integrated, multilevel security	• User authentication • Server certification, data integrity, and message encryption • Digital certificate support

Vendor Strengths. Last but not least, look carefully at the supplier — at their focus and commitment to their clients' success (Exhibit 22.4). Many vendors have backed into the EC market as a spin-off from a previous generation of products or services. Their loyalties are divided and electronic commerce is not their bread and butter.

The dynamics of the Internet and Internet-based electronic commerce require 100 percent of a vendor's attention. No less will do if clients are to receive the service and support required for a lasting, mutually profitable relationship.

CONCLUSIONS

"Suppliers that successfully integrate supply-chain and customer-facing systems ... will better understand the value chain for their market. These electronic links will allow companies to build to order, focusing on their core competencies while cooperating with channel partners to meet the rest of the customer's needs."

The Internet represents an exciting new Fourth Channel for conducting business. Established companies that transition quickly and well will gain

Exhibit 22.4. Qualities of an E-Commerce Supplier

Comprehensive services	• Pre-installation capabilities assessment and plans review
	• Installation support and service
	• Product training
	• EC application design and implementation
	• User training
	• Help desk, product and operational support
	• Back-end systems integration
	• Fast-track programs
	• Incubator services
Demonstrated track record	• Proven staying power
	• Guaranteed results
	• Successful referenceable clients
	• Market visibility and coverage
Commitment	• To customer success
	• To adapting to future customer needs
	• To market leadership
	• To supporting widely accepted EC standards
Knowledge and experience	• Electronic commerce and its business models
	• Internet technologies and standards
	• Legacy systems
	• ERP and supply change management systems
	• Integration technologies and techniques
	• Business process reengineering

market share, grow revenues, lower costs, and solidify their market grip. At the same time, the Internet is reshaping markets and creating new ones. This opens almost unlimited opportunity for small, entrepreneurial enterprises with vision and focus.

Interesting research from Northeast Consulting[6] uses a Future Mapping® technique to evaluate the likelihood and desirability of Endstate scenarios brought about by the Internet in the year 2000. Two rose to the top. First, the role of supply change intermediaries will change, if not invert. Buyers will "pull" products from the market rather than accept what suppliers push on them. The second is a concept embodied by the term "smart products." It predicts an extension of the integrated supply chain right down to chips embedded in products in the home, car, or office. On-board detection of a low-toner condition on a laser printer initiates shipping of a new cartridge. A failing tube in a consumer's TV prompts a call from the manufacturer to schedule a service.

These are just two utterly believable, but still somewhat futuristic, examples of things to come. These specific scenarios may not play out exactly; there will likely be some twists and turns. What is clear is that whatever changes are coming will be dramatic, and every enterprise must be prepared. Gaining hands-on experience in today's electronic commerce environment is the critical first step.

Establish a Sound Foundation with the Right Electronic Commerce Product

A high-quality packaged solution can help do that fast and profitably, and can turn a corporation's order processing, management, and fulfillment operations into an electronic ordering channel — one that directly links internal and external selling organizations' supply chain partners and purchasing managers to information in back-end systems over the Internet. And, it positions the enterprise for the unlimited opportunities that the next century will bring.

Author's Bio

Liz Sara has over 15 years of marketing experience, most of which has involved companies in the business-to-business market sector. Specifically, her career has focused on managing the marketing operations for companies in the electronic information industries. Sara joined SpaceWorks as a co-founder at its inception in January 1993. She developed the company's marketing strategy and manages the corporate marketing, sales, and public relations group.

Prior to joining SpaceWorks, Sara held executive positions at America Online, United Press International, and LEXIS/NEXIS, to name a few. She is a frequent speaker at industry conferences geared to electronic commerce issues and holds an M.A. in Journalism.

Notes

1. Technology Management Forum, December 1996. Presentation by Bill Bluestein.
2 "ROI in the Internet World," Research Note January 6, 1998, ECEA Service.
3. "EC Applications: Defining the Marketplace," Electronic Commerce & Extranet Applications Service, October 9, 1997.
4. "Taxonomy of Internet Commerce Functions," *Planning Assumption,* June 1997.
5. "The Dollars and Sense of the New Electronic Commerce," July, 1997.
6. Mapping the Future of eBusiness Strategy, Northeast Consulting Resources, Inc., April, 1998.

Chapter 23

Relationship Commerce: Beyond Online Transactions

Jeet Singh

THE RAPID GROWTH OF THE INTERNET AND CHANGING CUSTOMER LIFE-STYLES have accelerated the emergence of online commerce. Today's consumers have less free time to visit stores and shop because of family responsibilities or longer working hours. As a result, more consumers are going online because they want a shopping experience that is faster, more convenient, and provides them with individualized service and information. Online retailers that can satisfy these needs can excel at electronic commerce by establishing preemptive online customer relationships. These companies have the opportunity to provide a premium service to their existing customers, acquire new customers, and capture long-standing customer relationships held by their competitors. It is necessary to understand the opportunities and challenges of electronic commerce and how to work with retailers who want to build online consumer experiences that create loyal customer relationships. Companies moving into electronic commerce must understand that they have to think beyond the transaction and build personal relationships that gain and retain customers.

RELATIONSHIP COMMERCE

In the past, successful retailers and salespeople got to know their customers personally, establishing relationships that lasted for years and even generations. These personal relationships are the basis for Relationship Commerce. Many successful companies already engage in Relationship Commerce by collecting detailed information about customers' preferences and interests in order to personalize all of their interactions with them and anticipate their future needs.

For example, Levi Strauss's latest Relationship Commerce innovation is the mass-marketing of custom-fit Personal Pair™ jeans that are individual-

0-8493-9987-4/00/$0.00+$.50
© 2000 by CRC Press LLC

ly tailored for customers by using laser technology. Customers' exact measurements are taken at Levi Strauss retail outlets and their custom-manufactured jeans are shipped to them from the factory, 3 weeks later. Customers have responded very favorably to this extra level of service with increased brand loyalty, repeat purchases, and a willingness to pay premium prices. As a result, Levi Strauss is positioned to benefit from higher customer lifetime value, reduced marketing costs, and lower customer acquisition costs. Companies that want to implement Relationship Commerce online require a software solution to recreate the personalized attention that salespeople give their valued customers. These companies seek ways to provide value beyond the transaction itself by providing customers with individually tailored offerings, promotions, and "one size does not fit all" customer service.

MANAGING CUSTOMER RELATIONSHIPS ONLINE

Retailing on the World Wide Web provides the organization with the ability to penetrate new markets, target more affluent customers, provide better customer service, deliver more up-to-date information, lower operating costs, and earn higher profits than in existing, conventional distribution channels. However, the key to successfully implementing an online storefront comes from managing all customer interactions online, not just the basic ability of executing online transactions.

Retailers who want to implement Relationship Commerce on the World Wide Web need a framework for managing customer relationships online that reflects the Relationship Commerce sales cycle. In Relationship Commerce, all customer relationships progress through the stages shown below. During each stage, the retailer collects information about each customer's interests and preferences. Each interaction represents an opportunity to learn about the customer's needs, likes, and dislikes. Using this information, the retailer can personalize and target the information they present to each customer in subsequent contexts in anticipation of the customer's needs and deliver beyond expectations. Customers' needs for convenience, personalized service and relevant information are satisfied and the retailer benefits from a faster sales cycle and significantly reduced operating costs.

Awareness

In first stage of an online customer relationship, customers develop increased knowledge and awareness of the retailer's brand and product offerings. Each time the customers visit the retailer's Website, the retailer collects information about them, their interests and preferences, and stores this information in each customer's profile. In exchange for this information, retailers can tailor the information a customer sees, limiting it to products they have expressed an interest in. For example, the online book retailer Amazon.com provides registered customers with an Eyes & Editors Personal Notification Service that sends customers an e-mail message when new books by their favorite authors are published. This convenient, personalized service saves customers' time and encourages repeat purchases by anticipating their needs.

Targeting

When a customer revisits a retailer's Website, the retailer can deliver targeted advertising or personalized promotions to them based on the information stored in their customer profile. These promotions are assembled dynamically for each customer, based on business rules defined by store or marketing managers without extensive technical training. For instance, an online music store could present each member in their Music Club with personalized daily or weekly specials featuring new CD releases from their favorite artists. Personalized promotions and online targeting technology help guarantee that each visit to the retailer's Website will be rewarding and unique, encouraging customers to come back again and again.

References

Before making a purchasing decision, customers frequently seek the advice of their friends. Retailers can satisfy this need by providing virtual meeting places for people with similar tastes or interests. For example, people who like mystery novels read book reviews and purchase books that match their tastes or are recommended by a favorite reviewer. An online book retailer could provide customers with an online book review section where other customers post reviews of recent books that they've read, or a chat room where customers can discuss their favorite authors in real time. Customers can check these reviews each time they visit the retailer's Website and purchase books by their peers.

Shopping

Retailers can make it faster and more satisfying for customers to complete regular purchases by remembering personal information about them. For example, when a regular customer buys a dress shirt at a clothing retailer's online store, the retailer can automatically fill in their collar and sleeve length sizes based on information stored in the customer's profile.

Transaction

When a customer is ready to pay for items, the retailer can eliminate the tedious process of filling out method of payment, credit card, and expiration information for regular customers by automatically filling in the payment options stored in their customer profile.

Up-Selling and Cross-Selling

As the customer's experience with a product evolves, they become more educated about related products or higher-quality items. For instance, customers who purchase fly-fishing equipment online, might be interested in taking a salmon-fishing vacation in Alaska or Scotland. When a fly-fishing customer returns to the retailer's Website, a vacation cross-selling promotion can be offered to them, based on the information in their customer profile and purchase history.

Customer Service

Customers shop online because they can find the products they want quickly. Online customer service should also be fast and easy to use. Customers should be able to self-service their information needs online, such as checking on the status of back-ordered items or their account history. Similar self-service capabilities have been shown by Federal Express to be very effective online and can result in significant costs savings by online retailers.

Education

After a customer has purchased a product, a retailer can add significant value to it by providing customers with information that would normally be hard to distribute through other more conventional distribution channels such as retail outlets. For example, customers who purchase power tools online would be interested in expert tips or detailed plans for home construction projects.

Advocacy

Doing business the Relationship Commerce way will turn customers into advocates for the organization's business. This growing community of customers will return to the store again and again, recruiting new customers for the organization from their friends and family and significantly lowering customer acquisition, marketing, and operating costs.

BUILDING BLOCKS FOR ONLINE RELATIONSHIP COMMERCE

As retailers move their storefronts onto the World Wide Web, they need to find cost-effective ways to create and maintain customer relationships online. The key building blocks of online Relationship Commerce on the World Wide Web are dynamic content, personalization, and online targeting.

Dynamic Content

Most Websites show the same Web pages and content to every visitor, no matter how frequently they visit. The problem is that these sites get boring very quickly and people stop visiting. One solution is to continuously update the Website with new content. While this provides customers with a reason to visit again, it is very expensive to keep up over time, and isn't personally tailored for individual visitors.

A simpler, less expensive solution uses dynamically generated Web pages that are created and assembled on the fly when customers visit a Website. Dynamic Web pages are better than static HTML pages because retailers can easily change what visitors see when they visit. By using dynamic content, retailers can personalize the content each visitor experiences based on their preferences and interests, create targeted promotions and online boutiques, or adjust the look of their stores seasonally. Dynamic content keeps the content in the online storefront fresh, relevant, and entertaining, but it is just the first step. Imagine getting a catalog with just the stuff you're interested in.

Personalization

Personalization technology is a revolutionary new component of online Relationship Commerce that lets retailers develop a higher level of customer intimacy and continuously capture new kinds of information about customers that visit their online stores. Forrester Research predicts that the ability to deliver compelling, dynamic content based on customer history and preferences will be a major technology and market requirement for electronic commerce by large retailers and corporations.

With personalization, retailers can collect information about customer interests or lifestyle preferences. This information is stored in a database and can be used to determine which products or product categories are shown to the customer. In large online stores with thousands of items, information about customer preferences is used to help customers navigate through the store and reduce the number of pages they need to view to find the items they want. Customers who can find what they are looking for quickly are more likely to stay in a store longer and make a purchase.

In Relationship Commerce, the key to increasing the lifetime revenue captured from each customer depends on the ability to anticipate their future needs. Over the course of multiple store visits, customers will become interested in other product areas. More advanced personalization servers let retailers observe which new products or content areas customers view. This information can be stored in their customer profile and helps the retailer to anticipate additional product areas that the customer is interested in.

Targeting

Imagine having the ability to change the contents of the shop's front window displays, on the fly, for every customer who walks by. New online targeting techniques let you do just that. When the information stored in individual customer profiles is combined with promotional rules defined by store or marketing managers, it is possible to create personalized promotions designed to expedite a purchasing decision.

For example, a customer has previously purchased a Sony Walkman at an online stereo components store. It is known that customers who purchase this item also purchase batteries, battery rechargers, and blank cassette tapes. The next time this customer logs into the store, the store can dynamically create a personalized cross-sell promotion that offers these items on the first screen page. By constantly anticipating this customer's needs, it is very possible to boost the lifetime revenue collected from him or her. You save your customers' time by matching their needs with your products and you demonstrate to them that you are invested in maintaining a relationship with them — the cornerstone of Relationship Commerce.

ATTRIBUTES OF AN ADVANCED PERSONALIZATION SERVER

The optimum solution for creating relationship commerce systems is a server which has the ability to create online storefronts and personalized consumer shopping experiences that are highly scalable and can be rapidly deployed. Something that can provide retailers with turnkey store management capabilities and a flexible open environment for integration with existing back-end business systems. Dynamic content, personalization, and targeting capabilities need to be fully integrated, making it easy to manage online customer relationships and build online stores with thousands of items. Reporting and analysis tools must be provided to enable management to set goals and benchmark online promotions, improving the store's effectiveness and providing more control over customer relationships than possible using conventional distribution channels.

This "advanced" solution would ensure that each online storefront built is structured as a set of individually branded boutiques linked to a main store. Within each boutique, you may create dynamic product catalogs which can be broken down into any number of categories, subcategories, sections, and product pages for ease of navigation. Each page in a product catalog may be dynamically generated for each customer based on product information and media components stored in the product database, up-to-the-minute pricing information, promotional rules, and the customer preferences. This unique architecture has the effect of significantly reducing the cost of keeping the content in the store up-to-date, while providing each customer with a unique personalized experience.

Customers who visit stores can become members or visit the store as a guest. Profiles are created that store demographic information about them, their purchasing history, and preferred payment options, as well as psychographic information about their interests and preferences. This information is used to dynamically personalize all the products and promotions they see in the store.

As customers browse through the store, they can use powerful search tools to locate products that they're interested in. When customers decide to buy a product, it is placed in a virtual shopping basket which automatically keeps a running total of all the items they've chosen. When the customer is ready to purchase the items in their shopping basket, they review their order and specify payment preferences. Fully integrated customer self-service capabilities let them check on outstanding orders or review their account history at any time.

This optimum solution permits store managers and marketing managers to define the online store's business logic. This includes the definition of new customer profiling attributes and affinity groups, rule-based promotions, sales reports, and visitor activity reports as described below.

Personalization

Customer Profiling and Affinity Groups. Business managers can specify any number of customer attributes that can be collected when customers register at their store or by analyzing which products or information they view. Managers can also define affinity groups that segment your customer base along demographic or psychographic characteristics. These affinity groups and customer attributes are used to define the criteria for offering customers different personalized promotions.

Rule-Based Promotions. Business managers can define a wide range of personalized promotions, including sale pricing, featured products, member and affinity group discounts, and cross-selling and up-selling promotions based on customer profile information.

Sales Reports. A point and click interface makes it easy for business managers to define new sales reports that list sales by product, product category, boutique, or for the entire store for any time period. All reports can be printed or easily exported to third-party analysis tools such as Microsoft Excel.

Visitor Activity Reports. Activity reports can be defined to analyze the characteristics of people who visit your store and which product or content areas are most popular. This information is strategic because it can tell you what parts of your store are performing the best and where to invest additional effort.

Flexible Branding. Content developers and graphic designers may deliver unique brand identities at the store level or for individual boutiques and products. Multimedia text, audio, video, and graphics can be easily included in your store to attract shoppers, enable rapid product recognition, and support branding and storefront identify.

Predefined Page Templates. Predefined Web page templates enable the developer to quickly deploy professional-looking online storefronts. New pages templates can be created using your favorite Web page authoring tools and can be easily integrated with the store.

Content Staging. All new content and design elements can be staged off-line in a separate copy of the online store, eliminating the need for "under construction" signs in the store. Built-in previewing capabilities allow the developer to check the quality of the newest version of the store before it goes live.

Website Development Considerations. You should have to reengineer your existing business systems and legacy applications to open a new online store. In a recent study, IDC reports that 20 percent of Website development funds are spent on hardware and off-the-shelf software and 80 percent is spent on custom software development and integration.

Rapid Deployment. The storefront solution must be easy to install and can be rapidly deployed in the organization. Its interface must be easy to use by business managers, content developers, and graphic designers alike.

Integration with Legacy Applications

The software must easily integrate with a wide variety of transaction processing back-ends, legacy applications, and third-party service providers through a well-documented set of open APIs including:

- Product and inventory management
- Tax, shipping, and handling computation
- Payment processing
- Order fulfillment
- EDI and fax systems
- Credit card authorization
- Customer address verification

Performance and Scalability

The solution's architecture must be able to be partitioned across multiple application and database servers that can support millions of customers and still maintain performance.

Internet Standards and Security

The solution must adhere to industry standards such as those for Web developers: HTML and Java; and those for security: SSL, SHTTP, and SET.

CONCLUSION

Increasingly, the Internet is where people will do business. Internet shoppers represent a rapidly emerging market segment. Recent surveys of customer demographics on the World Wide Web show that the Web is the growing channel of preference for affluent, high-income consumers. The number of active Web shoppers has more than doubled in the past 18 months, and continues to grow unabated.

On the Internet, the phrase "Location, Location, Location" is replaced by "Relationship, Relationship, Relationship." The answer is a highly scalable, rapidly deployed, online storefront solution that provides the organization with built-in dynamic content, personalization, and promotional targeting capabilities. These are the cornerstones for Relationship Commerce on the World Wide Web. These should be at the foundation of your decision to set up shop on the Web.

Author's Bio

Jeet Singh *cofounded Art Technology Group with Joseph Chung in 1991. Since then, Singh has been responsible for the business strategy at ATG and, along with Chung, has led all the strategic design and development projects at ATG.*

Prior to founding ATG, Singh held positions in project management, product marketing and management, product planning, market management, and new business planning and development in start-up medium and large business environments. He was one of the first employees and product/marketing manager for the primary product line at Boston Technology, Inc., a manufacturer of highly advanced voice processing computers. Reporting to the president/CEO and to the vice president of marketing, Singh's responsibilities included development of pricing strategies and structures, maintenance and support plans, contract negotiations, product planning, competitive evaluation, new account penetration strategy, and development of marketing materials. Annual product revenues scaled from zero to more than $25 million between fiscal years 1988 to 1990.

Singh also has worked as a management consultant with Team Technologies, a Washington, D.C.-based consulting firm specializing in workgroup productivity, and as a marketing consultant with Groupe Bull/Bull Corporation of America. He received a B.S. in political science from MIT.

Chapter 24

How "Internet Bill Presentment" Changes the Deployment Strategy: Homebanking and Online Payment

Richard K. Crone

AS A BUSINESS TOOL, THE INTERNET IS RAPIDLY TRANSFORMING THE WORLD OF COMMERCE AND BANKING — making us faster and more efficient, and allowing us to provide more personalized services to the end user or customer. As a result, financial service providers now have a battery of completely new ways to add value and distinguish themselves from the previous generation of commoditized financial transactions.

The advantage of the Internet compared to existing proprietary online connections and banking services is that the Net allows financial institution to combine "content" from multiple sources onto "one" computer desktop. This capability is now considered one of the key enablers for accelerating the use of homebanking programs. By delivering billing content, namely statements, remittance notices, and other recurring bills directly to consumers, banks can attract more electronic consumers to their virtual banking storefronts.

Internet bill presentment and payment does indeed change the value proposition for homebanking and supports the customer movement from physical branches and paper transactions to electronics. In the bill pay-

0-8493-9987-4/00/$0.00+$.50
© 2000 by CRC Press LLC

ment world, if you present a bill in paper, you get paid with a paper check. Thus, it stands to reason that if you present your bill electronically, you will most likely get paid electronically. Purveyors of homebanking programs know that if they are to achieve the exponential increases projected for homebanking they must get the "billing content" incorporated into the bill payment and homebanking services.

It's the biller's bills and they own the content. All this is very good news, but there is an important caveat. One of the realities that banks must face in the pursuit of bill presentment services is that it's the biller's bills. Billers generate and own the billing content. Similarly, consumers don't owe the money to the bank; they owe it to the biller. And it's unlikely that billers are going to easily let go of their billing content without clearly understanding how such an action will impact their own relationships with their customers. After all, the billing touchpoint is one of the most guarded and protected assets of a business, primarily because brand reinforcement is at its most critical point when the customer pays. For most service companies, "the bill is the brand" — as consumers, we don't think "Ah, PG&E or ConEd" each time we snap on a light, but we sure do when we pay our electrical bill and thus guarantee service for the coming month.

The billing touchpoint not only maintains a customer's ongoing commitment to the biller's service, but also sets the stage for cross-selling more services that can be used to deepen the customer relationship. This creates what strategist and author Michael Porter calls a "barrier to exit." No wonder savvy billers look at billing as a sales and customer bonding opportunity, not just the mere collection of receivables. And the Internet takes this a step further because an Internet-presented bill can be used as content to draw a customer into a regular interactive electronic dialog.

In certain electronic billing scenarios, competitors are trying to break into this touchpoint as customers contemplate either extending their commitment or ending it with the original service provider (OSP). To maximize the benefits of this precious touchpoint, billers are looking to craft their electronic billing and payment receipt process in a way that enhances their own branded, one-to-one, direct interaction with their customers. The introduction of a competitor's offering or interloping agent can dilute the direct interaction and leave the OSP vulnerable to losing this customer to a competitor.

How does this impact financial institutions? We know that having access to billing content is critical to catapulting homebanking programs into exponential growth. So how does a bank ride the Internet billing tide and expand the use of its homebanking program without appearing to be poaching the content of billers?

A NEW POINT OF COLLECTION IS ON THE BILLER'S BILL, REGARDLESS OF WHERE IT IS PRESENTED

The answer is relatively simple. The emerging new point of Internet bill collection requires the cooperation and collaboration of billers, and it just so happens that the wholesale side of banking has the perfect processing model waiting in the wings. This is the unbranded lockbox and cash management services now provided to billers. It is the wholesale bank's existing relationship with billers that can be used as a new leverage point to extend the payment system franchise beyond the retail bank's current homebanking customer base.

Essentially, the wholesale bank needs to get its payment service embedded on the biller's online statement, and by doing so they will create a new acquisition channel for the retail side of bank. Both sides of banking have much to gain from this. For example, the wholesale bank not only serves billers; but also does so anonymously by not putting its brand on a bill or on the remittance processing service. There's no need to because wholesale banks are well compensated through serving the biller as the repository and cash management solution. As wholesale banking's single largest customer segment — accounting for as much as 50 percent of some banks' profits — major billers have a lot of weight to throw around and it is a good idea for banks to remember their heritage of serving billers anonymously.

Homebanking, on the other hand, is viewed as a retail banking initiative. It hinges on gaining a commitment from consumers for a bank-sponsored service that may include, among other things, electronic bill payment. Internet bill presentment and payment involves consumers, billers, and their respective banks. And, first and foremost, it requires the development of a new delivery channel and a new customer service interface point for billers. Bankers, armed with an understanding of what billers must do to "electrify" the billing and collection process, can begin to objectively analyze the various business models offered for Internet bill presentment and payment.

THREE P'S OF INTERNET BILLING

To achieve the benefits of Internet billing, billers must invest in the development of their own interactive billing and online payment capabilities whether they outsource the function or develop the capabilities in-house. In either case, billers will be obliged to address the three P's of interactive billing: presentment, payment, and posting.

Presentment: Added Value for Customers Builds Better Barriers to Exit

The presentment component involves taking static statement data, which is now directed to printers, and hosting that information on an interactive Web-based bill presentment server. With the Web, billers can customize the user interface to each individual customer. It is the user interface, custom layout, and navigational components that billers build into their interactive sites that can be used to differentiate them from the competition and leverage the billing touchpoint.

For example, the interactive presentment function has spawned a whole new form of billing functionality that can be called "statement analytics." Statement analytics are Web-based functions that can be used by individual consumers to analyze their billing data in ways that are personally meaningful to them. For example, a consultancy may wish to arrange its phone bill by phone numbers in order to analyze how many calls were made to a particular location. Providing this capability via the Web can be a true added value for a telephone company's customers. Along the same lines, American Express' small business customers are using its credit card interactive billing capabilities as a cash management tool, creating highly individualized review processes for themselves. In this way, American Express has turned the interactive statement into a daily touchpoint that didn't exist before   building loyalty not only before and during the purchase, but after the sale too.

Linking Presentment and Payment: Cost Savings and Instantaneous Settlement

Internet billing also provides billers with direct cost savings and cash management benefits. The critical assumption for the second P of interactive billing is that once customers have reviewed their bills online they can also pay online, thus fulfilling their financial obligations to the OSP. Linking presentment and payment is a critical component, not only for deepening a biller's customer relationships, but for also realizing the cost reductions originally promised to billers by homebanking.

It is estimated that the fully bundled costs to the biller averages between $0.75 to $1.50 per retail remittance. The major components in the fully bundled costs include the computer production runs, statement rendering, printing, statement stuffing, mailing, mail receipt from customers, envelope extraction, sorting by payment type (full, partial, multiple, white mail), workstation processing (assuming OCR stub and check), data entry, reject handling, balancing, posting, and account update. Billers driving customers to their own Website and securing online payment can cut their costs by approximately 50 percent even if they continue to send out paper statements. Obviously, if they can eliminate the distribution of paper statements, billers' costs can be reduced even more dramatically.

Role of Electronic Checks in Securing Electronic Payment

The key to Internet payment is providing a cost-effective payment mechanism that can be securely implemented and easily used by a biller's customers. Consumers are used to fulfilling recurring payment obligations with checks while billers prefer this form of payment because it is the least expensive form of remittance.

The equivalent of a paper check now exists on the Internet in the form of electronic checks. Subscribing to an electronic check service allows the biller to securely accept and process these electronic checks on their own Website. Cash register software provides a connection[1] to the biller's bank for depositing and settling electronic checks while providing the electronic payment information needed to update the biller's accounts receivable system.

Electronic checks provide consumers with the benefits of convenience and safety while allowing billers to maintain their existing depository relationships with their banks. Unlike many homebanking programs, the consumer and the biller can initiate the electronic check directly to the bank without third-party intermediation. This, in turn, lets the biller control the other key component of interactive billing, which is posting.

Posting: Maximizing Cash Management Benefits

The final P of interactive billing is posting. Once the statement is presented and payment is secured the biller must post to their accounts receivable system and update the customer's account. Unlike the manual check and list process or the proprietary connections that characterize many homebanking services, this is an automated connection that the biller can control and maintain for its own gain, without any dependency on a third party. Because the biller is making the connection itself to its own account receivable systems, it can do so without having to make changes or conforming to someone else's presentment, payment, or posting standard. Additionally, because the biller is not dependent on an outside third-party processor, the biller can establish its own posting algorithms for providing credit to its customer accounts. The biller can also maximize the cash management benefits of accelerating electronic check deposits directly to its depository institution.

THREE WAYS TO PRESENT AND PAY BILLS VIA THE INTERNET

Using this the P's framework as a backdrop, bankers can more easily evaluate the pros, cons, risks, and costs of each of the various approaches to Internet bill presentment and payment. There are essentially three ways to present and pay bills using the Internet:

- Directly on the biller's Website: Biller registers its own customers to come to its Website to view and pay bills. This is known as "biller-direct."
- Billers deliver their bills to a third-party concentrator: Biller sends all its statement and remittance detail to a service bureau that present

bills on behalf of many different billers. This is known as a "closed delivery" concentrator.
- Links to consumer magnets: Using the full power of hypertext links, billers maintain billing detail on their sites but cooperate with consumer magnet sites that provide directional pointers for consumers to retrieve, view, and pay their bills online. This is known as a "shared link" concentrator.

None of these approaches is mutually exclusive. However, the economic model and fees charged by the purveyors of each approach will most definitely affect how fast each achieve critical mass and breakeven processing volumes. For example, the biller-direct approach is generally approached from an in-house processing standpoint, thus the marginal cost for making all the billing records available on the site is relatively small. This is in sharp contrast to the "closed delivery" concentrator model that charges anywhere between $0.32 to $0.60 per presented bill. The concentrator's pricing model sets the marginal cost for presenting each new bill at a very high level. This motivates billers to minimize and limit the bills presented through this proprietary channel to those customers that request to see their bills at a location other than the biller's own site.

Banks must be sensitive to the decision-making process that billers go through in selecting and timing the deployment of each of the various bill presentment channels. Just as banks had to make a decision in selecting which channel to deliver homebanking services, so too with billers. Whether it's a bank selecting a homebanking channel or a biller selecting a bill presentment channel, the same set of criteria is used in the decision to select an information-based electronic distribution channel:

- Access and reach to the target markets and customer segments of the financial institution or biller
- Ability to enhance, manipulate, and personalize the informational content for the financial institution customer or biller
- Point of presence processing (POPP) capabilities and statement analytics that allow value creation to occur when the customer is interacting with the institution's system or the biller's bill or statement
- Connection effort, speed of accessing information, and overall ease of use from the consumer's perspective
- Integration cost with existing data processing systems, especially the biller's Accounts Receivable systems
- Security, privacy, and control of data flows

Again, these were the criteria that many banks applied to their homebanking decisions and the formulation of their electronic retail delivery strategies. Many of those decisions focused on selecting between proprietary and nonproprietary electronic connections with customers.

Obviously, the best channel combination maximizes access to the greatest number of desired customer segments at the least cost, and with the greatest branding and control at the faceplate (computer screen) level. In considering electronic banking options, banks chose primarily between proprietary (private) and nonproprietary network (Internet) connections. Billers will face the same decisions, choosing between connections that are closed and controlled by third-party providers vs. open and direct interfaces with consumers on their own Websites.

BILLER-DIRECT: THE NEW POINT OF COLLECTION

One the easiest decisions a biller can make regarding Internet bill presentment and payment is to host the bills on its own Website. It offers the simplest way to regain customer touchpoints lost to other payment methods offered by homebanking services and captures the cross-sell opportunities by leveraging the one-to-one interaction power of the Internet. Billing and payment can be used to reinforce the relationship with the original service provider through the biller's own site, e-mail, and "subscribe" technology. In each of these approaches customers are allowed to view billing obligations online and authorize payment directly over the Internet securely from their checking accounts. Examples of this service in operation today can be found at the Internet Websites of NUI Corporation (www.nui.com), Kansas City Power & Light (www.kcpl.com), and American Express (www.americanexpress.com).

The biller-direct empowers billers to use their own customer statement data as compelling content to drive traffic to their own storefronts and service displays. An electronic cash register service allows the biller to accept and track all three forms of electronic payment: electronic cash, credit card, and electronic checks. Billers are able to genuinely reduce their backend processing costs since all of the functions are under the control of the OSP and its bank.

In addition, the biller-direct model enables one-to-one communications for mass customization of client messages. This important capability allows billers to deepen their customer relationships through personalized electronic dialogs, weaving the billing process into the other cross-sell content on their Websites.

Electronic presentment and payment also provides a biller with a new way to distinguish themselves competitively by packing valuable new information-based or statement analytic services into their customer interactions. For example, account history, item sorting, and instantaneous answers to customer questions can be integrated into the interactive billing and payment process, further reinforcing the relationship between the biller and its customers. The key benefit is that this can all be accomplished without being disconnected from the biller's proprietary account statement nor relying on or being intermediated by third parties.

VIEW FROM THE WEBTOP

Critics of this approach cite the drawback of having to go to several individual Websites to view and pay bills. However, features in the leading browsers, such as bookmarks, make it very easy for consumers to accumulate their payment obligations on their own computer desktops, or "Webtops," as opposed to relying on a third-party service. When it is time to pay some bills, it is simply a matter of going to the "bill payment folder" and opening the obligations the consumer wants to meet at that time. Even newer technology allows Web users to "subscribe" to specific Websites. Once subscribed, specified information such as bills can be downloaded at predetermined intervals so consumers can automatically receive and review all their bills once a day, once a week, once a month, or whenever they specify. In this way, credit card and cellular phone bills can, for example, appear every Friday morning as you prepare your weekly expense report.

In this manner consumers can now participate in homebanking, one biller and one payment at a time, without the disturbance of changing bill-paying habits and without investing time in learning a third-party software package or incurring the ongoing cost of a homebanking service. You have the immediacy and security of making an electronic payment without giving up the control to someone else. For many consumers — perhaps the vast majority — Internet bill presentment and payment at the biller's own Website makes optimum sense. From the consumer's point of view, it certainly represents another avenue of customer service and convenience, unburdened by the shackles of paper and free from the timing and lack of control issues that plague other bill delivery channels. Not to provide the biller-direct option to that segment of consumers that value convenience, timing, and control leaves the door dangerously open to competitors that do — just as banks that didn't jump on the ATM or debit card bandwagons early on soon regretted their lack of competitive advantage.

PRIVACY MATTERS: WHO'S LOOKING AT THE BILLS?

Internet billing also presents a major privacy challenge. As billers assess the value they place on their customers, they need to also assess the value of ensuring customer privacy. Consumers expect billers to maintain the confidentiality of their statement data and payment obligations. The current paper-based method of paying recurring bills supports the preexisting covenant of trust between biller and consumer. For example, consumers expect billers to send the "sealed" envelope to only them for opening. The only thing viewed by anyone else is the address in the window envelope that the Postal Service uses to deliver the mail. When it is opened, consumers are not watched as they review the bill or statement stuffers, and they fill out their checks in complete privacy. The privacy covenant is further maintained in the consumer's mind when the sealed envelope is returned via the Postal Service directly to the biller. Why should it be any different on the Internet? Consumers are going to expect, and even demand, that billers honor the privacy covenant on the Internet — that their bills are delivered only to them and that their payments go directly to the biller.

The biller-direct model comes the closest to emulating the existing paper-based billing world that consumers experience today, but without the paper. In the biller-direct model, billing information is controlled and secured by the biller. This makes it fairly easy for the biller to self-regulate while deploying its own verified security measures to guard against misappropriation of information, mishap, and mischief. It is also relatively easily to verify and enforce the integrity of the billing data throughout the payment process.

CONCENTRATOR: SENDING THE CUSTOMER SOMEWHERE ELSE TO PAY

With billers moving quickly towards the Internet for presentment and payment, it is certain that *some* entity, either a bank or a third party, is going to reap the payment processing rewards. Billers interested in interactive billing and payment are already falling into two camps   those whose banks can support them with direct billing and payment services, and those that are looking towards third-party payment concentrators. In the first instance, the biller is empowered to accept payment directly at its own Website. Those that fall into the concentrator camp, on the other hand, delegate their direct billing opportunity to become ciphers on another company's bill payment list. Lumped together with a consumer's other payment obligations, they have little or no opportunity to strengthen customer bonds. In fact, it is typically the intermediating party's logo and corporate identity that is reinforced.

However, some billers will be tempted to achieve the cost savings without considering the important customer relationship issue discussed above. As a result, they will delegate the customer interaction function to a concentrator that aggregates the billing obligations of many different billers on one site. The other billers aggregated on the site may be both friend and foe. To understand the magnitude of the risk we need to compare the communication touchpoints of the both the biller-controlled and concentrator models, as shown in Exhibit 24.1.

The items on the left-hand side of Exhibit 24.1 are functions primarily under the control of the biller, including the customer interaction and branding of the billing process, payment, and other ancillary services. The items

Exhibit 24.1. Biller-Controlled Vs. Concentrator Model of Bill Payment

Biller-Controlled Billing Chain	Concentrator Billing Chain
Biller prepares electronic statement and sends electronic notice directly to customer	* Biller prepares electronic statement and sends directly to concentrator
Consumer uses PC to access the Internet and securely enters biller's Website	> Consumer securely enters concentrator's Website or uses a Microsoft, Intuit, or bank-branded interface to retrieve bills
Consumer reviews custom presentment of the entire statement with analytics including a rich array of cross-sell content completely controlled by the biller	* Consumer reviews only the "amount due" portion of the bill or statistic statement
	* Concentrator charges biller to present banner advertisements on their own bill
Consumer writes an electronic check directly to the biller for BOTH bill and cross-sell content; sale and collection complete customer service: biller	> Consumer authorizes third party to make payment to the biller which may or may not include payment for the items promoted through banner advertisements

shown with a greater than sign (>) are new functions introduced by the concentrator into the billing and remittance process and are controlled and branded by outside third parties. The items shown with an asterisk (*) represent either the negotiated or unconscious sharing of the customer interface and branding by the biller with third parties. Remember, you are looking for the items on the left side of Exhibit 24.1.

As you can see, the concentrator model portends forced co-branding and minimal biller control of the customer interaction session.

Banks must realize if a biller sends its customers to a concentrator to pay, the biller's bank loses the opportunity to be the depository institution and processing entity for the bills being presented. Even if the bank is hosting bill concentrating services, if they are relying on a third-party service bureau to operate the service, they are truly not the one garnering the fee income, advertising revenues, and other benefits that come from serving billers — that has been delegated to the third-party service bureau. The information learned from tracking consumers is gained by the concentrator, not the bank or the biller, since the concentrator is the entity tracking the cookies planted on consumer's PC.

Banks should look back on how bankcard draft processing evolved to clearly see that the strategy is completely the same for payment concentrators in the Internet billing market. Compared to when banks received the physical bankcard draft, electronic draft capture made it much more difficult for banks to maintain their customer relationships. Instead, billers could shop nationally for processing and no longer had to interact with their local bank when depositing bankcard drafts. As a result, nonbanks now process 75 percent of all bankcard transactions. And when banks gave up the customer contact and allowed their merchants to deposit electronically to nonbank third-party concentrators, they gave up the depository relationship by default.

With Internet billing and payment, the peril is even more profound. We are not talking about ancillary credit services, we are talking about the life-blood of the bank: demand deposit accounts. Standing by while third parties inject themselves into this picture will lead not just to a strategic retreat, but to a total rout that jeopardizes a bank's profitable DDA customer relationship while leaving the lucrative Internet field to the nonbank victors, perhaps for good.

CONSUMER MAGNETS AT HIGH TRAFFIC SITES

The third method of bill presentment is a hybrid of the first two models. In the third approach, content aggregators merely provide navigational services for finding, grouping, and viewing various billing obligations. Instead of requiring billers to ship all of their billing data and service content to a third party service bureau for publication and distribution, they point customers back to the individual Websites of the original service providers. This model offers the best of both worlds, providing customers with a single site for the identification and aggregation of billing obligations without intermediating the content of the biller.

One example of this is the bill presentment and payment offering of Intuit in their latest release of Quicken and Quicken.com. In each case the biller registers with Intuit. Then, using the point-to-point connection capabilities of the Internet, Quicken relies on the biller to display billing detail directly to the Quicken user through the use of an embedded browser inside of the Quicken software.

Banks can follow suit by providing biller identification and "pointing" services as well. What this portends, however, is that the battle for homebanking shifts from the banks to the billers. This realization dramatizes the need for collaboration between the wholesale and retail sides of the bank.

SERVING THE BILLERS

In most banks, there is a longstanding wall between wholesale and retail banking. Now is the time for banks to tear it down. It's incumbent on the wholesale side of the bank to take the leadership role and show the retail side how to deal with billers. Implicit in this is helping billers register consumers to pay their bills directly over the Internet at a biller's own Website in the same way they signed up the biller's customers to direct debit services and other Automated Clearing House Preauthorized Payment or Deposit (ACH PPD) services.

By offering billers electronic lockbox services, not only at a bank site but also at the biller's own Website, banks can now provide a new cash management service without intensive capital investment, labor, or the logistically bound infrastructure inherent in the paper-based remittance process. Plus, banks can do it as anonymously as their billers' desire, and without the costly check and list remittances that characterize traditional home-banking programs. A bank can even offer a managed ACH Preauthorized Payment Debit (PPD) service for a premium, warehousing the PPDs using an electronic cash register service and providing yet another value-add to the biller's business.

Taking this approach has huge implications for the DDA base of retail banks. For example, DDA customers that have at least one ACH PPD link to their account maintain higher idle balances, making ACH PPDs the single greatest contributor to the increasing profitability of demand deposit accounts. Banks also immediately inherit quasi-DDA relationships with every Internet bill-paying consumer and thus can extend their reach far beyond their traditional boundaries by capitalizing on these potential new retail customer touchpoints. It doesn't matter if the bill-paying consumers are retail customers of the bank or not. And it doesn't matter where they live. Thus, taking an aggressive stance with Internet bill presentment and payment can open new doors for a bank, even as it deepens a bank's existing DDA relationships with its most prized depositors: billers and electronic consumers.

HOW DOES THE BANK MAXIMIZE ITS INVOLVEMENT AT EACH NEW POINT OF COLLECTION?

The key strategy is embedding the electronic lockbox service not just at the biller level but at the individual statement level. Banks must link their wholesale payment services to each electronically presented statement, regardless of where the electronic statement is rendered or delivered in order to protect and extend a new retail relationship with the bill-paying consumer.

By the same token, banks providing direct debit programs to billers sit in the enviable position of being able to provide billers with the lowest-cost form of remittance over all other forms of payment. It is from this launch pad that banks possess a competitive advantage. Internet billing and payment, combined with "customer-initiated direct debit" or electronic check, extends this competitive advantage to the Internet bill presentment and payment arena. But it does so only as long as the bank can embed its electronic check capability on each electronic bill. As long as the bank has woven its electronic check capability into each electronically presented bill, the bank can be assured of participating in and adding value to the bill payment process, regardless where the bill is presented and paid. Embedding payment one biller and one payment at a time will ensure that the bank protects its prized commercial depository relationship with its billers, regardless of whether the biller collects payment directly on its own Website, customer magnet site, or through a "closed delivery," third-party concentrator.

This said, banks must recognize that it is in the biller's best interest to quickly provide a biller-direct option at its own Website, no matter what other channels it eventually employs. This allows the biller to realize maximum value from customer-initiated direct debit, while fully leveraging the interactive one-to-one marketing capabilities inherent to the Web. Once established on the Internet with a biller-direct capability at its own Website, a biller is in the optimal position to extend the number of its electronic channels or connections and thus capture more low-cost, high-value online payments. Implementing a biller-direct model is a step that can be taken *now* while payment concentrators, which rely on critical mass and standards to attract consumers to deliver a meaningful ROI, ramp up and come on stream.

IMPLEMENTING AN INTERNET BILL PRESENTMENT AND PAYMENT STRATEGY

Here is a suggested roadmap that banks can follow when establishing an electronic lockbox service that will maximize the value of Internet bill presentment and payment for both banks and their billers.

Develop the Solution

As discussed above, the first step to establishing an electronic lockbox service is to determine whether to offer just payment and posting, and thus leave the choice of presentment solutions to the billers, or to offer a complete presentment, payment, and posting solution. It is possible to do both by selecting partners to recommend to billers for the presentment piece. As the solutions are rolled out, the bank will gain experience integrating these partners and will then have multiple complete solutions.

Create the Business Model

There are many ways to package and price an Internet bill presentment and payment solution. These should be evaluated and the chosen one(s) carefully outlined so the sales force can articulate the benefits to the customer. Sales targets, incentives, and profit and loss goals should be set.

Develop the Sales Message

A bank's message to its biller customers will be a simple one. As the bank is already the biller's trusted custodian of the cash management, physical lockbox, and A/R service relationships, it should be the automatic choice for operating and consolidating the electronic lockbox relationship. A bank's sales point should be that, no matter where the biller goes to find partners for its electronic bill presentment initiatives, the bank's electronic lockbox solution should be used to consolidate and enable payments to the biller (and thus directly to the bank).

Additionally, this service will enable the biller to create a *totally* electronic back-end posting system in conjunction with bank services already being provided. This should set the expectation in the biller's mind that when dealing with any bill presentment vendor, they should bring their bank in on any meetings as the payment and lockbox provider.

Train the Sales Force

For the biller, the Internet bill presentment and payment decision involves strategic decisions about customer relationships, as well as issues surrounding marketing, customer service and support, cash management, and information systems. As such, it can be a long and complex sell. It can take up to 1 year for a biller to choose a solution.

Much of the sale process is education about alternatives. Bank sales personnel need to be trained in the benefits of the solution, the pitfalls, and the overall process.

Banks have a significant advantage in this arena; they are currently a trusted agent carrying out lockbox services. Banks should leverage this advantage by beginning to sell to current customers and then branch out to nonbank billers.

Set Goals and Establish a Measurement Process

Internet billing and payment is not for every biller initially. Early adopters can by identified relatively easily. They are usually early adopters of other types of technology and pride themselves on being first in their industry. They should have a relatively "wired" customer base. Certain areas of the country, such as the East and West Coasts are further along the online curve. The current account manager will be able to assess the predilection of a particular biller to consider Internet bill presentment and payment.

Initially, a bank's sales force will learn a great deal about the sales process. Feedback loops need to be in place to disseminate this information rapidly to other calling officers. This is an emerging market and it changes very quickly.

Identify Early Adopters among Current Customers

Pick several good customers with the right attributes. Price the solution so they receive an advantage for being first.

Conduct Several Pilots

Develop a test site, which can also serve as a demonstration site for customers. Pilot several different customer types to ensure that the software is completely exercised. If multiple presentment solutions are to be integrated, try to pilot one of each.

Launch

Like any new product or service launch, Internet bill presentment and payment requires visibility, marketing support, and so on. Electronic billing is a hot topic. Visibility is relatively easy to come by and most of the nation's billers are evaluating it in some way, shape, or form.

MANY HAPPY RETURNS ON INVESTMENT

As we've seen, Internet bill presentment and payment offers a significant opportunity for a bank to enhance its current cash management services, decrease its costs, and develop new revenue streams while deepening its relationship with its wholesale and retail customers. Additionally, this increased functionality helps create higher barriers to exit.

How does one go about projecting a return on investment from Internet billing? To begin with, creating an electronic lockbox service opens a new point of collection for the bank. The bank is no longer geographically restricted to offering lockbox services only where it maintains locations. Additionally, with electronic lockbox, profitability can be achieved with low volumes because there is little capital investment required.

Banks taking such a course can expect higher profit margins due to reduced paper processing, with cost savings somewhere between $0.75 and $1.25 for each paper check that is eliminated, according to the National Automated Clearing House Association (NACHA).

Additionally, an electronic lockbox service can represent a new source of fee (non-interest) income from billers. These fees can supplement current fee income.

There are also one-time revenue opportunities. An electronic lockbox service allows a bank to create a further revenue stream by marking up a third-party electronic check service upon resale to a biller.

Branding opportunities are also available by co-opting the biller as a value-added reseller (VAR) of bank services and generating new customer touchpoints for retail customer acquisition. A consumer paying his/her bill on the biller's Website through a bank's electronic lockbox creates a new touchpoint, which can bring in new retail customers.

For the first time, the wholesale side of the bank can create a competitive advantage by tracking new retail accounts. The opportunity exists to use the accounts registered with billers to expand homebanking services. A bank could even issue a digital debit card against registered accounts held by other banks and start garnering new fees.

FINANCIAL BENEFITS OF INTERNET BILL PRESENTMENT AND PAYMENT

Potential Hard Dollar Benefits to Banks

- Increase bank's deposit base
- Decrease processing costs
- Increase fee income
- Increase number and diversity of services offered to retain customers
- Increase bank's earning capability
- Decrease clearing and settlement costs
- Increase click stream revenues
- Increase access to funds
- Increase one-time revenue opportunities in the resale of the electronic check services to billers

Potential Soft Dollar Benefits to Banks

- Increase new customer acquisition opportunities
- Increase issuance of bank-branded digital debit cards
- Increase brand positioning
- Increase market penetration
- Increase perception in the marketplace as an industry leader in service and innovative service technologies
- Increase point-of-collection channels to expand collection bandwidth
- Decrease geographical dependence of paper-based lockbox services
- Increase customer loyalty

CONCLUSIONS

Electronic bill presentment and payment is here to stay. Industry projections indicate that 10 percent of all bills will be paid via the Internet by 2003 (source: MSFDC). This translates to approximately 2.5 billion electronically submitted lockbox items.

Every bank has a choice. A bank can leverage its current trusted relationships with billers to take ownership of the emerging bill presentment and electronic lockbox to protect its commercial deposit base. Or it can wait for nonbank entities to intermediate its relationship with it most profitable customers — billers.

Deploying a secure electronic check service to enable biller-direct bill payments creates an electronic lockbox that has several significant benefits for any bank:

- Extend existing services to new markets — enhance current lockbox and cash management services without adding processing facilities, equipment, and operations. This is accomplished by embedding a bank's payment capabilities on every statement generated by a biller over the Internet.
- Create a defensible perimeter by protecting a bank's depository relationship with billers at the electronic remittance level — by providing this service, a bank is assured of processing the payments regardless of where the bill is rendered or presented electronically on the Internet. This approach protects the depository relationship at the originating point, namely the electronic remittance statement.
- Establishes the bank as the payment vehicle of choice, regardless of where the bill is presented — billers will present bills at multiple Websites to reach their consumers. A bank's wholesale banking services group runs the risk of being intermediated by third-party payment concentrators in the same way that banks were intermediated by credit card processors more than a decade ago. Embedding online payment in the online bill ensures that all funds flow to the bank directly, not via a third party that may or may not be another financial institution.
- Create a tool for the retail homebanking market — when a retail customer pays a bill on a biller's Website, they will, if the enabling bank wishes, always see the bank's brand. This provides additional visibility and cross-selling opportunity for the retail side of the house.
- Positions the bank as a biller-centric solution — billers are a bank's natural wholesale customers. The electronic lockbox is bought and paid for by billers. An aggressive approach to Internet billing allows a bank to retain its place in the payments business.
- Finally, by empowering billers to accept payments directly at their own Websites, and directly on their own bill for that matter, a bank doesn't have to wait for new retail customers to walk into its branches, visit its ATMs, or sign up to its homebanking programs anymore. Instead, a bank gains the universal Internet as a channel into a new customer base, courtesy of its billers utilizing its electronic lockbox services.

There's not a lot of time for hesitation. Both billers and nonbanks are moving quickly. Banks still have the inside track with their existing biller relationships. By not moving resolutely, a bank runs a major risk of being disassociated from its billers — its bread and butter clientele — and of being edged out of much of the emerging electronic bill payment process. By the same token, billers stand to lose the marketing benefits inherent to Internet billing as they become disassociated from their own clientele to whom they act as the original service provider. Will they thank their bank for allowing that to happen? Doubtful. It's up to bankers to take the lead in order to preserve and extend their bill payments leadership.

E-COMMERCE MANAGEMENT

Author's Bio

Richard K. Crone *is Vice President and General Manager at CyberCash, Inc. He is responsible for the development and release of the PayNow™ Secure Electronic Check Service. Prior to joining CyberCash, Crone led the nation's largest savings bank at the time, Home Savings of America, as Senior Vice President and Co-Director of Electronic Banking, in their successful launch of online banking with Microsoft Money and Intuit's Quicken.*

Before HAS, he spent 8 years with KPMG Peat Marwick's Financial Services Consulting Practice, where he played an instrumental advisory role in the formation of business plans for both private and public funding of several Internet-based new ventures. He has been sharing his research on Point of Presence Processing (POPP) over the last several years in customized workshops and presentations for financial institutions, industry associations, and others concerning the inevitability of total electronic banking and online payment options over the Internet. Crone also spent nearly 9 years in the financial systems division of Unisys, a major hardware/software data processing supplier. As a marketing manager, he was responsible for developing, negotiating, and consummating agreements for data processing systems and services.

Crone has published over 100 articles, including authoring the "Notes From the Infobahn" column in the "Management Strategies Magazine" of the American Banker. *His most recent publication appears in the* Billing World Magazine, *titled "Advantages of Having Bills Paid at Your Own Web Site." Additionally, he has been the keynote speaker for the Bank Administrative Institute's Retail Delivery Conference, Treasury Management Association, and the American Banker's CyberBanking Conferences. He holds B.S. and M.B.A. degrees with honors from the University of Southern California.*

Notes

1. Instead of delivering cash and check deposits to a physical bank branch, an electronic check service uses advanced encryption to securely deliver EFT requests directly to a bank's systems for processing.

Chapter 25
XML-Based Business-to-Business E-Commerce

Michael Blank

MOST COMPANIES HAVE ALREADY RECOGNIZED THE BENEFITS of doing business electronically. E-commerce takes many forms and includes supply chain integration, procurement, online banking, and shipping and logistics. Solutions such as Enterprise Resource Planning (ERP), Electronic Data Interchange (EDI), and the Web have formed the foundation for E-commerce today. These applications link groups of departments, divisions, and companies that want to buy, sell, and exchange services and products, and that depend on seamless information access.

However, in order to remain competitive, companies will have to find solutions to extend their electronic trading networks among companies of all sizes. The technological hurdle to overcome is to find ways to access data that may reside in other complex systems, such as legacy databases, ERP, EDI, and the Web.

The goal of this chapter is to explore how XML (Extensible Markup Language) technologies allow businesses to rapidly and easily engage in business-to-business (B2B) E-commerce. It explores how companies can achieve application-to-application integration across highly heterogeneous environments by leveraging existing investments in legacy and Web-based products and technologies.

COMMERCE COMPONENTS

In order to fuel the growth of electronic trading networks beyond the enterprise, three major sources of information must be unlocked — EDI, ERP, and electronic commerce on the Web. A B2B integration solution must allow these disparate systems to communicate with each other, without requiring changes to the systems themselves.

0-8493-9987-4/00/$0.00+$.50
© 2000 by CRC Press LLC

EDI

EDI is based on a set of computerized forms that automate common business transactions such as package orders, invoices, shipping notices, and requests for proposals. EDI lets companies send and receive purchase orders, sales orders, invoices, and electronic payments.

EDI messages consist of agreed-upon data elements that typically appear in commercial business forms: names, addresses, prices, dates, and item numbers. Standardized lists of these data elements comprise forms such as purchase orders, invoice, ship notices, and medical billing forms. Hundreds of these forms have been developed over the past 20 years or so by a committee called X.12 of the American National Standards Institute (ANSI). International EDI standards have been coordinated by a United Nations organization called UN/EDIFACT.

EDI documents are essentially flat text files. They must be translated out of and into trading partners' internal systems, often at great cost. The widespread acceptance of EDI historically has been hampered by the prohibitive development and maintenance costs. Because EDI is a rigid standard, it requires complicated, proprietary translation and integration software. Furthermore, EDI is typically carried over private value-added networks (VANs), which requires expensive hardware as well as a transaction- and volume-based subscriber fees.

As such, EDI solutions have been limited to large companies, while excluding any trading partners that may not have the purse to play along. Because EDI is so expensive, cumbersome, and proprietary, Forrester Research estimates that only 2 percent of electronic transactions are done via EDI.

The Internet, with its low cost of entry and ease of use, could change all that; EDI over the Internet currently allows organizations to access a wider range of trading partners. Even though Internet-based EDI would eliminate the need for proprietary VANs, it does not address the need for costly translation software and integration with enterprise applications.

Traditional EDI vendors, such as Sterling Commerce, Harbinger, and GE Information Services, have allowed smaller companies to participate in EDI activities by providing Web-based forms for manual entry of EDI information, which is translated to an EDI format and forwarded to a larger trading partner. Internet-based EDI is still very interactive, and allows very little automation in comparison to direct automated VAN access from one company's system to another's. Other forms of Internet-based EDI include sending data through encrypted e-mail.

While Internet-based EDI is offered by several vendors, they are not interoperable, again due to the lack of standards. Large trading companies have coerced EDI standards to conform to their business processes, making it hard for smaller companies to compete. With different standards between trading partners, a company might have to support as many EDI implementations as they have trading partners, making it too costly for smaller companies to participate.

While the Internet expands the network reach of EDI, there is still a market requirement for seamless information exchange among *all* trading partners that extend the reach of proprietary EDI networks. As we'll see, EDI combined with XML-enabled integration solutions holds the promise of leveling the playing field and achieving a high degree of interoperability.

ERP

The Enterprise Resource Planning (ERP) system is another form of electronic commerce. It seeks to automate business process that span the organization, incorporating functions such as sales and materials planning, production planning, warehouse management, financial accounting, and personnel management into an integrated workflow of business events. ERP applications provide universal access to information across heterogeneous networks and data sources throughout the enterprise.

While automating key internal business processes is an important step towards integration, integrating processes and information with the information systems of key customers and suppliers is a real competitive advantage. Sharing ERP data among business partners can streamline value chain processes, automate purchasing or customer service applications for real-time processing, and reduce the cost of order processing and financial transaction management.

SAP, one of the leading vendors in the ERP space, has already recognized the need to extend R/3, their ERP solution, to address supply chain management. Unlike ERP systems, supply chain systems must cope with the complexity of integrating information from any number of disparate information systems spanning the entire length of the supply chain. In response, SAP has exposed business components within the R/3 system to applications compliant with open standards such as DCOM and CORBA.

Like EDI, ERP installations are not only proprietary but also involve substantial investment, which limits these solutions to larger companies. Because they focus on the enterprise, there are even fewer standards that link the ERP systems of *different* companies. Technologies and standards that bridge the gap between ERP and EDI or Web-based systems are virtually nonexistent.

XML has the promise to extend ERP beyond the bounds of the enterprise to achieve higher levels of intercompany and multivendor interoperability.

THE WEB

The Web has changed the face of business. Advertisements now feature URLs, and many organizations support sales over the Internet. Consumer Web users can browse catalogs, select items, and make purchases from the comfort of their living rooms. But Web-based shopping is only the tip of the electronic commerce iceberg. While much of E-commerce has been consumer oriented, the Internet can also be used to drastically improve efficiency, reduce costs, and increase sales for an organization by automating the business-to-business relationships with suppliers, distributors, and other partners.

Without realizing it, organizations have already established a viable set of services, available on the World Wide Web and addressable by URLs. Existing Web services span the spectrum from package tracking and online banking to procurement and supply chain integration.

Companies have looked to the open standards of the Web as a common means to communicate with their trading partners. Legacy databases, mainframes, and even EDI systems have been exposed via HTTP and HTML. The Web has truly become an integration platform.

However, HTML-based applications assume that a human is interacting with the system through a Web browser, browsing catalogs and placing orders. While this approach is appropriate for a casual shopper, it is not the most efficient design for business process-driven applications such as supply chain management. For greatest efficiency, the intercorporate supply chain should be automated to work without human intervention. For example, as inventory levels are depleted, the ERP system should automatically query suppliers for inventory levels and delivery schedules, and automatically place orders for replacement stock. Although the information and processes to query and place orders might already be integrated with the Web, they aren't designed to support external automated interfaces. Therefore, new interfaces need to be created to support Internet-based supply chain automation.

THE NEED FOR BUSINESS-TO-BUSINESS INTEGRATION

Solutions such as EDI and ERP focus only on providing software for automating operations within tightly coupled organizations. For an organization to achieve full benefits from electronic commerce, a solution must automate the operations *between* trading partners.

An integration solution must cope with the complexity of integrating information from any number of varied information systems, spanning the entire length of the E-commerce continuum. A solution must provide a secure and reliable mechanism to communicate between applications; the message format must be open and flexible enough for different applications to understand, process, and respond to it.

Some users are looking towards XML to solve the problem of business-to-business integration. XML may be the emerging standard that promises to bridge the communication gap between enterprise resource planning, electronic data interchange, and Web-based systems. Its real significance may emerge as a means for making it easier to create, deploy, and manage integration solutions over the Internet.

WHAT IS XML?

XML (eXtensible Markup Language) is a universal standard for data representation that can encode documents, data records, structured records, even data objects and graphical objects. XML documents are ASCII files that contain text as well as tags identifying structures within that text.

This enables XML to contain "meta data" — data about the content in the document, including hierarchical relationships. As such, XML is a standalone data format that is self-describing.

The following example illustrates how a purchase order might be represented using XML.

```
<?xml version= 1.0 ?>
<PurchaseOrder>
    <OrderNumber>1001</OrderNumber>
    <Status>Pending</Status>
    <Company>The ABC Company</Company>
    <LineItem>
        <SKU>45669</SKU>
        <Description>Modem Cable</Description>
        <Price>9.95</Price>
    </LineItem>
    <LineItem>
        <SKU>35675</SKU>
        <Description>Modem</Description>
        <Price>99.95</Price>
    </LineItem>
</PurchaseOrder>
```

A business application can locate a particular element and extract its value, regardless of the order of the elements within the document, and regardless of whether it recognizes all of the elements.

INTEROPERABILITY WITH XML

XML offers a lot more flexibility and extensibility than traditional messaging. The application that publishes the XML document could add a new attribute to the document, such as "Quantity," to support the requirements of another application. The original applications that used the document would be unaffected by the additional attribute since they may only be interested in the SKU, Description, and Price of the Item.

An XML document may be fully described by a Document Type Definition (DTD). An XML DTD specifies the format for a particular XML document type and identifies what tags must or may appear within the document. An XML document may contain or reference a DTD, in which case the DTD may be used to validate that the document matches a specific format.

DTDs may be utilized to define standard vocabularies, designed for specific communities of interest. For example, the messaging formats for partners along the supply chain could be specified by a common DTD.

XML Alone Is Not Enough

XML is an open standard, which leads us to a Utopian perception of automatic interoperability. However, XML alone does not provide a complete integration solution, but it represents a central piece of the puzzle. Integrating applications with XML actually requires a fair amount of work. Applications have to be able to understand, process, and respond to XML message formats.

Although the two applications do not need to agree on a specific message format, they still must reach consensus on the meaning of the data being passed. The two different applications are very likely to use different DTDs, and they must establish a way to match elements and attributes from one DTD to the entities and attributes in the other DTD.

In most circumstances, it is not enough to simply pass information from one application to another. The sending application has to tell the receiving application what to do with the data. Therefore, the two applications need to agree on a mechanism for specifying what should be done with the data.

A complete B2B solution would supply mechanisms that relate one application's data structures to those of another. And it would provide a mechanism for requesting specific services to act on the information. Combining XML and integration software brings us closer to a B2B integration solution.

AN XML-BASED B2B INTEGRATION SOLUTION

Although it is extremely powerful, XML by itself cannot deliver application integration. Application integration involves much more than self-describing, extensible message formats. The application must be adapted to learn to communicate using XML. It must be able to route requests, manage tasks, and translate between messages conforming to different DTDs.

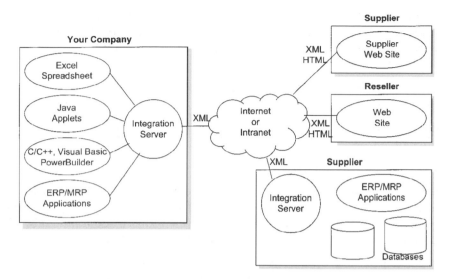

Exhibit 25.1.   Integration server connecting applications to applications and applications to Websites, over the Internet or an extranet, enabling the integration of business processes between trading partners.

A complete solution must also provide the integration between other internal or external systems. We'll refer to the application that implements such a solution as an "integration server." The integration server exposes a collection of integration services to XML-enabled clients. An integration service in the most generic sense is addressable by name, and it has a set of inputs and a set of outputs. The integration server provides the mapping of XML messages in and out of integration services.

Exhibit 25.1 illustrates how such a solution might support Web and application integration between multiple corporations based on an XML messaging mechanism. The environment provides a central integration point to support XML-enabled client applications and provides access to both internal and external resources.

XML AS THE RPC MESSAGE FORMAT

An application that requests a service of another application must issue a message to the other application. For the purposes of this discussion we'll refer to such a message as a Remote Procedure Call (RPC). An application issues an RPC by packaging a message, sending the message to the other application, and then waiting for the reply message.

Integration servers can combine the power of RPC middleware with the flexibility of XML to build a highly extensible, intercorporate integration system. XML RPC passes data as self-describing XML documents, unlike traditional RPC middleware systems that use a fixed, predefined message format. Formatting the messages using XML makes all B2B integration solutions highly flexible and extensible.

XML RPC performs all communications over HTTP using standard HTTP *get* and *post* operations. The contents of the XML RPC messages are standard Internet traffic: XML documents. XML RPC obviates the need to open firewalls to traditional middleware protocols such as DCOM or IIOP.

MAPPING BETWEEN DIFFERENT DTDS

The integration server must be able to map between different XML data formats, or DTDs. WIDL (Web Interface Definition Language)[1] provides such mapping capabilities and allows applications to communicate with each other via XML, regardless of the DTD they conform to.

WIDL provides document mapping by associating, or *binding*, certain document elements with application variables. Data bindings may be used to extract some or all of the information in an XML or HTML document. The following example illustrates the use of a WIDL binding with the XML document presented in the earlier example.

```
<OUTPUT-BINDING NAME= PurchaseOrderData >
<VALUE NAME= OrderNumber >doc.OrderNumber[0].text
</VALUE>
<VALUE NAME= SKU  DIM= 1 >doc.LineItem[].SKU[0].text
</VALUE>
</OUTPUT-BINDING>
```

An application would apply this binding to the XML purchase order document in the first example to map the order number and the list of SKU numbers to the variables *OrderNumber* and *SKU*. Only the variables defined by the WIDL binding are exposed to the application.

The variables within a WIDL binding abstract the application from the actual document reference, even from the XML data representation itself. An integration server would be able to apply similar bindings to a variety of XML formats to achieve the mapping between different DTDs.

Exhibit 25.2 illustrates the benefits of this capability. Here, industries and businesses have defined a variety of DTDs to which different RPC encodings conform. The interface defined with WIDL captures a superset of the services and data available through the DTDs. Although different client applications speak different XML encodings, the integration server is able to bridge these differences and to make the application universally accessible.

This approach enables different organizations to construct loosely coupled application integration schemes. One organization may want to estab-

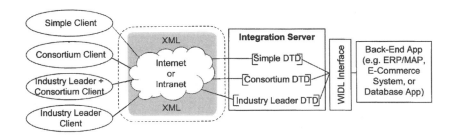

Exhibit 25.2. Using WIDL to make different XML messages interoperable.

lish electronic integration among many different partners. Each partner maintains electronic relationships with many other partners. It's extremely difficult for such a loose partnership organization to reach agreement on a single set of message formats. But XML DTD mapping bypasses the need to reach total agreement. Each organization can define its own DTD. An integration server would automatically resolve the differences and deliver information to an organization in the format that the organization requires.

EXPOSING APPLICATION SERVICES

Application services provide access to certain resources, which the integration server exposes to other XML RPC-based applications. The integration server decodes the XML RPC request, identifies the service requested by the RPC, and passes the request on to the service in a data format it understands. It then encodes the output of the service as a properly formatted XML RPC reply that the client is able to understand.

The application service provides the actual integration with internal or external resources, such as the Web, databases, EDI, or ERP systems. The implementation of a service, therefore, is completely abstracted from the message format. XML-based integration solutions actually XML-enable the systems they are integrating.

For example, an integration solution might support the direct integration of different ERP systems across the Internet. A manufacturer running SAP R/3 can integrate its procurement system with the order processing system at a supplier running Baan. The integration solution is implemented separately from the application systems. No modifications are required within the back-end ERP application systems.

In addition to providing a centralized switching system to support intercorporate communications, an integration server might also host business logic modules that tie the entire environment together or that add additional services to the integrated applications.

EXPOSING WEB SERVICES

An integration solution must also be able to leverage the vast quantities of information available on the Internet. It must provide unmanned access to Web resources, without a browser, and allow applications to integrate Web data and services. Programmatic access to the Web may also be referred to as *Web Automation*.

WIDL enables Web Automation by defining Application Programming Interfaces (APIs) to Web data and services. By using its data bindings, WIDL is able to extract data from fields in an HTML or XML document and map them to program variables. WIDL abstracts the application from the actual document references (that is, where the data being mapped actually exist in a page). Web Automation makes complex interactions with Web servers possible without requiring human intervention.

An integration server exposes Web services as regular integration services. With an XML RPC, client applications are able to invoke a Web service, provide a set of inputs, and receive a set of outputs. The client is abstracted from the actual implementation of the service and is not concerned whether data were derived from a Website, a local database, or remote ERP system.

AN INTEGRATION STRATEGY

Companies must be able to achieve application-to-application integration by leveraging existing investments in legacy and Web-based products and technologies. An integration server provides a transitional strategy for integrating the systems and processes of trading partners into the corporate infrastructure.

Let's look at an example. A manufacturer aims to integrate with a number of suppliers. If a supplier does not yet have a Web presence, it would be free to choose a Web-enabling technology that best suits its environment. By deploying an integration server, the manufacturer can incorporate its suppliers' Web services into its procurement process, for instance. To accomplish even tighter integration, the supplier could expose internal data by adding XML markup to its existing Web offering. The final step in achieving complete application-to-application integration occurs when a supplier also deploys an XML-enabled integration server.

CONCLUSION

Business-to-business integration delivers significant cost savings and operational efficiency through business process automation and just-in-time supply-chain management. Traditional EDI is cost prohibitive for most organizations, so the industry is turning to Internet-based B2B E-commerce. XML is a tremendous enabler. Using XML, applications can implement loosely coupled integration services that are flexible and extensible. But XML by itself will not provide automatic interoperability. Application integration requires infrastructure services to support reliable and secure performance. An integration server provides the infrastructure services that XML lacks.

The growth of electronic trading networks depends on access to diverse data and information sources that reside in various formats in electronic catalogs on the Web, legacy databases, EDI, or ERP systems. Suppliers who can provide solution which interoperate with multiple and diverse trading networks will become the dominant players in the electronic commerce arena. And their customers will become the earliest winners in the extended enterprise.

Author's Bio

Michael Blank *is a Senior Engineer at WebMethods, Inc., the leading provider of Web Automation and business-to-business integration solutions for the Global 2000.*

Prior to joining WebMethods, Blank was a founding member of the Web integration team at America Online, where he was instrumental in engineering www.aol.com, currently one of the most trafficked sites on the Web. With BDM Federal, he led some of the major reengineering efforts for the SEC's EDGAR electronic filing system. Blank holds a Master's degree in Computer Science from the College of William and Mary.

Notes

1. In September of 1997, WebMethods, Inc. submitted the original WIDL specification to the World Wide Web Consortium (W3C). In October the W3C acknowledged WIDL for its significance as an IDL and for its significance as a technology for programmatically accessing the Web. The W3C makes the submission available at the URL <http://www.w3.org/Submission/1997/15/Overview.html>.

Section V
Managing Internet Application Development

ALL IT MANAGERS MANAGE DEVELOPMENT PROJECTS. These have specific goals and objectives and require the use of various technologies. That's what this section is about — how to use some of these newfangled Web technologies.

As mentioned in the Preface, Internet development necessitates the use of the same techniques and methodologies as traditional IT development. While Internet development is the same as traditional development, for the most part, it's different enough that the differences warrant some attention.

Enabling databases on the Web is a whole other ball game, so we've included a brief primer in this section so you can see what your programmers are going to have to do to get that corporate database uploaded to the Web.

We've all heard of Java by this time and you're probably wondering whether or not it's worth exploring. In this section we include a chapter on developing and deploying server-side applications with Java so you can see what you're getting yourselves into if you decide to push ahead with Java development.

While we're all used to getting e-mail, management of it for the corporation is probably one of your new requirements. This, too, is included in this section.

When you were developing systems for internal use you didn't have to worry about folks from outside your country. Today's Internet sites had better be multilingual or your company will lose out in the competition for global dollars. In this section we'll learn how to do this as well as how to work for the various "masters" (i.e., marketing, legal, CEO, customer, supplier …) that Internet development fosters.

Building Websites requires us to honor the tenets of productivity and quality, which we cover in depth in this section, as well as the concepts of system integration.

Finally, this section will introduce a radically different approach to systems engineering (on and off the Web) that you really need to understand. Development Before the Fact (Chapters 30 to 33) is an approach to development that negates the necessity of programmers and requires almost no coding at all (take that, held-coded HTML).

Chapter 26

A System for Enterprise Web Production: Objectives and Requirements

Richard Petersen

THIS CHAPTER DISCUSSES THE OBJECTIVES AND REQUIREMENTS for a system for Enterprise Web Production, or EWP. The Web manager reading this chapter should find information that will help him or her to better analyze the organization's objectives for an EWP system, and to more accurately specify the technical requirements for such a system.

Many large firms spend tens of thousands of dollars to just to analyze and specify their Web production objectives and requirements. Other firms waste hundreds of thousands of dollars on inappropriate technology due to the lack of such an investigation, or an investigation that was driven more by the latest industry buzz than objective planning. It is hoped that this chapter will help the reader avoid such strategic errors.

What is Enterprise Web Production, and why is a system necessary to manage it? EWP is the underlying structure that supports and coordinates the myriad functions performed by the people who develop, test, edit, approve, and deploy any content relevant to one or more of an organization's internal and external Websites. It encompasses content management, application development, and workflow management. It touches not only all content that resides on a Web server, but also content that is related to the Web server, including dynamically accessed data in connected systems, business rules for personalization of the Web experience, and even any

0-8493-9987-4/00/$0.00+$.50
© 2000 by CRC Press LLC

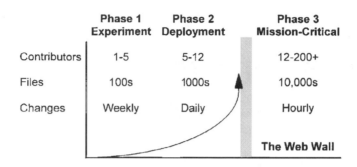

	Phase 1 Experiment	Phase 2 Deployment	Phase 3 Mission-Critical
Contributors	1-5	5-12	12-200+
Files	100s	1000s	10,000s
Changes	Weekly	Daily	Hourly
			The Web Wall

Exhibit 26.1. The stages of Enterprise Web Production.

---

non-Web content that plays a role in the development of the files deployed via the Web server.

Why is an EWP system necessary? As the Web grows in strategic importance to your organization, your operations will grow in terms of the number of contributors, the volume of content being managed, the types of content your site uses, and the systems with which your Website will interface. These factors may grow in a linear manner, but because they will all increase simultaneously they can create exponential complexity, and at worst, chaos (see Exhibit 26.1).

Many organizations trace their Web strategy through three stages: experiment, manageable deployment, and business-critical resource. It is the transition from the second to the third stage that mangers refer to as "the Web wall."

The mission-critical stage is the point where ad hoc communications and management processes no longer suffice, sequential project management gives way to parallel development, and bottom-line business objectives focus senior management attention on the performance and functionality of the organization's sites. The "Web wall" is also the point of breakdown for the Web team — adding more developers to the team won't help, because the problem is one of coordination, not manpower. Firms that have hit the "Web wall" do not lack talented Web developers; rather what's missing is a system to enable them to work concurrently and collaboratively, and with maximum efficiency.

OBJECTIVES FOR AN EWP SYSTEM

When organizations begin to implement an EWP system, they first define their objectives for their Web operations. In most cases, three general categories emerge: growth, efficiency, and quality. While these seem straightforward, defining them more precisely is the first step in establishing a robust specification for the EWP system and its supporting components.

Growth

At very large organizations, the EWP system must already accommodate simultaneous development by more than one hundred contributors, and the Web manager must be prepared for growth into thousands of contributors over time. In such an environment, the number of Web components will easily increase from several thousand to hundreds of thousands. Your organization may not yet be at that stage, but it is likely that even 20 contributors working concurrently will require robust process control to prevent chaos. When counting the number of contributors you expect to support, consider whether they are all working in a single location, multiple locations, or distributed across a number of remote access points. Also, don't forget to count outside contractors and agencies. They should also be supported by your system.

Perhaps the greatest challenge to the Web manager is the need to plan for extensibility. Which new languages, protocols, and APIs will be essential to your Web operations two years from today? Will your management process need to support XML DTDs or JavaBeans components? Further, will your EWP system scale beyond the production Web server and enable you to manage the application servers, databases, and other components of your entire Web operation?

Efficiency

Compared to growth, efficiency is a much less quantifiable objective. Most organizations only identify an efficiency problem when they discover their competitors have built much more sophisticated and functional Websites, or their Web team members have quit in frustration. Organizations that have achieved efficiency in their Web operations tend to have a number of common advantages:

- Empowered knowledge workers contribute Web content directly
- Established rules expedite Web workflow processes
- Administrative control maintains security and site integrity
- Regular operations are automated, saving the time of skilled workers

The clearest sign that a Web operation has achieved enterprise scale is that the number of contributors is greater than a small core Web team. Many organizations already consider most of their employees Web contributors. At a major software developer, product managers not only define product specifications, but also manage their online data sheets and technical information. At the same firm, the support team has improved end-user support by designing and updating its product support section. Site visitors receive better product information, more up-to-date FAQs, and the most recent product updates.

What is the core Web team doing while the contributors develop their components of the Website? They are supervising overall site operation and functionality. Are all components being produced with the appropriate look and feel? Is the site's search engine accurately guiding visitors to the correct information? Are localizations and expansions of the site proceeding according to plan? In a highly efficient Web operation, the EWP system allows the Web team to focus on site strategy by enabling knowledge workers to develop and test everyday content.

Most people involved in EWP are familiar with a workflow management issues. Developers with background in publishing understand editorial sign-off processes, and marketing professionals review materials regularly. Engineers have QA cycles and bug reporting systems. The EWP system workflow is likely to include components of all these processes, plus others that are unique to the Web space. What kind of workflow structure should the EWP system provide? Quite simply, *the one that maintains site quality and minimizes the time it takes for content to be approved and deployed*. A more detailed answer to this question will depend greatly on the nature of the organization and its business objectives for its Website.

Security is a primary concern for all Webmasters, and it is a large enough topic for a considerable number of books. However, it deserves mention in this chapter as it is a fundamental challenge to the Web production system. There are two basic concerns to the manager — how to prevent intentional or inadvertent corruption of site content, and how to recover the site once content has been corrupted. An EWP system that cannot address these two concerns is probably not worth investigating. Security is the one component of an EWP system where cutting corners can be disastrous.

Finally, the most obvious means of improving operational efficiency is automation of frequent operations. Among other functions, an EWP system should enable Web managers to easily monitor site activity, regularly deploy site updates, and automatically test site content for errors such as broken links, corrupted files, etc. A number of inexpensive tools provide these functions for small Websites, and experienced managers will use a combination of readily available tools and custom-built applications for enterprise-wide operations. A complete EWP system will comprise a combination of best-of-breed solutions, including standard tools, custom-developed applications, and hopefully, a comprehensive infrastructure.

Quality

Assuming the EWP provides the Web manager efficiency and growth, the final critical requirement for the system is to ensure that site content is improved as the site grows larger and is updated more frequently. A few measures of site quality are

- Site integrity
- Content accuracy
- Appropriate use of new technology
- Protection against disaster and disaster recovery

Site integrity means that the site's thousands of interrelated components interact correctly to provide every site visitor the intended experience. In the days of plain HTML, this meant checking for broken links and orphaned files. HTML remains the foundation of the Web, and most Webmasters have a number of favorite links checkers. However, as organizations adopt new types of content and link their Websites with combinations of application servers, testing site integrity becomes a much more complex operation. The only means to truly ensure site integrity is to enable all contributors to stage and fix their content in the context of the Website in real time, rather than waiting for a separate QA stage to identify problems.

Similarly, as the Website evolves from a collection of static text and images to a sophisticated application for the input and output of information, traditional content checks fail to provide a complete picture of the visitor's experience and potential areas of miscommunication. The editorial review process from print publication is useful for sites that have a limited size, are revised according to a regular schedule, and consist primarily of text and graphics similar to a print publication. However, leading-edge sites that communicate vital information to thousands of visitors daily have long outgrown the editorial model, and instead must depend to a much greater degree on the Web contributors to identify and correct content errors. This reinforces the requirement for immediate, in-context staging by all contributors.

Another trend in the growth of the Web is the greater diversity of content types that may be used to communicate with site visitors. While this is a boon to site designers, the implementation and testing of new technologies in the context of the Website can be a massive undertaking. How can an organization maintain the ongoing development of a Website comprising tens of thousands of files, while synchronously implementing a new technology in the same site? Without a rigorous means of parallel development, new development efforts would be based on content that rapidly becomes obsolete.

A critical concern for any organization is the recovery of content in the event of loss or corruption. A basic EWP system should enable recovery of any previous version of a file, much in the same manner that software tools and document management systems provide access to earlier versions of files. Due to the interrelated nature of Web content, a complete EWP system should provide access to saved versions of the entire site, with each site version available for review and recovery at any time. Unlike standalone documents, a single Web file is relatively useless. The Web team must be able to revert to a previous version of the site in its entirety.

REQUIREMENTS

Having drafted the objectives for your Web operation, you should develop a detailed specification for your particular requirements. You may find good ideas in industry publications about tools and products that are available. Keep two criteria at the top of your mind as you prioritize requirements: be sure to design a comprehensive system that can incorporate a combination of best-of-breed tools, and build a system based on your operations, not on vendor promises. The single most common mistake made by Web managers is selecting an "end-to-end" solution based on a number of "nice to have" capabilities, then discovering that it is incapable of integration with some of its "must have" tools.

Structure

How should you design the structure of your EWP system? The best starting point is a thorough analysis of your current operations. Your current operations are the best indicator of your requirements for development, review, testing, and deployment. Additionally, honestly identifying the trouble spots in your current processes will help you to better specify your EWP requirements. What bottlenecks do you hope to remove? What kinds of mistakes do you wish to prevent? What kind of information does the management team require?

Having looked at your current operations, consider your future plans. Do you hope to incorporate databases and legacy systems in your intranet or extranet? Will you build parallel versions of your Internet site in multiple languages for an international audience? Will you incorporate personalization, templating, traffic analysis, and other application servers into your site operations? Again, keep in mind that you may need to prioritize these plans, and predict the future of various technologies, from VRML to DHTML to XML.

You should require a high degree of configurability from your EWP system. How will workflow and administrative control functions be performed? Will other systems be tightly integrated, or will there be an awkward handoff between Web operations and other functions? Will configuration be based on standard technologies, or will it require expensive consulting for implementation and ongoing maintenance?

Open Solutions

These questions lead to one of the fundamental conclusions of this chapter: *an EWP solution must provide an open structure to support your on-*

going requirements. What is an open EWP system? Essentially, it is one that can answer "yes" to the following questions:

- Does the system allow contributors to use any tools on any client platform?
- Does the system manage any kind of file, without parsing or tagging?
- Does the system maintain and present content in a file system structure?
- Can the system be configured according to standard tools and scripts?

The most obvious advantage of an EWP system that meets these requirements is that you and your contributors will not have to give up any tools or platforms as you implement the EWP structure. The tools you use today, and those you will use tomorrow to manage and deploy Web content will continue to work. For enterprise-wide applications, it is imperative that Web contributors be able to use their tools of choice for the development and testing of Web content.

Similarly, your Website is most likely already connected to a number of systems and databases. As your objectives expand, will your EWP system facilitate the expanded connectivity of your Website, or will it impede your integration of critical systems to your Website? An open EWP system is the most secure means of protecting yourself against future compatibility problems.

Scalability, Performance, and Reliability

Ironically, some basic enterprise-system benchmarks can be difficult to specify and measure in solutions designed for Web production. When measuring system scalability, consider whether you are loading the production server or the development environment. Does the site enjoy very heavy traffic? If so, you will require a highly scalable, load-balanced production server operation. On the other hand, is your problem one of too many simultaneous developers? If so, you may have to measure the performance of your development environment as hundreds of clients simultaneously access, modify, and stage content on it.

Even an analysis of site size can be confusing. Cover all the bases. Can the EWP system manage tens of thousands of files in RAID arrays containing tens of gigabytes of data? Does your site have particularly disproportionate components such as extensive CGI or server-side scripting, or single directories containing tens of thousands of image files? If so, you will need to test these particular requirements as well.

Of course, you require high performance for site visitors and a standard file system structure for content on the production Web server is the surest means of ensuring this. However, performance is also an issue for those contributors who spend their working hours accessing, modifying, and staging Web content. They may be working on a high-speed LAN or accessing the EWP system from a remote location. Again, consider your operations and define your performance requirements accordingly.

Among enterprise systems, reliability and availability are critical points of comparison, and in Enterprise Web Production they are equally critical. What is the cost of one hour's downtime to your Web development? Looking "under the hood" at the design of an EWP system can help illuminate its reliability. Are operations transactional or could clients fail to communicate with the server? Is the server design multithreaded or do sequential system operations place user operations in a queue? Answering these questions will help you evaluate a system's ability to provide constant support for 24×7 Web development.

Ease of Use

If a solution's greatest advantage is that "you don't have to understand the structure of your Website to manage it" or "you don't have to understand HTML to author Web content," you should look carefully at how this "ease-of-use" fits with your EWP requirements. The truth is that nontechnical users have long had templates and WYSIWYG tools, and site managers have a variety of site mapping and management tools to choose from.

What is more critical to administrators and contributors is ready access to Web content and information about the site. Ease-of-use for an EWP system means that users can stage and share content through an intelligible interface and a system interaction that parallels their natural work processes. The tools they use to develop and test content must be supported; and again, if the system is an open one, they will have their choice of tools at their disposal.

Advanced users will similarly want the power to access and modify content, and they may require access through sophisticated tools that run from a command-line interface. Requiring programmers and advanced users to perform all their work through a GUI may be far less convenient than direct file system access.

While ease-of-use is critical to Web developers, it is also imperative that the EWP system minimize the effort required for the Web management team to do its job. Managers need to monitor system activity, test content, assign tasks, and recover content in a straightforward manner through the EWP system. By providing ready access to virtually any kind of system information and administrative functions, the EWP system can greatly improve the efficiency of the complete operation.

Security

Once again, in this brief chapter it is not possible to comprehensively discuss the details of a Web content security policy. However, your requirements for an EWP system should address the following issues:

- What is your disaster recovery policy and procedure?
- How will you control access to prevent accidental or intentional disruption?
- Can your deployment process be automated and safe?

Like many IS contingencies, disaster recovery in Web operations is not a question of "if" but "when." Minor errors such as lost or corrupted files will occur on a regular basis, so file-specific versioning and recovery should be an everyday function of your EWP system. On a larger scale, the only means of ensuring recovery in the event of a massive site corruption is to perform frequent, regular backups of the entire site. This process should be easy, automated, and comprehensive to ensure that when disaster strikes you can recover a recent, complete version of your entire site in a few minutes. The specification of an EWP system should plan on this kind of disaster happening and detail a testable process for immediate recovery.

The need for recovery is greatly reduced if your EWP system supports the organization's rules for access control, password protection, and group permissions. The EWP system should complement the security policies of your network operating system with additional functionality, rather than replacing it wholesale. File access permissions, group memberships, and passwords should be respected. Additionally, remote logins may need to be encrypted, firewall policies should be respected, and sensitive content may require encryption for secure transport over the Internet.

Deployment is a key security point, as it is the stage where problems are most painfully public. Any production server residing outside a firewall is exposed to danger. Continual monitoring of the production server will identify problems, and a rapid, secure deployment process can ensure that any corruption is immediately resolved. Of course, most deployment takes place over unsecured Internet connections, so once again encryption may be necessary. Automated deployment can be configured to perform basic checks to ensure that inappropriate content is not deployed from the production environment.

CONCLUSION

As your organization's Web production grows more extensive and incorporates a greater number of contributors, you will find a greater need for a robust structure in which those contributors can collaborate and coordinate their efforts. That is the heart of Enterprise Web Production. You will find that there are an infinite number of possible requirements to prepare for, and your most difficult task will be to prioritize them correctly. If you select an open, scalable system that fits your requirements and workflow, you are likely to develop a successful plan and provide your organization a foundation for a successful Web operation.

Author's Bio

Richard Petersen *is the manager of the Customer Marketing Group at Interwoven, Inc., the leading provider of systems for Enterprise Web Production. Interwoven's premier product, TeamSite, is used by Fortune 1000 firms such as FedEx, Ford Motor Co., and First Union Bank, as well as high-technology companies such as Bay Networks, Symantec, and GeoCities. He has helped these and other companies define their Web production requirements and better understand the advantages of TeamSite in Enterprise Web Production.*

Petersen has previously worked as a product manager at Insignia Solutions, where he managed development, localization, and distribution of compatibility solutions for the Macintosh, UNIX, Windows 95, and Windows NT platforms in the Asia–Pacific and Latin American regions. He holds a B.A. with high honors in Linguistics from Michigan State University and an M.B.A. from the Haas School of Business at the University of California, Berkeley.

Chapter 27
Developing and Deploying Server-Side Application with Java

Madison Cloutier

JAVA'S ORIGINAL POPULARITY WAS ITS ABILITY TO ENHANCE CLIENT-SIDE INTERNET BROWSERS, but developers have discovered that it can bring even greater business benefits to the development and deployment of server-side applications. There is no disputing Java's growing popularity as a server-side programming language and platform. IS shops worldwide are moving to Java for server-side applications because it solves the very real problem of building applications that run across several different operating systems, and Java offers some genuine programming efficiencies which helps with two ever-present issues: development productivity and software quality.

In this chapter we will look at some of the key issues surrounding the development and deployment of server-side Java applications. The focus is on demanding business-critical, server-hosted applications that are driving the Internet, intranet, and extranet sites for E-commerce and Net-business. First we will look at the benefits and some shortcomings of using Java on the server-side application development. We will then review the characteristics and requirements of server-side applications. Next we will look at the development issues and key decisions you will have to make. Finally, we will look at the deployment issues associated with moving server-side Java applications into enterprise production.

BENEFITS OF USING JAVA FOR SERVER-SIDE APPLICATIONS

While the market hype and platform-independent nature of Java will cause an IS shop to take a closer look at this new programming environment, it is its development efficiencies that is driving its rapid adoption as a server-side application programming language. Some IS shops have reported up to 10 times productivity gains using Java over C++. This is easily

0-8493-9987-4/00/$0.00+$.50
© 2000 by CRC Press LLC

understandable in light of the fact that a majority of the problems program-mers encountered with C++ deal with memory management, which is auto-matically taken care of by Java. Java's automatic memory and easy thread management means programmers can create an application faster and with fewer bugs. Because the syntax of Java is similar to C++ programmers can migrate to it with some ease and confidence. Collectively, this makes Java an excellent language for building the new generation of server-side net-enabled applications.

A key benefit of Java is that the language is based on a pure object model which enforces pure object-oriented programming techniques. Unlike C++, which supports object-oriented programming but does not enforce it, Java programmers can develop higher quality software because they cannot cir-cumvent the object model. This makes applications easier to test, debug, and maintain over time. Another benefit of the pure object model is that programmers will find it easier to use existing components and frame-works (which we will talk about shortly) encouraging software reuse which contributes to higher development productivity.

Another aspect of Java that contributes to programming efficiencies is the notion that development and deployment is decoupled (Exhibit 27.1). This is the fundamental basis for Java's "Write Once, Run Anywhere" ben-efit. Java source code can be quickly compiled into platform-independent "bytecode" classes and executed immediately, using an interpreter, which can make the edit-compile test cycle very short. Once the program has been functionally tested and is ready for production deployment, the plat-form-independent bytecode can be easily moved onto the appropriate server platform for execution. This means Java is both a rapid application development (RAD) language and a deployment language. By decoupling development and deployment, programmers can stay focused on the fea-tures, functionality, and capabilities of the application during develop-ment, and at deployment time deal with the performance and throughput issues of the application on the targeted server platform.

JAVA SHORTCOMINGS

Even though there are a number of real and tangible benefits to using Java for server-side application development there are some shortcomings you will need to take into consideration. Performance is usually the first criti-cism raised against using Java on the server. While it is true that bytecode interpreters cannot deliver the performance necessary for demanding serv-er-side applications, advanced just-in-time compilers and optimizing native Java deployment compilers are becoming available that allow Java applica-tions to execute at the performance levels of C++ applications.

Java standards and its uncertain future are other issues that critics will raise. It is important to remember that there are two elements to Java: Java,

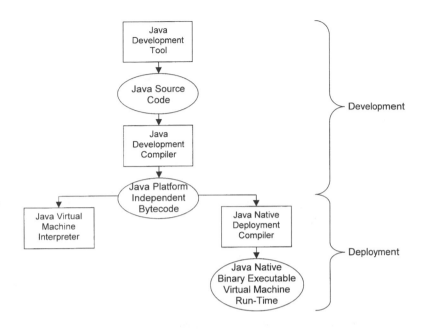

Exhibit 27.1. Decoupling development and deployment.

the platform, and Java, the language. Where Sun, Microsoft, and others battle over the Java platform especially in regards to the desktop, Java, the language, is stable. The idea of 100 percent compatibility across all client platforms may never be truly achieved; however, it is clear that there can be high compatibility of the Java language across server platforms. Using Java as a programming language, along with good object-oriented application design and architecture, will allow for a level of cross-platform compatibility higher than any previous programming language. Because of the industry momentum behind Java, the standards issue will be resolved in time and Java is destined to surpass Cobol, C++, and Visual Basic in popularity and usage.

Java development tools are currently immature compared to development tools for the more established languages, and the availability of quality components and frameworks are limited today. However, the industry acceptance of Java is strong and many of these shortcomings are being addressed because the language provides long -term benefits for the software industry.

We should note here that Java by itself is not a silver bullet. In order to achieve the full benefits of Java, IS shops must develop competencies in object-oriented design and programming along with other modern software engineering practices.

SERVER-SIDE APPLICATION REQUIREMENTS

Developers who are familiar with client/server systems will already know that the characteristics and requirements of client-side and server-side applications are different. In a typical client/server system, the client handles the graphical user interface (GUI), the server contains the data, and the application logic is spread across the two. The Internet is driving a trend toward multitier client/server systems which introduces the concept of application servers. In a typical multitier client/server system, the client handles the GUI, the database server contains the data, and the application server contains the application logic. An Internet multitier client/server architecture also introduces other types of servers such as HTTP servers and connection servers. We should briefly review the differences between client-side and server-side applications because we will need to consider these differences as we address the Java development and deployment issues.

In client/server environments, the client typically handles the GUI for such things as input forms and information retrieval. In a Java-based system this usually involves the execution of small Java "applets" which are downloaded from a server to the client as needed. Client-side Java applets support a single user on a single computer typically containing a single CPU. Java applets are usually updated "passively," meaning that should an input form or information retrieval display change, a new applet can be downloaded the next time the client accesses the particular application server. The application availability on a single client is not critical because only one user is affected should there be a problem. Because there are an array of different client platforms accessing Internet servers, Java applets need to be represented as bytecode, the platform-independent code that allows the applet to execute on any platform with a Java Virtual Machine (JVM)-enabled browser. The Java promise of "Write Once, Run Anywhere" has not been fully realized on the client side because of the different implementations of JVMs on the different client platforms used on the Internet, especially in the way GUI functions are handled. However, when you are dealing with a known client base as in intranet/extranet environments Java can be highly beneficial for client-side applications.

The servers are the real workhorses of the Internet, intranets, and extranets. This is where the processing logic is executed for business-critical E-commerce and Net-business applications. These are typically sophisticated and demanding applications that must support a large number of users simultaneously. Availability is critical because applications must be accessible 24×7×365. This requires "hot" application updates, or the ability to update an application without having to stop, reload, and restart. Large-scale server applications will typically execute on hardware that contains multiple processors or a cluster of processors. In some cases multiple applications may be running on a single piece of hardware requiring the ability to performance tune and manage them on an application-specific basis. Even though it may be desirable to deploy server-side Java applications as platform-independent bytecode, the need for execution, performance, and manageability will typically overshadow portability once the application is put into production. Because server-side applications usually do not require GUI support, the notion of "Write Once, Run Anywhere" is more realistic, assuming your applications are properly designed and developed.

DEVELOPING SERVER-SIDE APPLICATIONS WITH JAVA

Your first major decision will be choosing a server-side development strategy from an array of competing APIs, middleware, and architectural approaches. Because of the object-oriented nature of Java, the notion of acquiring existing frameworks and/or components as a starting point for custom applications is a realistic approach. Using existing software can provide significant benefits to an IS shop by reducing in-house development efforts and risks while improving application quality and flexibility.

For larger applications the selection of middleware will be critical. The middleware framework will become your strategic infrastructure responsible for connecting clients, databases, application servers, and transaction processors. There are currently three major connection models, as shown in Exhibit 27.2:

1. CORBA (Common Object Request Broker Architecture) — the industry standard for connecting heterogeneous systems.
2. RMI (Remote Method Invocation) — the Java standard for connecting Java-based systems.
3. COM (Component Object Model) — the Microsoft standard for connecting Windows-based systems.

There are multiple existing middleware products available that support one or more connection models. In addition, most of the new generation of

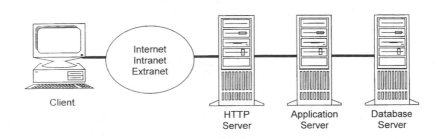

Exhibit 27.2. Typical multitier environment.

middleware products also provide database connectivity, transaction processing, security, and other infrastructural support. The supported features and capabilities of these middleware products vary considerably and you will need to thoroughly understand which are important to your overall strategy and application plans. Some of these products are completely written in Java such as WebLogic's Tanga, Visigenic's Inprise, or Novera Epic. Others such as Progress Apptivity or Netscape's Kiva are primarily written in C/C++ with a Java interface layer. Your ultimate decision should be based on fundamental business reasons such as strategic fit, features and capabilities, support and pricing. However, Java-based frameworks appear to provide better long-term flexibility.

After deciding the middleware infrastructure strategy, your application strategy will need to be addressed. As with middleware strategy, you should seriously consider existing application components and frameworks. This will allow you to acquire base capabilities and then develop only the specialized capabilities you need. There are currently two major competing component models on which Java frameworks are being built: Enterprise Java Beans (EJB) from Sun and Distributed Component Object Model (DCOM) from Microsoft. Where DCOM has been around somewhat longer and is mature, it currently only works with Microsoft Windows. EJB is gaining industry support and has a good chance of becoming the predominant model for heterogeneous enterprise environments because of its more open nature. Application frameworks provide an environment in which components interact to create a complete application. At some point in the future, components from different vendors may be easily integrated with each other. Currently, most components are part of an existing application framework. The most ambitious application framework to date is the IBM San Francisco project that is building an extensible framework for building and deploying serious enterprise business systems.

A key element of your development strategy will be your decision for platform independence vs. platform-specific development. Even though Java is touted as a platform-independent development environment, it is possible to design and develop server applications which are not platform independent. If your strategic objective is to maintain platform independence of your applications, use caution in your use of special operating systems services provided by platform vendors because by doing so you may be tying yourself to a specific server platform and lose future deployment flexibility.

You will find a number of Java development tools to choose from. Most include a rapid application development (RAD) environment which allows for the quick development of Java code and components. Currently, the popular tools include: Sun's JavaWork Shop, Inprise JBuilder, Microsoft Visual J++, IBM VisualAge for Java, and Symantec's Visual Cafe. Your choice of development tool should be made after other strategic development issues have been addressed and decided. It will not be uncommon for an IS group to use multiple development tools.

DEPLOYING SERVER-SIDE APPLICATIONS WITH JAVA

Deploying sophisticated server-side applications involve a whole new set of problems in the areas of distribution, updating, testing, performance tuning, and real-time system management, whether they are written in Java or some other language. In the Java world there are two options to executing deployed bytecode; one is based on interpreter technology, the other on native deployment compilation.

The standard Java virtual machine implementation works by interpreting bytecode that is generated off-line by a Java development compiler. The execution speed of the Java Development Kit interpreter correlates closely with the number of bytecode instructions executed. This clearly limits execution performance, making interpreters good for RAD and small applications but unsuitable for deploying demanding server-side applications. Currently, all major server vendors offer a Java interpreter on their platforms.

Just-In-Time (JIT) compilers are a step up from interpreters. They are virtual machine subsystems that convert byte code to native code on the fly during execution. Code optimization is done rapidly and only on a subsection of code at a time. While this can enhance the performance of small applications, the speed-up is limited on larger, more demanding programs. JITs vary in performance and scalability, but even the best ones are slower than comparably coded C++ server applications. Most major server vendors offer a JIT on their platforms.

A step up from JITs are smart interpreters which utilize "dynamic adaptive" techniques that convert only selected portions of the bytecode into optimized native code based on execution patterns. The idea is to begin the execution of bytecode in an interpreted mode, monitoring the execution to find frequently executed code segments or "hotspots," converting these hotspots into optimized native code and then patching them into the system. Where this approach can, in theory, provide high-performance execution for certain types of Java applications, it is unproven in demanding server-side applications. Because of the monitoring and optimization overhead, this approach requires additional computer resources during application execution, making it unsuitable for CPU-intensive systems. A bigger concern for business-critical systems is that this approach makes it extremely difficult, if not impossible, to fully certify a system or to reproduce the exact circumstances when a bug occurs. This is due to the fact that "on-the-fly" changes are automatically being patched into the system during execution. Sun has been the primary proponent of the "dynamic adaptive" approach via the marketing of its Hot Spot compiler, and currently only a few server platform vendors have announced their intention to offer this type of advanced interpreter.

The interpreter approach and its variations (i.e., JITs and Dynamic Adaptive) are not suitable run-time architectures for the demanding server-side Java applications which will be required to scale for high throughput. This approach also complicates the management of enterprise applications by separating the application from the run-time, thus adding another variable to version control. An alternative approach is to use native compilation that allows the Java Virtual Machine and run-time to be embedded in the applications as part of a self-contained native executable. This approach can significantly enhance execution performance, reliability, and manageability.

There are different flavors of Java native compilers, but in all cases they allow you to create a native executable off-line prior to the application execution. The key advantage of this is the fact that extensive performance optimization can be performed prior to execution, thus enhancing performance and reliability. Also, application-specific performance tuning can be accomplished more easily because the virtual machine run-time is part of the application executable.

Standard native Java compilers will generate binary executables directly from Java source code. If you have access to all the source code associated with your application and do not care about platform independence you can consider this approach. However, it is more likely that you will not have all the source code and some level of platform independence will be important. In this situation a "native deployment compiler" will be more appropriate because it will allow you to generate binary executables directly from previously generated bytecode.

There is also the notion of "closed" and "opened" native compilers. "Closed" or static native compilers, as they are usually referred to, do not allow the binary executables to be modified once they have been generated. In some cases this is fine, but if you need to perform "hot updates" to high-availability applications you will need an "open" native compiler. An "open" native compiler allows the generation of native DLLs (or shared libraries for UNIX) from bytecode off-line which can then be dynamically loaded into a running application. This is sometimes referred to as "Ahead-Of-Time" compilation. If you are required to dynamically update a running application directly with bytecode, the executable will need access to a Java interpreter which a full "open" native compiler and run-time environment support.

The ultimate Java deployment architecture for demanding server-side Java applications is an full "open" native deployment compiler and run-

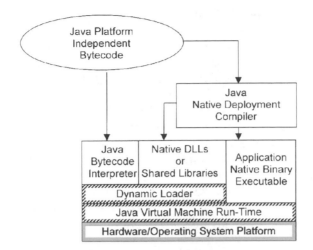

Exhibit 27.3. Full "open" native deployment compiler and run-time architecture.

time environment as shown in Exhibit 27.3. A key benefit of such an architecture is support for "programming in the large," or the ability to rapidly make safe changes to high-availability systems. This allows developers to better manage and evolve sophisticated systems. Using RAD approaches, developers can test new application features and capabilities in bytecode form and safely commit them to the system as native code as they become stable. This approach allows high performance and throughput to be maintained in high-availability enterprise systems during constant modifications. Commercially available full "open" native deployment compilers for Java are available for all the major server platforms.

One final issue to address is that of Java application management. This is likely to become a growing problem for enterprise system administrators as the number of deployed Java applications increases. When evaluating and choosing your application deployment options, be sure to consider the application management aspects and how Java applications will be managed within your system management framework. Rapidly changing distributed server-side Internet/intranet/extranet applications, whether written in Java or some other language, will be a challenge to manage. Due to the object-oriented nature of Java, properly engineered Java applications should be easier to manage and it is inevitable that suitable Java management tools will appear over time.

CONCLUSION

There is no question that Java is here to stay. Developing and deploying server-side applications in Java is not completely unlike developing and deploying server-side applications in other languages, however, Java does provide some real benefits. It solves the problem of building applications that run across several different operating systems, and it offers genuine programming efficiencies, which helps development productivity and software quality. Because of the object-oriented nature of Java and its rapidly growing popularity there will be many opportunities available for you to acquire existing frameworks and components which will significantly reduce your overall development efforts and resource requirements, reduce risks, and improve time to market. As with most new software technologies you have probably dealt with in the past, use good business sense when planning your use of Java for business-critical server-side applications. Java represents a new paradigm for the software industry, so be sure you have appropriate development and deployment strategies in place. A pilot project or two will prove invaluable. Good luck.

Author's Bio

Madison Cloutier has more than 23 years experience in the software industry. He has held technical, marketing, and business executive positions in Fortune 500 and start-up companies. Cloutier is currently the vice president of marketing at Tower Technology Corporation, a leading provider of technology, products, and services targeted at the enterprise use of Java. Prior to Tower, he was president of a management consulting firm helping an international clientele develop competitive advantage through information technology. Prior to that, Cloutier spent over a decade developing, marketing, and deploying business-critical systems used in the airline and travel industry. He has a computer science degree augmented by broad real-world experience in the software industry. At Tower, Cloutier has helped pioneer the use of object-oriented technologies in enterprise systems development, and more recently for Internet/intranet/extranet development.

Chapter 28
A Primer on Quality and Productivity for Internet Developers

Jessica Keyes

IN TRACY KIDDER'S BOOK, *SOUL OF A NEW MACHINE,* he details the riveting story of a project conducted at breakneck speed, and under incredible pressure. Driven by pure adrenaline, the team members soon became obsessed with trying to achieve the impossible. For more than a year, they gave up their nights and weekends — in the end logging nearly 100 hours a week each! Somewhere buried in the midst of Kidder's prose we find that at the end of this project the entire staff quit. Not just one or two of them, but every single one!

The Information Systems (IS) field is ripe with stories such as this one. Software development projects are usually complex and often mission critical. As a result the pressure on staff to produce is great. And sometimes, as in the Kidder example, even with success comes failure.

Successful software development projects (i.e., get the product done on time — and *not* lose staff members) have something in common. Each of these projects, in some way, shape, or form, followed one or more principles of quality and productivity. This chapter focuses on "expert" advice that can be used to achieve this ideal.

Productivity is extremely important to Hewlett-Packard because HP relies on new product development to maintain its competitive strength. HP introduces an average of one new product every business day. Some 70 percent of HP's engineers are involved in software development. Half of all R&D projects are exclusively devoted to software development.

It was this significant investment in software development that prompted HP's president to issue a challenge to achieve a10-fold improvement in software quality within 5 years. He also asked that new product development time be reduced by 50 percent.

0-8493-9987-4/00/$0.00+$.50
© 2000 by CRC Press LLC

An early outgrowth of this response was a process assessment program called Software Quality and Productivity Analysis (SQPA), according to SQPA team member Barbara Zimmer.[1] A few words about the company's general organization and history will help put the discussion in context.

HP's corporate structure is built on many different divisions or operations which operate more or less autonomously. These separate entities are organized into various groups based on product types. At the top levels of the hierarchy are product group sectors and, finally, corporate management.

At the entity level, a division or operation will normally include manufacturing, marketing, and administrative functions as well as a research and development laboratory. The lab manager, who reports directly to the division manager, will have responsibility for several section managers, who in turn oversee project managers. The labs vary greatly in size, ranging from 50 to 150 personnel.

The roots of the current software quality and productivity effort are in the Corporate Software Quality Council that grew out of a task force which was initiated in 1983. The council set some software development guidelines involving the use of Total Quality Control methods.

SQPA's original charter was based on the need to leverage HP's software development efforts in response to the evolution from a total technological approach, to software development, to one that includes consideration of quality and productivity with special emphasis on culture, change agents, methodologies, and human factors.

SQPA's major objective is to develop and implement a software engineering review process and a software management decision support system. Its tactic is to assess the state of each HP lab and draw comparisons with other HP labs and the rest of the industry. It focuses on eight key areas which impact software development:

- Methodologies
- Staff Variables
- Project Management and Control
- Programming Environment
- Tools
- Defect Prevention and Removal
- Physical Environment
- Measurement

After measuring variables in each of these categories, the program identifies strengths and weaknesses, pinpoints areas for improvement, makes recommendations, and provides follow-up measures to show progress over time. In the process, a quantitative and qualitative baseline of key factors impacting software development is established.

The SQPA methodology is based on a set of standardized questions which have been checked for validity and reliability. The questionnaire has continued to evolve, reflecting HP cultural anomalies, changes in technology, and HP management priorities, and incorporating what has been learned through SQPA team experience.

The SQPA process begins with a request from a lab, and a subsequent scheduling and information exchange. After the request the lab will generally be asked for demographic data, organization charts, and product descriptions. The formal interviews with lab and section managers, a representative sample of project managers, productivity and quality managers (if appropriate), and a representative sample of engineers take place next, usually over 2 days, depending upon the size of the lab. One engineer from the SQPA team conducts each 1- to 2-hour interview using the questionnaires discussed above.

After the interviews, the SQPA team does an analysis, including a statistical comparison with HP and industry data and a narrative summary of key findings. This is presented within a day or two to the R&D manager and anyone else he or she invites. The 2-hour presentation consists of a description of strengths, constraints, and weaknesses, graphs comparing the lab with HP and the industry in the eight key measurement areas, and recommendations for improvement. It is important that this immediate feedback session be interactive to clarify any misinformation or misperceptions and prepare managers for the written report to follow.

Over the next 3 to 4 weeks, the SQPA team confers on quantitative and verbal responses and consults with experts as appropriate to diagnose or prescribe specific activities. The final results are summarized in a formal written report containing graphs, text, and statistics and is sent to the R&D manager. The level of detail in the report can provide sufficient information on which to base specific improvement strategies. Finally, the database containing all the HP data collected to date is updated to allow for HP-wide trend analysis.

The last step in the SQPA process is follow-up analysis to measure and report changes and improvements, a step which normally takes place a year to 18 months later.

THE SEARCH FOR QUALITY

Although quality and productivity are foremost on the minds of management, few understand as well as HP how to correlate the tenets of quality to the process of information systems.

Total Quality Management, or TQM as it has come to be known, was actually born as a result of a loss of competitive edge to countries such as Japan. In fact, the father of TQM, W.E. Deming, finding no forum for his radical new ideas on quality in the U.S., found eager listeners in Japan. Today, Deming's ideas on quality are considered the basis for all work on quality in this country as well as Japan.

Deming's studies were only the start of a flood of research in the field. For example, Y.K. Shetty, a professor of management at Utah State University's College of Business and the coeditor of *The Quest for Competiveness* (Quorum Books, 1991), suggests that even though most corporate executives believe that quality and productivity are the most critical issues facing American business, many do not know how to achieve it. Particularly in the area of IS.

Essentially, IS quality can be defined as software that exhibits the absence of flaws and the presence of value. At the current time, over 70 percent of the software development budget is spent on "maintenance." The art of detecting bugs and errors of ommission or commission, as well as an accurate interpretation and implementation of user requirements, is still an aspiration seemingly just beyond the reach of many software engineering departments.

According to Tom DeMarco, author of *Software Systems Development* published by Yourdon Press, in 1984 15 percent of all software projects with more than 100,000 lines of code failed to deliver value. And in 1989, according to Capers Jones,[2] of all software projects with over 64,000 lines of code, 25 percent failed to deliver anything; 60 percent were significantly over budget and behind schedule, and only 1 percent finished on time, on budget, and met user requirements.

Since early TQM programs were largely manufacturing oriented, Information System (IS) researchers, academicians, and consulting firms were required to interpret and extrapolate TQM tenets and create quality paradigms that could be used to significant advantage. As a result, there is no single TQM methodology in use today that has garnered wholesale industry acceptance. All of these methodologies, however, are based on TQM tenets and all, if used properly, will provide organizations with a clear path towards better quality in their systems.

Be warned though, one size does not fit all. In report by Ernst & Young,[3] the notion was challenged that quality programs were universally beneficial for all organizations. Based on a study of 584 firms in North America, Japan, and Germany, the report noted that Total Quality Management practices are not generic. What works for some organizations may well turn out to be detrimental to the performance of others.

Instituting a quality program requires a careful study of techniques available as well as being applicable to the organization in question. While IS/Analyzer can't tailor a specific quality program for each of our readers, what we can offer is a bird's eye view of "tried and true" quality techniques.

THE COMPONENTS OF PRODUCTIVITY AND QUALITY

Productivity is indelibly linked to the concepts of quality although sometimes achieving both becomes something of a Catch-22 situation.

Most systems folks would agree with the notion that the more code a programmer churns out the more productive he or she is. However, introducing quality to the mix might, in fact, serve to reduce the amount of code a programmer can produce in a day. But so too would system complexity. That is, a real-time missile launch system, for example, demonstrates a much higher level of complexity than a batch Accounts Payable system. Therefore, the number of lines of code produced daily in the missile system would more than likely be lower than in the A/P system. Does that make the programming staff working on the missile system less productive?

Productivity is truly a quantitative term. It's insufficient to claim a percentage increase in productivity without having an appropriate method of measuring that increase.

It's also insufficient to measure productivity without taking into account the many factors affecting productivity, such as system complexity and addition of quality monitoring. But there are other more subtle factors affecting productivity that unfortunately receive little attention but pack a big punch.

The factors affecting software engineering productivity and quality fall into three broad categories: methodology, measurement, and nontechnical factors or "peopleware."

Although many organizations tackle each of these independently, in fact, they are indelibly intertwined. Where methodology provides the "roadmap" the organization will use in developing its systems, metrics provide the gauge used to measure mileage. Finally, peopleware ensures that everybody arrives on time, well-rested, and in good spirits. Ultimately, in the productivity game, the whole is indeed greater than the sum of its parts.

A CHOICE OF METHODOLOGIES

It probably comes as no surprise that the majority of software development shops are using no discernable methodology. Those that do dabble are, for the most part, divided into two camps: those that practice "safe computing" or the tried and true structured techniques and those that carry the information engineering banner. Then there are the explorers who have ventured forth into the unchartered territory of object-oriented methodologies.

Structured methodology is really a series of competing methodologies, all of which have their devotees. Notable among these variations are Gane-Sarson, DeMarco-Yourdon, and the Warnier-Orr (or LBMS) approach.

Structured methodology is probably the most widely used of all methodologies, it's also the most misunderstood since it has long since been pronounced "dead." Interestingly, it continues to thrive and even evolve. Where the 1970s version of structured methodology provided only data flow diagramming (DFD) as a tool, today's version has evolved to deal effectively with real-time systems by adding control flows and control processes to the DFD as well as adding an entirely new modeling tool — the state transition diagram. But as Ed Yourdon[4] admits, even the best methodologies don't guarantee the technical success of most systems development projects and technical success can't save a project from the larger issues of corporate politics in these whirligig days of mergers and downsizings.

Information Engineering (IE) was born out of the desire to accommodate software development to this rapid-fire pace of change. In 1981 James Martin and Clive Finkelstein published their now seminal work in the area. *Information Engineering*[5] paved the way for a whole new way of thinking about software development.

Long since gone their separate ways, Martin and Finkelstein are now the forebears of two separate IE movements. The first variant uses the existing functions of an organization as the starting point, data needed by the functions are then defined. In this DP variant, business knowledge is incorporated from users often by interview, but significantly there is subjective interpretation of the users' input by DP personnel. This is sometimes referred to as application IE, or DP-driven IE. It is supported by many of the IE software products on the market today.

The second variant starts with the strategic plans set by management at all levels of an organization. From these plans are defined the data, and later the functions, needed to support those plans. This approach is more user-driven than the DP variant and is referred to as enterprise Information Engineering, or business-driven Information Engineering. It is defined, according to Clive Finkelstein,[6] as follows:

> Information Engineering is an integrated set of techniques, based on corporate strategic planning, which results in the analysis, design, and development of systems which support those plans exactly. Information Engineering is applied by managers and users with no knowledge of computers, but instead with an expert knowledge of their business

— in conjunction with expert systems which provide rapid feedback to management for refinement of the strategic plans.

But of all the methodologies on technologists' plates today, the object-oriented variety seems to garner the most interest — if the least use. OO methodologies are still quite new, and many do not address all the concerns of the IS analyst. Especially in the area of productivity and quality.

When Margaret Hamilton[7] was director of software development for NASA's Apollo and SkyLab projects at MIT during the late 1960s and early 1970s, she began an empirical analysis of the massive amounts of information generated by these critical missions. As a result of this analysis, Hamilton, a recipient of the Augusta Ada Lovelace award for Excellence in Computing, spearheaded an extensive effort to minimize software errors in future critical software projects. The result was the embryo of a theory of systems engineering and software development that, if used correctly, could be a way to eliminate the majority of errors in a system before it is implemented. Twenty years and much research later this embryonic theory has fully matured and is known as "Development Before the Fact."

Development Before the Fact is a paradigm that fosters productivity and reliability. According to Hamilton, we fix most systems after the system has been implemented. This, in fact, is the reason our maintenance budgets often exceed our development budgets. Development Before the Fact is a way to make sure that errors are eliminated before the system is delivered.

Preventative development under the Development Before the Fact scenario requires that systems, whether they be in the area of simulation, missile systems, mission planning, integrated computer-aided manufacturing, battlefield management systems, communications, or even worldwide banking funds transfer, be created, building-block fashion, on a foundation of reusability and integration.

Development Before the Fact enables developers to create blocks of error-free code that can be continually reused. The best part of it is that these error-free blocks can be integrated to create new and increasingly more complex systems. Unfortunately, today's object-oriented paradigm concerns itself with the reusable components only. But what about the mechanisms that integrate these blocks of code? The Development Before the Fact paradigm is a software methodology that ensures that these mechanisms, or the infrastructure of the system under construction, is reliable and error-free as well.

MCDONNELL DOUGLAS

Creating a robust design environment is not easy under any circumstances. But when the company is McDonnell Douglas and the target is commercial as well as military avionic systems, the task is particularly complex.

But this was the task that Ed Lanigan,[8] then Electronics Unit Chief at Mc-Donnnell Douglas, chose to undertake. Lanigan wanted a set of methodologies and tools that would allow McDonnell Douglas to smoothly evolve all the avionic systems from the customer requirement to the delivery of the product. With that goal in mind the team at McDonnell Douglas set out to find a way to allow the marriage of technology with the philosophy of reliability and traceability.

What initially attracted McDonnell Douglas to the Development Before the Fact approach, according to Lanigan, was that its approach was very similar to the one that electronic engineers use. That is, you develop low-level reliable components and then you build your reliable systems based upon those component structures.

What also attracted Lanigan was that the Development Before the Fact methodology was rooted firmly on an object-oriented infrastructure. But, according to Lanigan, Development Before the Fact goes several steps further.

Lanigan contends that the design approach from the onset needs to be object-oriented in nature, and here Development Before the Fact is way ahead of the pack. With this methodology, according to Lanigan, the architects of the system can talk the same language as the detail designers.

Lanigan was dealing with a host of complexities in attempting to build a general design environment which would ultimately be shared by all departments within McDonnell Douglas. Capturing the requirements for a task of this magnitude required a methodology that exhibited a high level of quality and productivity. According to Lanigan, Development Before the Fact is the only modern methodology that fits that bill.

DELOITTE & TOUCHE'S MISUSES OF METHODOLOGY

It probably comes as no surprise but you can misuse as well as use any methodology. Ken Horner[9] is a partner in the Management Consulting practice of Deloitte & Touche. From his experience, as well as an informal survey of over 50 of his customers, all of whom have used one or more methodologies at some point, there seems to be several common benefits and problems. At least five common denominator methodology "misuses" are identifiable:

1. **Religious Fanaticism** — This is the situation where an organization holds to the theory that there can be nothing else but the methodology. A "methodology-centric" view of the world, if you'll permit the use. Such rigidity is seldom useful or productive. It may also be a symptom of other poor management practices.

2. **Bureaucracy** — Here the methodology gets wrapped up in a less than effective organization which adds yet another layer of protection and excuse as to why no products are produced. Using a methodology in an organization which may already have top-down communications problems and multiple management layers between the programmers and the management will not help. It will just cause people to push more paper.

3. **The end in itself** — Very similar to misuse #2 is the failure resulting from the total focus on the process of developing systems and not on the end results. Personnel are indoctrinated into the process and become wedded to the idea that step "16" must come after "15" and before "17," and that every last step must be completed and documented, even when it is obvious that performing the activities in a step will add no value to the result, or that what they are doing has no real business benefit.

4. **Using the wrong one** — This is rare but is sometimes seen. The few cases Horner has seen personally seem to arise because a methodology in place has failed to keep up with the times. For example, having no methods that focus on JAD or on structured testing or, trivially, a customer's methodology which still requires the use of a paper screen layout form when screen painters and prototyping provide far faster and more effective user interaction. A methodology incorporating no guidance in data modeling would be of little help in implementing a system using a modern relational database system.

5. **Lack of organizational penetration** — The most common problem is still lack of consistent use, starting with lack of commitment by management. Project leaders who get trained and start off by trying to conform will tend to fall by the wayside if not encouraged and coached to do better.

RATING METHODOLOGIES

Ultimately, the IS analyst must choose between a wide variety of methodologies. One size does not fit all. Choosing the best one for your organization is a lengthy and tedious process. Sam Holcman,[10] a vice president at CASE vendor KnowledgeWare, has devised a series of questions that will start you off on the right foot in your search for the right methodology.

1. Does the methodology identify the steps necessary to produce each deliverable of systems development/evolution?
2. Does the methodology house and deliver the details necessary for developing/evolving systems?
3. Does the methodology simplify the systems development/evolution process?

4. Does the methodology encourage and provide the means to implement a standard approach to systems development?
5. Can any aspect of the methodology be customized to meet specific standards and practices of the using organization?
6. Can changes to the methodology be verified as correct?
7. Does the methodology support current techniques and technology or is it based upon dated practices?
8. Does the methodology cover all aspects of systems activities?
9. Can the methodology be realistically followed by the systems organization or does it present overwhelming details?
10. Can cohesive pieces of the methodology be extracted for use on focused projects?
11. Is the methodology driven by the production of deliverables?
12. Is the methodology organized in terms of discrete methods that are linked by the deliverables they produce?
13. Does the methodology provide techniques that describe how to conduct its methods?
14. Can the methodology embody the standards and practices of the using organization?
15. Does the methodology identify the roles (types of job functions) that are involved in each method?
16. Does the methodology identify the support tools appropriate for the execution of each method?
17. Does the methodology allow for predefined paths that accomplish specific objectives?
18. Is the methodology expressed using formal models whose structural integrity can be automatically verified?
19. Can the methodology be expediently searched to retrieve methodology information?
20. Can select pieces of the methodology be published as project handbooks?
21. Can the methodology be ported to external software (tools)?
22. Is the methodology supported by a complete line of educational services?
23. Are services available to integrate the methodology with the standards, practices, and conventions of the using organization?
24. Is the vendor capable of demonstrating any aspect of the methodology on a real project?
25. Are services available to customize the methodology to incorporate the using organization's experiences?
26. Are services available to guide an effective roll-out of the methodology?

MEASUREMENT PROGRAMS

When an organization institutes a long-term productivity and quality improvement plan, one of the first tasks they usually undertake is to put a measurement program into place. Although, according to research performed by the author (New Art Technologies, Inc.),[11] less than 10 percent of software-producing organizations worldwide have any kind of ongoing measurement program, more and more organizations are realizing that measurement is an inexorable part of the productivity/quality equation.

In answer to the question, "Why should an organization measure?" there are two proverbs that truly characterize the state of software engineering today: "If you don't know where you are going, any road will do" and "If you don't know where you are, a map won't help!"

Howard Rubin[12] is a full professor and former chair of the Department of Computer Science at Hunter College, and CEO of Howard Rubin Associates. Through his experience and research, Dr. Rubin has collected data on more than 13,000 software projects as a basis for analyzing software productivity and quality trends. Dr. Rubin recommends that the first step that an organization should take in putting a measurement program in place is to assess "measurement readiness." He offers up these eight questions as a quick assessment:

1. How intense is the organization's desire to improve its performance?
   (0) No Desire   (5) Intense

2. Is the organization willing to invest time and money to improve systems performance with measurement?
   (0) No   (5) Funds and people are allocated

3. What is the current level of the systems skills inventory in regard to being able to use metrics?
   (0) None   (5) Already in wide effective use

4. To what extent are measurement concepts known and understood by the systems staff?
   (0) No staff has been exposed   (5) 100 percent trained

5. Is the systems culture adverse to using measurements at the organizational and individual level?
   (0) 100 percent against   (5) Anxious to implement

6. To what extent is a support structure in place to foster measurement practices and perform metrics technology transfer?
   (0) None   (5) In place

7. Are tools and repositories for acquiring and analyzing metrics data in place?
   (0) No   (5) Full suite available

8. Does the systems organization understand its role in the business processes?

(0) No

(5) Yes, the business processes are documented and tracked through metrics

If the answers to all of these questions are at the low end of the scale, the organization's measurement readiness is quite low. Radical change, according to Rubin, will be needed to get things going. A good starting point is to contact professional societies so that experiences in measurement can be shared and exchanged. Good contacts can be made through the IEEE Computer Society and the Quality Assurance Institute.[13]

There are as many metric systems as there are firms using them. The author has supplied the following list of those most frequently encountered:

- Lines of code
- Pages of documentation
- Number and size of tests
- Function count
- Variable count
- Number of modules
- Depth of nesting
- Count of changes required
- Count of discovered defects
- Count of changed lines of code
- Time to design, code, test
- Defect discovery rate by phase of development
- Cost to develop
- Number of external interfaces
- Number of tools used and why
- Reusability percentage
- Variance of schedule
- Staff years experience with team
- Staff years experience with language
- Software years experience with software tools
- MIPs per person
- Support to development personnel ratio
- Nonproject-to-project time ratio

Most organizations that measure still use a simple source-lines-of-code (SLOC) metric. Even with this metric, however, there is room for variation. In their 1986 book, *Software Engineering Metrics and Models,* published by the Benjamin/Cummings Publishing Company, the authors (Conte, Dunsmore, and Shen)[13a] proposed this definition of SLOC: "A line of code is any line of program text that is not a comment or blank line, regardless of the number of statements or fragments of statements on that line. This specifically includes all lines containing program headers, declarations, and executable and nonexecutable statements."

The SLOC metric is often further redefined into distinguishing the number of noncomment source lines of code (NCSLOC) from the lines of code containing comment statements (CSLOC).

Along with SLOC measurements, the weekly time sheet provides other gross statistics often used for productivity measurement. The total number of labor hours expended, divided by the total number of NCSLOC, provides an overall statistic that can be used to compare productivity from project to project.

One problem with the SLOC measurement is that it does not take into account the complexity of the code being developed or maintained. Lines of code and man-months hide some very important things. For example, the SLOC measurement for a name and address file update program might be 600 lines of code per day.

On the other hand, the output for software that tracks satellites might be in the range of 40 to 50 lines of code per day. To look at this output on a purely gross statistical level, one would conclude that the name and address project was more productive and efficient than the satellite project. This conclusion would be wrong.

So starting from this base, two researchers at the Massachusetts Institute of Technology's Center for Information Systems Research examined this complexity issue. Chris F. Kemerer and Geoffrey K. Gill[14] studied the software development projects undertaken by an aerospace defense contracting firm.

The Kemerer and Gill team began their research by reviewing the original measure for complexity as developed by Thomas McCabe, now president of McCabe & Associates, a Columbia, MD consulting group, in his article, "A Complexity Measure" in *IEEE Transactions on Software Engineering,* 1976. McCabe proposed that a valid measurement of complexity would be the number of possible paths in a software module. In 1978, W.J. Hansen in his article, "Measurement of Program Complexity by the Pair (Cyclomatic Number, Operator Count)" in *ACM SIGPLAN Notices*, March issue, interpreted McCabe's mathematical formula into four simple rules that would produce a numerical measure of complexity (i.e., the higher the number, the more complex):

Add 1 for every IF, Case or other alternate execution construct.
Add 1 for every iterative DO, DOWHILE or other repetitive construct.
Add 2 less than the number of logical alternatives in a Case.
Add 1 for each AND or OR in an IF statement.

The results of the Kemerer and Gill study showed that increased software complexity leads to reduced productivity. They recommend the use of more experienced staff and a reduction of the complexity of the individual software module. To reduce complexity, they suggest the establishment of a complexity measure that could be in use as the code is written, and adherence to this preset standard.

The goal of these studies is to transfer the generally accepted processes of measurement from the manufacturing arena to the software arena. The problem with the software industry is that we think everything we're doing is new.

In 1983, A.J. Albrecht, with IBM at that time, first proposed the function-point concept in a paper for *IEEE Transactions* on Software Engineering called "Software Function, Source Lines of Code and Development Effort Prediction: A Software Science Validation." This metric is a combination of metrics that assesses the functionality of the development process.

Most people are using function points because it is the only metric that comes close to matching the economic definition of productivity, which is costs or services produced per unit of labor and expense. Of 400 companies studied by Capers Jones, the national average was calculated to be five function points per person-month; IS groups averaged eight function points per person-month.

These numbers can dramatically increase with productivity tool usage (i.e., CASE) to the degree that it is possible to achieve 65 function points per person-month with a full CASE environment and reusable code. This metric will decrease when the development environment is new, but will regain momentum when familiarity with the toolset increases.

Jerrold M. Grochow,[15] a vice president of American Management Systems, Inc. (AMS), Arlington, VA was an early believer in the function-point concept. With over 2200 systems professionals, and supporting 28 product lines, AMS needed a metric system that worked. The company has been measuring productivity for over 10 years. The firm found that its traditional metrics of lines of code and work-months was hiding some very important information: not all work-months are created equal.

There are experienced people and not so experienced people, expensive people and not so expensive people, according to Grochow. If the company could find a way of optimizing this mix, then it would find increased productivity. To this end, AMS needed a measure that would foster economic productivity. Function points filled the bill.

Function points, however, are one of the most difficult of metric systems to successfully implement. IS analysts seriously interested in this measurement system are urged to contact the International Function Point Users' Group for more complete information.[16]

THE IEEE STANDARD DICTIONARY OF MEASURES

Organizations will find that the road to measurement success is littered with potholes. There is no such thing as a perfect metric, function points notwithstanding. The best approach, the author believes, may be to employ a variety of metrics.

The IEEE is no doubt familiar to most IS analysts. But what most don't know is that the IEEE has painstakingly gathered together some of the most robust of metrics and published them as the "Standard of Measures to Produce Reliable Software."[17]

The IEEE standards were written with the objective to provide the software community with defined measures currently used as indicators of reliability — and, hence, productivity and quality. What follows is a subset of the IEEE standard which we found to be the most easily adaptable by the general IS community.

Fault Density

This measure can be used to predict remaining faults by comparison with expected fault density, determine if sufficient testing has been completed, and establish standard fault densities for comparison and prediction.

$$F_d = F/KSLOC$$

where:

F = total number of unique faults found in a given interval resulting in failures of a specified severity level

KSLOC = number of source lines of executable code and nonexecutable data declarations, in thousands

Cumulative Failure Profile

This is a graphical method used to predict reliability, estimate additional testing time to reach an acceptable reliable system, and identify modules and subsystems that require additional testing. A plot is drawn of cumulative failures vs. a suitable time base.

Fault-Days Number

This measure represents the number of days that faults spend in the system, from their creation to their removal. For each fault detected and removed, during any phase, the number of days from its creation to its removal is determined (fault-days). The fault-days are then summed for all faults detected and removed to get the fault-days number at system level, including all faults detected and removed up to the delivery date. In cases where the creation date of the fault is not known, the fault is assumed to have been created at the middle of the phase in which it was introduced.

Functional or Modular Test Coverage

This measure is used to quantify a software test coverage index for a software delivery. From the system's functional requirements a cross-reference listing of associated modules must first be created.

$$\text{FUNCTIONAL (MODULAR) TEST} = \underline{\text{FE}}$$
$$\text{COVERAGE INDEX FT}$$

where:

FE = number of the software functional (modular) requirements for which all test cases have been satisfactorily completed

FT = total number of software functional (modular) requirements

Requirements Traceability

This measure aids in identifying requirements that are either missing from, or in addition to, the original requirements.

$$TM = \frac{R1}{R2} \times 100 \ \ \text{percent}$$

where:

R1 = number of requirements met by the architecture

R2 = number of original requirements

Software Maturity Index

This measure is used to quantify the readiness of a software product. Changes from a previous baseline to the current baseline are an indication of the current product stability.

$$SMI = \frac{M_T - (F_a + F_c + F_{del})}{M_T}$$

where:

SMI = maturity index

M_T = number of software functions (modules) in the current delivery

F_a = number of software functions (modules) in the current delivery that are additions to the previous delivery

F_c = number of software functions (modules) in the current delivery that include internal changes from a previous delivery

F_{del} = number of software functions (modules) in the previous delivery that are deleted in the current delivery

The Software Maturity Index may be *estimated* as:

$$\frac{SMI = M_T - F_c}{M_T}$$

Number of Conflicting Requirements

This measure is used to determine the reliability of a software system resulting from the software architecture under consideration, as represented by a specification based on the entity–relationship-attributed model. What is required is a list of the systems inputs, its outputs, and a list of the functions performed by each program. The mappings from the software architecture to the requirements are identified. Mappings from the same specification item to more than one differing requirement are examined for requirements inconsistency. Additionally, mappings from more than one spec item to a single requirement are examined for spec inconsistency.

Cyclomatic Complexity

This measure is used to determine the structured complexity of a coded module. The use of this measure is designed to limit the complexity of the module, thereby promoting understandability of the module.

$$C = E - N + 1$$

where:

C = complexity
N = number of nodes (sequential groups of program statements)
E = number of edges (program flows between nodes)

Test Coverage

This is a measure of the completeness of the testing process from both a developer and user perspective. The measure relates directly to the development, integration, and operational test stages of product development.

$$TC(\%) = \frac{(\text{implemented capabilities})}{(\text{required capabilities})} \times \frac{(\text{program primitives tested})}{(\text{total program primitives})} \times 100\%$$

where:

- Program functional primitives are either modules, segments, statements, branches, or paths
- Data functional primitives are classes of data
- Requirement primitives are test cases or functional capabilities

Data or Information Flow Complexity

This is a structural complexity or procedural complexity measure that can be used to evaluate the information flow structure of large-scale systems, the procedure and module information flow structure, the complexity of the interconnections between modules, and the degree of simplicity of relationships between subsystems, and to correlate total observed failures and software reliability with data complexity.

$$\text{weighted IFC} = \text{length} \times (\text{fanin} \times \text{fanout})^2$$

where:

IFC = Information Flow Complexity
Fanin = local flows into a procedure + number of data structures from which the procedures retrieves data

371

Fanout = local flows from a procedure + number of data structures that the procedure updates

Length = number of source statements in a procedure (excluding comments)

The flow of information between modules and/or subsystems needs to be determined either through the use of automated techniques or charting mechanisms. A local flow from module A to B exists if one of the following occurs:

1. A calls B.
2. B calls A and A returns a value to B that is passed by B.
3. Both A and B are called by another module that passes a value from A to B.

Mean Time to Failure

This measure is the basic parameter required by most software reliability models. Detailed recordkeeping of failure occurrences that accurately track time (calendar or execution) at which the faults manifest themselves is essential.

SEI's Process Maturity Framework

The Systems Engineering Institute (SEI) at Carnegie-Mellon is the bulwark of engineering productivity research. In their studies of thousands of firms they've discovered some common characteristics that can be used to measure how progressive a firm is in terms of its maturity in the quest for productivity and quality.

SEI has developed a five-level framework that can be used to assess the quality of the software development process in an organization. It is disheartening to note that SEI has determined that over 86 percent of companies assessed fall in Stage 1, while only 1 percent of firms achieve Stage 5.

Level one (initial) is characterized by a software engineering department that does things in an ad hoc way. There is little formalization (i.e., no measurement system in place, inconsistent or nonuse of methodology), and tools are informally applied to the process. To move to the next level of "process maturity" requires the organization to initiate rigorous project management, management review, and quality assurance.

A level two (repeatable) organization has achieved a stable process with a repeatable level of statistical control. Firms in this category can improve (i.e., get to the next level) by establishing a formal process group or committee charged with establishing a software development process architecture and ultimately introducing software engineering methods and technologies.

Level three (defined) organizations have achieved a foundation for major and continuing progress. The key actions for these organizations to

progress to the next step are to establish a basic set of process manage-
ments to identify quality and cost parameters; establish a process database and then gather and maintain process data. Process data, when used
in conjunction with metrics, can be used to assess the relative quality of
each product.

Level four organizations, of which there are few according to SEI's Watts
Humphrey, are characterized by substantial quality improvements and implementations of comprehensive process measurement systems. Although
level four is a much vaunted stage, even these organizations can improve.
To do so they must support automatic gathering of process data and then
use those data to analyze and modify the process. It is only then that these
organizations have any chance at reaching the much sought after level five
of process maturity — optimized.

NONTECHNICAL FACTORS IN PROMOTING PRODUCTIVITY

Quality and productivity are obviously tightly linked; the approaches
used to address these issues — metrics, methodology, and tools — must
be interconnected. Yourdon suggests that simply throwing technology or
methodology at the problem is not enough. Information Systems (IS) departments must also use peopleware solutions.

For example, one way to improve development is to hire better developers. Rather than spend lots of money trying to bring in a new methodology,
why not just bring in better people? According to Yourdon, there is a 25 to
1 differential between the best and the worst people, and a 4 to 1 differential between the best and the worst teams, maybe the best way to improve
productivity and quality is just to improve hiring practices.

If you take a random group of 100 people and put them in a room with a
complex programming exercise, one of them will finish 25 times faster than
the others. Another peopleware improvement to productivity is to help
managers improve their skills, as well as to foster a teamwork approach
among developers. Peopleware solutions boost productivity and quality
more than any tools or techniques. This may very well be the surest path
to productivity.

Given the enormous variance in the productivity of programmers, there
is a large opportunity for improvement. According to statistical measures
by Barry Boehm,[18] when the experience of a programmer increases from 1
month to 3 years (36-fold increase), productivity is improved by only 34
percent. This appears to show that experience seems to have no effect on
software project costs. In another study by Boehm it was shown that the
difference in productivity between a programmer who uses no tools at all
and one who uses the most up-to-date, powerful tools available, on the
most powerful machines, is no larger than 50 percent.

Motivating Programmers

Studies have also shown that programmers have a motivation pattern which is different from that of their managers and from workers in other industries. This difference might well explain why some well-intentioned software managers fail to motivate their programmers. Motivation factors that affect productivity include:

- *Recognition* — The reaction of the organization to the programmer's performance. Indifference leads to a drop in motivation which leads to a decline in productivity.
- *Achievement* — The satisfaction that the programmer gets from doing a challenging task. This implies that the organization must keep supplying the programmer with challenging tasks to maintain motivation.
- *The work* — The nature of the tasks that must be executed is a powerful tool to motivate a programmer.
- *Responsibility* — This is derived from basic management theory. That is, if you want something to happen, make someone specifically responsible for it.
- *Advancement* — A programmer who feels that he or she has the possibly of career advancement in the organization is more motivated than one who does not.
- *Salary* — A programmer who feels that he or she is being paid adequately, and who anticipates that salary increases will continue on par with performance, will be more motivated than one who does not.
- *Possibility for growth* — This factor measures the possibilities for professional growth within a programmer's company.

Interpersonal Relations with Subordinates

- *Status* — This measures the importance of the worker in his or her company, such as participation at meetings, participation in decision making, ceremonial functions, usage of restricted services and privileges of the corporation.
- *Interpersonal relations with superiors* — This is controllable to the extent that the manager has latitude in assigning group leaders.
- *Interpersonal relations with peers* — Since teamwork is a key ingredient for the success of any group effort, the manager should take care in dividing staff into working groups.
- *Technical supervision* — This measures the willingness of the programmer's supervisor to help the programmer solve technical problems, orient efforts, and make choices.
- *Company policy and administration* — This factor measures how clearly the command structure of the company is defined, how rational it is, and how easy it is to determine who each worker reports to.
- *Working conditions* — This factor represents working conditions in the traditional sense such as office space, light.

- *Factors in personal life* — Given that the programmer's personal life influences motivation and job performance, the manager can assign key positions or tasks to those that have the best conditions.
- *Job security* — This factor is very important.

Management Factors

Peopleware is really a two-edged sword. The employee (i.e., programmer) is not solely responsible for productivity. The actions of the manager are a big part of the equation as well. Poor management produces a host of woes including:

- Unrealistic project plans are due to poor planning/scheduling/estimation skills
- Staff can lose motivation due to inability of management to manage a creative staff
- A lack of teamwork can develop due to inability to build and manage effective teams
- There can be poor project execution due to inadequate organization, delegation, and monitoring
- Technical problems can develop due to lack of management understanding of disciplines such as quality assurance, configuration management
- The danger of maintaining an inadequately trained staff due to a short-sighted rather than a long-term perspective

There are some possible solutions to poor management problems. Some organizations have had much success with the definition of dual career paths for technical and managerial staff. Training managers to be good managers is just as important as training programmers to be good programmers. Some organizations make an active practice out of mentoring and supervision of staff by senior managers. Finally, increasing delegation of responsibility and matching authority is a definite step in the right direction.

THE QUALITY IMPERATIVE

Quality is as much of a mindset as anything else. Utah State's Professor Y.K Shetty[19] found some characteristics that quality-oriented organizations have in common. She refers to these as the Seven Principles of Quality.

Principles of Quality

Principle 1: Quality Improvement Requires the Firm Commitment of Top Management. All top management, including the CEO, must be personally committed to quality. The keyword here is *personally*. Many CEOs pay only lip service to this particular edict. Therefore, top management must be consistent and reflect its commitment through the company's philosophy, goals, policies, priorities, and executive behavior. Steps management can take to accomplish this end include: establish and communicate a clear vision of corporate philosophy, principles, and objectives relevant to product and service quality; channel resources toward these objectives and define roles and responsibilities in this endeavor; invest time to learn about quality issues and monitor the progress of any initiatives; encourage communication between management and employees, among departments, and among various units of the firm and customers; and be a good role model in communication and action.

Principle 2: Quality is a Strategic Issue. It must be a part of a company's goals and strategies and be consistent with and reinforce a company's other strategic objectives. It must also be integrated into budgets and plans and be a corporate mission with planned goals and strategies. Finally, quality should be at the heart of every action.

Principle 3: Employees Are the Key to Consistent Quality. The organization must have a people-oriented philosophy. Poorly managed people convey their disdain for quality and service when they work. It is important to pay special attention to employee recruitment, selection, and socialization and to reinforce the socialization and quality process with continuous training and education. It is also a good idea to incorporate quality into performance appraisal and reward systems and to encourage employee participation and involvement.

Effective communication throughout the department, between department, and throughout the organization is required to reinforce the deep commitment of management and creates an awareness and understanding of the role of quality and customer service.

Principle 4: Quality Standards and Measurements Must Be Customer Driven. It can be measured by: formal customer surveys, focus groups, customer complaints, quality audits, testing panels, statistical quality controls, and interaction with customers.

Principle 5: Many Programs and Techniques Can Be Used to Improve Quality. Examples are statistical quality control, quality circles, suggestion systems, quality-of-worklife projects, and competitive benchmarking.

Principle 6: All Company Activities Have Potential for Improving Product Quality, Therefore Teamwork is Vital. Quality improvement requires close cooperation between managers and employees and among departments. Total quality management involves preventing errors at the point where work is performed and ultimately every employee and department is responsible for quality.

Principle 7: Quality Is a Never-Ending Process. Quality must be planned. Quality must be organized. Quality must be monitored. Quality must be continuously revitalized.

MOTOROLA'S SIX SIGMA DEFECT REDUCTION TECHNIQUE

In 1987 Motorola took some of these principles to heart and set in motion a 5-year quality improvement program. The term Six Sigma is one used by statisticians and engineers to describe a state of zero defects. The result of this program has produced productivity gains of 40 percent as well as winning Motorola the Malcolm Baldridge National Quality award in 1988.

Benefits to Motorola included increased productivity by 40 percent, reduced backlog from years to months, increased customer service levels, shifted IS time from correcting mistakes to value-added work, more motivated staff, and, finally, Motorola saved $1.5 billion in reduced cost.

Six Sigma Defect Reduction is easily reproducible by IS analysts:

1. Identify your product. Determine what is the service or product you are producing. IS must align what they do with what the customers want.
2. Identify customer requirements. IS must determine what the customer perceives as a defect-free product or service. The unit of work that the user is dealing with must be considered. For example, in a general ledger system, in which the user worries about defects per journal voucher and not defects per thousand lines of code.
3. Diagnose the frequency and source of errors. Four categories of metrics were established to target defect reduction: new software development, service delivery, cycle time, and customer satisfaction which is composed of a detailed service metric with the intent of validating the first three metrics.
4. Define a process for doing the task. Motorola refers to this process as mapping but closely aligned to the reengineering process. The process involves using personal computer-based tools to determine flow-through of processes and answering the following questions: which processes can be eliminated, which processes can be simplified?
5. Mistake-proof the process. By streamlining a process and eliminating any unnecessary steps, it is possible to make the process mistake proof. By using metrics a process control mechanism is put into place so that problems can be addressed before it affects output.
6. Put permanent control measures in place. Once Six Sigma is reached, this level must be maintained.

At this step, the Six Sigma metrics are set up to be used to continuously monitor the process. Monthly quality review meetings are held where each person gets up and discusses their metric, its trend, diagnosis of source cause of errors, action plan to correct.

COOPERS & LYBRAND'S SQM STRATEGY[20]

Coopers & Lybrand has taken appropriate elements of Total Quality Management (TQM) and successfully applied them to software delivery organizations. It has developed a specific four-phase methodology, dubbed Software Quality Management (SQM) which provides a framework for managing continuous improvement for software delivery.

1. Assessment

The purpose of the assessment phase is to evaluate the organization's current environment and determine how well the organization meets or is likely to meet its customers' software quality requirements. In any assessment phase, a measurement system must first be designed as a tool and to establish a quality baseline.

During assessment, it is important to understand the activities involved in the software development process as well as the organizational roles and responsibilities. The measurements currently being used by the organization must also be identified and assessed. Whenever possible, existing measures should be used as part of the quality assessment to promote familiarity and acceptance.

2. Planning

The analysis of the data collected during the assessment provides the foundation for the quality improvement plan. The assessment defines the organization's quality profile and identifies opportunities for improvement. The objectives of the planning phase are to establish strategic and tactical direction, as well as consensus and commitment for improvements identified in the assessment. A process improvement plan is the final outcome of this strategic planing effort.

The organization's vision of what quality software means and where it expects to be must be agreed upon early in the planning effort. Most organizations find that there are several areas where improvement efforts can be focused; however, trying to do too much at once is not a good idea. Priorities should be assigned to targets based on the following criteria:

- Criticality
- Cost
- Resources
- Timing
- Risks
- Opportunity for near-term success

The projects that are selected as top priorities will require further discussion and decisions regarding the manner in which the improvements are to be implemented. The result will be a prioritized statement of quality objectives, the process improvements to be achieved, and the measurements that will demonstrate success. In addition, each quality improvement project should have:

- A mission statement that includes improvement goals
- Schedules and resource and cost estimates for each project
- An organization structure responsible for quality management
- Measurement procedures to validate the meeting of goals

3. Implementation

Introducing measurement systems and the concept of continuous improvement will require far-reaching changes to an organization. During the implementation phase, these changes begin to occur. Implementing the quality improvement plan means incorporating the measurement and improvement efforts into the organizational culture and discovering which behavioral changes need to occur. This effort, therefore, requires a corresponding change in the reward structure. A reward system should motivate the staff to change development procedures in a way that is consistent with the goals of the improvements efforts.

Once a new reward system is in place, implementation should turn to those short-term projects that were identified in the planning phase. These may include:

- Project tracking techniques and tools
- Formalizing reviews and walkthroughs
- Implementing Joint Application Design (JAD) sessions
- Applying new approaches to testing

4. Institutionalization

Institutionalization requires that the lessons learned during implementation be captured and transformed into organizational assets to form the basis of a continuous improvement culture. As a first step, the experiences gained in near-term improvement projects should be analyzed, packaged, and communicated to everyone in the organization. Successes must be validated and publicized. The experience is packaged into self-contained units including approach, results, techniques, tools, manuals, and training, to transform the knowledge gained into the organization's culture.

The basic techniques for institutionalizing continuous quality improvement include:

- Analyzing the results of short-term projects and comparing the results with the targets defined in planning

- Synthesizing the experience into lessons learned, domain expertise, rules and models
- Packaging the experience as products that can be delivered to the organization

Author's Bio

Jessica Keyes is president of New Art Technologies, Inc., a high-technology software development firm. Keyes has given seminars for such prestigious universities as Carnegie Mellon, Boston University, University of Illinois, James Madison University, and San Francisco State University. She is a frequent keynote speaker on the topics of competitive strategy using information technology and marketing on the information superhighway. She is an advisor for DataPro, McGraw-Hill's computer research arm as well as a member of the Sprint Business Council. Keyes is also a founding Board of Director member of the New York Software Industry Association. She has recently completed a 2-year term on the Mayor of New York City's Small Business Advisory Council.

Prior to founding The Company, Keyes was Managing Director of R&D for the New York Stock Exchange and has been an officer with Swiss Bank Co. and Banker's Trust, both in New York City. She holds a Master's from New York University where she did her research in the area of artificial intelligence.

A noted columnist and correspondent, with over 150 articles published, Keyes is the author of 12 books.

Notes

1. Barbara Zimmer, HP Corporate Engineering Department, 1801 Page Mill Road, Bldg. 18D, Palo Alto, CA, 94304.
2. Capers Jones can be contacted at Software Productivity Research, One New England Executive Park Drive, Burlington, MA, 01803, (617) 273-0140.
3. More information about the Ernst & Young Quality Studies can be obtained from Paul Kikta, National Performance Improvement Office. Paul is located in Ernst & Young's Cleveland, OH office and can be reached at (216) 861-5000, ext 5128.
4. Ed Yourdon is the author of a multitude of books including *Structured Design,* published in 1979 by Yourdon Press/Prentice-Hall, Upper Saddle River, NJ.
5. The seminal work referred to here is *Information Engineering,* written by James Martin and Clive Finkelstein and published by the Savant Institute in 1981. The Savant Institute is located in Carnforth, Lancs, U.K.
6. Clive Finkelstein is the founder of Information Engineering Systems Corp. Since he is located in Australia, interested readers can contact the president of the firm, Glen Hughlette, for more information on Information Engineering. He is located at IESC, 201 North Union Street, 5th Floor, Alexandria, VA, 22314, (703) 739-2242.
7. Margaret Hamilton is president of Hamilton Technologies, Inc. which is located at 17 Inman Street, Cambridge, MA, 02139, (617) 492-0058.
8. Ed Lanigan has since departed McDonnell Douglas and is now president of The Lanigan Group which is located in St. Louis, MO, (314) 725-0980.
9. DRT Systems is a joint venture between Deloitte & Touche and a Japanese firm. DRT Systems is located at 1633 Broadway, New York, 10019.
10. Sam Holcman is a vice president at KnowlegeWare, which is located at 39555 Orchard Hill Place, Suite 450, Novi, MI, 48375.
11. Jessica Keyes is president of New Art Technologies, Inc. which is a high-technology consultantcy and software development firm located at 200 West 79 Street, Suite 8H, New York, 10024, (212) 362-0559.

12. Howard Rubin is president of Howard Rubin Associates located at Winterbottom Lane, Pound Ridge, NY, 10576, (914) 764-4931.
13. The IEEE Computer Society is located at 1730 Massachusetts Ave., NW, Washington, D.C. 20036, (202) 371-0101. The Quality Assurance Institute is located at 7575 Phillips Blvd. #35, Orlando, FL, 32819, (407) 363-1111.
13a. Conte, Dunsmore, and Shen. *Software Engineering Metrics and Models*, Benjamin/Cummings Publishing, Menlo Park, CA, 1986.
14. Information about this study can be obtained through Professor Chris Kemerer who is located at the Sloan School at MIT, Cambridge, MA 02139, (617) 253-2971.
15. Jerry Grochow can be reached at his offices at AMS, 4050 Legato Road, Fairfax, VA 22033, (703) 841-6498.
16. IFPUG is located in the Blendonview Office Park, 50008-28 Pine Creek Drive, Westerville, OH 43081-4899, (614) 895-7130.
17. This section references the IEEE Standard of Measures to Produce Reliable Software. Standard 982.1-1988. More information can be obtained from the IEEE Service Center, 445 Hoes Lane, Piscataway, NJ 08854, (908) 981-0060.
18. Barry Boehm is a giant in this area. Readers interested in more on this subject should read Boehm's book, *Software Engineering Economics,* which was published in 1981 by Prentice-Hall, Upper Saddle River, NJ.
19. Y.K. Shetty can be reached at Utah State University's College of Business, (801) 750-2369.
20. Bill Smillie works out of several Coopers & Lybrand offices. He can be reached at (410) 323-2468.

Chapter 29

Getting the Most Bang for Your Buck: Designing and Maintaining a Website Using the 80/20 Rule

Dennis Laughren

THE WEBSITE MY TEAM MAINTAINS encompasses ~50,000 pages of static and dynamic data, over several servers at several locations. We average 220,000 hits a day and 12,000 visitors to our home page. Some companies employ teams of Web developers for such a daunting task, yet I am one of only three full-time personnel dedicated to our site's design, graphic look, and maintenance. Our home page's look and feel changes completely every couple of weeks, and its not unusual for 200 pages to be posted in 1 day, yet you won't find any of those "under construction" pages on our site. You also won't find many errors or broken links. Your Website may not be this large, but there are design and maintenance methods and tools you can use that will allow you to post and maintain a consistent, well-designed site, while keeping the content fresh and your department heads happy.

The overriding concern in the maintenance of our Website is time and project management. At any given time, my team may have 15 to 20 projects in our work request database. Some projects have been there for months and some a few minutes. When prioritizing tasks for my team (and myself), I almost always fix existing mistakes first, like spelling errors or glaring errors. After existing mistakes are corrected, I try to identify the

0-8493-9987-4/00/$0.00+$.50
© 2000 by CRC Press LLC

cause of the problem and eliminate it. After existing mistakes are correct-ed, then time-dependent information, like press releases, is addressed. Every other request made of the Webmaster can be classified using a version of the "80/20 rule." When prioritizing tasks, always ask yourself, "which projects will affect the most people, the most entry points for the Web page, and have the greatest exposure to the public?" Those projects get 80 percent of my team's time. There is one section of our Website linked right from our front page, but it only gets 1/1000th of our traffic. Consequently, it doesn't get much attention. This rule also applies to the way I address the maintenance of the site. I want my team to spend 80 percent of its time producing results, not figuring out where to place the file, what to name it, and what sort of font should be used for the title.

This might seem like common sense, but Webmasters and Web managers are by necessity micromanagers. Our job is an endless stream of "little issues" always distracting us from the wider implications of our work. Imagine being so obsessed with your lapel pin you forget to put on your trousers. The lapel pin that isn't what your next visitor is going to notice, even if cool animated flames shoot out of the top. This chapter will show you how to design a site that will be easy to maintain and give you leads on tools and strategies that won't waste your time or break the bank.

THE RIGHT TOOL FOR THE RIGHT JOB

The most important consideration for you to make immediately is the way you will be accessing and editing your Web page. Whether you're host-ing in-house, with a Windows NT server hooked to your LAN through the firewall, or using FTP to upload and download files to your Web hosting ser-vice, the choice of the right editor can save you immeasurable amounts of time. The perfect editor should be useful to both the beginner and the ex-pert, with automated wizards, a text editor, browser, and FTP retrieval built into the product. This means you'll be able to open remote files with one click, rather than switching between several applications to accomplish a change. Many of the heavyweight applications like MS FrontPage or PageMill have these capabilities to varying degrees, but I prefer to use Homesite 3 (Exhibit 29.1), from Allaire Software (www.allaire.com). It has simple remote file management, configurable tag assistance, tag color-cod-ing, and point-and-click wizards for frames, tables, DHTML, objects, and anything else you might need for Web management.

The software is under $100, and Allaire's Website frequently offers up-grades and trials of their other products. They also offer a free 30-day trial — ample time to get you hooked.

If your site uses ASP or other database-driven content, and you have over $1000 to spend, MS Visual Studio (Exhibit 29.2) is probably the best editor for you. It is certainly not for beginners, but shares the same look

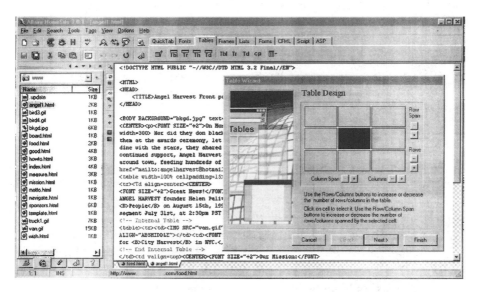

Exhibit 29.1. Homesite 3.

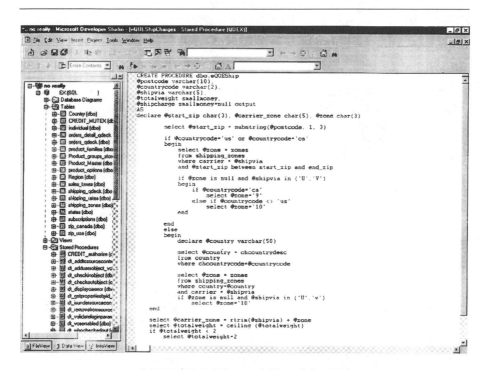

Exhibit 29.2. Microsoft Visual Studio.

and feel of Homesite, while offering full integrated access to FrontPage, SQL queries, advanced object wizards, source control, and complete VB and J++ development environments. I used this suite of applications to learn ASP/SQL and can produce an online store in about 1 month.

If you want to try other Web editors, you can find dozens of trial versions on the Internet at places like www.download.com, www.shareware.com, www.winfiles.com, and www.jumbo.com.

TEMPLATE-DRIVEN DESIGN

Whether you're running a five-page static site or a database-driven tech support wunderkind, you need to train yourself to be *consistent* or face the prospect of spending all your free time at work. Each page should have several elements that are identical: the header and header graphic, footer and footer graphic, and navigation buttons should look virtually the same on every page. Not only does this make your life easier, it takes much less time to load additional pages, increasing user page views.

Graphics should all be based on the same theme/colors, and all header graphics/text should have common traits to give the site a sense of order. If you are using text for your headers instead of graphics, font choice is important. You may be tempted to use a "cool" font, but if the user doesn't have that font installed on their system, you've lost control of your look and feel. Use Arial, Courier, and Times New Roman fonts in all text.

Headers and Footers

The top and side navigation bar graphics should be consistent throughout the site, and all are linked from this directory. Footer graphics, like the company logo, are also stored in this directory. Footers should be at the bottom of every page on your site. The footer should contain only necessary information, like a legal copyright notice and a Webmaster e-mail address (Exhibits 29.3, 29.4, and 29.5); it should appear exactly the same on every page. (If you use an NT Web server, you can use FrontPage extensions to call out all footer text from one file with the <! INCLUDE ...> tag, saving yourself time later if there are changes.)

For questions about this site, contact Webmaster
Copyright 1997-8 Systems, Inc. For more information, contact info@.com

Powered by

Exhibit 29.3. Webmaster e-mail message.

Exhibit 29.4. Sample headers or footers.

Similarly, navigation buttons (Exhibit 29.6) should reflect the same color scheme.

Navigation

There are two major schools of thought at the present time about navigation. Some designers prefer a consistent top or side navigation bar that appears on every page in a frame or table layout; others prefer a hierarchical navigation, relying on train of thought (and a browser's "Back" button) to guide users. My favorite design is a hybrid of these two ideas. The top navigation bar is small and unobtrusive, providing links to a few major sections of the site. Once inside one of those sections, a larger left-hand navigation bar provides specific options for that subject. Each section also uses a primary color scheme to differentiate itself from other parts of the site. For example, a serious part of the site like Investor Relations might use grays, while an online contest uses bright, fun colors to attract visitors.

MANAGING FILES ON YOUR SERVER FOR EFFICIENCY

As with any work endeavor, organization leads to efficiency (Exhibit 29.7). Organizing the layout of your Website behind the scenes will make maintenance much easier, and using a logical layout at the beginning or taking the time to convert existing layouts will save time down the road.

Exhibit 29.5. Sample headers or footers.

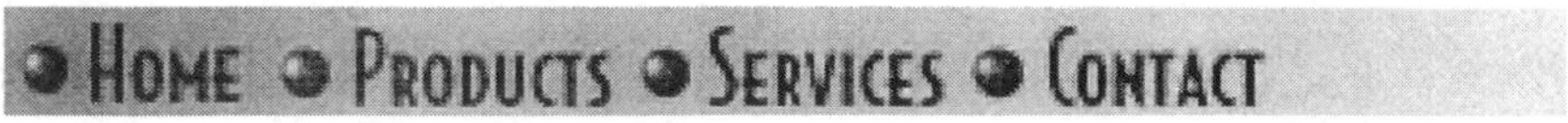

Home
Products
Services
Contact

Exhibit 29.6. Navigation buttons.

web
downloads
info
cust serv
images
images
media rel
images
sales
images
products
product1
images
product2
images
product3
images
secure
services
service1
images
service2
images
support
images

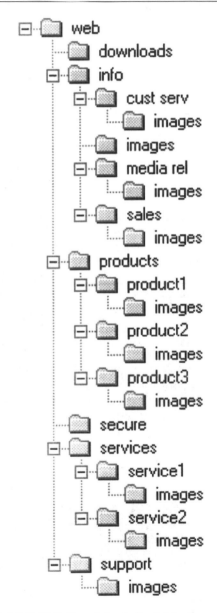

Exhibit 29.7. Consistent site folder layout.

You'll know if you've succeeded when your new hire doesn't have to ask where the newest product section should be placed.

Naming

Names for all folders and files should consistently be in lower-case or upper-case letters for convenience. If you're using an NT server, this is less important, but it's good form to stick to a standard; it's also easier for users to type "www.mypage.com/products/acme" instead of "www.MyPage.com/Products/ACME/." Forming new links will be easier, and adding new folders and files will produce fewer questions from your team. If your team ever has to migrate a large amount of existing Web content from an NT site to a UNIX site, for example, you'll appreciate the simplicity of case conformity. Abbreviations are another time waster. You may think you're saving typing time by calling your new product folder "bglngprdnm," but "biglongproductname" is much more descriptive to user and Webmaster alike. Unless an abbreviation or acronym is widely accepted, don't use it to name files or folders on your site unless you love answering e-mail and fixing broken links. The biggest cause of broken links on your site, however, will probably be the Web page extensions ".htm" and ".html." Choose one of these standards and stick to it. Some servers aren't as strict about Web filenames, but my Web server won't display "acme.html" if the link calls for "acme.htm."

Graphics

There should only be one instance of each identical graphic on your server; when it's time to change the graphic, you simply replace one file and you've saved immeasurable time. For example, all primary images on our server reside in http://www.ourserver.com/images/. Every graphic on the Website resides in an "images" directory. Product-specific images, like box shots, reside in the /products/specificproduct/images/ directory, so that each main part of the Website has its own repository for images. If your site is small, you may be tempted to place all of your images in one directory, but Websites rarely stop growing. Save yourself time creating graphics by using graphic template files. A graphics editor like Adobe Photoshop, or some of the better shareware titles out there will support layers. Layers allow you to create one background and use it for many different graphics without degrading quality or editing out old text for new text. You can save a file with many layers, then turn layers on and off to create different, but consistent, effects. This allows you to maintain a consistent look and feel while adding new and distinct parts of your site, with a minimum of additional work.

BROWSER COMPATIBILITY

Though designing Websites for as wide an audience as possible is much easier today than it was a couple of years ago, there are still vexing problems associated with Web design and the two major (and several minor) browsers out there. The conscientious Webmaster will design a site that is immediately compatible with 95 percent of the browsers out there: Netscape Navigator 3/Communicator and MSIE 3 and 4. This means that at least part of the Website (and certainly the front page) should not contain complex Java, require downloading plug-ins, or use such a large layout that a 14" monitor at 1024×768 resolution will not see everything. It is difficult, with all of the interesting technologies (like DHTML, new flavors of JAVA, and formats like Shockwave or MBED) not to design a whole site around them. After all, if a site is not visually stimulating from the start, it may never matter what's behind the curtain. However, some consideration must be given to the hapless 28.8 baud user whose download of your 100 kb plug-in could take 10 minutes on their bandwidth-starved large ISP, and who will most likely click off before giving you their money.

The best course to take is a creative treatment of the existing HTML 3 layout. Design critique sites like High Five (www.highfive.com) almost always favor a well-designed and compatible introduction to a splashy multimedia blitz requiring the latest version of IE and five different plug-ins. It is also bad form to "drop a cookie" on your home page unless it is absolutely necessary. If you have ever been to a Geocities or fly-by-night merchandising site with browser security turned on, you understand the frustration of canceling past 15 cookies to get to the home page.

A creative use of frames or tables can create very interesting and creative looks without discouraging someone without the latest browser. Though some people still use browsers that are nonframes compatible, it is a very small percentage. This is where the 80/20 rule comes back into play — you can't please everyone, so seek to please most of the people most of the time. If you must use a format that requires a plug-in or excludes a large class of users from your site, be sure to include alternate display text informing the user of the problem, and providing them a direct link to the site where a new browser can be downloaded.

It's a constant challenge keeping a Website interesting and up-to-date, but planning makes the difference. As with any project, a good management strategy will result in fewer emergencies, less e-mail, and happy supervisors.

Author's Bio

Dennis Laughren is the Webmaster for Quarterdeck Corporation, headquartered in Marina del Rey, CA. Quarterdeck can be found at www.quarterdeck.com. Quarterdeck makes "HelpWare" software that makes your PC run better and communicate more efficiently. Well-known titles like CleanSweep and Procomm Plus continually win industry awards for excellence in their categories.

Chapter 30

"Less is More" Management: A System-Oriented Object Environment for Managing and Developing Internet-Based Applications

Margaret Hamilton

OVERNIGHT OUR LIVES CHANGED WITH THE ADVENT OF THE PHONE, just as with the radio and television. Now its the Internet, with the software industry being forced to undergo yet again a rapid and rocky transition, more so than ever before, resulting in even further impact to all of us. It's necessitated by distributed client server technologies with volumes of traffic as typified by the Internet, and users are demanding much more functionality and flexibility in their systems than before.

Given the nature of problems to be solved, their systems must be error-free. These environments sound like the earlier days of real-time, distributed environments where complexity gave rise to new kinds of problems, including those having to do with interface and integration issues. The difference now is that the playing field is orders of magnitude larger than before.

0-8493-9987-4/00/$0.00+$.50
© 2000 by CRC Press LLC

This is compounded by the introduction into the marketplace (and often blind acceptance) of a plethora of new products, many having less to do with the Internet than how persuasive a particular vendor is in selling his wares or how much "safer" it is to go along with the others, much of which is accelerated and proliferated with the use of the Internet.

This phenomenon is not unlike the fifties, with street vendors on every corner selling Hadacol, claiming it would cure all ills. Of course Hadacol did not live up to its claims but its vendors made tons of money selling it. Now vendors are in board rooms selling their products on Websites throughout the world.

The software marketplace responds to the media frenzy by rushing to standardize. For reasons similar to those above, many gravitate to standards just for the sake of having them, not realizing their potentially negative impact. Once popularized, an entire new set of products is released centered around such standards, again forcing another round of dubious transitions. What seems to be hard for many is avoiding the temptation of always going along with the "latest" and "greatest" when it could in fact ultimately be compromising the bottom line.

Transitions, whether for the Internet or new products, must be managed properly. Most important is knowing whether they should be made and when and how to make them. Often transitions are made ignoring lessons learned from previous experiences. Yet, we are surprised to see problems resurface that were in earlier generations of software.

A transition does not have to be a bad experience. It in fact can present a major opportunity — an opportunity to take a step back and examine the underlying process used to manage, design, build, and deploy software, and examine where Internet products truly fit within the *systems* development framework.

For despite the continuing pronouncements of Internet software, two things remain constant. One is that systems and software fail more often than necessary; the other is that change is inevitable. The question management should ask is "Are these new tools and techniques addressing these issues or are they making things worse or, at best, no better than before?"

Software fails when either the application being developed or the process of building it fails. The application fails when it doesn't work as intended. The process of building it fails if it takes too long or costs too much to build that application.

Software fails because we do not learn from history. The Internet with all of its new tools and techniques does not alleviate this problem. It makes it worse. Many new players have entered into this arena without the experience of other software arenas. Incompatibility, traceability, timing, and integration problems proliferate.

But, isn't learning what is meant by true reuse? Talk about the virtues of reuse abounds in the industry, so why is this (not learning from history, that is) an issue? Certainly there is an abundance of methods and tools centered around reuse. Even companies are formed around these methods.

THE BALL IS IN MANAGEMENT'S COURT

The problem begins and ends with management. Management's responsibility is to select the processes, methods, and tools involved in software development and make sure that they are executed properly. Given today's systems to build and the predominately accepted practices, this task is daunting. Managers who have been around for awhile do not need to be reminded about hours of communication blackouts affecting companies worldwide, recalls of thousands of products involving human lives, aborted missions, failing businesses, or ruined careers to know what can happen when software fails.

But it does not have to be this way. And, management can do something about it. To stop long enough to think about it instead of jumping in with the latest and most popular fads is the first step. It would become clear that "management" along with its associated development can be performed differently. For example, advanced methods and tools based on formal foundations (in the mathematical sense, that is) are available today that would allow us to automatically (or inherently) capitalize on true reuse and develop systems instead of just supporting their development or supporting management of development. Problems would be minimized. Much of what was needed before would be eliminated. Tasks would become obsolete, as well as the tasks up and down the chain that support them.

What, then, becomes left for management is leadership. As a leader, a manager's first and continuing role is to minimize his own role or at least relegate it outside of the human realm, in essence replacing himself. Leadership begins by first understanding an organization's business, i.e., its goals. Once this process is completed it is up to management to take action and take the necessary steps to fulfill its goals, keeping in mind that this process is dynamic and, therefore, is never over.

After having analyzed many software companies (or projects), it became clear that for each set of company goals there was a strong dependency between most of them (if not all of them) and the software approach it uses; or, putting it another way, a strong dependency on the properties in the software it develops.[1] What this suggests is that decisions made today about the company's software methods and tools could be the deciding factor as to whether it will succeed or fail in the future.

In the majority of companies, it becomes evident that what is really needed is a way to create *durable* systems. It is only then that one is free to safely make the key decision of when and how we transition what one has today to what one needs tomorrow. Durable because they incorporate a structure and process for the continuous evolution of any or all parts of a system. Durable because they provide a way to productively, instead of destructively, manage change to a system — change in the businesses they support and change in the technologies used to implement them.

Change in the software industry needs no introduction. But it is this facet of our industry which has provided at best a foundation of quicksand for the systems that we have deployed to date.

The good news is that many continue to strive for ways to make software that is both reliable and affordable, resulting in *better, faster, cheaper* software. This means the degree of failure of both the software and the process that develops that software is minimized. Encouraging are the attempts to revamp entire enterprises by bringing in truly modern technologies, ones with paradigms that will significantly change business as it is now conducted. The case studies in succeeding chapters are illustrations of this transformation.

In this chapter we explain the properties of better, faster, cheaper software and how to manage and develop it in terms of the Development Before the Fact (DBTF) preventative approach[2-6] and its automated development environment. [7] Using this approach over a traditional one consistently shows dramatic improvement; not only are DBTF systems more reliable but they are developed with lower cost and with accelerated time to market, be they high or low level, large or small, complex or simple.[2,8-14]

This chapter serves as an introduction to help understand how the DBTF approach was used to develop applications deployed for the Internet. Three of these applications are described in subsequent chapters.

WHY SOFTWARE FAILS

The reason that software fails is not so much that the technology is new, as some would argue, or old, as others would argue. Rather, it's related to the very reason that so much else in the world seems to fail: we do not take advantage of what we have learned in the past. In software development environments as in life, knowledge is not gathered intelligently, not analyzed appropriately, nor put to intelligent reuse. In short, wisdom is lacking.

That intelligence-gathering deficiency is part and parcel of conventional development techniques — even today, in an era of great advances in computer technology and computer science. Under the conventional development scenario the probability approaches zero that a software-based system will be reliable, let alone durable, and that it will be developed within a reasonable time and within budget.

The broader in scope and more complex the system, the less likely it is that it will be reliable. It doesn't seem to matter that developers expend enormous resources on prototyping, design, performance analysis, and testing.

FAILURE COMPOUNDED BY THE NEW

Unfortunately, things have not really changed with newer types of applications, whether they be client server, Internet-based, or object-oriented using whatever mix of approaches and tools. And to add to the confusion, with each new generation of developers and users comes new popularized terms and disjunct tools to deal with these terms and camouflage "old" ideas, both good and bad, and old solutions — whether good and bad. A new set of "experts," often with lack of real systems expertise, is born around these terms and tools. "New," less-proven ways of doing things, often based on misguided rationales surface.

How often have you heard: "We have to go in that direction because everyone else is doing it; if everyone else is using it, it must be good; it is inferior if we build it this way but we'll get there faster and make more money; or let's use that software we got for free." The latest buzz words take the masses off to the latest set of tools to respond to the latest fads. Again, a new generation of designers and developers reinvents the wheel, often throwing out the baby with the imperfect bath water. Is it any wonder that familiar problems, already solved, arise again?

Meanwhile "old experts," having become "hard wired" to one way of doing things, take the path of least resistance by always using the same tools and techniques even if they don't work as well as some newer approaches for the project in question because that is what they learned in school or on their first assignment and it is too late to teach an "old" programmer new tricks. "All the other applications in the organization use this technology, therefore every new application in the organization should use it."

Conversely an organization's response to a nontraditional technology that does show real promise includes things like, "we just don't have time, we don't have the budget, or we tried such things as structured approaches, CASE tools, object-oriented techniques, and they do not meet promised expectations." "First we had to learn C++, now this is being replaced by Java. Why bother learning anything new at all?"

Just as there is a need to have openness within the software to be successful, there is a need for its developers, both old and new, to have openness when dealing with the complexities of developing software. And to compound things we have the ever-lasting software development culture with which to contend. Consider some typical scenarios.

On one project, everything that could go wrong did go wrong. The prime contractor was unable to deliver a working system and everyone agreed that the root problem was the prime contractor. Yet, when it came time to try again, the same prime won the bid to build the new system. According to the customer it was because the prime contractor was more experienced than the other bidders with building this kind of system! This is the norm, not the exception.

When things go wrong a typical solution is to throw more people on the project and more managers on the project to manage the people. The new managers still cannot deliver and more managers are added to manage the new managers. The end user is forced to play the "telephone" game. His set of requirements are given to one of the higher tiers of management who pass it down to the next tier(s) of management until it reaches the lowest level tier for development. The user's requirements become implemented as a system which is "exactly what he did not want."

Now is the time for Quality Assurance (QA) to come in and attempt to understand what went wrong "in the software." More time, energy, and dollars are wasted. Once again management takes the "safe" path by throwing more people and "experts" on the job. Hence, the failure is of the software whether it be for the Internet or anything else.

Another solution when things go wrong is to place blame when not understanding the problem and to take action without knowing the consequences. How familiar is this scenario? An entire management team is thrown out to show strong action by its management. Replaced by an inferior management team just after the previous organization got its act together, the new management discards all previous work (both good and bad) as well as the lessons learned. Now they will go through the same process themselves, losing months of lead time.

There are those who insist that the software be delivered on the scheduled date at all cost; again, without understanding the problem or knowing the consequences. The choice: deliver a system that does not work or deliver a system that worked before, instead of the new one, and suffer the consequences.

Of course, some systems "work" — but usually at the cost of compromised functionality, wasted dollars, lost time, and missed deadlines. For businesses, this often translates into lost opportunities and a competitive disadvantage.

Poor management can also bring about casualties when things are going well in the software. One venture group ousted all the technical people when the product in one small company reached production-ready status, leaving only marketing and sales people in the company. No one was left that was technical enough when real technical issues surfaced. Not only was it now impossible to make changes, but there were many nuances about the product that could only be answered by those who were no longer in the company.

Clearly, it's more complicated than simply blaming systems developers. After all, most are forced to think and design in ways that are governed by the limitations of the methodologies available to them. This is where leadership is needed to change things.

"FIXING WRONG THINGS UP"

Over the last decade, and even longer, a "quality" movement has swept the industry. It's mantra: do things right the first time. But this movement has largely bypassed systems engineering and software development. In those environments, the norm is one of "fixing wrong things up." What do we mean by this?

The problems start with the definition of requirements. Developers rely on many different types of mismatched methods to capture aspects of even a single definition. Typically, use cases are defined using one method, data flow another, dynamics another, state transitions another, object types yet another, and structures using still another method. The result is disaster waiting to happen, because once these aspects of requirements are defined there is no way to integrate them.

Unfortunately, requirements definition is only the beginning of the problems. Integration of object to object, module to module, phase to phase, or type of application to type of application becomes even more of a challenge than solving the business problem at hand. And this is compounded by a mismatch of products used for requirements, design, and development. Integration is left to the devices of myriad developers well into the development process. The resulting systems are hard to understand, and objects cannot be traced. At best, the system corresponds only a bit to the real world.

Often, developers are forced to codify requirements or design in terms of specific implementation technologies such as those that describe a database schema or are used to build a graphical user interface (GUI). More often than not, a system's key requirements and design information are buried or lost deep in a tangled Web of thousands of lines of manually constructed program code — or worse yet, left trapped in the mind of the original developer and never successfully transferred to those left to maintain or evolve the system.

Bad enough is to attempt an evolution of such a system; worse yet is to use parts of it as reusables to build a new system. In one project, upper management decided that an existing developed system was "very much like" another system that needed to be developed. The developers knew better. Nevertheless the developers were instructed by management to take the already developed system implemented in one language and reuse major portions of it, translating it line by line to a different implementation language, losing sight of all requirements for the new system. This insanity was instigated in large part by management up and down the chain who panicked because they could not see "real code" early into the project. These are the same managers who cannot understand why that same "real code" does not work, well after final release date.

We would go so far as to argue that these traditional methods actually encourage the ambiguous and ultimately incorrect definition of systems, which leads to incompatible interfaces and the propagation of errors throughout the development process. Again, to be fair, the developers inherit the problem.

SYSTEMS AND DEVELOPMENT ARE OUT OF CONTROL

To their credit, many systems developers define requirements that concentrate on the application needs of users. But users change their minds. Computing environments change. What about taking these into account?

Under the traditional development scenario, flexibility for change and handling the unpredictable are simply not dealt with up front. Requirements definitions take little note of the potential for the user's needs or environment to change. Unfortunately, porting to a new environment becomes a new development; for each new architecture, operating system, database, graphics environment, or language. Critical functionality is avoided out of fear of the unknown. Maintenance — because it is risky and the most expensive part of a system's life cycle — is left unaccounted for during the development phase. And when a system is targeted for a distributed environment, it is often defined and developed for a single processor environment and then redeveloped for a distributed environment.

From there, insufficient information about a system's run-time performance — including the information about decisions to be made between algorithms or architectures — is incorporated into a system definition. This results in design decisions that depend on analysis of outputs from exercising ad hoc implementations and associated testing scenarios. A system is defined without considering how to separate it from its target environment.

With this typical approach, developers have no way of knowing whether their design is a good one until the system is implemented and either fails or works. Any focus on reuse is late into development, during the coding phase. Compounding the problem, requirements definitions lack properties to help find, create, and make use of commonality. Modelers are forced to use informal and manual methods in their effort to find ways to divide a system into components natural for reuse. This makes redundancy a way of life, and provides little incentive for reuse. Errors proliferate.

Add to all this the problem of automation, or lack thereof. The typical requirements and development processes are needlessly manual. Today's systems are defined with insufficient intelligence for automated tools to use them as input. As a result, most automated tools concentrate on supporting the manual process instead of doing the real work.

Developers manually convert definitions into code. A process that could have been mechanized once for reuse is performed manually over and over. And even when automation attempts to do the real work, it is often incomplete across application domains or even within a domain, resulting in incomplete code (such as shell code). The generated code is often inefficient or hard-wired to an architecture, a language, or even a version of a language. In many cases, partial automations need to be integrated with incompatible partial automations or manual processes. Manual processes are then needed to complete what was left unfinished.

HOW THINGS GOT TO WHERE THEY ARE

While developers may think they can overcome any problem through sheer skill, managers need to know that development tools and practices themselves have a tremendous impact on the quality of software, and the expense of creating that software. Most of today's design and programming environments contain only a fragment of what is really needed to develop a complete system; sometimes they even make things worse.

For a good example of this phenomenon, take the traditional computer-aided software engineering tools — which were earlier designated as traditional CASE and many of these more recently recast and renamed in different forms. These tools were developed to help manage the development of large software applications. Focused on supporting the traditional paradigm with an evolving sophistication of user friendliness features (such as going from text to pictures), these tools added more enhancements as hardware and software advanced. But they didn't solve the root development problems.

There are tools available that handle analysis and design and tools used for generating some code. But there are few integrated tools available that handle the spectrum of "upper," "middle," and "lower" system functionality. Even fewer can be integrated with other support tools such as simulators, debuggers, and database managers. A seamless integration of the components of these tools is an even rarer phenomenon. And any choice of keeping up with new components as they enter the marketplace is all but nonexistent.

In many respects, things got worse with the move to GUIs. With the movement of systems from a host-based environment to the workstation and/or PC, we saw the introduction of a plethora of GUI development programs in the marketplace. The vast majority of these do not support the development of the entire system. Largely ignoring the core processing requirements of a system, they focus solely on the front end. This has created a new generation of systems, more sophisticated but ultimately just as fragmented and error-prone as those of the past.

Many of these earlier tools have had incorporated into themselves object-oriented features, "after the fact." While it may prove that to master object orientation is to provide increases in productivity, there is a significant downside risk. Done inappropriately, object-oriented development can cause problems more profound than those that flow from other development techniques. While languages such as C++ and Java can create hierarchies of many neat little packages called objects, the code used to define the interaction between the objects can easily resemble spaghetti (reminiscent of the "old" days), thus jeopardizing reliable reuse.

Today's migration to distributed technologies such as client/server (where the organization's data can be spread across one or more geographically distributed servers while the end user uses his or her GUI of choice to perform local processing) disables most of the utility of earlier and traditional methodologies.

Client servers, including those that are Internet based, are characterized by their diversity. In these models, a client initiates a distributed activity and a server(s) carries out that activity. One organization may store its data on multiple databases, program in several programming languages, and use more than one operating system — hence, different GUIs.

Since the complexity of software development is increased a hundred fold in this new environment, the need for a better methodology is heightened. Given the complexity of such things as client/server, code trapped in programs is not flexible enough to meet the needs of this type of environment.

Unfortunately, there are no conventional object-oriented methodologies with associated tools to help developers develop systems that hit the better, faster, cheaper mark. As a result, most of today's systems still require more resources allocated to maintenance than to the original development effort.

It is to their credit that many of the people in the software engineering field are attempting to rectify the causes of declining productivity and quality that accompany the conventional systems development approach. But their efforts continue to fall short because the core paradigm on which their work is based treats symptoms rather than the root problem. Current software engineering approaches fail to see the software development process from the larger perspective that is so critical. They continue to travel the traditional path.

A PLAN FOR SYSTEMS THAT BUILD THEMSELVES

The first step is to understand the impact that software and its development (good or bad) has on an organization. But for this to happen the organization itself needs to be understood. One way of understanding an organization better is to define its goals.

A business plan (or project plan) should reflect a true understanding of an organization's goals and therefore a means to accomplish them (what the true business plan should be). If goals (the organization's requirements) were better defined, business plans (specifications) and its associated operational plans (detailed designs) would be more realistic and the company in question would have a much better chance to be on the right track. Otherwise what is the system (the company) that is being developed or transitioning to and who are its users (the marketplace)?

We have worked with several organizations (including commercial and government agencies) to define goals and to determine how each organization can best meet its goals. These goals were defined as part of an enterprise model using DBTF and a system design and development environment based on it.

Part of defining goals is to show how they relate to each other; for example, if a goal is not accomplished with some success, those dependent on it have less chance of being accomplished successfully.

Interesting things surface during such a process. For example, it quickly becomes clear how dependent the bottom line can be on seemingly unrelated or distantly related areas. A decision such as who is chosen to manage the software; what software processes, methods, and tools are selected; what axioms are at the very foundations of the methods selected; how one module in the organization is designed; or what the properties of an object are in one of the applications would be taken more seriously by upper management if they realized the significance of such a decision on the bottom line. Even before this kind of exercise, one would no doubt conclude that such decisions could impact somewhat the quality and cost of building the software. What is not so apparent is that it affects the organization in many not so obvious ways, ranging from what kind of people are attracted to your business to what kind of business you will ultimately have.

MANAGING A SOFTWARE DEVELOPER ORGANIZATION

Today, a typical software company is at a crossroads and must decide whether to keep things the way they are now or whether it should change its way of doing business. It builds reasonably complex to complex systems having both real-time distributed and database requirements. Until now the company has been building systems the traditional way such as using a commercial proprietary GUI builder for screens, competing database products for database portions, and handcoding in C or C++ and perhaps Java for the rest of its software development process. These systems reside on several platforms including UNIX, PC, and mainframes.

Standards are not in common use at this company and every project does things differently. When standards are put in place, they are not necessarily standards that will benefit the company. The company is growing too fast and is having trouble delivering on time. When it does deliver, the systems are not working and it takes months longer than anticipated to turn them into production quality for its users. Everything depends on a handful of experts and there are not enough experts to go around.

One software developer company we learned a lot about was the market leader in its vertical market, bringing in new business at a startling rate. But, it was losing money, also at a startling rate. It was in jeopardy of losing market share to a company who had less baggage to cope with. Some hard decisions needed to be made, particularly in how to build its software. Changes were needed in order to avoid such problems in the future. The question was what to do to get from here to there.

Options for the Software Developer Organization

This software company has several options, ranging from one extreme to the other: (1) keep things the same; (2) add tools and techniques that support business as usual but provide relief in selected areas; (3) bring in more modern but traditional tools and techniques to replace existing ones; (4) use a new paradigm with the most advanced tools and techniques that formalizes the process of software development while at the same time capitalizing on software already developed; or (5) same as the previous option except start over from the beginning.

Certainly, it is high risk for this company to keep doing things the way it has been. As with any organization, change is not easy, but this company knows that change will be necessary in order to save itself. Option 1, therefore, should not be an option. To do so would compromise reaching the company's highest priority goals. The second option of applying a more or less quick fix would at best address only some of the problem areas and then only on a temporary basis. Maybe worse yet is bringing in an entirely "new" but traditional approach. Not only does it take the time and effort to transition from one approach to another but the new approach still suffers from the basic core problems of the one being used by the company today.

Choosing an option becomes an easier task once a company's goals are understood and agreed upon. Exhibit 30.1 contains a summary of goals we defined for and with this company. Here is contained a sketch of goals and their direct and indirect relationships (including dependencies) as types of objects in this company's enterprise model. Here we begin to make use of reusables to express the goals, sketched with a partially filled in Type Map (TMap). The TMap, a tree of objects and their relationships, is one form of model using DBTF's system language. The models are created with the use of a systems design and development environment, an automation based on DBTF.

In this TMap sketch, the top node type is Maximize Profit (see upper left-hand corner). This sketch has been decomposed a few levels in order to illustrate some of the types of relationships in this system. The types on all of the other nodes are needed to define how to Maximize Profit. Several other TMap sketches are contained in this model, each of which is a reusable for at least one TMap sketch. See, for example, Be the Best which is used in Maximize Profit, Handles Fast Growth, and Prepare for the Shortage of Good People.

One of the interesting findings in examining this model is that every goal, if you drive it down to a low enough level, is dependent on the strategic technology goal, including itself since it is recursive. Similarly, all of the goals are dependent on the reuse goal, including itself. Clearly, if they are not already, the reuse and technologies strategies used within the corporation should be the highest of priorities in determining if the company is in fact meeting the requirements that are important for all of its goals including maximizing short- and long-term profits for the corporation.

In order to reach these goals, we learned during the process the importance of the company's choosing the fourth or fifth option of evolving to the use of tools and techniques that formalize, preventatively, the company's process of software engineering. The fourth option is probably most practical from a short-term consideration. The fifth option, although most desirable from a long-term view, would take more time and should be chosen if such time, including lead time, is available on the project that will first apply the new technology.

How the Goals Impact Each Other

Each company goal was better understood if its relationships to other goals were understood. For example, it quickly became apparent that high-

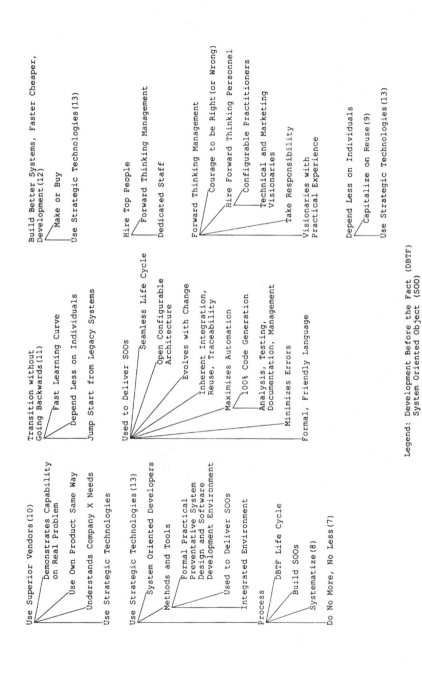

Exhibit 30.1. TMap sketch of goals.

404

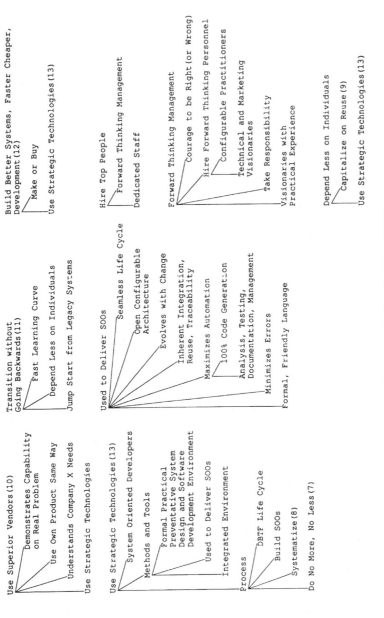

Use Superior Vendors (10)
 Demonstrates Capability on Real Problem
 Use Own Product Same Way
 Understands Company X Needs
Use Strategic Technologies

Use Strategic Technologies (13)
 System Oriented Developers
 Methods and Tools
 Formal Practical Preventative System Design and Software Development Environment
 Used to Deliver SOOs
 Integrated Environment
Process
 DBTF Life Cycle
 Build SOOs
Systematize (8)
Do No More, No Less (7)

Transition without Going Backwards (11)
 Fast Learning Curve
 Depend Less on Individuals
 Jump Start from Legacy Systems

Used to Deliver SOOs
 Seamless Life Cycle
 Open Configurable Architecture
 Evolves with Change
 Inherent Integration, Reuse, Traceability
 100% Code Generation
 Maximizes Automation
 Analysis, Testing, Documentation, Management
 Minimizes Errors
 Formal, Friendly Language

Build Better Systems, Faster Cheaper, Development (12)
 Make or Buy
 Use Strategic Technologies (13)

Hire Top People
 Forward Thinking Management
 Dedicated Staff

Forward Thinking Management
 Courage to be Right (or Wrong)
 Hire Forward Thinking Personnel
 Configurable Practitioners
 Technical and Marketing Visionaries
 Take Responsibility
 Visionaries with Practical Experience

Depend Less on Individuals
 Capitalize on Reuse (9)
 Use Strategic Technologies (13)

Legend: Development Before the Fact (DBTF)
        System Oriented Object (SOO)

Exhibit 30.1. *Continued.*

405

level goals such as making a profit and preparing for the future are directly dependent on which methods and tools are used for building the company's software.

It is important to understand the spirit of a goal and not just pay it umbrage. For example, coming up with an arbitrary set of standards just to have standards is not within the spirit of the standards goal. Mandating a standard of using the same vendor's tools as those used by a neighboring project when such tools do not support the project as well as other tools could, is an example of not satisfying this goal. Subgoal constraints such as the standard of using the same language, tools, etc. for all aspects of definition help to prevent a loose and misguided interpretation of this goal, illustrating the importance of formally defining these goals.

Everything Is Relative

To truly understand a system, be it a company as an enterprise or a payroll software system, means to understand it in terms of its relativity. Everything in the world in any of these systems is relative. One person's requirements are another's implementation; one person's application is another's operating system.

On one project, two development groups argued for weeks about which definition for requirements was the correct one. Upon further analysis, they were both correct since they were each talking about a different target system. One was a system for the end user. The other was a system about that system used for developing the end-user system. Like the difference between a simulation and a simulator.

No More, No Less

An important goal for any organization is the one which follows the no more, no less principle. This means doing what is necessary to reach the company's goals, but not anything unnecessary. Unnecessary work happens when meetings or paperwork are created for walk-throughs of results from manual tasks that could have been automated (such as the manual creation of code and its analysis); learning more than one language for different phases or for different tools when it is not necessary; doing extra work because of being locked into the wrong tool; doing redundant work because one tool cannot be transitioned over gracefully to another tool needed to complete a task.

Satisfying this goal also means not making things more difficult than necessary. Most everyone learns from their own experiences — whether developing real world systems or just getting through each day — that there are difficult solutions to a problems and very straightforward solutions to the same problem. For example, it is more difficult to perform long division with Roman numerals than with the Arabic number system.

When possible, it is usually best to tackle the source or cause of a problem instead of just removing its symptoms. Sometimes things can be simplified by creating solutions that will help recover from what *appears* to be the *effect* and not the *cause* of a problem, but, in fact, is the source relative to the problem being solved. For example, recovering from the loss of computer memory is simpler than dealing separately with all of the things that might cause such a thing to happen such as lightning, the computer being mishandled by the user, etc. Here relativity becomes a consideration in simplifying the solution. In this case the direct source of the problem that is being solved resides with the computer, not the outside world which has lightning and careless users. In a sense, this is the ability of an object to have self preservation.

Often, a solution derived for one problem solves other problems. The trick is to recognize when you have solved more than one problem with a solution. For example, we developed a system that could be reconfigured in real time to more effectively respond to and recover from errors and to deal with changing priorities by going from a synchronous to an asynchronous operating system. We then realized we had also found a much better and less error-prone way to have the same kind of flexibility with the development of that system. It worked because the actual system being developed had been evolved into a more modular system to accommodate the asynchronous processes of development, where a change to a process or functional area was separate and apart from another process. This significantly accelerated the application's development and maintenance process.

Reducing unnecessary tasks is not only a savings in time and money, but it also eliminates a dependency on processes, methods, and tools that are no longer needed. More importantly, there is no longer a dependency on what could become for some businesses armies of people needed to support obsolescence. And today armies of people are hard to find.

Reuse in the Large

Another goal that is important to all organizations is the reuse goal. Part of meeting the reuse goal is to mechanize by standardization and effective automation, both inherent forms of reuse. Sometimes what is explicit reuse in traditional methods is implicit with more advanced methods. For example, with traditional object-oriented methods one needs to work at being object oriented. This is not the case, however, with more advanced object-oriented methods.

Reuse in the true sense of the word is a systematic process. It starts from the beginning with requirements that allow for diverse projects with an option for different specifications where each specification allows for different implementations (for example, one project with code generated to interface with Informix and another with Oracle; or one project with client server and another with mainframe).

To be successful, reuse needs to be an intelligent and formal process, under control. A mechanism can be set up by management to support all development projects in the sharing of a common set of reuse modules, itself a system. This could be a core product from which all applications could jump start their developments (what NASA refers to as reusable productization).[15,16]

Even the vendor chosen can impact a company's reuse strategy. If a vendor actually uses its own technology and products to do for itself what it is selling to the customer this should be an excellent sign, since it illustrates reuse of common experience.

Avoiding a Rocky Transition

To transition to new methods and tools without taking a step backwards (see transition goal) — no time or money lost and less risk than before — by its very nature depends on what the new methods and tools are and how they are applied. Many things need to be taken into consideration. A learning curve that fits into a project's schedules is important, but if the benefits, such as the productivity gained using the new methods is great enough, then a longer learning curve may be justifiable. To counter risk, it is also important to have a means to evolve from the existing methods to the new ones at a safe pace should it become necessary or desirable to do so. It is important, for example, that the new approach provides a means to reuse what has already been developed in the company. With a strategic technology, with features like an open architecture, risk is minimized.

To make sure that the transition is a smooth one, it helps to start off with one or more forward-thinking technical leaders at the company. They will inspire others and can help train them as well. In addition it helps to define a process for the others that shows one way to get started, using a company project as an example of how to accomplish this.

The Strategic Technology Goal is the Sleeper

With the strategic technology goal, "point" products are used only if they can become an integral part of the strategic technology and products. Such technology and products should be used only if they support the philosophy of preventing as many things as possible that could go wrong before they do go wrong. All objects in a system whether they be for hardware, peopleware, or software (or some combination thereof) should be treated systematically from the start to the deployment of that system following the systematic goal. Such a technology solution inherently capitalizes on following the reuse goal and applying the "no more, no less" goal and can be used at any phase of development.

This technology should be formal so that its semantics and the semantics of the system it is used to develop are well understood. Although the properties of being formal are inherently part of the methods and associated tools, it must also be "friendly" enough to be placed into practical use.

What does not often surface in the beginning, that should when considering a technology, is its durability, i.e., its ability to adapt to changing technologies, market conditions, and requirements. It is safe to say that never should a technology be adopted that locks a corporation in. A product that locks you in compromises your choices of functionality, hardware, and software products you can use (including your own reusables) both now and in the future.

With a "lock-in" product, the result could be at best a significantly greater effort if you want to change your mind in the future. An example is a product that can only generate to client server applications but not to mainframe based applications. Another is a product that can only use its own GUI environment but does not allow its users to take the advantage of additional capability from another GUI environment, when there is a requirement to do so. Or a product that once it automatically generates its application for one database environment cannot turn around and automatically generate that same application for another database environment.

A strategic product should be able to interface to other technologies (call or be called by or generate to other technologies) as they come into the marketplace, and to existing legacy code on an as-needed basis. It should provide a means to evolve from and with legacy code, now and later, to newer technologies and application requirements as they become available; it should provide a means to automatically generate (and then reconfigure and regenerate) diverse implementations and architectures from a given set of requirements.

A strategic product should be able to evolve and allow one to continue to build on top of it and in terms of it, maintaining the same formal properties. It should allow one to integrate with old and new developments should one choose to add to the vendor's environment.

What is important is that the product automatically does the real work, instead of automatically supporting unnecessary manual processes, sometimes actually creating extra work. In addition, it should provide the ability to build effective reusables that will evolve with change. With properties such as these, the reliability of the software is maximized and the cost to build it and the time to market it is minimized.

A RADICALLY DIFFERENT APPROACH FOR STRATEGIC TECHNOLOGIES

The means to fulfill the strategic technology goal may well be found along nontraditional paths, through innovation — which means creating new methods or new environments for using new methods. In fact, the road to success may well exist within past mistakes. If this is the case, the company for whom the goals were defined is in the right place at the right time to take advantage of such a moment.

The first step to a new approach is to recognize the problems that are truly at the root, and categorize those problems in terms of how they might be prevented in the future. Deriving practical solutions comes next, and the process can be repeated again and again as we look to solve new problems with the benefit of what we know from our new solution environment. With the company discussed above, for example, this was accomplished by saying what is needed (defining the goals), realizing, therefore, what is missing, and filling in the void by satisfying the goals, including coming up with the right methods and tools.

What if management adopted a different kind of thinking that governed systems development? What if the kind of thinking needed to satisfy the strategic technology goal would govern the above company's development? What if there were a different way to build systems that would significantly and positively affect a company's financial picture, one that concentrated on preventing problems that surface in a typical development environment rather than fixing them after they've surfaced at the most inopportune and expensive point in time (see Exhibit 30.2). How might it work? Wouldn't it require a radical revision of the way this company does its software?

Radical, indeed, because it would have to provide a formal framework for doing things right the first time. And that is precisely what we have with Development Before the Fact (DBTF).

The DBTF paradigm is about beginnings. It was derived from the combination of steps taken to solve the problems of traditional systems engineering and software development. What makes DBTF radically different is that it is preventative rather than curative.

We can make an analogy to a human system to explain the difference. John goes to the dentist because he has a cavity in his tooth, and the dentist determines that a root canal is needed. Had John gone sooner, the dentist might have been able to simply fill the cavity, which — because it would have been that a root canal was necessary — would have been curative with respect to the cavity and preventative with respect to the root canal. Had John eaten properly and brushed regularly, he might have prevented not only the root canal, but the initial cavity as well.

Exhibit 30.2. Problems of Traditional System Engineering and Software Development Environments

Too late, if at all	Compromised quality, Late to market, $$$ ... wasted
Integration: Mismatched methods, objects, modules, phases, application types, architectures and products.	Left to devices of a myriad developers well into development. Hard to understand. Cannot trace objects. No correspondence to real world.
Elimination of errors: Methods encourage systems to be defined as ambiguous and incorrect.	System out of control, incompatible interfaces, propagation of errors throughout development.
Flexibility/unpredictability: Systems not defined to handle open architectures/processes, changes, or error recovery.	Porting is new development. Maintenance is costly and risky. Critical functionality avoided for fear of the unknown.
Reusability: No properties in definitions to find, create, and use commonality. Focus is on implementation.	Redundancy a way of life. Errors propagate accordingly.
Automation: Supports manual process instead of doing the real work. Limited, incomplete, fragmented, disparate, and inefficient.	Most of the development process is manual and, therefore, error prone and inefficient. Manual processes needed to complete unfinished automations.

If we add in the cost of dental care, this analogy becomes particularly instructive with respect to systems development. To treat a cavity with a root canal — that is, after the fact — is expensive. To fill a cavity on time is far less expensive. And to prevent the cavity in the first place — that is, before the fact — is far less expensive again.

Another illustration comes from our own experience developing systems. A few years ago, one of the students in training in our group was in awe of one of the developers because he could "program so fast." But this developer's stuff was full of bugs and impossible to understand. In fact, we spent a lot of time redeveloping his application to make it work, because it wasn't done right in the first place.

There was another developer in the group who was not nearly as fast, but almost everything he did worked and was easy to understand. The time we spent redeveloping the "fast" developer's work exceeded the time this "slower" developer spent on his stuff.

A third developer in the group got little attention from this student. He was always deep in thought, looking for ways to abstract, looking for ways to build more generic software. He often took even longer to program than the "slower" developer above. On more than one occasion, he found out that it was not necessary at all to develop the program in question because he had already created reusables.

411

In the end, the third developer was really the "fastest," because his approach was more "before the fact" than the others.

The first developer — the one with whom our student was in awe — might learn to develop modules for the rest of us to reuse. But what would be missing without the benefit of the right experience, or reusable knowledge, is that deep thought the third developer put into his work.

The DBTF Philosophy

Reliability is at the heart of DBTF, which treats all objects as complete systems. It provides an initial and logical framework using mathematics within which objects, their structure, behavior, and interactions with other objects may be captured. The philosophy behind DBTF is that its objects are recursively reusable and reliable. Reliable systems are defined in terms of reliable systems (see Exhibit 30.3): only reliable systems are used as building blocks, and only reliable systems are used as mechanisms to integrate these building blocks to form a new system. The new system becomes reusable for building other systems. All levels and layers of a system have to be reliable for a system to be reliable.

DBTF is based on a set of axioms and on the assumption of a universal set of objects. Each DBTF system is defined with properties that control its own design and development throughout its life cycle(s), where the life cycle itself is an evolving system that could be defined and developed as a target system using this approach. The emphasis on defining things with the right methods the first time prevents problems before they happen. An integration of function and object oriented, DBTF is based on a unique concept of control of a system's objects (including control of organization of objects, timing, priority, resources, data flow, and data).

Reliable Systems
are Defined in Terms of Reliable Systems

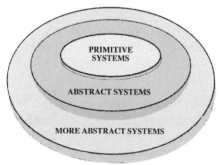

- Use only reliable systems

- Integrate these systems with reliable systems

- The result is a system(s) which is reliable

- Use resulting reliable system(s) along with more primitive ones to build new and larger reliable systems

Exhibit 30.3. Reliable systems are defined in terms of reliable systems.

From the very beginning, a DBTF system inherently integrates all of its own objects (and all aspects, relationships, and viewpoints of these objects) and the combinations of functionality using these objects. A DBTF system maximizes its own reliability and flexibility to change; capitalizes on its own parallelism; supports its own run-time performance analysis; and maximizes the potential for its own reuse and automation. It is defined with built-in quality, built-in productivity, and built-in control.

The concept of automation is central to this whole discussion. When you think about it, automation itself is an inherently reusable process. If a system can not be reused, it certainly can not be automated. Consider, for example, the process of software development used within a particular organization. Were that process mechanized it could be reused again and again. That in itself implies the process could be automated.

Again, a DBTF system achieves its high level of quality through a preventative rather than curative approach. Whereas the curative approach requires continuously testing the system until the errors are eliminated, the preventative approach of DBTF means not allowing those errors to appear in the first place. Whereas accelerating a particular design and development process under the curative scenario means adding resources, be they people or processors, the preventative approach finds a more efficient way, capitalizing more on reuse or eliminating parts of the process altogether.

DBTF is centered on doing things right in the first place by using a unique yet straightforward way of definition. A starting point is concept formulation and requirements definition, done in a way that eliminates many of the common problems of traditional software development.

This method concentrates on how one can define a system model that captures — to the greatest extent practical — goals such as reuse, portability, and interoperability. Engineering judgment is useful in determining when to use which type of modeling, and how these sides of a system should play together depending on the requirements of the target system. Under this scenario, "design" and "programming" become relative terms. Higher-level "programming" becomes design to lower layers. The focus is a systems viewpoint, keeping in mind that even lower levels of a program can be defined as a set of models.

With DBTF, we model objects from the real world with a formal but friendly graphical language and then use that model to build an implementation-independent design around those objects. We describe a set of system-oriented concepts and a modeling technique that can be used to analyze problem requirements, design a solution to the problem, and then automatically implement that solution in terms of an architecture of choice (e.g., choice of operating system, programming language, graphical user interface, communications protocol, database, or legacy code).

413

We see effective reuse itself as an inherently preventative concept. Reuse can be successful only if the system is worth reusing. First, the functionality requirements of the system to be reused must be equivalent to the candidate system for using that resusable. Reusing something that has no errors, to obtain a desired functionality, avoids the errors of developing a system from scratch as well as the time and money wasted in developing it.

This does not mean reusing code from an earlier system which is "kind of like" the new system and which has to be changed in a "few places" to force-fit the reuse. It means starting from the beginning of a life cycle, not its end — as is typically the case with traditional methods. From there, a system can be reused for each new phase of development. No matter what kind, every 10 reuses saves 10 unnecessary developments.

Because DBTF systems can be developed with properties that control their very own design and development, the methodology results in the creation of reusable systems that promote automation. Each system definition models both its application and its life cycle.

It has been our experience that the requirements definition for a software-based system determines to a great extent the degree to which the development of that system is a success. Not only should the requirements be defined to state the user's explicit intent, but they should also support the process of defining themselves and the systems implemented from them. These are underlying concepts of DBTF.

With an automation of DBTF, the same concepts and same notation can be used throughout the entire systems design and software development process. There's no need for the software engineer to translate into a new notation at each development stage.

The DBTF approach includes a language, a set of methods and tools, and a process — all of which are based on a formal theory.

Formal, but Friendly Language

Once understood, the characteristics of good design can be reused by incorporating them into a language for defining systems. The DBTF language — meta-language, really — is the key to DBTF. It can define any aspect of any system and integrate it with any other aspect, whether it is used to define highway, banking, library, missile, or enterprise systems; Internet-based, real-time, client server, or database environments; across industries, academia, or government. The same language can be used to define system requirements (where the language supports and accelerates the collective thinking process before concepts are well understood), specifications, design, and detailed design for functional, resource, and resource allocation architectures throughout all levels and layers of seamless definition, including hardware, software, and peopleware.

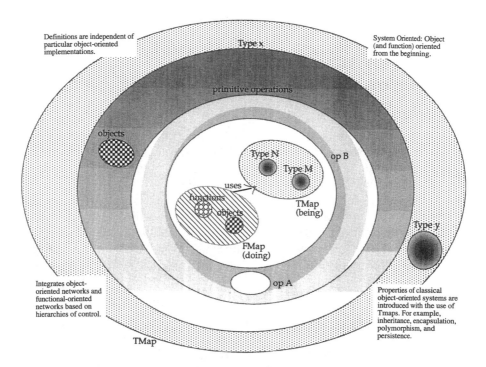

Exhibit 30.4. Every object is a system, every system is an object.

Although syntax independent, every syntax shares the same semantics. Overarching this is that all of these aspects are directly related to the real world and that the language inherently captures this.

DBTF's language is used to define system-oriented objects. A system-oriented object (SOO) is a system that is both object oriented and function-oriented. Its function oriented definitions are inherently integrated with its object-oriented definitions. With SOOs, every object is a system, every system is an object (Exhibit 30.4).

Unlike traditional approaches, DBTF concentrates on delivering formal and reliable systems as its main focus. Whereas traditional tools support a user in managing the process of developing software, DBTF's automation develops the software. In fact it develops itself.

DBTF is used throughout a life cycle, starting with the formulation of concepts and interviewing the user and continuing with the definition of requirements, analysis, simulation, specification, design (including system architecture design), algorithm development, implementation, configuration management, testing, maintenance, and reverse engineering. Its users include end users, managers, system engineers, software engineers, and test engineers.

MODELING A SYSTEM-ORIENTED OBJECT

Every SOO model is defined in terms of functional hierarchies (FMaps) to capture time characteristics and type hierarchies (TMaps) to capture space characteristics (Exhibit 30.5). The TMap, a static view of the structure of the objects in a system, describes the types of objects in a system and the relationships between them. The FMap describes the functions in a system and the relationships between them — including the potential interactions among objects in the system as they change state and transition from function to function. Exhibit 30.6 contains an example of a very small view of a company's enterprise model which has only one FMap and one TMap. In this model the TMap defines the objects having to do with kinds of employees and departments and the FMap is used to determine if a given employee is full time or not.

Using an FMap, the functional model describes the dynamics or aspects of a system that change over time, including data flow, control flow, and the functional mappings (data transformations) that take place within a system. An FMap is a hierarchical network, or graph, whose nodes are functions, any of which could be assigned to a process. A parent's relationship to its children is defined in terms of a function structure. A function structure is a type of function with unspecified function nodes in its definition, but when the structure is used, the nodes — as with the TMap — are specified or filled in.

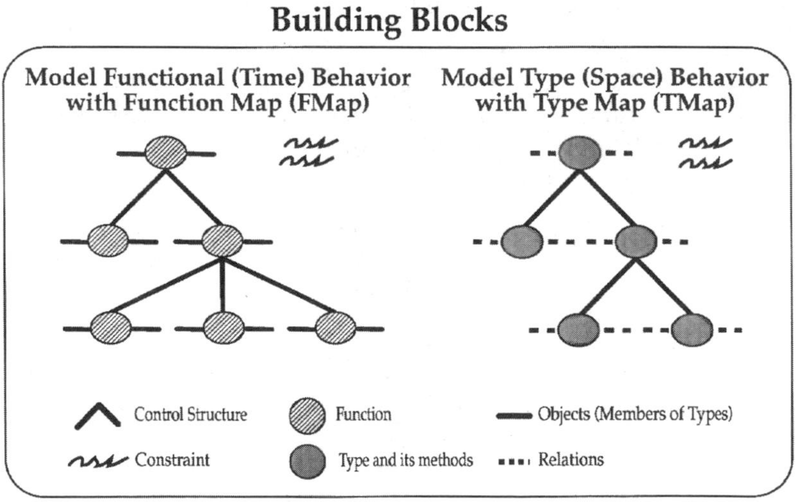

Building Blocks

Exhibit 30.5. Building blocks.

A System: the Integration of FMaps and TMaps

Type Map

Function Map

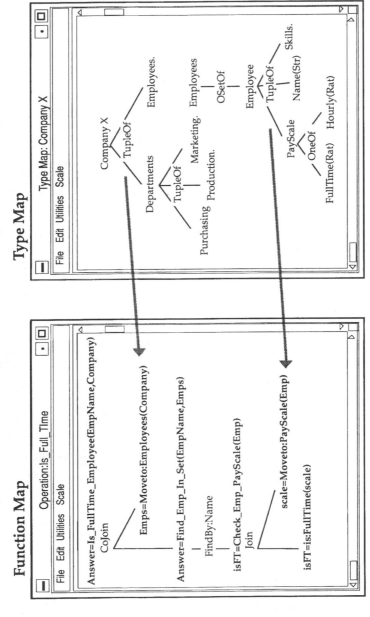

Specific Abstract Types inherit methods from Parameterized Types and are applied as leaf functions in FMaps

Exhibit 30.6. A system: the integration of FMaps and TMaps.

417

FMaps and TMaps guide the designer in thinking through his concepts at all levels of system design. With these hierarchies, everything you need to know (no more, no less) is available. All model viewpoints can be obtained from FMaps and TMaps, including those mentioned above: data flow, control flow, state transitions, data structure, and dynamics. Maps of functions (FMaps) are inherently and naturally integrated with maps of types (TMaps).

Each function on an FMap node is defined in terms of and controls its children functions. For example, the function "build the table" could be decomposed into and control its children functions "make parts and assemble." Each function on an FMap has one or more objects as its input and one or more objects as its output. All inputs of any function in an FMap as well as all outputs are members of types in a TMap. On a TMap there is a type at each node that is defined in terms of, and controls, its children types. For example, "type, table," could be decomposed into and control its children types, "legs and top."

A TMap is a hierarchical network (control hierarchy or networked relations between objects), or graph, whose nodes are object types. Every type on a TMap owns a set of inherited primitive operations. For every function (operation) within an object's domain there is an associated function control hierarchy (i.e., an FMap). Each object type node, as a parent, controls its children types; as a child, each is controlled by its parent. A parent's relationship to its children is defined in terms of a type structure. A type structure is a type of object with unspecified type nodes in its definition; when the structure is used, the nodes are specified or filled in.

The relationship between a parent and its children is determined by the type structure chosen to define it. A type structure encapsulates a set of operators to be applied to the relationships between the parent objects and their children objects. A type structure may also include other encapsulated object types. Every type has a set of operations associated with it.

There are other types of control hierarchies for SOOs. For example, an object map (OMap) — which is an object control hierarchy — is an instance of a TMap. John's "green truck" represented by an OMap could, for example, be an object instance of object type "truck" represented by a TMap. In Exhibit 30.7 Joe, in one of the OMaps, is an instance of person on the TMap and Sam, on the other OMap, is an instance of the same type. Each object (a member of a type from a TMap) is an instantiation of a TMap type and resides in an object hierarchy (OMap).

FMaps are inherently integrated with TMaps by using these objects and their primitive operations. FMaps are used to define, integrate, and control the transformations of objects from one state to another state (for example, a table with a broken leg to a table with a fixed leg). Primitive functions

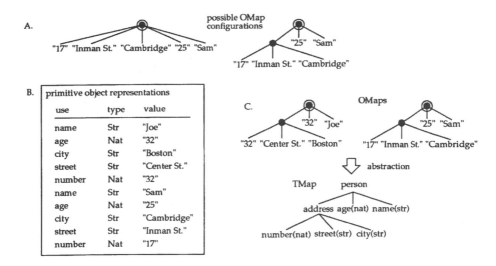

Abtracting OMaps into TMaps

Exhibit 30.7. Abstracting OMaps into Tmaps.

---

corresponding to primitive operations on types defined in the TMap reside at the bottom nodes of an FMap. Primitive types reside at the bottom nodes of a TMap. Each primitive function (leaf node) on an FMap is a primitive operation of a member (object) of the TMap.

In this context, primitive does not imply low level; rather it is a term that describes the encapsulation of behavior and data behind a well-defined interface, raising the level of abstraction of a system. New primitive types are defined and recursively reused in new DBTF systems. Primitive types are also used to define boundaries between a DBTF system and other existing systems (such as database managers or existing legacy systems).

When a system has its input object states instantiated with values plugged in for a particular performance pass, it exists in the form of an execution hierarchy (EMap).

A way to begin designing a SOO is that an observer (or modeler) compares the behavior of real-world objects to the known tools that support the DBTF object modeling theory (Exhibit 30.8). Objects and their behaviors are represented in the object modeling theory in terms of OMaps, each of which is an instance of a TMap, and EMaps, each of which is an instance of an FMap, as tools. An OMap is a hierarchical network of objects and their relationships. An EMap is a set of functions, instances, and their relationships.

A history of instances of OMap and EMap model constructions (which are really based on an underlying control theory upon which the modeling

419

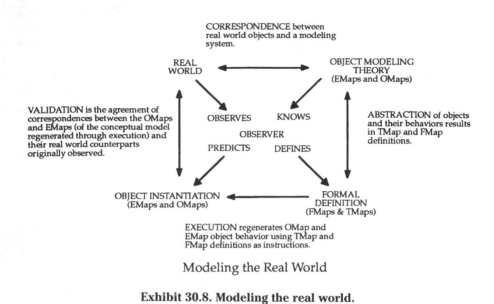

Modeling the Real World

Exhibit 30.8. Modeling the real world.

theory is based) can be simplified by abstracting them into formal definition as TMaps and FMaps, respectively. An OMap derives the control of its objects from a TMap. Likewise, an EMap derives the control of its actions from an FMap. Once a modeler has a formal definition, it is then used to run (or regenerate the OMap and EMap instances of) the system. Since the object instantiation is to be a prediction of the original real-world correspondence that was defined, it is validated by comparing it to the original real world with the object instantiation. If it matches, it is an accurate depiction of the real world — and the observer's intent has been satisfied.

Models and Their Integration

Relative to OMaps and EMaps, TMaps and FMaps are reusables for capturing an object's structure and behavior. Whereas an OMap depicts an actual instance of an object's behavior, a TMap depicts one of a possible set of instances of an object's behavior. Whereas an EMap depicts an actual execution instance, an FMap depicts one of a possible set of execution instances. An object is an instance of a type. An action is an instance of a function.

Conversely, when one executes a definition consisting of FMaps and TMaps, the FMap abstract definition is instantiated as one or more EMaps and the TMap abstract definition is instantiated as one or more OMaps.

An FMap (Exhibit 30.9A) is a definition of a system of object events and their possible interactions. The FMap integrates with the TMap to specify

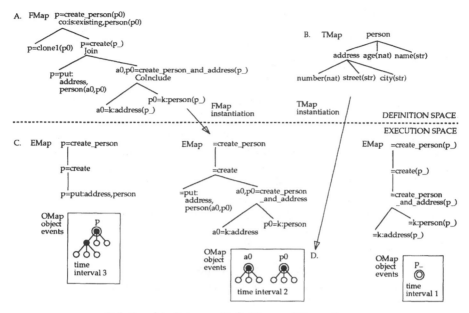

Relationship Between Definition and Execution

Exhibit 30.9. Relationship between definition and execution.

---

the event types and the specific function (as an instance of a primitive operation of a TMap type) to be performed on each object. The FMap controls the sequencing and activation of events — the event structures — in terms of what we call primitive control structures, which define all the possible ways in which events may functionally interact. As we discussed earlier, the concept of a structure is applied to both FMaps and TMaps.

A TMap (Exhibit 30.9B) defines the potential organization of objects for its OMap instances, the potential relations, and the interactions which an object may have with other objects. The TMap is sometimes thought of as a blueprint for object construction. These potential interactions are defined for each parent type as a set of primitive operation definitions. When used in an FMap, a primitive operation defines how the parent may interact with other objects in a particular functional context as with a primitive function.

An EMap (Exhibit 30.9C), an instantiation of an FMap, indicates within a particular time interval the lines of active control over actions that are in force for a set of co-occurring events and their associated OMap objects. Primitive functions of an FMap become primitive actions on an EMap. An action, once activated with its input events, transitions their associated OMap objects to output events. As new events come into existence, new

421

lines of control are formed to bring future actions under control. When events and actions are no longer needed and they recede into the past, their lines of control are withdrawn. An EMap is always only in the present, while the FMap represents all the potential activations of the system of events and actions over all time.

An OMap (Exhibit 30.9D), an instantiation of a TMap, indicates the current state of interrelationships of the set of objects of which it is in control. OMap objects and their relationships are subject to the actions of the EMap. As actions in response to object events are managed by the EMap, their corresponding OMap objects (referenced by an event) evolve, appear, change (having relations with other objects and severing relations), and disappear. OMap objects take on a shape or structure as constrained by the blueprint of combinations which are allowed in the TMap.

A Design Scenario

Typically, a team of designers will begin to design a system at any level (this system could be hardware, software, peopleware, or some combination) by sketching a TMap of their application. This is where they decide on the types of objects (and the relationships between these objects) that they will have in their system. Often a Road Map (RMap), which organizes all system objects (including FMaps, Tmaps, and other RMaps) will be sketched in parallel with the TMap (Exhibit 30.10).

As we've been told by several SOO designers: "the FMaps begin almost to fall into place once a TMap(s) has been agreed upon by the design team because of the natural partitioning of functionality (or groups of functionality) provided to the designers by the TMap system." The structure of a TMap by its very nature defines several universal mechanisms that support its life cycle. For example, a TMap has an inherent way to be instantiated, to be populated using a GUI, to be stored persistently, etc. The TMap provides the structural criteria from which to evaluate the functional partitioning of the system (for example, the shape of the structural partitioning of the FMaps is balanced against the structural organization of the shape of the objects as defined by the TMap). With FMaps and Tmaps, a system (and its viewpoints) is divided into functionally natural components and groups of functional components which naturally work together; a system is defined from the very beginning to inherently integrate and make understandable its own real-world definition.

All FMaps and TMaps are ultimately defined in terms of three primitive control structures: a parent controls its children to have a dependent relationship, an independent relationship, or a decision-making relationship. We say "ultimately" because, more abstract structures can be defined in terms of the primitive ones to accelerate the process of defining and understanding a system.

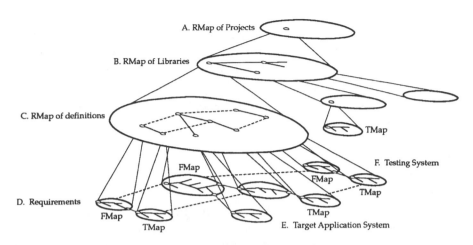

A. RMap of Projects

B. RMap of Libraries

C. RMap of definitions

D. Requirements

FMap

TMap

FMap

TMap

FMap

TMap

F. Testing System

E. Target Application System

An RMap Defines the Architecture of a System

A. RMap of projects.
B. RMap of libraries within a project.
C. RMap of definitions within a project library.
D. Requirements for target system being built.
E. The target application system being built.
F. A testing system for the target application.

Exhibit 30.10. An RMap defines the architecture of a system.

Nonprimitive structures can be defined for both FMaps and TMaps. They can be created for asynchronous, synchronous, and interrupt scenarios used in real-time, distributed systems such as those found in Internet applications. Similarly, retrieval and query structures can be defined for database management systems within a client server environment. Nonprimitive structures can also be created for more vertical market-driven reusables, for example for a cash management or accident reporting system.

A formal set of rules is associated with each primitive structure. If these rules are followed, interface errors — which typically account for up to 90 percent of all system errors — are "removed" before the fact (that is, during the definition phase) by preventing them in the first place. In traditional development most of these errors would not even be discovered until testing. Using the primitive structures and their derivatives supports a system to be defined from the very beginning to inherently maximize its own elimination of errors.

The TMap provides universal primitive operations of type, Any, which are used for controlling objects and their object states which are inherited by all types. They create, destroy, copy, reference, move, access a value, detect and recover from errors, and access the type of an object. They provide an easy way to manipulate and think about different types of objects.

With the universal primitive operations, building systems can be accomplished in a more uniform manner. TMaps and OMaps are also available as types to facilitate the ability of a system to understand itself better and manipulate all objects the same way when it is beneficial to do so.

TMap properties ensure the proper use of objects in an FMap. A TMap has a corresponding set of control properties for controlling spatial relationships between objects.

PROPERTIES OF SYSTEM-ORIENTED OBJECTS FOR BETTER, FASTER, CHEAPER SYSTEMS

The goals defined for a company are the requirements for its enterprise as a target system. Since DBTF is a systems theory for defining, designing, and developing software systems in terms of SOOs, it can become part of the specification for meeting the strategic technology goal of the software company discussed above.

Properties of SOOs are summarized in Exhibit 30.11 as part of a TMap-like definition. For example, the object "affordable" has children objects "reusable" and "optimizes resources in operation and development." Whenever a property in the table is underlined it refers to a section that is a reusable. A more detailed discussion of these properties can be found in the *Handbook of Technology in Financial Services.*[1]

The properties of system-oriented objects include those which the object-oriented world has come to expect (the desirable ones, that is), and more. As shown here, above all, a system-oriented object is about quality. And quality systems are systems that are both reliable and affordable.

Whether a system or application is viewed as an object with its functions or as a function with its objects is not the issue. One person's object can be another person's function. Either can be viewed as a system; it's just a matter of perspective. What *does* matter is how these objects and their functions (or functions and their objects) are put together and, ultimately, how they will work together as a family of systems — both now and for future reuse.

An Embodiment of DBTF

To capitalize fully on the properties of a SOO a suite of automated tools based on DBTF is needed to manage and develop it. One such automation is a full life cycle requirement, systems design and engineering and software development environment encompassing all phases of development starting with the definition of the meta process and the definition of requirements. Part of this environment concentrates on developing the system by working with the definition space of a system in terms of FMaps and Tmaps, and the other part concentrates on understanding a system in terms of its

Exhibit 30.11. System Oriented Object Properties of Development Before the Fact

Quality (better, faster, cheaper)
• Reliable
• Affordable

Reliable (better)
• In control and under control
• Based on a set of axioms
– domain identification (intended, unintended)
– ordering (priority and time)
– access rights:incoming object (or relation), outgoing
– object (or relation)
– replacement
• Formal
– consistent, logically complete
– necessary and sufficient
– common semantic base
– unique state identification
• Error free (based on formal definition of "error"
– always gets the right answer at the right time and in the right place
– satisfies users and developers intent
• Handles the unpredictable
• Predictable

Affordable (faster, cheaper)
• Reusable
• Optimizes resources in operation and development
– in minimum time and space
– with best fit of objects to resources

Reusable
• Understandable, integratable and maintainable
• Flexible
• Follows standards
• Automation
• Common definitions
– natural modularity
■ natural separation (e.g., functional architecture from its resource architectures);
■ dumb modules
■ an object is integrated with respect to structure, behavior, and properties of control
– integration in terms of structure and behavior
– type of mechanisms
■ function maps (relate an object's function to other functions)
■ object type maps (relate objects to objects)
■ structures of functions and types
– category
■ relativity
■ instantiation
■ polymorphism
■ parent/child
■ being/doing
■ having/not having
■ abstraction
■ encapsulation

replacement
relation including function
typing including classification
form including both structure and behavior (for object types and functions)
■ derivation
deduction
inference
inheritance

Handles the unpredictable
• Throughout development and operation
• Without affecting unintended areas
• Error detect and recover from the unexpected
• Interface with, change, and reconfigure in asynchronous, distributed, real-time environment

Flexible
• Changeable without side effects
• Evolvable
• Durable
• Reliable
• Extensible
• Ability to break up and put together
– one object too many: modularity, decomposition, instantiation
– many objects to one: composition, applicative operators, integration, abstraction

Exhibit 30.11. System Oriented Object Properties of Development Before the Fact (*Continued*)

- Portable
  - secure
  - diverse and changing layered developments
  - open architecture (implementation, resource allocation, and execution independence)
  - plug-in (or be plugged into) or reconfiguration of different modules
  - adaptable for different organizations, applications, functionality, people, products

Automation
- The ultimate form of reusable
- Formalize, mechanize, then automate
  - it
  - its development
  - that which automates its development

Understandable, integratable, and maintainable
- Reliable
- A measurable history
- Natural correspondence to real world
  - persistence, create, and delete
  - appear and disappear
  - accessibility
  - reference assumes existence of objects
  - real time and space constraints
  - representation
  - relativity, abstraction, derivation
- Provides user-friendly definitions
  - recognizes that one user's friendliness is another user's nightmare
  - hides unnecessary detail (abstraction)
  - variable, user selected syntax
  - self teaching
  - derived from a commong semantic base
  - common definition mechanisms

- Communicates with common semantics to all entities
- Defined to be simple as possible, but not simpler
- Defined with integration of all of its objects (and all aspects of these objects)
- Traceability of behavior and structure and their changes (maintenance) throughout its birth, life, and death
- Knows and able to reach the state of completion
  - definition
  - development of itself and that which develops it
    - analysis
    - design
    - implementation
    - instantiation
    - testing
    - maintenance

Note: All underlined words point to a reusable.

Source: Hamilton, M., Software Design and Development, Chap. 122, *The Electronics Handbook*, CRC Press, IEEE Press, 1996.

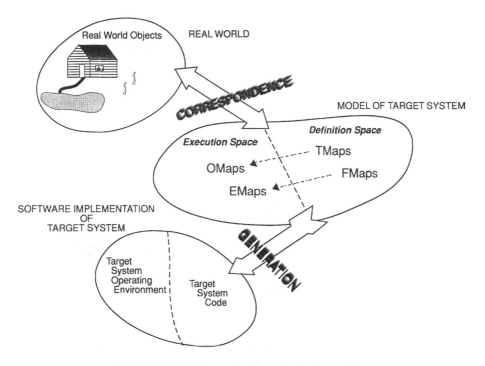

Exhibit 30.12. Representing the real world.

---

execution space, OMaps and EMaps (see Exhibit 30.12). With this environment, anything can become a SOO. It could be an individual software module for a turnpike application, or it could be the entire turnpike system which might include, hardware, software, and human operators.

Formal Definition

Using FMaps and Tmaps, any kind of system can be designed and simulated; and any kind of software system can be automatically developed, resulting in complete, integrated, and fully production-ready target system code (or documentation) configured for the language and architecture of choice. Also provided is a means to observe the behavior of a system as it is being evolved and executed in terms of OMaps and EMaps (Exhibit 30.13).

Every system developed with this environment is a DBTF system, including itself. This is because it was used to define and generate itself. Although a full life cycle design and development environment, it can coexist and interface with other tools. It can be used to prototype a system and/or to develop that system fully.

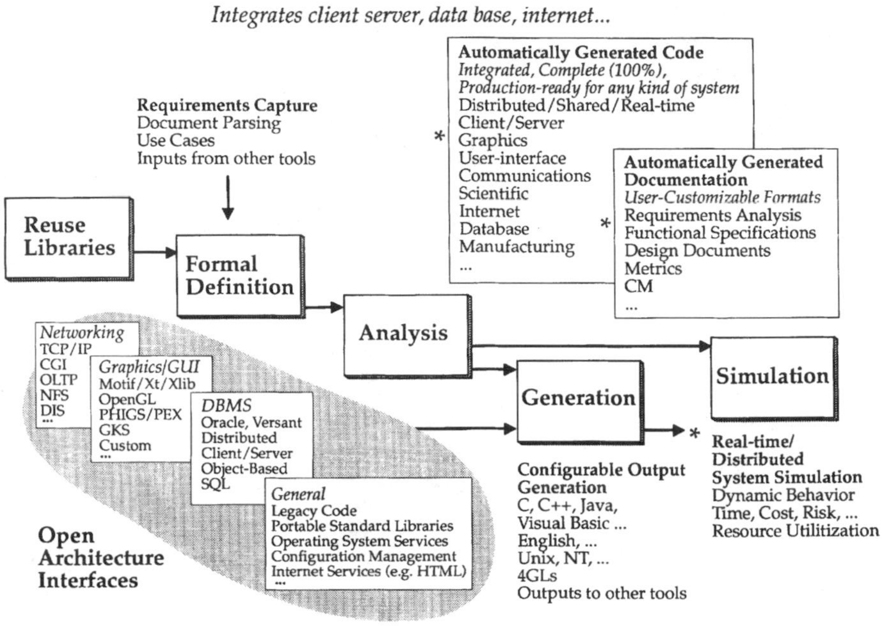

Integrates client server, data base, internet...

Automatically Generated Code
Integrated, Complete (100%),
Production-ready for any kind of system

Requirements Capture
Document Parsing
Use Cases
Inputs from other tools

* Distributed/Shared/Real-time
Client/Server
Graphics
User-interface
Communications
Scientific
Internet
Database
Manufacturing
...

Automatically Generated Documentation
User-Customizable Formats
Requirements Analysis
* Functional Specifications
Design Documents
Metrics
CM
...

Reuse Libraries

Formal Definition

Analysis

Generation

Simulation

Networking
TCP/IP
CGI
OLTP
NFS
DIS
...

Graphics/GUI
Motif/Xt/Xlib
OpenGL
PHIGS/PEX
GKS
Custom
...

DBMS
Oracle, Versant
Distributed
Client/Server
Object-Based
SQL

General
Legacy Code
Portable Standard Libraries
Operating System Services
Configuration Management
Internet Services (e.g. HTML)
...

Open Architecture Interfaces

Configurable Output
Generation
C, C++, Java,
Visual Basic ...
English, ...
Unix, NT, ...
4GLs
Outputs to other tools

* Real-time/
Distributed
System Simulation
Dynamic Behavior
Time, Cost, Risk, ...
Resource Utilitization

**Exhibit 30.13. Integrated, seamless, configurable environment for systems
engineering and software development.**

Analysis

All models within this environment are defined with the DBTF formal systems language resulting in SOOs. This modeling process could be in any phase of the life cycle, including problem analysis, operational scenarios (use cases), and design. Models are submitted to a dataflow structure calculator to automatically provide the structures with an analysis of the local data flow for a given model. The analyzer can then be used to ensure that each model or set of models was defined properly. This includes static analysis for preventative properties and dynamic analysis for user intent properties.

Generation

Once a model has been decomposed to the level of objects designated as primitive and analyzed successfully, it can be handed to the generator. The generator automatically generates a fully production-ready and fully integrated software implementation for any kind of application, consistent with the model, for a selected target environment in the language and architecture of choice.

The generator is generic; it can be configured to interface with language, database, graphics, client/server, legacy code, operating system, communications systems, Internet-based systems, and machine environments of choice. If the selected environment has already been configured, the generator selects that environment directly, otherwise, the generator is first configured for a new language and architecture.

The type part of the generator generates object-type templates for a particular application domain from one or more TMaps. The code generated by the functional part of the generator is automatically connected to the code generated from the TMap and code for the primitive types in the core library, as well as — if desired — libraries developed from other environments.

Once the generator is configured for a new environment, a system can be automatically regenerated to reside on that environment. This open architecture approach provides more flexibility to the user when moving from an older technology to a newer one.

To illustrate the power of an open environment, on a DBTF elevator system, C was automatically generated for one part of an the system, Ada for another part, and FORTRAN for another. The system was then executed with executables generated from three different languages all executing concurrently, communicating via TCP/IP protocol to perform a coordinated multiprocessing task.

The user-configurable generator has been configured for several languages including C, FORTRAN, COBOL, Ada, APL, Lisp, and English and soon to be available with Java and Visual Basic.

This environment's completely open architecture allows a user to put wrappers around a set of capabilities so that it can be configured to automatically generate to an architecture of choice. It can be configured to interface to a system at all levels, from high levels such as a DBMS API to low levels such as operating system calls (e.g., POSIX). With a user-configurable open architecture for interfacing to databases (e.g., Oracle, SQL Server), operating systems (e.g., UNIX, NT, OpenNT), user interface (e.g., Motif, Windows), communication protocols (e.g., TCP/IP, SNMP, SNA), and Web packages such as Front Page and legacy code of choice, there is no need to lose time to market and spend unnecessary resources to port to a new environment.

Examples of interfaces currently available are UNIX, Motif, NT, and TCP/IP as well as cross targeting from UNIX to Windows console applications. With this facility, there is a choice of code generation using a single solution specification (also user configurable). Once the generator is configured for a new environment, it will automatically regenerate the new system to reside on that environment. Thus, the generator becomes an agent of reuse across its target code implementations.

The generated code can be compiled and executed on the machine where the DBTF environment resides where those platforms have been configured or it can be sent over to other machines for subsequent compilation and execution. User-tailored documents — with selectable portions of a system definition, implementation, description, and projections such as parallel patterns, decision trees, and priority maps — can also be configured to be automatically generated by the generator. Once a system has been generated, it is ready to be compiled, linked, and executed.

To maintain traceability, the source code generated by the generator has the same name as the FMaps and TMaps from which it was generated. Once generated, a system is ready to be executed. If it is software, the system can undergo testing for further user-intent errors. It becomes operational after testing.

Verification and Validation

Although the correct use of the language together with the analyzer inherently or automatically finds the majority of errors, there are still the remaining ones to find, those that fall into the user-intent category.

As part of the execution and testing phase, an OMap editor is provided a run-time system which automatically creates a user interface based on the data description in the TMap.

Run-time constraint tests that validate correct object manipulation and construction, as well as unit test harnesses for testing each object and its relationships, are automatically generated. The automatic user interface is provided with the OMap editor for populating and manipulating complex objects, including storage and retrieval for persistent objects. This provides the ability to test the target system at any input/output interface with predefined object test data sets.

The generator automatically generates test code that finds an additional set of errors dynamically. For example, it would not allow an engine to be put into a truck that already had one, nor allow an engine to be removed from a truck with no engine.

To support testing further, the developer is notified of the impact to his system of any changes; those areas that are affected (for example, all FMaps that are affected by a change to a TMap) are demoted.

GUI INTEGRATED WITH APPLICATION

The GUI environment (as well as its interface to the Internet) is tightly integrated with the development of an application. The user interface is graphical and displayed in terms of RMaps, Fmaps, and TMaps (using a tree-like representation of models). RMaps at a library and project level are used as a high-level organizational tool to support user coordination and support user understanding of the organization of the system.

GUI (e.g., Motif) support is provided while preserving traceability, interface integrity, and control seamlessly between the GUI part of the application and the other parts of the application. Its automatic data-driven interface generator supports rapid program evolution. Layers of loosely to tightly coupled GUI integration are provided. At the lowest level of integration, a set of primitive data types is provided to access the power of Xlib, Xt, and the Motif windowing system. Each of these layers is defined with primitive operators and types that match the API for that layer. At this layer, all of the raw power of the windowing system may be accessed.

An intermediate layer above these base level API's (called GUI and GUIELEMENT) is provided that encapsulates most of the repetitive operational aspects of Widget management and construction of X widgets. Since this layer was defined as SOOs, it's object editor can be used to specify and view information about the window hierarchy. In addition, the GUI objects may be persistently stored as OMaps to be used during the initialization, modification, or analysis stages of GUI development.

The highest layer is tightly integrated with the TMap system. It is at this layer that the object editor is always available to an application to populate and manipulate objects based on the TMap. The object editor has standard default presentations as well as a set of primitive operators that allow a user to use the OMap editor presentation features to develop interactive GUIs that are tightly coupled to the TMap (e.g., automatic generation of a system of menus from a TMap description).

Other screen description technologies (e.g., WYSIWG GUI builders) may also be used in conjunction with a translator of their export capabilities to a DBTF GUI specification. An example translator was developed to go from Motif UIL as an output of ICS's Builder Xcessory product.

In addition to the above GUI layers, users can define their own primitive type interfaces to user-chosen API's, providing the end user with freedom and flexibility of choice. Throughout all of these choices the API's are integrated with the use of FMaps and TMaps, a part of DBTF's systems language.

Simulation

FMaps and TMaps can be executed directly by a system analysis component that operates as a run-time executive, as an emulator, or as a simulation executive. A definition is an executable specification in that it has information in it for its simulator to understand its behavior and dynamically analyze it for things such as risk, timing, and cost; and a higher-layer operating system to execute it. For software that same definition can be used as input to the automatic code generator. The result is a rapid prototype for a system designer or a production-ready system for a software developer. That which is simulated by the DBTF simulator can be integrated with that which is automatically generated by the generator to a very fine or loosely grained level.

As an executive, resources are scheduled and allocated by the systems component to activate primitive operations. As an emulator of an operating system, it dispatches dynamically bound executable functions at appropriate places in the specification. As a simulator, it records and displays information. It understands the real-time semantics embedded in a SOO definition by executing or simulating a system before implementation to observe characteristics such as timing, cost, and risk based on a particular allocation of resources. If the model being simulated has been designed to be a production software system, then the same FMaps and TMaps can be automatically generated for production.

The analysis component can be used to analyze processes such as those in a business environment (enterprise model), manufacturing or software development environment (process model), as well as detailed algorithms (e.g., searching for parallelism).

The documentation environment is tightly integrated with the definition of the system. In fact documentation can be automatically generated from a SOO definition by the generator, wrapping in the user's own comments should it be desirable to do so; and that same definition can itself become part of that same generated document. Documentation from the various model viewpoints of a system can be collected and integrated into the documentation of the system. This means, for example, that a resulting document could also include descriptions of the requirements, the testing, developer's issues, and developer's decisions made about the design of a system.

The baseliner facility provides version control and baselining for all RMaps, FMaps, Tmaps, and user-defined reusables, including defined structures. The build manager configuration control facility's primary role is to manage all entities used in the construction of an executable. This includes source files, header files, and context information about the steps taken to produce the executable. This facility also provides options for controlling the optimization level, debugging information, and profiling information of the compiled code.

Requirements Analysis

The requirements component provides users with more control over their own requirements process. In addition to generating metrics, it allows users to enter requirements into the system and trace between those requirements and corresponding FMaps and TMaps (and corresponding generated code) throughout system specification, detailed design, implementation, and final documentation.

With the requirements component a user can define any relationship between objects and describe the complex dependencies between these objects. This allows the user to query, for example, on the relationships between a set of requirements and its supporting specifications and implementations.

Management

A session manager component is provided for managing all sessions, the project manager for managing all projects, the library manager component for managing libraries within one project, and the definition manager component for managing definitions within a library.

The project manager component is the system management interface for all projects and users. It lets the user create, enter, and delete projects, and maintains a list of file system mount points on which projects may reside, watching them for adequate space. For each project, the project manager component also maintains a list of users who may access the project and enforces these access privileges.

The library manager component is the system management interface for a single project, where each object it manages is a library. The library manager allows the user to create, enter, and delete libraries within that project. Libraries may also be linked together into subtrees; this enables one library to use the definitions in another. Library utilities work on the currently selected library to provide error recovery, environment configuration, searching, and other useful support.

The definition manager component is the system management interface for a library, where each object it manages is a definition. Maps may be created, edited, and deleted, as well as taken through their respective life cycles.

The definition editor component of the definition manager component is used to define FMaps and TMaps in either graphical or textual form. Each manager manages an RMap (Road Map) of objects, including other managers, to be managed (refer again to Exhibit 10). An RMap provides an index or table of contents to the user's system of definitions; it also supports the managers in the management of these definitions, including those for FMaps, TMaps, defined structures, primitive data types, objects brought in from other environments, as well as other RMaps. Managers use the RMap to coordinate multi-user access to the definitions of the system being developed. Each RMap in a system is an OMap of the objects in the system used to develop that system within each particular manager's domain. The Road Map editor is used to define RMap hierarchies.

THE PROCESS IN ACTION

Using the DBTF automated environment, an organization can select a management process that works for its type of environment. For example,

433

some projects may wish to manage the process of managing the development of a system by following the traditional waterfall model. Others may choose a spiral development model. Below we discuss aspects of a system design and software development process which can be applied in either type of management model.

Requirements Capturing

A typical development process begins with the capturing of requirements, which are usually in the form of a customer-supplied English document. The requirements can then be modeled with FMaps and TMaps to match the initial set of English requirements. The automatic import facility reads the user's requirements document and builds an RMap of FMaps matching the requirements, to get a head start on the development of these FMaps and TMaps.

The requirements component automatically parses the requirements document for key expressions (for example, "cash management system") and key words (for example, "shall"). An RMap is then automatically generated which essentially is an outline of the sections in the requirements document. Each node in the RMap corresponds to an FMap and its automatically generated functions, which continue to outline the paragraphs of a section of the requirements document. A sentence may contain one or more requirements. An FMap leaf node function under a parent function associated with a paragraph is associated with a requirement. Each requirement is uniquely identified and is numbered with a requirements identifier used to make correspondences to the target system which will be defined by the user during the design process.

The requirements (each of which is derived from a statement with key words or expressions) are attached to functions in an FMap belonging to a node in the RMap (which corresponds to a section in the original requirements document) along with information the user chose for the purpose of establishing traceability and gathering metrics throughout the life cycle. As part of the design process, reusables can be used to fulfill some of the requirements associated with the nodes on the RMap. For others, some FMaps and TMaps may already have been defined for this system. Others are yet to be defined.

A requirement in a definition (e.g., the currently selected requirement in an FMap or a TMap) can be graphically connected (via RMap model relationship connectors) by the system designer to other definition nodes (e.g., another set of requirements, a set of tests, or a target system model) for the purpose of tracing that requirement to the other models. A traceability matrix is automatically generated based on the relationships between the different model types.

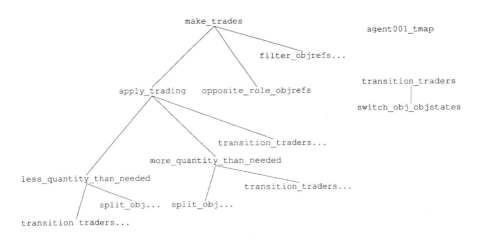

Exhibit 30.14. RMap sample from agent001db.

The requirements editor allows the user to specify, query, and report on a database of information about a model (and its relationships) as well as about its development (and its relationships). This information, together with its formal definition, is used for gathering metrics about the system and its development (such as who is responsible for the object in question, constraints, TBDs, requirements from the user, issues, and information about the contents of the model itself), providing a mechanism to trace from requirements to code and back again, ensuring that the implemented system meets the requirements. The generator can use this information to generate reports on the progress or state of the development of the current target system and its relationship to the original requirements.

A Trading System Example

Following is an RMap excerpt taken from the system, agent001db (Exhibit 30.14); agent001db is used to manage the interaction of agents and objects being traded between them. Within this system there are producers and consumers. Consumers can specify objects (and their characteristics) that they need and producers can identify objects (and their characteristics) that they can provide. The agent database automatically provides a trading service which matches supply and demand. When a producer specifies the items that it can provide, a listing of all potential consumers is provided to the producer so that it has the option of selecting the consumer; agent001db automatically selects a consumer for the producer, if he does not select one. In addition to providing trading services, agent001db provides general purpose search and presentation services.

435

Requirements Tracing

For requirements tracing, RMap relations are automatically and visually drawn between model types on the RMap which is then printable as an RMap diagram. A traceability matrix can be automatically generated for any combination of RMap model relationships to provide traceability information.

Code Coverage

The need for code coverage testing is minimized with the use of SOOs. The use of the formal language for defining the system ensures no interface errors, which means that there will be no logic in danger of not being used properly due to interface problems in the models since the model, if it had an interface error, would be caught by the SOO analyzer before the code was automatically generated from that model. This eliminates the need for wire-tracing-oriented tests that analyze generated code.

Since all of the code is automatically generated from the FMaps and TMaps of the target system by the generator, the chance for a human to miss either creating the code for part of a model or interface incorrectly to the other code in the system is eliminated.

Additional test coverage analysis can be performed by configuration of the generator to generate coverage analysis FMap calls to provide user-definable monitors in generated C code. Decision information inherent within FMaps and TMaps can be used for test case initialization for these numbers.

Software Design Modeling

With this development environment, complete life cycle development is based on formal methods using a formal language, from requirements to code generation.

Following are excerpts of FMaps, Tmaps, and OMaps taken from the agent001db system as well as an excerpt of C code that was automatically generated by the generator from the set of FMaps and TMaps that these were taken from (Exhibits 30.15 through 30.18). Notice that the FMap, apply_trading , is an FMap node on the excerpted RMap.

Debugging

We have already discussed above how run-time constraint tests, as well as unit test harnesses for testing each object and its relationships, are automatically generated by the generator. In addition, an automatic user interface is provided by the OMap editor which provides the ability to test the target system.

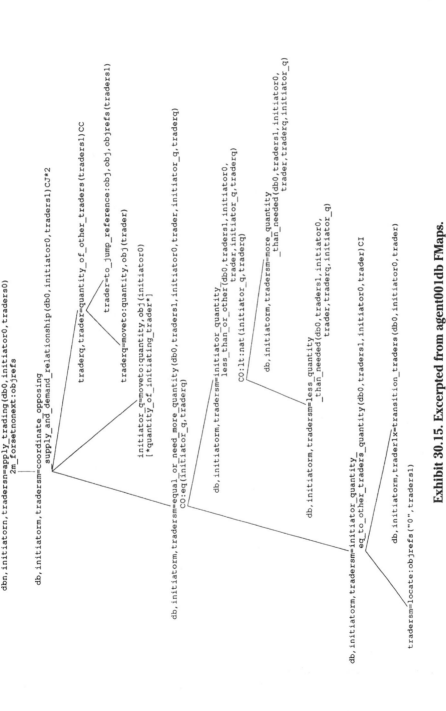

Exhibit 30.15. Excerpted from agent001db FMaps.

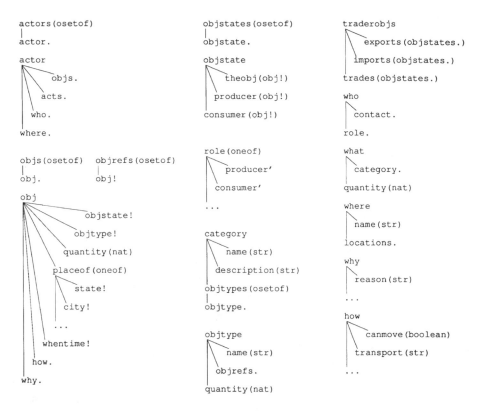

Exhibit 30.16. Excerpted from agent001db TMaps.

Debugging can be performed at the code level with the user's native debugger. The code is generated with variable and function names that closely match to their corresponding name in the design specification. The debugger is used to set breakpoints and examine values of simple object variables. The OMap editor (with a Motif windowing interface) is used to examine complex OMap objects (from within the debugger) and to modify their values or load other OMaps having test values. Testing is also supported by ASCII output generation of OMap objects from the debugger.

FMaps and TMaps can also be used to model the testing system. Test cases are stored as OMap files providing pre and post conditions for the testing of FMaps in the target system. Just as with the target system, code is automatically generated from the FMaps and TMaps in the testing system. The tests are then ready to run. The results are captured as OMap files. Special analysis functions can be developed in terms of FMaps and TMaps as part of the test system to analyze the results (e.g., to analyze the

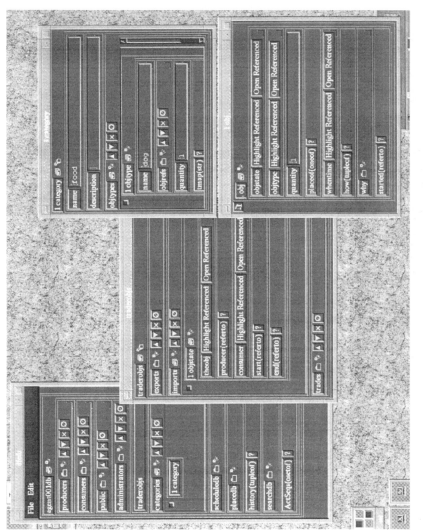

Exhibit 30.17. Excerpted from agent001db OMaps.

```
/*   001-Generated C code for functional specification 'APPLY_TRADING'
        VERSION: 3.2.3.9 C-RAT
         AUTHOR: Hamilton Technologies Inc. Copyright 1991.
      OPERATION: APPLY_TRADING
      GENERATED: Wed May 27 15:58:38 1998
         SCCSID: @(#) %M% %I% of %G%.
*/
#include "AGENT001DB.h"
...

fAPPLY_TRADING(V0DB0,V0INITIATOR0,V0TRADERS0,
               V0DBN,V0INITIATORN,V0TRADERSN)
IDECLARE_AGENT001DB(V0DB0)
...
{                   /* __LOCAL_VARIABLE_DECLARATIONS__ */
DECLARE_NAT(C1)
...
                    /* __FUNCTION_SOURCE_CODE_BEGINNING__ */
...
rec1_0REPEAT=1;
while(rec1_0REPEAT--){
   ATNULL_OBJREFS(V0TRADERS1,V1_0ATN)
   COPY_BOOLEAN(V1_0ATN,D1_D10)
     if(D1_D10<1)
 {if(D1_D10 == REJECT_BOOLEAN) {REJECT_TEST_BOOLEAN()}
   MOVETO_OBJ_OBJREFS(V0TRADERS1,V2_PO)
   CONVERT_OMAP_OBJ(V2_PO,V2_POOM)
   JUMP_REFERTO_OMAP(V2_POOM,V2_OBJOM)
   CONVERT_OBJ_OMAP(V2_OBJOM,V0TRADER)
   MOVETO_QUANTITY_OBJ(V0TRADER,V0TRADERQ)
   MOVETO_QUANTITY_OBJ(V0INITIATOR0,V0INITIATOR_Q)
   EQ_NAT(V0INITIATOR_Q,V0TRADERQ,D0D7)
     if(D0D7<1)
 {if(D0D7 == REJECT_BOOLEAN) {REJECT_TEST_BOOLEAN()}
   LT_NAT(V0INITIATOR_Q,V0TRADERQ,D0D8)
     if(D0D8<1)
 {if(D0D8 == REJECT_BOOLEAN) {REJECT_TEST_BOOLEAN()}
   fMORE_QUANTITY_THAN_NEEDED(V0DB0,V0TRADERS1,V0INITIATOR0,
                              V0TRADER,V0TRADERQ,V0INITIATOR_Q,
                              &V0DB,&V0INITIATORM,&V0TRADERSM);
}/*FALSE*/
else{/*LESS_QUANTITY_THAN_NEEDED*/
...
}/*FALSE*/
else{/*0INITIATOR_QUANTITY_EQ_TO_OTHER_TRADERS_QUANTITY*/
   fTRANSITION_TRADERS(V0DB0,V0INITIATOR0,V0TRADER,
   &V0DB,&V0INITIATORM,&V0TRADER1X);
   LOCATE_OBJREFS(C1,V0TRADERS1,V0TRADERSM)
...
return;
}
/*  -------------- end of source ------------------*/
```

**Exhibit 30.18. Excerpted from code automatically generated from
agent001db FMaps and TMaps.**

output OMap objects and the input OMap objects to see whether or not a particular function behaves as expected for a particular test).

Code regression testing can be defined in FMaps to perform comprehensive analysis of any subsystem portion of the system at the granularity of an FMap model. A unit test harness interface is automatically generated upon request for any FMap operation in the system. This test harness provides access to data sets corresponding to the inputs of the FMap in order to drive the regression testing. The resulting outputs of these test data sets can then be validated for correctness.

Much of the testing is no longer needed when using this environment since the semantics of the formal systems language not only supports the user to think, design, and analyze his system's requirements in an organized manner, but its correct use eliminates errors from the very beginning and its analyzer automatically ensures that the language was used correctly, so that such errors are indeed eliminated. All objects in a system are under control and traceable; again, obviating the need for another set of tests that are needed in a more traditional setting.

GENERATING AND REGENERATING THE CODE

Code is automatically generated (or regenerated) for any part or type of model in a system (and for any part of the system that has been changed, obsolete code is automatically replaced and integrated into the new and changed code) whether it be GUI, database, Internet based, communications, real time, distributed, client server, multi-user, or mathematical algorithms. There is no manual work to be done to finish the coding task. The generator is accessible to a user to tailor it for his own brand of generated code, if needed. This generator can be used to provide output information that can be used as input by other tools or as output for testing (such as showing all of the decision points in the system). This feature can also be used as another means of rapid prototyping for systems design studies.

The quality of the generated code has been given high marks by its users since it inherits all of the SOO qualities including interface correctness and traceability, from and to the requirements and design from whence it came and within the code layer itself.

While the task of configuring the generator is in process, the user can develop his systems using a current generator configuration to automatically generate his applications. Once the new configuration of the generator is prepared the user can automatically regenerate his system for the newly configured architecture. Once this new configuration is completed it can be used over and over again as a reusable for other projects.

Detailed Design Document Generation

Because DBTF's documentation environment is tightly integrated with the definition of the system, a new document or portion of a document can be automatically generated by the generator from a specification that has changed. Documentation (e.g., detailed design documents generated from the SOO models) can be automatically generated (when analysis is completed or when needed) from those same specifications, making them always consistent with the generated code.

Documents can be generated to match document templates or document artifacts corresponding to those for other phases. This documentation (partial or complete) can then be imported, for example, into WORD for processing and/or direct incorporation into the other phases.

Mapping Changes to Code

Changes to the requirements can be made to the original requirements or to the requirements FMaps and TMaps. If a user makes incremental changes to the requirements document and then re-imports it by generating a new RMap of FMaps for those requirements, the requirements component will allow for requirements document changes and then re-import those requirements with a minimum of disturbance to the established RMap of FMap requirements models and their associated links to other models (e.g., testing systems or the target system under development).

If a user makes changes to the requirements at the level of FMaps and TMaps, a formal and consistent representation for the requirements, they are in the form where the analyzer is able to automatically determine if all of the requirements are consistent and logically complete and traceable.

Any relationship connections between models are automatically maintained. For example, if a requirement FMap has a dependency relation to a supporting target system (software) model and the requirement FMap is deleted, then the dependency relation is removed. Test models can be evolved as needed and regression tests performed as needed. The new design information is extracted and placed into the document based on the document configuration of the generator.

A change in a DBTF specification is followed by an automatic regeneration of the code that has been impacted with the change using the generator in order to guarantee that the code matches the specification.

Target changes are made to the definition or model, *not to the code*. Target architecture changes are made to the configuration of the generator environment, *not to the code*. All changes are traceable. If, for example, a TMap is changed, all of the FMaps impacted by that change are demoted. With traditional products, after the shell code or partial code has been generated, it is necessary for programmers to add or change code manually; as more code is written, it becomes less possible to regenerate the shell or partial code from changes in the requirements because the manual code would be destroyed or made obsolete. The maintenance process using traditional products becomes increasingly manual and, therefore, error prone as the software evolves. With the DBTF approach, the user doesn't ever need to change the generated code, only the specification, and then regenerates (automatically) only that part of the system that has changed. Once again, the system is automatically compiled, linked, and executed without manual intervention.

INTEGRATION WITH LEGACY SYSTEMS

Because the architecture of the DBTF environment is open, it allows for interfacing to existing or future legacy code. Several options exist for such an interface. Wrappers can be placed around existing or legacy code to create primitives for the generation environment to automatically interface to; systems can be defined to have FMaps that directly call legacy code, and legacy code can send input to DBTF-generated code at execution time; the generator can be configured to generate language-specific statements that interface to the legacy code; or shell scripts within the environment are open to end-user modification (e.g., modification of link and compile scripts).

PROTOTYPING

A DBTF system can be presented before the fact to end users as a rapid and evolving prototype starting with a skeleton "show and tell" or "mock up" of what is to come for the user. This could be for any system, since DBTF enables design and modeling of any concept that humans can envision. For example in addition to the target system, it could be the testing system including the user model and the operational model (or use cases,), a model of the development process for building target systems, a model of the end-user's enterprise, or the enterprise of the developer organization itself.

MEETING THE COMPANY'S GOALS WITH DBTF

As these scenarios illustrate, the DBTF environment automates the development process within each phase and between phases, beginning when the user first inputs his thoughts and ending when testing his ideas. The same language and the same tools can be used throughout all phases, levels, and layers of design and development. There are no other languages or tools to learn. Each development phase is implementation independent. The system can be automatically generated to various alternative implementations without changing its original definition.

Traceability exists throughout from the beginning of the life cycle, to implementation, to operation, and back again since the DBTF process is seamless. A primitive in one phase — say, requirements — becomes the top node for a module in the next lower-level phase, specifications. The environment takes advantage of the fact that a system is defined from the very beginning to inherently maximize the potential for its own automation.

If the real system is hardware or peopleware, the software system serves as a simulation upon which the real system can be based. Once a system has been developed, the system and the process used to develop it are analyzed with tools such as simulation to understand how to improve the next round of system development.

It may not always be considered realistic for a project to develop a particular application from the standpoint of a pure systems viewpoint where, in the ideal world, the requirements are understood first as a system before later phases of development. Should this be the case, this approach has the flexibility of either supporting its users in defining such an application from its beginning or in starting to use it in a later phase of development, such as with one of its software module subsystems in a detailed design phase. The software implementation would then be automatically generated from the design of this subsystem.

A new set of alternatives is provided for the different disciplines associated with the traditional development process. Take, for example, reverse engineering. Redevelopment is a more viable option, since a system can be developed with higher reliability and productivity than before. Another alternative is to develop main portions of the system with this approach, but hook into existing libraries at the core primitive level and reuse portions of existing legacy code that are worth reusing, at least to get started. In the future, for those systems developed within the DBTF environment, reverse engineering becomes a matter of selecting the appropriate generator configuration or of configuring the generator environment of choice and then generating to the new environment.

Motivating the Staff

With a DBTF environment, managers (and their developers) can be proud of their accomplishments and more motivated since they can deliver. With the current critical programmer shortage aflicting our industry today, it is clear that a company is not as dependent on individuals with an environment such as this at their disposal, in particular since it can be set up to not only do a major part of the work (for example, generate 100 percent of the code), but to make it easy to reuse as well.

FOLLOWING THE "NO MORE, NO LESS PATH"

The formalism behind DBTF enforces the "no more, no less rule," a prime example of which is reuse. With one formal semantic language to define and integrate all aspects of a system, diverse modeling languages (and methodologies for using them), each of which defines only part of a system, are no longer necessary. No longer is there a need to reconcile multiple techniques with semantics that interfere with each other.

No longer is there a need to continue to learn new languages or techniques each time a new one becomes popularized. Why, for example, learn C, followed by a replacement of C with a more modern C++, followed by a replacement of C++ with Java? Each is a major step which requires significant training and reverse engineering. One could instead use — and continue to use — a single definition language and automatically generate the latest implementation environment.

The fact that DBTF-developed systems will not lock an organization in means that unnecessary work can be avoided. They incorporate a structure and process for the continuous evolution of any or all parts of a system. Not only can the models as well as their automatically generated implementations be reused, but new implementations can be regenerated from any model and this can be done by using reusable architecture configurations.

The fact that the DBTF approach does not lock an organization in to process, architecture, design, or implementation becomes even more important with today's rapidly changing technologies. The user has designer freedom without compromising the integrity of the system. The only constraints imposed are those that support the designer in making a reliable system. In fact, the designer can abstract to as high (or as low) a level as he would like.

Techniques and tools for transitioning from one phase of the life cycle to another become obsolete. Dealing with all of the paperwork that is either manually or automatically generated to support the manual processes of development when these processes could be automated can become a thing of the past. Techniques for maintaining source code as a separate process are no longer needed, since the source is automatically generated from the system specification.

Verification, too, becomes obsolete. What good is an automatic wire-tracing tool if there is nothing left to trace?

Techniques for managing other paper documents give way to entering requirements and their changes directly into the requirements specification database. Testing procedures and tools for finding most errors are no longer needed because those errors no longer exist. Tools developed to support programming as a manual process are no longer needed when all programming becomes automated.

No longer needed are tools that focus on the measurement of complexity. Instead of measuring it, it becomes minimized. Complexity does not increase with the size of the system since all objects are under control, integrated, and traceable.

No longer is it necessary to do what is unnecessary over and over again or to keep adding on after the fact when there is a way to do it right the first time.

SATISFYING THE REUSE GOAL

Reuse succeeds only if what is reused works and is under control. Such is the case with SOOs. Every defined model becomes inherently a candidate for reuse. Reuse is supported in FMaps by operations, universal operations (those containing polymorphism), and user-defined FMap structures (functional templates with or without polymorphism). Reuse in TMaps is supported by the automatic generation of abstract types using a set of predefined parameterized types (i.e., type templates); leaf types defining: container extension, external references or relations (pointer-like), recursive objects; user-defined primitive types (at code level or layered onto FMap and TMaps); user-defined layered types, and user-defined parameterized types.

Reuse naturally takes place throughout the DBTF life cycle. Objects, no matter how complex, can be reused and integrated. Environment configurations for different kinds of architectures can be reused. A newly developed system can be safely reused to increase even further the productivity of the systems developed with it.

Inherent reuse with SOOs recursively and safely raises objects to a new and higher level, seamlessly integrating aspects such as the GUI, database, and communications side of a system with all of its other parts.

Learning from history is a form of reuse. Towards this end, reuse with SOOs exists from the start, culminating in automation itself.

AVOIDING A ROCKY TRANSITION

The learning curve of DBTF is relatively short. A week's introductory course proves sufficient to start using its environment. Internships are typically used to teach in-depth techniques that are applied to solving problems in a particular application area. Internships reinforce that which is taught in the introductory course. One can become quite productive after a month of regular use. This is because the process is intuitive, there is only one language and only one set of integrated tools to learn for the life cycle, it is straightforward, everything else is derivable from the core concepts, its formalism enforces the "no more, no less rule," and the modeler concentrates on the objects in a system and how to relate and use them, not on how to make them be object oriented.

Transitioning from one environment to a new one can be done in several ways; for example, by creating wrappers around legacy code including application code already developed in an organization or code generated by other tools, and turning it into DBTF primitives which can then be automatically generated to by the generator. If other chosen tools support openness, the code generated by the generator can be integrated with or accessed by these other tools.

INTEGRATING THE PARTS

With respect to choosing a strategic technology, integration in all forms is key. One of the problems that can occur with traditional systems, including the object-oriented ones, is the difficulty in integrating all the parts. The process is error prone and time consuming. This is not the case with DBTF since all of its parts are by their very nature formally integrated. The result is an integrated, seamless design and development environment. There is no longer an additional expense for integrating diverse products for developing different parts of a system, phases of the system, or for integrating the modules or views (e.g., data flow, timing, state transition, and object types) of a module created with or resulting from these disparate products.

Systems are defined to handle changes both during development and operation, since all objects are system oriented, under control, and traceable. All aspects of system design and development are integrated with one systems language and its associated automation.

THE BOTTOM LINE

Collective experience strongly and consistently confirms that quality is maximized, and cost and time to market are minimized with the increased use of DBTF's properties and its automation. Its preventative philosophy — to solve a given problem as early as possible — means finding a problem statically is better than finding it dynamically. Preventing it by the way a system is defined is even better. Better yet, is not having to define (and build) it at all. Only then have we satisfied the reuse goal, the other one (in addition to the strategic technology goal) that needs to be satisfied to successfully achieve all of the other goals in the business.

When we carried this analysis further, we discovered that productivity was higher the larger and more complex the system — the opposite of what one finds with traditional systems development. This is in major part because of the high degree of DBTF's support of reuse and, therefore, the use of reuse on larger systems. Measuring productivity becomes a process of relativity, relative to the last system that was developed. Older methods for measuring productivity are no longer applicable.

But there are other reasons for this higher productivity as well, such as the savings realized and time saved due to tasks and processes that are no longer necessary with the use of this approach. For beginners there is less to learn and for everyone less to do — less analysis, less testing, less to manage, less to document, less maintenance, little or no implementation, and less to integrate since a major part of all these areas has been automated or they inherently take place because of the nature of DBTF's formal language.

DBTF APPLICATIONS DEVELOPED FOR THE INTERNET: THREE CASE STUDIES

In the following three chapters of this Handbook are case studies of Internet-based applications developed using the DBTF automated environment: an accident reporting system for state highway departments; a remote query system for librarians; and an adaptable systems architecture for building and integrating enterprise-wide applications. These applications use middleware library reusables, available as options with the DBTF automated environment, as their foundations; these reusables include client server, CGI, session server, agent001db, datetime services, and view server[17,18] developed in terms of a unified systems model based on the DBTF Escher and VSphere foundations.[19] With these middleware libraries, the first spiral of an application can be jump started and up and running in an early stage of development. Each application was defined in terms of SOOs. Each was automatically generated and automatically integrated by the DBTF environment.

CONCLUSION

The availability of quality application systems software capable of handling the various aspects of daily corporate commercial operations has reached a crisis level which will likely create economic chaos on a global scale if current trends are not halted and eventually reversed.

At the end of the day the known impact that a technology has on the bottom line will become less subtle. The current trend of enforced "versionism" and obsolescence (not to be confused with legitimate obsolescence stemming from the "no more, no less" goal) requiring continuing re-equipment by end users, while profitable for those vendors promoting it, is unsustainable and will bring about the demise of businesses unable to control the chain of supply; i.e., those corporations faced with constantly increasing infrastructure costs and constantly decreasing margins.[20]

An approach should not be selected because it answers to the latest fad or because it is part of the "safety in numbers" syndrome (everyone else is using it so if it doesn't work, there will be no blame); it should not be selected because it has properties of a particular paradigm such as being "object oriented" especially if it does not inherently provide such properties, forcing managers and developers to go to great lengths to have a system become object oriented. Instead it should be selected because it will be what is needed to meet the highest priority goals of the organization.

A transition to a formal, before the fact, systems approach forms the foundation for better, faster, cheaper software, the answer to success in business, certainly in a business which delivers software. With this approach durable systems can be developed. A company is then free to safely make the key decision of when and how it transitions what it has today to what it needs tomorrow.

Such a transition, as would take place with Option 4 or Option 5 for the company we discussed earlier, presents a major opportunity — an opportunity to take a step back and examine the underlying process used to design, build, and deploy software and examine where the next introduction of modern (in the real sense) technologies and products truly fit within the company's systems development framework.

Although change is difficult for any organization, changing from a traditional environment to an environment like Development Before the Fact is like transitioning from the typewriter to the word processor. Certainly the initial overhead is needed for learning the new way of doing things, but once having used word processors would we ever go back to the typewriter?

The three systems described as case studies in the following chapters were developed with DBTF and its automated development environment. All of these systems are examples of Internet-based systems that demand the type of functionality and flexibility typical of Internet-related applications. Common themes were shared among these systems as well as with the other systems developed with this paradigm. For example, not only did these systems work, but a significant amount of time and money was saved when comparing for each system its DBTF development experience with what would have been a traditional development experience. This is in large part due to the fact that many of the processes, methods, and tools considered necessary within the traditional life style are no longer necessary with DBTF.

Following the "no more, no less" rule becomes the deciding factor. Yet, if we think about it, it is a matter of common sense. Not only does it result in using the best strategic technologies, but it makes sure that they are used the way they should be, capitalizing, for example, on reuse and relativity and treating everything systematically. One result is that of removing the requirement for people that are no longer needed to support obsolescence. This brings freedom, both for the people who should not be locked into using obsolete methods and to the corporation that should not be losing profits by doing unnecessary work. Is not freedom the most valuable commodity of them all; for without it we lose control of our destiny?

True, many software companies today are doing quite well using traditional, informal, and after the fact development techniques. Relatively speaking, that is, when it comes to making a profit. But how long will this last? As with anything it is usually a matter of time and timing. And as we said earlier, every system is relative. What works for success today may not work tomorrow, especially if there are known weaknesses in the system.

Others will catch on that there is a better way to do business after all. Especially those who have less to lose. They could well leave the so-called successful ones behind in the dust. Once each organization begins to understand the degree to which a technology affects it, software will be given its due respect.

In software today the going gets tough on a nonstop basis. Unlike a manager who is not a leader, a manager who is a leader has wisdom that he or she applies when the going gets tough, or better yet, before the going gets tough, before the fact. And, isn't wisdom the highest form of reuse, with the exception of that which reuses wisdom already applied?

Author's Bio

Margaret Hamilton (mhh@htius.com) is the founder and CEO of Hamilton Technologies, Inc. (HTI), based in Cambridge, MA, (17 Inman Street, Cambridge, MA 02139, 617-492-0058). She is a pioneer in the systems engineering and software development industry. Hamilton's mission has been to bring to market a completely integrated and robust tool suite that is based on the unique systems theory paradigm which she created, called Development Before the Fact (DBTF). In bringing her product to market, her company leveraged the power of reusability and the reliability of seamless integration to provide a tool that sharply decreases errors while simultaneously increasing productivity. The result is an ultra-reliable system at a fraction of the cost of conventional systems. Hamilton's goal was to embed this formal and completely systems-oriented object (SOO) framework into a highly efficient, high-performance, completely graphical portable workbench of smart tools which the systems engineer and software developer could use throughout the entire design and development life cycle. Today this ideal has been surpassed with the 001 Tool Suite.

Earlier in her career, as the leader of the Software Engineering Division at MIT's Charles Stark Draper Laboratory, Hamilton was the director of the Apollo on-board flight software project and created Higher Order Software (HOS), a formal systems design theory.

Hamilton later founded and was CEO of Higher Order Software where she was responsible for the development of the first comprehensive CASE tool in the industry. This tool, called USE.IT, was based on her formal design theory, HOS.

Notes

1. *Handbook of Technology in Financial Services,* Jessica Keyes, Ed., Auerbach Publications, Boca Raton, FL, 1999.
2. Hamilton, M., Development before the fact in action, *Elec. Des.,* June 13, 1994, ES.
3. Hamilton, M. 1994. Inside Development before the fact. *Elec. Des.,* April 4, ES.

4. Hamilton, M., "Zero-Defect Software: The Elusive Goal," *IEEE Spect.*, 23:3, 48–53, 1986.

5. Hamilton, M. and Hackler, R., "001: A Rapid Development Approach for Rapid Prototyping Based on a System that Supports its Own Life Cycle," IEEE Proc., First Int. Workshop on Rapid System Prototyping, Research Triangle Park, NC, June 4, 1990.

6. Hamilton, M. and Hackler, W.R., *Object Thinking,* McGraw-Hill, New York, 2000.

7. The 001 Tool Suite Reference Manual, Version 3, Hamilton Technologies, Inc., Cambridge, MA, 1998.

8. Krut, B., Jr., "Integrating 001 Tool Support in the Feature-Oriented Domain Analysis Methodology" (CMU/SEI-93-TR-11, ESC-TR-93-188), Software Engineering Institute, Carnegie-Mellon University, Pittsburgh, PA, 1993.

9. Software Engineering Tools Experiment — Final Report, Vol. 1, Experiment Summary, Table 1, Pg. 9, Department of Defense, Strategic Defense Initiative, Washington, D.C., 20301–7100, 1993.

10. Ouyang, M. and Golay, M.W., "An Integrated Formal Approach for Developing High Quality Software of Safety-Critical Systems," Report No. MIT-ANP-TR-035, Massachusetts Institute of Technology, Cambridge, MA, 1995.

11. Schindler, M., Computer Aided Software Design, in *From Spaceship to G-Train, Courtesy 001,* John Wiley & Sons, New York, 1990, 284–294.

12. Huang, M., Ariel Technologies Technical Demo, July 1998.

13. Customer Profiles & What Others Say about 001, http://world.std.com/~hti.

14. McCauley, B., Software Development Tools in the 1990s, AIS Security Technology for Space Operations Conference, July 1993, Houston,TX.

15. Hornstein, R.S., "A Cross-Cutting Agenda for Achieving a *Faster, Better, Cheaper* Space Operations Infrastructure," AIAA Workshop on Reducing the Costs of Space Operations, Arlington, VA, 1995.

16. Hornstein, R., Willoughby, J., Hamilton, M., Heuser, W., LoPinto, F., and Hawkins, F., From Space Systems R&D to Commercial Products: Technology Transfer Initiatives to Benefit Small Satellite Missions, NASA Headquarters, Fall of 1997.

17. Hamilton Technologies, Inc., HTIDOC #IR3298-3 Internet Reuse Library and Architecture, March 4, 1998.

18. Hamilton Technologies, Inc., 001 Internet Reuse Components, November 1996.

19. Hamilton Technologies, Inc. (HTI), "Final Report: AIOS Xecutor Demonstration," Prepared for Los Alamos National Laboratory, Los Alamos, NM, Order No. 9-XG1-K9937-1, November 1991.

20. Severino, R., Application Systems Software and Information Technology Infrastructure Background Paper, Toldark Pty. Ltd., August 3, 1998.

The following are trademarks of Hamilton Technologies, Inc.: [001, 001 Tool Suite, Function Map, FMap, Type Map, TMap, Object Map, OMap, Execution Map, EMap, Road Map, RMap, Xecutor, OMap Editor, 001 Analyzer, System Oriented Object (SOO), Resource Allocation Tool, RAT, AntiRAT, Object Editor, Primitive Control Structures, Development Before the Fact (DBTF), RT(x), 001 AXES, agent 001db, VSphere, and 001Escher.

Chapter 31
Managing the Development of an Accident Record System for State Highway Departments: Case Study

Margaret Hamilton
William R. Hackler

CURRENT STATE ACCIDENT REPORTING SYSTEMS used by U.S. state highway departments are notorious for their problems, not the least of which is that they comprise interoperational systems that are not interfaced to work together cooperatively. This is compounded by the fact that approximately one-half of all accidents reported each year are difficult to track because operators provide incomplete information to government agencies. Most notably, state highway departments find it quite difficult to analyze accident volumes and recommend mitigation actions because of poor information about accident locations. And because systems do not include a specific and direct interface to traffic records volume data, computation of accident rates — when it does happen — must be done manually.

Many local jurisdictions have more current computerized accident information than state agencies, leaving the state highway department in a vulnerable, reactive stance to local construction requests; and systems do

0-8493-9987-4/00/$0.00+$.50
© 2000 by CRC Press LLC

not include a specific interface to traffic records volume data directly, leaving the accident rate computation (accidents/traffic) an unintegrated, manual function.

There is also a direct fiscal consequence. The federal Intermodal Surface Transportation Efficiency Act, administered by the Federal Highway Administration (FHWA), mandates that a standard accident record system be used in all states. Federal funds for highway safety improvements must also be based on accident/crash data. When states cannot meet this criterion, acquisition of these funds is threatened.

The overall result is that state-wide traffic records users' needs are not met, and the Highway Safety Improvement Program is not based on accident/crash data as is federally mandated, threatening acquisition of federal highway funds by the individual states.

To address these problems, we developed a generic Accident Reporting System (ARS) as a reusable that can be tailored to meet each individual state's needs using Development Before the Fact (DBTF) and the 001 Tool Suite (see Chapter 30 for a more detailed discussion on DBTF and 001).

ARS was developed for state highway departments within the U.S. It supports Traffic Operations to comply with the Intermodal Surface Transportation Efficiency Act (ISTEA) of the FHWA federal mandates, to provide standard accident record systems in all states across the U.S. Versions of the ARS are currently operational within state highway department traffic operations.

To understand our approach to developing the ARS, think of a system of roads — a complex organization of *interacting* systems for a network of roads, management and planning, accident report collection, accident analysis and reporting, traffic monitoring systems, and road maintenance. The ARS sits within this system, with a primary focus on supporting traffic safety engineering objectives: identifying hazardous road locations, diagnosing crash problems, selecting appropriate countermeasures, ranking design plans in terms of treatment and preparation, programming and implementing countermeasures, and evaluating those countermeasures. To facilitate meeting these objectives, the ARS provides access to accident reports, the road network topology, physical road characteristics, and traffic monitoring information. In addition, it supports analysis of traffic engineering problems and generation of analysis reports.

"ARS supports an evolutionary approach to accident investigation and road system analysis as part of the road safety engineering process. It provides for the exploration of accident data to hone in on road system sites with a demonstrated need for treatment." Using the DBTF graphical and formal modeling language, Function Map (FMap) and Type Map (TMap)

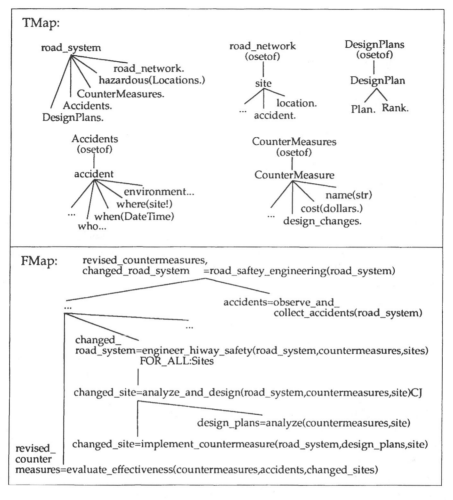

Exhibit 31.1. Traffic engineering process.

models were used to provide a formal statement of the road safety engineering process as described by K. W. Ogden in Safer Roads.[1]

The TMap defines the relationships established between an accident and the other objects which characterize an accident and which can be used for future analysis by ARS users. A *road_system* object (in the TMap of Exhibit 30.1) contains a *road_network* object and a set of *CounterMeasures*. The FMap is used to describe the functionality of what is being done by the objects and how they are interacting with each other. For example, the countermeasures object is interacting with the *road_system* object when they are input to the function "engineer_hiway_safety."

This ARS requirements model drives the decisions made in the ARS architecture. The ARS is an ideal example of how the DBTF environment can be used to evaluate system requirements as well as provide formal specifications that can be used to develop the target system automatically (in this case, the ARS itself).

The details of how the ARS was developed demonstrate the power of DBTF. To understand the development process best, though, requires some background on the road safety engineering process.

ROAD SAFETY ENGINEERING PROCESS

The central object in the road safety engineering process is an accident. When an accident happens, it is recorded in an accident record. To ensure effective future traffic engineering analysis, accident data used for road safety engineering purposes must be as accurate, consistent, and complete as possible. Standard information such as time (when), location (where), contributing factors (why and how), and results of an accident (what) are captured about the accident from several key perspectives so correct accident analysis can be performed.

A traffic engineer is provided with information about the accident site (e.g., location and cause), road network, and road characteristics (e.g., physical road features, traffic monitoring data). This information can then be used to determine if changes need to be made in the road and/or road network within the road system.

Traffic engineering analysis implies the ability to examine the road system objects at different levels of detail. This means there needs to be a basic framework within which accidents can be located: at an intersection, say, or on a section of a road (between an intersection and another intersection or a road endpoint, as illustrated in Exhibit 31.2. From a traffic engineering point of view, it is this framework that provides information that can be used to answer basic questions about where an accident occurred.

Given this abstract view of the road network, road characteristics need to be accessible if an accident is to be analyzed. The road system topology evolves over time. As the road system changes — as new roads are added to the road system or older roads are being repaired — time must be recorded. A segment needs to have a time associated with it because an analysis may be performed on accidents that happened at different times during the evolution of the road system. In the road system, an inventory of each segment is maintained to keep track of the changes to a piece of road.

The road maintenance and monitoring subsystems store physical road characteristics as well as road monitoring information in the road inventory and associate it with a segment. For example, the average daily traffic is a traffic monitoring attribute associated with a segment.

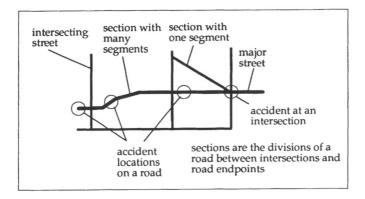

Exhibit 31.2. Traffic engineering view of road network.

Several other pieces of information must be kept. For example, the official street name of a road may change. In the ARS a history of official street name changes are maintained as a list of aliases so that accident reports that use any of the names may be correctly correlated with the official name. In addition, two physically different streets may have the same name. Because of these facts, a street name is not used to uniquely identify the road within the road system. A road is uniquely identified within the road system by a road inventory record that corresponds to the real physical road object.

The accident record has data that indicates the location of the accident site. These data capture the location with numerous methods of location including major and intersecting street names, landmarks, and linear referencing methods (e.g., mile markers, street addresses). Any of this information may be partial, missing, or incorrect. The *ARS* supports the resolution of imprecise location data provided by the accident recording function. There are two basic methods that can be used to identify an accident site given the type of location information in the accident records: street name pattern matching methods or geographic analysis using coordinate systems, including linear referencing. (In fact, one challenge for the *ARS* was to raise the percentage of locatable accidents based on accident record data, given these basic methods of location resolution.)

A global positioning system (GPS) can be used to resolve the accurate accident location issue, given that the accident observer/recorder has a GPS device. Even when GPS becomes the norm there is still the need to analyze imprecise information for all of the other characteristics that are not being captured accurately. The human observer will always relay information in an imprecise way and there will always be a need to resolve information based on the mix of the recording instruments of the observer/recorder of the accident as a road event.

With an accurate road location, a traffic engineer can use the ARS to obtain the road characteristics needed to perform accident/traffic analysis. In order to perform this analysis both physical road assets and geographical information come into play. To support the traffic engineer in these two areas, the ARS locates all accidents within some geographical area and is able to gather road characteristics from the road inventory that correspond to the identified set of accidents.

Accident analysis is the key process which is used to obtain information about accidents and their relationships to the road system and other systems. These relationships may be direct or indirect: while driving a car has a direct relation to the road system, the consumption of alcoholic beverages is indirectly related to the road system.

Safety analysis implies the need to qualify the road characteristics based on the type of analysis being performed. An analysis might need to examine the rate of traffic at all intersections of a particular road for a city (for example, examine the rate of traffic at all intersections of Alameda Ave. in Denver).

For safety engineering to occur at all, it is mandatory to maintain a historical record of countermeasures that have been applied to hazardous accident sites as road design changes, so their impact can be evaluated in terms of a road system design strategy. Take a road safety countermeasure such as reducing vehicle speeds on a road by stationing a police car with a radar gun at peak traffic volume times on the most highly traveled roads with the most speeding accidents. In order to determine where to place the police cars, the ARS needs to maximize the multiple objectives of speed-caused accidents against traffic rates and minimize the number of police cars.

THE ARS SYSTEM

The functional architecture of the ARS (e.g., what is to be done) is defined with FMaps and TMaps independent of how it is implemented (e.g., which database or what machines are used). It takes into account those systems with which it must interoperate by identifying their interfaces and functionality.

These interfaces — as well as its own functionality in response to these interfaces — help define the constraints to be placed on a design. For example, the ARS resides within the safety engineering system and so must respond to inaccurate accident location information resulting from the way accident records have been documented in the past.

Thus, one of the major functions of the ARS is to resolve the inaccurate locations so as to be as accurate as possible. The ARS can then correlate the rest of the accident information (e.g., weather) with road characteristics maintained in the road inventory database (e.g., type of pavement) to support road safety engineering analysis.

Also, the ARS supports requests for accident analysis by external agencies involved in the road system. The services provided to these agencies range from legal services, to road construction engineering support, to the physical maintenance of the road system itself.

The ARS system architecture is divided into two levels of inter/intrasystems. An intersystem is one in which two systems participate; an intrasystem is one in which a set of components or individuals within a group participate equally and locally. The first inter/intrasystem boundary is between state external systems and the state highway department as a system. For example, the FHWA or another state agency having interfaces with the state highway department would be considered to be part of the intersystem boundary. The next level of detail in the state highway department intrasystem is used to distinguish the interface boundaries between the ARS intrasystem participants (e.g., different functional groups within the state highway department, such as Traffic Operations, Information Technologies, IT, and Transportation Planning Development, TP&D).

The ARS system functional architecture (operational) model includes the following functional areas:

- The import of accident record data from a Registry of Motor Vehicles (RMV) or from an existing legacy system
- Accident site location resolution using data cleaning strategies to validate accident record information (e.g., text cleanup of street names based on valid street names)
- Update of the ARS database as new accident records are imported (connecting accident records to other databases, such as road network information from TP&D)
- Access to information in the ARS database as well as related information that may be accessible via other databases
- User interface query and reporting facilities on the ARS database
- ARS maintenance and building of tailored query/report templates

Input to the ARS can come from an RMV, a legacy system, or interactively from an authorized ARS user. Accident information is validated and cleaned if necessary and possible. The focus is on accident location resolution, since any analysis is valid only if the data are accurate. The ARS database is then updated with this accident information as are any interconnections to other database information. Once authorized by Traffic Operations, the official external view of the ARS data is available by the connected intra- and intersystems. ARS users have access to validated accident information to perform accident analysis using the set of predefined query/reports and an all purpose ad hoc query/report. On an ongoing basis and as needed, the ARS system administrator configures new query/report templates and imports new accident record information into the system.

Each of the above functional areas indicated will be associated with an ARS system component that has the capability to support one or more of these areas.

DESIGN FOR CHANGE/EVOLUTION/MAINTENANCE

We had several key design objectives for the ARS. It had to be easy to maintain. It had to incorporate the use of cross-platform standards for a high degree of platform independence. It had to provide an open architecture. It had to allow integration of future implementation technologies. It was imperative that it improve on the imported data (e.g., the resolution of accident locations for imported accident records), allow for large volumes of accident record data, and be reliable.

The effort needed to maintain any system is measured by the ease, speed, and level of difficulty of responding to changes in ways of doing business and their supporting technologies. While it is difficult to forecast future changes that can impact a system, it is necessary to try to anticipate the potentially affected areas (functional as well as developmental) during the design phases of that system's development. Maintainability is clearly one of the areas a design must consider(see Exhibit 31.3).

Maintainability is a continuum between maintenance requiring design modifications at the FMap/TMap level and maintenance requiring configuration of a component by a user of the system. The goal was to design and implement the ARS so that it is positioned close to the user maintenance end of this continuum.

In addition to maintainability, choices of targeted implementation technologies were based on other design constraints such as legacy systems, level of user acceptance, and political objectives.

We met the design objectives for the ARS by using the strengths of the DBTF development environment coupled with its ability to adjust to a supporting cast of current business technologies (e.g., Internet, client/server). Thus, the DBTF development environment became an integrator of technology foundations upon which to develop the ARS system.

THE SPIRAL DEVELOPMENT PROCESS WITH FMAPS AND TMAPS

Unlike a traditional waterfall development approach which saves the implementation (build) functions to the end of the project, we used a spiral development technique — for which DBTF is uniquely suited. This means that analysis, design, build, and testing tasks took place in parallel through-

Exhibit 31.3. Maintainability Goals

MAINTENANCE AREA	MAINTAINABILITY GOAL
Report output formatting options (both detail and summary reporting requirements).	Provide the ability to create or change report output formats and to target alternative output rendering choices (allow, for example, the ability to generate straight text vs. HTML vs. Postscript vs. RTF) with no programming changes to ARS.
Data summarization options.	Give the user the ability to summarize any valid combination of accident data to any number of levels with a single pass through the accident data. Provide parallel processing options to allow the summary process to scale easily as additional CPUs are available.
Allow additional data from outside sources to be integrated into ARS so that it can be included in ARS reports.	Allow data stored in an external database (e.g., Oracle) to be included in ARS reports at both a summary and detailed level.
Ability to move ARS reporting data to other application environments.	Provide the ability to export ARS report data to alternative application environments (such as spreadsheets, word processors, statistical analysis packages, etc.)
Definition of query criteria screens.	Be able to define input query screens based on the requirements of a newly defined ARS report.
Input and validation of query data.	Input choices are defined by the data available within ARS and external tool and database linkages. Validation of this data is defined by the TMap model of the ARS and its associated data. This will be a very stable approach provided the TMap always models a real world view of the ARS data. The objective is to allow query of data to be dynamically defined based on the ARS TMap model and to be validated to prevent invalid queries from being processed.
Selection and display of detail data.	Provide basic search and data display/entry capability for detailed accident data which is dynamic based on the ARS TMap.

out the ARS development life cycle. As the system evolved, each spiral in development results in an operational system with increasing functionality as the system evolves.

The requirements analysis, specification, and design models of the ARS have been defined and refined throughout several iterations using the same modeling language. These evolving models will continue to serve as the master from which satisfaction of objectives are gauged. The models of the ARS are defined with evolving FMaps and TMaps. The prototype ARS FMaps and TMaps served as a starting point.

FMap and TMap models are automatically analyzed by the analyzer to check for errors, including ambiguities, inconsistencies, and redundancies. Evolving, working, executable developer versions/releases of the ARS were automatically generated from the FMaps and TMaps during the analysis and design phase.

Completing an evolution of the FMaps and TMaps is an important milestone. Since complete running code can be automatically generated from FMaps and TMaps, it means that the user can be shown a running system at an early stage of spiral development. The FMaps and TMaps created during analysis and design are used to create what is required in the build phase of development — automatically. As we've learned, this process is possible because a complete system can be automatically generated or regenerated (or only those portions of the system that are impacted by a change are selectively generated), including Graphical User Interface (GUI), database, communications, and mathematical algorithms, as the system continues to evolve.

In the case of the ARS, as with all systems developed using DBTF and its development environment, all of the automatically generated code is production ready, including the code for GUI, database (e.g., Oracle), and the mathematical algorithms. For testing, run-time constraint test cases are automatically generated to validate correct object construction and unit test harnesses for any user function, providing an automatic user interface for the testing of data sets with an object editor for any of the objects in the systems to be tested. All of the changes to the ARS were made to the specification instead of the code (and will be done so for the future). That part of the system which is changed can then be regenerated automatically. All parts of the system that are affected by that change are traceable. As a result, maintenance of the system becomes a very straightforward, reliable, and efficient process — not only for the ARS project, but for state highway department systems as they evolve over time. Once the basic components are in place, maintenance costs see a significant reduction.

To support a state highway department, interfaces consistent with this open architecture approach were reused from the DBTF reuse library. More sophisticated types or interfaces to preexisting services can be constructed using primitive types which are available with the DBTF development environment. As explained in the previous chapter, each primitive data type has a set of primitive operations. A primitive operation (with some number of inputs and some number of outputs) behaves like an object-oriented method or action that can be performed on an object of its type. Each primitive type has an associated implementation that contains the interfaces relevant to each of the primitive operations of the primitive type. The implementation can be C code that either calls an API or calls code that was generated from an FMap. Examples of primitive types that were reused in the ARS are basic core types available with the development environment; database types such as SQL and Oracle Call Interface (OCI) types, Geographic Information System (GIS) types, Client/Server types for distributed processing, Internet functionality with types to support Common Gateway Interface (CGI) processing, and GUI types.[2,3]

The above set of data types allows the development environment to have access to the technologies needed to support the smooth evolution and extension of the ARS as needed. With the use of the DBTF automated environment along with the spiral development process, the ARS system is inherently flexible to changing requirements, ensuring that changes in the future are straightforward.

Because of this approach, testing is minimized. The reasons for this are many. Correct use of the language eliminates approximately 75 percent of the errors up front that would have been still around after implementation with a traditional approach. The analyzer ensures that the language is used correctly and, therefore, eliminates all interface errors. The code generator automatically generates a set of run-time constraint test cases with the code. Then, when the code is executed these tests find an additional set of errors automatically. Test harnesses for functions are also automatically generated for unit testing of the different objects in the system. Other tests are developed as systems, themselves, using the DBTF environment in the same way as it is used for developing the ARS system.

Testing is performed by the developer and the end user. Whereas the focus of testing for the developer is "inside out" testing, the focus of testing for the end user is "outside in" testing. For testing, the end user supplies test data, the developer enters the test data and tests the system, and the end user reviews the results for technical content.

The ARS was developed with 001 on UNIX workstations and automatically generated for UNIX and/or the PC depending on the requirements of the particular state highway department environment.

SYSTEM ARCHITECTURE

A system architecture is the integration of a functional architecture (what is to be done) that has been allocated to a resource architecture (how it is to be done) using an allocation architecture. The allocation architecture is the result of a design process during development which makes a set of resource component implementation choices based on the options of both the developer and those of the target system (here, the ARS) deployment environment of the user.

A resource component in the software arena is considered to be a composite of the software and hardware needed to support a particular capability. A component will typically raise the level and simplify the domain technology upon which it is layered. For example, the client/server reusables are layered onto TCP/IP which is provided as a standard for internetworking of systems.[2,3]

Exhibit 31.4. Component Implementation Options

System Component	Implementation Options
Client software	C using Win32, browser
User interface	HTML, Win32, Motif
Report formatting	HTML, Postscript, Win32, Motif
Application server	C alone, C combined with SQL, either option with Web server
Data server(s)	Oracle, 001 Persistent OMap objects

The ARS system resource architecture is designed to maximize flexibility and scalability and to minimize maintenance costs through an open and extendible architecture.

The design goals and constraints provide the criteria for the selection of appropriate technologies. For example, flexibility and scalability are goals that can be used as selection criteria to decide on the use of an n-tiered parallel and distributed client/server processing implementation architecture rather than a simplified two-tier architecture. Our goal again was to make the ARS easy to adapt and evolve as system and business needs change.

Each component was designed with alternative implementation choices (and their relationship to future trends) such as Internet browsers and *n-*tier client/server architectures (Exhibit 31.4 outlines allocation choices we considered).

Given a set of resource implementation options, the DBTF development environment is used as the integrator by providing the technology to interface to the technologies listed in Exhibit 31.4.

ARS configurations use the implementation options of Oracle/DBTF persistent objects, Hypertext Markup Language (HTML), C with SQL, and client HTML browsers. The ARS resource architecture (Exhibit 31.5) was chosen because of a key ARS requirement: the need for an open environment that is relatively easy to support. All of the components of this architecture have been designed to work with the DBTF environment using the open standards: HTML, POSIX, CGI, SQL, and Classic C language. Using these standards provides a high degree of flexibility for implementing ARS under a number of different run-time environments.

All parts of the ARS system between the CGI interface boundary and the OCI interface were developed using FMaps and TMaps and generated as high-performance C code to run on the UNIX host. The standard C and POSIX compliant run-time libraries are used to provide UNIX host platform independence.

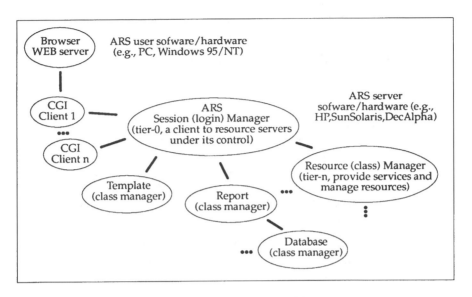

Exhibit 31.5. ARS resource architecture.

On current installations, the ARS user interface allows users to use PC-based machines for their interface while using ARS services that are provided on Unix hosts. The ARS services could as well be configured to reside on NT. This was accomplished by the DBTF environment's integration to Internet technology. User presentation and interaction is provided by a browser using HTML and a WEB/CGI server (both of which are accessed through primitive types) to provide network connectivity to the UNIX host, with C programming capability to access ARS services (via the code generation capability). Database technologies were used to provide storage and backup facilities (via the OCI primitive type reusables), and GIS support tool capabilities already in place at state highway departments were used to provide support for the processing and display of geographic information. The ARS Session Manager coordinates and validates ARS user connections. The Template Manager defines the data display and user interaction characteristics.

USER INTERFACE

The ARS uses templates to drive the user interface screen presentation engine. This architecture allows for designing and building report templates that are independent of the presentation engine, e.g., HTML (browsers or Postscript-based printers). These templates provide ARS users with flexibility to create and modify report presentation formats as business needs dictate — without additional modifications of the ARS FMaps and TMaps.

For Internet technology, this consists of HTML (to define the presentation) with embedded 001 query statements (to define the content). The embedded query statements select the content using control statements (e.g., to select a set of elements to be gathered) and object selection paths (OSP) to identify some location in an Object Map (OMap), the tree of objects instantiated from a TMap. The OSP is a unique path down the tree (based on the node names of the TMap) to some descendent child object node. These query statements, in essence, target the information content to be retrieved from the ARS database. The ARS generates dynamic HTML based on these embedded OMap query statements and associated OSPs to be used for query and report presentation by a browser.

These templates are maintained by the ARS template server. They are then used by the ARS output processing to mix in the HTML screen presentation with the specific report information gathered as a result of the ARS user's request for accident information. This is done by indicating which accident criteria they are interested in (Exhibit 31.6). The HTML screens are tightly coupled with the ARS query system TMaps (Exhibit 31.7). For example, the HTML screen contains a field having "[majorStreet]." This is an OSP indicating that when the user enters information in this field it will be interpreted as the name of the major street and will be put into an OMap that mimics the users screen at the leaf node in the TMap "majorStreet(str)." The "(str)" indicates that the entry is string data.

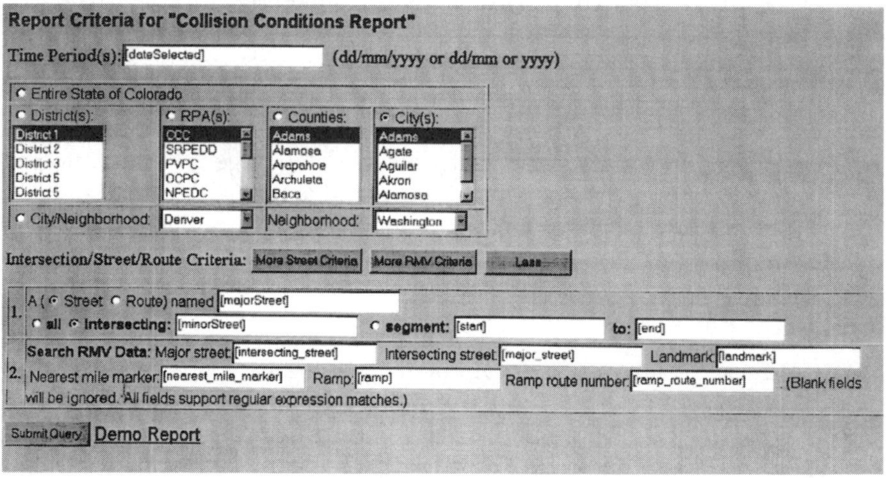

Exhibit 31.6. Accident selection criteria.

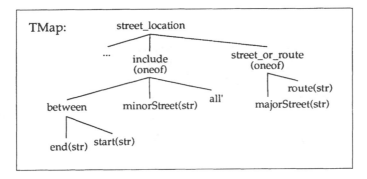

Exhibit 31.7. TMap for street_location criteria.

The specification of these templates is accomplished using an HTML editor. We chose to use Microsoft's FrontPage HTML editor which is tightly integrated with most http servers and provides a WYSIWYG (What You See Is What You Get, as seen in Exhibit 31.6) interface for HTML editing. Our choice of Front Page came after a review of several possibilities, all of which would have been integratable with 001: Netscape Navigator GOLD, HotMetal Pro, and several shareware products. Our choice was an ergonomic one: HTML statements could have just as well been written manually in a normal text editor.

The ARS Internet user interface is supported by a standard HTML browser (e.g., one from Netscape or Microsoft). The advantage of the Microsoft Browser is its support for OLE (Object Linking and Embedding). This means that the ARS can make use of embedded documents (such as Excel for charting) or ActiveX components to integrate new tools and capabilities into its environment.

EXAMPLE QUERIES/REPORTS

There are two basic information gathering strategies in the ARS: summary and detailed for queries/reports. Detailed reports display attributes from individual accidents and summary reports which provide multilevel summaries of accident data. Exhibit 31.8 illustrates an ARS summary report as displayed on a browser. Again, this report output can be seen to closely correlate to a TMap. The TMap in Exhibit 31.9 shows excerpts of some of the information that is associated with an accident.

Queries/reports are qualified by filtering, or limiting, the information to be gathered through selection criteria at the user interface. For example, the user is able to specify a range of dates, a town, or a specific highway segment or intersection; the resulting report includes only the information

Accident Reporting System (ARS) Report Date: 09/21/1996
Page 1

Highway Department
Traffic Operations Section

COLLISION CONDITIONS REPORT
City=DENVER;Period=01/01/1995-01/31/1995

Road Surface Conditions	Accident Type							
	All		Fatal		Injury		Property Damage	
	Count	%	Count	%	Count	%	Count	%
No Defects	13		2		5		6	
Holes Ruts Bumps	4		0		3		1	
Foreign Matter on Surface	5		2		2		1	
Defective Shoulder								
Road Under Construction								
Other								
Unknown								

©1996 by Hamilton Technologies Inc.

Exhibit 31.8. Collision conditions report output.

meeting the stated criteria. A user is also able to specify ad hoc reports, including the creation of columns for calculations using ARS toolkit functions. The following are typical reports that provide statistics for a specified reporting period:

•*All Road Traffic Accident Reports:* for a specified city or town, and specified street or intersection, the details related to each accident, including the date, hour, number of vehicles, number of injured, number of fatalities, collision types, collision objects, vehicle actions, traffic controls, and environmental conditions

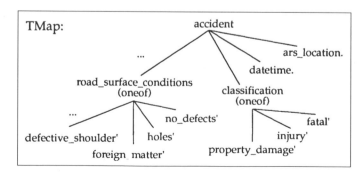

Exhibit 31.9. Excerpts of accident Tmap.

- *Top (n) Accident Sites:* for a state or city, the *intersections*, *sections*, or *locations* having the highest number of accidents (based on a weighted average of injuries and fatalities)
- *Type of Accident by Intersection, Section, or Location:* a summary of the type of accidents, weather, road conditions, and collision factors
- *Contributing Factors Report:* a summary of the number of accidents in which weather, light, pavement condition, or time of day played a contributing role
- *Accident Rate Report:* the number of accidents, injured, fatalities, and a weighted average for the intersections, segments, or locations with the highest accident rate

001 CLIENT/SERVER SUPPORT LAYER

The ARS was layered on top of 001's general purpose client/server layer that uses TCP/IP, the Internet Reuse Library, and Architecture.[2,3] This layer provides an *n*-tiered networked client/server model which can be thought of as a management hierarchy of controllers with a parent being a client to its child as a server (Exhibit 31.5). Parent and children can communicate up and down the hierarchy and a parent can interrupt its children. Controllers can also communicate to other controllers in a networked fashion outside of the standard lines of control as long as they have been authorized to do so by their parent controllers. Each controller can perform local functionality as well as delegate functions to be performed by their children controllers. Each node is also thought of as an active class dispatcher where the controller is the agent that performs the methods of that class.

In the ARS Internet version, a CGI client initiates or attaches to the SessionManager as a server. Multiple CGI clients are managed by the SessionManager. The SessionManager controls access to the ARS system resource class services (via a child controller). If the CGI client is recognized, then the SessionManager as a client initiates or attaches to one of its children controllers as a server to service the request. The child controller could in turn activate or connect to other controllers under its control. This architecture provides for a very high degree of scalability since any number of ARS servers can be targeted to run on any number of networked UNIX hosts or CPUs.

Excerpts from the client/server layer of the ARS show how the generic client/server model described in Exhibit 31.5 is instantiated. The first FMap in Exhibit 31.10 shows the SessionManager making a connection to one of the resource managers that it controls. The subfunction "connect_to_report_manager" starts (or attaches to) the "arsreports" server. When this completes, the send and receive function performs generically to provide communication between a client and its server. Any OMap object constructed from a TMap can be passed between the client

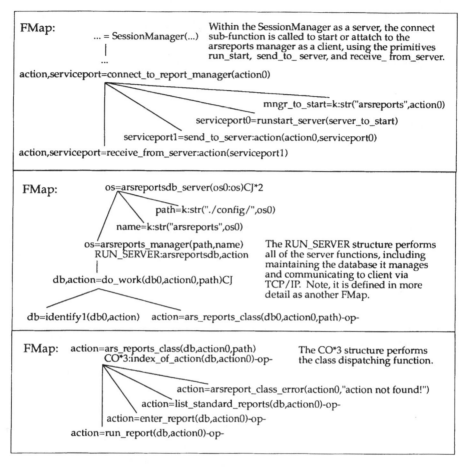

Exhibit 31.10. SessionManager (as a client) to report_manager (as a server).

and server via automatic marshaling of data. For example, the action parmeter to the communications functions indicates the TMap type of the OMap to be communicated.

The second FMap is the arsreports_manager, that is, the server being connected to. It uses a RUN_SERVER structure that does all of the client server protocol and database management functions. The "do_work" function is the function that it applies to all of the report requests that it handles for the SessionManager or other clients that may call it. This server may be on a different networked machine than that of the SessionManager. The "arsreportsdb_server" FMap implementation is automatically generated by 001 as a C function.

470

Excerpts of the code generated by 001 can be seen in Exhibit 31.11. Note that the system is designed to append "db_server" to the name of the server "arsreports" internal to the function "runstart_server." The third FMap "ars_reports_class" is called from the leaf function of the second FMap and dispatches the specific types of requests as primitive operations (or methods) on the action class for the different report requests.

Any number of different WEB servers can be used to support ARS internetworking needs. Possible choices can be either the standard NCSA or CERN httpd servers or commercially available servers. The only constraint imposed is that it must support CGI.

DATABASE DESIGN

The TMap design takes into consideration the tradeoffs between a real-world view of an accident and several other factors: the need to incorporate information via interfaces from interacting systems (e.g., provided by the RMV, TP&D); the need to access or provide access to this information via a common storage technology (e.g., Oracle); and the immediate query and reporting needs of ARS users.

Further, the TMap was defined with special care to use type names that closely resemble objects recognizable to a traffic engineer. Because of this, user queries are able to be validated and specified by the user directly from the TMap. This also makes the job of training end users easier.

The ARS TMap provides more than enough information for the Oracle table design implemented as Oracle schemas to allow access to ARS information. In some cases, we had to limit the use of TMap constructs, since Oracle was not able to handle these more complex structural mechanisms.

The first installation used only persistent OMap objects. Later versions of the ARS use both Oracle and persistent objects from the DBTF environment. Oracle was introduced to provide access to existing Oracle database information (e.g., GIS roadway information from TP&D) and to support external intersystem connectivity (e.g., to insurance company databases).

Access to Oracle was provided by the DBTF environment's reuse library interface to Oracle's OCI interface, which is a cross-platform, high-performance API for accessing Oracle data using standard SQL. The DBTF environment takes advantage of the OCI array processing to maximize throughput when performing queries against Oracle.

Maintenance is supported by the automatic demotion of the status of an FMap if the TMap has been changed and that change could affect that FMap. Information structures may be added to a TMap at the end of Tuple-Of grouped information (similar to a record structure) and new abstract

Exhibit 31.11. Excerpts of C Code Automatically Generated by 001 for FMap: arsreportsdb_server

```
/*001-Generated C code for functional specification
     'ARSREPORTSDB_SERVER'
     VERSION: 3.2.3.9 C-RAT
     AUTHOR: Hamilton Technologies Inc. Copyright 1991.
     OPERATION: ARSREPORTSDB_SERVER
     GENERATED: Sat Jun 7 19:41:11 1997
     SCCSID: @(#)  %M% %I% of  %G%.
*/
#include "ACTION.h"
#include "OMAP.h"
#include "SERVICEPORT.h"
#include "CPORT.h"
#include "PORTADDR.h"
...
#include <stdio.h>
...
fARSREPORTSDB_SERVER(V0OS0,
     V0OS)
IDECLARE_OS(V0OS0)
ODECLARE_OS(V0OS)
{
     /* __LOCAL_VARIABLE_DECLARATIONS__ */
DECLARE_ACTION(V0A1)
DECLARE_STR(V0FNM)
...
     /* __ITERATION_VARIABLE_DECLARATIONS__ */
int rec1_RUN;
DECLARE_OS(R121_OS0)
DECLARE_OMAP(R121_SVOM1)
DECLARE_STR(R120PATH)
     /* __CONSTANT_DECLARATIONS_AND_ASSIGNMENTS__ */
NEWSTACK_TRACE_IDSC("ARSREPORTSDB_SERVER");
...
DOT_K_STR(".omap",C44)
     /* __FUNCTION_SOURCE_CODE_BEGINNING__ */
...
     fDEBUG_SERVER(V0PATH,V0NAME,V1_OS00,&V1_B);
     CLONE_OS(V1_OS00,V1_OS0)
     fLOADOMAP_SERVER(V0PATH,V0NAME,&V1_SVOM0);
     ISREJECT_OMAP(V1_SVOM0,D1_D6)
          if(D1_D6<1)
     {if(D1_D6 == REJECT_BOOLEAN) {REJECT_TEST_BOOLEAN()}
          fSTARTUP_SERVER(V1_OS0,V0PATH,V1_SVOM0,&V1_SVOM1);
     R121_OS0=V1_OS0;
     R121_SVOM1=V1_SVOM1;
     R120PATH=V0PATH;
     rec1_RUN=1;
     while(rec1_RUN -- ){
```

**Exhibit 31.11. Excerpts of C Code Automatically Generated by 001 for
FMap: arsreportsdb_server** *(Continued)*

```
fTRY_CONNECTING_TO_CLIENT(V1_SVOM1,&V1_CPA0,&V1_CLIENT0,
&V1_SVOM3);
        ISREJECT_CPORT(V1_CLIENT0,D1_D11)
        if(D1_D11<1)
{if(D1_D11 == REJECT_BOOLEAN) {REJECT_TEST_BOOLEAN()}
READTMAP_ACTION(V1_CLIENT0,V1_TM)
fRECEIVE_FROM_CLIENT(V1_TM,V1_SVOM3,V1_CPA0,V1_CLIENT0,
        &V1_CLIENT,&V1_CSP,&V1_RQOM0,&V1_SVOM4);
fGET_DATA_SERVER(V1_SVOM4,&V1_DBOM0,&V1_SVOM5);
CONVERT_ACTION_OMAP(V1_RQOM0,V0A0)
CONVERT_ARSREPORTSDB_OMAP(V1_DBOM0,V0DB0)
K_STR(C3,V0A0,V0FNM)
K_OS(V0FNM,V2_OS)
READTMAP_ACTION(V2_OS,V2_TM)
NODENAME_TMAP(V2_TM,V2_TYPENM)
K_STR(C44,V2_TYPENM,V2_OMF0)
MERGE_STR(C42,V2_TYPENM,V2_OMF0,V2_OMFNM0)
MERGE_STR(C40,V0FNM,V2_OMFNM0,V2_OMFNM1)
CASE_STR(C38,C37,V2_OMFNM1,V2_OMFNM2)
STORE_ACTION(V2_OMFNM2,V0A0,V2_B)
CLONE_ACTION(V0A0,V0A1)
fARS_REPORTS_CLASS(V0DB0,V0A1,V0PATH,&V0A);
CLONE_ARSREPORTSDB(V0DB0,V0DB)
CONVERT_OMAP_ACTION(V0A,V1_RQOM)
CONVERT_OMAP_ARSREPORTSDB(V0DB,V1_DBOM)
fPUT_DATA_SERVER(V1_DBOM,V1_SVOM5,&V1_SVOM6);

fSEND_TO_CLIENT(V1_SVOM6,V1_CLIENT,V1_CSP,V1_RQOM,&V1_SVOMN);
    rec1_RUN=1;
    V1_OS0=V1_OS0;
    V1_SVOM1=V1_SVOMN;
    V0PATH=V0PATH;
}/*FALSE*/
else{/*TIMEOUT_EXIT_SERVER*/
    fTIMEOUT_EXIT_SERVER(V1_OS0,V1_SVOM3,V0OS);
}/*TRUE*/
}
V1_OS0=R121_OS0;
V1_SVOM1=R121_SVOM1;
V0PATH=R120PATH;
}/*FALSE*/
else{/*CLONE1_OS*/
    CLONE_OS(V1_OS0,*V0OS)
}/*TRUE*/
ENDSTACK_IDSC(); /* STR Garbage Collector */
return;
}
/* — — — — — — — — end of source — — — — — — — — — — */
```

types may be added to the TMap without affecting any of the FMaps in the ARS application. The ARS developer also has the ability to use this environment to define transformation functions to convert one information structure to another when the organization of the information changes significantly.

In some configurations of the ARS, typical database administration functions are performed using the Oracle database administration tools provided with the Oracle software together with the DBTF environment, whereas other versions use only the DBTF environment.

CONCLUSION

The technical details above provide confirmation of the value of using DBTF and its automated environment to develop the Accident Record System. We made some other observations and drew some further conclusions from this effort which we'd like to share. Following are some observations and conclusions that were made as a result of designing and developing the ARS with this environment.

Since FMaps and TMaps are used as a model and not directly as a programming language, they were able to be used at all stages of the life cycle process. For example, they were used to define the engineering processes and they were also used to model the ARS tool. The ARS code was then automatically generated from the model. Providing a model allows one to select alternative implementations while maintaining an accurate description of the system at a higher level of abstraction, one that is more consistent with the actual physical components of the real-world aspects of the system.

The Development Before the Fact methodology embedded within its language and the development environment led to a reliable construction process for building the ARS. This ranged from sketching FMaps and TMaps early in the requirements and user interviewing process to later in the life cycle when a concrete solution had to be completely modeled in terms of FMaps and TMaps. The thinking process and the reliability of the solutions generated were significantly enhanced by the abstraction capabilities of the DBTF systems language. For example, the ability for a user to define reusable structures and generic universal functionalities allowed developers to hide unnecessary details, thus enhancing reliability. The DBTF automated environment provided much needed coordination among members of the development team.

DBTF's object orientation and its support for persistent objects significantly simplified many of the modeling areas. For example, patterns of objects could be stored as a persistent OMap object to be used later in many different ways (e.g., to verify against another object or to use as a default starting pattern). The ability to use the range of strong typing (e.g., an object as type accident) to weak typing (e.g., the accident object as type OMap) allowed for generic FMaps that would work with accident objects as well as vehicle objects. This generic capability along with the ability to switch between these two different ways of treating the same object made it possible to use the strong points of each view when appropriate.

Our use of the DBTF library of reusables simplified the design of the ARS. Having the reusables available also significantly shortened the time to complete the first prototype and successive evolutions of the ARS. Some of the contributing reusables that helped make the difference included: the generic client/server reusables with automatic marshaling of OMap objects between machines, seamless integration of external database facilities via the DBTF environment's OCI primitive type reusables, and CGI primitive types and other Internet-related reusables

Putting all this together — coupled with the understanding of the objectives of the system and the ease with which changes were able to be made — allowed the team to develop functionality well beyond what was originally thought to be reasonable. In essence, 001 made the difference.

Authors' Bios

Margaret Hamilton (mhh@htius.com) is the founder and CEO of Hamilton Technologies, Inc. (HTI), based in Cambridge, MA, (17 Inman Street, Cambridge, MA 02139, 617-492-0058). She is a pioneer in the systems engineering and software development industry. Hamilton's mission has been to bring to market a completely integrated and robust tool suite that is based on the unique systems theory paradigm which she created, called Development Before the Fact (DBTF). In bringing her product to market, her company leveraged the power of reusability and the reliability of seamless integration to provide a tool that sharply decreases errors while simultaneously increasing productivity. The result is an ultra-reliable system at a fraction of the cost of conventional systems. Hamilton's goal was to embed this formal and completely systems oriented object (SOO) framework into a highly efficient, high-performance, completely graphical, portable workbench of smart tools which the systems engineer and software developer could use throughout the entire design and development life cycle. Today this ideal has been surpassed with the 001 Tool Suite.

Earlier in her career, as the leader of the Software Engineering Division at MIT's Charles Stark Draper Laboratory, Hamilton was the director of the Apollo onboard flight software project and created Higher Order Software (HOS), a formal systems design theory. Hamilton later founded and was CEO of Higher Order Software where she was responsible for the development of the first comprehensive CASE tool in the industry. This tool, called USE.IT, was based on her formal design theory, HOS.

William R. Hackler is Director of Development at Hamilton Technologies, Inc. (HTI) based in Cambridge, MA. As part of his responsibilities, he is the lead engineer for the development of both current and future versions of the 001 tool suite using 001 to define and generate itself. In addition Hackler has been responsible for many areas of the DBTF technology. Hackler has been responsible for many other 001 designed and de-

veloped systems including the development of a simulator for the University of California Los Alamos National Laboratory; a missile tracking simulation for a large aerospace company (HTI was nominated for SBA Subcontractor of the Year as a result of this effort); several asynchronous real-time distributed applications for SDI; a factory model for an aerospace manufacturing plant; and several Internet-related applications including an accident record system for state highway departments.

Prior to HTI, Hackler was Director of Advanced Concepts at Higher Order Software, Inc. where he spent many years defining and developing technologies based on research using the foundations of the HOS methodology. Here he was responsible for many applications applying this methodology and its automation, USE.IT (many components of which he was responsible for designing and developing). These applications included the development of systems in the areas of battle management and aerospace manufacturing. Prior to this, he studied composition with composer Martin Brown in Charles Ives lineage of music and applied music theory to the objects of mathematics.

Notes

1. Ogden K.W., *Safer Roads: A Guide to Road Safety Engineering,* Avebury, Brookfield, VT, 1995.
2. Hamilton Technologies, Inc., HTIDOC #IR3298-3 Internet Reuse Library and Architecture, March 4, 1998.
3. Hamilton Technologies, Inc., 001 Internet Reuse Components, November 1996.

The following are trademarks of Hamilton Technologies, Inc.: 001, 001 Tool Suite, Function Map, FMap, Type Map, TMap, Object Map, OMap, Execution Map, EMap, Road Map, RMap, Xecutor, OMap Editor, 001 Analyzer, System Oriented Object (SOO), Resource Allocation Tool, RAT, AntiRAT, Object Editor, Primitive Control Structures, Development Before the Fact (DBTF), RT(x), 001 AXES, agent 001db, VSphere, and 001Escher.

Chapter 32

A Remote Query System for the Web: Managing the Development of Distributed Systems

Steve Dolha
Dave Chiste

DESCRIPTION OF THE RESOURCE LIBRARIAN REMOTE QUERY SYSTEM:

> The Resource Librarian Remote Query system allows Internet (and intranet) users to query an online resource catalog and subsequently make requests for these resources via e-mail to employees of the ERC. This case study describes Cadeon's experience designing and developing this system using the 001 systems engineering product (refer to Chapter 30) from Hamilton Technologies Inc. of Cambridge MA.

INTRODUCTION

Internet-based systems are fast becoming the way to disseminate information across a wide geographic region at a very low cost. Early in 1996, Cadeon Strategic Technologies, Inc. (WWW.CADEON.COM) was approached to provide a remote query capability for the Education Resource Centre for Continuing Care of Alberta, Canada. The ERC is a resource library that provides materials such as books and videos to healthcare professionals across Western Canada. An existing system had been used to provide online public access to the ERC catalog of resources but was proving to be costly to operate because of its dependency on a public X25 network. In addition, the software had to be manually loaded and configured on each client machine, a process that was a costly administrative head-

0-8493-9987-4/00/$0.00+$.50
© 2000 by CRC Press LLC

ache. What was needed was a solution that provided all the power of a distributed client-server system without the associated overhead of the existing solution. The pervasive client-server technologies and low cost structure associated with the Internet proved to be the perfect solution for development of an Internet-based system that would better position the ERC to meet its key business objectives.

Despite the pervasive nature of the Internet and the apparent ease with which Internet-based systems can be built, the distributed nature of Internet-based systems requires careful management of such a project to achieve the appropriate level of quality and architectural stability in the final product. If one examines the state of systems development implemented using Internet technologies, one will realize how much in its infancy is the development of such systems. Therefore, it was doubly critical that a clear project scope be maintained.

As a first step, it is important to establish the key project principles. The principles we used to guide this project were (1) ensuring the system could evolve as Internet technologies rapidly matured and as business objectives changed, and (2) providing for the ability to scale the system as the volume of data and demand for the system's use increased. We were struck by the tendency of the software industry to dramatically oversimplify the effort to design, build, and maintain Internet-based systems. While technologies such as HTML, Java, and ActiveX certainly provide powerful capabilities to rapidly implement Internet software, it became clear to us that much more was needed to develop what are complex, distributed client-server-based systems.

These systems are more complex than traditional systems for a couple of reasons:

- The distributed nature of components of these systems means that managing them is much more difficult than a traditional "connected" straight-line application. This is due in large part to the lack of completely defined connectivity between all parts of the system (everything from requirements models right through to the actual system components). Such connectivity is necessary to ensure that all interfaces within a system are consistent and that change to parts of the system can be made without introducing errors (in other words, easy impact analysis).
- These systems have a higher number of interfaces between distributed components. This means that there are more places for such a system to break.

So despite the relative strengths of Internet technologies to implement distributed client-server systems, many challenges remain:

1. Model a system independent of Web technologies or any other existing or yet to exist technologies.
2. Provide a fully connected model of all the distributed components of the system.
3. Ensure that all interfaces between distributed components are correct and reliable.
4. Provide high levels of reuse and reliability.
5. Evolve systems easily as either technology or business requirements change.

This is where the use of a sophisticated systems engineering environment called 001 from Hamilton Technologies Inc. of Cambridge, MA fits. 001 provides the means to seamlessly model the pieces of a distributed system in a highly connected manner, 001 essentially provides the modeling infrastructure "glue" that binds all these distributed pieces together, and 001 excels in providing the full end-to-end integration lacking in most systems designed and built without 001. 001 is based on a management principle that the best way to achieve extremely high quality is by adopting a "before the fact" philosophy to systems engineering. This is achieved with a process defined to prevent defects before they happen or as early in the process as possible to ensure that their removal is fast and cheap (and automatic). We believe that this Deming-style philosophy along with a supporting tool (001) is unique in the systems engineering industry.

THE DEVELOPMENT STRATEGY

This project was defined by first developing a clear set of design and strategic objectives to guide the development of the software solution to meet the ERC's immediate needs as well as give the ERC a well-defined strategic position for the evolution of the solution into the future. These objectives were addressed in a way that we believe defines the best way to design, build, and deploy Internet or intranet systems for any business — large or small.

To provide a clear view of our development strategy, we present first our strategic development objectives, followed by a description of the actual development process. The design objectives for the ERC project are described following this review of the development approach.

The development approach used on this project was been designed to support the following strategic development objectives:

- Be able to incorporate and take advantage of the best of what others have created. This is done by designing well-defined interfaces to existing products and components and providing place in the system architecture to incorporate that interface while minimizing the impact on the remainder of the system architecture — 001 provides a strong

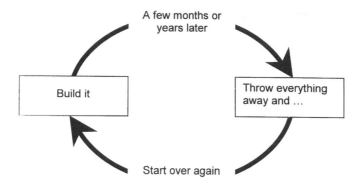

Exhibit 32.1. The "boom and bust" approach to software development.

integration capability to incorporate these interfaces in a consistent manner that "objectifies" the interface. An example of this kind of interface is the Oracle Call Interface used to interact with all the capabilities of Oracle databases.

- Be able to build on the successes of the past and continually reduce the impact and cost of business and technology change.
- For all of our projects, we have a process and the basic architectures that provide a solid basis for building evolutionary systems. Our key objective is to avoid the "boom and bust" approach to software development, as shown in Exhibit 32.1.
- Evolutionary software development must be done on a reliable and secure foundation.

Strive Toward Error-Free Systems

It goes without saying that we all would like to achieve error-free systems. Our experience is that this is only going to be possible through the adoption of a "Development Before the Fact" philosophy and by continually striving toward the improvement of processes that allow errors to be introduced into a system. This includes the automation of complex processes that are error prone when performed manually. 001 has taken a large step towards this with its analyzer capability that examines a 001 specification and reports on errors early in initial development which typically are not discovered until well into implementation of a system using traditional system development methods (whether object oriented or structured systems analysis).

Continually Drive Down the Cost and Complexity of Building Systems

Strategically it is important to focus on driving down the cost and complexity of systems in an iterative manner. The use of system architectures and well-defined, reliable, and reusable software components provides the opportunity to make systems development less expensive and less difficult to do successfully.

Ensure an Accurate Design Based on User Objectives and Requirements

Although it often goes without saying that one must build appropriate software solutions, without a clear understanding of user objectives and requirements this is an impossible task. We prescribe to the use of a contextual inquiry and design approach, which ensures information is collected that is able to provide appropriate and accurate software solutions.

THE DEVELOPMENT APPROACH

The software development process used to develop the ERC Remote Query System is designed to balance the immediate needs of a system with the long-term objective of providing for reuse and the evolution of a system. This balance is managed on every project by applying appropriate levels of effort to both the specific requirements for the project and the supporting system architecture.

It is important to recognize the higher initial cost associated with building reusable system architecture at the same time as one is producing a specific system. Within any project, hard decisions must be made to keep projects costs in line without sacrificing long-term needs. However, it is equally important to make this decision based on the total lifetime cost of a system. It is our experience that the lifetime cost of a system will be substantially lower by using an evolutionary development and maintenance approach to software. Without an evolutionary approach, one reaches a point much sooner where a software solution must be redeveloped entirely from scratch — at that point, an extremely costly proposition. This is a sharp contrast to the evolutionary approach of performing less costly and "safer" incremental improvements of software solutions designed from the start to be durable. With this approach we are clearly targeting a significant reduction in the cost of the activity after the initial development, which traditionally consumes 70 percent of the lifetime cost of a system — maintenance and update of a software solution. "Creating durable, reusable software is more expensive initially, but less costly over the long haul."[1]

It is critical that the development process support an evolutionary approach from the start. Evolution is only reasonable when a system is structured to allow for it to happen easily. The methodology that 001 implements (called Development Before the Fact, or DBTF) provides strong support for the evolution of systems because:

- The graphical representation of 001 models improves the visualization of structural or data flow changes in Function Maps (FMaps).

These are graphical representations of the specification and function calls implemented in a system.

- The entire 001 system model is fully connected. Thus change can be better managed because the impact of any change (especially interface changes) can be immediately traced through the 001 system model. Since every 001 module requires clearly defined inputs and outputs, changes become obvious and are reported to the developer immediately for EVERY component of the system that will be affected. This prevents any part of the system from being overlooked or forgotten by the developer making the change. This greatly increases the reliability of the system being delivered.

- 001 provides an object model that, through encapsulation, allows functional implementation to be hidden behind well-defined interfaces. This significantly reduces the impact of changes in this implementation on the rest of the system.

- The 001 analyzer traps interface errors (75 percent of the errors are fixed after the fact in traditional systems) before parts of a system are deployed.

The following is a description of the primary phases of the development process to build the ERC Remote Query System:

1. Determine user requirements along with system and business objectives (requirements model). We prescribe to a customer-centered design methodology called "Contextual Inquiry and Design" from Incontext Enterprises of Harvard, MA (www.incent.com). This method discovers and captures detailed information about how people work in context while they work at real tasks in their workplace. It guides the development of a system design and provides the means to prototype and test designs with customers before any system development occurs. By involving the users in the design process, we (as designers) "participate in the users' world, [and] we want it shown to us so well that we know it — we want our feet to be sore when their shoes pinch."[2] Only then can we be assured that we have captured the correct design.

2. Design additions or changes to the system architecture to provide the foundation to meet key long-term system and business objectives. This includes making strategic implementation choices to support systems of this type. The supporting system architecture is reviewed as part of every project to determine the scope of changes to support requirements for this particular project, as well as for other similar projects. Additions or changes to the system architecture are prioritized based on the likelihood and impact of a future change in the applications supported by this part of the system architecture. Those parts of a system which have a high likelihood of change and where such change will have a dramatic impact on the system are

supported within the architecture using a design that provides both powerful and intuitive customization capabilities. In the ERC system, the template mechanism where dynamic data are merged with a static defined HTML template is an example of such a component.

3. Prototype using Type Maps(data definition)and Function Maps combined with static HTML pages to illustrate both user interface and functional flow.

4. Build/revise the system architecture based on the design(s) from Step 2.

5. Build the project-specific components using the completed system architecture.

This process is applied in an iterative manner using a spiral development cycle. This spiral approach acknowledges that development is most successful when applied in an iterative evolutionary fashion until a level of stability is reached that meets the existing objectives. This is the initiation of a lifelong evolutionary process that supports the software solution through its entire lifetime, not just its initial creation.

This iterative evolutionary development process is summarized in Exhibit 32.2 as it relates to the continuous improvement process of Plan, Do, Check, and Act.[1]

Having put the "cart before the horse" in terms of explaining the development process before the objectives that it supports, we now turn our attention to describing objectives for this project and describing how this development process supports successful achievement of the objectives.

REMOTE QUERY DESIGN OBJECTIVES

In addition to the development approach supporting the already described strategic objectives, each project has unique design objectives to meet the client's particular needs. Each of ERC's objectives is listed below with a description of the supporting part of the development strategy used to address the objective:

The System Must Be Easy to Learn and Use

The key objective is the ability for ERC clients to easily locate and request appropriate ERC resources. The use of Contextual Inquiry and Design (see the earlier description of Contextual Design) ensures a clear understanding of the underlying process and a review of the usability of the resulting design.

Nontechnical Administrators Can Support the System

The use of technologies that are easy to set up and provide powerful yet intuitive management facilities are key to meet this objective. We feel it is

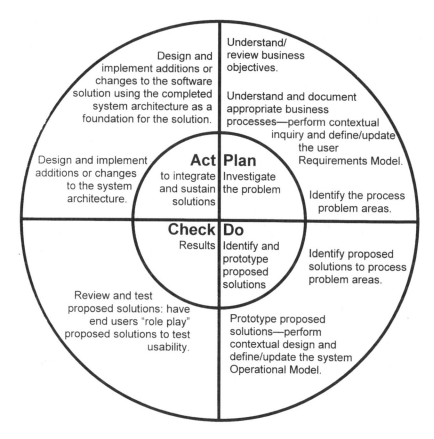

Exhibit 32.2. An iterative evolutionary development process.

important to design automation that allows nontechnical administrators to make changes, such as those changes required in the user interface using the HTML view template process. The key here is innovative and well-defined designs based on the contextual inquiry and design methodology.

The System Must Have Low Operational and Administration Costs

The use of the browser client along with automation of the various regular operational activities contributes to keeping these costs low or virtually nonexistent.

The System Must Have Low Development Costs

The power of 001 and its large library of software components allows the development costs to remain low. In total, the entire system through phase II was developed with a total of eight person–months of development activity. Our expectation is that future similar systems will require 10 to 20 percent of this effort because of the number of "reuseful"[3] and reusable components produced within this project.

The System Must Be Available Worldwide on a 24-Hour, 7 Days a Week Basis

By its very definition, the Internet is a 24 hours a day, 7 days a week operation. The operational environment relies on the stability of the various supporting hardware, software, and network pieces of the system. Thus far, the system has run for 6 months with only one power-related outage.

The system must provide timely availability of new or updated resource catalog data and integrate seamlessly with the existing operational system. This objective requires a clear definition of the data shared between the existing and new system and the appropriate times to perform the updates to keep the parallel systems synchronized as required by the supported business processes. With the ERC system, it was sufficient that an automated batch update process would provide updates to the system. These updates could easily be done in a timely manner to meet the end user requirements. This batch update is currently done weekly, although the design accommodates more frequent updates if desired.

The existing system from which the resource catalog data is drawn has been interfaced to the new Remote Query system by combining an export utility with an automated load process. This batch load process automatically updates the query database and requires no scheduled downtime of the Remote Query system. The automated load process watches a specific export file and when it's modified or its date and time is changed, a load is triggered for some future configurable time frame. This allows the initial export to be done anytime and act as the trigger to start the load, but it also ensures that the load is automatically scheduled outside of the prime time for query activity. When a load is successful, the load process then informs the administrator, who can then switch the active query database to the newly loaded query database.

THE SYSTEM ARCHITECTURE

Any system can be defined using components defined in layers that build upon each other to provide larger and more complex systems. It is critical that each layer and its components be well defined to support reliable interaction between them. Equally important is the need to define each layer and its components to ensure that a layer can be evolved with minimal impact on the rest of the system.

Software makes up a significant part of the architecture needed to make computers effective and powerful tools. As such, and considering the in-

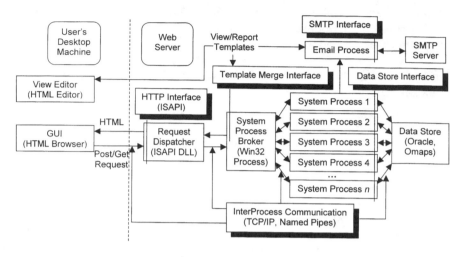

Exhibit 32.3. Web system architecture.

---

creasing complexity of computer systems, it is, more than ever, important to first architect, then build, then evolve systems.

As part of this project, we defined system architecture (Exhibit 32.3) to support the development of the ERC system and all similar Web-based systems. In fact, the architecture shown here can be used to support many dynamic and scalable Web or distributed client/server-based systems. The following text describes the various components of this architecture including the particular implementations chosen to support the various parts of the architecture.

Graphical User Interface (HTML Browser)

This component fulfills the role of client-side interaction. Any HTML browser can provide simple user interface capabilities using standard HTML forms. Further complex user interaction is available with certain browsers (such as Netscape or MS Internet Explorer) using Java or ActiveX-based components and browser scripting with VBScript or JavaScript. The 001 resource allocation tool (RAT) could be configured to generate from Function Maps to any of these languages — this was not done in this project since no scripting was required to satisfy the user interaction requirements of the ERC Remote Query system.

HTTP Interface

The typical Web-based system will use either the CGI interface or one of a number of propriety interfaces such as Microsoft's ISAPI interface for processing POST or GET requests from the HTML browser. A key conceptual view of this interaction is that the traditional workstation event loop has been replaced with a workstation <-> HTTP server loop. This is sufficient for the simplest user-GUI interaction (for example, actions associated with push buttons). It has the disadvantage of increased network interaction and, thus, may not be appropriate for certain types of GUI interaction (typically microlevel interactions such as field level edits or "drag and drop" support). The ISAPI interface was chosen for the ERC Remote Query system to coincide with the choice of Windows NT/IIS as the supporting WEB server platform.

View Editor (HTML Editor)

Flexibility of the user interface and report output process is provided by a series of View Templates. The editing or modification of these templates is accomplished using an HTML editor.

Request Dispatcher and System Process Broker

The Request Dispatcher will take the input provided by the user and pass it on to the "System Process Broker." The System Process Broker will either attach to the appropriate process that is already running, or it will spawn a new system process to handle the user's request. The ability to dynamically create then attach to new processes which can run as services on any number of hosts is important to allow the system to automatically scale up as demand on the system increases.

System Processes

A system process is either already running on the server or is created by the System Process Broker. Each process will handle a user's request and pass the results of the request back. Each system process will be for a unique action on a set of data passed in from the user. After a process has been "idle" for a while it will terminate. It is up to the System Process Broker to decide if it can attach to an idle process or if it needs to create a new one.

Template Merge Interface

The objective of the template/view processing component is to provide a means of defining dynamic HTML pages that integrate data from data stores (such as Oracle) based on user-supplied data and actions — in other words, define the GUI. This part of a system is the primary control of both the look and feel of a system from the end-user perspective. As a result, it is one of the components of the architecture to be highly impacted by change in user needs or ERC business requirements. Rather than developing dynamic HTML pages using a program-driven, hardwired approach — an approach which complicates change to the pages — a simple template language was developed which is embedded within the HTML describing each page of the system. This language is simple to use, yet does not in any way limit the capability to support complex user interaction within the Web browser environment (including the use of VBScript or JavaScript). This approach is similar to the concept of server-side technology and includes Microsoft's "Active Server" technology.

The template language provides for the following:

1. The substitution of data values passed from a previous POST or GET request into the page.
2. The creation, alteration, or transformation of data merged in the output by calling predefined 001-generated functions — predefined functions such as one to support the specification of a SQL-based query.
3. Allow formatting of multiple-row query results in an iterative manner by specifying a single "row section" around specific HTML tags.
4. Define the flow of the pages using "next template" commands that include conditional logic processing to decide which page to display next.

In the second phase of the ERC project, some work was done on the template language to align the template language closer to the concept of a 001 Type Map and corresponding Function Map. This has resulted in a template language which is able to automatically apply the concepts inherent in the 001 types (such as an OSetOf implying iteration over all of its elements).

These pages can be easily constructed using any HTML editor. We designed and built a utility program to parse, error check, and load a new or updated template. The templates are stored in a 001 OMap format consistent with the definition of the Type Map of a template page. As data or other results are passed back to the user, it is combined or "merged" with a particular template so that the data can be presented in many different customizable ways. Typically, these templates will consist of HTML for the browser to interpret and display. Note that this is an implementation similar to the Smalltalk Model/Controller/View (MVC) architecture. The key advantage of this architecture is that the views can be customized without affecting the "model" or core functionality, that is, GUI-independent parts of the system.

Exhibits 32.4 through 32.7 illustrate the results of some of the pages dynamically generated using this template component in the Resource Librarian Remote query system.

Exhibit 32.4 shows the simple query page used to initiate queries. The user can enter Boolean syntax into any of the four fields (Title keyword, Series, Author, or Subject Heading) and request a count or display matches found. Exhibit 32.5 shows the dynamically formatted table output of query

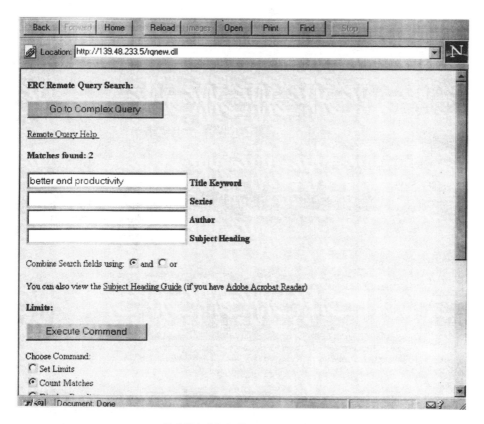

Exhibit 32.4. Simple query.

results. It includes a checkbox to allow the user to select desired resources for inclusion in the following request page.

When submitted, the data from the request page on Exhibit 32.6 are formatted using the template facility to generate an e-mail format of the message sent to ERC staff. This is possible because the template mechanism is not tightly coupled to HTML as a formatting language, thus it can also be used to format data into simple text messages appropriate for e-mail.

The user administration page shown in Exhibit 32.7 is an example using the newer (and simpler) template language which is more aligned with the concept of traversing 001 OMaps than the original template language used to generate the previous pages.

Our goal for future versions of this mechanism will allow default views to be automatically generated from 001TMap definitions. Automation of such tasks will ultimately allow systems to be created extremely quickly

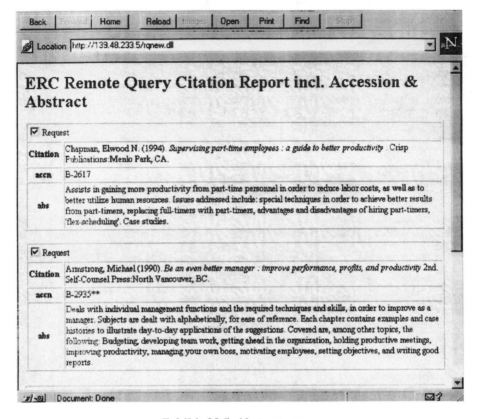

Exhibit 32.5. Abstract page.

without losing the customization abilities needed to meet a particular system's requirements.

DATA STORE (ORACLE, OMAPS)

The first phase of the ERC Remote Query project used the 001-Oracle interface to query data stored in an Oracle database. The queries were defined using an SQL-like syntax defined in the template language. It allows queries to be customized based on input provided by the user. In the second phase of this development project it was realized that by taking advantage of the power of the 001 environment we could replace the implementation of the database component of the architecture with our own custom built database engine — at an extremely low incremental cost. In fact, the cost was the same as the licensing fees charged by Oracle to provide unlimited database access on the Web. This approach provided several advantages:

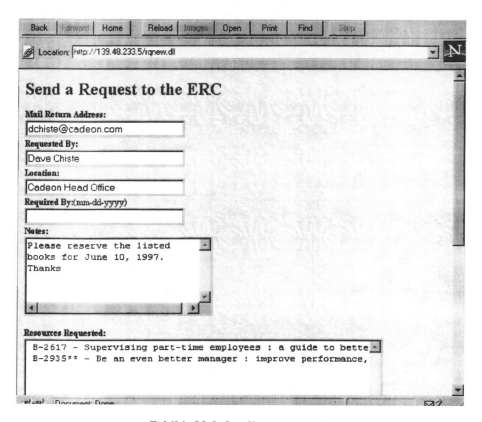

Exhibit 32.6. Sending a request.

1. A significantly reduced cost to deploy the system by eliminating Oracle licensing costs.
2. Implementation of a set of efficient algorithms for searching that are easily tailored to the type of data in this system and are reusable in future systems.
3. Complete control over the design and implementation of the data store and retrieval components of the architecture (keep in mind that software developed using 001 is ultra-reliable).

The decision to build a custom data storage and query mechanism was possible only because of the inherent power and reliability of 001-defined systems. With 001 it is possible to consider the option of building custom complex systems in a fraction of the time — placing them on equal footing with the option of using product-based implementations (such as Oracle). It is this ability of 001 that expands the viable choices to implement systems. The result is an increased competitive edge over those who do not use 001.

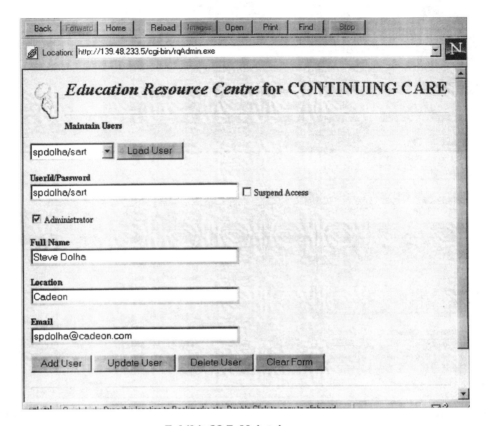

Exhibit 32.7. Maintain users.

InterProcess Communication (Named Pipes, TCP/IP)

InterProcess Communication is that infrastructure component of the architecture which supports the interaction between the various "services" (or system processes) defined in the system. Named pipes were chosen for this system implementation. It should be noted that 001 supports standard IPC mechanisms based on Berkley sockets on UNIX and WinSock on Windows NT platforms.

INNOVATIONS AND CHALLENGES

To put the scope and level of sophistication of the final Resource Librarian Remote Query system into perspective, here is a list of the key innovations/challenges that were encountered during the project:

1. Designed and developed an HTML/SQL query template language, parser, and run-time engine.

2. Developed using 001 on UNIX and deployed the system under Windows NT. The deployment of the 001 produced C code required porting of the 001-primitive library to WIN32. Because it is POSIX and C run-time compliant, the 001 primitive library required very little effort to successfully port it to Windows NT. Other than that, the 001-produced C code was simply copied to the Windows NT machine and compiled without any changes.
3. Developed an 001 interface to the Microsoft ISAPI and named pipe WIN32 functions.
4. Developed an 001 interface to Oracle's "Oracle Call Interface" (OCI) API. This demonstrated to us the ease of incorporating vendor product interfaces as primitive layers in 001. We actually were able to go a step further and architect this interface to allow future support for other SQL database or Object database interfaces.
5. Developed generic bitmap, hash table, and binary tree indexing capabilities for 001 OMaps. This allowed us to provide a fast and easy way to define database structures using 001 OMaps instead of Oracle databases — a choice which we feel was more appropriate for this particular system.
6. Designed a Boolean search language and implemented a parser for the language that uses the indexing capabilities described above to search OMaps. This is similar to the parsing and execution of a dynamic SQL statement as provided by Oracle.

All of this was performed by a team of two people with a total manpower effort of 10 months. We believe it is significant that with a relatively small effort a substantial base of powerful and reusable capability has been produced for building Internet and intranet systems. It is our belief that without 001, this effort would have been several (6 to 10) times longer and would not even come close to the level of architectural sophistication and reliability present in the Remote Query system.

SUMMARY

This case study illustrates an approach used by Cadeon to architect and build robust, reliable, and scalable systems based on Internet technologies. The Resource Librarian Remote Query Project demonstrates how 001 can be used to develop such systems while also accommodating the important strategic objectives of systems development — software evolution and reuse.

With 001, one is modeling systems in the pure Function Map and Type Map form, then choosing to implement those systems with the distributed client-server technologies used to drive the Internet (and intranets). None of these technologies alone is anything radically new (except, of course, 001 itself) — it is the pervasive and open use of Web technologies across much different hardware and networking platforms that is significant. Web technology is the closest that the IT industry has come so far to a set of standard client-sever protocols that are supported consistently across many different desktop, server, and network hardware platforms. HTML is used to drive the client GUI, CGI is used to define the server request interface, TCP/IP provides a reliable packet transport mechanism, and HTTP serves hypertext document requests. This pervasive nature makes Web technologies the best choice yet for a highly stable implementation.

Still the major challenge remains to be able to model a system independent of this or any implementation and provide a "connected" model of all the distributed components of a system. This is where 001 fits. It is the glue that defines as well as binds together all the pieces of a distributed system. It provides a level of integration and reliability missing in systems designed and built without 001. Regardless whether a system is implemented using traditional mainframe technologies or the latest and greatest Web technologies mixed with traditional client-server technologies such as SQL databases, 001 is a constant and stable foundation that allows one to build, maintain, and evolve complex systems in an unprecedented manner.

Authors' Bios

Steve Dolha *(spdolha@cadeon.com) is president of Cadeon Strategic Technologies Inc.*

Dave Chiste *(dchiste@cadeon.com) is a senior systems analyst with Cadeon Strategic Technologies Inc. Cadeon provides software strategic planning and development services throughout Canada and the U.S.*

Notes

1. Arthur, L.J., *Improving Software Quality: An Insider's Guide to TQM,* John Wiley & Sons, New York, 1993.
2. Holtzblatt, K. and Beyer, H., "Making Customer Centered Design Work for Teams" Communications of the ACM, October 1993, p. 93.
3. "Reuseful" is a term which recognizes that it may not be possible to initially create designs or software components as fully reusable because of the constraints of cost or time for a specific project, but acknowledges that future work is justified to evolve the designs or software components towards a stronger "reusable" condition.

The following are trademarks of Hamilton Technologies, Inc.: 001, Development Before the Fact (DBTF), Function Map (FMap), Type Map (TMap), and Resource Allocation Tool (RAT).

Chapter 33
Simplifying Systems Integration

Michael Huang
Marc Beaulieu
Norman Beaulieu

SYSTEMS INTEGRATION AND BUSINESS APPLICATIONS are becoming more and more complex due to continuous changes in business processes and increasingly swift market evolution. Because of this, enterprise software providers will need to more rapidly develop and integrate totally reusable, user-defined, application-specific solutions that are cost-effectively modifiable. Unlike today's "force-fitted" solutions, profitable vendors will need to create and maintain a massive library of reusable software that will be intelligently and strategically deployed to more accurately meet the needs of new clients and to better service existing clients.

To achieve this, traditional development rules and practices will need to give way to more consistent and logically complete modeling approaches in order to more rapidly respond to increasingly complex, ever-evolving business needs. This trend of change is evidenced by increasing demand for a more common or universal method of building software systems to avoid problems of interpreting semantics of varied languages; to facilitate maintenance, upgrades, and changes; and to reduce costs by increasing a product's life cycle. Based upon these improved solution methodologies, fixed price and fixed schedule product implementation contracts will become the rule, not the exception. This will be a critical success factor because the speed at which an organization must adapt and evolve to simply remain competitive is staggering. And no one wants to be left behind.

BACKGROUND TO A SOLUTION

This technological revolution and transformation became very evident a few Internet light-years ago — about 4 calendar years — as our company began integrating its first database with the Internet. It was a systems integration project related to our vision of better using technology to more

0-8493-9987-4/00/$0.00+$.50
© 2000 by CRC Press LLC

productively impact the operations of nonprofit organizations — including educational institutions, hospitals, and charitable and government organizations. We quickly encountered the fact that integration between the rapidly expanding Internet, database systems, and applications presented some interesting challenges. The main challenge seemed obvious: *reliably* integrate the Internet, various databases, and applications in a more rapid, cost-efficient manner.

To meet this challenge, our company began carefully examining the traditional ways of building and integrating systems. Not surprisingly, we soon concluded that commonly used methods, products, and tools did not offer a complete solution. A major problem we found, which still is rampant today, is that products and systems are built to solve a particular problem and, therefore, are not adaptable when hardware, software, or the business processes change.

Given these issues, the rapid pace of technological change and increased competitive pressures spurred by a more global business community, it was glaringly apparent that a more productive and cost-efficient approach to building and integrating enterprise-wide solutions was more than overdue. The future, it seemed, would belong to those organizations that could best harness technological advancements to their advantage in the most time-effective and cost-efficient manner.

ENTERPRISE MANAGEMENT ARCHITECTURE (EMA)

Software developers are under intense pressure to deliver a product within a certain time frame which makes adhering to strict development practices (like those proposed by Software Engineering Institute (SEI) nearly impossible. Teams of project engineers using traditional development methods attempt to manually integrate thousands of lines of manually produced code which is time consuming, highly error prone, and has suspect documentation. Shortcuts are taken and functionality is often compromised to get the product out the door. Unfortunately, it is the client who suffers in the end because initial expectations are rarely met, product implementation is typically delayed, modifications are costly and tend to propagate errors, and the life cycle of the product is, therefore, significantly reduced. In order to address these issues, our company sought a more effective way of delivering software solutions to significantly improve client satisfaction, cut costs, and extend the life cycle of the software. The result: Enterprise Management Architecture (EMA).

EMA delivers an adaptable systems integration framework designed to more productively build and integrate enterprise-wide applications for the entire lifetime of a total system. "Framework" refers to the EMA architecture — a real-time distributed approach that enables the integration of various applications, databases, and the Internet through open distribution between clients and servers. It has the ability to be able to integrate with most hardware, software, and databases available today, and it is designed to integrate with the products of the future. This chapter will focus on the integration solution aspects of EMA (and not its application building aspects) that our company has developed to assist us in delivering integrated solutions to our clients.

COMPONENTS

EMA consists of a group of independent software components. The main components are the kernel, communication server, CORBA/DCOM interface, and ODBC/JDBC interface.

EMA Kernel

The EMA kernel is the main component or the control center of the whole system. The kernel is implemented using the state-driven approach. Each state represents the current status of the system. State changes depend completely on the incoming request message and the current state. Therefore, the control sequence will be implemented by the state-driven method.

Basically, there are three main state diagrams (modes) in the EMA kernel according to the available EMA running modes: csstate (client/server state), nbstate (network browser state), and slstate (standalone state). Each state contains different control sequences.

CSSTATE (Exhibit 33.1). Begin from the *start* state; right after EMA start-up, the system goes into the *Initialize* state. Then, the EMA server will try to start up and the system will be in the *waitConnection* state to wait for the client to request a connection.

Once the request arrives, the system will get into the *securityCheck* state to check the end users authentication. If the user at the client site doesn't have enough authentication to use the server, the server will get into the *Alert* state. Otherwise, EMA will be in the *waitMessage/Object* state to wait for the incoming messages and objects.

Once the message or object comes in from the client site, EMA will get into the *Action state* which includes a sequence of control commands to the other EMA components for the incoming client request. After EMA completes the task, it will get into the *sendMessage/Object* state in order to send the message or object back to the client site.

When the message/object is out, EMA will go into the *WaitAcknowledge* state to wait for client to send back the acknowledgment. If the acknowledgment arrives, EMA will get back into the *SecurityCheck* and repeat the process loop. Otherwise, if the acknowledgment doesn't arrive before a

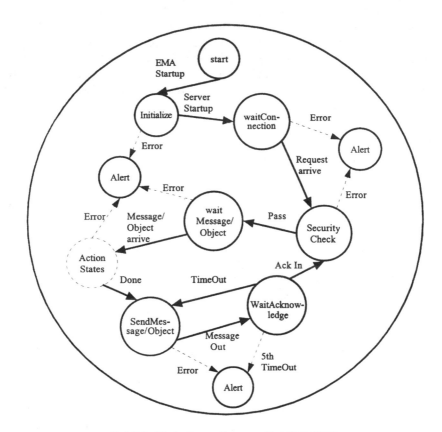

Exhibit 33.1. State diagram for CSSTATE.

certain time, EMA will go back to *SendMessage/Object* state and resend the message and object to the client. This will continue until the timeout happens more than five times.

One more thing to point out is that every state has an exception handling mechanism. Once the error or exception happens, EMA will get into the *Alert* state. This applies to the other two modes as well.

NBSTATE (Exhibit 33.2). Again, we begin from the *start* state; after EMA startup, the system goes into the *Initialize* state. Then, the EMA server will try to start up and EMA will go into the *CheckHttpd* state in order to check whether the http daemon is running in the system. If the daemon is there, EMA will be in the *waitHttpdConnection* state to wait for the client to request an http connection.

Once the http request arrives, the system will get into the *securityCheck* state to check the end-user's authentication. If the user at the client site

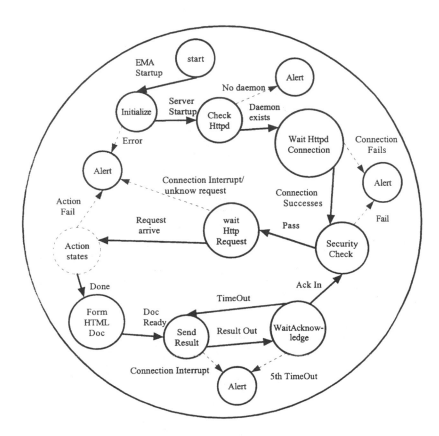

Exhibit 33.2. State diagram for NBSTATE.

doesn't have enough authentication to use the server, the server will go into the *Alert* state. Otherwise, EMA will be in the *waitHttpRequest* state to wait for the incoming http request.

Once the http request comes in from the client site, EMA will get into the *Action state* which includes a sequence of control commands to the other EMA components for any incoming http requests. After EMA completes the task, it will go into the *FormHTMLDoc* state in order to prepare the return HTML document which includes the result of the task.

Once the document is ready, EMA will be in the *SendResult* state to send the resultant HTML document. When the result is out, EMA will go into the *WaitAcknowledge* state to wait for the acknowledgment to arrive. If the acknowledgment arrives, EMA will get back into the *SecurityCheck* and repeat the process loop. Otherwise, if the acknowledgment doesn't arrive before a certain time, EMA will go back to the *SendResult* state and resend the mes-

499

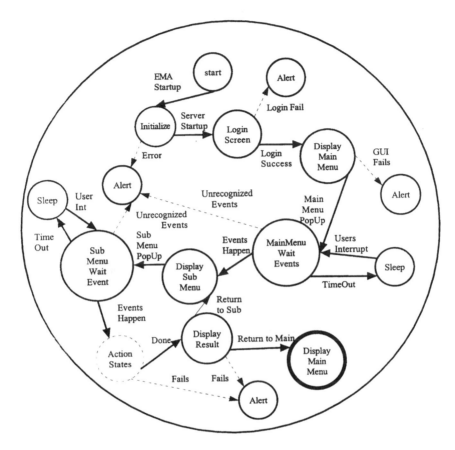

Exhibit 33.3. State diagram for SLSTATE.

sage and object to the client. This will continue until the timeout happens more than five times.

SLSTATE (Exhibit 33.3). We begin again from *start* state; after EMA start-up, the system goes into the *Initialize* state. Then, the EMA server will try to start up and the system will be in the *LoginScreen* state to wait for the end user to do a password login.

Once the login process is finished, the system will go into the *Display-MainMenu* state to display the system main menu. Once the main menu is up, EMA will be in the *MainMenuWaitEvents* state to wait for any possible desktop events (*Mouse clicks, keystrokes, and so on*). Once the event happens, EMA will be in the DisplaySubMenu state to display the submenu. When the submenu pops up, EMA goes into the Action state which includes a sequence of control commands to the other EMA components for the end-user's request.

After EMA completes the task, it will go into the DisplayResult state in order to display the process result. EMA then has the option to go back to either the DisplayMainMenu or the DisplaySubMenu state depending on the need of the end user.

Communication Server

The Communication Server is the EMA communication center — our version of a standard Application Programming Interface (API). Its main task is to manage the different types of communication protocols including Telnet, Ftp, TCP/IP, UDP (Universal Data Protocol), and RTP (Real Time Protocol). The communication server is based upon the OSI standard and is designed to meet the requirements of abstraction, encapsulation, modularity, and hierarchy in order to make EMA flexible and heterogeneous.

The communication server is EMA's door to the outside world. It simplifies the communication process between varied applications that share the aforementioned protocols so that integration is greatly facilitated. When implementing large enterprise-wide systems that can have multiple applications from various vendors, writing separate interfaces for one to speak with the other is time consuming, costly, and error prone — especially when vendors do application upgrades. By using a protocol-based communication center, many of the conventional integration problems are more effectively addressed.

CORBA/DCOM Interface

CORBA/DCOM interface is the EMA distributed computing center. The main task is to connect to the existing CORBA or DCOM standard applications by transferring objects. The typical system integration model includes the 6 levels: standard architecture (level 6); frameworks (level 5); distributed objects (i.e., CORBA) (level 4); Mature Remote Procedure Calls (i.e., OSF DCE) (level 3); Miscellaneous Mechanisms (level 2); and commercial off-the-shelf solutions (level 1).

With the CORBA/DCOM standard embedded in EMA, EMA begins at level 4. Usually, a CORBA/DCOM interface will include four components: Dynamic Invocation, IDL Stub, ORB Interface, and ORB core. Dynamic Invocation allows for the specification of requests at run-time. This is necessary when the object interface is not known at run-time. Dynamic Invocation works in conjunction with the interface repository.

IDL Stub consists of functions generated by the IDL interface definitions and linked into the program. The functions are a mapping between the cli-

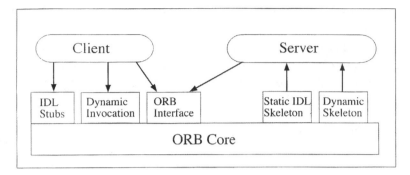

Exhibit 33.4. Example of ORB core.

ent and the ORB implementation. Therefore, ORB capabilities can be made available for any client implementation for which there is a language mapping. Functions are called just as if it was a local object.

The ORB interface may be called by either the client or the object implementation. The interface provides functions of the ORB that may be directly accessed by the client (such as retrieving a reference to an object) or by the object implementations. This interface is mapped to the host programming language. The ORB interface must be supported by any ORB.

ORB core is an underlying mechanism used as the transport level. It provides basic communication of requests to other subcomponents. A common ORB architecture is shown in Exhibit 33.4.

The request and the response (either return values or an exception) both pass through the Object Request Broker (ORB), which is responsible for mediating all the differences between the systems. Specifically, the process steps of an ORB are

1. Marshal arguments for the call: that is, assemble them into the proper format.
2. Locate a server for the object.
3. If necessary, transmit the request, via RPC or sockets or some other mechanism.
4. If necessary, create a process at the server end to handle the request.
5. Unmarshal the arguments into the format required by the server process.
6. Marshal the return values or exception information constituting the response.
7. If necessary, transmit the response.
8. Unmarshal the response at the client end.

Overall, the CORBA/DCOM interface is a component that facilitates integration of disparate object-oriented applications.

ODBC/JDBC Interface

The ODBC/JDBC interface is EMA's database connection center. Its main task is to connect to database systems such as Oracle, Sybase, DB2, mSQL, MS Access, etc. The current standard and most popular ODBC/JDBC version is 3.0. It contains performance improvements for more flexibility, better memory management through binding enhancements, client-side result set searching, and an improved error model through diagnostics. The ODBC/JDBC API is implemented in terms of a vendor-specific driver that then uses a vendor-specific Net library in order to get across the Internet.

001 EXAMPLE OF EMA KERNEL

We will use the *State Diagram Driver* as an example to show how we use 001 as a tool to implement the EMA kernel (see Chapter 30 for a detailed description of 001 and its modeling environment). The purpose of the *State Diagram Driver is* to control the state transmission during the EMA process cycle. It will basically wait until the next event happens and transfer to the next state according to the current state. In order to make it more flexible (it can be modified in the future), the state transmission table will be built into OMap files. The structure of the state transmission table TMap file contains four fields: *current_state, event, next_state,* and *actions* (where actions is oSetOf type of action). Exhibit 33.5 shows the state transmission table TMap structure:

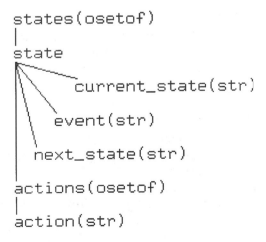

Exhibit 33.5. State transmission table TMap structure.

Exhibit 33.6. State Transmission for CSSTATE

current_state	event	next_state	actions
Start	EMA startup	Initialize	—
Initialize	Server startup	waitConnection	—
Initialize	Error	Alert	—
waitConnection	Request arrive	securityCheck	—
waitconnection	Error	Alert	—

For example, part of the state transmission table for *csstate* according to the csstate diagram is shown in Exhibit 33.6.

After the table structure is determined, the operations of the *State Diagram Driver* will be built on top of it. These operations can be categorized into three functionalities according to their purposes — EMA kernel setup functionalities, EMA kernel debug functionalities, and EMA run-time functionalities.

EMA kernel setup functionalities are only used by Ariel Technologies, Inc. to set up the EMA kernel for the client and it shall stay unchanged after the setup. EMA kernel debug functionalities are used for debugging purposes. EMA run-time functionalities are used during EMA run-time to keep tracking the current state of EMA so that the kernel can control the EMA components. Only seven functions are chosen to demonstrate the 001 FMaps: *create_state, insert_state, delete_state,* and *display_state* are EMA kernel setup functions; *show_current_state* and *show_next_states* are EMA kernel debug functions; and *store_current_state* is the EMA run-time function.

Create State OMap File (create_state)

This FMap creates a new OMap file to store the state diagram for EMA kernel. Its input (str) is the filename of state diagram (Exhibit 33.7). The output *done* (Boolean) could indicate whether the function is done without any problems.

Insert One Record Into State (insert_state)

This FMap inserts a new record into a state OMap file. Input *filename* (str) is the state diagram OMap filename. Input *c_state* will be stored in the current_state field. Input *event* (str) will be stored in the event field. Input *next_state* (str) will be stored in the next_state field. The output *done* (Boolean) could again indicate whether the function is done without any problems (Exhibit 33.8).

```
done:boolean=create_state(filename:str)CJ
```
```
        state=create_skeleton:states(filename)
```
```
   done=c_storeomap:states("/usr/local/EMA",filename,state)
```

Exhibit 33.7. Create CSTATE.

Delete One Record From State (delete_state)

This FMap deletes one record from a state OMap file. Input *filename* (str) is the state diagram OMap filename. Input the *current_state* (str) and *event* (str) indicates which record is going to be deleted. The combination of value of *current_state* and *event* shall be unique in the OMap file (Exhibit 33.9).

Display All Records from State (display_state)

This FMap displays every record in a state OMap file. Its input *filename* (str) is the state diagram OMap file. All records in *filename* will be displayed on the screen (Exhibit 33.10).

Show EMA Current State (show_current_state)

This FMap shows an EMA user's current state which is saved in a file called *username_state* under the directory /usr/local/EMA. For example, if user John is using EMA, his current EMA state will be saved in *john_state*. This FMap will read this file and display it. Its input *username* (str) indicates the name of the EMA user. The output *current_state* (str) displays the user's current state. The output *exist* (Boolean) indicates whether *username* exists in EMA or not (Exhibit 33.11).

Exhibit 33.8. Insert state.

Exhibit 33.9. Delete state.

Show Next Possible States (show_next_states)

This FMap finds all next possible states for an EMA user according to his/her current state. Its input *username* (str) indicates the name of the EMA user. Its output *next_state* (str) shows all next possible states (Exhibit 33.12).

Store Current State (store_current_state)

This FMap saves the current state for an EMA user in the file *username_state* under /usr/local/EMA based on the input *username*. The other input *state* (str) tells what state shall be saved. The output done (Boolean) indicates whether the save is done without a problem or not (Exhibit 33.13).

506

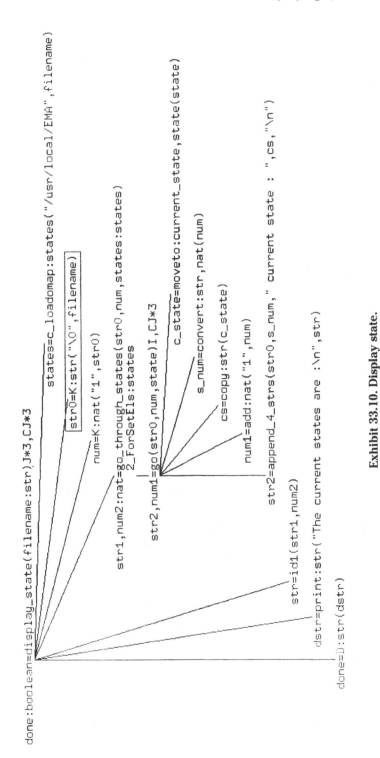

Exhibit 33.10. Display state.

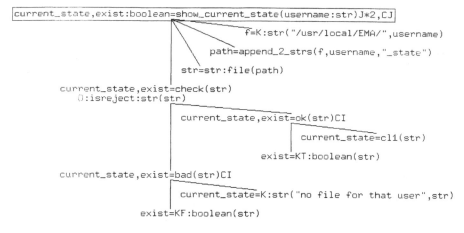

Exhibit 33.11. Show current state.

EMA BENEFITS

Integrating complete systems such as the client/server, database(s), and the Internet, is a complex task for traditional systems, in part because of different languages and various interfaces. Traditionally, the integrated code is done manually by one or more programmers and if that same group is not available on an ongoing basis, new people must be hired to interpret the code.

EMA was crafted to significantly advance and make more expeditious this integration process. Combined, the aforementioned EMA components make up a solution set of engines that do the real work, behind the scenes, for one part or for the entire enterprise system. With EMA, IS departments significantly reduce the complexity of integrating the Internet, databases, and client/server systems because the real work to accomplish integration is already done. Therefore, by using EMA, organizations have a single, core framework from which new applications can be built or plugged in, and existing systems can be fully utilized and integrated.

The result is a system that most accurately and most productively meets existing needs and is fully engineered to be adaptable to evolving needs. This is critical given the rapidity with which the business processes change and the speed at which data must be managed for a business to stay ahead of the competition. Overall, the EMA solution improves quality, is less time consuming, and less costly.

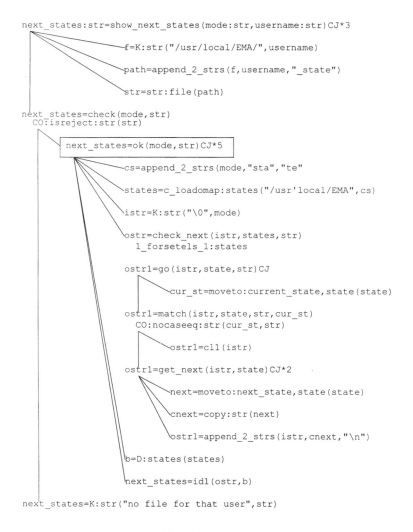

```
next_states:str=show_next_states(mode:str,username:str)CJ*3
            f=K:str("/usr/local/EMA/",username)
            path=append_2_strs(f,username,"_state")
            str=str:file(path)
next_states=check(mode,str)
  CO:isreject:str(str)
        next_states=ok(mode,str)CJ*5
            cs=append_2_strs(mode,"sta","te"
            states=c_loadomap:states("/usr'local/EMA",cs)
            istr=K:str("\0",mode)
            ostr=check_next(istr,states,str)
              1_forsetels_1:states
            ostrl=go(istr,state,str)CJ
                  cur_st=moveto:current_state,state(state)
            ostrl=match(istr,state,str,cur_st)
              CO:nocaseeq:str(cur_st,str)
                  ostrl=cll(istr)
            ostrl=get_next(istr,state)CJ*2
                  next=moveto:next_state,state(state)
                  cnext=copy:str(next)
                  ostrl=append_2_strs(istr,cnext,"\n")
            b=D:states(states)
            next_states=idl(ostr,b)
  next_states=K:str("no file for that user",str)
```

Exhibit 33.12. Show next states.

CONCLUSION

Technologically speaking, it has been a long time since our initial quest began for a more reliable way to build and integrate solutions with the Internet and various databases and applications. During that time, one thing is for sure; the Internet has spurred a sweeping technological revolution. Major changes are evidenced not only with businesses embracing the Internet and the surge of database technology, but corporate culture is being jarred as well. More and more CEOs and Executive Directors view technology as mission critical and are themselves becoming technologically com-

509

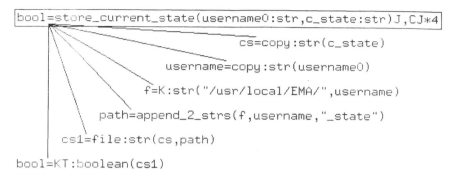

Exhibit 33.13. Store current state.

petent and savvy, thus putting pressure on IT managers to locate solutions that are more reliable and cost effective.

This trend is of major significance. As organization leaders take an active, participatory role in information technology, we should witness a far less forgiving temperament with products and integration services that do not make the grade. Today's market-driven technology behemoths have been providing products and services catered to a conservative mainstream marketplace which have not always been "best of breed." Interestingly enough it appears as though this very market — with many CEO's leading the charge — may be realizing that waiting too long or compromising in any way on technological solutions can no longer be tolerated.

Coinciding with this new cultural trend are the initially described technological challenges which are critical success factors in the increasingly competitive global marketplace. A solution to meet these technological challenges must reliably interconnect various databases and applications with *n*-tier levels of access and control in multiple locations via the Internet. The solution must also be cost effective to build and maintain, and most certainly must adapt to any changes in hardware, software, databases, or even in the business process itself. EMA offers a framework foundation for an integration solution that addresses these needs.

Gone are the days of force-fitting products and costly, time-consuming manual intervention to keep these products and their error-prone integration working. Today, leadership is demanding reliability and expectations for it will be commensurate. Fortunately, solutions are available because the new reality is that technology is fast becoming the fulcrum — the focus for solutions to remain competitive in an increasingly global economy.

Authors' Bios

Michael Huang, *(Ph.D.) is the Chief Technical Officer for Ariel Technologies, Inc. and is principal architect for EMA. He is a computer scientist who has written four books:* Data Processing, Fundamental & Advanced Programming Language, Data Structure, *and* Database Management Systems. *Huang has extensive knowledge in various modeling tools, Java, JavaScript, C++ programming, as well as substantial system administration experience. He currently is a part-time professor at Boston University teaching object-oriented programming.*

Marc Beaulieu *is cofounder and Managing Principal of Ariel Technologies, Inc., a leading-edge consulting and systems integration firm based in Boston, MA. He is a chief technologist in research and development for new EMA applications. Prior to cofounding the company, Beaulieu managed expansive financial services database applications and customer service database systems for Fidelity Investments and Liberty Financial. He received a BS from Cornell University in Ithaca, NY in 1991.*

Norman Beaulieu *is cofounder and Managing Principal of Ariel Technologies, Inc. a leading edge consulting and systems integration firm based in Boston, MA. He is chief marketing and development officer and has served on panel discussions and spoken on technology-related issues. Prior to cofounding the company, he was a financial consultant for American Express. He received a BA, cum laude, from Wesleyan University in Middletown, CT in 1989.*

Notes

Enterprise Management Architecture and EMA are trademarks of Ariel Technologies, Inc.
001, OMap, TMap, and FMap are all trademarks of Hamilton Technologies, Inc.

Chapter 34
Managing Corporate E-Mail and Website Feedback

Deborah Galea

HOW OFTEN HAVE YOU SENT AN E-MAIL TO A COMPANY and received a reply only after 2 weeks or maybe never? To me it happens regularly, and I always wonder why companies advertising their Website or e-mail address if they are so obviously ill prepared for its use? To me this indicates an important lack of customer service and will not give me much confidence in their product or service. It seems as if companies recognize the importance of the Internet but do not realize that this new medium automatically involves a completely new communication method: e-mail.

And this in an era where e-mail usage is growing exponentially: by the year 2000, the Electronic Messaging Association (in conjunction with Wilkofsky, Gruen and Associates) projects that there will be 108 million e-mail users — double today's number (Exhibit 34.1). Not only will the number of users double, the number of e-mail messages is expected to grow exponentially: the 108 million users are expected to receive more than 7 trillion messages a year! What companies need is a tool to be able to cope with this surge in e-mail. And this tool is E-Mail Management, a concept which was virtually unknown until only 1 year ago.

WHY E-MAIL MANAGEMENT IS NECESSARY

The days are past when companies thought that the design of their Web page was the be all and end all. By now we all know that designing a Web page is only half of the work and that the second, probably more essential, part is to create that all-important traffic to your site. However, after creating the interest in your Website, in a sense, things are only beginning.

What most companies do not foresee is that when traffic to their Web page starts to increase, the amount of e-mail they receive will also start to

0-8493-9987-4/00/$0.00+$.50
© 2000 by CRC Press LLC

E-mail Messages in the U.S.

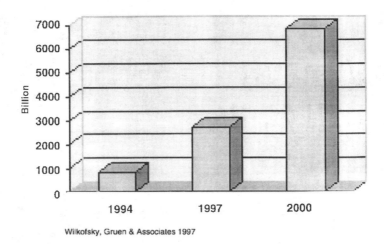

Wilkofsky, Gruen & Associates 1997

Exhibit 34.1. E-mail use is growing exponentially.

increase. When at one time a company was pleased to receive 10 e-mail messages a day, employees are suddenly overwhelmed by 50 to 100 messages a day and are not ready to deal with this new means of communication. The result is that the sudden work overload often cannot be handled efficiently, customers' e-mail correspondence are not answered quickly enough, and consequently customers look elsewhere for their requirements. But it is not only the workload that stops the majority of companies from answering e-mail efficiently. It seems that there is still a lack of "respect" for e-mail, something that is present for the "more traditional" means of communication such as telephone or fax. A self-respecting company would never leave a telephone unanswered or not follow up a telephone message. The same is true for faxes. However, companies seem to be quite unashamed about simply not answering e-mail.

Furthermore, apart from a growing amount of e-mail, the company Website also opens up new possibilities such as ordering or requesting information via the Internet. These online order forms and information request forms change the way organizations work and many companies turn out to be ill prepared or even completely unprepared for these changes. This is where E-Mail Management comes into play. E-Mail Management helps companies prepare for the changes that a Website brings and helps companies deal with the changed and often increased workload.

E-MAIL MANAGEMENT

E-Mail Management is a system whereby companies manage, track, archive, distribute and automate their corporate Website e-mail, such as sales@yourcompany.com, support@yourcompany.com, or info@yourcompany.com. You could compare it to a call center where all incoming calls and responses are tracked, and individual activity can be monitored. Instead of just leaving it up to chance whether an e-mail is actually answered, and what answer is given, companies actually "manage" their incoming and outgoing e-mail. With the help of software applications, companies can archive all incoming and outgoing e-mail and subsequent answers, view reports on average response times and other e-mail statistics, distribute mail amongst different persons, and send automatic acknowledgments with tracking numbers.

Another concept in this area is E-Mail Automation. Not only should you manage your e-mail, but you should also try to automate it as much as possible in order to reduce workload, and in that way again improve the management of your corporate e-mail. Examples of automation are the automatic archiving of Web forms (order forms, information request forms) into databases, sending automatic personalized followups, and triggering possible workflow processes.

COMPONENTS OF E-MAIL MANAGEMENT

Keeping Track of E-Mail

First of all with E-Mail Management (Exhibit 34.2) companies can keep track of their e-mail messages. For instance software packages can archive all e-mail (sent and received) into a central ODBC database and staff can track e-mail by searching for names, keywords, or tracking numbers. For example, in case of a telephone inquiry, staff can instantly see whether an e-mail has been received, whether it was answered and what the answer was, even if it was answered by someone else. This can be particularly useful when customers complain that their e-mail has not been answered, because with an E-Mail Management application staff can instantly verify whether their claim is correct. Furthermore, archiving of e-mail allows managers to keep an eye on the content of messages and, therefore, manage the e-mail image and consistency of the company.

Apart from searching for a specific e-mail, staff members can also view a complete history of the e-mail exchanged with a certain customer. For instance in the case of a complaint, managers will be able to view the "thread" of e-mail messages that led up to it, including those received from the customer and the replies from different staff members. Furthermore, this can also be used when billing customers for services. The tracking sys-

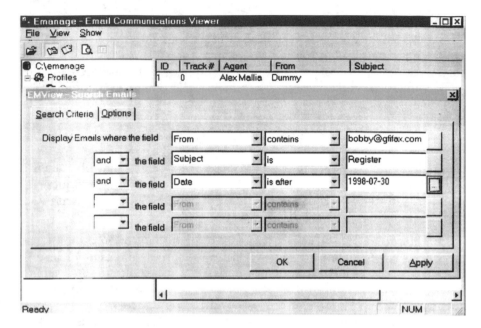

Exhibit 34.2. E-Mail Management viewer.

tem shows exactly how often customers have received consultancy, support, or any other service.

Finally, keeping track of e-mail is a useful way for managers to stay in touch with their customers. Most managers normally will not see much of the incoming sales or support e-mail. However, by periodically looking through, for instance, sent and received sales e-mail, managers will get an idea of what customers are asking for, who the perceived competitors are, and how their product or service is being rated. In the case of technical support e-mail, managers could find valuable information about repetitive problems, or possible defects in the product.

Quick Responses to E-Mail

Because it is important that your staff members act on leads while interest is still high, quick response times of corporate and Website e-mail are essential for any business. Therefore, keeping an eye on the amount of e-mail received and average response times is an important part of e-mail management. With the help of software packages, managers can view instant reports on the amount of e-mail received per e-mail address and the average response time per mail agent (person that answers e-mail within a company). With a workflow system it is also possible to automatically alert mail agents when an e-mail has not been answered.

There are also tools that can help mail agents answer their e-mail quicker and more effectively. For instance, mail agents can use a kind of "clip book" with predefined answers. When answering an e-mail, they just select a predefined text and send the message out. This not only ensures a faster response, but also allows managers to dictate certain contents for e-mail, thus ensuring the quality of the responses and the consistency of the company's image.

Sharing the Workload

E-Mail Management also entails distributing the e-mail workload evenly. Instead of letting only one person answer all e-mail to a generic address such as sales@yourcompany.com, with e-mail management companies distribute this mail among several designated mail agents. For instance, if your company has five sales persons, the generic sales e-mail could be divided among these persons (Exhibit 34.3). This enables a company to spread the workload, but it also gives more persons within the organization the opportunity to stay in touch with what customers are asking and requesting.

Automating Follow-Up

Sending your customers personalized acknowledgments after receiving their e-mail gives your company a professional image and lets customers know that their e-mail has been received. This acknowledgment can include important information about when the e-mail was received (useful for time zone differences), who is dealing with it, and when the customer can expect an answer. Each acknowledgment can also include a unique tracking number for customer reference purposes. In case of an inquiry, staff members can search for the e-mail using the unique tracking number.

Another way of automating followup is by sending custom replies whenever an online Web form is filled out. For instance with e-mail management software you can automatically send out an e-mail a week after a customer orders a product on your Website, asking whether they have received their product and whether they are satisfied with the service they received. Another example is an information request form. As soon as a customer fills out the form, you could send an e-mail saying that the request has been received and that the information will be mailed out within a couple of days. A week later you could automatically trigger an e-mail asking whether the information has been received and if they are interested in the product or service. By using merge fields, the e-mail text can include any information that was entered in the Web form. In this way, you can optimize your customer service with hardly any effort on your part. By automatically archiving the Web form output into an ODBC database, you also have a valuable backup for accounts or marketing purposes that can be of use at a later stage.

Finally, you also can automate tasks by sending out scheduled personalized e-mail by querying ODBC databases. For instance, you could query

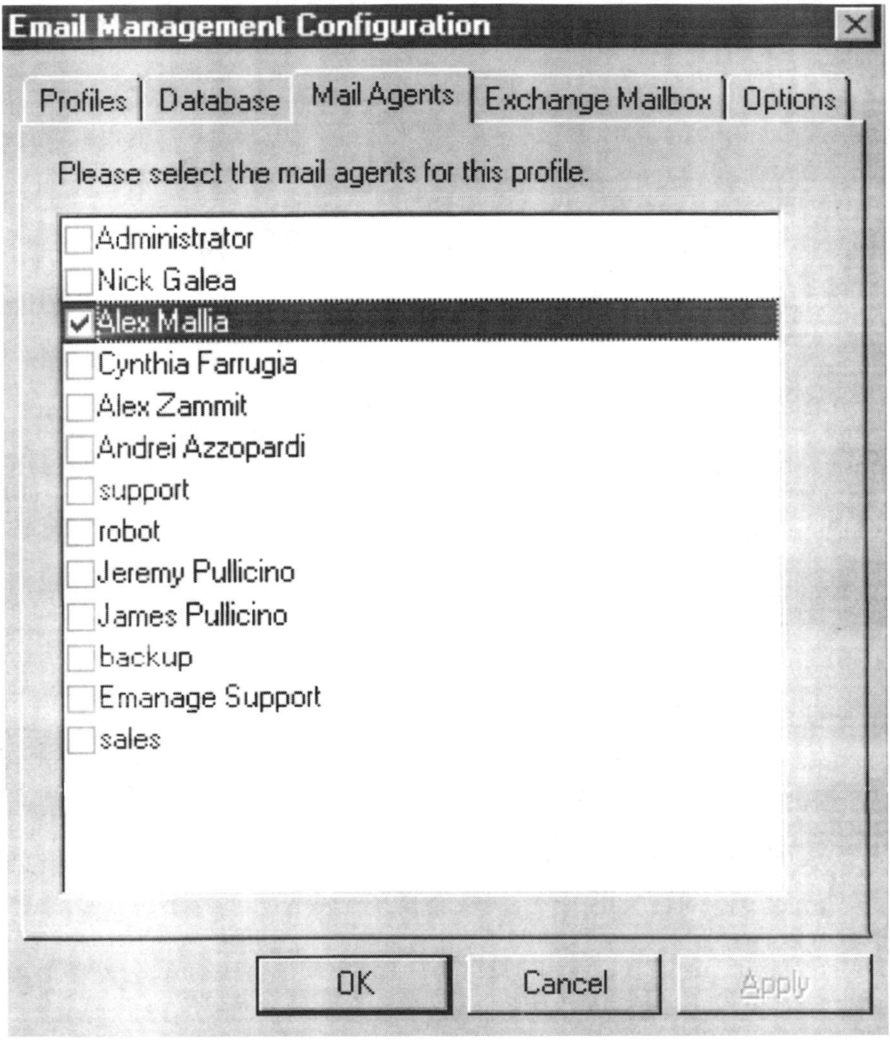

Email Management Configuration   ☒

Profiles | Database | **Mail Agents** | Exchange Mailbox | Options

Please select the mail agents for this profile.

- ☐ Administrator
- ☐ Nick Galea
- ☑ **Alex Mallia**
- ☐ Cynthia Farrugia
- ☐ Alex Zammit
- ☐ Andrei Azzopardi
- ☐ support
- ☐ robot
- ☐ Jeremy Pullicino
- ☐ James Pullicino
- ☐ backup
- ☐ Emanage Support
- ☐ sales

| OK | Cancel | Apply |

Exhibit 34.3. Distributing e-mail automatically.

your invoice database each month and send an e-mail reminder to each company with payment arrears. By using merge fields, you can also automatically include the outstanding invoice number and invoice amount.

Analyzing E-Mail Traffic

With detailed reports on e-mail (Exhibit 34.4), such as average response times and the amount of e-mail received per mail agent and department, you can determine whether your Website is producing enough feedback,

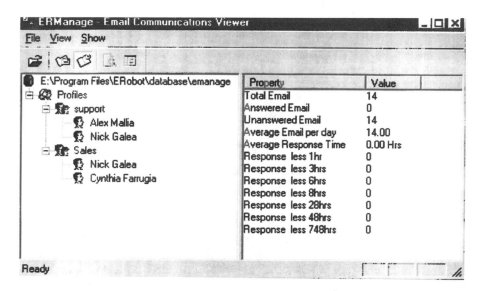

Exhibit 34.4. Detailed e-mail reporting.

whether your mail agents/departments are responding quickly enough to their e-mail, and whether their workload is still manageable. This information can help companies detect staffing and communications problems at an early stage. Furthermore, managers can compare the amount of e-mail each address receives. For instance, is the support e-mail growing out of hand compared to the sales e-mail? Also, is mail agent A taking much longer to answer than mail agent B, C, and D?

Custom Management

Sometimes companies have an e-mail task that is specific to their company. For instance when an e-mail sent to a certain address is received, a company might want to automatically send out a fax. Or a multinational company, in order to maintain international consistency, might want to have a Web page where all standard replies are stored so that mail agents can use these replies to answer their e-mail.

Another company might want to automatically include a disclaimer at the bottom of each outgoing e-mail. E-Mail Management systems can also cater to these specific requirements by providing the possibility to create scripts that can be totally unique to a company.

WHAT KIND OF BUSINESSES NEED E-MAIL MANAGEMENT?

Any company that does business or provides customer service via the Internet basically needs e-mail management. This is virtually irrespective of a company's size. For instance a small company might be operating in a heavily competitive environment, where speed is of the utmost importance. An e-mail management system can help such as company keep track of its e-mail and average response times and increase its competitive edge over others. Furthermore it would decrease the workload by automating some parts of the e-mail process and by providing an important backup system for e-mail and received Web forms.

In medium- to large-size companies, speed will also be of importance, but because of the company's size, a good tracking system for its e-mail would be just as essential. First, managers would be able to view all messages in order to keep an eye on what employees are communicating and the volume of their workload. Furthermore, in the case of a customer complaint or inquiry, managers would be able to track the exact string of e-mail that was sent back and forth concerning the matter before coming to a proper decision. Finally, employees need insight into each other's e-mail. What if employee A is out sick and a customer rings about an e-mail which should have been answered a long time ago? Without e-mail management the employee would have to go into his or her colleague's system, to which he or she might not even have access. With e-mail management, the e-mail will be instantly trackable from the employee's desktop.

CASE STUDY

To illustrate the possible implementation of E-Mail Management, we will describe two situations: companies with and without E-Mail Management. For both case studies we will use the same fictional company: Flora Direct, a company with 10 employees that offers a flower delivery service by telephone and fax, and has recently started offering this service on the Internet. The company has five sales persons, an accountant, a part-time Webmaster, a secretary, a marketing/PR manager, and a managing director. When an order comes in by telephone or fax, one of the sales persons takes down the order and passes it on to the nearest flower shop to arrange for delivery. Since Flora Direct put up the company Website, customers can also order flower deliveries on the Internet by filling out the online order form.

Apart from the single flower deliveries, the company also provides a party/occasion delivery service for corporate and private customers. In the past, these deliveries where mainly received by fax because each order involved several instructions that needed to be followed closely. With the company Website, Flora Direct has noticed that corporate customers like to make use of e-mail to order the flowers for their occasions, and, consequently have been faced with an important increase of e-mail and Internet orders.

Flora Direct without E-Mail Management

Before they used E-Mail Management, Flora Direct assigned the answering of the sales@floradirect.com e-mail to one of the sales persons in the company, Julie Smith. Julie answered all questions such as how much the service costs, how it works, how quickly the flowers can be delivered, etc. Sometimes, orders were also received by e-mail. However, Julie also had to answer the telephone and when it became busy, Julie had to put off answering e-mail. The next day Julie often forgot to answer the e-mail messages of the day before as she now had a whole new load of e-mail to answer.

Sometimes customers phoned to say that their e-mail had not been answered. But if the phone was answered by one of Julie's colleagues, they could not check whether this e-mail had actually been received or whether it was answered.

Mike Winter was put in charge of receiving Internet orders. As soon as an order came in, Mike had to enter the order into their "normal" order system and then handle the order just as a normal telephone order. In fact, an Internet order took more time than a telephone order.

Flora Direct also made use of two more e-mail addresses, info@floradirect.com and complaints@floradirect.com, which were answered by the secretary, Kim Edwards. Sometimes Kim did not always know the answer to an e-mail inquiry and would forward the e-mail to her boss, Barry Thompson. However, Barry was out of the office a lot and did not always remember to pick up his e-mail. He sometimes even forgot to answer his e-mail.

Flora Direct with E-Mail Management

With E-Mail Management, Flora Direct now distributes all sales e-mail among the five sales persons. Julie was quite relieved that her increasing e-mail burden could now be shared with her colleagues. Now, when a customer sends an e-mail to Flora Direct, he or she instantly receives notification that the e-mail has been received and which mail agent is dealing with their question or request. Moreover, the acknowledged e-mail includes useful information about pricing, delivery times, and opening times, and includes a unique tracking number to which the customer can refer if they have any queries. The Flora Direct representatives can bring up the particular e-mail in an instant.

A large part of the Internet orders has now been automated. An Internet order is automatically entered into an ODBC database for invoicing purposes. The credit card is automatically processed and, according to the place and time of the delivery, the e-mail is forwarded to the appropriate flower shop for the fulfillment of the delivery.

The managing director, Barry Thompson, can now keep an eye on the average response times and the amount of e-mail received. Also, E-mail Management has enabled Barry to periodically review all the e-mail complaints received within a specific period. Sometimes he notices that complaints are centered around a particular area. In this case, he can follow up the complaints and call the responsible flower shop. In some cases, this has led him to choose another flower shop for the particular area.

The accountant, Steve Burke, has now started using e-mail for sending automatic payment reminders. With E-Mail Management, each month the invoice system is automatically checked and all outstanding accounts are sent an e-mail including the invoice number, date, and amount.

The marketing/PR manager is also pleased with the new tool as press releases can now automatically be distributed via e-mail by querying the press contacts database. Also, a regular e-mail newsletter is being sent out to customers, including useful information about the service.

Author's Bio

Deborah Galea is Marketing Manager at GFI FAX & VOICE, developers of E-mailrobot (e-mail manager and automater), FAXmaker (fax server for Windows NT and Exchange), and E-mailflow (e-mail-based workflow product), with offices in the U.S., U.K., Germany, and Malta. She has written for various publications including those of the European Commission and various magazines. Before her position at GFI FAX & VOICE, she was Account Manager at public relations agency Hill & Knowlton and Deputy Publisher at Informatiebank.

Chapter 35
Multilingual Websites

Deborah Tyroler
Elana Yellin

INTERNATIONAL WORLD WIDE WEB USAGE IS ON THE RISE. Between January 1997 and January 1998, the total number of people accessing the Internet worldwide rose from 57 million to 102 million, and that number is expected to top 700 million by 2001.[1] While the U.S. and Canada currently make up 61 percent of Web users worldwide, the scales are poised to tip by the end of 1999.[2]

Reduced connectivity and hardware costs and improved infrastructure continue to lower barriers to access worldwide. Analysts expect that by the end of 1999, 1 out 10 households in the U.K., Germany, and Denmark will be online, and similar percentage rates are anticipated for Italy and the Netherlands by the year 2000.[3] Nearly 10 percent of the Japanese population accesses the Internet[4] and growth in emerging markets such as Brazil, China, and Korea is taking off. E-commerce is fueling the growth of the global Web, principally in the area of business-to-business commerce. Currently, an $8 billion industry, analysts project E-commerce will reach $327 billion by 2002.[5] By that time, non-U.S. commerce will account for 37 percent of E-commerce worldwide.[6]

Paralleling the growth of the public Internet is the spread of intranets and extranets throughout the global enterprise. Businesses are enabling their information systems, moving mission-critical business applications to powerful private networks based on Web technologies. Systems for order processing, inventory tracking, supply chain management, and invoicing are moving to the Web. Enabling systems to tap the power of the Web offers a key competitive advantage to global companies who need to conduct business across geographies and time zones. In a global marketplace where customers, suppliers, and co-workers are international and located worldwide, multilingual content is integral to effective, efficient, communication.

As Internet technologies permeate the enterprise and the Web continues to evolve into a global mass medium, the profile of the international Internet user is rapidly changing. There is a direct correlation between increased international usage and decreased viability of the English-only

0-8493-9987-4/00/$0.00+$.50
© 2000 by CRC Press LLC

Web. Illustrating this trend, Brazilian ISP Universo Online (UOL), reported that the percentage of Brazilian Internet users who understood English dropped from 62 percent in 1996 to 58 percent in 1997.[7] Today users are coming online with all levels of technical and linguistic aptitudes, making multilingual content a key ingredient to a successful global Web strategy.

GLOBALIZATION PLAN

Providing multilingual content will augment the benefits and cost savings you already derive from your Website. However, few companies have an unlimited development budget, and innovations and enhancements to a site must be cost justified. To ensure maximum return on your localization[8] dollars, the first rule of thumb is fairly obvious: don't create multilingual content that won't be relevant to international users. To assess what is most relevant to international users, the litmus test must be tempered to specificities of your site as well as to the objectives and mandates of your organization. You need to determine what will be pertinent in each market as well as what will be possible.

Budgeting constraints generally prescribe a phased approach to localization. You'll need to set priorities both with respect to content and to target markets, and these will shift over time. The Web is a medium of change and innovation. Your Website is in a constant state of evolution, progressing toward greater usability. Adding multilingual content is an important enhancement in this direction. It helps you reach a broader audience and at the same time makes your site more specialized and personal.

Whether your Website is a corporate marketing site, an E-commerce site or an intranet, it is likely to reach out in multiple directions to different audiences. Think through how the various aims of your site — supporting existing customers, global branding, recruiting, linking to suppliers, training employees, tracking orders, transacting sales, attracting investors — relate to each of the language markets you intend to target. For example, if products and services will vary from market to market, you will want to reflect this in your site by customizing the content. Even if the content remains ostensibly the same, local tastes, preferences, and conventions may also influence how you position products or services. The degree to which cultural nuance impacts how you handle content depends on your assessment of how important cultural differences are to your target markets. This will vary greatly depending on whether your audience is consumer-based, business-to-business, or within your organization.

CONTENT MANAGEMENT

Multilingual, multilocal sites are Websites that have country-specific content. These sites often contain content that is uniform across languages as well. A well-managed and well-conceived multilingual, multilocal site

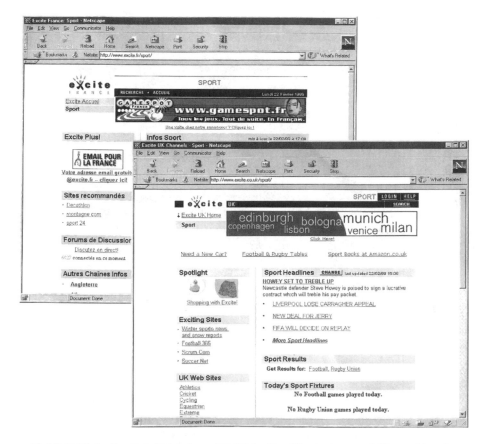

Exhibit 35.1. Excite's French and British sites illustrate a multilingual/multilocal approach where content has been tailored to local preferences.

will succeed in providing local flavor without forfeiting brand identity. Major search engines such as Yahoo!, Lycos, and Excite offer a good case in point. They all allow for multilingual searching and the content within search categories is tailored to the interests of each market. A sampling of sports categories from Excite's French site (Exhibit 35.1) include the Tour de France, the French Decathalon, and the World Cup '98. In contrast, Excite U.K. includes cricket, rugby, and equestrian events.

While the content has been tailored to local tastes, two core elements of the site have been preserved: the features and functionality, and the look and feel. As a result, whether a user is searching Excite in French or in U.K. English, the experience is authentically French or British, and at the same time brand identity is promoted.

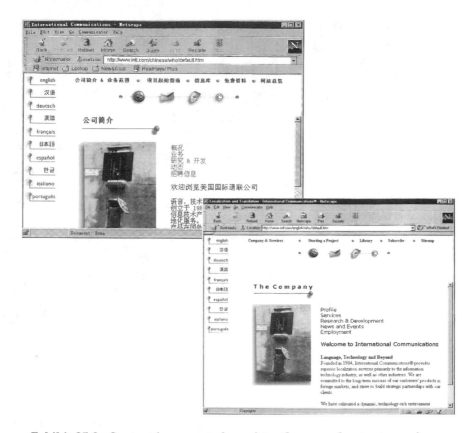

**Exhibit 35.2. Content is presented consistently across language versions
of Intl.com satisfying global branding objectives. Multilingual navigation is structured to let visitors change languages at any point.**

If global branding is a central aim of your international campaign, then a
more uniform treatment of content across language versions of your site may
prove a better approach. International Communications (Exhibit 35.2) has
done this on their site, www.intl.com, which is localized into 10 languages.

The site producers have prioritized key portions of the site to translate
based on their target audiences and have chosen to leave other portions in
English. For example, the company's services, profile, and resource information is translated, while job listings and news and events have been left
in English. The localized pages maintain the same look and feel across languages. A unique feature of this site is that the language navigation bar appears on every page, allowing visitors to move between languages from
any point in the site.

Whatever the configuration of content on your site, you will need to address content management issues. A pivotal decision will be whether to apply a centralized or decentralized model. Corporate mandates will be an important determinant. You will need to assess where corporate aims and local concerns overlap and where they diverge. The challenge is to determine what must remain uniform for consistency and global branding and what is open to local flavor and interpretation.

The basic architecture of your site will also impact how you prioritize what to localize and for which markets. Your site may be database-driven, static, application-rich or more likely some hybrid. It may contain frequently updated content posted at predictable intervals, or it may incorporate erratic or constant data streams. You will need to architect a system to manage updates and data streams across languages. For some companies, it makes sense to localize the static portions of a site first and tackle frequently updated content in a later phase. As with other considerations, be sure to weigh the relevance of your content to your target before you architect your content management system.

INTERNATIONALIZATION

English is not going to serve you effectively in every market the world over. However, you may not be able to cost-justify localization of your Website into 30-plus languages. More likely than not, you will want to leverage the English version of your site beyond a North American audience. Your English Web content can serve multiple purposes. Most obviously, it can target English language markets outside the U.S., such as India, Australia, or Singapore. It can be used to target smaller markets for which you may never have the budget to localize such as Norway or Finland, where local language content would be preferable, but English may be acceptable. Additionally, the English language version of your site can provide a short- to mid-term solution for second- or third-tier priority markets you intend to localize at a later date. Ideally, you will begin to think of the English language version of your site as the "international" version, the foundation upon which the entire site is built.

Creating an internationalized site consists of taking the original language version and looking at it as yet just another language. Considerations generally entail removing cultural references and colloquialisms, enabling time and date functions, and implementing double-byte character support[9] for Asian languages. Bringing an international perspective to your site helps you keep the design and architecture open and flexible enough to accommodate and anticipate new markets. Taking this step ensures that your content will be accessible and acceptable to your international visitors, allowing them to utilize your site, while also preparing it for possible localization.

TEXT AND IMAGES

Ad copy and company slogans, common on marketing and E-commerce sites, are notorious for being difficult to introduce into a foreign market, whether or not they are translated. Popular examples of *faux pas* made by large corporations making the foray into the international market include the Pepsi slogan "Come alive with the Pepsi Generation" that was translated for the Taiwan market as "Pepsi will bring your ancestors back from the dead." Salem cigarettes' slogan, "Salem — Feeling Free," was translated for the Japanese market into "When smoking Salem, you feel so refreshed that your mind seems to be free and empty."

When looking at your copy and images remember that specific cultural references may confuse or offend those outside your target market. If later in the game you do decide to target a specific market with localized content, you may add cultural images, references, and slang to create a local flavor (Exhibit 35.3).

The same holds true for images and color schemes. Although there may not be universal colors or images there are certainly cultures that identify more closely with some than others. For example, a picture of a woman of Japanese origin on a site targeting U.S. visitors would probably be considered multicultural and open-minded. But if a U.S. company tried to bring their site into the Japanese market with images of stereotypical American-looking people, it would probably be considered inauthentic by Japanese visitors.

TECHNICAL ISSUES

Apart from marketing-related issues such as images and copy, there are also various technical considerations to take into account when providing internationalized content for your visitor. One of the most important considerations is to be aware of how the visitor interacts with your site to find the information he needs. If a visitor can fill out a contact form, order items generated by a database, or simply track down your e-mail and phone number, you need to make sure you can glean the information that you need from them, as well as effectively respond to their inquiries.

Providing contact information for your company or asking visitors to provide you with various bits of information may seem very straightforward, but there are certain query fields that need to be properly internationalized. Names, addresses, and phone numbers may not follow the same format conventions in other countries as they do in the U.S. For instance, telephone numbers may not be grouped as xxx-xxx-xxxx, "State" may not exist, and a surname may be quite lengthy. Hard-coding form fields to allow only a limited number of characters, or requiring certain fields, can frustrate the international visitor (Exhibit 35.4).

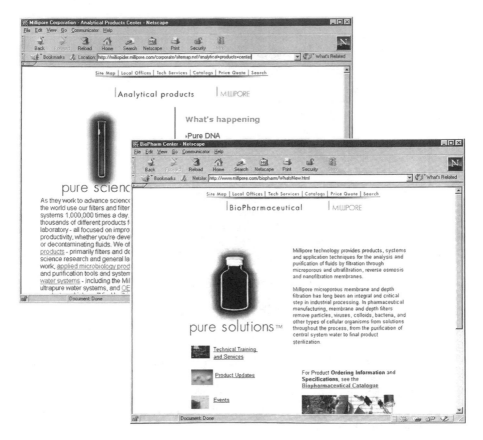

Exhibit 35.3. Millipore uses universal images such as eyeglasses, a computer chip, a test tube, and a vial to illustrate their global branding campaign. These images are widely understood, even when copy is not translated.

Other considerations include:

- Toll-free numbers are not accessible from outside the U.S. Make sure you include an alternate phone number including the country code.
- Time and date formats are generally formatted differently than in the U.S. Not everyone knows what PST or EST means. It's helpful to also mention your time in relation to Greenwich Mean Time. Date format can also vary from country to country. For example, the date 1/5/99, understood as January 5, 1999 in the U.S., would be understood in Europe and elsewhere as May 1, 1999. To avoid confusion, it would be more appropriate to show the date as January 5, 1999.
- If you're targeting a particular market, make sure you are able to effectively answer foreign language e-mail inquiries with an internal em-

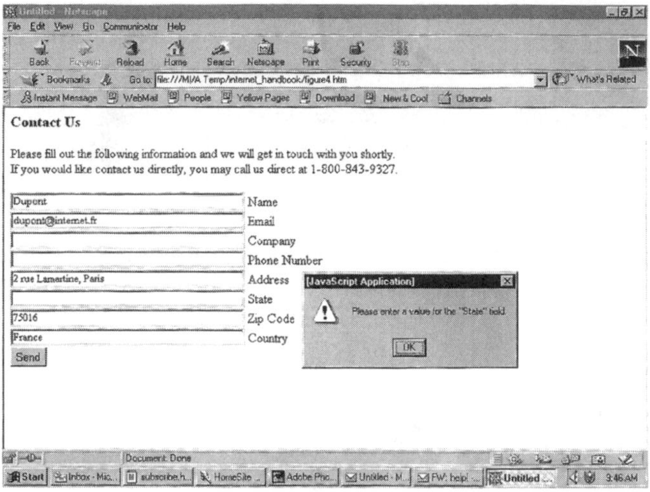

Exhibit 35.4. This form prompts the user to enter in a State, where "State" is not valid outside the U.S. A more appropriate field label would be State/Province.

ployee, a partner office, or a translation partner. To help reduce overall costs it can be beneficial to build a multilingual FAQ from the inquiries received over a period of time. Visitors can then be encouraged to seek answers on your Website, reducing the need for individual tech support.

If you do decide to localize your site, there are also backend issues to consider, especially if you are targeting the Asian market. Unlike English and European languages which are handled by single-byte (8 bits) character sets, Asian languages (Chinese, Korean, Japanese) require double-byte (16 bits) or multibyte character sets. If you will allow your Japanese customer to order through your online form using Japanese characters, you'll need to determine whether your back end is available in double-byte versions and/or are double-byte enabled.

Your database may need to accept double-byte characters, but this does not mean you will need to completely localize all of the content within. For example, a database used for online ordering that stores the sizes, colors, and styles of various shoes, would not require localization. The user interface (where the visitor chooses the items he wishes to purchase) would have to be translated into the target market language, but the items the user is selecting — the items that are being referenced in the database — would remain in English.

BANDWIDTH/DOWNLOAD TIME

Large images, video clips, and Shockwave™ can take an inordinate amount of time to download for any users who are still using a 14.4 or 28.8 kbps modem. In addition to a slow modem, add poor telephone lines and costly Internet access fees, and you suddenly have a very frustrated user. These issues are still real considerations in many countries outside the U.S. Kenyan users have to accept speeds as slow as 9.6 to 14.4 kbps[10] and must pay an average of US$65 per month for Internet access.[11] A recent report showed that 88.9 percent of Internet users in China complained of slow connections and 61.2 percent said online fees were too expensive.[12] Good Web design takes these issues into account, whether creating a site for a domestic or international market (Exhibit 35.5).

Exhibit 35.5. ChinaConnect makes use of graphics with limited colors and complexity to cater to its high percentage of visitors originating from a low-bandwidth market.

INTERNATIONAL SITE PROMOTION

"If you build it they will come" is a slogan now well known to be inaccurate by savvy Web marketers. Simply building a Website does not ensure the traffic, and this certainly holds true for your multilingual versions as well. Web users will first search for content in their native language and will switch to English (provided they know English) only if they can't find the information they are seeking.

A recent survey by SiteMetrics[13] examined 31,000 U.S.-based sites run by companies in 14 different industries with annual revenues from $10 million to more than $1 billion. Only 30 percent included the Meta keyword tag used by the largest search engines to catalog Websites. Only 27 percent of those surveyed included the Meta description tag.

The above statistic is surprising, considering the abundance of promotional information available on the Web. Not only is Meta tag usage[14] important for your English pages, but it is also equally important for your translated site. Although every search engine doesn't utilize Meta tags, they can help your site get indexed in the foreign language engines. Additionally, Meta tags may increase the searchability of your site in the English engines by bringing up your site when users enter in foreign language keywords.

If your site offers goods, services, or information to the foreign market, but isn't yet multilingual, translating some Meta key words within your English pages for your target markets can be a cost-effective first step that helps drive foreign language speakers to your site. Make sure your site is internationalized for these visitors to ensure it delivers relevant and useful content, products, or services.

Translating Meta tags is only part of promoting your site to non-English speakers. There are other forms of promotion to consider, whether or not you will be creating a global marketing campaign.

- The search engines need to find out about the multilingual or internationalized versions of your site. This step involves manually entering in URLs and site description into search engines and language directories.
- If your traffic to the English version of your site has benefited from reciprocal links for the English version, this can also be an effective form of promotion for your multilingual versions.
- You can announce your site to the international press using companies that specialize in distributing online press releases. These companies often have an international module, as in the case of the Internet News Bureau (www.newsbureau.com). They maintain international affiliates while also providing translation services for worldwide press distribution.

- Multilingual banner ad campaigns can be created by an internationally savvy advertising firm, or your preexisting ads can be localized for each market. LinkExchange (www.linkexchange.com), a popular banner exchange program, recently added an option to categorize a site based on language categories, enabling the exchange of banners with other sites of the same language.

GLOBAL WEB TEAM

As you decide to target an international market and begin to grapple with these many issues, the capability of your team will become essential to the success of your localization strategy for the Web. You will draw on expertise from within your own organization, supplemented and strengthened by experts external to your company. For example, Web developers with strong internationalization experience will consider issues such as double-byte-enabled databases and optimizing graphics for the Web. A knowledgeable localization partner will use native translators, familiar with your target market's own cultural nuances, as well as technical, project management, and publishing specialists who will be able to republish your site with all the features and functionality of the original kept intact. E-marketing firms will work with you to develop a successful international e-marketing campaign for your global Website. In addition to your central team of experts, make multilingualism and internationalization a priority within your company so internal staff will view it as a critical and worthwhile step in the overall success of your company.

CONCLUSION

The global nature of the Web has rapidly accelerated the need for well-thought-out international Web strategies. Traditionally, companies introduced their products market by market. Now via the Web, information, products, and services are instantaneously available around the world. The Web provides companies with constant and immediate global exposure, heightening the need for careful attention to global branding and international product marketing. The question is no longer when or whether to go international, it's how to plan and manage the process to derive the greatest benefit from your global Web presence.

As you map out your global Web strategy, which sections to localize and which language markets to target first will fall into place. Whether you opt for a multilingual, multilocal site or a site that is uniform across language versions, multilingual content adds a layer of richness and functionality to your site. If you approach site design with an international mindset, taking structure, aesthetics, and content into account, you will ensure an architecture that can support any language direction you want to go. The World Wide Web is a global medium and if you don't address an international, non-English-speaking audience, the efficacy of your Web presence will be diminished. Creating a multilingual Website for your overseas target markets is one of the best ways to transcend linguistic barriers and "speak" your customer's language.

Authors' Bios

Deborah Tyroler is a Director of Webstream & Interactive Services, International Communications and works closely with clients to develop customized solutions and ensure that project execution is smooth and tailored to the clients' requirements. She has more than 10 years international and technical experience. A leading spokesperson for International Communications, Tyroler has presented at Internet-related seminars and written on global Web strategies for publications such as Software Developer *and* Publisher *and* Language International. *Prior to joining International Communications in 1992, she was one of the pioneers in the field of electronic news and data retrieval as a researcher at the Latin America Database. Tyroler also taught Spanish and Portuguese at the University of New Mexico. She received her Bachelor of Arts degree in Classical Liberal Arts from St. John's College and a Master of Arts degree in Latin American Studies from the University of New Mexico. Deborah was a Fulbright Group Fellow in India and a Mellon Inter-American Intern.*

Elana Yellin is Website Producer at International Communications. She is primarily responsible for producing intl.com, the corporate Website, and Headcount.com, a resource of statistics of Internet populations worldwide. In addition, she manages the localization of intl.com into 10 languages, serves as editor of the monthly e-mail bulletin, GlobalConnect, *and has helped to define GlobalSubmit, the multilingual search engine submission service. Yellin has written Internet-related articles for publications such as the* Internet Marketing Report *and e-mail bulletins such as WebPromote.com. Prior to working at International Communications, she maintained the Israel Trade and Investment Website at the New England Israel Chamber of Commerce. Yellin holds a B.A. degree from Brandeis University.*

Notes

1. Headcount.com, http://www.headcount.com, June 1998.
2. "Is the World Wide Web Really Worldwide?" *EMarketer*, July, 1998, http://www.emarketer.com.
3. Jupiter Communications, http://www.jup.com, August, 1998.
4. Jupiter Communications, http://www.jup.com, August, 1988.
5. "CEOs Feel Internet's Global Impact," *Internet Week,* May 25, 1998, http://www.internetwk.com.
6. Headcount.com, http://www.headcount.com, January 1998.
7. Brazil Net Use Diversifying, *News.com,* April 3, 1998, http://www.news.com.
8. Localization: the process by which all elements of a product are customized to the local culture and characteristics of a particular target market. This generally includes translating the user interface, altering time/date formats and ensuring images and terms are culturally sensitive and make sense to the end user.
9. Double-byte character enabling (DBCE): Chinese, Japanese, and Korean are written in complex systems of thousands of ideographic and syllabic characters. An advantage of ideograms is that one character may have a single meaning but a different spoken word in another dialect. Other characters may present similar sounds with vastly different meanings. There are so many characters that two bytes are required to specify them in computer operating systems, hence the term "double byte." That is, Roman characters can be

easily represented in 128 characters using 7-bit ASCII, while East Asian languages require 16 bits to represent roughly 32,000 double-byte characters. Some programs are not written with these double-byte character sets in mind, and so are not able to handle the input, output, and internal manipulation of words or strings that include double-byte characters. Double-byte enabling is the process in which the program is altered to allow the proper handling of double-byte characters.

10 "Kenya on an Information Dirt Track," Fox News, June 12, 1998, http://www.foxnews.com.

11. "A Picture of Africa," Sagonet, April 15, 1998, http://demiurge.wn.apc.org/.

12. "1.2 Million Chinese Now Online," Techserver, July 13, 1998, http://www.techserver.com/.

13. SiteMetrics, Web Content Survey, April 1998, http://www.sitemetrics.com/contentsurvey/byindustry.htm.

14. Meta tags: A special HTML tag that provides information about a Web page. Unlike normal HTML tags, Meta tags do not affect how a page is displayed. Instead, they can provide a summary, title, and key words for a page, as well as information about the author, how often the page is updated, character encoding, and its audience rating. Many search engines use this information to help build their indexes. For more information on search engine ranking and Meta tag usage, view http://www.searchenginewatch.com/.

Chapter 36
Serving Many Masters

Kay Palkhivala
Anne Anderson-Lemieux
Charles Mappin

DOES THIS SCENARIO SEEM FAMILIAR?

Scene: Your cubicle, in the technical writing department of a software company.
Enter your boss, accompanied by the vice president of R&D.
Boss: "Have you seen the Website they've set up for us at Head Office?"
You: "Yes, our network guru showed it to me a while ago."
VP of R&D: "What did you think of it?"
You: "Well, it seems cute, but it's full of 'Under Construction' notices."
Boss: "Do you think you could do better?"
You (innocently): "How hard could it be?"
VP of R&D (with a gleam in his eye): "We'll be back!"
45 minutes later ...
Re-enter the boss, this time accompanied by the network guru, who is grinning.
Boss: "Congratulations, Webmaster. The corporate Website is now in-
    stalled on your departmental UNIX box. Chris here will show you how
    to get at it. We're looking forward to seeing great things!"
Exit the boss, hastily ...

That's how some people become Webmasters. Two or three years pass,
then the battle-scarred Webmasters get asked how they did it. Why didn't
they scream and run out of the room the minute those guys showed up?
No, really, it's a cool job and we've learned a lot, some of which can appear
in a respectable publication.

WHAT IT'S ALL ABOUT

You're taking up the challenge of managing a corporate Website — starting from scratch, or building it up. Your goal is to support and enhance both
the internal and the external activities of your organization. Initially, most
Websites are seen simply as PR and advertising vehicles. Management has

0-8493-9987-4/00/$0.00+$.50
© 2000 by CRC Press LLC

heard that "there's gold in them thar Webs," but has no idea how to mine it. Soon, however, every department will get ideas about what your Website can do, and they won't hesitate to tell you. As a point of first contact, the Webmaster is not without influence, and you may be surprised to learn how many diverse goals you can meet, plus a few that nobody expected.

GATHER THE TEAM

A Website needs a variety of skills. There are hundreds of publications about Web technology, graphics, coding, interactivity, writing style, and so on. The advice changes every day, so you'll never stop learning. As a brief framework, here are the kinds of resources you'll need:

- Toasterheads — technical gurus to set up the Webserver and connections, acquire software tools, troubleshoot, make backups, tell you about cool stuff they've seen.
- Writers/editors — to create and update the words about your business, products, and services. No matter what you may have heard, content IS king. Fast turnaround is essential. Edit ruthlessly for formality, brevity, and reading level.
- Artists — effective layout and creative graphics are what make your site a pleasure to visit. Make each pixel count; go easy on the bandwidth requirements.

It's easy to forget how fast everything changes on the Web — not just the message, but the tools that say it. Keep renewing, revising, and rebuilding; your site will never be finished.

FACE THE MUSIC

If you think of all the people you must keep happy, you'll hyperventilate, so let's talk about the care and feeding of your many masters in the order in which they might come through your door.

CORPORATE PR

The first person to call on the Webmaster may well be the public relations officer. PR professionals appreciate the value of low-cost media that can be carefully managed. From your point of view, it's a good place to start because both content and photographs are usually ready. Make sure you're crystal clear about the corporate image and settle any approval requirements before the material goes live. Don't chain yourself to a detailed sign-off for every page; establish your credibility and professionalism right away. While you're talking to the PR officer, get items like these:

- Corporate mission statement
- Offices or factories (how to get there and what they do)
- Press releases and coverage in the news

Think of the corporate information from the surfer's perspective, which is probably the reverse of how executives see things. News comes first then the products or services you offer. Don't include too much about individuals, it facilitates headhunting and can expose people to junk mail. That mission statement should be simple, short, sweet, and last.

MARKETING

Right behind the PR officer, the Marketing department will bring their list. The digital age has made the Web a key element of any marketing strategy. Your site should say, "Here's what our stuff is like; how can it help you?" Chat with the marketers often so you'll get their orientation plus ideas about future strategies.

Earn some respect from marketing management by being specific about how your Website can work for them. Support lead tracking by setting up interactive pages where interested visitors can provide contact information. Popular features include:

- Visitor guest book or survey with space for comment
- A contest about your company, possibly with a freebie prize
- White papers or product demos
- E-mail to the president, marketing, or product development chief

When marketing has a special campaign, support it with new custom-designed Web pages. In your direct mail and advertising material (in print or on the Web), mention the URL of the new pages. For example: "For more info, visit www.mycompany.com/campaign/." You'll be able to address these pages to their own specific audience and include a form to retrieve information from visitors.

SALES AND PRODUCT DISTRIBUTION

Sales will naturally follow marketing to your door, since a Website can be a great sales and distribution channel. If your product or service can be delivered electronically, your Website can do the whole job. But even if you sell live aardvarks and deliver them by helicopter, the Website can still receive and process your orders. Many E-commerce products available now will let you quickly set up a complete online shop.

However, when the sales manager asks you to open a store on your Website, take a minute to talk about issues like these:

- *Global reach.* It's a World Wide Web. Can you provide contact information for potential customers around the globe? How will you fill orders in remote locations? Who pays for shipping, handling, duties, and taxes?
- *Pricing.* It's unlikely that you'll have one price list for the whole world, and your prices may be negotiable. Can you give a price range? Should

you omit prices, but include an e-mail link and phone numbers for your sales offices?

- *Payment.* Electronic payment is more feasible now that the Web offers better security and people are getting used to online shopping. What payment methods will you be able to handle?
- *Delivery.* Can you deliver your product via the Web? Software, travel reservations, translation, and financial services are successfully sold and delivered online. Other products, like books, music, computer hardware and accessories are sold on Websites and delivered by traditional methods. Can you make a profit with your product that way?
- *Existing sales function.* Can your sales organization support this new channel? How will Web orders be passed to your order processing system? Which part of the sales team will handle these orders?

INVESTORS

If yours is a public company, current and potential investors will come to your site looking for the scoop. Probably your least technical users, these visitors are nevertheless accustomed to getting financial data like stock quotes online and they expect to find more than window dressing. Investor information can be judiciously selected from your corporate and marketing pages. Investors often don't want to buy your product, they just want to be sure that lots of other people do.

Fill your investor pages with background data about the company, financial results, product direction, success stories, market recognition, etc. Add a link to a stock quote service and an e-mail link to the executive suite. Some of these data may be sensitive, so senior management will want to review it and you'll want to conform to any legal rules about what and how much to include.

CUSTOMER SUPPORT

The people who man the hot lines and talk to troubled customers all day will be among your most enthusiastic clients. For them, you offer a reliable central source of the information that they're repeating endlessly over the phone, and giving them a way of making customers feel special. You can easily set up a Customer Support Site, with password access, that supplies restricted information for customers only. It could include:

- A database of known problems and solutions, hints and tips, troubleshooting advice
- An e-mail link to the support coordinator
- Previews and demos of new products
- A suggestion box
- Freebies for faithful or frequent users
- A link to a user group Website
- Discussion groups or newsgroups

Once you start, the list will grow. You can use one general customer password, or add a bit more programming to give each registered customer a unique password.

SALES STAFF AND FIELD SUPPORT

The folks in the field should always get the latest news, but they often feel isolated and out of the loop. Since they can't come to you, offer them a Field News Site as a reliable, informed source, containing:

- Current product data, proposed product direction
- Background and competitive information and related Websites
- Multimedia demos and ready-to-use sales presentations

Encourage field staff to use the site by offering an incentive, even if it's just recognition as Best-Informed Representative of the month.

Make sure that your Field News, especially if it promises future goodies, is ready for possible leakage to the world. You could create problems for your company if you downplay current products and hype the dreamware that may never become reality. And, of course, talk to sales and product management to review and update the content frequently.

TRAINING

You probably distrust computer-based training; you've tried glitzy software tutorials and you're not sure they do the job. But don't overlook the potential of your Website to support internal and external training programs.

- For starters, post your course schedules, prices, descriptions, and locations, how to sign up and how to get more information
- With some programming input, set up online registration, administer precourse qualifying quizzes, and accept feedback from students and instructors
- Eventually, complete the back end to process your training statistics, monitor training cash flow, and print your course certificates automatically

If you're intrigued by online training, your company may have material you can adapt. For example, suppose accounting has a training booklet called *"Making sure we always get our discounts."* You could convert it into a Web tutorial that employees can follow on a Web browser and submit quizzes via e-mail.

DOCUMENTATION

If you can print it, you can put it on the Web. Your Website is a great place to keep all the documents that everyone needs but hates to find space for.

- Start close to home, with your employee handbook and directory, policy manuals, insurance and expense forms, local holiday calendar, messages from the CEO ... you get the idea
- Turn your attention outward and make a place for press releases and success stories, marketing collateral, product documents or manuals, data sheets, white papers, and so on and on
- Provide online versions that can be downloaded and printed by the recipient, plus a list of printed publications that people can order

Your documentation mother lode on the Web should attract regular visits from the people who create the publications you're offering, so you can receive updates as they occur. Pass the requests for printed copies along to the originators, too; you don't want to be taken for a printing service along with all the other new tasks you're rapidly acquiring.

INTERNATIONAL

Although English dominates the Web, more sites are now appearing in other languages. If you do business in foreign countries, you should consider translating at least parts of your Website. But be forewarned; multilingualism may induce migraines at update time. Will your Spanish, French, Japanese, Farsi, or Tagalog translator be available when you need her? Some recommendations for this thorny field:

- Unless you speak in many tongues, you'll need outside translators, preferably volunteer; your foreign offices and distributors should pitch in; the work is for their benefit
- Don't forget the need for timeliness and fast turnaround; translations always lag your main site but they can't wait forever
- Always have someone in the target location review translated material; languages grow and jargon varies in different places
- If you solicit feedback in other languages, make sure that someone on the receiving end can read the messages and respond appropriately.
- If you have satellite Websites, make sure there are reciprocal links between them and your main site

LEGAL

Beware the fine print. Sooner or later your legal advisors will ask you to add copyright notices, disclaimers, product warranties, or licensing information. Put the legal jargon on a separate page linked to your home page. Don't forget to claim copyright on your own Web pages, and equally don't forget to acknowledge the authorship of material you liberate from other Websites. Everyone copies from the Web and you will too, but a corporate Webmaster must uphold the copyright law.

EMPLOYEES

Within your organization, the corporate Website can enhance the social environment and build team spirit. If you already have an employee newsletter, publish a Web version; if not, create a space for company news with an employee focus. The bowling team and the softball league will enjoy seeing their schedule and pictures on the Web. Then there's long-service awards, community achievements, weddings, babies, promotions, and retirements.

Don't forget potential employees either; the Web is an active recruiting medium. Post job opportunities at your company and accept online applications. It's much less expensive than print advertising and may significantly extend the reach and success rate of your recruitment efforts. Also think about Web-based recruiting services, who will usually be happy to set up reciprocal links between their Websites and yours.

INTRANET

Think big about the internal services that your Website can handle; you're creating an "intranet." The personnel department already has forms for expense reports, timesheets, insurance claims, vacation allocations, performance evaluations, employee address book, and the like. It's a snap to put these paper forms on your Website as HTML pages and set a password to keep them private. When you have the resources (bribe your programmer with chocolate at regular intervals), code the forms so they can be filled out and submitted electronically. Tell the financial folks how an intranet system for personnel services can quickly pay for itself in increased accuracy and reduced manual processing.

If you link the intranet services to your employee news pages, as in Exhibit 36.1, you'll increase readership and participation. Assuming that you have in-house e-mail, you could send each update of the intranet password along with a snippet of company news or the latest additions to the Website.

PRODUCT DEVELOPMENT

Many organizations keep R&D and product engineers far in the back room, well away from real people. Without speculating on the reasons for that policy, we suggest that your Website can help bridge the gap without disturbing anyone's way of working. When the Website becomes a channel for interdepartmental communication, everyone benefits. Planning and product management could maintain project schedules in various levels of detail, and product package definitions could itemize what is to be delivered in what format. Don't add to anyone's workload; just offer a central place to post the information that's already being used.

Exhibit 36.1. The employee news page.

No matter what business you're in, there will be corporate standards that you can post on the Web for employee reference. For example, list the rules about the corporate logo: size, color, spacing … for people sending mailers or making slide presentations. Create an archive of great graphics and packaging design, or boilerplate about company history and product features. These items are always being requested, so you'll save everyone's time and achieve better quality results.

PRODUCT TESTING

Manufacturers who conduct off-site testing, whether by employees or favored customers, know that contact and follow-up is a major challenge.

Your Website can be an efficient, low-cost way to handle beta test recruiting, managing, and reporting. Furnish your Beta Test Center with:

- Testing paperwork and reports
- Backgrounders on the products being tested
- Test announcements, plans, and schedules
- E-mail link to the testing coordinator
- Chat line or newsgroup for tester feedback and discussion
- A coffee mug or other prize offer for conscientious testers.

If your product can be distributed electronically, set up a download center where testers can get the beta versions they will be working on.

BUSINESS PARTNERS

Your Website can keep your main office in touch and in favor with far-flung business partners. A password-protected Partners section on your site could provide company news and product information. The Webmaster can be a clearinghouse for questions that a partner might not know where to direct, so include an easy way for partners to request information and to update their own records.

On the public side, use your Website to help generate additional business activity and attract new partners to your program. A partnership directory can list your partner businesses and describe their services. Encourage initial contact through a simple online application form. If you like, you could offer to host small advertisements from your partners as a membership bonus.

USER ASSOCIATIONS

Visitors will come back to your site if you focus on their interests. To support your customer base, list the user group meetings, upcoming seminars, and trade shows. As always, update the pages regularly, provide a channel to contact you, and offer incentives such as conference discounts, to encourage use of the site.

Many user associations suggest setting up an e-mail List Server or automated group mailing list so your customers, employees, and partners can exchange ideas, solve problems, announce events, and hold ongoing discussions on relevant topics. These mailing list programs register subscribers and let them send e-mail to the whole list or to specific members. Check your local college or Internet service provider for a List Server program you can use.

AARDVARKS

Finally, don't forget that everyone needs some fun. Web surfers despise a vanilla cone; they crave a banana split with cherries, sprinkles, and fudge sauce. Hard information is why you're there, but don't underestimate the value of entertainment or surprise. Animation is cool, provided it doesn't clog transmission, and a light and lively editing hand makes technical data less painful. Many sites hide an Easter egg — an unadvertised link to a cool Web gizmo, a quick game or a bit of culture. Try a quiz or contest with answers somewhere on your site, and offer a nice trivial prize.

We know of at least one site that includes fake advertising slogans about the company — insider amusement for the Webmaster at least. And since you're doing all the work, you and your gang can bury a few special features about yourselves deep in the bytes. Where else could you publish that novel of yours or display your vacation photos so easily? And why an aardvark? Got your attention, didn't it?

THAT'S ALL, FOLKS

If you've decided that climbing Mount Everest sounds like a restful afternoon compared to the life of a Webmaster, you obviously haven't spent enough time training a puppy. Veterans will tell you how maddening it all is, but they'll fight like tigers to keep the job. If we've managed to give you just a few ideas about managing the insanity, that's our contribution to a better Web for us all.

Authors' Bios

Kay Palkhivala is currently Director of Technical Documentation and Education at Speedware Corporation in Montreal, Canada. She is a survivor of a dozen years as an educator and another dozen as manager of technical writing for various software companies. Having spent one third of her adult life as a parent and another third in high schools, she has found happiness among software manuals and thinks everyone should understand why she keeps a battery-powered plush pterodactyl in her bottom desk drawer.

Anne Anderson-Lemieux is an Electronic Publications Specialist with Speedware Corporation. She dabbles in "painless" drawing and painting. Many of her skills were acquired through the study of "what to see" and the rest was transferred to her by her parents through osmosis.

Charles Mappin is a Technical Writer and Associate Webmaster (a.k.a. Webslave) at Speedware Corporation. He prepared for this career with degrees in Linguistics and Urban Planning, which seems about as good a background as any to write all day long about computers.

Chapter 37
A Brief Introduction to Enabling Simple Databases on the Web

Jessica Keyes

DATA COMES IN MANY FORMS. Some of it's in files. And some of it's in databases. Some of it may even be in data warehouses. In essence your goal is to broadcast some, or all, of that data on the Web. I like to refer to it as datacasting.

Datacasting requires you to make some very important decisions. The first decision is a big one. Do you need a database at all? There is a definite downside to hooking the corporate database to the Web. The primary goal of Web-database connectivity is to get as much done in one connection as possible. But the more efficient the system is in doing this, the slower the results are returned to the user. Another thing to think about is data integrity. While the concept of commits, backups, and restores is what database administrators cut their teeth on in the corporate environment, it's a whole new frontier for Webmasters. Then there's the question of whether you permit access to the corporate datastores themselves or copies of these datastores. And how best to optimize those copies. Given the agonizingly slow response of more than a few database-driven Websites I've been visiting lately, it seems these lessons have not yet been learned by more than a few Webmasters.

So what's a Webmaster to do? The first thing to do is to recognize that there's more than one way to skin a cat. Coincidentally, there's more than one way to datacast. This chapter, also known as "Datacasting Light," will discuss some rather straightforward and simple ways of getting data on the Web.

DATA PUBLISHING USING A FLAT FILE

One of the easiest ways of updating data on the Web is through the use of a flat file (i.e., ASCII/TEXT). This method is most expedient if the amount of the data is small and not too many people are expected to be

0-8493-9987-4/00/$0.00+$.50
© 2000 by CRC Press LLC

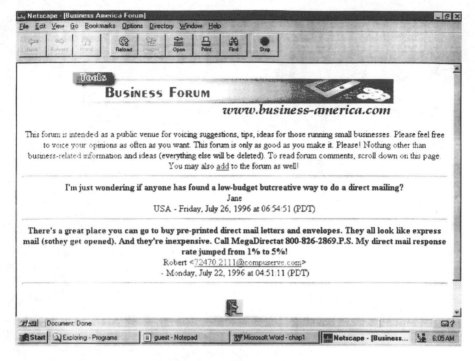

Exhibit 37.1. The guest book.

updating the system at the same time (folks just don't appreciate that "server busy" notice).

A good example of this is the now ubiquitous guest book. Everyone's got one. In fact, they probably have the same one. Matt Wright is owner and proprietor of probably one of the most popular sites on the Web. His archive contains scripts for every purpose — from search engines to the guest book discussed below (www.worldwidemart.com).The guest book demonstrates the principles behind using CGI and a text file to permit end users to update and then view data on the Web, as shown in Exhibit 37.1.

Notice the comments from visitors. Essentially, it takes two HTML pages and one CGI script to perform the function of using CGI to move data between the end user and the Web server. The first HTML page is the "add" page which is a hyperlink to the HTML page above. Exhibit 37.2 shows a typical guest book add input form.

The HTML for this form follows:

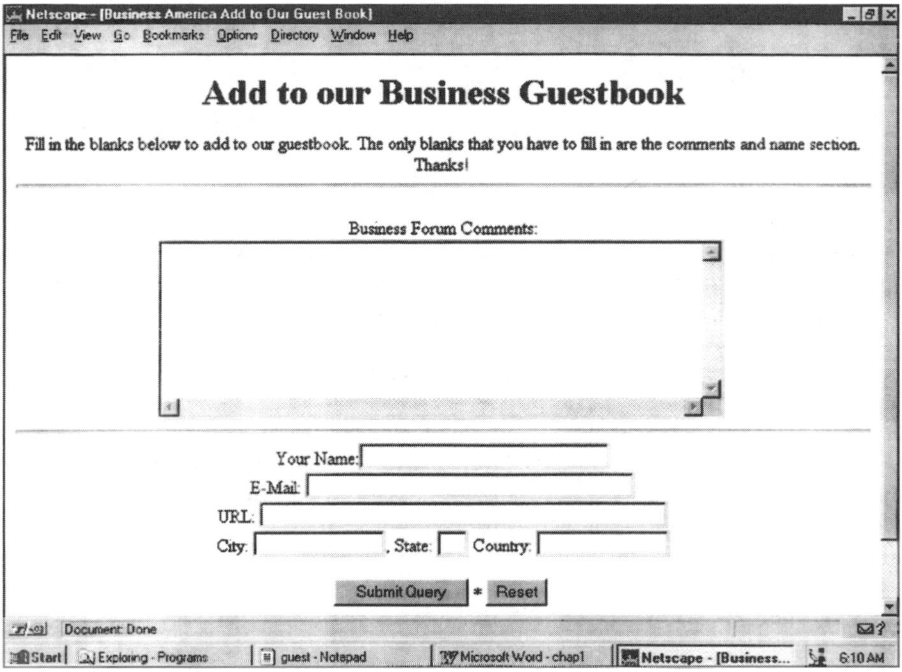

Exhibit 37.2. A typical add form to a guest book.

```
<HTML>
<TITLE>Business America Add to Our Guest Book</TITLE>
<body bgcolor= #ffffff  text= #000000  link= #342567
><center>
<body>
<h1>Add to our Business Guestbook</h1></center>
Fill in the blanks below to add to our guestbook. The
only blanks that you have to fill in are the comments
and name section. Thanks!
<hr><form method=POST action= /cgi-bin/guest.pl >Busi-
ness Forum Comments:
<br><textarea name=comments COLS=60 ROWS=8></textarea>
<hr>Your Name:<input type=text name=realname size=30>
<br>E-Mail: <input type=text name=username size=40>
<br>URL: <input type=text name=url size=50>
<br>City: <input type=text name=city size=15>, State:
<input type=text name=state size=2> Country: <input
type=text name=country size=15>
<p>
<p>
<input type=submit> * <input type=reset>
```

549

```
</form>
<hr><a href= guest.htm >Back to the Guestbook En-
tries</a>
<br>
</body>
</html>
```

Once the visitor clicks on the submit button, control is passed to a program in the site's cgi-bin directory. A Perl program called guest.pl then processes the input, does some light error-checking to make sure certain input fields are present, and then writes the input to the output file which is called guest.htm and displays a "thank you for adding your comments" message. This last message is dynamically generated as an HTML file directly from the Perl program.

I'm not going to get into the details of this Perl script (Matt has extensive instructions on his site at: http://www.worldwidemart.com/scripts). Suffice it to say, it is a simple but effective way to get quasidynamic data out to the Web.

LEVEL 2 DATACASTING — EXPORT TO HTML

There are many instances when it just isn't necessary to integrate a "live" database to the Web. If your application calls for "read-only" and your volume of data is not too large, then exporting database data to HTML just might be your ticket to Web-database integration.

Many reporting tools, such as Crystal Reports, include an "export to HTML" option. Some of these tools also contain a scheduler that permits you to automatically generate HTML for Web publication on a regular basis.

A good example of this is Microsoft's Access 97. With Microsoft Access, you can output two types of HTML files: static or dynamic. The static HTML files you output are a "snapshot"' of the data at the time you publish your files. In general, you use static HTML files for reports and datasheets that you update and disseminate as part of your regular business cycles, such as weekly stock-level reminders or monthly sales reports. Microsoft Access creates one Web page for each report page and one Web page for each datasheet that you output. When your data changes, you need to publish your files again, so that your users can view the new data on the Web.

Those of you with access to Access 97 (and who doesn't have it) can follow along with this minitutorial using the now famous sample Northwind database. The Northwind report called "Alphabetical List of Products" lists each product, the category it belongs to, the quantity per unit, and the current stock level.

The HTML pages you output will simulate the report's page orientation, margin settings, and other attributes such as color, font, and align-

Clicking **Export** will display the **HTML Output Options** dialog box.

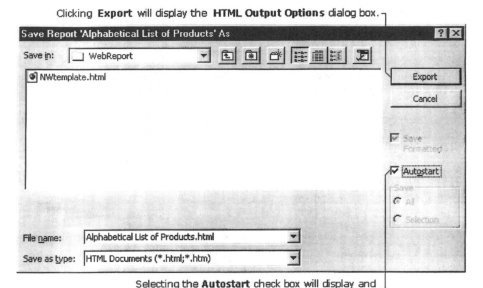

Selecting the **Autostart** check box will display and verify your output in your default Web browser.

Exhibit 37.3. Access export to HTML.

ment. You can output most controls and features of a Microsoft Access report to HTML.

Open the Northwind sample database, Northwind.mdb (located by default in C:\Program Files\Microsoft Office\Office\Samples). In the Database window, on the Reports tab, click Alphabetical List of Products, and then on the File menu, click Save As/Export. In the Save As dialog box, click HTML Documents (*.html;*.htm); select the Autostart check box so that you can use your browser to verify the generated output; and then click Export as shown in Exhibit 37.3.

It's really as simple as that. Microsoft typifies the "big vendor" approach that is building Web portability right into their database products. You'll read much more about how to do this in a dynamic way in the later chapters of this book.

THE ONE TOOL, MANY DATABASES APPROACH

Corel, once known solely for their Drawing software, has gotten itself a good reputation as a provider of Web-building tools. Corel Web.DATA is an excellent approach for those with limited database or Internet knowledge, or those folks who simply don't want to bother with more complex approaches.

Corel Web.DATA's fully graphical user interface leads you through the steps to gather the information you want to use, organize and determine the layout, and include additional text and codes to enhance it. Web.DATA automatically adds other standard HTML codes that will complete the formatting of your Web page. Then, with a simple push of a button, your HTML page containing your data is created and published to the Web.

All of the instructions on how to create your Web page are stored in a file called a recipe — somewhat akin to a macro. You can use the recipe over and over, or modify it to create different recipes or a different look to the page. If your data changes, all you need to do is open the recipe and press the Process button and your data is immediately updated on your Web page.

Corel Web.DATA uses Open Database Connectivity (ODBC) drivers to connect to a wide variety of databases on SQL servers such as Oracle — and at less than $300 the price is definitely right. The feature set is definitely right too. For instance, Web.DATA can join tables from the same type or different types of data sources, to create complex new views. It can join an Excel spreadsheet to a local dBASE file, and extend the view with data from an Oracle table. You can create lookups between a large number of tables from the same or different database files. Let's take a look at how Web.DATA works.

Web.DATA EXAMPLE

In order to access an SQL database, we must access or create a file that has ODBC connect information. For example: CONNECT = DSN = NORTHWIND; UID = Dan; PWD = prince; SQL=SELECT * FROM CUSTOMERS. This connect string specifies the data source name (DSN), the user ID (UID), and the password (PWD), while the SQL string requests all information from the CUSTOMERS reference. We can also use Common Gateway Interface macros in the ODBC SQL statement to optimize SQL queries. The data source must be defined in the ODBC.INI file, in order to be accessible. The ODBC.INI file can be edited through the ODBC application in the Control Panel.

A recipe is a Corel Web.DATA file that contains the instructions for setting up the database publishing process. Once we create a recipe, we can use it repeatedly to produce a particular publication, or modify it to change the publication's style and format.

To build a recipe we must perform four mandatory steps: Select Database, Publishing Options, Field Selection, and Output Setup. With these steps we select and format our database information for publication. Corel Web.DATA has four optional steps for further customizing and formatting: Record Selection, Record Sorting, Field Attributes, and Global Attributes.

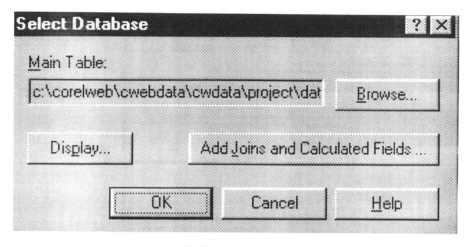

Exhibit 37.4. Specifying a database in Web.DATA.

When designing a recipe, we need a place to store the recipe information. In Corel Web.DATA, we'll save all this information in an .RCP file. To create a new recipe file:

1. Click File, New.
2. Click File, Save As.
3. Browse through the Save In list to find the default directory in which you want to save this recipe file, in this example, C:\COREL-WEB\CWEBDATA\CWDATA\project\recipes.
4. In the File Name box, we type MyCDHome.
5. We now select Recipes in the Save As Type list.
6. Finally, we click Save.

The next step in creating a recipe is specifying the database (or databases) we'll use, as shown in Exhibit 37.4.

Now we need to specify how we would like these data published. Since we'll be publishing our recipe file to HTML, we need to specify the extension and the processing method. The extension list allows us to specify the browser that will open when we publish our document. Since the Internet browsers available have minor differences in their capabilities, we will customize our document to take advantage of our browser's characteristics. Here, we will be selecting HTML 3.0, as shown in Exhibit 37.5, so we can publish our document using any browser which supports HTML 3.0. In selecting the Processing Method, we are given the option of having Corel Web.DATA publish our document in a standardized table format, or of creating a custom format ourselves. Here, we'll use Web.DATA's table formatting capabilities.

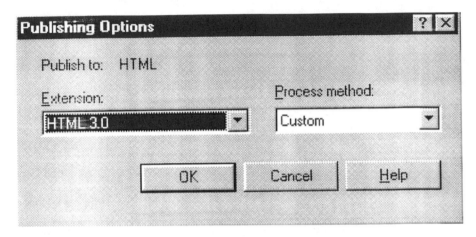

Exhibit 37.5. Publishing to HTML.

In the next step, which is shown in Exhibit 37.6, we'll select the fields that we want to appear in our recipe. Web.DATA provides us with different areas in our document (heading blocks and the document body block) to which we can assign different fields. In this example, we will assign the fields to the document body.

As we assign attributes to the fields, notice that each field begins with the prefix t0. It indicates that these fields belong to the main database. When we join other tables to the main table, their fields are prefixed by tn, where n is 1 for the first joined table, 2 for the second, and so on.

The t0.LOGO field is the product's filename, we will use this field twice. The first occurrence will be used to reference the product's graphic file; the second will be used to reference the product's text file.

In Exhibit 37.7, we see the dialog to set the field attributes. Although, in our example we will not be setting any of these attributes, the process provides Web.DATA with details on how we would like to use the fields in our table.

Now, we will add a second database (again, see Exhibit 37.4) to the recipe file. This second database will be a Microsoft Access database. We will also create a join between the two databases to add information to our recipe. To create a join, as shown in Exhibit 37.8, we do the following:

1. Accept the default Look-up, in the Join As section.
2. Select t0.LOGO in the Fields Joined To list and LOGO in the Lookup Fields list.
3. Click Create Join.
4. Click Display in the Views section to see the result, which is shown in Exhibit 37.9.

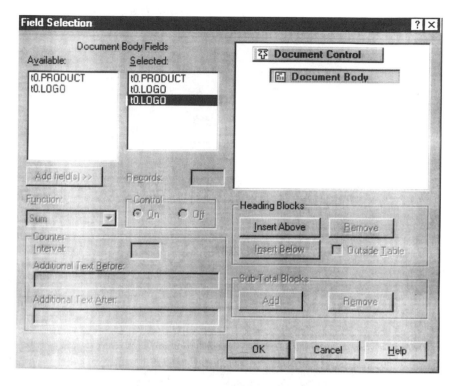

Exhibit 37.6. Selecting report fields.

Corel Web.DATA also offers a leg up on delivering merely static HTML. It can also be used as a CGI server application, enabling us to provide dynamic access to our databases. All we need do is install the program on the Web server and include CGI macros in the Record Selection section of the recipe, which is somewhat akin to a macro. As a CGI server, Web.DATA receives the request from the Web server and retrieves the information from the database. It then enhances and formats the data, and sends the results back to the Web server, which in turn passes it on to the Web browser.

Two Web.DATA macros handle the CGI function:

- CGI DATA:[variable names]: Passes a list of variables from an HTML form to Corel Web.DATA running in server mode using CGI
- CGI ENV:[environment variable names]: Inserts the values of the specified system environment variables

CONCLUSION

Thus far, we've discussed simple and/or static methods for getting data to the Web. While this simplistic approach will be sufficient for many data

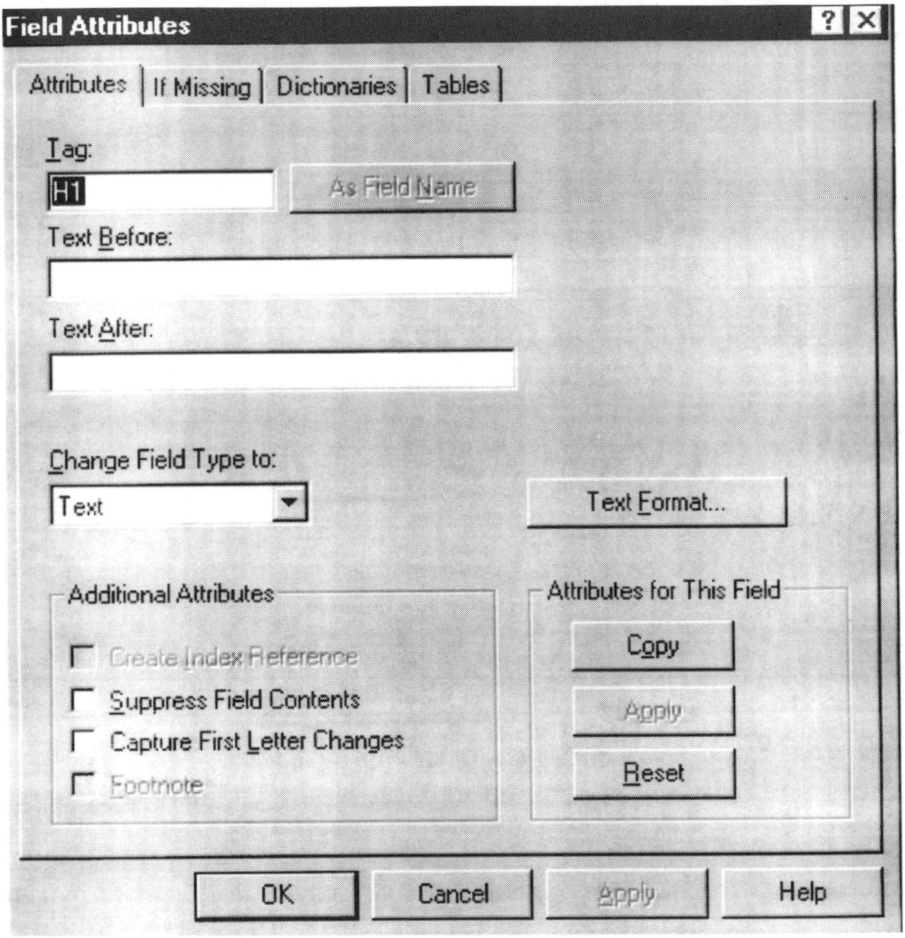

Exhibit 37.7. Web.DATA field attribute selection.

applications, it's no match for the requirement of bringing the corporate database to the Web. For this, the developer needs the help of one or more tools to assist in the creation of dynamic, database-driven Web pages.

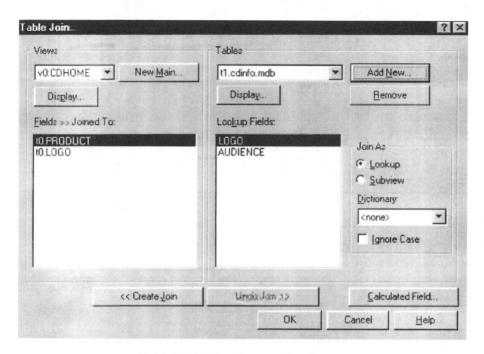

Exhibit 37.8. Joining two databases.

	t0.PRODUCT	t0.LOGO	t1.LOGO	t1.AUDIENC
1	The Interactive Alphabet	Alphabet	Alphabet	1
2	Corel Classic Books	Clasbook	Clasbook	3
3	Arcade Mania	Arcade	Arcade	2
4	Blue Tortoise	Bluetort	Bluetort	1
5	Wild Board Games	Wildbord	Wildbord	2
6	Adventures with Edison	Edison	Edison	1
7	Green Bear	Grbear	Grbear	1
8	The Complete Herman Collection	Hermlogo	Hermlogo	2
9	Bernard of Hollywood's Marilyn	Marilyn	Marilyn	3
10	Corel All Movie Guide	Movie	Movie	2
11	NN'n N Toy Makers	Nnnnlogo	Nnnnlogo	1
12	Red Rhino	Redrhino	Redrhino	1
13	Wild Cards	Wildcard	Wildcard	2
14	Yellow Hippo	Yelhippo	Yelhippo	1

Exhibit 37.9. The resulting output using Web.DATA and CGI.

Author's Bio

Jessica Keyes is president of New Art Technologies, Inc., a high-technology software development firm. Keyes has given seminars for such prestigious universities as Carnegie Mellon, Boston University, University of Illinois, James Madison University, and San Francisco State University. She is a frequent keynote speaker on the topics of competitive strategy using information technology and marketing on the information superhighway. She is an advisor for DataPro, McGraw-Hill's computer research arm, as well as a member of the Sprint Business Council. Keyes is also a founding Board of Director member of the New York Software Industry Association. She has recently completed a 2-year term on the Mayor of New York City's Small Business Advisory Council.

Prior to founding the company, Keyes was Managing Director of R&D for the New York Stock Exchange and has been an officer with Swiss Bank Co. and Banker's Trust, both in New York City. She holds a Master's from New York University where she did her research in the area of artificial intelligence.

A noted columnist and correspondent, with over 150 articles published, Keyes is the author of 12 books.

Section VI
Managing Advanced Application Development

IN SECTION V WE COVERED MORE TRADITIONAL APPLICATIONS of Internet development. In this section we will cover the aspects of Web development that are a bit more esoteric.

While we've always measured the performance of our computers, today we need to measure Web traffic across our site — for both performance as well as to glean marketing insight out of who is visiting our site. Find out how to do this in this section.

Another challenge to your technological prowess will be in connecting your corporate LAN to the Internet and the sticky problem of directory integration.

This book's experts dispense advice in this complex area as well.

Also in this section you'll find information about adding multimedia and audio/video to your site. This is the "fun" part of the business. Go from being an IT manager to a movie producer!

Chapter 38
Web Server Monitoring

Pete Welter

THIS CHAPTER INTRODUCES WEB SERVER MONITORING, explaining the importance of monitoring, describing monitoring concepts, and discussing various types of monitoring. A set of common Web server problems are enumerated, along with methods of monitoring to detect and/or prevent these conditions. Finally, automated monitoring systems are discussed, along with two of their primary advantages — immediate notification of problems, and the gathering of historical data. Although the focus of this chapter is on Web server monitoring, the concepts generalize for other types of Internet servers, including Mail, News, FTP, and application servers.

THE IMPORTANCE OF MONITORING

In today's information age competition, a well-designed and smoothly operating Website provides a distinct competitive advantage . On the Internet, the only hard currency is attention. A Website that fails to deliver its content, either in a timely manner or at all, causes visitors to quickly lose interest, wasting the time and money spent on the site's development. Ensuring that all of the elements of a Website are functioning properly is critical to maximizing a company's Web investment. If an irate customer call (or even good-natured e-mail) provides the first indication of a Website failure, then many other potential users have certainly been turned away.

When the inevitable failures do occur, minimizing downtime reduces the impact of the problems. Failure of a corporate Website quickly transforms visitors from potential customers to disinterested passers-by. One of the primary advantages of a corporate Website is its ability to reach customers around the world 24 hours a day, 7 days a week. A broken Website does not fulfill that potential.

Intranet Web server failures sever important lines of intracompany communication. Common and prolonged failures can change a corporate culture to depend less on these highly effective communications tools, thus minimizing the return on Intranet investments.

0-8493-9987-4/00/$0.00+$.50
© 2000 by CRC Press LLC

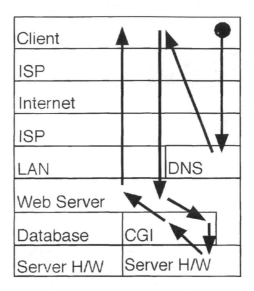

Exhibit 38.1. Typical Web page request. Each section represents a major component in a typical Internet/Web server architecture, starting from the client (browser) and progressing over the network to the Web server.

THE GOALS OF WEB SERVER MONITORING

After a Website has been designed, created, and deployed, it must be maintained and operated. Web server monitoring performs several functions critical to the smooth day-to-day operation of a Website. Monitoring:

- Verifies that all components of the Website are functioning properly
- Enables quick and accurate diagnosis of problems when they do occur
- Measures performance to quantify the user experience and to provide hard data for capacity planning
- Aids in predicting possible problems or needs for increased resources

Because of the distributed nature of the Internet, failures can occur at many points, some of which are outside of a Web administrator's control. Exhibit 38.1 shows a simplified view a single Web page request; note the number of complex components that are required to fulfill the request. Being able to quickly ascertain which components are functioning and which have failed can dramatically reduce the time taken to diagnose the problem. Once the Website is back up and functioning, hard data can be used to inform customers and management of the causes of a given failure.

Monitoring can prevent problems by revealing patterns of resource usage and performance that might otherwise go undetected. For example, full disks typically cause a host of problems for applications and operating systems. Simply knowing that a disk is nearing capacity may save a Web administrator hours of time fixing the problems caused by a full disk, not to mention heading off the inevitable flood of user reports.

MONITORING STRATEGY

A "monitor" is a test, typically a diagnostic command or emulation of actual use of the system, whose results are recorded so that they can be stored and/or acted upon. Monitoring systems or processes check services and components on a periodic basis, frequently enough to catch failures in a timely manner, but not so often as to significantly impact system resources. Monitoring systems typically consist of a set of monitors, mechanisms for alerting administrators if failures occur, and a historical log of data collected by the monitors. The focus of various monitor types covers a broad spectrum, from "deep" monitors that simulate user actions and that test many components of a Website simultaneously, to "shallow" monitors that measure a single aspect of a single component.

Tests performed by deep monitors involve a large number of components (see Exhibit 38.2), and often simulate a typical user transaction; results are measure in "user units," such as the number of seconds to complete a common task. Deep monitors indicate whether a large set of components that provide a given service are functioning properly (in

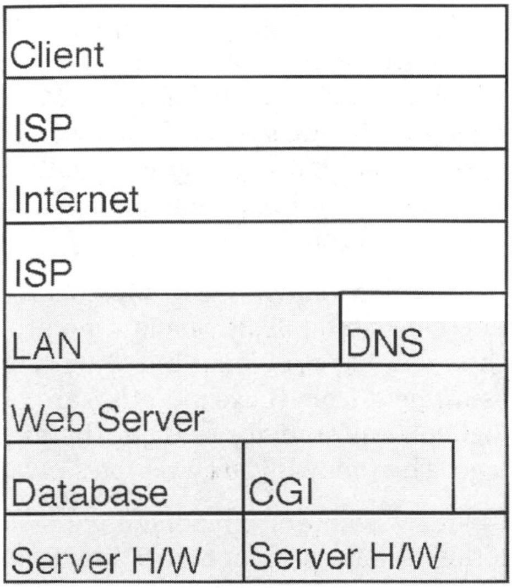

Exhibit 38.2. Deep monitoring coverage for a URL monitor. Shaded areas are covered, meaning that a failure in any of the components will be detected by testing the URL.

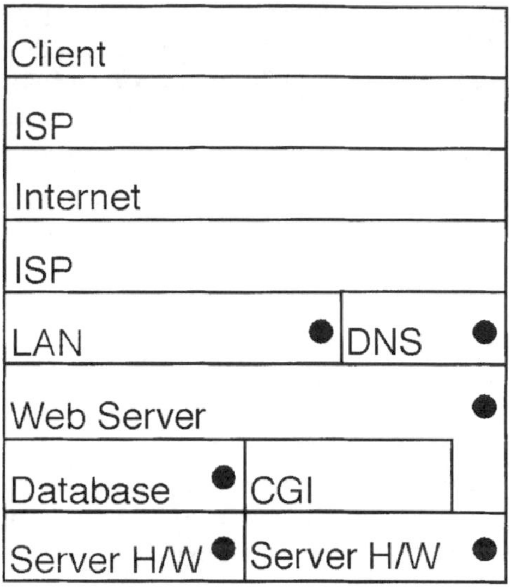

Client		
ISP		
Internet		
ISP		
LAN	● DNS	●
Web Server		●
Database ●	CGI	
Server H/W ●	Server H/W	●

Exhibit 38.3. Shallow monitoring coverage, which uses monitors focused on specific parts of the architecture.

which case the performance data represents what a user would see) or if something is wrong with at least one of the components (although a precise diagnosis may be difficult). One common example of a deep monitor is a monitor that periodically attempts to retrieve a URL, recording any errors that may occur and the amount of time the retrieval took. This procedure can be performed manually, using a browser to retrieve the page, or automatically, using a monitoring system. Other examples of deep monitoring include filling in and submitting a series of Web forms (a common E-commerce activity), sending and receiving an e-mail message, or downloading a file from an FTP server.

In contrast, shallow monitors test one or more aspects of a single component of the system (see Exhibit 38.3). Shallow monitors indicate precisely when a given component has problems, but often lack the context of real system usage. Measurement from these monitors are typically in the units of the component being monitored; for example, bytes per second, or CPU utilization percentage. The following are examples of shallow monitors:

- Ping Monitor — tests whether a machine is reachable over the network, and whether the target machine is functioning well enough to send a simple reply
- Domain Name Server (DNS) Monitor — tests whether a machine's name (for example, www.freshtech.com) can be mapped into a network address

- Process Monitor — ensures that a process is still active and using an acceptable amount of system resources
- CPU Monitor — measures the utilization of the CPU to flag chronic overloading
- Memory monitor — measures memory usage and paging activity

In practice, a combination of deep and shallow monitors gives the most effective and understandable picture of a Website's current state and allows the quickest diagnosis of problems. To create good overlapping coverage for the deep URL test, a URL monitor can be combined with several shallow monitors such as a process monitor, DNS monitor, a CPU monitor, and several ping monitors. The URL monitor verifies that a page can be retrieved from the server in a timely manner, while the process monitor verifies that the Web server process is still running. The CPU monitor ensures that processing resources on the server aren't overloaded, while the DNS monitor tests whether the host name portion of the URL can be resolved. Finally, the ping monitors check network connectivity between the Web server and the router, the ISP, the backbone, and several remote sites on the Internet (Exhibit 38.4).

INTERNAL VS. REMOTE MONITORING

Remote monitoring are tests done by machines that are outside a site's internal network. An example of a remote monitor would be a monitoring

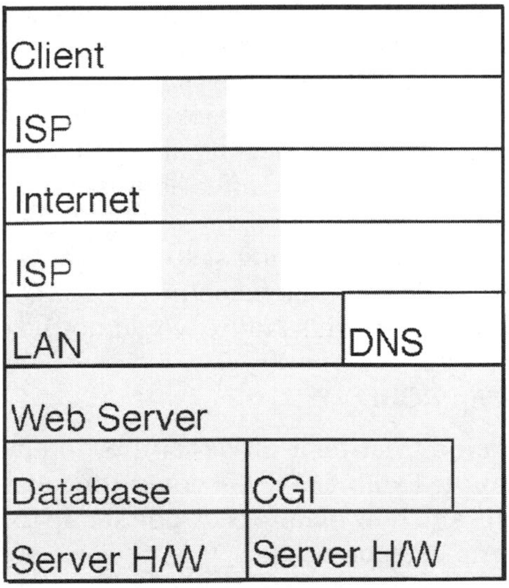

Client	
ISP	
Internet	
ISP	
LAN	DNS
Web Server	
Database	CGI
Server H/W	Server H/W

Exhibit 38.4. Local monitoring coverage showing the ability to cover the local components well, decreasing in effectiveness in testing the network components.

machine in New York that fetched a public Web page from a Web server in San Francisco. Internal monitoring occurs on a Web server itself, or from a machine on the internal network. The advantages of internal monitoring are

- It is closer to the source of addressable problems — internal monitoring keeps confounding factors such as ISP or backbone failures from obscuring site-specific problems (see Exhibit 38.4). Because of the finer granularity of measurements possible, more precise problem diagnosis can be achieved. Problems detected by internal monitoring can generally be corrected by people at the site because they control the machines and the networks.
- It allows automatic corrective actions to be taken — internal monitors, especially those running on the servers they are monitoring, have the direct access required to take actions. Remote monitors usually don't have the security access required to initiate actions.
- It is more reliable — internal monitoring doesn't depend on other networks to monitor and deliver data.
- It is easier to administer — internal monitoring software and configuration are on directly accessible machines.

Remote monitoring has its own set of benefits.

- It provides truer access time measurements — access time measurements taken remotely are a truer reflection of the end user's experience than measurements taken from internal machines
- It detects configuration errors that affect external users — configuration errors in Web servers, firewalls, proxy servers, and routers may permit access from internal machines to internal sites, but may prevent legitimate external users from reaching a Website.
- It detects problems with ISP and backbone links — testing connectivity from sites out on the Internet can also help detect failures in ISP or backbone links which may be affecting users' ability to access the Website (Exhibit 38.5).
- It serves as a backup monitoring system. A catastrophic event could crash and/or disable all of the machines at a site. Without some monitoring from the outside, this failure would not be detected.

COMMON WEBSITE PROBLEMS

Although a detailed treatment of Website problems could itself comprise an entire chapter, Exhibit 38.6 will cover the most common points of failure for a Website, and how monitors can be set up to detect them. These fall into three general categories:

1. The client cannot connect to any Websites.
2. An error occurs at the Web server and is returned to the user.
3. The connection times out or fails.

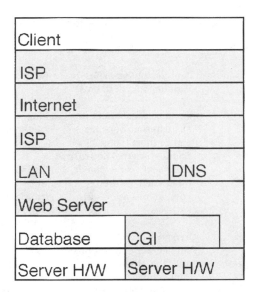

Exhibit 38.5. Remote monitoring coverage. A large number of components are covered by a remote monitor, although if an error occurs, pinpointing the problem component can be difficult.

This discussion will proceed from the points architecturally most distant from the Web server (and hence less under an administrator's control), and move towards the Web server itself (top to bottom in Exhibit 38.6).

AUTOMATED MONITORING SYSTEMS

There are several ways to implement a Web monitoring strategy. Most simply, a person or group of people can manually check various aspects of the Website on a periodic basis. Self-monitoring is better than relying on visitors to do the monitoring; however, people can forget, and they probably won't be around 24 hours a day. The results of manual monitoring are rarely recorded in a form that permits historical and quantitative analysis. Information gathered by hand also does not generally get broadly disseminated, so the status of the site is only known to a few people.

Automated monitoring tools run these tests 24 hours a day, 7 days a week. These tools exist in a large number of forms: commercial products, shareware, freeware scripts, and home-grown solutions. A number of commercial remote monitoring services also exist. They all share the common abilities of periodically measuring some aspects of the system and recording these data. Most have a variety of shallow monitors, some also allow deeper levels of monitoring. By keeping historical records, trends that will lead to problems can be nipped in the bud. Knowing that a disk is nearing

Exhibit 38.6. Common Website Problems

Problem/Failure Point	Symptoms	Monitors
Client software or machine	Client machine crashes, or cannot connect to any Website	None
Network connection between client and Internet	Client cannot connect to any external Websites, can connect to machines on their internal network	Ping monitors from an internal machine to major ISPs and routers
Internet backbone connection	Some clients can connect, other can't, or the connections are very slow	Ping to remote locations on Internet that use different backbones, remote ping and URL monitoring to Web server
Server ISP connection	All remote clients cannot connect, or connections are slow, although connections from internal machines work OK	Ping all routers between server and the Internet, some remote locations, and remote ping and URL monitoring
Document file is missing or HTML link is broken	Web server returns a "document missing" (404) error.	Local or remote URL monitor
Document file has improper permissions	Web server returns a "forbidden" (401) error	Local or remote URL monitor
CGI or other server-side process broken	Web server returns a "server error" (501 or 500) error, Web page displays error message or improper output (when HTTP headers or HTML are returned), or "no data" is returned	Local or remote URL monitor, with HTML content matching
DNS is misconfigured	"Host not found" error returned to remote and internal clients	Use nslookup-type monitor, or other monitor that requires a name lookup, such as a ping or URL monitor
DNS configuration has not been propagated	"Host not found," or wrong host, returned to remote clients, but internal clients are OK	Use remote nslookup-type monitor, or other remote monitor that requires a name lookup, such as a ping or URL monitor.
Firewall is misconfigured	Remote clients cannot connect, internal clients connect OK	Use remote monitor for each service that will be accessed through the firewall
Service process, such as HTTP (Web), FTP, database, etc. is down	One or more services do not function, other work OK	Use a deep monitor for each service of interest to verify proper operation

Exhibit 38.6. Common Website Problems (Continued)

Problem/Failure Point	Symptoms	Monitors
Services are performing inadequately	Services time out, or perform too slowly	Monitor CPU and memory (paging) usage for each service of interest, monitor performance of system overall
Web server or back-end services/applications have occasional errors	An error condition is being triggered in the server that may not be detectable externally.	Monitor service/application log files for error messages
Web server returns "Server Busy" errors	Too many simultaneous connections to a Web server	Monitor service periodically to detect patterns and determine whether additional resources are warranted
Web server crashed	Machine is totally unreachable	Remote ping or other network monitors, or ping monitors from other internal machines
Server is overloaded	Client requests time out frequently	Use deep monitors for each service, with reasonable timeout limits. Also monitor system resources, such as CPU and memory for the system and key processes, to correlate with performance of service

capacity allows some quick file cleaning or additional storage to be added, before the system comes to a screeching halt.

MANAGING PROBLEMS WHEN THEY OCCUR

After the detection of a problem, the persons responsible for the equipment or function in question should be notified, typically via e-mail or pager messages. The faster the notification, the greater the chance that the problem can be fixed without affecting customers or users. When implementing a notification scheme, remember that if the scheme can be disabled by the same problems that are being monitored, notification may not succeed.

For example, if e-mail is used to trigger a pager message, and the e-mail server, or the connection to the e-mail server, has problems, the pager message won't get sent. Also consider the "cry wolf" syndrome; if alerts are sent out too often, and for unimportant events, then when real problems occur the chances of the notification being ignored are high.

Notification is fine; automatically correcting problems is even better. A hung Web server process can be automatically restarted, a nearly full disk can have temporary files automatically erased, or a flaky machine can be automatically rebooted. Automatically fixing as many problems as possible ensures minimum down time, and reduces the need for human intervention.

COLLECTING AND USING HISTORICAL DATA

Historical data allows the correlation of several sets of monitor readings, leading to a quicker diagnosis of problems. For example, if the CPU utilization of the Web server machine is very high, then failures to retrieve URLs during that period of time may be related to Web server overload rather than the failure of the Web server process itself.

Historical data can also uncover trends that are useful in preventative maintenance. If a disk space usage monitor indicates a disk is filling up, steps can be taken to determine the root cause well before the problem becomes critical. Cyclical patterns of usage may also be revealed. A nightly maintenance process might be creating temporary files that bring the disk perilously close to capacity, and then delete those files before anyone notices.

Here's an real-world example that illustrates the usefulness of having a history of a server's performance. A Web administrator who had been running automated monitoring software was sure that there was something wrong with the monitoring setup — requests for Web pages from his server were shown as timing out at the top of every hour, and he hadn't heard any complaints from his users. However, later on that week, when he had a chance to try out his site manually with a browser, sure enough, at the top of the hour, the server response was incredibly slow (as in minutes to load a Web page). It turned out that there was a scheduled job being run on the hour, whose resource requirements slowed the server to a crawl. Without historical data, the few percent of users who would have eventually reported this problem would have had to give quite accurate time information for this pattern to have ever been found.

CONCLUSION

If you've taken the time and money to create and maintain a Website, then monitoring can protect that investment from the inevitable failures and performance problems that accompany the complex array of software, hardware, and network connections that comprise Web servers on the Internet.

Author's Bio

Pete Welter (pete@freshtech.com) is a senior software engineer at Freshwater Software, Inc. (http://www.freshtech.com) in Boulder, CO. He spends his days talking to Web administrators about monitoring their Websites and developing commercial Web monitoring tools.

Notes

Spainhour, S. and Spainhour, V., *Webmaster in a Nutshell,* O'Reilly and Associates, Sebastopol, CA, 1996.

Nemeth E., Snyder, G., Seebass, S., and Hein, T.R., *UNIX System Administration Handbook,* Prentice-Hall, Upper Saddle River, NJ, 1995.

Welter, P., Why is my web site down?, *Sys. Admin.,* April, 1998.

Chapter 39
Multimedia Impact on Web Pages

Valerie Taylor
Chris Ammen

COMMUNICATION ON THE INTERNET CAN TAKE MANY FORMS. For most of us, the communications model that applies to Websites is that of publishing. You make information available. Your audience will seek out your Web pages and access the information. Attracting and holding the interest of the reader or viewer is critical. Unlike traditional print publishing, the audience is just a mouse click away from thousands of other sites with interesting content. However, there is a big advantage for you, the publisher. The Web supports multimedia and hypertext links within the text-based page framework. Incorporating these additional information resources can greatly enhance your ability to attract and inform your audience.

For the purposes of this discussion, the Internet and the World Wide Web are the same. Actually, the Web is a subset of the Internet. The Internet has been available for many years but access was restricted to university and government research facilities using unfriendly user interfaces. In late 1993, Mosaic was the first Web browser that was easy to use. Finally, the Internet was accessible by the rest of us. Mosaic supported multimedia and was distributed free. Others soon followed. Netscape, Microsoft, and many others created and distributed Web browsers.

The Internet and the World Wide Web are expanding at a rate of 50 percent or so a month. This explosive growth is having a profound effect on everything associated with the Web. In fact, the Web works so well as a publishing media that many corporations and organizations are using private networks and restricted access to communicate with employees, suppliers, and customers via intranets and extranets. The pages, files, and media are delivered to user desktops using the same software and communications links, but the content is just not universally accessible as it is for information published to the Internet and World Wide Web.

0-8493-9987-4/00/$0.00+$.50
© 2000 by CRC Press LLC

WEBSITE DESIGN

Website design is key to putting together a coherent, informative, memorable Web presence. The Web is becoming more crowded. Standing out and attracting attention is becoming increasingly important. Once the user finds your site, the real process of communications begins. As users navigate through your pages, they are finding information (or not) and developing an image of your company as well as your products and services. This may be your only chance to get your message to a potential customer. It must be memorable as well as productive. Your message must be clear, concise, and complete. Adding appropriate multimedia will help get your message across.

Multimedia is not just text and graphics. Multimedia includes video, audio, and animations. The bandwidth exists today to allow the inclusion of all multimedia object-types on Web pages. The technologies already exist for creating and distributing multimedia over the Web. Business, education, consumer product marketing, scientific research, and art can benefit from the addition of multimedia on Web pages. These new developments are constantly changing the playing field for anyone planning to use the Internet for business, education, or recreation.

DIALOG, DISCUSSION, AND DELIVERY

In textbook terms, there are three basic forms of communication — dialog, discussion, and delivery. These apply whether communicating in person or via electronic media such as the Internet. Each form is characterized by the number of participants and the direction or directions of information flow.

A dialog takes place between two parties. The communication flows in both directions between the parties and both participate in the exchange. E-mail exchanges are dialogs. The individual messages are only transmitted in one direction but the interchange is a dialog. In the early days of the Web, pages were static. The viewer could select from a list of links or hyperlinked text but that was about all. With the use of background programs or scripts, Web pages can be sufficiently interactive or responsive enough to be considered a true dialog.

Marketing visionaries saw this capacity for dialog as the greatest strength of the Internet for sales and marketing. Buyers and sellers interact directly, one on one, without cumbersome relaying of information through second and third parties necessitated by traditional retail distribution channels. Some of the companies that successfully pioneered selling goods and services over the Internet include Cisco Systems (telecommunications products), computer manufacturer Dell Computer, Virtual Vinyards (wine and food merchant), Amazon (books), and CDNow (music CDs), just to name a few.

A discussion involves more than two participants. Electronic bulletin boards and newsgroups are good examples of this many-to-many communication. Specialized software is available to provide chat discussions on the Web. Developing communities has become increasingly important for attracting new audiences and providing a valuable service to friends and customers alike. The Internet, through discussions and chats, is bringing geographically separated groups of individuals together through common interests.

Most Websites fall into the category of delivery-type communications. The communication is one way. The Web page contains the information accessible by any and all who seek it out. However, unlike broadcast, this delivery is passive. It just sits there until someone requests the information.

This presents a problem for getting your message out. You do not incur huge printing, postage, and distribution costs associated with selling magazines or sending out catalogs and brochures by the thousands. However, aggressively sending e-mail solicitations to potential customers is considered a breach of "Netiquette." Every direct marketer knows that sending out thousands of pieces to well-qualified leads is a productive source of new customers. Some recipients call it junk mail, but it works. In theory, direct mail ought to work even better electronically. Actually it works too well. Generating millions of e-mail messages costs almost nothing. Some early marketers sent so many messages to everyone with an e-mail address that it became disruptive, counterproductive, and much publicized. The term spam refers to unsolicited and usually unwanted e-mail. The government is even considering making "spamming" illegal.

How are you going to get people to come to your Website? Multimedia can play an important role in attracting visitors to a site and keeping their interest. It makes your message attractive and memorable. Including particularly interesting multimedia may get you noticed in the trade press or in *The Wall Street Journal*. If nothing else, your customers and prospective clients will benefit from an engaging multisensory presentation of your information and that is the primary objective.

Today, there are few technical limitations to multimedia inclusion and playback. Development effort and resources are being focused on providing solutions. The appeal of multimedia on the Internet has generated tremendous public interest and raised expectations for global communications and information exchange.

TEXT

Web pages are inherently text-based as defined by the HTML language used to construct Web pages. HTML stands for Hyper Text Markup Language. Several markup languages have been around for many years and are used extensively in documentation for government projects. Using a consistent set of identifiers or tags embedded in the document to standardize the structure and content of long, complex documents helps readers locate key components within the document.

Some of the earliest browsers only supported text and hyperlinks. It is easy to put together an interesting and informative set of text-only pages. The display of text is entirely dependent on the display capabilities of the browsers and user settings of selectable parameters. This is good news and bad news. The HTML files are small — usually a few kilobytes each. However, a page that looks great on your computer may not be what the viewer sees. The text is all there but the formatting can look completely different.

There are many different audiences for your Web pages. Try to accommodate a broad range of connectivity and interests — the techie, the consumer, the power user. Unlike print or broadcast, you are rarely limited in the amount of content that you can provide on the Web. Viewers appreciate having access to detailed product specifications, frequently asked questions, back issues of newsletters, etc. So long as the navigation through the site is well laid out, the more information you provide, the better.

GRAPHICS

The addition of graphic element display by the Mosaic browser was the first enhancement of HTML. Graphics are the easiest and most visible additions to any Web page. A splash of color, a dramatic image, or an identifiable logo can be included easily on Web pages. Virtually all browsers have the ability to display pictures in a variety of file formats. GIF format image files are compact for downloading quickly. JPEG format images are also displayable by most browsers. A large JPEG image can be displayed as separate page of its own.

Images and graphics files can be large if color and resolution are important. A 640×480 24-bit color image is about 1 Mb uncompressed. Illustrations and photographs can be much larger. A large format photo like those taken from a satellite can be 60 Mb. JPEG format files can be compressed to reduce the amount of data transferred and speed downloading times. Visitors with slower connections appreciate seeing a small version or "thumbnail" of a large image before choosing to download a very large picture.

The overall appearance of your site can also make you stand out from the competition. While it is important to have a consistent look to your site, variations on the theme are important to distinguish between the pages, especially if there are large numbers of pages. Viewers appreciate visual cues as navigational aids. A family of brightly colored graphics based on a theme or a logo style can help to present a consistent image across a large number of Web pages in a site.

Web page design is an evolving art form. Regular surfing is the best way to stay current on new capabilities and to find exciting uses of the technology. New Web-related technology can significantly enhance your Website experience.

INTERACTIVITY

Hyperlinks are the most exciting feature of the World Wide Web. The ability to electronically reference other pages located anywhere on the planet is a great concept. Visitors like to be involved and control how they navigate through information. It is this interconnectivity that led to the name World Wide Web for the part of the Web that can be accessed and linked through Hyper Text Transport Protocol (HTTP) and Universal Resource Locators (URL).

Hyperlinks are particularly useful for linking references to related information and Web pages of interest wherever they are located, regardless of the source — other authors, documentation sources, resources, or program files. It is considered polite to inform a site you reference that you have made this link. Most sites are delighted to have these references, and may even provide information about other areas of common interest. Be sure to validate links periodically, especially links to outside sources. Pages are frequently changed, moved, or renamed without warning and without forwarding addresses.

Additional interactivity is achieved through Common Gateway Interface (CGI) scripts or programs that can be linked to Web pages. Forms are one common way to encourage communication. CGI scripts or programs attached to Web pages also can be used to access databases, customize Web pages in reply, and a host of other applications. Forms are also used to promote interactivity through survey questionnaires, registration forms, and structured feedback requests. More about programs and scripts later.

STYLE AND LAYOUT

Layout, fonts, graphic placement, and image detail can be as important as the text content. Newspapers, magazines, and forms rely on exact layout to convey image, present material, and comply with information input requirements. These rich text documents can be created and distributed on the Web. The HTML standard has evolved over time. From its very primitive text and hypertext beginnings, the HTML standard has undergone several major revisions and browsers have been updated to include style and enhanced layout information.

Adobe Acrobat was one of the first rich document standards used on the Web. Each Acrobat page file contains explicit formatting information to display the exact layout and fonts of the original document. The Web versions of *The New York Times,* an Amherst College humor magazine, and the Federal government forms archive are a few examples of sites utilizing Acrobat files. Acrobat files are much larger than an HTML version of the same text and graphics. However, this may be a reasonable trade-off if layout is important. Acrobat documents always display exactly as created regardless of the platform used for display. Many browsers include Acrobat PDF format display.

The HTML standard is evolving under the direction of the World Wide Web Consortium (W3C), an international standards body. Additions and changes to the HTML standard include font and layout information that provide these rich text format capabilities. Introduced in the HTML 2.0 standard, the FONT tag made it possible to control the size, color, and position of text.

With the adoption of HTML 3.0, three main technologies make up Dynamic HTML (DHTML) — HTML, JavaScript, and Cascading Style Sheets (CSS). As Web technologies have evolved, so has the definition of the term Dynamic HTML. Originally it was used to describe the customized pages built with information received about the user's browser and operating system or in response to a viewer request. Search results, form posting verification, and displayed database records are all examples of Dynamic HTML. Scripting languages, such as JavaScript and VBScript, allow changes to be made to a document after it leaves the server, but before it was displayed by the browser.

Today, Dynamic HTML refers to technologies that allow documents to be changed after their initial display, without server access, through user interaction and client-side scripting. Page elements can be displayed selectively, then modified, moved, or replaced. This ability to move and replace objects allows for the animation of text and graphics. Selective display and replacement can be used for database record retrieval. Pages look and feel like applications, with more of the actual computing performed at the browser end. More information on Dynamic HTML is available at http//webreference.com/dhtml/about.html.

CSS

Cascading Style Sheets (CSS) define the presentation and style of the document. Style sheets work by separating style (CSS1) and layout (CSS2) from the structure of content. Style rules can be embedded inside a page, but are ideally stored in a separate referenced HTML document — a style sheet. It is this separation that gives style sheets their power.

One of the fundamental features of CSS is that style sheets cascade. Authors can attach a preferred style sheet, while the reader may have a personal style sheet to adjust for human or technological handicaps. The overall look of an entire page or even entire Websites can be changed by changing one style rule or style sheet. The rules for resolving conflicts between different style sheets are defined in this specification.

Style sheets are engineered with the future in mind. Style sheets' independence of style from structure makes it easier to adapt the Web to different technologies and ways of experiencing those technologies. The blind, for instance, could have a special sound-oriented style sheet that specifies speech parameters, intonation, reader style, and preferred speech plug-in. Set-top Net boxes like WebTV could invoke special TV-optimized style sheets that enlarge letters, shrink wide tables, and simplify layouts.

JavaScript

JavaScript is not Java. Although there is a similarity in naming, Java is a more powerful language which requires a compiler (more about Java™ later). JavaScript is used exclusively on the Web, whereas Java can be used to create software programs. JavaScript is the cross-platform, object-based scripting language for client and server applications. Browsers can interpret JavaScript statements embedded in an HTML page. When a user requests such a page, the server sends the full content of the document, including HTML and JavaScript statements, over the network to the client. The browser then displays the HTML and executes the JavaScript, producing the results that the user sees.

JavaScript is used to manipulate the Document Object Model (DOM). Document objects include windows, text, images, and other display elements. JavaScript statements embedded in an HTML page can respond to user events such as mouse clicks, form input, and page navigation. For example, you can write a JavaScript function to verify that users enter valid information into a form requesting a telephone number or zip code. Without any network transmission, the HTML page with embedded JavaScript can check the entered data and alert the user with a dialog box if the input is invalid.

Some of the nifty special effects you see on pages are produced with Java-Script. Images change color as you roll your cursor over them, pages display the current date and time, scrolling text; these are just a few of the things that JavaScript can do.

More information on JavaScript can be found at JavaScript World, http://www.jsworld.com/.

XML

Other areas of evolution within the Web content and delivery are likely to make use of XML (Extensible Markup Language). XML is not a markup language but a set of rules for defining special-purpose markup languages.

XML is used to create custom TAGS and elements using a subset of SGML, the grandfather of HTML. The tags themselves provide information about the content within the tags. In HTML the <H1> actually denotes the primary level of structure within the document. It has come to be interpreted by most graphical browsers to display the text as 24-point proportionally spaced font. With XML, authors can create tags like <BYLINE> or <PRODUCT> with associated rules about contents and display.

In theory, XML is a great way to really separate style from data and even from HTML. An XML page handled by the XML-capable browser is displayed using the styling format for the page in a special style sheet, or XSL. How well browsers will handle these author-defined tags remains to be seen. For details see the WebDeveloper.com Guide to XML at http://www.Webdeveloper.com/categories/html/html_xml_2.html.

MULTIMEDIA

We live in an information-rich society. Via the Internet, the audience for any content published on the Web is global. Multimedia — audio, video, and animation, influence a broader audience with more information in more formats. Using multiple appropriate media types adds interest, reduces customer support costs, improves sales productivity, and provides another opportunity for product and service information distribution.

Adding multimedia elements to Website design and implementation requires planning. Video, sound, and animation files are usually large and require a lot of data to be transferred to the user. Compression techniques help to reduce file sizes significantly, but compared with text, all these media formats require large numbers of bits for even short clips.

Multimedia files provide impact to a Web page. Used sparingly and appropriately, multimedia can enhance the visitor experience, convey important additional information, and add entertainment value to Web pages.

VIDEO

Video is the most powerful of all media objects and should definitely be included in every developers repertoire of cool Web stuff. Video formats used on the Web include AVI, ActiveX, ActiveMovie, ASF, Microsoft Office, MPEG1, MPEG2, QuickTime, and RealVideo. However, video files are huge and require special high-speed data transfer capabilities to display properly.

The storage and distribution of digital video files over the Internet is an important addition to any Website. In this video-rich world, video plays a key role in selling products and services, communicating complex information, bridging cultural gaps, educating young and old, and informing and entertaining us. Video also represents the most challenges in terms of digitization, compression, storage, and distribution.

We are not talking about feature-length movies yet. Traditional business to business communication often includes a video tape or a slide presentation. Many applications can be effective with small, lower resolution video using new or existing video (and audio) to enhance text-based Web pages. The intended audience and message is key to determining which format is appropriate.

Major corporations are using video to promote their products and services. Video clip demonstrations are helping promote concepts to employees, resellers, and clients around the world. For example, video clips dramatically show the simplicity of product user interfaces, which seem extremely complex when described in text only. Joint Venture, a Silicon Valley organization that brings together businesses and local government to promote the region, has effectively used digital video on their Website. Landmarks, local industry luminaries, working environments, high-tech know how, and quality of life are all featured in the video clips. The video has prompted many inquiries from outside the U.S. as well as from businesses considering relocation to the San Francisco Bay area. Most entertainment companies provide previews of their latest releases and interviews with stars as attractions for potential box-office business.

There are two distinct type of video media — streaming and download-then-play. Choosing which is appropriate will depend on the connectivity speed of the intended audience, acceptable quality of presentation, and in some cases, copyright issues. Depending on the situation, both streaming and download-then-play media have their place in delivered multimedia.

Streaming Video

In order to play audio or video on a computer, the information must be available as it is required to form the picture and sounds. Video, and to a lesser extent audio, requires thousands to millions of bits of data per second to present acceptable playback of the content. Video is considered "full motion" when 24 to 30 frames, or individual images, are presented per second. Insufficient data transfer can result in missing information leading to poor sound quality, blurry or jerky movement, and small picture size.

Streaming means that video, animation, and/or sound files start playing immediately while media downloads in the background. The host server delivers the interactive information with little or no waiting. The information is transferred directly to the viewer or listener and then it is gone. On the Internet, this receive-view-discard model is known as streaming. The goal of sending enough information continuously from the host site to the viewer's desktop on demand has not always been realized. Protocol limitations, file size, and modem speed can adversely affect the quality of audio, video, and animations playback.

Most streaming implementations allow the user to determine which part of a file to transfer and play. The user can start at the beginning or in the middle. The transfer time is approximately the same as the play time so there is no long delay between starting the transfer and playing. However, with streaming, the quality is limited by the available data rate.

One way to compensate for the lack of data transfer speed via the browser is to download the entire audio or video file, then play the file. All the information is on the viewer's computer hard drive before play begins. Once the entire file has been transferred, the browser then launches a player application to play the file from the user's computer. This arrangement has several serious limitations — transfer time, lack of browsing/preview capability, and copyright issues. Video files can be especially large — 10 Mb/min even when the file is compressed. For slower modems, these files take hours to download. However, as modem speeds increase and other faster telecommunications sources become available, file size and transfer rate will not be the impediments they are now.

With streaming players, copyright holders are more confident that their rights are not being violated. The user never gets a complete copy of the material. Most streaming players are reusing the same disk space as they play the material, overwriting the previously played portion of the file. With download-then-play, the entire file must be downloaded (at least temporarily) onto the user's hard drive before the player is launched. Adequate free hard drive space must be available to hold the entire downloaded file.

RealNetworks' Real Media Architecture (RMA) has become the de facto standard for streaming media over the Internet. Media types supported include audio, video, text, 2D, and even 3D graphics through partnerships with content creation tool developers like Macromedia.

SMIL (Synchronized Media Integration Language) makes it possible to deliver multiple streams to a single Web page simultaneously. There continues to be tremendous interest and development in this area.

Download-Then-Play Video

There are some advantages to the download-then-play format. Once the files have been transferred to the user's computer, the user does not have to be connected to the Web to view or hear the material. However, this may raise some copyright issues. The user has a copy of the material for distribution, for use in derivative works, or for archival purposes.

However, video files can be huge. For MPEG1 and QuickTime/Cinepak video, files are about 10 Mb/min. These formats provide good quality video at frame rates of 12 to 15 frames per second (fps) — fine for talking heads or moderate action. Fast action or quick scene changes will probably suffer

Movies – Downloads by File Size

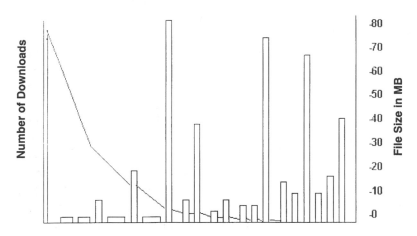

Exhibit 39.1. Video file downloads — file size and download count.

some loss of quality. MPEG2 and higher data transfer rates are required for broadcast television quality playback at files sizes of 30 Mb/min or more.

Exhibit 39.1 illustrates some interesting choices being made by Web surfers. The vertical bars represent individual videos. The height of the bar indicates the size of the video file — the taller the bar, the bigger the video file. The videos are arranged from most frequently downloaded on the left to least frequently downloaded on the right. The shaded area behind the bars shows the number of downloads for the video. The left half of the chart is pretty clear. Small video files are downloaded more often than large video files.

However, the right half suggests that size is not as important as some other factors. Other influencing factors include video content and location in the list of videos available. If users want the information, they are prepared to download relatively large files (some of these files are more than 30 Mb).

The connection and bandwidth capabilities of Web users vary tremendously. The Web may be universally accessible but not all access is equal. Users with 28.8 kbps connections wait more than an hour to download a one minute video clip. The same file can be downloaded via a T1 link in just over a minute. What is intolerable to some users is just fine for others. From some remote region of the country or world, just having access to information can be well worth the wait — however long that may be. This broad spectrum of users can be accommodated by offering choices of file size and format.

Here are some guidelines for using video on Web pages. Many of these suggestions apply to any multimedia files. These are not intended to represent a definitive work on digitized video. These are intended to get you thinking about some of the issues associated with digitizing video.

Although there are other video and audio formats, MPEG and QuickTime are emerging as the best choices. QuickTime is an Apple extension for Macintosh and Windows to integrate time-based data into applications. MPEG (Moving Pictures Experts Group) is a family of ISO (the International Standards Organization) standards for digital video (sequences of images in time) and audio compression that define a compressed bit stream, which implicitly defines a decompressor.

We encourage you to provide video in both QuickTime and MPEG1 formats. Specialized video-compression/decompression (CODEC) hardware is still relatively expensive so offering software-only playback is advisable. In general, QuickTime files can be played with software on most computers being used to access the Internet today. MPEG1 plays back at better quality but requires a high-end computer or additional hardware to assist in the decoding process. By choosing both QuickTime and MPEG1 for your video presentation, you can reach and empower the broadest range of users.

All links to files should include file size, play time, and a description of the content to help users determine if they really want to download this file.

QUICKTIME

Apple Computer's QuickTime is a widely used video format on the Internet. QuickTime is an Apple proprietary software for Macintosh and Windows creating and playing time-based data including sound, video (MPEG, Cinepak), animation, data produced by scientific instruments, financial results, music information (MIDI), and other similar data types.

QuickTime is well suited for use. Software-only QuickTime players can be downloaded from the Apple Website and, therefore, are readily available to anyone with access. QuickTime players are available for Macintosh and Windows platforms. QuickTime video creators have a lot of control over the options that ultimately determine download times and video playback quality, enabling them to meet a broad range of requirements. Quarter-screen or smaller images and low frames rates (2 to 15 fps) work best at slower modem speeds. Larger images and higher frame rates can be selected when data transfer rate is not a limiting factor.

QuickTime is a software architecture that supports the inclusion of many different compression/decompression schemes to play specific file formats. MPEG files can be played by QuickTime software with the appropriate decompressor. Cinepak video compression is SuperMac's software

584

video CODEC technology under the QuickTime™ system-software architecture and is widely supported. Currently, most references to QuickTime really refer to QuickTime with SuperMac's Cinepak or some other widely distributed compression algorithm such as Apple video, animation, or JPEG. MPEG usually refers to files that conform to the MPEG1 standard. Both MPEG and Cinepak video compression technology use interframe compression to achieve high compression rates.

There are different compression algorithms for specific content types — JPEG for still pictures, video, animation, playback from CD-ROM (Cinepak), Intel's Indeo, and others. The resulting file sizes can vary widely depending on the source video, image size, audio and video quality parameters chosen, and the compression method selection.

The compression and playback characteristics can be varied by the encoding software. The average compression ratio is 60:1 compared to original source material. The exact compression ratio depends on the complexity of the video content and the quality desired in the video playback. The data rate for a quarter-screen video with audio can be 10 Mb/min. That is as large as an MPEG file but the QuickTime file is more universally playable today. A 30-s video that is a series of still images with narration could be as small as 1 Mb. The file of the same video produced with another compression method might be as large as 5 Mb. If the content of the video is very complex and has a large number of changes between frames, then more space will be required to store the needed information. The more complex the content, the more space it requires, and the lower the compression ratio. There are lots of choices depending on the desired results and necessary trade-offs.

Cinepak video compression is SuperMac's software video CODEC technology that has been adopted by Apple, Microsoft, 3DO, Sega, Atari, Creative Labs, and Cirrus Logic. Cinepak video compression technology allows authors and publishers to create one version of their video products for the entire group. Cinepak video compression technology uses 320×240 pixels (1/4 screen) of video displayed from 12 to 30 fps. The technology is scalable and takes advantage of whatever power the system can provide.

There are professional QuickTime encoding services available as well. Several software developers are introducing products and services to enhance the quality and playback of QuickTime video. Very good results can be achieved by these professionals using sophisticated software tools.

Windows and DOS do not recognize the resource forks in Macintosh files. To run QuickTime movies created on a Macintosh computer on a Windows computer, files must be "flattened." Utilities are available to do this.

Player applications or plug-ins for most computer platforms are available from the Apple Computer Website.

MPEG

The Motion Picture Experts Group standard, MPEG1, is also an important video format for use on the Internet.

MPEG (Moving Pictures Experts Group) meet under ISO (the International Standards Organization) to generate standards for digital video (sequences of images in time) and audio compression. In particular, they define a compressed bit stream, which implicitly defines a decompressor. The compression algorithms are up to the individual manufacturers, and that is where proprietary advantage is obtained within the scope of a publicly available international standard. There are actually a family of MPEG standards. MPEG1 is the more compressed version. MPEG2 delivers much better quality but the files are at three to six times larger. For most users, the sacrifice of quality for a smaller file size is acceptable.

With MPEG1 files, VHS or better playback is possible — full screen, 30 fps, with CD-quality audio. The compression algorithms are sophisticated and require lots of computing power or hardware assistance for playback. Selecting MPEG1 format reduces the size of the files but burdens the user with considerable decompression processing for viewing.

MPEG1 is a good choice for delivered video. The various hardware and software decoding systems offer MPEG format video and audio decompression with output to standard VGA and audio cards as decoded video, audio, or system streams. Full-motion frame rates of 30 fps can easily be achieved on these systems. The compact video stream plays back as full frames (640×480 pixels) with CD-quality audio. The resulting file size is approximately 10 Mb/min.

MPEG1 is designed for data rates from 1 to 5 Mb/s or 125 to 625 kb/s. Image size, although variable under the specification, is usually set to 320×240 at 30 fields per second or SIF resolution. Most MPEG players display a full-screen presentation by line-doubling the data to 640×480 pixels. Within MPEG there are variations, specifically VideoCD and CD-i. The MPEG hardware manufactures all support VideoCD, which specifies image size, data rate, and audio formats. Data rates that are higher or lower than specified in the VideoCD standard will not play back consistently on all systems.

High-quality MPEG1 encoded files compare well with VHS tape when played back. For business-to-business presentations, videographers, and video production companies, MPEG1 is the best choice in video file formats. MPEG encoding is still relatively expensive. Recreational MPEG encoding systems start at $4000. High-end cinematic quality MPEG encoding suites with sophisticated prefiltering software can cost hundreds of thousands of dollars. Highly skilled compressionists can do scene-by-scene encoding optimization which delivers superior results over the less expensive systems.

586

Decoding is processing intensive. While it can be done with a fast computer and software alone, the addition of a hardware assist is desirable. There are 20 to 30 MPEG decoding boards, priced from $300, available for Windows machines. Few Macintosh MPEG hardware decoders are available. Software decoders can play MPEG1 without additional hardware on Pentium-class PCs with Mediamatics player built into Win95, OS2, and Win98 for Pentium class PCs. Most high-end UNIX workstations also play MPEG1 video, although some play only the video portion without the audio.

For those applications where broadcast quality video is required, MPEG2 can deliver, but the data files are huge (more than six times larger than MPEG1). Because MPEG2 is designed to deliver production quality video, it does not support reduced frame sizes or frame rates. Therefore, it requires data rates of 4 to 10 Mb/s which is not suitable for most implementations of distribution.

Although originally specified in the MPEG family of media standards, MPEG3 has been abandoned. It was intended for High Definition TV (HDTV) but was subsequently folded into MPEG2.

More recently, the MPEG4 standard was developed to be scalable in both frame size and frame rate to perform at modem data rates of 56 and 112 kb/s. As the MPEG4 standard is finalized and promoted, we expect it to be widely adopted as a good compromise of low data rates and good video quality for Internet delivery.

OTHER VIDEO CONSIDERATIONS

For Internet use, compression is essential to reduce the amount of data transferred. Cinepak, MPEG, and JPEG are good choices.

The color depth has a direct impact on file size. For QuickTime and Apple's video compression, using 256 colors or even 4 or 16 grays can significantly reduce the file size. However, some compressors like Cinepak and MPEG only work with millions of colors. If you are trying to save file size by reducing colors, be sure to chose a compression method that works with a reduced color palette.

Audio compatibility is a significant problem for software codecs like QuickTime/Cinepak and software MPEG players as they rely on the audio subsystem in the computer to decode the audio. Many multimedia systems cannot handle CD-quality audio (44 kHz/16-bit audio) and the audio track of the video may be lost. This does not apply to MPEG hardware decoders. MPEG hardware decoders are well standardized so compatibility is not a problem.

Even small video files can add impact to a Web page. A 20- to 30-s clip to add a personal note, or to introduce a guest speaker or a corporate officer, can be very effective. A 30-s demonstration of a complex procedure — like installing a printer toner cartridge — is more effective than many pages of diagrams and text explanation.

Use video to do what video does best — show motion, demonstrate complex concepts visually, or add sound and music. Remember, someone has to download this video before they play it. Be sure it is worth their while. Users do not want to wait for a 5 Mb file to download just to see a corporate logo fly about the screen.

Digitizing existing video for inclusion into a Web page works, and is a good way to start using Web-delivered video. Editing and clip selection are critical. Rely on the text to provide the linear framework. Use video to add interest. Make every second count.

Several companies are developing technology for interactive hot spots within video. As the video plays, the user can click on a car in the scene to find out more about the make and model. In an instructional video about insects, click on the head to see the electron microscope image of its eye.

AUDIO AND SOUND

Audio, sound, music, and narration can all add impact to a Website experience. There is less standardization in sound file formats than in other areas of multimedia. AU, WAV, and AIF are file architectures for storing sound. They support various compression codecs. For example, a WAV file can be saved in MPEG1, layer 3 codec.

The AU sound format is the most portable and can be used on all platforms. However, most Windows sound files are in WAV format. Macintosh sound files are usually in AIF format. These sound files are downloaded then played. Microsoft is promoting its WAV format. The MPEG family of audio and video standards are gaining in popularity. Many music files are available in MPEG1, layer 3, or MP3 format. MP3 codecs are available from Microsoft with Microsoft's NetShow player.

RealNetworks (originally called RealAudio) was one of the early entrants into the streaming or browsing audio player software arena. Their proprietary audio formatting and compression software for the host server has become the Web de facto standard. The client or user player software is available free from Websites using these technologies and from the vendors. RealNetworks player technology is included within many browsers, eliminating the need for a separate helper application or plug-in.

Audio is a good media addition to a Web page. Hearing a voice or music or sound provides more information than text alone. The file size and bandwidth for audio is minimal compared to video. Audio-only can be just as effective as a talking head video.

Audio can be used in conjunction with a graphic image. For example, a client wanted to include a complex satellite image on a page. In order to see the detail, the image needed to be displayed on the full screen. However, that covered the description of the image. An audio file describing the image that played while the image was on screen resolved the problem.

ANIMATION

There are several ways to provide animation to Web page viewers. The simplest is with animated GIFs. The animation is a series of individual GIF image files that are linked together. When the viewer's browser detects an animated GIF, it displays the series of images in sequence. A file option determines the number of times the sequence is repeated. Several animation authoring tools are available.

There are other proprietary file formats for delivering animation. Shockwave from Macromedia is one of these. Shockwave is a series of players that let you view high-quality, streaming content in a Web browser. It is included with many popular browsers and services such as Netscape Navigator, Microsoft Explorer, and AOL. Macromedia's Website is http://www.macromedia.com/shockwave/.

JAVA

While not a media type itself, Sun Microsystems' Java is a multimedia authoring system. Java components include object-oriented applications that run on the user desktop, an authoring language, and additional server functionality to support these concepts. Java applets are being used to deliver interactive animation, dynamic stock quotation updating, online training, and almost any other type of application.

Java software runs in many places, on many kinds of computers and devices, and is not limited to the Internet. Java applets are written, compiled, and place on a Web server, ready for use. References to Java applets are embedded on a Web page. When the Web browser sees these references, it loads the Java applet and the user gets an interactive Java applet running in a browser. The same Java applet runs in browsers on PCs, Macs, UNIX® workstations, Network computers, and elsewhere.

Java allows Website developers to incorporate a lot of interactivity into their sites and provide services such as customer support, electronic commerce, entertainment, and online education without having to create versions of these applications to run on each of dozens of difference types of computers. Sun Microsystems' Website is http://java.sun.com/nav/whatis/worksinbrowser.html.

BROWSERS, PLUG-INS, AND HELPER APPLICATIONS

Originally, Web browsers recognized just HTML text and GIF format graphic files. However, when the viewer clicks on a reference that points to one of these other files, the browser downloads the file and launches the appropriate application program for the file. These are known as helpers or helper applications.

Support for additional commonly accessed file types has been added to Netscape Navigator and Microsoft Explorer to allow access to every type of file on the Internet. When the browser encounters a sound, image, or video file, it hands off the data to other programs, called helper applications or plug-ins, to run or display the file.

For most multimedia types, there are one or more helper applications available. Some helpers are programs that a user may already have — Powerpoint, Word, QuickTime MoviePlayer, and Windows Media Player. Other helpers such as Adobe Acrobat, Sparkle, and RealNetworks can be downloaded from various sites. Others can be purchased from computer vendors and retailers. MPEG decoding boards and associated application software are usually offered as a package. Once the software is installed, helper applications in the Preferences options in the browser can be launched automatically.

Most browsers have additional configuration options available. To maximize file transfers, increasing the size of buffers and cache settings in the Network and Cache options menu can significantly improve data transfer rates. This allows the computer to gather bigger chunks of the file during download.

BANDWIDTH

The issue of bandwidth comes up in most discussions of the use of multimedia on the Internet. So here is our perspective. If bandwidth is an issue for users now, it will not be for long. Modem speeds are increasing, prices are falling, and many other modes of data communication are becoming available including cable, wireless, and satellite communications.

There have been dramatic changes occurring in the growth of bandwidth and traffic on the Web since 1991. As the interest and demand goes up, so does the bandwidth.

Statistics of video file transfers from sites all over the world show that the server speed directly impacts the transfer time. Transfer delays over the Net are never more than 5 to 10 ms in hundreds of samples. The bandwidth is there if both the sender and receiver are capable of reasonable transfer speeds.

If the viewer only has a 28.8 kbaud modem, server speed has little effect. For business-to-business information distribution, server speed is critical.

Today, there are hundreds of thousands of T1 lines installed and the number is growing by thousands per month. Frame relay and partial T1 lines are being installed in even larger numbers. These users can download files in the time it takes to play them, and streaming video playback is possible at this file transfer rate.

Homes and businesses everywhere are getting connected with ISDN lines. While ISDN is not fast enough for broadcast-quality full motion, full-screen video-on-demand, it is adequate for most demonstrations, conferencing, and learning applications.

Telephone companies and cable providers have the connectivity to the users home and office. With changing regulations, both groups see delivery of data from the Internet to desk- and set-tops as important to their long-term growth (or even survival).

FUTURE OF MULTIMEDIA ON THE INTERNET

Generally speaking, the quality of information published on the Internet is improving. The level of professionalism in Web page design is evident everywhere. Major corporations are producing Websites with great graphics, interesting audio and video, and sophisticated interactivity. For example, Silicon Graphics has great graphics. Oracle is demonstrating how customized Web pages can be produced from a database of information to fit the requirements of a single user on demand. Sun Microsystems and its clients have developed a number of Java applications for sales and marketing, product demonstrations, customer support, and interactive learning.

The quantity of information published on the Internet is growing. Sites are expanding. Having a Home Page is a start. However, many sites now have hundreds of interconnecting pages describing the company, products, and services and are offering online technical support through frequently asked questions — FAQs — for most customer problems. Apple, HP, and Sun all maintain large, complex sites.

Commercial distribution of information is beginning to take off. Some of the early adopters are financial and stock quotation services, specialized industry-specific newsletters, software retailers, and other electronic commerce applications. Some are offering information as a one-time charge. Others are using the subscription model — pay one price for multiple issues of a magazine. The entertainment industry is keenly aware of the potential of the Internet as a new outlet for its products and services and as a distribution channel for its content.

Because there is so much information, it is often difficult and time consuming to sift through all the apparently related information to find the reliable sources of information. Editorial and Review Services are beginning to make their mark. Although they do not create the information, they review it and summarize and/or identify the best sources. Users are willing to pay to have this culling done. The time saving can be well worth the money.

Many of the most active sites provide free service to users. Some, like Yahoo, categorize site listings, and InfoSeek offers extensive search and retrieval capabilities. These services now charge for advertising on their popular sites. Charging for advertising appears to be the most successful way to make money for providing content and navigation-related services.

The advent of the World Wide Web technology has enabled millions of content owners and users to provide and retrieve information. As the Web matures, more multimedia objects will be added to text and graphics-based messages. People all over the world are promoting products and services, educating themselves and others, and forging new relationships with the power of video, audio, and animation.

Communication in text and pictures works. It has for centuries. When more senses and communication styles can be integrated, the process improves. You may not be able to read all the words in a foreign language text but you hear the enthusiasm in the voice and see the smiles and gestures in the video. Multimedia can add impact to any message. Try it. You can see and hear the difference!

Authors' Bios

Valerie Taylor's 20 years of data processing and multimedia experience include a comprehensive background in high-technology product development, management, customer service, and marketing. She has a proven track record in multimedia production, product design, and management for a variety of products and services for CD-ROM titles and educational software, information publishing, and World Wide Web promotional services. Taylor directed the development and marketing of multimedia projects for clients that included NASA Ames Research Center, Stanford University, Sun Microsystems, The Learning Kingdom, and The Tech Museum of Innovation, and is currently researching and developing Web-based learning technologies for K-12 education.

Chris Ammen has been involved in video production technology for all of his 25-year professional career. He has pioneered technological developments in analog and digital video production, and was awarded the prestigious Joey Award for New Technologies for his work in Synchronization Services. Ammen has continued to expand his expertise into the computer-to-video scan conversion process area.

He is Vice President of Advanced Technologies for Television Associates (TVA) of Mountain View, CA. TVA is one of Silicon Valley's leading video production facilities. Ammen is responsible for assembling and perfecting TVA's Compression Services that include multimedia presentations, MPEG, and QuickTime encoding, DVD-video authoring, and other digital video services.

Chapter 40
Web Traffic Analysis: Analyzing What Is Happening on Your Site

Michael McClure

THE WEB TRAFFIC ANALYSIS MARKET BARELY EXISTED A FEW SHORT YEARS AGO and is already a multimillion dollar segment of the e-business industry. Web traffic analysis growth is being driven by the growth of the World Wide Web and the desire to know as much as possible about visitors through self-identification, registration, and Web server logs. According to a recent report by International Data Corporation, the Web traffic analysis market will break $100 million by the year 2002.

Web traffic analysis tools take Web server traffic information and try to make sense of it so intelligent business conclusions can be drawn. Simple things like how many total files were requested can be easily calculated and reported. By looking for multiple requests from the same computer during the same timeframe, more complex things can be calculated, like the number of total visitors and visits that were made to a site. By adding other information to the analysis, such as advertising information, ad impressions, and click-through rates also can be calculated.

Two types of Web traffic analysis are described below, namely Web log analysis and Web mining.

WEB LOG ANALYSIS — TRADITIONAL WEB TRAFFIC ANALYSIS

Web log analysis software reports basic traffic information based on Web server log files. Tools in this category use calculations and assumptions to create a maximum amount of log data relationships for inclusion in reports.

0-8493-9987-4/00/$0.00+$.50
© 2000 by CRC Press LLC

The main purpose for Web log analysis has traditionally been to gain a general understanding of what is happening on the site. Webmasters and system administrators who are responsible for keeping the site up and running often want to know how much traffic they are getting, how many requests fail, and what kinds of errors are being generated. This information is typically used for Website management purposes.

Recently Web log analysis has become more popular with Web marketers. By adding information such as advertisement names, filters, and virtual server information, log data can be further analyzed to track the results of specific marketing campaigns. Product managers and marketers who are responsible for allocating budgets in the most efficient manner require this type of information to make intelligent business decisions. Web log analysis can be used to answer questions like:

- What companies are visiting your site?
- What pages are the most and least popular?
- What sites are your visitors coming from?
- How much bandwidth does your site utilize?

WEB MINING — ADVANCED WEB TRAFFIC ANALYSIS

Rather than look at Web traffic data as its own island of information (Exhibit 40.1), Web mining integrates Web traffic information with other databases in the corporation such as customer, accounting, profile, and e-commerce databases. The resulting reports not only use advanced relationships between log data, but also draw from these external databases as well.

The main purpose of Web mining is to analyze online investments of the entire enterprise, in an effort to maximize return. Executive management and Chief Information Officers are typical candidates for this type of information.

Many Web miners base their offers on visitor profiles and, more importantly, create new products that match the results of their analysis. Web mining is typically used to answer more complex Web-related questions like:

- How do visitors' demographic and psychographic information correlate with their Website browsing behavior?
- What is your Website's return on investment?
- Which advertising banners are bringing the most qualified visitors to your site?
- Which sites refer the highest number of visitors who actually purchase?

An Overview of Web Traffic Analysis Software

To accomplish its goal, Web traffic analysis software must be able to collect Web traffic data from multiple Websites, store it into a data ware-

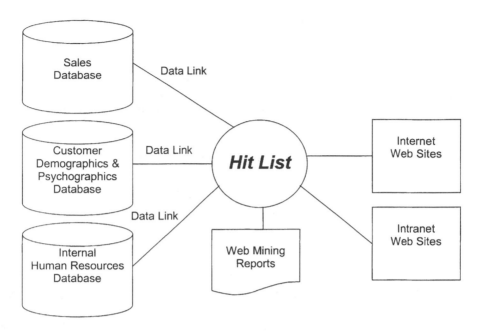

Exhibit 40.1. Web mining tools integrate Web traffic data with other corporate data from sales, customer, and human resources databases.

house, integrate it with other sources of information, and then analyze and report the results quickly and accurately. The ideal Web traffic analysis system is also both completely programmable and extensible to support customization and scalability with the enterprise. This section goes through an overview of the technology typically used to accomplish each of these tasks. Good Web traffic analysis software is available today and ranges in price from free to over $20,000. The most popular packages are priced at around $300.

DATA COLLECTION

Web traffic analysis tools must first be able to collect Web traffic information, often from multiple Websites deployed throughout the world. This can be accomplished through reading Web server log files or more recently through TCP/IP packet sniffing techniques.

Web Server Log Files

Web server log files are undoubtedly the most common source for Web traffic information. Behind every Website is a Web server, whose purpose in life is to respond to visitors by locating and sending the requested files.

After each request, the Web server logs the results of the exchange in a "log file." A typical log file is ASCII-based and contains information about which computer made the request, for which file and on which date.

These log files contain useful Web traffic information. By looking for multiple requests from the same computer during the same time frame, conclusions can be drawn about the total number of visitors and visits that were made to a site.

Data Collection through Packet Sniffing Technology

Packet sniffing technology has recently been introduced into the traffic analysis market which eliminates the need to collect and centralize log file data entirely. This technology gets its information directly from the TCP/IP packets that are sent to and from the Web server.

The advantage here is

- Data are collected in real time rather than being read in from a log file after the fact. This keeps the data warehouse up-to-date on a continuous basis.
- Data are continuously being read into the data warehouse rather than being collected from huge log files. This increases the data warehouse capacity.
- Companies with distributed Web servers can easily and automatically collect information in a centralized data warehouse. This solves the problem of collecting all the latest log files from sites located throughout the world.

Packet sniffing technology (Exhibit 40.2) watches network traffic going to and from the Web server and extracts information directly from the TCP/IP packets. The data collector must be installed on a computer located on the same network segment as the Web server that it is supposed to monitor, in order to "see" the network traffic as it goes by. Most packet sniffing tools are priced over $10,000.

DATA INTEGRATION

For Web mining applications, Web traffic data must be linked to other traditional business and marketing databases within the company. These databases might include E-commerce, profile, accounting, and customer registration databases, for example.

A typical way to perform this is through the computer IP address, as all requests to your Web server will include this information. Once you link an IP address to a particular company or person, you will be able to correlate future visits from the same IP address. This method is not perfect, however, as it is common for IP addresses to be shared among multiple users.

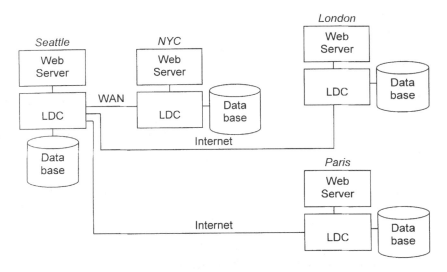

Exhibit 40.2. Packet sniffing allows for multiple distributed Web servers to send traffic information over the Internet to a centralized data warehouse. Here, Live Data Collectors (LDCs) are used in New York, London, and Paris to form a data warehouse in Seattle.

This is done by larger organizations, such as Microsoft, as well as by Internet Service Providers such as America Online.

A more accurate method of creating this link is through the use of "cookie" technology. This ensures that the same computer is connected to your site, independent of the IP address that is used to make the connection. Both cookies and computer IP addresses are covered in more detail in the next sections.

DATA REPORTING AND ANALYSIS

This is a typical area that Web traffic analysis tools overlook. It is important to keep in mind that the end goal of Web traffic analysis is to allow for online investments to be quickly analyzed and business decisions to be made. These reports, therefore, must include real data that can be acted on, rather than just reams of detailed technical information. If you can't easily analyze this information, put it in a presentation-quality format, and quickly get it to the right decision maker, then there isn't much purpose to collecting the information in the first place.

A quality Web traffic analysis package will include features like multilevel filtering, remote reporting, and will support multiple output formats.

597

These features make Web traffic information easy to obtain for everyone in the organization.

EXTENSIBLE AND PROGRAMMABLE

The final essential feature for Web traffic analysis tools is the ability to easily program the tool to integrate it with other Web applications you may have, or extend its capabilities. This is a key requirement for any organization that has had to wrestle with a tool that couldn't grow with the organization's needs and eventually needed to be replaced — an extremely painful and expensive process.

The ability to program a tool, through a standard scripting language, makes it easy to add custom functions. This might be used, for example, to remotely administer advertisements through user-created ASP pages.

Beyond programmability, the ability to add plug-ins is a requirement if you need to purchase or integrate your own custom functions. This can be used to extend data collection capabilities to other file types such as advertising servers and streaming-media logs, for example. It can also be used to create custom output types that might be necessary for proprietary data analysis systems.

Some Important Web Traffic Analysis Concepts

To better understand Web traffic analysis software and what visitor information can be obtained from a Website server, it is useful to have a basic understanding of how a Web server collects and logs visitor data.

To illustrate this, we will use the Marketwave Web server as an example. When visitors enters the URL "http://www.marketwave.com/default.htm" into a Web browser, they are asking the Marketwave Web server to send a file to them called default.htm which is located in the root directory. The Marketwave server responds to this request by sending the file and logging the results of the exchange in a server "log file."

In Marketwave's case, the default.htm file has references to 2 other HTML files and 23 other graphic files, which are needed to fully display the page. These files will also be automatically sent by the Marketwave Web server to the computer making the request and will be logged by adding lines to the Marketwave Web server log file. This means that a visit to the Marketwave home page will result in 26 total files (3 HTML files and 23 graphic files) being transferred and 26 lines being added to the server log files.

This example illustrates some key definitions that are imperative to understand when analyzing Websites:

- *Hit or Request.* A "Hit" or "Request" refers to an individual file request made to the Web server. This can be measured very precisely by simply counting the number of lines contained in the Web server log file. Measuring requests, however, is not a very accurate measure of Website popularity, as each visit to a site can generate large numbers of file requests. The way a Website is designed and the number of graphics it has will both significantly affect the number of file requests a site receives. In the example above, there are 26 requests.

- *Page View.* A better measurement of site traffic can be found by counting page views. A page view is simply the transfer of a specific HTML file. Page views can also be measured precisely by simply counting the number of requests for HTML files. Page views are a better measurement of Website popularity, but are still imprecise when multiple HTML files are required to display a page (when using frames on a site, for example). In the example above, there are three page views, due to the use of frames on the Marketwave home page.
- *Visitor.* A visitor is defined simply as a unique computer "IP address." This measurement is less precise, due to the fact that IP address are sometimes shared by many people, as is the case with large corporations and online service organizations. This precision can be improved by using other information as well, such as the browser type or a persistent cookie (more on this technology later). Visitors are a much better measurement of gross Website traffic than page views or requests. In the above example, there is only one visitor.
- *Visit.* A visit is a collection of requests that represent all the pages and graphics seen by a particular visitor at one time. The total number of visits is usually more than the total number of visitors because each visitor can visit the site more than once. Visits are more difficult to measure precisely, because there is no way to be certain that a series of requests actually belongs to the same person, or, for that matter, to the same person during the same visit. Measuring visits is also a good measure of gross Website traffic popularity. In the example above, there is only one visit.

It is important to realize that measuring Website popularity is an imperfect science. The art of good Web traffic analysis includes the ability to draw business conclusions using data that are imperfect. Having an understanding of the data, how they are collected, and what limitations exist, is key to drawing the proper business conclusions. As demonstrated in our example, one must understand and trade off between PRECISION (Requests and Page Views are precise but less accurate) and ACCURACY (Visits and Visitors are more accurate, but less precise) before drawing conclusions.

MORE DETAILS ON LOG FILES

This section is included to give you the detailed background needed to understand how Web traffic data are collected and analyzed. A typical Web server log file is ASCII based and contains information about which computer made the request, for which file. Additional information can be recorded including the date, the browser type, the requesting computer's IP address, any error codes, and the referring site, to name a few.

LOG FILE FORMATS

Different Web servers record this information in different log file formats. Most formats have similar information — they simply store it in different ways. Common log file formats include NCSA, W3C, Microsoft IIS, and O'Reilly. Here is a portion of a log file from the Marketwave Website. This file was created by Microsoft's Internet Information Server, Version 4.0, which stores its log output in W3C format.

This log file shows 54 log files entries (requests), 10 HTML file request (page views), and 1 unique IP address (visitor). Lets analyze it in more detail and explain each piece of the data to demonstrate what can be learned from this information.

The first thing to notice is that there are 18 unique fields (columns) in this log file, each representing a different piece of the Web traffic puzzle. In this respect, Web log analysis is a lot like music composition — there are only a few basic pieces of information (notes) to build from, yet by putting this information together in different ways, it is amazing what can be derived.

LOG FILE FIELD DEFINITIONS

The definitions of these fields are as follows:

- *Request date.* This is the date that the request was made of the server.
- *Request time.* This is the time the request was made of the server. Some Web servers will include the time, as well as the offset from Greenwich Mean Time. If you are analyzing data from multiple Websites located around the world, you will want to account for date and time-zone changes.
- *Request IP address.* This is the IP address of the computer that made the request. Every computer on the internet has a unique IP address so that other computers can find and connect to it. An IP address is made up of a series of four numbers separated by dots (206.129.192.10). Because humans have a difficult time remembering long strings of numbers, the Internet Domain Name System (DNS) was created, allowing these IP address to be associated with more readable domain names (e.g., marketwave.com).
- *Authenticated user name.* This is for sites that require a user to fill in a name and password before accessing a page. Whatever the visitor types in as their username is added to this field in the log file. This is typically used to restrict content on your site to only a few select users who know the password.

- *Server name.* This is the name of the server that responded to the request. It is useful for individually tracking multiple sites that are hosted on one computer (called virtual servers). For example, a publishing company might have a different Website for each of its magazines, but host them all through one computer and one Webmaster. The term virtual server comes from the fact that there is only one computer behind the scenes, but to the outside world there appears to be multiple "virtual" Websites, one for each magazine. This field allows the publishing company to analyze each site individually, as well as create aggregate statistics for the entire Web operation.
- *Computer name.* This is the name of the computer that responded to the request. It is useful for larger sites that require more than one computer to handle the number of requests being made (sites like Netscape, Microsoft, and Yahoo). This field could be used to calculate the "load" on each of the Web server computers and help determine when it is time to add additional resources or perform "load balancing" among the computers.
- *Server IP address.* This is the IP address of the server that responded to the request. In Marketwave's case, the Web server's IP address is 206.129.192.10, which is the computer hosting the Marketwave Website.
- *Method.* This is the method that was used to respond to the request. GET is the most common command to retrieve HTML documents. Another commands you may see include HEAD, which is used to retrieve just the header portion of a file, and POST, which passes data to the server directly without being displayed in the URL (usually for security reasons).
- *Requested file name.* This is the path and file name that was requested relative to its root directory location on the Web server.
- *Query string.* This field includes any "query" text that was entered along with the URL. For example, in the URL "http://www.marketwave.com/default.htm?MWUID=info@marketwave.com" the text after the ? (MWUID=info@marketwave.com) is referred to as a query string. You will notice these strings being used on dynamically generated sites like search engines and may sometimes see them embedded in hyperlinks to better track marketing campaigns. By intelligently using query strings, you can improve the trackability of your site.
- *Error code.* This is the Web server error response code. A "successful" request (meaning the visitor's browser loaded the entire HTML/GIF/JPEG, etc.) generates a response code of 200. Codes in the 200 and 300 range are generally OK, while codes in the 400 range are bad and in the 500 range are really bad. Server codes are grouped into ranges as follows:
  - 200 Range — successful delivery of the requested file
  - 300 Range — successful re-direct to another file

- 400 Range — failure to deliver the file
- 500 Range — server error
- *Bytes received.* This is the number of bytes of data that were received by the Web server.
- *Bytes sent.* This is the number of bytes of data that were transferred to the client during the visit.
- *Time taken.* This is the time the server took to respond to this request.
- *Version.* This is the format and version number of the request protocol, in this case HTTP, Version 1.0. A protocol is simply the "language" that computers use to communicate with one another. HTTP is the standard protocol of the Web and stands for HyperText Transfer Protocol. Another protocol you may run into is FTP, which stands for File Transfer Protocol.
- *Agent.* This is a code that identifies which browser and operating system made the request. "Mozilla/4.04" refers to the Netscape browser, and Win95 refers to the operating system, which in this case is Windows 95.
- *Cookie.* This is any cookie information from the browser (more on this later).
- *Referring page.* This is the page and site our visitor was on immediately prior to making this request. This is very useful information if we want to determine how visitors are finding our site.

INTERPRETING THE LOG FILE

Looking at our example log file tells us quite a bit about what is happening with our Website. The first line is a request for the Marketwave home page (default.htm). We notice a couple of useful pieces of information in this line, including the referring site (www.uu.se) and the referring page /software/analyzers/access-analyzers.html. This immediately tells us that this visitor came from a site based in Sweden (from the .se extension) and indicates that this site probably has a link to the Marketwave site on the /software/analyzers/access-analyzers.html page. If we go to this site ourselves, we find out that this is a university and the page in question has lots of links to different Web traffic analysis software packages.

The error code of 304 is also interesting. It tells us that this visitor already had access to cached version of our home page. Rather than send the file again, the Marketwave Web server responds with a status 304, indicating to the visitor's browser that it should go ahead and use the version of the page it already has.

The next 25 requests are all related to the home page. These are the additional 2 HTML frames and 23 graphics files (GIFs) that make up the remainder of the Marketwave home page. Notice that all of these requests resulted in an error code of 304, meaning that this visitor already had up-to-date copies of these files available. No files needed to be exchanged to display the Marketwave home page, frames, and graphics, as this computer has been to our site before and has our pages cached locally.

The next request is for a file called hitlist/live/default.htm. Odds are, this visitor clicked on a link to the Hit List Live page. This resulted in an error code 200, meaning the file was transferred and received successfully. The next 21 lines are the frames and graphics associated with the Hit List Live page. Notice that all of them were transferred successfully (error code 200) and the file sizes range from a few hundred Kbytes to almost 5000 Kbytes.

The next request was for a file called /downloads/frames-default, which is the Marketwave download page. Great! This prospect hit our home page, then hit our Hit List Live page, and then went right to the download page. You can't ask for much more than that from a Website!

As can be seen, a lot of information is available in the log file. Understanding how your Website is designed will really help with interpreting these data. If you didn't know that the Marketwave home page used frames, for example, you might think that the first three lines of the log file referenced three separate pages on the site. By knowing how the site is designed and looking at the data in the Web server log file, we can start to draw conclusions about visitors who can to the site.

Don't Waste Your Time Manually Interpreting Log Files!

Don't misinterpret the intent of the previous section! I highly recommend that you DON'T waste your time manually trying to interpret your log files. There are plenty of good software packages on the market that will do this job for you, including many of them that are offered free of charge. You can get a reasonably complete list by going to any search engine and looking for "Web traffic analysis" or "log file analysis."

The intent of the last section was to give you enough of an understanding of what is happening in the background of this process so that you can better interpret the results you get from these packages. As with any type of data analysis, understanding what is behind the data is a key part of interpreting the results. The more details you understand, the better choice you'll make when buying Web traffic analysis software and the better job you will do interpreting the results.

Getting Fancy with Web Traffic Information

The last section shows how simple conclusions can be drawn directly from the information in the log file. With this information alone we could easily calculate things like:

- Which browsers and operating systems are the most common (through the agent field)

- How many bytes are being transferred by the server (through the bytes sent field)
- Which files and directories are the most popular (through the requested file names)
- What sites are visitors coming from (through the referring pages)

But wait! With a little more work, there's still more information we can add to this analysis.

CONVERTING IP ADDRESSES BACK TO DOMAIN NAMES

We know this particular visitor was using a computer connected to the internet with IP address 193.237.55.144. Remember that every IP address has a corresponding domain name associated with it and these are linked through the Domain Name System (DNS). When a visitor entered www.marketwave.com into their browser, it was the DNS system that converted this name into the appropriate IP address (206.129.192.10) so that the computers could connect with each other. We can use the DNS system in reverse (called a reverse DNS lookup) to convert our mystery visitor's IP address back into a domain name. In this case, after doing a reverse DNS lookup, we find that the IP address 193.237.55.144 belongs to the domain issel.demon.co.uk. With this information we surmise that our visitor was using a computer owned by a company name Issel (due to the first part of the domain name) which is based in the U.K. (due to the .uk extension in the domain name).

You can either have your Web server perform this DNS conversion for you, or have your Web traffic analysis software do it. I generally recommend that you have your Web traffic analysis software do it, so you don't slow your Web server with this task. In addition, if someone else hosts your site, you may not have a choice in the matter, as most service providers don't want to slow their servers down to perform reverse DNS lookups. That's OK, simply get the log files from your provider and have your Web traffic analysis software do it for you.

CONVERTING FILE NAMES TO PAGE TITLES

A well-designed site will have a title (using the TITLE HTML keyword) for every page on the site. Rather than simply report the file names that were requested, we can easily look at these files and determine the corresponding page names. In general, page names are much more human-friendly in terms of communicating information. By simply extracting the page names from the files that are listed in our Web server logs, we can end up with a report that contains actual page names, rather than simply the file names themselves.

CALCULATING VISITORS AND VISITS

If we make a simple assumption that any log file entry with same IP address and same browser is probably the same visitor, we can easily calculate the number of visitors on our site. Note that this assumption is not perfect, as it is certainly possible that two different visitors happen to have the same IP address and browser type (from an online service provider for example). In general, however, this is unlikely to happen enough to significantly change the results of your analysis.

We can also calculate the number of visits to the site by assuming that if we don't see any more requests from that same visitor in 30 minutes, that the visit has ended. If we then see that same IP address and browser sometime in the future, we can assume that the same visitor is back for a second visit.

PATH ANALYSIS

By linking log file entries and then sorting by time and date, we can also start to see the path that a visitor took through the site. This is what we did in our example above. The log file shown only included requests from IP address 193.237.55.144 on 7/19/98. If we did this for each individual visitor, we would be able to calculate the most popular paths taken through the site as a whole.

GROUPING INFORMATION

By grouping information together, we can start to draw conclusions. For example, if we group all Netscape Browser and all Microsoft Browser information together we could calculate which company's browser was the more popular on our site. Using this same technique with referrer information, and looking for any referring URL with the word "Yahoo" in it, we could see how many of our visitors came from Yahoo as a whole.

COUNTRIES

By looking at the extensions on our visitors domain names, we can also estimate where in the world our visitors are coming from. Example extensions include:

.ca — Canada
.au — Australia
.se — Sweden
.uk — United Kingdom

FILTERING INFORMATION

By filtering information, we can answer very specific questions about the site. For example, to calculate how many visitors we got from Microsoft this week, we would only look at information from this week, and only look at visitors that have the word "Microsoft" contained in their domain name. This could be compared to our overall traffic to determine what percentage of our visitors presumably work for Microsoft.

CORRELATING INFORMATION

By correlating and cross-tabbing information, we can answer questions like, "Of the visitors I get from Germany, how many of them use Microsoft Windows 98 as their operating system?" This kind of detailed information can be useful for both site management and marketing segmentation purposes.

QUERY STRING PARSING

A piece of information we have glossed over is the query string field, which was blank in our example above. Query strings are typically used on database-driven sites and consist of all of the data at the end of a URL (usually delimited with a "?"). For example, the following referring URL is from Yahoo: http://search.yahoo.com/bin/search?p=Web+Traffic+Analysis.

By looking at the data after the "?" we see that this visitor searched for "Web Traffic Analysis" on Yahoo before coming to our site. Yahoo encodes this information with a query parameter called "p" and separates each search keyword with the "+" character. In this example, "p" is called the query parameter and "Web," "Traffic," and "Analysis" are each referred to as parameter values.

This information would normally be stored via the query field in the log file, and by looking at it in detail we can draw conclusions about what our visitors was searching for before hitting our site. This is useful information when trying to design the site to come up higher on the list of search engines, or when trying to determine what visitors are looking for before coming to our site.

VIRTUAL SERVERS

If you host multiple sites, another useful piece of information is contained in the site name field. By using this information intelligently, we could perform a separate analysis for each of the sites that you host. This would tell you which of your sites is responsible for the most traffic.

ADDING COOKIES INTO THE PICTURE

Another field we glossed over was the cookie field, which is a topic that has received much attention and debate in the press. Up to this point, we have not actually been tracking people, but are instead tracking Internet (IP) addresses as they come to our site. Cookies were invented to attempt to do a better job of tracking people, rather than simply IP addresses.

This technology was developed by Netscape and is really pretty ingenious. A cookie is merely a unique identifying code that the Web server gives to the browser to store locally on the hard drive during the first visit to the site. The intent of a cookie is to uniquely identify visitors as they come to the site.

Cookies benefit Website developers by making individual "requests" much more trackable, which results in a greater understanding on how the site is being used and, therefore, a better Website design. Cookies also benefit visitors by allowing Websites to "recognize" repeat visitors. For example, Amazon.com uses cookies to enable their "one-click" book ordering. Since the company already has your mailing address and credit card on file, they don't make you reenter all of this information to complete the transaction. It is important to note that the cookie did not obtain this mailing or credit card information. This information was collected in some other way, typically by the visitor entering it directly into a form contained on the site. The cookie merely confirms that the same computer is back during the next visit to the site.

Unfortunately, cookies remain a misunderstood and controversial topic. Contrary to many beliefs, a cookie is not an executable program, so it can't format your hard drive or steal private information from you (note that languages like Java CAN do either of these things, but for some reason Java doesn't get the negative "security" press that cookies do). The second objection regarding cookies is that some people feel that it is a violation of their resources to be forced to store information on their computers for the benefit of the Website's owner. In reality, the amount of disk space that a cookie takes up is trivial. Regardless of how you feel about cookies, modern browsers all have the ability to turn this feature off and not accept cookies.

If your site uses cookies, this information will show up in the cookie field of the log file and can be used by your Web traffic analysis software to do a better job of tracking repeat visitors.

Now comes the time to put all this log file information together into a readable report that we can draw conclusions from. Next is an example report showing the types of information that can be obtained from simply running your log files through a typical Web traffic analysis program.

WEB MINING — GOING BEYOND WEB SERVER LOG FILES

As mentioned at the beginning of this chapter, Web mining can be used to incorporate other information along with Web server log files into your analysis. This allows for information to be correlated to Web browsing behavior, such as accounting, profile, demographic, and psychographic information. Complex questions like the following, therefore, can be addressed:

- Of the people that hit our Website, how many purchased something?
- Which advertising campaigns resulted in the most purchases (not just "hits")?
- Do my Web visitors fit a certain profile? Can I use this for segmenting my market?

Exhibit 40.3. A Worldwide Distribution Report of Top Sales Prospects Who Hit the Website Yesterday (Jana Winslow — VP, Domestic Sales)

Company	Contact	E-mail	Telephone	Visits
Microsoft	Seth Longo	Sethl@microsoft.com	206-962-1200	3
Tango Designs	Suzanne Gayaldo	Sgayaldo@dirk.tango.net	509-323-6027	3
Intel	Sanford Arnold	Sa@intel.com	212-865-8584	2
Lucent	Larry Rubin	Larry_rubin@lucent.com	201-386-4200	2
Volvo	Yasim Kinneer	Ykinner@vd.volvo.se	206-765-1008	2
ESPN	Michael Louis	Orioles@espn.com	203-585-2000	1
USDA	Tom Bianchi	Tommyb@dc.usda.gov	202-548-2435	1
Apple	Mark Sojic	Mark@apple.com	301-255-7500	1

Note: This information has been generated by matching Web traffic data stored in the Hit List database with information stored in the Marketwave customer registration database.

As an example of this technology in action, we will again use the Marketwave Website (www.marketwave.com). When you download a Hit List product from our Website, we ask you to register it. During this registration process we ask you for information including your name, company, phone number, e-mail address, and state/country. This information (along with your IP address, the date, and the product you downloaded) is automatically stored in a contact management software package. All Marketwave personnel use this centralized database to handle any interactions we have with you. This includes our sales, marketing, public relations, and support departments.

Our contact management database is linked to the Hit List Web traffic database through "DataLink" technology using your computer's IP address as the key field. Combining Hit List information with sales and marketing data opens up a whole realm of one-to-one marketing possibilities. In our case, every time we see your computer (the same IP address) on our site, we can pull up your registration information and take appropriate action. Often, this action is personalized to your particular situation.

One of the first things we do with the information we collect from you is to sort it by territory and send it to our worldwide distribution network (Exhibit 40.3). On a daily basis, we automatically e-mail a report to the appropriate Marketwave personnel. This report shows Web activity for the previous day, as well as product downloads. We sort these by territory to make it easy for our territory managers to personally follow up on the leads in their area. We also link our database of actual contact names and phone numbers into the report, rather than only including domain names which, by themselves, aren't as useful to our distribution channel.

TRACKING E-BUSINESS SALES

Marketwave recently added the ability to order Hit List directly from our Website using a credit card. Our marketing department and management staff now receive a daily report with e-business information in DOLLARS (not just hits, page views, or visits). This is accomplished by linking to our e-business database. The report shows how many online sales were made the previous day and how many dollars were involved. More importantly, we also report on the number of sales that were not completed and who they were. This helps us track down prospects who had trouble with the online ordering process, as well as those who simply need a bit more information before making a purchase decision.

The Way We Manage Our E-Mail Campaigns

When we release new product versions, we first go back and market to our existing installed base of users. Generally, this is done through e-mail. In this e-mail, we add a link that looks something like: http://www.marketwave.com/default.htm?CAMPAIGN=date&MWUID=email.

The query string characters you see in this URL after the "?" are for tracking purposes. In this case, the campaign you are responding to (CAMPAIGN) is filled in with today's date and your Marketwave User ID (MWUID) is your e-mail address. When people click on this URL, these parameters end up in the query field of the log file. This means that we cannot only find out how many visitors we got as a result of our marketing efforts (through the CAMPAIGN parameter), but we can also tell who those visitors were (through the MWUID parameter).

Measuring Marketwave Print Advertising

In addition, Marketwave directs visitors to our site through print advertising campaigns. These ads point people to our Website for more information on our product and free evaluation software. The URLs we give in our print ads usually look something like: http://www.marketwave.com/adname.

This allows us to measure how many people responded to the campaign, by simply looking for how many people came from this URL. For example, by adding an entry page filter set to "adname*" to any of our reports, we would be able to see how many visitors we had to the site that clicked on the above URL.

I suggest keeping "adname" to just a few characters, as many people won't type long strings of text into their browsers. Also, like most marketing information, the data we get are not perfect. Many of our visitors will not type the "/adname" portion of the URL into their browser, so your actual response rate is probably higher than what is reported through your Web traffic analysis software.

Measuring Marketwave Banner Advertising

Marketwave also is currently running multiple banner advertising campaigns. We also use query strings to track these. When we submit the ads to the sites we want to run them on, we also submit click-through URLs for each ad that look something like these:

http://www.marketwave.com/default.htm?AdName=ad1&
    AdSource=sitename1
http://www.marketwave.com/default.htm?AdName=ad2&
    AdSource=sitename1
http://www.marketwave.com/default.htm?AdName=ad2&
    AdSource=sitename2

We then run reports filtering on AdName as the query parameter when we want to know how each ad is doing relative to the other (ad1 vs. ad2). To compare our ad sites, we use filters that look for different AdSource as the query parameter (sitename1 vs. sitename2). These data not only are used to make future advertising decisions, but also to check the validity of the data we get from the sites we choose to do business with.

Measuring Return on Investment

The ultimate measure of an advertising campaign is return on investment. On a periodic basis, we report the cost of each of our ad campaigns and impressions. This is then compared to our e-business database to calculate a total return for any particular campaign.

We then shift our promotional budget towards those ad campaigns that perform the best for us — in dollars returned, not visitors returned. As you may already suspect, it is not always true that the least advertising CPM (cost per thousand impressions) is the best value.

OTHER EXAMPLES OF WEB MINING TECHNOLOGY

This section demonstrates some other real-world applications that Web mining technology is currently being used for within other major corporations.

Qualifying Leads

Web mining can be used to not only collect and distribute leads, but also qualify them as well. For example, imagine using the Dun and Bradstreet SIC database to integrate corporate information along with your Web traffic information. Leads could be sorted by territory, then by company size, and distributed worldwide to the proper sales territory. This

Exhibit 40.4. Most Popular Pages by SIC Code

Page Name	SIC Code	Total Requests
Home Page.htm	3454 — Manufacturing	4090
	5466 — Software	3000
	8745 — Real Estate	3500
Pricing Page.htm	0343 — Construction	10,057
	2354 — Insurance	1300
Ordering Page.htm	6404 — Banking	3700
	2111 — Manufacturing	2300
Reseller Page.htm	9999 — Financial Services	3516
	6854 — Telecommunication	5400

Note: Shows which pages are most commonly requested by companies with the following SIC codes and SIC descriptions.

process can be completely automated, distributing Web leads as often as you would like.

In addition, these data can be used in a marketing report showing what pages are the most popular by industry (SIC code), as shown in Exhibit 40.4. This information could then be used to better target site information to particular industries.

Performing Marketing Segmentation

When combined with a profiling system, Web mining can be used to perform marketing segmentation. This allows Web marketers to better target campaigns and messages to each target group.

For example, an online music company using a profiling system could easily create reports detailing the differences in browsing behavior based on age ranges. They might find that most of their actual purchasers are in their twenties (Exhibit 40.5). An understanding of what information was attractive to other visitors would be invaluable in designing the Website to appeal to a wider audience. This information could then be used to expand content and quickly direct visitors to the right place.

FEATURES USERS LOOK FOR IN WEB TRAFFIC ANALYSIS TOOLS

If you are in the market for a good Web traffic analysis software package, this section covers specific features you should consider when comparing tools.

Basic Log Analysis Features (The Basic Stuff)

Product Architecture. We start with product architecture, as it is probably the single biggest difference in the leading Web traffic analysis tools

Exhibit 40.5. Report Showing Browsing Profiles by Age Range Per Page

Page Name	Age range	Requests
Home Page	0:9	1
	10:19	3
	20:29	23
	30:39	13
	40:49	11
	50:59	8
	60:69	3
Product Page	0:9	1
	10:19	4

Note: Shows the age ranges, in 10-year increments, of visitors to each page.

and significantly impacts what can be done with the product. Some tools parse log file information directly into memory and then produce reports, all in one step. Others, first create a database of Web traffic information, then use this database to create Web traffic reports.

The main advantage of the "parsing" approach is speed for the *first* report, as writing data to a database is a step that is completely avoided. The main disadvantage of this approach is flexibility. Every change you need to make to a report (like a simple filter or query) will require that you reread all the log files and recreate a report from scratch. Not only does this take time, but it also eliminates the possibility of using the product with extremely high-traffic sites.

The main advantage to the database approach is that once a database has been formed, detailed reports can be generated by making simple queries to this database. In addition, having these data available is *fundamental* to the ability to perform one-to-one marketing and Web mining. Using a standard database opens up a realm of possibilities to effectively data mine your Web traffic information. This allows Web visitation information to be integrated into the rest of your organization, rather than having Web traffic analysis be its own island of information within your company.

Reporting Speed. When comparing Web traffic analysis tools for speed, I have two suggestions:

1. Make sure you are comparing "apples to apples." Some products don't store their results in a database and don't perform IP address lookups. For an "apples-to-apples" comparison, make sure you store the results and turn on IP-lookup capability, if it is available.
2. Make sure you compare multiple reporting sessions rather than simply running one report. Products that parse log files into memory

will be faster on the first pass, as they don't store any data, so save the time of this step. The downside to this is that a *second* report with a simple change (like a filter or query) will require that you re-read all the log files and recreate the report from scratch.

Predefined Reports/Elements. This is the No. 1 requested feature by users — predefined reports that already perform the most common analysis tasks. Look for products that already include reports on advertising, marketing, technical analysis, proxy server, long-term trends, virtual server, and management summaries.

Flexible Filtering. Look for products that make it easy to get more detailed information, usually through the use of filters. Overview reports are fine, but you will soon find yourself asking for more detailed data, like how many visitors am I getting from each of the search engines? Sophisticated filtering includes the ability to apply filters to individual reports and individual reporting elements.

Easy Creation of New Reports and Customization of Existing Reports. Look for products that are easy to use and are intuitive, especially when creating your own reports. You want to spend your time analyzing the data, not creating the report.

Report Output in Common Formats Like HTML, ASCII, CSV, Word Processor and Spreadsheet Formats. Look for a product that produces reports in the formats you need and use. Another nice feature is the ability to automatically post reports on a network or Website.

Support for Multiple Web Servers. Make sure the product reads and understands all of the Web server formats you use in your organization. Often companies will have multiple formats around the world that will need to be combined for reporting purposes.

Automated Event Scheduling. Look for a solution that lets you automate the creation and distribution of reports. For example, you may want a daily report to be created every night and automatically e-mailed to your sales force

Automatic LAN and FTP Retrieval of Compressed Log Files. If you have Website located remotely, look for a product that can automatically retrieve compressed log files from any FTP site or LAN.

Language Manager for Customization. Look for support for foreign language as well as support for company-specific terminology.

Advanced Log Analysis Features (The Fancy Stuff)

Search-Engine Keyword Reporting. Look for software that intelligently uses the query string information. This is useful for tracking marketing campaigns, as well as understanding what visitors are searching for both on and off your site.

Advertising Banner Campaign Analysis

If you run advertising campaigns, look for the ability to track them through measurement of impressions and click-through rates. In addition, you may consider a package that can link to your accounting database, so that results can be measured in terms of expenses and revenues generated, as opposed to just "Hits."

Virtual Server Reporting. If you run multiple sites, look for a package that can report on individual (real or virtual) servers separately. This allows you to understand how each server and site is doing.

Detailed Visitor Path Analysis. Some packages include the ability to analyze the most common paths that visitors take through the site. This is useful for optimizing the site to direct visitors towards certain areas, such as the ordering page or the technical support page.

Link Checking Capability. Web traffic analysis can highlight any error or broken links that visitors are encountering. This is useful for Webmasters to understand the details of what errors users are encountering on the site.

Remote Reporting with Security Manager. Remote reporting allows any authorized user to obtain Web traffic information with nothing more than an Internet connection and browser. This makes it easy to get data to the people who need it, without having to install custom software or design individual reports for them. Making Web traffic data easily accessible to the nontechnical business specialists will improve an organization's efficiency in a distributed decision-making environment.

Database-Driven Site/Query Reporting. If you run a database-driven site, you will need the ability to parse your query strings into the parameters and values that are called from the integrated database. When combined with DataLink, query parsing results of dynamic site activity can be linked back to tables within the actual dynamic site generator to provide more meaningful information, such as a page title or content description.

Custom Columns and Calculations Including User-Defined Variables and Formatting. Much like a spreadsheet, look for the ability to add a column to any report table with custom calculations and formatting. This could be used by an ISP, for example, to calculate customer bills based on bytes transferred and display the result in dollars. When combined with DataLink, billing rates could even be read from another database.

Web Mining Features (The Really Fancy Stuff)

Plug-In Architecture for Extendibility. If you have custom needs, you should look for the ability to extend the software to perform the tasks you wish.

Web Mining for Combining Web Log Data with Information from Other E-Business Databases. This means that Web traffic information does not have to be yet another island of data within your organization. For example, reports can incorporate detailed customer information like real names, e-mail addresses, and phone numbers. For complex users, look for SQL statement support for ultimate information flexibility. This allows more complex questions to be answered based on Dollars and ROI, rather than just Hits and Visits.

Integrated Programming Language and Editor. Many companies will need the ability to customize their Web traffic analysis tool to meet specific needs or integrate with other e-business applications. Look for extendability through a standard programming language such as Visual Basic and Visual C++.

Remote Administration from Any Connected Computer. If you work for a larger organization, consider the ability to administer your software from any network connection. This makes maintenance and administration in distributed environments extremely easy from any location.

Real-Time Data Collection Via TCP/IP Packet Sniffing and Web Server Plug-Ins. Packet sniffing eliminates the need to collect and manage multiple distributed server log files by automatically collecting traffic information in real time directly from the TCP/IP network packets. The resulting database is always up-to-date and available for reporting. The benefit here is not only the real-time aspects of data reporting, but also the complete elimination of log file administration. This feature is especially useful for companies with multiple Websites located throughout the world. Packet sniffing allows data to be collected and stored in a centralized data warehouse, completely automatically and in the background.

CONCLUSION

The Internet is the most significant technology the world has seen since the computer and has the potential to revolutionize business and marketing techniques. If you are serious about your online investment, the first step is to get a better understanding about who is visiting your site and what they are looking for.

Knowing this information allows you to make better business decisions by catering to your best customers and delivering the information they are looking for. With today's powerful Web traffic analysis software, this analysis can be performed easily and inexpensively.

Author's Bio

Michael McClure *is currently Vice President of Marketing at Marketwave Corporation, a leader in the Web traffic analysis industry. He is responsible for all aspects of the Hit List product line including pricing, promotion, distribution, and future product development.*

Prior to joining Marketwave, McClure was Vice President of Marketing at Chronology Corporation, a Redmond, WA-based company and focused on electronic design automation software. Before that, he was Vice President of Strategic Development at Virtual Vision, a manufacturer of virtual head-mounted displays. McClure has also held senior marketing positions at Data I/O and Honeywell Corporations.

McClure received his MBA degree from the Stanford School of Business with concentrations in entrepreneurship and marketing. He also holds a BSEE degree from the University of Washington. In his spare time McClure enjoys hiking, biking, softball, and spending time with his kids. His e-mail address is mikem@marketwave.com.

Chapter 41

Connecting Your LAN to the Internet: Understanding Network Address Translators (NATs) Vs. Proxies

Richard Lamb

THE WEALTH OF RESOURCES AVAILABLE ON THE INTERNET today make it necessary for almost any business to provide access to them for their personnel. These resources may range from simple package tracking information to specific data available from government and corporate sites. To offer this connectivity to your employees requires that your Local Area Network (LAN) be connected to the Internet in some fashion.

This can be accomplished in a number of ways. The first and most general approach is to make your LAN a part of the Internet by allocating a unique Internet address (IP address) for every PC or workstation in your company and then connecting your internal network to the Internet via a general purpose router. Although viable and useful for certain situations, this approach has two major drawbacks for the vast majority of companies. The first drawback is security. With every node fully "visible" to the Internet (Net) at large, it becomes a trivial matter for a hacker to access company records that may reside, even temporarily, on a machine. It is even easier for the malicious hacker to simply disable or render useless the Internet-connected machine by overwhelming it with carefully crafted

0-8493-9987-4/00/$0.00+$.50
© 2000 by CRC Press LLC

traffic patterns. The second drawback is a bit more subtle, but equally problematic — IP address management. Every time a machine is moved, replaced, or added, the network administrator must ensure that duplicate addresses do not get assigned and that there are a sufficient number of them to cover all the machines. Since these machines are full members of the Internet, the choice and availability of these addresses is not under the control of the company but rather by a centralized authority called the InterNic. The InterNic is a single company located near Washington, D.C. that manages all the IP addresses on the Net. Typically, you will make address requests to your Internet Service Provider (ISP), but in the end it is this organization that decides who get which addresses and how many.

Although both of these drawbacks can be overcome, the security issue with a firewall and the address management issue with a cooperative ISP and some tools (DHCP — an IP management protocol),[1] they require a level of expertise and effort that may not be practical for most businesses. This led network designers to develop another method of connecting corporate LANs to the Net, one that addressed both of these drawbacks in one step. The method, which has been in engineering environments in some form or another since 1993, has in recent times been termed Network Address Translation or NAT.

In this chapter we are admittedly focusing on machines that have gained widespread popularity such as the PC and MAC. The operating systems that run on these machines almost universally support DHCP and can derive their IP configuration from a DHCP Server. There are some special cases of devices that may not (or you would like not) use DHCP. In these cases you may statically assign the information to these units without affecting NAT operation. In a mixed environment you may want to exclude the assigned IP addresses from the pool assigned on the NAT/DHCP server to avoid conflicts.

As the name suggests a NAT simply translates all the IP addresses used on your internal network or LAN into different IP addresses on the Internet. This simplifies the IP management problem by allowing the Network Administrator to choose ANY IP address. Since the internal IP addresses are not visible to the Internet (i.e., the core routers which control the flow of all traffic on the Internet do not have a route to them), a hacker cannot send data and, therefore, cannot gain access to any of the machines connected to your LAN. Meanwhile, your personnel may still access the resources on the Internet since his/her packets will get rewritten by the NAT to appear as if they came from the company's valid Internet address. As described below, products that modify this NAT technology and supplement it with some IP management tools result in a solution that all but eliminates the drawbacks and maintenance issues associated with connecting to the Internet.

Exhibit 41.1. TCP/UDP/IP Protocol Stack

Application Layer — Web, E-Mail, FTP, Telnet, VideoConferencing Data
TCP or UDP Header — from and to Port Number
IP Header — from and to Internet Address

$\rightarrow$ Ethernet, PPP (Dial-Up), or Other Media Access Layer Header

Start of Packet

NAT DESCRIPTION

In recent times the popularity of the NAT has equaled or exceeded that of other traditional methods of connecting LANs to the Internet. The NAT is an Internet connection solution that was designed from the ground up to address the drawbacks of such a connection. Many of the traditional approaches to solving the security and management problems, such as filtering routers and proxy servers, were implemented as modifications of existing products.

The NAT uses the simple concept of address translation to protect and simplify connecting multiple computers on a LAN to the Internet by hiding the address of the internal machines. It does this by rewriting the addresses in the header of each outgoing (LAN to Internet) packet to reflect a new address and keeping track of this change so that it may route incoming packets back to the correct machine. Since the networking protocol used on the Internet is exclusively TCP/IP, the address we are referring to is found in the IP portion of the packet (Exhibit 41.1).

To maintain data integrity, every packet has a checksum which will alert to an error if any portion of the packet has been corrupted or modified. Therefore, the NAT must recompute the checksum after address modification AND test the incoming checksum for every packet that it handles. It is imperative that the incoming packet be checked since not doing so might cause a corrupted or illicitly modified packet to be considered good by all subsequent devices. This process is applied to packets traveling in both directions, to and from the LAN, and also affects the checksum component of the TCP and UDP headers. Algorithms have been developed to perform the checksum modification in an efficient manner so as to avoid full recalculations for every packet. This maintains the throughput, and thus is one of the key advantages of the NAT implementation over the Proxy (see Proxy Description).

Since each new machine requires a new (fake) internal address as well as a new (real) external one, various methods were developed to make these selections from a pool of addresses initially configured for the NAT. The simplest method is to statically assign on a one-to-one basis an internal address to the external address. For example, 24.128.50.48 (a real address on the Net) might be associated with 192.168.1.1. When the internal machine with the single address 192.168.1.1 attempts to connect to some outside resource such a as a Website, its packet first hits the internal side of the NAT, which, for example, has the address of 192.168.1.2.

The choice of internal IP addresses for use with a NAT is completely up to the network administrator; however, there is the pathological case in which the IP addresses chosen may correspond to servers on the Internet to which you may want access. In this case, since the address of the external server and the address of some node on your internal network are the same, any attempt to access the external server connects you to this local node. All other sites shall be fine, it will just be this one. To avoid this problem the InterNic has set aside a generous block of addresses that are guaranteed not to be found on the Internet and, therefore, can be safely used on your LAN. These numbers[2] are displayed in Exhibit 41.2.

The NAT (Exhibit 41.3) uses the source address of the packet to look up what its external source address should be and finds 24.128.50.48. It replaces the source IP address with this, corrects the checksums, then sends the packet out its external side which would have as one of its many addresses (often referred to as multihoming) 24.128.50.48. When the remote Web server replies to this packet, it thinks it came from 24.128.50.48 and therefore sends the reply with destination address 24.128.50.48. The Internet and its cooperating components routes this packet faithfully back to the external interface of our NAT. It then looks up the destination address of this packet in its table and finds 192.168.1.1. The NAT replaces the destination address in the IP header with this, corrects the checksums, and sends the packet out the internal interface. Subsequent packets follow the same path. If another machine were added to the internal network with an address of 192.168.1.3, another external address would have to be also allocated, 24.128.50.49. The external interface of the NAT would now have both 24.128.50.48 and 24.128.50.49 as addresses and would respond to both.

Processing for the 192.168.1.3 machine would be the same as for the first one and may happen simultaneously. This basic NAT operation is what was described in early drafts by the Internet Engineering Task Force (IETF) in

---

Exhibit 41.2. Block of Addresses which Can be Used for LANs

Characteristic	Proxy	NAT
Web page caching	Yes	No
Transparent to clients	No	Yes
Throughput	WAN speeds	LAN speeds
Maximum client count	500	5000

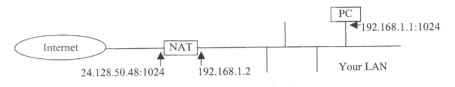

Exhibit 41.3. NAT example.

its recommendations.[3] The key fact to note here is that the NAT operations are COMPLETELY invisible to the Internet. There is no way for the outside world to determine what your internal IP address is or that any modifications were ever performed on the packet. This effect is important for two reasons: (1) it protects your internal network from attack and (2) it allows the internal machine to have any address so long as it appears in the NAT's translation table. In an efficiently designed NAT implementation, the replace and correct operations are performed in place, i.e., data are never copied from one buffer to another, further enhancing the throughput of NAT technology.

Now that basic NAT operations have been explained, let's look at another method for associating internal and external addresses, namely dynamic. In this case, when an internal machine attempts to connect to an external resource, i.e., sends a packet, the NAT automatically creates an association in its translation table using the source address of the original packet and the next free external address it can obtain from the pool (or range) of address it was configured with. This simplifies NAT configuration and when supplemented with a time-out or aging mechanism for table entries, permits the external addresses to be shared by a larger number of internal addresses or machines. This is based on the assumption than not all machines will be actively using the Internet at the same time. The ability to share addresses is another critical component of a NAT implementation. Since external real IP addresses are limited and have, if not a specific dollar value, a management and maintenance cost associated with them, it is important to conserve and minimize the number of these used. Sharing real addresses using a NAT helps achieve this goal.

Dynamically sharing addresses is one way to conserve addresses on the Internet; however, in many cases your ISP may severely limit the number of addresses you may use. This is often the case for many of the new low-cost, high-speed access technologies such as Cable Modems, ADSL, or Satellite. More importantly, it is often difficult to control user access patterns to the Internet to assure the idle periods for the dynamic approach described above to work, particularly in medium to larger organizations. For this reason, NAT manufacturers have developed another approach referred to as Port Address Translation or PAT. Versions of this have been available since

1994 under various names. Even the term "Proxy" has been used to describe it in an effort to piggyback on the name recognition of the older, but well-known capabilities these technologies bring to networking.

PAT (Exhibit 41.4) allows for a much greater number of internal machines to share limited external IP addresses. In fact, a single real IP address can theoretically be shared among 64,000 machines. As the name suggests, PAT accomplishes this feat by controlling and modifying elements in the next layer of the packet, namely, TCP and UDP port numbers. Both IP addresses (source and destination) and TCP/UDP ports (source and destination) are modified and the final checksum appropriately (and efficiently) corrected. The 64,000 theoretical limit comes from the fact that the port number in the TCP and UDP headers is encoded as a 16-bit number and, therefore, ranges from 0 to $2^{16} - 1$. A unique endpoint in a TCP/UDP/IP protocol-based network is defined by IP address and port number; therefore for a single IP address there are only 64,000 endpoints (often referred to as sockets) for each protocol (TCP or UDP) that can be unambiguously distinguished from each other. Tracing the life of a packet using a PAT capable NAT we find the following scenario.

When an internal machine with IP address 192.168.1.1 attempts to connect to an external resource, say a Web server, it sends a TCP packet to the NAT. Assuming we have only one real IP address (such as 24.128.50.48) to share among all internal machines, the NAT finds the next unused TCP port number (say 2001) associated with the real IP address. Then an association is created (on the fly) in the NAT table consisting of this port number (2001), the source IP address of the packet (192.168.1.1), and the source TCP port number (say 1024) of the packet. The source IP address is changed to the real one (24.128.50.48), the source TCP port number is changed to the unused one (2001), the checksums for IP and TCP headers are corrected, and packet is sent through the external side of the NAT into the Internet. When the reply returns, it will be addressed to the external interface IP address 24.128.50.48 and have a destination TCP port number 2001. The NAT looks up 2001 in its table and finds IP address 192.168.1.1 and port 1024. Using this information it replaces the destination address and destination TCP port number, recalculates the IP and TCP checksums, and sends the packet out the internal interface to the internal machine that

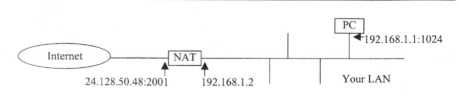

Exhibit 41.4. PAT example.

initiated the connection. Subsequent packets follow the same path, unbeknownst to the Internet at large or to the LAN. By way of extension, other internal machines or additional connections from this same machine will simply take up additional external port numbers and slots in the NAT table.

As in the dynamic method described previously, some form of aging mechanism must be imposed on the NAT table to ensure that slots (memory) will be available for new connections and machines. Given the large number of slots available (64,000), the chances of running out of slots before any age themselves out (via simple time-out), is unlikely for a reasonable number of machines. An ancillary feature that some NAT/PAT implementation have to further maintain the table is the ability to inspect the flag element of TCP packets. If the TCP flag indicates that a connection will be closed, the slot in the table may be freed or at least aged out faster. This is easily accommodated in the NAT implementation since TCP headers are already being inspected for PAT. Unfortunately, UDP packets have no such element and, therefore, their slots must be aged using standard time-out techniques. Studies have shown that the average peak number of simultaneous connections per machines is less than 10, hence a conservative estimate for the number of machines that a NAT should be able to support per real IP address would be 5000.

Depending on implementation details, hardware limitations, and most importantly the bandwidth of your WAN connection to the outside world, the maximum number of nodes you choose to connect may differ. Many small desktop NAT/PAT implementations simply do not have the memory and horsepower to provide unhindered access to the Net for this many machines, while most medium to large corporate sites with large internal networks and standard platform-based NAT implementations will have no degradation in performance. A draft of an updated IETF NAT document[4] includes more information on PAT.

As demands on the Network and Internet have increased, NAT technology has progressed. With each new Internet application, additional functionality, which is often difficult to implement in a Proxy, can always be supported, often with little or no modification, in a NAT implementation. This is due to that fact that the whole network stack is accessible to the NAT from the MAC (Ethernet) layer through the application layer. To take advantage of its location in the networking stack, a few advanced NATs have made use of information from all layers and coined the name Stateful Multilayer Packet Inspection. Here, instead of simply modifying the IP and TCP/UDP headers of a packet, the application portion of the packet may also be inspected and modified. Most advanced implementations use this to control usage patterns for their employees and to further shape traffic.

Typical examples include URL blocking which controls which sites a user may or may not access from the corporate LAN, and prioritization which attempts to offer the WAN bandwidth to critical applications first. However, there are a growing number of new applications, as well as a few old ones such as FTP, that require multiple simultaneous connections through the Internet. Examples of this are videoconferencing, network games (a growing industry at time of writing), chat, and virtual private networking, to name a few. To retain the simple transparent nature of a NAT for these applications, a good NAT implementation must also support these by inspecting and possibly rewriting application information.

Oftentimes this is information concerning the other simultaneous connections for this application which must be kept consistent with all the address and port translations going on. Doing this requires intimate knowledge of the application protocols and in some cases, such as standards-based videoconferencing,[5,6] requires partial implementation of the application itself. Currently most of this support is done in proprietary circles, however with NAT deployment on the rise, IETF members, as well as application vendors, are describing and implementing new protocols that are more aware of the Internet environment in which they operate and, consequently, will often just work out of the box in a NAT-connected network.[7]

An example of an application that requires the full range of access to the protocol stack is a Virtual Private Network protocol called Point to Point Tunneling Protocol or PPTP. Made popular by Microsoft by including it in every copy of its operating system, this suite of applications and drivers allows secure access of the company LAN from the road or home via any Internet connection. It requires that packets be sent via the IP layer, TCP layer, and application layer. At least one implementation[8] successfully exploits its access to all protocol layers to synchronize and translate the various PPTP streams to simultaneously allow all internal machines to run as PPTP clients. Although this requires intimate knowledge by the NAT of the PPTP protocol, such a function would not have been possible in an Proxy environment.

The PAT approach may appear to be getting "something for nothing," and you should be suspicious. There is one aspect of Internet connectivity that is given up for the ability to reuse a single IP address for so many machines. Since a TCP/UDP/IP endpoint is defined only by IP address and port number, machines on the Internet wishing to initiate a connection with a specific machine on the inside may not. For the majority of users this is not an issue and in fact is the primary protection that using a NAT affords. However, for specific cases such as the desire to make an internal server visible to the Internet, this can cause a problem. Fortunately, modern NAT implementations offer a way to redirect specified port numbers on the outside to specific machines on the inside. In the case of a Web server using standard port 80, a static entry in the NAT table could be configured to always forward packets for 24.128.50.48:80 (IP:Port using the previous example) to some internal machine at 192.168.1.1:8000.

Even though there could be many internal servers on different machines, there can only be one unique IP:Port pair on the Internet, so in this example there can only be one Web server on the inside visible on the standard TCP port for Web server (port 80). If you feel you will encounter a situation that will require multiple servers for similar services, such as a Web server farm, or any setup with multiple real IP addresses, such devices should be placed on the outside interface with respect to the NAT.

Until now, we have not discussed how the IP address information gets assigned to each of the internal machines. Although it is beyond the scope of this chapter, we will provide a short overview here since modern implementations of NATs[8] have mechanisms to simplify this task as well. Each machine requires an IP address, network mask, gateway address, and DNS address. For purposes of example we shall use 192.168.1.1, 255.255.255.0, 192.168.1.2, and 18.62.0.6, respectively. In the rudimentary case, a network administrator could manually enter this information on each machine, with the first item, IP address, being different for each machine. However, with each new machine, changed machine, or moved machine he/she runs the risk of assigning duplicate addresses, not to mention the possibility of some item such as DNS (Domain Name System) address (18.62.0.6) being changed which would require changes on every machine. Granted, with a NAT in place the specifics of what IP address is chosen are all but eliminated, but it would be nice to eliminate completely any network administration on individual machines. Solving this problem is simple using a DHCP (Dynamic Host Configuration Protocol) server.

Once such a server is configured with some basic information about the range of addresses you want to hand out, the rest is automatic. DHCP servers come built in with many standard platforms (NT Server, Unix) and using one of these is satisfactory, however certain simplifications can be derived when such a server is incorporated directly into a NAT implementation. The NAT typically must be configured with the range of addresses it will translate (network mask can be usually derived from this). By its very operation it is itself the gateway for these nodes. Finally, when configured as a DHCP client itself, or directly connected to the Internet, it has knowledge of working DNS addresses.

Since the NAT has all the information required for the DHCP server, the user of a combined NAT/DHCP implementation would only need to configure one piece of network equipment to get his whole internal LAN connected to the Internet. This is a major advantage for the small- to medium-size company that may not want to expend the resources to keep a full-time network administrator on staff.

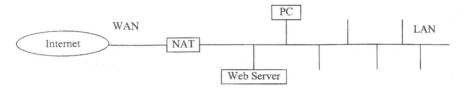

Exhibit 41.5. Standalone NAT application.

NAT APPLICATIONS

The NAT may be used standalone, with an existing connection, or in conjunction with other networking devices. The following figures show some typical applications. Exhibit 41.5 is a standalone example. NAT by its very nature operates at the packet level, specifically, at the IP and TCP/UDP packet level. This means that NAT implementations most often have routing functionality built in, allowing it to replace the router, as shown in Exhibit 41.5.

As mentioned in the NAT Description section, some modern NAT implementations have a built-in DHCP server, further simplifying setup and making the network depicted in Exhibit 41.5 completely automatic, requiring no individual machine configuration. The same modern NAT often has the capability to designate specific servers on the inside to also act as a server to the Net at large. In Exhibit 41.5 the Web server port (80) is redirected from the outside interface toward the internal Web server. If the NAT implementation is a good one, it will also include standard protection mechanisms for your internal servers (such as denial of service or SYN attacks).

Exhibit 41.6 shows an application to an existing Internet connected network. Here the router serves as the connection to the Internet and existing servers (visible to the outside) and workstations may operate as before; however, the addition of a new business unit with Internet access requirements has been added. Only a single IP address is needed for this new network (or an existing one from an existing server may be shared) and all members of the new network shall have access to the corporate servers and vice versa. Once again, employing DHCP will all but eliminate any maintenance for adding new machines on the new network.

Exhibit 41.7 shows how a NAT may be incorporated in an existing network to supplement an existing Internet-connected network. This may be useful as a simple way to provide Internet access to more machines without having to get more IP addresses. Note that nothing about the existing network is changed other than the addition of the NAT. Both internal and external interfaces are connected to the same network segment and packets with both real and fake IP addresses flow on the same segment. At first

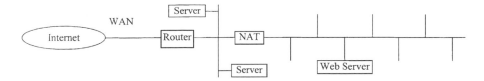

Exhibit 41.6. Adding a new business unit.

this may seem a bit odd, but this situation arises often where an investment has already been made in creating and protecting, either via a firewall or firewall/router, an Internet-connected network. Instead of starting over or changing the Internet service to provide more or different addresses, adding a NAT instantly adds the capability to add thousands of machines. In this case DHCP is probably preexisting and, therefore, not needed from the NAT device[9] as was an early shareware product which addressed this common scenario using only a single interface.

In Exhibit 41.8 we show how the IP address translation aspect of NAT can be used to simplify and manage a large organization with multiple departments, in this case accounting, marketing, and quality assurance. Each one of these departments is free to add, remove, or change machines without coordinating with the other departments. Here, the inherent protection from external connections that NAT provides maintains separation between say Q/A and accounting departments while still allowing shared access to companywide servers.

PROXY DESCRIPTION

The Proxy was developed by the UNIX community originally as a simple solution to the increased number of attacks brought on by the explosive growth of the Net. Initially, it was designed for only for handling Web requests. It works as follows. When a machine on the internal side of the Proxy needs to connect to a machine on the outside, e.g., a Web server, instead of sending packets requesting the connection directly to the external

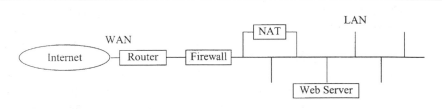

Exhibit 41.7. Adding more nodes to an existing network.

627

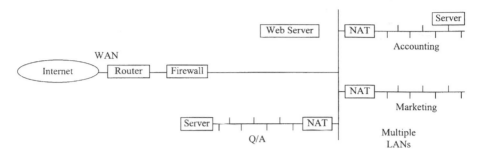

Exhibit 41.8. Separating departmental networks.

machine, it must send them to the Proxy. The Proxy answers the connection request and simultaneously initiates a connection request to the destination machine through its external port. Once the connection to the destination machine is established, data are copied to and from the internal and destination connections until the transaction is complete. At this point both connections are closed and whatever resources they consumed on the Proxy machine (e.g., memory) are released. Since the only machine connected to the outside is the Proxy machine itself, connection attempts to any of the internal machines is blocked, thus protecting the internal machines from attack.

Machines working with a Proxy require special functionality to be included in every browser as well as some additional configuration. But due to the early introduction of the Proxy and the close ties that both browser and Proxy developers had with each other (via CERN), such functionality was and continues to be built into every major browser available. As the needs of the Net expanded, Proxies were called upon to do many more tasks. First, support for more than just Web browsing was required. The support for basic Internet applications such as Telnet, e-mail, and FTP are now supported by most Proxies and is built into most browsers. Although not general, this satisfied most users at the time.

Within a short time a problem other than security started plaguing the Internet. Due to the popularity of the Web and the large amounts of information that drive it, the bandwidth required for acceptable download times became difficult or too expensive to obtain. Using Proxy technology, the UNIX community was able to devise a solution to this problem, too. As Web pages became fancier and larger, browsing became unbearable or limiting for many sites due to the long time it took for a page to get transferred. Since the Proxy was already in the middle, copying every byte between browser and Web server, it was in a prime position to also make a copy of the page being transferred from the server.

This functionality is called caching, where a copy of every page is kept on the local Proxy server in the hopes that a popular site will have multiple requests and thus can be served up instantly from the local copy, as opposed to retrieving the page again over the bandwidth-limited Net. To make this process truly useful (no one wants OLD data), today's Proxies with caching capability have mechanisms to timeout or purge old copies of pages as well as interpret codes embedded in the pages themselves that determine a page's longevity in the cache (e.g., you would not want stock data or transactions to be cached at all).

With the increase in new Internet applications, the straightforward Proxy has little value without additional functionality. Some implementations have kept up with new applications by including special software for each. Most have opted for some combination of low-level address translation functionality, so that new applications can be supported with little or no modification, and traditional Proxy technology. Microsoft Proxy Server[10] is one such example. Doing this may extend the life of Proxies, although from current trends it appears that NAT-based solutions (and its variants) to Internet connectivity are surpassing Proxy-based ones, with the caching function being relegated to a separate device when its function is needed (as in a ISP).

Some Terminology

The term Proxy can be applied to any device which acts on behalf of another. Specifically, anytime a product maintains two separate connections for each transaction, one from the internal machine and the other to the destination machine, it is a Proxy. Often time the terms Proxy, NAT, and Gateway get misused in marketing literature. This is frequently an effort to capitalize on the history and name recognition of the one term over the other (e.g., Proxy and NAT). We point this out here to alert the reader to the fact that in searching for a solution, be aware that Proxy, NAT, and Gateway will be used interchangeably by many. The term Gateway applies to any device which may or may not act on behalf of another and may or may not maintain multiple connections for each transaction but WILL translate data to and from one machine and another. Examples are e-mail gateways where one mail format, say ATT-mail, gets translated into Internet or MIME mail, which is usually implemented as a file conversion. Another example are TCP/IP to SNA gateways where the equivalent functions in each protocol world (Internet and IBM Mainframes) get translated. For this case an example would be the translation of FTP or File Transfer Protocol in the TCP/IP world to FTAM in the IBM Mainframe world. This would allow users in either world to transparently transfer files from machine to machine.

DIFFERENCES BETWEEN NAT AND PROXY TECHNOLOGIES

Exhibit 41.9 lists the primary differences between the two technologies. The major difference between NATs and Proxies is the Web page caching

Exhibit 41.9. Distinguishing Features of NATs and Proxy Servers

10.0.0.0 — 10.255.255.255	16 million addresses
172.16.0.0 — 172.31.255.255	1 million addresses
192.168.0.0 — 192.168.255.255	65,000 addresses

feature found in most (but not all) Proxies. By making copies of Web pages that users request onto a local disk, subsequent requests for the same page may be satisfied immediately from the local disk instead of pulling the page through the WAN connection again. This avoids the use of the precious WAN bandwidth, and gives subsequent users what appears to be instant access to the page. This is definitely an advantage for scenarios where multiple users may all wish to retrieve the same page off the Net simultaneously.

A classroom environment would be one such example. In most cases, however, such as in the corporate environment, the only pages that would (or should) be frequently accessed are ones on the internal corporate network (company home page, departmental information pages, Web/Java applications). So the gains here would be slight.

Other drawbacks include uncertainty as to the cached page's "freshness."[11] Unless Web pages are specifically coded with messages for proxies servers en route, the end user cannot be certain as to how recently the page and its data were updated. Stale information for a researcher would be useless. In addition, communication back to the Web server (e.g., "cookies" and hit counters) is not guaranteed to be delivered through a Proxy. Finally, with the number of low-cost high-bandwidth WAN options on the rise, such as Cable Modems, ADSL, and Satellite, the WAN bandwidth bottleneck argument becomes less of a concern. In fact, if all Web requests are sent to the Proxy server first it, too, becomes a bottleneck.[11] However, if carefully placed in a network, caching will provide performance gains. Therefore, except for special cases where either WAN bandwidth is critical (e.g., regular modem connection) or traffic patterns lend themselves duplicate requests (e.g., classroom or ISP), the caching component of a Proxy server may be more trouble than it is worth.

The next major difference between Proxy and NAT technologies are the requirements the Proxy approach puts on the client machines or workstations. Proxies require that each client machine be configured to encapsulate and send all its requests to the Proxy server. The additional software required to accomplish this is included in most, but not all, network applications and does require yet another configuration parameter in addition to the usual IP address, network mask, default gateway, or DNS address parameters. It also must be configured for each application. This is a major drawback of the Proxy approach and is one of the reasons much of the industry, including former Proxy manufacturers, are developing hybrid products that include some NAT functionality as well.

The final two items, throughput and maximum client count, are affected by the way NATs and Proxies are implemented. Due to the fact that Proxies typically run as applications on a host operating system, packets must traverse many more layers of software before being operated on. This comes from the fact that the original Proxies were designed this way based on the original free reference implementations set forth by the UNIX community. Traversing these extra layers of code not only slows the process down and affects throughput, but also consumes the machine's resources in an inefficient manner. Using up resources, mostly memory, limits the maximum number of simultaneous connections that can be handled. Since each connection through the Proxy involves two connections (one inside and one outside), the maximum number of connections is on the order of a few hundred for a reasonable amount of memory. Similarly, since the packet must be copied between connections, the maximum throughput one can expect from a Proxy implementation is that of an application running on the Proxy machine.

SUMMARY/CONCLUSIONS

In this chapter we have compared two of the most popular methods used to connect a LAN to the Internet — the Proxy and NAT. We found the Proxy server approach to be somewhat outdated except in certain cases. The Proxy does have the advantage of being able to cache Web pages to speed up repetitive downloads. However, for the scenarios where caching would be useful, this function should be separated from the Internet connectivity problem. (Note: at the time of writing there are a number of caching-only devices making their way onto the market precisely for this reason.)

The NAT solution, being a second-generation solution to the Internet connectivity problem, simplifies and improves on the performance of the Proxy, basically by operating at a much lower level in the TCP/IP protocol stack. However, as Internet applications have become more complicated, the responsibility of modern NAT implementations has crept into the higher application layers. This overlap into Proxy space suggests that maybe some hybrid approach would yield the optimum solution. Caution must be exercised though in choosing such a system, to make sure that the whole process is still performed in an efficient manner and not as an application. Most products that have been rewritten from the ground up have avoided this pitfall. We also discussed the advantages of placing NAT functionality together with DHCP address management. This last step all but eliminates network administration on the individual machines.

MANAGING ADVANCED APPLICATION DEVELOPMENT

Author's Bio

Richard Lamb, Ph.D., is a cofounder of Nevod Incorporated and has served as its CEO since 1995. He is responsible for the company's strategic development programs as well as day-to-day operations. Prior to founding Nevod, Lamb served as VP of Engineering for XtcN, Ltd which pioneered the development of ISDN and Frame Relay Routers with built-in Telco interfaces for Internet and LAN interconnection. Their introduction of ISDN routers in 1992 preceded the proven success of this technology and market.

Previous positions include consultant to ATT, TRW, ON Technology, Cayman Systems, the U.S. Navy, and other leading corporations. Lamb earned a Ph.D., ScD, and Master's degree in electrical engineering from the Massachusetts Institute of Technology.

Notes

1. Droms, R., "Dynamic Host Configuration Protocol," RFC2131, Bucknell University, March 1997.
2. Rekhter, Y., Moskowitz, B., Karrenberg, D., de Groot, G., and Lear, E., "Address Allocation for Private Internets," RFC 1918 or its successor.
3. Egevang K. and Francis P., "The IP Network Address Translator (NAT)," RFC1631, Cray Communications, NTT, May 1994.
4. Srisuresh, P., "The IP Network Address Translator," INTERNET-DRAFT, Lucet Technologies, February 1998 (http://info.internet.isi.edu:80/in-drafts/files/draft-rfced-info-srisuresh-05.txt).
5. Reid, M., "Internet Videoconferencing Is Ready for the Prime Time," *Boston Business Journal,* July 17, 1998. (Videoconferencing article on the value of H.323 standards.)
6. ITU-R Recommendation H.323, "Visual Telephone Systems and Equipment for Local Area Networks Which Provide A Non-Guaranteed Quality of Service," May 28, 1966.
7. Private communication with Dan Kegel of Activision, Inc., Santa Monica, CA, May 1998. "Activision new Game Protocol with NAT Support."
8. Nevod NAT1000 Description — http://www.nevod.com/products/nat1000.html.
9. Nevod PIP Description — http://www.nevod.com/products/pip/index.html.
10. Microsoft Proxy Server description — http://www.microsoft.com/proxy/guide/features.asp.
11. Mendel, B., "Web Servers Become a Cache Cow," *LanTimes,* pp 40–41, May 11, 1998. (Also see "Getting Attention in the Enterprise," *LanTimes,* pp 1, 23, May 11, 1998.)

Chapter 42

Cracking the Directory Problem: An Introduction to Directory Integration and Meta Directory Concepts

Tony Mulqueen
Ian Goldsmith

MESSAGING FIRST ENTERED THE WORLD OF BUSINESS AS A SERVICE to "islands" of users. The earliest e-mail systems connected all the users on a LAN or on a corporate mainframe. The concept had yet to arrive that employees would want to communicate beyond the building they were in, let alone to users in other organizations. Even the culture that would welcome such ubiquitous access had yet to evolve. IT managers, and those who set their goals, could at first see little benefit in allowing messaging access outside their existing user groups.

In this cosy but confined world, managing the messaging infrastructure was straightforward. Two trends conspired to disrupt this scenario. The first trend was that corporate mergers and acquisitions brought the need to integrate various diverse forms of corporate messaging. In distributed or international organizations, IT managers had to respond to demands that, say, mainframe users, Notes users, Microsoft Mail users, and Internet users could all talk together. By the nineties, the average number of messaging systems in an organization had grown to around seven, causing quite a headache for the luckless system administrator with responsibility for mes-

0-8493-9987-4/00/$0.00+$.50
© 2000 by CRC Press LLC

saging connectivity. The problem created a market for "hub" style products. These complex and powerful messaging servers were expensive propositions, not just to buy, but to maintain at an acceptable level of reliability.

In general, the service offered by a messaging hub was basic connectivity. The thornier problem of maintaining consistent corporate address books was often addressed by manual techniques. If a change occurred in, say a specific Notes address book, it was propagated to other messaging sectors by means of phone calls, e-mail messages between system administrators, and finally, manual updating of diverse address books in different locations. Getting someone added to a number of systems, let alone deleting them in the event of relocation or departure, grew to become a notorious black hole of administrative effort.

The second major trend was that the Internet grew and grew in popularity and mindshare. This had a number of effects. IT strategists were exposed to the prospect of a world where messaging was ubiquitous, not confined to a corporate island or archipelago. Slowly, the idea gained acceptance that pervasive messaging capability provided essential competitive advantage. Furthermore, by offering a common standard for the formatting, addressing, and routing of messages, the Internet offered the prospect of universal connectivity. All that was required, it seemed, was for the various vendors of messaging systems to provide connectors to the Internet.

This happened in due course, and today it is safe to say that all major messaging systems come with Internet connectors, albeit of somewhat variable quality. What has happened, in fact, is that the Internet has replaced the role of the traditional hub. Unsurprisingly, the problems that haunted hub servers now continue to live on and plague the system administrator. The only difference is that now user numbers are larger, expectations are higher, and the demands for reliable connectivity — and consistent addressing and access — are louder and more strident.

Like the hub, the Internet is a lowest common denominator. It lacks universal implementation of some of the sophisticated features that are an accepted part of LAN-based mail, such as delivery and receipt notifications, or interactive scheduling. These shortcomings are being addressed by standards development, and so this problem is a transitory one. Because of the considerably more anarchic and unpredictable environment in which the Internet must run, reliability and quality of service are still a good deal short of LAN-based systems. Again, this problem is likely to be relatively transitory, responding to the development of business quality service agreements and the provision of increased bandwidth.

The most intractable and costly problem is actually the management of the messaging system. Just as the old style hub was only as effective as the network of address books that kept users pointed in the right directions, so the Internet stands or falls as a corporate facility on the effective maintenance of directory style information. Just as the hub's sophisticated connectivity features masked a world of phone calls and handmade updates, so also the Internet corporate connectivity often carries the price tag of expensive manual management.

For a message to pass between a proprietary system and the Internet, a mapping must be defined between the address on the proprietary system and the Internet address. The organization is faced with two unpalatable prospects. The complexity of the internal messaging structure may be exposed outside the organizations with addresses such as joe.bloggs@notes.acme.com and john.smith@exchange.acme.com, which has a negative effect on the corporate image, and results in much additional work if a user changes location or system.

Alternatively, an alias file can make the necessary mappings, for example, mapping joe.bloggs@acme.com against the necessary Notes addressing details. Once again, we are in a world of manual updates. The information in the alias file is not available to the general user population in the form of a White Pages service. Just like in the bad old days of hub management, changes to local address books still need to be propagated by the usual bush telegraph techniques every time a user is added, deleted, or relocated.

IT strategists are beginning to realize that the directory problem associated with mixed messaging systems is part of a much larger one. The more systems we use to automate our dealings with people, the more directories we spawn. In addition to potentially multiple e-mail addresses, an employee also has a phone extension, plus home number, mobile, and home fax — typically maintained on a PABX-based system. At a network level, the employee has network access and rights, perhaps even more than someone engaged in administration or software development. At the level of communications facilities, the employee may have specific rights for controlled or expensive media, such as X.25. At the application layer, the employee may or may not have rights to various sensitive lines of business systems: accounts, billing, inventory, human resources.

The list goes on, to the point where industry analysts, The Burton Group, estimate that there are more than 100 directories in use in the average medium-size enterprise. On the one hand, there are security benefits to be had from partitioning all this information, and keeping the control of the data distributed among various functions which jealously guard "their" areas. On the other, there is a security threat associated with this approach. When someone leaves, it is complex to disestablish all their rights, and the resulting open account can be attacked by a disgruntled former employee.

In a security audit, a company of 100,000 employees found that there were over 500,000 different accounts that had access to line-of-business applications. Alarmingly, many of the accounts had been assigned to individuals who were no longer with the company, and some of them were even dead. Yet these accounts were still being accessed on a daily basis. Further analysis showed that when a user transferred from one project to another, the account stayed behind and was used by the replacement employee.

The strategic direction for enterprises is to get to a point where local supervisors can grant an employee access to line-of-business applications, and instantaneously enable the employee with proper access facilities. In the same manner, corporate security or human resources can in a single keystroke disable an individual account. This would make it possible to terminate an employee and minimize the threat of retaliation. This facility is referred to as "single sign on."

Before arriving at such an advanced scenario, we must solve the more basic problems one at a time. Let's look back at what is required from our messaging and directory system. First of all, we want to get rid of those time-consuming manual updates, so software agents are no longer required to regularly inspect local address books for additions, deletions, or modifications. We require a repository for this information, and it would be ideal if this information could also be made widely available to people and applications.

Enter Directory technology! Directories based on open access standards such as LDAP can be used as a common repository for not just e-mail addresses, but all of the heterogeneous information about people and resources we are endeavoring to manage. This approach is referred to as "Integrated Directory," also known as "Directory synchronization." Open standards are available for methods such as replication and partitioning of information, which mean that data can be kept close to where they are most frequently required, or alternatively, distributed widely throughout an organization. The directory data can be exposed as a White Pages service, accessed via a Web browser, or made available to e-mail applications via an LDAP address lookup.

If addressing details are sensitive, security policies can determine which users and groups have access to certain parts of the address book. Secure messaging systems can be more easily implemented using open directories, since security details such as a public key can be easily associated with a user's directory entry, and obtained by a messaging application at the same time as it looks up the e-mail address.

But the real long-term benefit of the directory approach goes beyond messaging requirements, to potentially cracking the entire directory problem. The Burton Group has defined a term, Meta Directory, which is the conceptual "join" of all directories — a consistent, single, and highly managed view of the information held in directory-style resources. Who needs meta directory? Organizations of all sizes need to keep information up-to-date, synchronize messaging address books and legacy information sources, and make addressing information more readily accessible to end users. Meta directory capabilities also offer service providers many new opportunities: to provide White/Yellow Pages services, to run a cluster of servers as a single virtual service, to act as certification authorities for a secure e-mail service, and to leverage value added services such as I/P, telephony, and videoconferencing.

Interestingly, it is easier to demonstrate return on investment in a meta directory than in messaging itself. While it is difficult to demonstrate tangible revenue gain or cost savings from messaging, it is straightforward to place a cost on lost messages and other messaging inefficiencies.

The suggested way to calculate return on investment for directory deployments is to investigate the impact of the directory on specific applications. It is easier to get a handle on the potential cost savings of an individual application and then determine where the directory can help reduce this cost. It is very difficult to take the directory implementation as a whole and try to determine the impact on the entire information infrastructure.

The following examples all assume that the directory deployed is a meta directory providing a tight integration between Human Resources systems and the various applications described. This ensures that the deployed meta directory can be the foundation of the electronic business environment, by providing a reliable, accurate source of information about employees and contractors.

MESSAGING DIRECTORY SYNCHRONIZATION

Meta directory technology can integrate the functions found in traditional directory synchronization applications with the enterprise directory. One of the main benefits of synchronizing the address books of dissimilar messaging systems through the meta directory is that all corporate e-mail users will now be able to easily address messages to one another with fewer delivery errors.

The number of internal messages which are incorrectly delivered or not delivered at all can easily be determined from audit information from the various messaging servers. By making some assumptions about the time taken to recover from incorrectly addressed messages we can quickly come to a conservative estimate about the cost of nondelivered internal messages. This is a cost which can easily be eliminated with the deployment of an enterprise directory capable of dissimilar messaging system address book synchronization.

Some messaging products can also use the synchronized directory to provide a unified single Internet domain distributed across all the enterprise messaging systems. This can help to eliminate business lost when a user migrates to a different system.

Assumptions

Most of the following assumptions and estimates can, with a little investigation, be replaced with real numbers for your specific organization. The example below uses a fake corporation of about Global 2000 size.

Corporation X Mail Users: $n = 10,000$

Estimated percentage of internal messages that are incorrectly addressed	1 percent
Estimated number of internal messages per user per day	10
Estimated average time wasted per incorrectly addressed internal message	10 minutes
Estimated average loaded labor cost	$100,000 per year = $50 per hour

Cost of Incorrectly Addressed Internal Messages

Total number of messages per day	$(10,000 \times 10) = 100,000$
Number of incorrectly addressed messages per day	(1 percent of 100,000) = 1,000
Average time wasted per day	$(1,000 \times 10) = 10,000$ minutes
Average time wasted per year	(10,000 minutes $\times$ 200 days) = 2,000,000 minutes = ~ 33,000 hours
Cost of time wasted due to incorrectly addressed internal messages	$(33,000 \times 50) = \$1,650,000$/year

Note: The above calculation addresses only the cost of time wasted due to incorrectly addressed messages. It does not begin to try and calculate the costs associated with sending sensitive information to the wrong people. For example, it is not inconceivable that a message intended for a senior manager describing a possible organizational downsizing might end up in the mailbox of a junior employee with a similar name.

TELEPHONE NUMBER SYNCHRONIZATION

Many large organizations have studied the cost of maintaining a paper phone book. There are many costs involved with this ranging from a calculation similar to the messaging example presented above, to the physical manufacturing cost of producing a paper phone book. Other, less tangible examples, are the cost saving in having a receptionist who can quickly find the phone number and location of not only an employee who has a visitor, but also that employee's colleagues and administrative assistant.

A calculation for money saved by integrating a telephone system (PABX) with the directory follows:

Assumptions

Corporation X phone users	10,000
Estimated number of phone calls per employee each day that require a number lookup	1
Estimated average time to look up a number in a paper directory	1 minute
Estimated average time to look up a number in an electronic directory	15 seconds
Estimated percentage of times number looked up is wrong	2 percent
Estimated average time to find correct number	5 minutes
Estimated average loaded labor cost	$100,000 per year = $50 per hour
Estimated cost of materials in paper phone book	$1 per copy
Estimated cost of distribution of paper phone book	$0.50 per copy
Estimated number of issues per year	6
Estimated annual effort to maintain paper phone book	1 man year

Note: Most of the above assumptions and estimates can, with a little investigation, be replaced with real numbers for a specific organization.

Cost Saving With Electronic Telephone Directory

Cost of maintaining, printing and distributing paper phone book	$(10{,}000 \times 6 \times \$1.5 + 1 \times \$100{,}000) =$ $190,000
Total time looking up numbers in paper book	$(10{,}000 \times 1 \times 200 \times 1 \text{ min}/60) =$ 33,333 hours/year
Total time looking up numbers in an electronic directory	8,333 hours/year
Time saved with electronic directory	25,000 hours/year

Total time finding numbers that are wrong on paper	$(10,000 \times .02 \times 200 \times 5 \text{ min}/60) =$ 3,333 hours/year
Total time saved with electronic telephone directory	28,333 hours/year
Total cost saving with electronic telephone directory	$(28,333 \times \$50 + 250,000) =$ \$1,607,000/year

NETWORK OPERATING SYSTEM MANAGEMENT

The cost savings for using a meta directory to maintain and manage a network operating system fall into two main areas. The most obvious and easiest to calculate is the reduction in administrative effort required to manage NOS implementations. The second is in the area of improved security by ensuring that only authorized personnel have access to the NOS. This is potentially a much greater cost saving, but is very hard to calculate.

Many of the leading industry analysts have derived estimates for the cost of security breaches in most organizations. They also have determined that a large proportion of this cost is attributable to internal staff. One of the key factors involved in reducing this cost can be to ensure that only authorized employees have access to the Network Operating System. Many organizations have no way of automatically disabling or removing the accounts of ex-employees. In some cases ex-employees can have unauthorized access to corporate systems for many months after they leave.

There is a large difference between a good NOS directory and a bad one, and the cost savings that can be realized will depend on the current NOS environment.

Assumptions

Organization X NOS users	10,000
Estimated average loaded labor cost of NOS admin.	\$100,000 per year
Number of NOS users per full-time equivalent	500 (based on META Group analysis)
Estimated reduction in admin. effort with meta directory	25 percent

Cost Saving with Meta Directory Deployment

Cost of admin. before meta directory deployment	$(10,000/500 \times \$100,000) =$ \$2,000,000
Saving with meta directory deployment	(\$2 million $\times$ 25 percent) = \$500,000/year

MESSAGING SYSTEM MANAGEMENT

A very similar calculation to the estimates for NOS management can also be applied for messaging. Many of the arguments for security hold true in this example, and are equally difficult to calculate.

The following calculation considers only the cost of management and administration of the messaging environment.

Assumptions

Organization X e-mail users	10,000
LAN-based e-mail users (e.g., cc:Mail or MS Mail)	5000
Client server e-mail users (e.g., MS Exchange or Lotus Notes)	5000
Number of LAN-based e-mail users per full-time equivalent	200 (based on META Group analysis)
Number of client server-based e-mail users per full-time equivalent	750 (based on META Group analysis)
Average loaded labor cost of e-mail admin.	$100,000 per year
Estimated reduction in admin. effort with meta directory	25 percent

Cost Saving for Meta Directory Deployment

Cost of admin. of LAN systems before meta directory deployment	(5000/200 × $100,000) = $2,500,000
Cost of admin. of client server systems before meta directory deployment	(5000/750 × $100,000) = $667,000
Saving with meta directory deployment	($2,500,000 + $667,000 × 25 percent) = $792,000/year

The examples presented above for an organization with 10,000 employees, using dissimilar messaging systems, a paper phone book, and an enterprise-wide NOS infrastructure could expect to save $4,549,000 per year.

This addresses only the cost savings and does not include any incremental revenue or even the improved peace of mind and reduced cost of increased security.

The numbers presented above represent a very rough calculation of return on meta directory investment. The do provide a framework which can be used to support a business case for building these services. It is always difficult to justify investment in information infrastructure, especially with "background" applications like a directory.

It is clear from the rough numbers presented that a meta directory deployment can very quickly provide a very large cost saving and, therefore, have an immediate positive impact on the bottom line.

SUMMARY

Meta Directory holds the potential to solve many of the key issues that are holding back enterprise networks from achieving their full potential. From the system administrator's perspective, the task list associated with adding, moving, or deleting users is cut to a small fraction of its former size, even reduced to "single sign on." To users, it is much easier to reach people by a variety of media such as e-mail, fax, phone, video, and voicemail. To the designers of value-added services, it can provide the basis for advanced features such as user profile maintenance and enforcement. As expectations of what can be expected from the enterprise directory soar, we will all hear a lot more about Meta Directory.

Authors' Bios

Tony Mulqueen is a graduate of Trinity College, Dublin (English Language and Literature, BA Mod. and MA) and the University of Limerick (Grad. Diploma in Computing). After working as an academic in the areas of literature and applied linguistics, he entered the data communications industry with Retix in 1989, joined System Dynamics for 2 years, and has worked with ISOCOR since 1994.

Mulqueen is responsible for the series of ISOCOR White Papers that describe open standards messaging and directory technologies, and ISOCOR's product range. He also presents on messaging and directory topics to seminars and industry forums. For the past 7 years, Mulqueen has contributed a monthly column on information technology trends to Irish Computer, *and has worked as a Visiting Lecturer at the University of Limerick.*

Ian Goldsmith joined ISOCOR in September 1997 as Business Manager, Strategic Products, with more than 10 years of experience in messaging and networking technology. He rapidly assumed responsibility for Directory Products as the Manager, Directory Technology and Products. Previously he was the Technical Manager, U.S. operations for NEXOR.

For more than 6 years prior to joining NEXOR, Goldsmith was a Technical Consultant with ICL Information Services Division. He was responsible for X.400, X.500, and SMTP deployments at major telecommunications providers around the world. Goldsmith holds an MA in Computer Science from Cambridge University, England.

Chapter 43

Audio and Video Production Values for Webcasters

Jessica Keyes

WEBCASTING IS THAT COMBINATION OF AUDIO, VIDEO, AND ANIMATION which makes for a dynamic Website. You don't have to be a professional movie maker and/or broadcaster to manage successful Webcasting projects. However, some of their expertise would be worthwhile to discuss. This chapter delves into some of the things that make good Webcasting — it's also an interesting read into an area that most IT managers never delve into but should.

There are some basics that I'd like to discuss right up front. Some people have it — some people don't. What I mean is that you should select with care those folks who will be your spokespeople online. Some people's voices are more suited to recording than others. Professional announcers are paid not only for their reading abilities, but also for their acting, dynamics, inflection, and most importantly vocal tone. Bear this in mind when choosing the person behind the microphone.

You might also want to surf over to http://hwww.broadcast.net which is a great jumping-off point for broadcast enthusiasts.

GUIDELINES FOR DIGITAL VIDEO

There is no commonly agreed-upon methodology to create digital video. Since the hardware and software invoked is continually evolving, the digital videomaker will have to keep on his or her toes to make sure that the videos produced are always on the "cutting edge."

The following discussion depicts a fairly common sequence of events that take place in the creation of a video on a PC (before encoding). Since the computer brings the creation process into the nonlinear age, none of

0-8493-9987-4/00/$0.00+$.50
© 2000 by CRC Press LLC

these steps really has to follow in exact sequence. Assuming that the story-boarding process has been completed, the following steps can occur.

Gathering Source Material

Production facilities and personnel may be employed to create new footage for editing and manipulation, or stock footage may be gathered. The effects of the nonlinear editing process are obvious here because it allows editors to play "what if" with the story line in an unprecedented manner. Thus, additional footage maybe shot at this stage, and more footage may be required later if the story line is allowed to evolve. The computer itself is capable of generating text, graphics, and even 2D and 3D animations.

Digitizing

Before any editing can take place, the source video must be converted into digital form by the computer and stored on disk. This process is known as digitizing. Video input can come from many kinds of input devices, from consumer-quality VHS machines to traditional high-end tape equipment. However, the quality of the digital image is directly dependent on the quality of the medium from which it comes. While there are several methods of digitizing, they all depend on the quality of the source device. Thus the rental or purchase of a high-quality deck should be factored into the overall cost of equipment. Still frames to be included in the production can be created on the PC or brought in through a high-quality scanner.

Editing Nonlinearly

The nonlinear editing process has many advantages. Most software products handle the editing process by facilitating the creation in an offline model of the final video, rather than by actually compositing the video themselves online.

This model contains information about how the video is to unfold over time. Various video clips are trimmed and then sequenced together with intervening transitions, wipes, and keys. Rather than manipulate the video files themselves, the model contains information about the files and pointers to them.

Since the computer is a general purpose tool, it can be used for more than just the editing process. Static graphic elements can be assembled by means of professional-quality graphics programs, text can be generated, and 2D and 3D animations can be created. Changes to all of these production elements can be made right up to the last minute.

The computer allows the editor to create and store a model of the video project without creating the actual video. Since this model can also be duplicated and the duplicate can be altered without altering the original, it is possible to create several different models or previews of the same project.

After the creation process has ended, the resulting video model must be used to create or render an actual video. During the rendering process the computer proceeds frame by frame through the model and performs all operations necessary to create a complete frame at the desired resolution and quality. This process can be quite time-consuming depending on the complexity of the model and the duration of the video.

Since many compositing and special-effect computations are very processor intensive, three ways to speed the rendering process are to (1) purchase a faster computer, (2) accelerate your current machine, or (3) take advantage of multiprocessor hardware and software to operate in parallel.

Broadcast-Quality Software

Software for personal computers and workstations now exists that can create stills, edit video nonlinearly, create transitions, perform composites, render special effects, animate in two and three dimensions, and so on.

No one package can do it all, however, so it is important to research the capabilities of different software from different vendors. The minimum feature-set necessary to ensure broadcast-quality output is comprised of 24-bit color manipulation, subpixel positioning, and anti-aliasing, Alpha channel support, and text generation that supports anti-aliasing of Postscript and TrueType fonts.

The most common representation of color in personal computers is familiar to video professionals as "component" video. Here, colors are composed of three channels: red, green, and blue. Each channel is represented by 8 bits (1 byte), for a total of 24 bits per pixel. Programs that generate 24-bit color output are essential to broadcast-quality work, because this color scheme can represent more than 16 million separate colors — more than the human eye can distinguish.

If your software has DVE-like features, subpixel positioning is essential for achieving smooth-looking motion of video layers and is important for compositing. To achieve broadcast-quality motion, it is necessary to compensate for the computer's limited screen resolution. This is created by the illusion that the number of screen pixels per inch is much greater than it actually is. Subpixel sampling is the frame-processing method that creates this illusion.

Anti-aliasing becomes important when the edges of any graphic object are diagonal to any degree, when rectangular shapes are rotated, or when smooth curves are desired as with character recognition. Like subpixel positioning, it is a method of compensating for the limited resolution of the screen. It accomplishes this by removing "jaggies," thereby smoothing diagonal lines and curves.

The Alpha channel contains transparency information for each pixel. Many video professionals are surprised to learn that some PC-based graphics software, such as PhotoShop, are more capable of creating and handling Alpha channel information than a more professional broadcast paint system. To the video professional this transparency information is a key signal that defines which parts of the video frame are transparent, which are opaque, and which are semitransparent.

The most common example of this may be seen on most newscasts. The character generator used to overlay the type on the screen contains an Alpha channel. The layering device uses the Alpha channel to determine which parts of the overlay (the letters) will be opaque and which parts will be filled with the background image (a reporter standing in front of City Hall). Uses for this include compositing 3D computer-generated graphic animations into 2D backgrounds.

RECOMMENDATIONS FOR VIDEO AND AUDIO CAPTURE

The basic shooting goals for compressed video are

1. Limit the amount of picture content that changes from one frame to the next.
2. Limit the amount of textured detail in the picture (clothing, backgrounds, etc.)

The following list of tips naturally follow from these two basic goals. If possible, always use a stationary (tripod-mounted) camera, especially for "talking heads," office interiors, even outside location shots. This is probably the single most important factor for high-quality compressed video. Plan for limited motion in and through the scene. For example, if you're shooting a talking head, put the person in a chair that can't rock back and forth. If your subject is particularly animated, shoot from farther back to reduce the amount of motion in the frame.

- Have your subject wear bright colors. Red, pink, yellow, and light blue solids are good. Black and navy are bad — dark colors generate video "noise" which gets interpreted as changing frame content and thus is unnecessarily encoded.
- Have your subject wear solids instead of patterns. Herringbone, checks, stripes, and prints all contain complicated edge details that must be encoded and compressed, taking precious bits away from the details you want to render, like facial expressions and moving lips. These color and pattern recommendations apply to background detail as well. It's much better to shoot your subject in front of a piece of uni-

formly colored seamless paper than sitting in front of a bookcase filled with books or a window covered by venetian blinds.

- Plan for "settle time" after transitions (e.g., titles, screen shots, cuts). Say you're creating a training video and shooting screen shots of a computer application. You show the mouse clicking on a menu item, and a submenu drops down. The submenu will be a bit blurry when it first makes its appearance. Wait a few seconds for the text to clear up.
- Use large, clear fonts for titles, credits, supers, computer screen shots, etc. The picture is going to be small to begin with and it will be difficult to read fine print in a compressed image. Larger text will make your viewers much more comfortable. Avoid rapid-fire "Music Video"-style cuts, dissolves, wipes, pans, zooms, special effects, etc. Images that aren't on the screen for more than a second or two won't have a chance to resolve themselves to clarity. If you have the flexibility, short depth-of-field is preferable — soft, out-of-focus backgrounds are easier to code than sharply defined, complicated details and textures. Choose a faster shutter speed and a wider aperture to reduce depth-of-field. Don't use automatic exposure controls — maintain constant brightness. For example, while shooting an interior location, as people move into and out of the scene the background light level should not change. Changing background lighting levels will be interpreted as changes in frame contents and will be unnecessarily encoded. Brighter lighting gets coded better — avoid dark frame contents, large shadows, etc. Areas that are dimly lit can generate video "noise" which will be interpreted as changing frame contents and will be unnecessarily encoded.
- Digitize video in uncompressed format. After connecting the video source to your computer's video capture board, capture digital video in uncompressed format. If your video is already compressed when you pass it to your digital composing software, the file that results will not be of as high quality as it should be.

AUDIO CONSIDERATIONS

Here are some tips for achieving high-quality compressed audio:

- Use a good microphone to reduce or eliminate background noise as much as possible. For "talking heads" use a wired (not wireless) clip-on Lavalier microphone. In crowded areas, use a shotgun or boom microphone, as directionally as you can.
- Do not use a camcorder's built-in microphone. These generally pick up motor noise in the camcorder itself, in addition to omnidirectional sounds in a noisy environment.
- Set microphone gain properly. If the gain is too high, clipping or distortion may result. If it's too low, the audio may be too faint to be encoded properly or heard upon playback.

- Understand the limitations of your audio compression algorithm. The audio heard at the far end, when decompressed, will be of telephone toll quality. The frequency range of the audio will be between 300 and 3400 Hz.
- Don't expect to hear high sibilant treble or booming bass sounds. G.723 audio lends itself quite well to a single human speaker, not as well to music, and somewhat poorly to a simultaneous combination of speech and music.
- Digitize audio at 8 kHz, 16-bit mono. When the time comes to perform audio capture from tape onto your computer, these settings work best for most of the PC-based audio compressors. Avoid higher sampling rates, avoid 8-bit samples, and avoid stereo sampling.

APPLICATIONS AND DESIGN CONSIDERATIONS IN USING AUDIO IN WEBCASTING

Several different types of audio output speech, music, and sound effects can be incorporated into audio on the Internet. To use each type effectively, developers need to learn more about how each of the types can be used to improve their content.

Speech

Two types of speech are available for use: digitized and synthesized. Digitized speech provides high-quality, natural speech, but requires significant disk storage capacity. Synthesized speech is not as storage intensive, but may not sound as natural as human speech.

Speech is an important element of human communication and can be used effectively to transmit information. One advantage of using natural speech is the power of the human voice to persuade. Another advantage is that speech can potentially eliminate the need to display large amounts of text.

Music

Music is also an important component of human communication. It is used to set a mood or tone, provide connections or transitions, add interest or excitement, and evoke emotion. Music, especially when combined with speech and sound effects, can greatly enhance the presentation of text and visuals.

Sound Effects

Sound effects are used to enhance or augment the presentation of information. Two types of sound effects are natural and synthetic. Natural sounds are unadorned, commonplace sounds that occur around us. Synthetic sounds are those that are produced electronically or artificially.

There are two general categories of sound effects: ambient and special. Ambient sounds are the background sounds that communicate the context of the screen or place. Special sounds are uniquely identifiable sounds, such as the ring of a telephone, that complement narration and/or visuals.

Narration

To produce high-quality recorded speech, a script should be written and professionally recorded. To provide balance, both female and male narrators should be used. Nonprofessional narrators such as corporate officers may be used to provide credibility. When content needs to be explained or information needs to be delivered accurately, a professional can be relied upon to follow the specifications of the script and deliver a professional-sounding audio track.

To be effective, a narrator should:

- Vary intonation to motivate, explain, provoke, exhort, or empathize
- Use a conversational tone
- Be amiable, candid, sincere, and straightforward
- Avoid sounding arrogant, pretentious, flippant, disrespectful, or sarcastic
- Avoid a lecturing tone

When you are recording narrative speech, be sure to eliminate background or ambient sound unless it is used to provide a realistic environment. On occasion, incorporating ambient sound can be effective, since it can be used to help establish a mood or to increase the feeling of reality.

Developing the Speech

Good writing techniques are essential to the development of successful Webcasting programs. Thus, to integrate speech as an effective tool, developers must learn to write an effective narration as part of a program script. General guidelines for this activity can be gathered from the techniques used for scriptwriting for other media:

- Write the way people speak
- Use language the audience can understand
- Write as if the narrator were teaching or speaking with one person
- Write in a clear, straightforward manner
- Write in short sentences that can be spoken in a single breath
- Use second-person pronouns — you and your
- Use contractions and other simplified forms that are used in speech
- Emphasize clarity and simplicity
- Omit needless words
- Avoid slang
- Avoid oral presentation of figures and statistics

- Use humor when appropriate
- Present information in small chunks
- Emphasize the objectives or goals of the Webcast
- Interpret what the user is seeing rather than simply describing it
- Make the visuals and narration go hand in hand; usually the visuals tell the story and the narration interprets, explains, or elaborates
- Adhere to time limits and length requirements
- Understand the capabilities and limitations of Internet hardware and software; especially as related to the use of speech

Narration should be read aloud and then revised if it sounds awkward, stilted, or boring To raise the level of user interest, quotes, conversations, and case studies could be included in audio scripts.

Selecting Music

Few articles or books have been written that provide detailed information or guidelines about the effective use of music in interactive programs. Some suggest that incorporating music begins with identifying the function of the music and making it an integral element or the script. Thus, the use of music needs to be considered as the program is being visualized and the script written.

Generally, music can be used to:

- Establish mood
- Set pace
- Signal a turn of events
- Indicate progress and activity
- Provide transitions and continuity
- Evoke emotion
- Accompany titles or introduction information
- Emphasize important points
- Support visual information
- Add interest, realism, and surprise

Music can have a wide variety of effects on its listeners. It is not only "background" but also works in conjunction with the visual message or provides interest, excitement, tension, and realism. Since music plays an important story-telling role, it should fit the pace and mood of the presentation and appeal to the audience's lifestyle, taste, and workplace position. Guidelines to accomplish this are

1. Make music an integral part from the start, rather than try to find music to "go with" imagery later.
2. Choose a music style that conveys the mood you wish to create.
3. Convey personality through instrumentation.

4. Use recurring themes as musical signatures to help the audience feel familiar with a characters, place or segment.
5. Use tempo, dynamics, and pitch to establish energy levels.
6. Use different styles of music and instrumentation to suggest time periods, cultures, locations, and sense of place.
7. Use musical genres to communicate to specific audiences: e.g., big band sounds for older audiences, or rap, metal, or pop for teenagers.
8. Know when to hold them, when to fold them. Music should not compete with the narration or overwhelm the message of the program

Selecting Sound Effects

Natural, ambient sounds are an integral part of our daily lives. We use them to help us interpret and assess our surroundings. For example, we listen to the thunk of a car door to find out if it has closed properly.

Sound or nonspeech audio can provide different types of messages, including alarms or warnings and status or monitoring messages. Alarms and warnings are sounds and signals that interrupt and alert a listener. These sounds, such as fire alarms and police sirens, normally are loud and easily identifiable.

Status and monitoring messages are sounds that give us information about ongoing tasks. The click of the keys on the keyboard is an example of these typically short sounds. Status and monitoring sounds fade rapidly from the listener's awareness and are significant only when they indicate a change; for example, when the sound does not occur.

There are several other categories of sound:

1. Physical events: we can identify whether a dropped glass bounded or shattered.
2. Invisible structures: tapping a wall helps us to locate where to hang a picture.
3. Dynamic change: as we pour liquid into a glass, we can hear when it is full.
4. Abnormal structures: we can tell when our car engine is malfunctioning by its sound.
5. Events in space: we can hear someone approaching by the sound of footsteps.

Not only can sound effects provide specific information about an environment or setting, they can also be used to accomplish the following tasks:

- Create atmosphere
- Add realism
- Emphasize important points

- Indicate progress or activity
- Increase interest
- Establish mood
- Cue or prompt users
- Increase users' motivation

Three significant considerations should govern the use of sound effects:

1. They must be clear and easily identifiable.
2. They should not overwhelm the primary message.
3. They should be appropriate to the intended audience.

General Guidelines

1. To maximize the use of audio, analyze carefully the target audience, delivery environment, and content.
2. Clearly define why and how audio will be used.
3. Whenever possible, integrate audio into the whole program, and do it from the start of the project.
4. Develop detailed scripts or storyboards.
5. Allow users to control the audio.
6. Make sound effects meaningful.
7. Use the highest-quality audio possible, given the storage constraints of the Internet.
8. Collaborate with others who have experience using different types of audio.
9. Learn more about the use of sound, especially music.

AUDIO HINTS

The staff of Progressive Networks (RealAudio) have become expert at squeezing the beat sound out of the limited bandwidth of the Internet. Here are some of their words of wisdom.

Use a Good Original Source

A high-quality audio source is probably the single most important variable in determining your final audio quality. They start with satellite signals, audio compact discs, or digital audio tapes. When creating sounds from scratch, they use professional-quality microphones. You can make sound files from low-quality analog cassettes, tiny condenser microphones, or anything else — but the hiss and distortion in the resulting sound file will have a substantial adverse effect on clarity after the file is encoded.

You should always encode from 16-bit (not 8-bit or *mu*-law) sound files. They also recommend digitizing at a 22,050 Hz sample rate.

Set Your Input Levels Correctly

Setting correct levels is absolutely crucial. When creating your original sound file, the input level should be set to use the full range of available amplitude, while avoiding clipping. Clipping is audible as a high-frequency crackling noise and is what happens if you try to send too much input to your sound card (or any other piece of audio equipment).

When digitizing with your sound card, first do several test runs and adjust your input level so the input approaches but does not exceed the maximum level. You can adjust this on the mixer page of your sound card utilities. Look for the Input Levels or Recording Levels option — most mixer pages have some sort of visual display where you can see how much sound is coming in. Make sure there are no peaks above maximum. These are generally indicated by a red light somewhere. Be conservative with your levels; you never know when someone will get excited and speak much louder, or when a great play at a sports event will make a crowd roar. Differences in volume levels can be evened out later.

Sound files that do not use the full amplitude range will produce poor-quality encoded files. If the amplitude range of an existing file is too low, you can use your audio editor's Increase Amplitude or Increase Volume command to adjust the range before encoding your levels automatically.

Note, however, that better quality will be achieved if the levels are set correctly at the time of recording. The good news is that once you set your input levels correctly, they generally will not need to be reset. If you are reasonably consistent with your recording practices, you'll save yourself a lot of trouble in the long run.

Use High-Quality Equipment

High-quality equipment will produce better results and save you a lot of headaches in the long run. Every piece of equipment in the audio chain, from the microphone to the sound card to the software, will have an effect on your encoded message. If you intend to make sound a big part of your Website, you should invest in professional-quality audio equipment. This need not be a crippling investment, but it does mean you will have to purchase from a professional recording equipment dealer, not your local computer/hi-fi/gadget store.

Select Appropriate Material

If you want to encode music for transmission over 14.4 kbps phone lines, remember that the simpler the source the better chance that the encoded version will be faithful to the original. There isn't enough bandwidth in a 14.4 line to do a harmonically complex signal (like a full orchestra) justice.

Many folks have used music successfully in their 14.4 clips as background, where fidelity isn't as important an issue.

Correct DC Offset

Sometimes when files are digitized, something known as DC offset creeps in. This is when the digitized waveform is not correctly centered around the 0 volts axis. Most of this is due to improper grounding of the sound cards. Some sound cards are worse than others; to see how bad your sound card is try recording silence. You should in theory see nothing in your waveform window, but you'll probably see a flat line just slightly above or below the 0 volts axis. This is DC offset.

This can wreak havoc when you attempt to process your waveform, and can add a low rumbling sound to the encoded file. Luckily, most editors have a built-in facility to take care of this. Some call it "Centering the Wave" and correct it automatically; others allow you to adjust DC offset manually (+/–). In this case you'll have to find out precisely what your DC offset is by running a "statistics" command or something similar. Then you'll have to correct it. For instance, if your average DC offset is 45 you'll want to offset the wave by –45.

Obviously if you are doing a live broadcast, you'll have to live with whatever DC offset you have. Proper balanced wiring between all of your audio components will help minimize this, as well as any ground loops.

Noise Gating (or Expansion)

Noise gating, or downward expansion, eliminates unwanted background noise which becomes audible during pauses in the audio (e.g., when an announcer pauses, or there is a gap between programs). Signals above a certain volume level are left alone, but below this level the signal is turned down or even off depending on how heavy the gating or expansion is. Setting up a noise gate or expander is straightforward. Most budget compressors have a noise gate built in.

To use noise gating, set the threshold control so that the gating or expansion occurs when there is no desired audio, but not so high that the beginnings of words or music that you want to hear are chopped off. It takes a bit of time, but remember to err on the side of caution just in case the next person in the program has a softer voice.

If your gate or expander has a range control, set this to around 5 to 10 dB. This means it will turn down the "noise" section a little, but not turn it off altogether. That way you'll hear if the gate is cutting something off that you want to hear, and you can then readjust the threshold setting accordingly.

Compression

One of the side effects of digital encoding is artifacts — sounds that weren't there before encoding. These can sometimes be heard as rumbling or distortion in the signal. These artifacts appear at a relatively constant low level, whether the original sound file was loud or quiet. Louder files tend to mask these quiet artifacts. So it is recommended to feed the encoder a loud signal. However, we are limited by the loudest section of the file being encoded. If we could turn up down the loudest section, we could turn up the overall volume of the sound file. A compressor helps us accomplish this.

Compression reduces the difference between the loudest and quietest sections of the incoming signal. Sections that exceed a user-defined threshold are turned down. Now that these loud sections have been turned down, we can turn up the overall volume of the sound file. How much the sections are turned up or down depends on how much compression you use.

How much compression should you use? The exact settings will be determined by experience and by referring to the manual that comes with your equipment or software. However, for speech it is recommended that you use moderate to extreme compression (4:1 to 10:1).

Equalization

Equalization (or EQ) changes the tone of the incoming signal just as you can on your home stereo or car radio. This is done by "boosting" (turning up) or "cutting" (turning down) certain frequencies. Using EQ, we can boost frequencies that we like (where the important content is) and cut frequencies where noise or unwanted sound is. By doing this, we can give the encoder a big hint about which sound information to keep. Encoding discards a lot of the high-end or treble information — this can make files sound dull. To compensate for this, it helps to boost the middle or midrange frequencies. This will also make speech sound more intelligible.

Most good mixing boards will have a midrange EQ knob. Sometimes you can choose which frequency to boost, other times this is preset at the factory. If not, or if you are using a graphic equalizer or audio processing software, you'll want to boost at around 2.5 kHz.

If your equipment does not have a midfrequencies EQ knob, you can obtain a similar result by turning the low and high EQ knobs down and then turning the overall volume back up (note, though, that this is not as effective as boosting the mids, which attacks the problem at its source).

The amount that you should turn up the midrange depends on your EQ equipment and source file. A little experimentation is necessary. Try adding some mids to a short section of a piece to be encoded and check it with the audio player. If it is a bit muddy or hard to understand, try adding a little more. You can keep going until the knob won't turn anymore, or until the result starts to sound too harsh.

For digital audio encoded at 14.4 kbps it is important to try and make the voice as full as possible in the middle frequencies. This is where the majority of speech information is contained. What we are trying to do is lift the voice away from any background noise.

Some signals can be improved by rolling off (turning down) the bass frequencies as well. Side effects of encoding are sometimes audible as a lower voice "shadowing" the original. This is particularly noticeable with women speakers. When this effect is too prominent, try rolling off the bass and encoding the result. The artifacts will not disappear, but sometimes they will be quieter. Be careful not to make the voice sound too thin or brittle.

For audio played back at 28.8 kbps, much more of the fidelity of the original recording is retained, so you won't need to worry about EQ as much. It still helps to boost at around 2.5 kHz to compensate for the high-frequency loss, but boosting too much will make music sound thin and tinny.

Normalization

Normalization is a process included in most audio recording software whereby the computer calculates exactly how much it can turn up the volume of a file without distortion. Because we always want to feed the encoder the loudest files possible, this is a very handy function. This is why you can afford to be fairly conservative with your recording input levels, and then let your program's normalization function take care of the rest. Normalization should be the last thing you do. If you normalize your file and then add some EQ, you'll end up with distortion.

Author's Bio

Jessica Keyes is president of New Art Technologies, Inc., a high-technology software development firm. Keyes has given seminars for such prestigious universities as Carnegie Mellon, Boston University, University of Illinois, James Madison University, and San Francisco State University. She is a frequent keynote speaker on the topics of competitive strategy using information technology and marketing on the information superhighway. She is an advisor for DataPro, McGraw-Hill's computer research arm, as well as a member of the Sprint Business Council. Keyes is also a founding Board of Director member of the New York Software Industry Association. She has recently completed a 2-year term on the Mayor of New York City's Small Business Advisory Council.

Prior to founding the company, Keyes was Managing Director of R&D for the New York Stock Exchange and has been an officer with Swiss Bank Co. and Banker's Trust, both in New York City. She holds a Master's from New York University where she did her research in the area of artificial intelligence.

A noted columnist and correspondent, with over 150 articles published, Keyes is the author of 12 books.

Chapter 44

Guaranteeing Internet Service Levels: TCP Rate Control

Bob Packer
Pat Thomas

TCP RATE CONTROL PROVIDES A UNIQUE TECHNOLOGY that differentiates it from other network applications or devices. To appreciate how TCP Rate Control can guarantee service levels, you need to understand the way it manages TCP packets and traffic flow.

BACKGROUND

The Transmission Control Protocol (TCP) provides connection-oriented services for the protocol's application layer; that is, the client and the server must establish a connection to exchange data. TCP transmits data in segments encased in IP datagrams, along with checksums used to detect data corruption, and sequence numbers to ensure an ordered byte stream. TCP is considered to be a reliable transport mechanism because it requires the receiving computer to acknowledge not only the receipt of data, but their completeness and sequence. If the sending computer doesn't receive notification from the receiving computer within an expected time frame, the segment is retransmitted. TCP also maintains a flow control window to restrict transmissions. The receiver advertises a window size, indicating how many bytes it can handle.

In summary, TCP provides the following reliability checks:

- Acknowledges receipt of packets; retransmits when dropped packets are detected
- Resequences segments, if necessary, if they arrive out of order

0-8493-9987-4/00/$0.00+$.50
© 2000 by CRC Press LLC

- Tosses packets if data became corrupted during transmission
- Discards duplicate segments
- Maintains flow control to manage a connection's transmission rate

THE BANDWIDTH CHALLENGE

TCP/IP was primarily designed to support two traffic applications — FTP and Telnet. With the growth of the Internet, network applications and user expectations have changed. Today, with more high-speed users, and bursty, interactive Web traffic, greater demand is placed on networks, causing delays and bottlenecks that impact a user's quality of service. Many of the features that make TCP reliable, contribute to performance problems:

- Retransmitting when the network "cloud" drops packets or delays acknowledgments.
- Backing off when it infers congestion exists. Conventional TCP bandwidth management uses indirect feedback to infer network congestion. TCP increases a connection's transmission rate until it senses a problem and then it backs off. It interprets dropped packets as a sign of congestion. The goal of TCP is for individual connections to burst on demand to use all available bandwidth, while at the same time reacting conservatively to inferred problems in order to alleviate congestion.

TCP uses a sliding-window flow-control mechanism to increase the throughput over wide-area networks. It allows the sender to transmit multiple packets before it stops and waits for an acknowledgment. This leads to faster data transfer, since the sender doesn't have to wait for an acknowledgment each time a packet is sent.[1] The sender "fills the pipe" and then waits for an acknowledgment before sending more data. The receiver not only acknowledges that it got the data, but it advertises how much data it can now handle — that is, its window size.

TCP's slow-start algorithm attempts to alleviate the problem of multiple packets filling up router queues. Remember that TCP flow control typically is handled by the receiver, which tells the sender how much data it can handle. The slow-start algorithm, on the other hand, uses a congestion window, which is a flow-control mechanism managed by the sender. With TCP slow-start, when a connection opens, only one packet is sent until an ACK is received. For each received ACK, the congestion window increases by one. For each round trip, the number of outstanding segments doubles until a threshold is reached.

In summary, TCP uses flow control determined by client and server operating system configurations, distances, and other network conditions. As you'll see in subsequent sections, TCP Rate Control provides rate control explicitly configured in user-defined policies.

BANDWIDTH MANAGEMENT APPROACHES

When faced with bandwidth constraints, a number of solutions come to mind. This section addresses the following potential solutions, focusing on their advantages and limitations:

- Adding Bandwidth
- Using Queuing Schemes on Routers
- Upgrading Web Servers
- Defining Precise Control (The TCP Rate Control Solution)

Adding Bandwidth

An obvious approach to overcoming bandwidth limitations is to add more bandwidth. As technology trends demonstrate, this is a short-term solution — as soon as bandwidth is increased, it is consumed. So, you're back to where you started — trying to manage the bandwidth that you have more efficiently.

Using Queuing Schemes on Routers

For the most part, network devices have kept pace with evolving high-speed technology. Routers provide queuing schemes such as weighted fair queuing, priority output queuing, and custom queuing in an attempt to prioritize and distribute bandwidth to individual data flows so that low-volume applications, such as interactive Web applications, don't get overtaken by large data transfers, typical of FTP traffic.[2-4]

Router-based queuing schemes have several limitations:

- Routers manage bandwidth passively, tossing packets and providing no direct feedback to end systems. Routers can only use queuing — that is, buffering and adding delay — or packet tossing, to try to control traffic sources.
- Router queuing is unidirectional — outbound traffic only.
- Queuing results in chunkier traffic and erratic performance because multiple, independent TCP sources compete for bandwidth, ramping up and backing off; and queues accumulate at the access link. Queuing, especially "weighted fair queuing," doesn't work well for chunky flows because packets arriving in chunks tend to be discarded.
- Routers don't allow you to set guaranteed rates for specific traffic types.
- Routers can't prevent "brown-outs," that is, they don't provide admission-control policies to dictate what happens when a link is oversubscribed.
- Rate specification is imprecise. You can't specify high-speed and low-speed connections separately and you can't specify speed in bits per second.

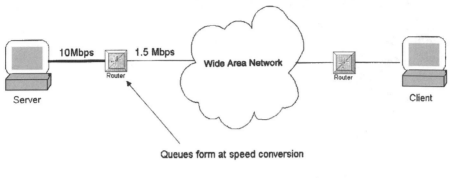

Exhibit 44.1. Access link bottlenecks.

- Traffic classification is too coarse. A router can't classify traffic by URL, treating all flows the same at the Website.

Upgrading Web Servers

On the Web server end, hardware improvements, server software, and HTTP protocols have caused the bottleneck to move away from the server, out to the access link. As illustrated in Exhibit 44.1, congestion occurs when data from a LAN's large pipe is passed to a smaller pipe on the WAN.

Defining Precise Control — The TCP Rate Control Solution

Traffic, by nature, consists of chunks of data that accumulate when multiple independent sources of data are combined. These data chunks tend to form at access links where speed conversion is handled. This is where TCP Rate Control makes a difference.

Imagine putting fine sand, rather than gravel, through a network pipe. Sand can pass through the pipe more evenly and quickly than chunks. TCP Rate Control conditions traffic so that it becomes more like sand than gravel. These smoothly controlled connections are much less likely to incur packet loss and, more importantly, the end user experiences consistent service.

As you'll see in the next section, TCP Rate Control takes advantage of TCP mechanisms to overcome TCP deficiencies and offer predictable performance. Where TCP relies on indirect network feedback from tossed packets to infer congestion, TCP Rate Control provides direct feedback to the transmitter by detecting a remote user's access speed and network latency and correlating these data with aggregate flow information. This results in smoothed traffic flow.

HOW TCP RATE CONTROL WORKS — RATE CONTROL VS. FLOW CONTROL

TCP Rate Control maintains state information about individual TCP connections, giving it the ability to provide direct, quality-of-service feedback to the transmitter. In addition, you can define TCP Rate Control policies to explicitly manage different traffic classes and partition bandwidth resources to meet your business needs. As a result, you gain precise control of your service levels.

TCP Rate Control provides several key functions that differentiate it from other bandwidth-management solutions:

- Controls the end-to-end connection, eliminating burstiness, so users experience smooth, even data displays.
- Classifies traffic for precise control and even can classify by a specific application or URL.
- Allocates bandwidth according to your policies.These features are discussed in more detail in the following sections.

Controls the End-to-End Connection

TCP Rate Control uses two methods to control the rate of TCP transmissions:

1. Detects real-time flow speed and then delays acknowledgments going back to the transmitter.
2. Modifies the advertised window size in the packets sent to the transmitter. TCP Rate Control changes the end-to-end TCP semantics from the middle of the connection. It calculates the round-trip time (RTT), intercepts the acknowledgment, and holds onto it for the amount of time that is required to smooth the traffic flow without incurring retransmission time-out (RTO). It also supplies a window size that helps the sender determine when to send the next packet. To see how this rate control mechanism works, refer to Exhibit 44.2 and the following data flow example.

A TCP Rate Control Data Flow Example. Exhibit 44.2 shows how TCP Rate Control intervenes and paces the data transmission to deliver predictable service. The following steps trace the data transfer shown in Exhibit 44.2.

1. A data segment is sent to the receiver.
2. The receiver acknowledges receipt and advertises an 8000-byte window size.
3. TCP Rate Control intercepts the ACK and determines that the data must be more evenly transmitted. Otherwise, subsequent data segments will queue up and packets will be tossed because insufficient bandwidth is available, as defined by this flow's policy.

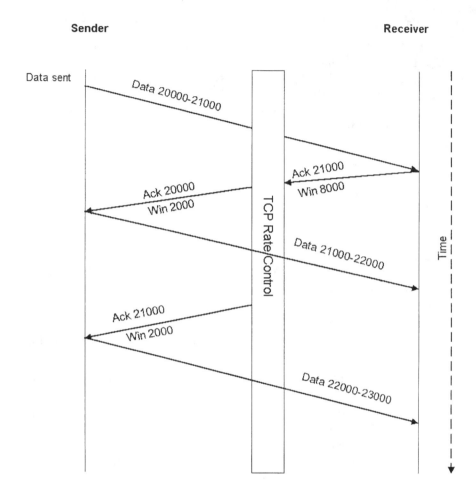

Exhibit 44.2. TCP Rate Control manages the connection.

---

4. TCP Rate Control sends an ACK to the sender, calculated to arrive at the sender to cause the sender to immediately remit data, i.e., the ACK sequence number plus the window size allows the sender to transmit an additional packet.

Smooth Traffic Flow With TCP Rate Control. Without the benefit of TCP Rate Control, multiple packets are sent; an intermediate router queues the packets; and when the queue reaches its capacity, the router tosses packets, which must then be retransmitted. Exhibit 44.3 shows bursty traffic when TCP Rate Control is not used, and evenly spaced data transmissions when TCP Rate Control intervenes. Note: independent of access-link con-

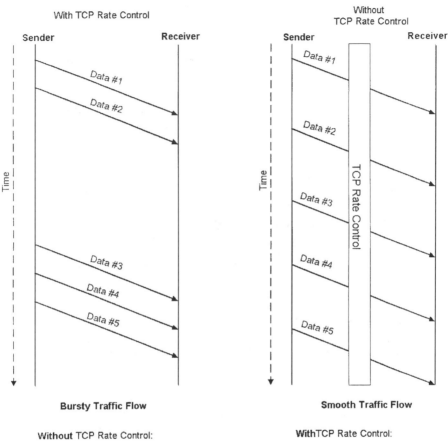

Exhibit 44.3. Traffic behavior: before and after TCP Rate Control.

gestion problems, traffic chunks are more prone to packet loss than evenly spaced traffic.

Classifies Traffic for Precise Control

TCP Rate Control uses a hierarchical tree structure to classify traffic. You identify the characteristics of the traffic types you want to control, such as traffic from a particular application (like Web traffic) or even a specific URL. You need not classify all network traffic — only the traffic that af-

Exhibit 44.4. A Typical Web-Browsing Session. (t45-1.doc)

User Action	TCP Rate Control Action
1. Click on a button to select a specific URL.	1. Classifies the traffic flow by URL — Is it an index? Is it an html file? Is it a gif?
	2. Maps the traffic class to a policy — the rules for rate control.
	3. Smoothes the data transfer, giving the user an even, nonbursty data display.

fects your business' quality of service. TCP Rate Control classifies a traffic flow by traversing the traffic class tree, attempting to match the flow to one of the classes you've defined. The final step in the classification process maps a flow to a policy. The policy defines the type of service you want a traffic class to get, for example, a guaranteed rate.

TCP Rate Control offers rich traffic classification by:

- Providing classification for specific applications and URLs, giving you precise control
- Maintaining a traffic class hierarchy to manage priorities and enable policy inheritance
- Ordering traffic classes automatically, yet allowing you to flag specific classes as exceptions, overriding the natural tree search order

A Web-Access Scenario. Anyone using a Web browser to access information on the World Wide Web communicates on the Internet using HTTP (Hypertext Transfer Protocol) over TCP. HTTP traffic tends to be bursty because HTTP transfers data for each user request. A typical Web-browsing session is shown in Exhibit 44.4.

Allocates Bandwidth

After you have created traffic classes for the traffic types you want to control, you define policies, which are the rules that govern how TCP Rate Control allocates bandwidth. Then, you apply the policies to appropriate classes.

As TCP Rate Control processes a traffic flow, it matches the flow to one of the classes in its tree structure and uses the class-assigned policy to set the quality of service for the flow. A traffic flow can be either a connection or an individual URL.

TCP Rate Control offers three policy types: rate-based, priority-based, and never-admit-that-you-configure-to-control-bandwidth. The following sections describe how TCP Rate Control determines how to divide bandwidth in accordance with the rules you've defined.

Assigning Rates for a Traffic Class. Designed to smooth bursty traffic, rate-based policies let you reserve bandwidth by assigning a guaranteed rate for a traffic class. The guaranteed rate sets a precise rate, in bits per second, for a connection. If bandwidth is available, the connection can use some of the unused or excess rate, according to the policy settings you've defined.

Controlling Admissions. You define what should happen if a traffic class' total guaranteed rate gets used up. For example, if the next connection for a class needs a guaranteed rate and no bandwidth is available, TCP Rate Control can handle the bandwidth request by either refusing the connection or Web request, redirecting the request, or squeezing the connection into the existing bandwidth pipe.

Scaling Bandwidth to Connection Speed for Efficient Bandwidth Use. TCP Rate Control monitors a connection's speed and adjusts bandwidth allocation as the connection speed changes. Low-speed connections and high-speed connections can be assigned separate guaranteed rates so that TCP Rate Control can scale bandwidth usage accordingly. For example, during a typical Web session, the wait period between clicks doesn't consume bandwidth, so TCP Rate Control frees up bandwidth to satisfy other demands.

Prioritizing Bandwidth Allocation. You can use priority-based policies for traffic that doesn't require a guaranteed rate, but that you still want to manage along with competing traffic. Priority-based policies are ideal for non-bursty traffic, for which you don't need to reserve a guaranteed rate. You assign a priority (0 to 7) to a traffic class so that TCP Rate Control can determine how to manage the aggregate flow. You don't have to classify all traffic. Any traffic that you haven't classified is treated as priority-based traffic with a priority of 3.

Denying Access. In some cases, you may want to deny access to users — perhaps traffic from a particular IP address. You can control access using a Never-Admit policy, which you can configure to always refuse access or redirect the user to another URL.

TCP Rate Control Bandwidth Allocation Order

TCP Rate Control uses the policies you've defined to determine how to allocate bandwidth. When determining bandwidth allocation, TCP Rate Control takes into account all bandwidth demands, not just the individual traffic flows. As shown in Exhibit 44.5, bandwidth is allocated based on the following basic allocation scheme:

- Traffic flows that have assigned guaranteed rates are satisfied first
- All other traffic — both traffic with assigned policies and unclassified traffic — competes for the remaining or excess bandwidth

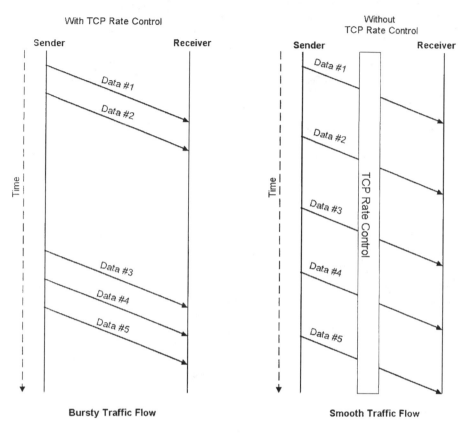

Exhibit 44.5. Bandwidth allocation.

- Excess bandwidth is allocated based on the priorities you've set in priority-based policies

Note that a flow may have both a guaranteed rate and some excess rate, as it is available. You determine an application's priority. For example, you could set PointCast connections to use excess rate at a low priority to keep it from interfering with revenue-generating activities (see Exhibit 44.4). How TCP Rate Control Allocates BandwidthThe TCP Rate Control AdvantageTCP Rate Control provides patent-pending technology that enables you to explicitly control TCP/IP bandwidth to keep your network under your control. This technology offers the following unique bandwidth management features:

- Explicit bits-per-second rate control, giving you the ability to specify guaranteed rates and to define how total bandwidth should be allocated
- Smoothed traffic flow — that is, evenly paced transmissions — eliminating the burstiness associated with Web traffic and ensuring consistent quality of service
- Precise traffic classification — even by URL or by application type
- Bidirectional traffic control, unlike routers, which control outbound traffic only
- Direct feedback to sender about transmission rate and flow status, rather than the indirect feedback provided by routers
- Admissions control for brown-out protection

Authors' Bios

Bob Packer *has been an independent consultant since 1987. He has pioneered telecommunications and networking technologies for a number of high-tech firms: Hybrid Networks (Remote Link Adapter for TCP/IP over cable), Metricom (protocols for the Ricochet microcellular TCP/IP network), IBM (OSI protocols), British Telecom North America (high-performance packet switch), and Raynet (Loop Optical carrier). Packer is a cofounder of Packeteer, Inc., providers of intelligent bandwidth management solutions and currently is Chief Technical Officer of Packeteer, Inc. He holds a B.A. in philosophy and political science from Swarthmore College.*

Pat Thomas *has been a technical instructor and writer since 1986 at several Silicon Valley companies: Unisys, Seagate Software, and Auspex Systems. She is currently the Technical Communication Manager at Packeteer, Inc. Thomas has a B.S. in education from Millersville University, with computer science credits from UCSC and Villanova University.*

Notes

1. Stevens, W. R., *TCP/IP Illustrated*, Vol. 1: The Protocols, Addison Wesley Longman, Reading, MA, 1994, 455.
2. Recent work in network engineering indicates that traffic has self-similar or fractal properties. This implies that queuing problems at access links are far worse than would be predicted by traditional Poisson modeling.
3. Paxson, V. and Floyd, S., Wide Area Traffic: The Failure of Poisson Modeling, *IEEE/ACM Trans. Networking*, Vol. 3, No. 3, June 1995.
4. Erramilli, A., Narayan, O., and Willinger, W., Experimental Queuing Analysis with Long-Range Dependent Packet Traffic, *IEEE/ACM Trans. Networking*, Vol. 4, No. 2, April 1996.

Chapter 45
Internet Telephony: Why Use A Low Bit-Rate, Parametric Codec for VoIP Applications?

Jeff Hill

IT IS WITHOUT QUESTION THAT INTERNET TELEPHONY SYSTEMS ARE HERE TO STAY, and their use and deployment will only increase as time progresses. Managers in high-technology companies must understand the nature of Internet telephony, its various components, that it means different things to different people and markets, and at least be familiar with the underlying technology that drives it. Internet telephony could mean two people communicating via voice on their respective PCs with no telephone used at all. On the other hand, a 75-year-old man who has never owned nor touched a PC could pick up a telephone manufactured and purchased in 1962 and make a call to his brother in England, also using a standard telephone, via a Voice-over Internet Protocol (VoIP) link. In the latter case, the elderly brothers would have no idea their call was being transmitted over a data network.

This chapter begins with an introduction to the concept of Internet telephony designed for the beginner, and eventually expands the discussion to include some standard calculations and system design issues. Some of the trade-offs forced upon the designers of Internet telephony systems are discussed, as are the many variables upon which system quality and performance depend. The chapter was designed to be readable, and a knowledge of math beyond arithmetic is not required.

0-8493-9987-4/00/$0.00+$.50
© 2000 by CRC Press LLC

Today someone in Butte, MT can call someone in London (or anywhere in the world), talk for hours, and pay less than a dollar (the cost of a local phone call) for the privilege. All that is needed is a multimedia PC,[1] any commercially available, inexpensive Internet phone software, and someone in London logged onto their computer (outfitted with similar items as well). Most people would confess that it sounds like a pretty good deal, especially when such a phone call from Montana to London could cost hundreds of dollars if made via more traditional means. So why does anyone use the telephone anymore? Tens of millions of people own PCs, and millions more are buying them every year.

The answer is simple and obvious: sound quality. The world is accustomed to a certain degree of clarity and naturalness when conversing via the telephone. Unfortunately, systems designed to enable two-way voice communications over data networks, e.g., Voice Over Internet Protocol (VoIP) systems, have yet to approach that quality plateau.

CIRCUIT- VS. PACKET-SWITCHING

When you pick up the telephone to call your mother on her birthday, you expect a reasonable delay between the time you finish dialing the number and the time the phone on the other end begins to ring. During this time the telephone company is finding an electronic roadway between your phone and your mother's. Once that path is established, it remains open for the length of the call and allows you to experience almost no perceptible delay. When you say "Happy Birthday, Mom," an electronic version of your speech travels over that dedicated path to your mother's ear. When she says "thank you," her speech travels back uninterrupted over that same highway.

This "circuit-switched" architecture has been the foundation of the world's phone system since the telephone was first invented, and it has served us well. The sound quality is very good, but you pay for that dedicated line in long-distance phone charges. If you use test instruments to actually measure the delay of a land-based coast-to-coast (U.S.) phone call, you would probably measure something like 40 ms of delay, where 30 ms is attributable to the "speed of light," for the electronic signal to travel the 3000 miles across the North American continent.

Recently, however, people have discovered that you can send speech information over a different kind of network: the Internet.[2] For years the Internet has been used to send text, but only recently has its function expanded to include real-time speech delivery. The manner in which speech is sent over the Internet is very different than that used in the standard public telephone network. For example, if you decided to place that phone call to your mother using your home PC, you would not be afforded the luxury of a dedicated electronic highway for your transmission. Indeed, far from it. You would, in fact, be sharing a massive electronic highway with the millions of other Internet users logged on at the time of your phone call. When you said "Happy Birthday, Mom," that speech stream would be divided and sent to your mother via potentially several different paths, depending on traffic conditions on the network at each moment. The "H-a" in "Happy" may travel through California before reaching your mother's house. However, if the California link became congested a moment later, the "p-p" might make its way through Texas. All or most of these little snippets of speech would eventually arrive at your mother's house to be reconstructed and played to her. But it might take some time to accomplish this. In fact, it may take one or two seconds from the time you begin saying "Happy Birthday, Mom" to the time she actually begins to hear it. This delay, or "latency," makes Internet voice communications cumbersome and tiring, and is likely one of the key reasons people have not abandoned their telephones just yet.

SOURCES OF DELAY

So what causes this delay? Actually, it is the collective result of the contribution of about 10 steps in the process by which voice information is collected and transmitted over the Internet. Those 10 steps are listed in Exhibit 45.1 in order of their chronological occurrence, and are explained below.

The first system delay is incurred when the first speaker begins speaking. Unlike the telephone network in which speech data are sent almost immediately and without extraordinary formatting, speech data must be carefully processed before transmission over the Internet. As a result, the system must record a certain amount of data to be processed before it does anything else. Picture yourself watering flowers on the weekend. You turn the hose on and fill the bucket with water, then you pour the water on the flowers. Before you can water the first flower, however, you must wait for the bucket to fill. Here you incur a delay, or latency, in which you're not watering any flowers and basically not accomplishing anything. You might start

---

Exhibit 45.1. Sources of Internet Transmission Delay

1	Transmitter recording
2	Codec (encode)
3	Compression
4	Transmitter modem
5	Internet
6	Receiver modem
7	Jitter buffer
8	Decompression
9	Codec (decode)
10	Playback

the project at 9:00 a.m. (by turning on the hose), but you don't actually start watering the flowers until perhaps 9:02 a.m. (when the bucket has filled).

A similar delay occurs when transmitting speech over the Internet. Let's say a speaker begins talking at exactly 1:00:00 p.m. The VoIP system might collect data for 1 s,[3] then begin processing that 1 s of data for transmission. It's now 1:00:01 p.m., and although speech has begun on the transmitter's end, on the other end of the connection the listener has heard nothing. This initial data collection delay is known as *transmitter record delay*, and can be reduced by minimizing the record time slice interval from 1 s in this simple example, to something much less than that — say 20 ms. Note, however, that reducing this recording period too much can adversely affect system quality in other ways that we'll discuss later. At this point it should suffice to say that there is a critical and delicate trade-off between recording time length and system latency.

One additional note is appropriate here regarding transmitter record delay. This discussion implicitly assumes a phone-to-phone call. That is, someone using their standard household telephone to call someone else with a standard household telephone. The call in this case, however, is connected not over a standard circuit-switched network as defined previously, but rather over a packet-switched network. The industry term for this type of VoIP application is "toll-bypass." In essence, the caller is placing a long-distance call which uses standard phone lines only to a certain point, then is handed off to the data network (e.g., Internet, VPN). This results in a long-distance connection for the price of a local phone call.

Since the telephone, as we've seen, is a low latency device, the transmitter record delay can be engineered to the minimum "chunk" or "bucket" of time acceptable to the next step in the VoIP system: encoding. This is typically in the range of 15 to 45 ms. However, if the call were placed using a personal computer, transmitter record delays would be much longer. This is because the current generation of personal computers (and PC operating systems) was not originally designed for low-latency record and playback. On today's PCs the minimum speech data bucket size that can be processed is much larger than the bucket size of a codec (between 150 and 300 ms). In the future we can expect low-latency PC sound drivers to be developed which will significantly improve the latency of PC–PC communications.

The second source of delay or latency is attributable to software that actually compresses the data before transmitting it. Speech data takes up a great deal of space electronically; this is why voicemail systems allow you to leave only a certain-size message before they cut off. Sophisticated software exists today that can compress speech before it is transmitted and decompress it when it arrives at its destination. To do this, the software, also known as a *codec* (short for coder/decoder), must hold up the data briefly so it can evaluate longer segments of it. For example, codecs work much better if they see the entire word "Hello" compared to just the "H-e" part of the word. Instead of compressing "H-e," the codec might wait for the entire word "Hello" before compressing it. Having seen what follows "H-e," the codec is much better able to code the "H-e." Thus, some small delay is incurred as the codec "looks ahead" during its mathematical computations.

Typical "low delay" codecs look ahead 15 to 45 ms for this purpose. However, it should be noted that if you engineer the VoIP system correctly, you size the recording delay to exactly meet the requirements of the codec. In this case no extra delay is introduced into the system by the look-ahead requirement of the codec. Finally, various sources use different terminology for the description of delay contributions. The reader should, therefore, be aware that the combination of *transmitter record delay* and *codec delay* is often called "algorithmic delay."

The codec does, however, introduce some additional delay while it conducts the actual computations that compress the speech for transmission. Those calculations are conducted on the computer processor on which the codec is running, e.g., a Pentium chip or a digital signal processor (DSP), and consume actual time; the process does not happen instantaneously. The faster the processor, the lesser the delay. The time required to conduct these calculations, and the system delay incurred as a result of it, are known as *compression delay*, the third of the 10 steps.

In addition to performing the compression calculations during this step, the speech data are also formatted for transmission over the Internet. Although that process introduces minimal system delay, it is a notable activity. In essence, the speech data are encapsulated in "packets" that the Internet can recognize and distribute appropriately. For example, the Internet needs to understand the final destination of the speech data packet so it can route it properly. These data are included in the packet built during this step. The composition of a typical packet will be discussed later in this document.

Once the speech data have been compressed, they are ready to be shipped over the Internet. If the terminal isn't directly connected to a network (which in turn is connected to the Internet), a connection must be set up, typically over a standard phone line. This is how most consumers access the Internet from their homes, and how many business travelers access the Net from the road.

Unfortunately, the data that a computer understands are quite different than the data understood by the public telephone network. Computers process "digitized" data, while the telephone network transports sound (analog signals). Thus, a device is needed to translate the computer's data format to sounds that can be carried over the public telephone network. This device is commonly known as a modem (short for modulator/demod-

Exhibit 45.2. PC-to-PC VoIP Call Modem Conversions

Modem Delay Occurrence	Data Conversion	From	To
1	PC format to PSTN format	Transmitter's PC	PSTN lines
2	PSTN format to Internet format	PSTN lines	Internet service Provider network
3	Internet format to PSTN format	Internet service Provider network	PSTN lines
4	PSTN format to PC format	PSTN lines	Receiver's PC

ulator). Like the codec, the modem must conduct calculations to enable this conversion, and those calculations take time to accomplish. For example, a 28.8 kbps modem can convert 28,800 bits of data to the telephone network's format in 1 s. Although that sounds very fast, when you're attempting to enable perceptibly instantaneous communications, every small delay counts.

In fact, this *modem delay*, the fourth step, can account for a nontrivial percentage of the end-to-end VoIP latency. Moreover, this modem delay occurs not only once during a VoIP PC-to-PC call, but four times, as detailed in Exhibit 45.2. It should be noted that Internet Service Provider (ISP) modems are typically substantially faster (able to process more data in a given period of time), and thus introduce considerably less delay than typical PC modems. Therefore, it would be somewhat inaccurate to calculate the modem delay associated with a 28.8 modem and simply multiply by four to obtain a figure for total end-to-end modem delay.

Note that similar to the transmitter record delay discussion, there are considerable latency implications whether the VoIP call is made via PC-to-PC or standard telephone-to-telephone. In a phone-to-phone or toll-bypass call (defined previously), there are no PC modems, so modem delay is nonexistent (as indicated previously, ISP modem delay is considered to be insignificant). Our example here assumes a PC-to-PC/modem access connection.

One of the most uncertain sources of VoIP packet delay is encountered when the data packets actually begin their journey over the network. As discussed previously, the Internet's packet-switched architecture moves packets from point to point in an unpredictable manner, and considerable delay is typically incurred for a significant percentage of packets sent via the Internet. Indeed, under very poor network conditions, up to 15 percent of the packets might not arrive at all, while it's not uncommon for a well-engineered network to lose, on average, 5 percent of those packets sent.

Given the nature of the transmission medium, it is nearly impossible to calculate this *Internet delay* (our fifth source of VoIP transmission delay), and even more difficult to control it. All data networks will introduce a minimum delay that cannot be reduced by the VoIP system. It simply takes a finite period of time for a packet to make its way from point A to point B. In a well-engineered network this fixed packet delay is unlikely to fall below 75 ms, and delays in the range of 90 to 120 ms are typical for well-engineered networks.[4] Such a fixed delay is tolerable, and VoIP system designers are more than capable of accounting for it as they design their systems. What is substantially more troublesome is the variation in this delay known as "jitter." A hypothetical data network that can guarantee its packets will arrive exactly 100 ms after transmission, and never more than that, is considered to have zero jitter. Thus, it is important to distinguish between Internet delay, a rather fixed quantity for a given network, and the variation in that delay (jitter). The sixth source of VoIP packet delay, *receiver modem delay,* is the inverse of the fourth.

This brings us to our seventh source of delay, *jitter buffer delay.* Jitter buffer delay is a response to the Internet's unreliability and volatility. It was mentioned above that when packet delivery is delayed by the Internet, the VoIP application developer is typically forced to wait for those late packets. The jitter buffer is the mechanism by which this waiting occurs. Let's say that someone in Texas is talking to someone in Boston using their PCs and a VoIP system, and the person in Texas says "Hello." The VoIP system takes the "Hello" data, processes them and places them in packets for shipment over the Internet. For the purpose of this argument, let's assume it can pack those data into three discrete packages or packets. In Boston packets #1 and #3 arrive on time, but packet #2 is delayed. When packet #1 arrives, it is stored in the jitter buffer while it waits for packets #2 and #3 to catch up. If the system doesn't wait for the slowed packets to arrive, it will be forced to play the "Hello" to the Boston conversation member with gaps in the speech; it will sound more like "He.....o." Thus, most VoIP systems incorporate a jitter buffer that fills and empties like a bucket of water. However, the larger the jitter buffer (the longer the system waits for delayed packets), the greater the delay introduced into the system. Later in this chapter we'll discuss ways in which jitter buffer delay can be reduced using state of the art technologies.

After waiting their turn in the jitter buffer, the speech packets must now be decoded. Delay sources 8 and 9, *decompression delay* and *decoding delay*, are the direct opposite of delay sources 2 and 3, *compression delay* and *encoding delay* and, therefore, will not be discussed further here.

Finally, the digitized packets must be converted one last time from digital format (the output of the decoder) to analog format so the sound can be played through the PC's speakers. Since our ears only understand analog signals, playing the digitized version wouldn't do us much good.[5] This final digital-to-analog conversion is accomplished by the PC's sound card and its core operating system. Unfortunately, as discussed previously, the management of the data by the PC's operating system through this device also introduces delay. This final source, *playback delay*, can also be significant, as today's sound cards and the software that controls them (known as "drivers") were not necessarily designed with the VoIP application in mind. This playback delay can be as large as 150 ms.

MINIMIZING TRANSMITTER RECORD DELAY

As discussed above, when a segment of speech data is sent over the Internet, it is first chopped into small time slices and compressed (or coded). The compressed output is organized into "frames," each of which contains the data to represent the individual time slice of speech. For example, if you say "Happy Birthday," the "H-a" may go in one frame, the "p-p-y" in the next, and so on.

However, the system can't simply send these naked speech frames alone. One or more frames (typically two to four) must be placed in small bundles (called packets) for shipment. The packets add some instructions about their destination, where they came from, a sequence number, etc. Remember, each of these packets may take a different path to the final destination (your mother's house in this case), and some may never arrive at all, so *each* one must have *all* this information. VoIP system lexicon refers to this information as the "header."

The header assures that each packet has the necessary information required for it to reach its destination and be reconstructed effectively. Unfortunately, data space is required to transmit this information. That is, to send this information the system must ship 320 bits of data *just for the header*, not including speech data. This overhead becomes significant when a system is sending thousands of packets. Given this, you might suggest sending as many frames as possible in each packet so the effect of the header overhead is minimized. Unfortunately, it's not that easy; don't forget about the *transmitter record delay* discussed earlier.

What does it mean to send more frames of data in each packet to minimize header overhead? Well, it means you must record more speech before you send it. Thus, instead of recording the "H-a" in "Happy Birthday" and sending it immediately, the system would record all of "Happy," stuff it into a single packet and send it. If you recorded just "H-a" and sent it, then "p-p-y" and sent it, you would have to send two headers (one for the "H-a" frame and one for the "p-p-y" frame). However, your mother would have to wait less time to hear you speak because she would be listening to the "H-a" playing back while you were recording and sending the "p-p-y." With a little luck, she might not be able to discern that two different packets were sent. On the other hand, if we send all of "Happy" in one packet, we would save 320 bits (the size of one header), but substantial "latency" would be introduced and mother would be waiting to hear us speak. So how do we resolve this problem? It seems that no matter what we do, we lose.

As discussed earlier, all speech is compressed, using a software product called a "codec," before it is placed in a packet and shipped over the Internet. All codecs are not the same, and the degree to which each compresses speech varies. One of the more popular codecs available today, the G.723.1, compresses speech to 6,300 bits per second. That means that if I speak for 1 s, the G.723.1 codec can record and compress my 1 s of speech and use only 6,300 bits to capture the information and ship it over the Internet. If I speak for 2 s, it would need 12,600 bits, and so on. Other codecs can compress the data further, requiring a smaller number of bits to send the same amount of speech. For example, Voxware's RT24 codec needs only 2,400 bits to send 1 s of speech data, less than half that of G.723.1. It's similar to the old "Name That Tune" game show. The fewer notes you need to name the song, the more you win.

Another important characteristic of a codec is the smallest frame size it can handle. Remember that a frame is a segment of speech data, and the smaller the chunk of data the codec can handle, the shorter the transmitter record delay. The frame size for the RT24 codec is 22.5 ms (there are 1000 ms in 1 s), while the minimum frame size for the G.723.1 is 30 ms. Interesting, but what does it mean for our current VoIP transmitter record delay conundrum?

Consider a packet of data with a single frame of speech. The RT24 packet would contain 22.5 ms of speech, while the G.723.1 packet would contain 30 ms. Before going any further, the G.723.1 system would have an additional 7.5 ms (30 ms – 22.5 ms = 7.5 ms) of transmitter record delay. But that's not the whole story. Given its lower bit rate, the RT24 can pack more data into a given amount of bits, and can use that bit savings to send more headers, and thus more packets, thereby reducing transmitter record delay. Exhibit 45.3 illustrates the comparative bandwidth requirements of G.723.1 and the RT24 for 1, 2, 3, and 4 frame-per-packet configurations. It also lists the transmitter delay comparison. Note that the RT24 reduces latency *and* requires less bandwidth, directly addressing the transmitter delay enigma described above.

Note from Exhibit 45.4 that for a given bandwidth, the RT24 codec can send packets with fewer frames. For example, for a constant bit rate of 9.8 kbps, G.723.1 would have to send 3 frames per packet, while RT24 could send 2 frames per packet for that same (actually less) bandwidth.

Exhibit 45.3. Bandwidth Requirements Vs. Transmitter Record Delay for G.723.1 and RT24

	G.723.1		Voxware RT24		Delay Savings with Voxware RT24	Bandwidth Savings with Voxware RT24
Frames per Packet	Required Bandwidth (kbps)[a]	Transmitter Record Delay	Required Bandwidth (kbps)[b]	Transmitter Record Delay		
1	17.0	30 ms	16.6	22.5 ms	7.5 ms	0.6 kbps
2	11.6	60 ms	9.5	45 ms	15 ms	2.1 kbps
3	9.8	90 ms	7.1	67.5 ms	22.5 ms	2.7 kbps
4	9.0	120 ms	6.0	90 ms	30 ms	3.0 kbps

[a] Calculated as follows: Bits/Frame = (6300 bits/s) × (1 s/1000 ms) × (30 ms/Frame) = 189 bits/frame; Required Bandwidth = ((# Frames/Packet) × (189 Bits/Frame) + 320 = Bits/Packet; (Bits/Packet) × (Packet/(30 × # Frames/Packet) ms) × (1000 ms/1 s) = (Bits/s) × (1 kb/1000 bits) = kbps.

[b] Substituted 2400 bits/s and frame size of 22.5 ms for 6300 bits/s and 30 ms in footnote #3 calculation.

MINIMIZING MODEM DELAY

Modem delay is one of the more substantial sources of delay encountered by VoIP systems primarily because it adds system delay not only once, but twice (and sometimes three or four times) during a packet's journey from one PC to another. Therefore, any successful reduction in modem delay can contribute substantially to overall system latency savings. Modem types are indicated by their speeds, or the amount of data they can process in a given period of time. For example, a 28.8 kbps modem can "capture" (that is, move into its buffers and ready for processing) 28,800 bits of data each second. Actually moving these data into the modem's

---

Exhibit 45.4. Bandwidth Requirements Vs. Frame Size For G.723.1 and RT24

Frames per Packet	G.723.1 Required Bandwidth (kbps)[a]	Voxware RT24 Required Bandwidth (kbps)[b]
1	17.0	16.6
2	11.6	9.5
3	9.8	7.1
4	9.0	6.0

[a] Calculated as follows: Bits/Frame = (6300 bits/s) × (1 s/1000 ms) × (30 ms/Frame) = 189 bits/frame; Required Bandwidth = ((# Frames/Packet) × (189 Bits/Frame)) + 320 = Bits/Packet; (Bits/Packet) × (Packet/(30 × # Frames/Packet) ms) × (1000 ms/1 s) = (bits/sec) × (1 kb/1000 bits) = kbps.

[b] Substituted 2400 bits/s and frame size of 22.5 ms for 6300 bits/s and 30 ms in footnote #3 calculation.

buffer is one of two modem delay sources. Once the data are moved into the modem, it must be processed (mathematical computations must be completed) to execute the conversion from digital to analog or vice versa. These computations require time to accomplish, contributing further to the system's overall delay.

As might be expected, the higher the modem bit rate (28.8 vs. 14.4 kbps), the faster it completes these calculations. The analysis that follows focuses exclusively on the first type of delay (moving data into the modem's buffer), but it should be noted that the second type of modem delay (call it calculation delay) can add as much as 25 ms each time data pass through the modem.

Additionally, because conversion of data is a function of bit rate, the more bits it must process, the higher the system's modem delay contribution becomes, highlighting yet another advantage of a low bit rate codec.

To determine the first type of modem delay, individual packet size must be calculated and considered. Since the smallest VoIP data chunk a modem "sees" is a packet, it must move at least one whole packet into the modem before it can begin processing. The time it takes to accomplish this is equal to its delay contribution. Thus, if a single packet is 1000 bits long, it will take a 28,800-bits/s modem 1000/28,800 s to move that single packet into its buffer, thereby introducing a delay equal to that time period.

In this 1000-bit-long packet example, the 28.8 kbps modem would introduce 35 ms of system delay. Note that in a PC-to-PC connection, data must pass through two modems, thereby doubling their overall delay contribution. In this example, total system modem delay (transmitter and receiver modem delay combined) would be equal to 70 ms (not including modem calculation delay, which is likely to add an additional 50 ms [25 ms $\times$ 2 = 50 ms]). Exhibit 45.5 compares the modem delay contributions of a system built with RT24 and one with G.723.1 for various modem speeds and multiple packet configurations.

As illustrated in Exhibit 45.5, the latency or delay savings achievable by employing a low bit-rate codec is substantial, even when using some of the highest data rate modems commercially available today. Again, note that this calculation includes a three frames per packet data payload configuration (highlighted above). Now, return to Exhibit 45.3 and note that a packet with three frames of G.723.1 not only consumes substantially more bandwidth than an RT24 packet with three frames (greatly increasing modem delay as illustrated in Exhibit 45.5), but the G.723.1 packet also incurs more transmitter record delay than does the RT24 packet. Thus, the low bit-rate RT24 codec provides system designers the best of both worlds — a lower bit-rate to enable faster modem processing, and a smaller frame size to allow the reduction of transmitter record delay.

Exhibit 45.5. G.723.1 Vs. RT24 Modem Delay (Does Not Include Modem Calculation Delay)

Modem Speed (kbps)	Frames per Packet	Bits/ Packet (RT24)	Bits/ Packet (G.723.1)	Single Modem Delay (RT24) (ms)	Single Modem Delay (G.723.1) (ms)	Single Modem Delay Savings with RT24 (ms)	Dual Modem Delay Savings with RT24 (ms)
14.4	1	374	509	26	35	9	18
	2	428	698	30	48	18	36
	3	482	887	33	62	29	58
	4	536	1076	37	75	38	76
19.2	1	374	509	20	27	7	14
	2	428	698	22	36	14	28
	3	482	887	25	46	21	42
	4	536	1076	28	56	28	56
28.8	1	374	509	13	18	5	10
	2	428	698	15	24	9	18
	3	482	887	17	31	14	28
	4	536	1076	19	37	18	36

MINIMIZING JITTER BUFFER DELAY

When a VoIP system designer chooses a low bit-rate, parametric codec, jitter buffer delay can be reduced substantially by exploiting a major feature of such a codec — the luxury of dropping delayed packets and synthesizing the missing speech data using the special properties of a parametric codec.

Recalling that the function of the jitter buffer in a VoIP system is to hold and temporarily store packets in an effort to "wait" for packets that have been delayed during their journey across the Internet, it would appear that little can be done to minimize this source of system delay. Indeed, no system can reliably control or affect the Internet's ability to transport packets (be they speech or data packets); one can only hope for the best. Right? Not necessarily. This rather fatalistic perspective is appropriate if the only option available to a VoIP system is to helplessly wait for delayed packets to arrive. But what if the VoIP system could drop delayed packets if they fail to arrive on time without appreciably sacrificing sound quality?

As it turns out, certain kinds of codecs have the ability to accurately reproduce the actual speech stream with only a partial amount of the originally coded speech. That is, if three packets are sent from Butte, MT to London and one of them is delayed for an unacceptable period of time, the codec in London can reconstruct or "synthesize" the missing data — "fake it" or "fill in the gap," if you will; it doesn't necessarily have to wait for the late packet. Those codecs with an inherent ability to accurately "fill in the

Exhibit 45.6. Hypothetical Packet Delay Example

Packet Number	Delay Beyond Baseline Delay
1	40 ms
2	70 ms
3	120 ms
4	80 ms

gaps" are known as "parametric"[6] codecs. A detailed discussion of the features of parametric codecs is beyond the scope of this chapter, and the ability of such codecs to effectively reconstruct speech streams with missing data can be truly appreciated only by listening to their performance.[7] However, given this attribute of a parametric codec, conclusions can be drawn with substantial ramifications for reducing VoIP system latency.

Let's assume for a moment that four packets are sent from Butte, MT to New York. We'll hypothesize a network with a baseline packet delay time of 80 ms (that is, the minimum time a packet needs to traverse this distance is 80 ms). Let's further assume that packet #1 arrives in 120 ms from the time it leaves Butte (40 ms beyond the baseline); the second packet takes 150 ms to traverse the Internet (70 ms beyond the baseline); the third needs 200 ms (120 ms beyond the baseline); and the last consumes 160 ms (80 ms greater than the baseline). Exhibit 45.6 presents the data in this hypothetical example.[8]

If the VoIP system were using a codec that was unable to accurately reconstruct gaps in the data, it would be forced to wait for all four packets to arrive, thereby incurring a delay of 120 ms waiting for, in this case, packet #3 to catch up. Another way to phrase this is to say that the "jitter buffer is 120 ms long" and, therefore, the system's "jitter buffer delay" is 120 ms. Now what if the codec were a parametric codec, such as Voxware's RT24? In that case the codec would have the luxury to drop packet #3 because it is late, and fill in the missing gap with completely synthesized speech. To reconstruct the speech, the RT24-based system would require a jitter buffer of only 80 ms (long enough to capture the longest delayed packet it wishes to wait for; in this case, packet #4). The jitter buffer delay of the RT24-based system is, in this hypothetical case, 40 ms lower than that of the system using a nonparametric codec (otherwise known as waveform or time-domain based).

Jitter buffer sizes vary appreciably from system to system, but it's not uncommon for them to be as large as 200 to 300 ms. Thus, considerable latency savings can be achieved if delayed packets can be dropped and their gaps reconstructed. In one recent test conducted at Voxware, it was determined that the jitter buffer size could be reduced by 50 ms if 33 percent of

Exhibit 45.7. Source of Internet Transmission Delay

Chronological Order	Delay Source Description	"Typical" Value (ms) PC-to-PC (Internet Phone)	"Typical" Value (ms) Phone-to-Phone (Toll Bypass)
1	Transmitter recording	150–300	20–150
2	Codec (encode)	5	5
3	Compression	5	5
4	Transmitter modem	5–38	0
5	Internet	70–150	70–150
6	Receiver modem	5–38	0
7	Jitter buffer	150–300	150–300
8	Decompression	5	5
9	Codec (decode)	10	10
10	Playback	40–300	0

the late packets were dropped.[9] While sound quality noticeably degraded under these conditions, resulting transmission was intelligible and rather impressive given the extraordinary dropped packet rate.[10]

Finally, it should be noted that systems built with waveform (nonparametric) codecs like G.723.1 and G.729 can also reconstruct missing speech to some degree, but techniques used by waveform-based systems are substantially less sophisticated than those employed by parametric codecs like Voxware's RT24, and the sound quality of such waveform reconstructions is considerably lower.

END-TO-END SYSTEM DELAY

Earlier in this discussion we listed and discussed the ten major VoIP latency sources, but purposely omitted estimates of actual delays introduced by each source. In Exhibit 45.7, we provide such characteristic values in absolute terms with the following strong caveat: absolute values for VoIP system latency vary not only from system to system, but also from time to time in the *same* system. Thus, it is nearly impossible to delineate a "typical" value, and for that reason we've placed "typical" in quotes throughout this section. The numbers in Exhibit 45.7 were derived from observations made by Voxware engineers during the development of several Internet telephone and conferencing products during the past 3 years. They are presented here only to facilitate discussion.

"TYPICAL" ACTUAL DELAYS

Based on a quick inspection of the data in Exhibit 45.7, it is clear that reducing transmitter recording delay, transmitter and receiver modem delay, and jitter buffer delay can substantially reduce the end-to-end delay encountered by typical VoIP systems. When one notes that a delay of 150 ms is perceptible to the average human, these results are even more compelling.

Author's Bio

Jeff Hill has spent the bulk of his career as a product manager for products as diverse as analytic scientific instrumentation and noise-filtering software and hardware. He joined Voxware in 1997 as Director of Product Management, and now serves as the company's Director of Marketing as well. Before coming to Voxware, Hill was the senior product manager for high-density speech products at Dialogic Corporation. He holds a B.S. in Aerospace Engineering from the University of Maryland, and an M.S. in System Engineering from Johns Hopkins University.

Notes

1. A multimedia PC is one equipped with a "sound card" (a hardware device that converts analog speech into the digitized data format that a PC understands), a microphone, and some speakers. Nearly all PCs shipped today are of the multimedia variety.
2. This discussion is relevant to not only Internet-based communications, but any data network, including LANs, WANs, and Virtual Private Networks (VPNs).
3. Transmitter record time slices are never 1 s long, and in fact are typically a fraction of that. The 1 s time frame used here was selected to illustrate the concept.
4. Some of this inherent delay is due literally to the speed of light; it simply takes a finite period of time for an electronic impulse to traverse a long distance.
5. Playing digitized speech through conventional speakers without first converting it to analog format would create the same sound you hear when you fax a document; that is, the high-pitched, screeching and annoying tones that indicate your fax machine is "talking" to the receiving fax machine. What you're hearing are digitized signals being sent over an analog network and played through the fax machine's speakers.
6. Also known as "frequency-domain-based" codecs.
7. Contact Voxware at (609) 514-4100 for a codec evaluator.
8. The example here is grossly oversimplified to illustrate that delayed packets can be dropped and a reconstruction accomplished. Actual Internet packet delay profiles are substantially more complex and comprise bursts of delayed packets. That is, a single packet is rarely delayed considerably longer that those adjacent to it. Rather, two, three, or more packets would likely encounter a congested router or other element of the Internet and be substantially delayed in a group. Voxware provides test software that enables customers to build custom loss profiles and test codec performance. Contact Voxware for a copy of that test software.
9. Test conducted on 9/8/97, California to Princeton via UUnet Network, 20 packets per second packet rate; 8 kbps bandwidth; 28.8 kbps modems on each end. Given that the packets were not required to exit the UUnet system, it is likely that this represents a reasonable best case test and that jitter buffer saving would be greater for the same packet loss rate under different conditions.
10. Contact your nearest Voxware sales representative for a demonstration of Voxware codec operation under these conditions.

Section VII
Appendix

Appendix
Internet
Development
Resources

APPLICATION DEVELOPMENT

Hamilton Technologies, Inc.

Address: 17 Inman Street, Cambridge, MA 02139
Phone: (617) 492-0058
Fax: (617) 492-1727
E-Mail: sales@htius.com
Website: http://world.std.com/~hti
Sales Contact Name: Hannah Gold

■ **Product: 001 (pronounced "double oh one")**

Version Number: 3.2.8
Pricing: seat and component based
Hardware Requirements: UNIX (HP, Sun, RS6000, Alpha), Windows (NT)
Software Requirements: Developer Package for hardware environment
of choice which includes C compiler and GUI environment (Motif or
Windows)

Description Summary. Hamilton Technologies, Inc. (HTI) was founded in
1986 to provide products and services to modernize the system engineering and software development process in order to maximize reliability, lower cost, and accelerate time to market. HTI's flagship product, 001, is based
on HTI's Development Before The Fact (DBTF) formal systems theory used
to develop systems in terms of System Oriented Objects (SOOs). This paradigm integrates systems and software engineering disciplines and transforms the software development process away from an inefficient and
expensive curative process to a preventative, more productive, reliable
process.

APPENDIX

001 is a completely integrated systems engineering and software development environment. It can be used to define, analyze, and automatically generate complete, integrated, and fully production-ready code for any kind of software application with a significantly lower error rate and high reusability. Since 001 has an open architecture it can be configured to generate (or interface to) systems at all levels including hardware platforms, software platforms, programming languages, databases, operating systems, Internet systems, embedded systems, communication protocols, GUIs, and legacy code of choice.

Product Feature List

- *Always number one when put to the test,* no matter how large or complex the system.
- *Inherently reusable,* all 001 developed systems are system-oriented objects (SOOs).
  - No interface errors
  - All objects are under control and traceable
- *Formal but friendly language,* the same language is used for defining any part of a system at any phase of development.
- *Integrated seamless design and development environment.*
- *Executable specification simulation.*
- *Integrated metrics for predictive systems,* with a mechanism to trace from requirements to code and back again
- *100 percent automatic code generation,* 001 automatically generates complete, integrated, fully production ready-to-run code for any kind of system whether it be GUI, database, communications, real time, distributed, client server, multi-user or mathematical algorithms.
- *001's generator is accessible to a user to tailor it for his own brand of generated code;* once configured, 001 will automatically regenerate the new system to reside on that environment. Complete flexibility is provided to the user to define his own primitive type interfaces to chosen APIs which 001 integrates with 001's formal definitions.
- *Maintenance performed at the blueprint level,* the user doesn't ever need to change the code, only the specification, and then regenerates only the changed part of the system.
- *GUI environment tightly integrated with the development of an application.*
- *Automatic testing.*
- *Automatic documentation,* 001's generator is able to automatically document reports for all phases of development since its documentation environment is tightly integrated with the formal definition of the system.
- *001 was completely defined and generated with itself.*

Interwoven, Inc.

Address: 1195 W. Fremont Ave., #2000, Sunnyvale, CA 94087-3825
Phone: (408) 774-2000
Fax: (408) 774-2002
E-Mail: info@interwoven.com
Website: www.interwoven.com

■ Product: TeamSite

Version Number: 2.0
Pricing: by server and seat
Hardware requirements: NT or Solaris-based server
Software requirements: any Web server

Description Summary. Interwoven TeamSite is the first and only open, scalable system developed specifically to manage the development and deployment of the large, dynamic Websites. Teamsite, an Enterprise Web Production system, supports Web content management, software configuration management, and workflow for enterprise Web development.

Product Feature List

- *Openness* — leverages existing IT investments, compatible with all tools and content
- *Ease of use* — empowers all contributors — from authors to IT professionals
- *Performance/scalability* — manages sites comprising hundreds of thousands of files
- *Branching* — enables massively parallel development on hundreds of simultaneous Web projects.
- *InContext QA* — provides each Web contributor a complete, fully functional copy of the site in which to develop and stage content.
- *Accommodates rapid change* — only TeamSite can handle the realistic challenge of Enterprise Web Production for a site with 50,000 files, and a team of 100 developers who have to build and release the Website every two hours. No other product can scale to meet these demands.
- *Deployment* — Interwoven OpenDeploy provides a secure and configurable solution for deployment of Web content to any number of production servers.

Speedware Corporation

Address: 9999 Cavendish Boulevard, St. Laurent, Quebec, Canada, H4M 2X5
Phone: (514) 747-7007

Fax: (514) 747-3380
E-Mail: Webmaster@speedware.com
Website: www.speedware.com

■ Product: Visual Speedware

Version Number: 1.01
Pricing: from $4995 U.S.
Hardware/software requirements: Visual Speedware is available for
Windows 95, Windows NT, HP-UX, and MPE/iX. Requires Visual Basic
5.0

Description Summary. Visual Speedware is the first true multi-user development environment built on Microsoft Visual Basic. With Visual Speedware, you can create and deploy complex, robust, graphical client-server applications quickly and efficiently. Visual Speedware significantly reduces the time and cost of developing your applications and helps you use client and server resources intelligently.

Product Feature List

- *Scaling VB to the Enterprise* — integrating Visual Basic with Speedware server-side technology offers a single, comprehensive working environment and extends the processing power of VB applications, scaling them up from the PC platform to back-end servers such as Windows NT, UNIX, and MPE.
- *Cutting Development Time* — simplifies application development by offering time-saving wizards and by letting you create client and server components in one process using one tool.
- *Eliminating Deployment Costs* — Auto-Deployment feature distributes the application client components from server to end-users.
- *Controlling Logic Partitioning* — allows the developer to control which parts of the application logic are executed on the client and which on the server.
- *Leveraging Existing Systems* — Visual Speedware lets you plug Windows applications into a Visual Speedware client or legacy applications into the server component.

■ Product: Speedware Autobahn

Version Number: 1.3
Pricing: from $6000 U.S.
Hardware/software requirements: Speedware Autobahn is available for
Windows 95, Windows NT, HP-UX, AIX, Solaris, and MPE/iX. Requires
Web server software.

Description Summary. Speedware Autobahn is a complete development environment for creating new Web applications and Web-enabling existing, mission-critical applications for Internet, intranet, and extranet environments. Autobahn is based on an *n*-tier scalable Application Server that openly supports all Web technologies.

Product Feature List

- *Industry's Highest Level of Security* — secure access to Web-based applications. Autobahn combines three distinct internal security features to ensure users are securely connected to their server-based applications.
- *Robust State Management* — no other product handles state-oriented applications more completely. Autobahnís architecture enables permanent and persistent binding between users and applications.
- *Scalable Distributed Computing* — two types of scalability: scaling software architecture to a large number of simultaneous users and hardware architecture to incorporate multiple machines.
- *Web-Enabling Existing Applications* — offers a variety of methods for tightly integrating legacy systems into Web-based applications, breathing new life into existing applications.
- *Easily Integrate Other Web Technologies* — supports an Open Web Architecture to facilitate the integration of current and future Web technology without having to regenerate applications.

■ Product: Media

Version Number: V3.0

Pricing: Media/MR Developer license is US$4995 per developer and $2000 per user. Server price from $23,400 for 20 users.

Hardware/software requirements: Client-supported platforms include Windows 95 and Windows NT. Server-supported platforms include Windows NT and UNIX (HP 9000, RS/6000 and Sun Solaris).

Description Summary. Media lets you access, graphically display, and analyze unlimited quantities of up-to-the-minute data, with lightning speed — and it's simple to deploy and maintain. Media is available for both Windows and the Web.

Media/M, a Multidimensional Online Analytical Processing (MOLAP) tool, accesses data from its own compact, multimatrix multidimensional database, offering unmatched performance. Media/MR is a Hybrid Online Analytical Processing (HOLAP) tool that rapidly accesses high-level aggregates from its multidimensional database, and vast amounts of detailed data directly from any relational database.

APPENDIX

Product Feature List

- *Excellent Performance* — precalculate aggregates in Media's compact multimatrix MDDB; cache results of relational queries on the server, and share them between users.
- *Analytical Flexibility* — slice and dice, drill down, perform sophisticated calculations, forecast, etc.
- *Real-time Data* — real-time access to detailed data from your RDBMS or data warehouse.
- *High Data Capacity* — dynamic dimensions donít limit you to a predefined multidimensional structure.
- *Leverages Data Warehouse* — connects to all RDBMSs, and supports all schemas.
- *Easy Development* — Dictionary Wizard guides you through the rapid construction of your multidimensional model by proposing indicators and dimensions.
- *Low Maintenance* — metadata-driven, keeps the multidimensional model in synch with the underlying RDBMS.

■ Product: Esperant

Version Number: V4.1
Pricing: from US$595 per user
Hardware/software requirements: IBM compatible PC running Windows 95 or NT.

Description Summary. Esperant is the fastest, most productive way to put corporate information into the hands of decision makers. Esperant is a powerful ad hoc query and reporting tool that empowers users with accurate information — the basis for sound business decisions.

The point-and-click interface removes the need to learn complex data structures or SQL. Only Esperant can generate the robust SQL you need to handle the widest range of business queries. Its patented SQL Expert ensures correct results. Esperant is available for both Windows and the Web.

Product Feature List

- *Intuitive, powerful queries* — English-like queries; transparent joins from multiple data sources; batch scheduling, custom prompted queries.
- *Complete reporting and charting* — drag-and-drop live-data report formatting; customizable report templates; OLE2 support; 24 chart and graph types.
- *Desktop integration* — export query results to spreadsheets and word processors; Executive Desktop for one-click access to queries and reports; programmable integration through OLE Automation.

- *Flexible administration* — transform complex database structures into business terms; import database structures from the RDBMS catalog; full hierarchical security with inheritance.
- *Aggregate aware* — a collection of tables can be marked as an Aggregate Set and displayed to the end user as a single category.
- *Partitioned Set capability* — useful for applications that store identcal fields in different tables, such as different time periods.

AUDIO

Voxware, Inc.

Address: 305 College Road East, Princeton, NJ 08540
Phone: (609) 514-4100
Fax: (609) 514-4101
E-Mail: vox@voxware.com
Website: www.voxware.com
Sales Contact Name: Jeff Hill

■ Product: Custom Compression and Signal Processing SDKs

Version Number: Varies
Product Feature List: Contact Voxware
Pricing: Contact Voxware
Hardware requirements: Pentium class microprocessors or a variety of DSPs and RISC chips
Software requirements: Windows, Unix, Java and others

Description Summary. Voxware's voice compression and VOIP software development kits offer users state of the art compression, voice-activity detection, comfort noise generation, frame loss concealment, automatic jitter buffer minimization, and other technologies accessible by well-documented and easy-to-use APIs. Voxware specializes in technologies that maximize the quality of real-time voice communications over PC-to-PC links via the Internet an intranets. Voxware's SDKs handle packetization and other network interface functions, as well as PC sound system interface, and data sampling conversion. They are available in Window NT, Windows 95, and many version are offered in other operating systems and with Java interfaces.

BANKING (INTERNET)

nFront, Inc.

Address: 1551 Jennings Mill Road, Suite 800A, Bogart, GA 30622
Phone: (706) 369-3779
Fax: (706) 369-8611
E-Mail: apowell@banking.com
Website: www.banking.com/www.nfront.com
Sales Contact Name: Alan Powell

■ **Product: nHome™**

Pricing: Based on Asset size of institution
Hardware requirements:
- Pentium 75 Processor or greater PC
- 16 Mb RAM or greater
- 28.8 BPS Asynch modem or greater
- CD ROM drive
- Monitor
- Keyboard
- Mouse
- Dedicated analog telephone line for dialup connectivity
- PC must be housed in a secure area of the bank and be available to receive daily ACH files and transmit nightly balance files (basically a PC running Windows 95 with 16 Mb RAM and an Asynch modem)

Software requirements:
- Microsoft Windows 95 Version 4.00.950 B or greater on CD ROM
- Microsoft Plus!

Description Summary. nHome™, the company's Microsoft NT-based Internet banking application, enables banking customers to open new accounts, apply for loans, view account balances and histories, pay bills, transfer funds, download images of cleared checks, customize reports, and download active statements into personal financial management packages at anytime, from any location, using any secure, browser-enabled device such as personal computers and televisions.

From the bank's perspective, nHome allows the financial institution to expand its reach to a broader market, primarily composed of the most profitable banking customers, while taking advantage of the least expensive delivery channel available today. Because customers are afforded greater access to and control over their account information, the bank's customer service overhead ultimately can be reduced. And perhaps most importantly, through the collection of data captured online in this fat server solution, the bank can target specific customers for more efficient and effective cross-selling and marketing campaigns.

Product Feature List

- Secure account and credit applications
- Account summaries and histories
- DDAs
- Savings
- CDs
- IRAs
- Mortgages
- Loans
- Equity lines
- Lines of credit
- Funds transfer
- Bill payment
- Immediate and future transfers
- Immediate and future payments
- One-time and recurring transfers
- One-time and recurring payments
- Custom reports
- PFM downloads
- Account type
- Date
- Check number
- Quicken™
- Transaction amount
- Transaction type
- Microsoft Money™
- Interactive calculators
- Personal Information Manager
- Retirement planning
- College planning
- PIN management
- Mortgage estimating
- Loan estimating
- Change of address, etc.
- Check imaging
- Administrative interface
- Internet branch reporting
- Data mining/cross-selling
- Update rates and product information
- Customer-specific reporting
- Download secure online applications
- Automatic sales message delivery
- View audit tables and customer stats
- E-mail notification system
- Online help
- Branded online demo
- … and more

CHAT

Acuity Corporation

Address: 11100 Metric Blvd., #725, Austin, TX 78758
Phone: (512) 425-2200
Toll Free: (888) 242-8669
Fax: (512) 719-8225
E-Mail: info@acuity.com
Website: http://www.acuity.com
Sales Contact Name: Mark Roycroft

APPENDIX

■ Product: ichat ROOMS

Version Number: 4.0
Pricing: Concurrent user pricing, starting at $595.
Hardware requirements: Depending on your system, approximately
32 Mb of available memory and a minimum of 20 Mb disk space is
required.
Software requirements: Available for Windows NT 4.0 and Solaris 2.5.1;
works with Microsoft IIS and Netscape Enterprise Web Servers.

Product Feature List

- *Event moderation* — advanced event moderation features simplify the
management of large, live discussions that can involve thousands of
simultaneous users.
- *Numerous client options* — Java, Netscape Plug-in, ActiveX control,
and HTML client interfaces provide numerous options for Windows,
Macintosh, and Unix users.
- *Intuitive user interface* — visitors enter a conversation simply by typing.
- *Private messaging* — support for public and private messages offers
users one-to-one and one-to-many communications channels.
- *Multimedia support* — ROOMS is multimedia-ready, supporting sound,
video, and VRML.
- *File transfer* — a convenient client-to-client file transfer capability in-
creases desktop productivity, allowing users to instantly share files.
- *HTML embedding* — messages may have embedded hyperlinks and
HTML formatting. Important notices or comments can appear in bold
text, or a URL can be conveniently displayed as a clickable link.
- *Collaborative browsing* — ichat ROOMS' support for collaborative site
navigation enhances customer service and group interaction.
- *Robust administration* — administrators have easy access to detailed
conversation and server status logs and configuration settings, which
can be modified remotely via a simple HTML interface.
- *API* — C++ extensions (servlets) enable administrators to add new
and unique features to ROOMS.
- *Seamless product integration* — with shared authentication functions, ROOMS functions as part of the ichat real-time enterprise
architecture.

■ Product: ichat Message Boards

Version Number: 2.0
Pricing: Message Boards starts at $2995 for 50 concurrent users
Hardware requirements: Intel-based Windows NT 4.0 or Sun Solaris
2.5.1; 32 Mb RAM and 20 Mb disk space (minimums)
Software requirements: Major Web server (Netscape Enterprise Server
or Microsoft IIS)

Description Summary. Message boards is a client-server software system that allows users to search for information and post questions and answers in a threaded, hierarchical format. Since Message Boards uses standard HTML and users access discussion forums right from their browser, no additional client software is needed. Server setup and configuration is conducted through an HTML interface, enabling robust forum management and remote administration.

Product Feature List

- *Browser based* — employees or customers can instantly access online discussion groups from within their favorite Web browser. No additional software is required.
- *Highly configurable interface* — a configurable HTML interface allows site administrators to easily create unique, branded user experiences. iHTML, ichat's interactive extension to the HTML standard, allows developers to embed ichat Message Boards functionality within their Website or intranet.
- *NNTP client support* — NNTP (Network News Transfer Protocol) client support allows network news users to connect and participate in discussion forums.
- *Organized discussions* — ichat Message Boards discussion groups are displayed hierarchically, allowing users to easily follow conversation "threads."
- *Moderated topics* — the moderation option allows administrators to effectively organize and lead discussions. Question and answer message areas can be regulated so that only approved responses are visible to regular users. Similarly, a moderated company information area can contain postings that are prescreened by site administrators.
- *Versatile administration* — Message Boards permits administrators to delegate message management to topic owners and forum moderators. An HTML interface enables quick and easy remote administration, with new topics and moderated threads established with the click of a mouse. Content filtering can also be controlled at the topic group level.
- *Text searching* — message subject and topic key word search support enables ichat Message Boards to serve as a document and information archive. Frequently asked questions can be quickly sorted or all messages referring to a particular project name can easily be found.

■ Product: ichat Paging System

Version Number: 1.1
Pricing: The Paging System starts at $1595 for 100 concurrent users.
Hardware requirements: Intel-based Windows NT 4.0 or Sun Solaris
2.5.1; 48 Mb RAM and 64 Mb disk space (minimums).

APPENDIX

Description Summary. The ichat Paging System™ delivers critical new real-time communications capabilities to the desktop. Users can instantly send high-priority messages or determine whether a colleague is online. With a clean, professional interface that displays messages on top of open windows, the Paging System enables individuals to exchange information with new levels of immediacy.

When phone calls are routed to voice mail and e-mails are lost in heavy traffic, ichat Pager users benefit from real-time, impossible-to-miss desktop communication. Additionally, by adding contacts to their list of associates, users can see when others are available for instant messaging, invitations to Netscape Conferences and Microsoft NetMeetings, or Quick Chat™ text conferencing.

Product Feature List

- Server Features:
  - *Global messaging* — connected to the ichat Global Message Router, individuals and groups can send and receive messages from users of remote Paging Systems. Messages sent to offline users are stored for later delivery.
  - *Scalability* — add multiple Paging Servers to your Website or intranet to support tens of thousands of simultaneous users.
  - *Notify your users* — with the ichat Paging Server's flexible administrative tools you can easily communicate with your users by sending instant messages, URLs, or links to live audio streams. Tools are provided to send messages to multiple user categories including all online users, users in specific interest groups, or to individual users.
  - *Display advertising/informational banners* — with an external ad server you can insert images into all user messages. Graphic image size is variable — you can include any size image and the client application will size to accommodate it. Using an intelligent background file caching scheme, client response is not slowed by the addition of banner graphics to instant messages.
  - *Customizable interface* — administrators can customize the Pager client interface to contain customer logos, links to Websites, links to ROOMS chat or Message Board discussions, or lists of other users.
  - *Server logging and monitoring* — monitoring server events, system messages, and server uptime through the HTML interface is straightforward. You can also track user activity, server load and usage, and message delivery systems.
  - Administrative controls — the ichat Paging System is easily administered via an HTML interface. Administrative functions include:
  - *System security* — encrypted passwords, IP restrictions.

- *Text filtering* — eliminate specified text or regular expression matches from message content.
- User management.
- Client configuration tools.
- Message gateway application
- Client features:
  - *Instant Messaging* — Send and receive instant messages from other users.
  - *Quick Chat*™ — Easily initiate a real-time chat session with one or more users.
  - *Privacy* — Optionally hide your user profile information, receive pages only from certain users, or ignore individual users.
  - *User Status Information* — Indicates when other users are on-line, idle or away from their computer.
- *Interest Categories* — Sign up for server-defined interest categories to easily find users

---

CONSULTING/SOLUTION PROVIDERS

Brainstorm Technology

Address: One Alewife Center, Cambridge, MA 02140
Phone: (617) 588 0840
Fax: (617) 588 0806
E-Mail: sales@braintech.com
Website: www.braintech.com

Description Summary. Brainstorm Technology, Inc., the leader in Groupware Tools and Professional Services, helps organizations design, develop, and deploy groupware applications, using platforms such as Lotus Notes and corporate intranets. Brainstorm has pioneered the development of a three-tiered Java Architecture for deployment of highly interactive database applications for the Web.

Customers include over 1500 organizations worldwide. Brainstorm's Groupware tools and Professional Services allow these customers to leverage their existing information technology infrastructure while adopting new technologies. Founded in 1993 by two MIT Alumni, Brainstorm has experienced triple digit growth each year. Brainstorm's customers include Federal Express, Arthur Andersen, General Motors, Hitachi, Price Waterhouse, Digital Equipment Corporation, and many other Fortune 500 companies.

Free Range Media

Address: 100 S. King Street; Suite 600, Seattle, WA 98104
Phone: (206) 340-9305
Toll-Free: (800) 570-3873
Fax: (206) 344-6028
E-Mail: info@freerange.com
Website: www.freerange.com
Sales Contact Name: Geoff Brown, Sales Director

Description Summary. Free Range Media is a full service online business solutions provider based in Seattle, WA, with regional offices around the U.S. An expert in Return on Internet Investment (ROI2)™, Free Range Media delivers bottom line results for companies looking to use the Web strategically. By combining business strategy, innovative design and technical expertise with client partnerships, Free Range Media has developed Internet, intranet and/or extranet solutions for numerous prominent companies nationwide including Swedish Medical Center, Hewlett-Packard Company, Dain Rauscher Corporation, and First Choice Health and Blue Shield of California.

International Communications, Inc.

Address: 492 Old Connecticut Path, Framingham, MA
Phone: (508) 620-3900
Fax: (508) 620-3999
E-Mail: info@intl.com
Website: www.intl.com
Sales Contact Name: Derek Perkins, Vice President of Sales

■ Product: Localization and translation services

Version Number: Localize into over 22 different languages

Description Summary. International Communications specializes in the localization of software, Websites, marketing materials, and interactive media. Committed to helping leaders in the IT industry achieve success in overseas markets, the company utilizes leading-edge tools and provides customized solutions for complex projects. U.S. offices are located in Boston, MA; Chicago, IL; San Francisco, CA; and Seattle, WA. Overseas offices are in Beijing, China; Paris, France; and Rendsburg, Germany.

DIRECTORY SERVERS

Isocor

Address: 3420 Ocean Park Blvd., Santa Monica, CA 90405
Phone: (310) 581-8100
Fax: (310) 581-8111
E-Mail: sales.info@isocor.com
Website: www.isocor.com

■ Product: Global Directory Server

Version Number: 2.3
Hardware requirements: GDS runs a wide variety of platforms from low
   end NT hardware up to very large UNIX environments

Description Summary. The ISOCOR Global Directory Server (GDS) provides the cornerstone of the electronic business environment. It is a world-
class directory server with support for LDAP version 3 and the X.500 protocols, setting the highest standards for performance and scalability. GDS
and its companion products offer all the benefits of open enterprise directory services: a single and consistent view of distributed data, tools for integrating different breeds of messaging and directory products, and secure
and controlled access to sensitive information. These directory services
can be managed and controlled remotely by an intuitive, centralized management console.

Product Feature List

- LDAPv3 support
- Unparalled scaling and performance
- Intuitive administration GUI
- Extensive security features
- Robust distribution mechanism
- Supports X.500 standards

■ Product: MetaConnect Family

Version Number: 1.0
Hardware requirements: Runs on a wide range of NT machines, UNIX
   ports available in '99.

Description Summary. The ISOCOR MetaConnect solution is the next-generation meta directory solution. It allows an organization to connect their
"islands of information." MetaConnect provides connectors for most common corporate information resources, and includes easy to use tools for
delivering custom connectors and to organize and unify the information.

APPENDIX

The MetaConnect controller offers a powerful and intuitive mechanism for unifying, or joining, information about a person or object from many different sources and securely publish selected information. Once the information is unified it can be selectively made accessible to an authorized community over the Internet to provide the foundation for corporate electronic commerce services.

Product Feature List

- Directory server independent
- Open access to connected directories and databases
- Open programming and scripting support
- Real-time updates to information
- High performance
- Scalable

DOCUMENT CONTROL

Trellix Corporation

Address: 51 Sawyer Road, Waltham, MA 02453
Phone: (781) 788-9400
Toll-Free: (800) 617-2876
Fax: (781) 788-9494
E-Mail: support@trellix.com
Website: www.trellix.com
Sales Contact Name: Bryan Semple

■ **Product: Trellix**

Version Number: 1.0
Pricing: $99
Hardware/Software requirements: IBM 486/66 MHz PC/compatible or higher, Windows 95 or Windows NT 4.X, 16 Mb RAM, 23 Mb hard disk space.

Description Summary. Trellix 1.0: The "Web" processor that makes it easy to communicate business information online. Trellix features an interactive document map as an easy way to create, modify, navigate, and present the contents and structure of your documents. Trellix also includes one-step linking and automatic navigation buttons that make it easy for your readers to get where they want to go. And, Trellix simplifies online delivery through a free Trellix Viewer or by using any HTML/Web browser. You can use Trellix to publish industry-standard HTML 3.2 files in a single step on the Net using the included Microsoft Web Publishing Wizard or integrate Trellix output with information from other sources using Microsoft® FrontPage®, HoTMetaL Pro, or NetObjects Fusion™ site management tools. Of course, you can alway print Trellix pages — including headers, footers, and footnotes that identify link destinations — when you need hard copy.

Product Feature List

- Interactive document map
  - Shows the whole document at a glance
  - Displays page titles as you move the cursor over each page icon
  - Identifies the current page with a yellow page icon
  - Presents the contents of any page when you click on its page icon
  - Organizes logical sequences of pages
  - Lets you add labels, rectangles, and images to organize and enhance your maps
  - Can export in HTML as part of Web pages
- One-step linking
  - Create new links with a simple highlight, point, and click
  - Link to URLs and files outside Trellix
  - Places navigation buttons on every page in a sequence
  - Create a list of links with titles of every page in a sequence from one menu choice
  - Add and organize pages knowing that your links will always be up-to-date
- Intuitive interface
  - Familiar, word-processor-like menus and toolbars
  - Look and feel of popular desktop applications
  - Ready-to-use page layouts
  - Includes attractive, structured way to present business information clearly
  - Takes its look-and-feel from any one of Trellix's attractive document designs
  - Includes formatting of text in the page body plus up to four borders
  - Works with text, images, and background images .BMP, .GIF, .JPG, .PCX, .PIC, .TGA, and .TIF formats
  - Offers optional and automatic scrollbars for easy browsing.
  - Publish to the Net
  - Creates industry-standard HTML 3.2 files in a single step
- Print Trellix pages
- Includes headers, footers, and footnotes that identify link destinations

E-COMMERCE

Art Technology Group

Address: 101 Huntington Avenue, Boston, MA 02199
Phone: (617) 859-1212
Fax: (617) 859-1211
E-Mail: info@atg.com
Website: www.atg.com
Sales Contact Name: Lauren Kelley, Director of Sales

Description Summary. Dynamo Application Server and Dynamo Profile Station offer the only market-proven E-commerce solution for rapidly developing, deploying, and running extensive personalization-driven Websites. Ranked the number one personalization solution by Forrester Research, Dynamo Application Server and Dynamo Profile Station are designed specifically to tackle the management of online relationships by applying personalization to each and every user experience.

Dynamo Application Server 3.5 ("Dynamo") and Dynamo Profile Station 3.5 ("Profile Station") provide enterprises with the platform and tools required to rapidly build and deploy scalable, high-volume Web applications utilizing dynamic HTML page generation, real-time user profiling, and personalized content delivery. Built to run together, Dynamo and Profile Station offer the industry's first true personalization engine that enables Websites to track visitors, dynamically target content, and tailor each user's visit in real time. The Dynamo product suite provides the engine for managing online customer relationships and drives several of the busiest personalization-driven E-commerce sites on the Web today including Sony (www.station.sony.com) and BMG Music Service (bmgmusicservice.com) Technical specs, hardware req's, etc. can be found at: http://www.atg.com/industry/products/d3/ and http://www.atg.com/industry/products/profile/.

CyberCash, Inc.

Address: 2100 Reston Parkway, Suite 430, Reston, VA 22091
Phone: (703) 620-4200
Fax: (703) 620-4215
E-Mail: info@cybercash.com
Website: www.cybercash.com
Sales Contact Name: Richard K. Crone

■ **Product: Electronic Cash Register for Internet payments credit card, electronic check, and electronic cash**

Version Number: 3.0
Hardware requirements: all platforms
Software requirements: all platforms

Description Summary. CyberCash is introducing a new Internet payment architecture for our CashRegister that will make it easier to integrate storefronts, operate payment services, and enjoy upgrades to new services, standards, and options as they become available. With the CR3 Series, we lower the technical and financial hurdles to secure Internet payments.

The CyberCash CashRegister connects a storefront or Website to the CyberCash payment services, enabling businesses to accept secure, real-time payments at their Website.

Product Feature List

- Secure credit card transactions (including both SSL and SET)
- CyberCoin service, for cash payments from $0.25 to $10
- PayNow electronic check service, for interactive billing applications

---

ICentral, Inc.

Address: 225 N. University Ave., Provo, UT 84601
Phone: (801) 373-4347
Toll-Free: (888) 373-4347
Fax: (801) 373-7211
E-Mail: info@icentral.com
Website: www.shopsite.com
Sales Contact Name: Jan Johnson, VP marketing

■ **Product: ShopSite Pro**

Version Number: v3.3
Pricing: $1295 (MSRP)
Hardware/Software requirements: These system requirements are for the average functional store.
- Operating systems
  - OpenLinux, Linux, Free BSD, or BSDI on Intel
  - Solaris on SPARC shipping; Solaris on Intel coming soon
  - NT and IRIX coming soon
  - 16 Mb RAM

- 10 Mb hard drive space (up to 25 Mb may be required for install only)
- Hardware platforms must be running
  - Stronghold, Netscape, or any NCSA-compatible, secure Web server software
  - PERL 5.003 or greater Sendmail
- Client side (Website Developer or Merchant)
  - Requires Netscape browsers or Microsoft Internet Explorer, versions 3.0 or later, running on the user's system of choice (PC, Mac or UNIX).
- Client side (Shopper)
  - Browser of choice

Description Summary. ShopSite Pro is a secure, online store creation and management application designed to meet the needs of site developers and merchants who are seeking to build a professional, yet affordable storefront. In addition to its site creation and management tools and secure shopping basket, ShopSite Pro includes real-time credit card authorization, a site search engine, and an Associates Tracking program.

Product Feature List

- Ported to several Unix OS and NT
- Client-side, any platform that supports a standard browser
- Foreign language support
- Unlimited simultaneous shoppers
- Online help
- Payment information encryption
- E-mail notification of orders
- Auto shipping and tax calculation
- First Virtual payment system
- Customizable order system
- Easily indexed by search engines
- Sales stats
- Traffic stats
- Page creation/site management tools
- Direct media upload
- Media library manager
- Database upload
- Order database download
- Credit card authorization
- Stats plus
- Associates tracking
- Site search
- Large database handling tools
- Interface to other applications
- SmartTags
- Discount calculation
- Automatic product upsell
- Global database editing

■ **Product: ShopSite Manager**

Version Number: v3.3
Pricing: $495 (MSRP)

Hardware/Software requirements: These system requirements are for the average functional store.

- Operating systems
  - OpenLinux, Linux, Free BSD, or BSDI on Intel
  - Solaris on SPARC shipping; Solaris on Intel coming soon
  - NT and IRIX coming soon
  - 16 Mb RAM
  - 10 Mb hard drive space (to 25 Mb may be required for install only)
- Hardware platforms must be running
  - Stronghold, Netscape, or any NCSA-compatible Web server software
  - PERL 5.003 or greater Sendmail
- Clientside (Website Developer or Merchant)
  - Requires Netscape browsers or Microsoft Internet Explorer, versions 3.0 or later, running on the user's system (PC, Mac or UNIX)
- Client-side (Shopper)
  - Browser of choice

Description Summary. ShopSite Manager is for the small- to medium-size business manager who wants to begin marketing and selling products on the Internet, or who currently has a Website, but wants to take the next step of selling products online.

For Website designers, it reduces the many tedious tasks involved in maintaining a Website, allowing them to concentrate on pure design. It empowers merchants by only allowing them to make day-to-day merchandising changes without impacting the site designer. For the do-it-yourself merchant, this person can use ShopSite Manager and build an entire site without knowing HTML.

Product Feature List

- Ported to several Unix OS and NT
- Client side, any platform that supports a standard browser
- Foreign language support
- Unlimited simultaneous shoppers
- Online help
- Payment information encryption
- E-mail notification of orders
- Auto shipping and tax calculation
- First Virtual payment system
- Customizable order system
- Easily indexed by search engines
- Sales stats
- Traffic stats
- Page creation/site management tools
- Direct media upload
- Media library manager
- Database upload
- Order database download
- Credit card authorization

APPENDIX

■ Product: ShopSite Express

Version Number: v3.3

Hardware/Software requirements: These system requirements are for
the average functional store.

- Operating systems
  - OpenLinux, Linux, Free BSD, or BSDI on Intel
  - Solaris on SPARC shipping; Solaris on Intel coming soon
  - NT and IRIX coming soon
  - 16 Mb RAM
  - 10 Mb hard drive space (up to 25 Mb may be required for install only)
- Hardware platforms must be running
  - Stronghold, Netscape, or any NCSA-compatible, secure Web server
    software
  - PERL 5.003 or greater Sendmail
- Client-side (Website Developer or Merchant)
  - Requires Netscape browsers or Microsoft Internet Explorer, ver-
    sions 3.0 or later, running on the user's system of choice (PC, Mac
    or UNIX).
- Client side (Shopper)
  - Browser of choice

Description Summary. ShopSite Express is a shopping basket software
application that allows a site developer to build a site using his or her
HTML tool of choice, then quickly and easily add "order" and "checkout"
buttons to the Website. Shoppers can click on these buttons and place an
order in the secure shopping basket.

ShopSite Express offers a simple point-and-click, fill-in-the-blanks interface.
Enter product information (name, price, ordering options) into ShopSite
Express through the browser interface. After configuring tax and shipping
(so it will be calculated automatically for shoppers), click on the "Create
Links" button and ShopSite will automatically generate "order" and "checkout" buttons for each product in the ShopSite database. These buttons can
be drag-and-dropped onto the HTML editing window.

Product Feature List

- A 25-product limit (no real-time credit card handling capabilities, but
  can capture and store credit card information securely in the orders
  database for manual processing later)
- Ported to several Unix OS and NT
- Client side, any platform that supports a standard browser
- Foreign language support
- Unlimited simultaneous shoppers

- Online help
- Payment information encryption
- E-mail notification of orders
- Auto shipping and tax calculation
- First Virtual payment system
- Customizable order system
- Easily indexed by search engines
- Basic sales stats

SpaceWorks

Address: 51 Monroe Street, Rockville, MD 20850
Phone: (301) 251-4136
Toll-Free: (800) 5 SPACE 5
Fax: (301) 738-9284
E-Mail: kwillard@spaceworks.com
Website: www.spaceworks.com
Sales Contact Name: Liz Sara, Co-founder and Vice President of Corporate Marketing

■ Product: OrderManager

Version Number: 4.0
Pricing: OrderManager starts at 100k
Software/Hardware Requirements:
- UNIX
  - HP/UX 10.x
  - Informix 7.x or Oracle 7.x
  - Web browser (NS or IE)
  - Netscape Enterprise Server 4.0 or higher
  - 20 Mb disk storage
- NT
  - MS Windows NT 4.0 Service Pack 3
  - SQL Server 6.5, OBDC drivers 2.5
  - SQL Service Pack 3
  - Web Browser (NS or IE)
  - Internet Information Server 3.0

Description Summary. The SpaceWorks OrderManager software application transforms traditional order processing into a self-service electronic channel ... one that directly links supply chain partners, resellers, customers, and procurement managers to information in the back-end system of your company and those of your suppliers. SpaceWorks OrderManager provides a company with a secure Internet electronic ordering, supply and fulfillment solution — all in real-time, 24 × 7.

Companies are looking for ways to gain a competitive edge via improved service and reduced costs. SpaceWorks offers OrderManager, a productivity solution that improves the ordering and purchasing process by providing a self-service Web-based system, 24 hours a day. OrderManager allows a company to significantly reduce the cost of processing orders, reduces order errors, and significantly improves the quality of service to a company's customer base. SpaceWorks, a leading electronic commerce vendor, is based in Rockville, MD and was established in 1993. For more information, visit the company's Website at www.spaceworks.com.

Product Features List

- SpaceWorks offers complete sell-side/buy-side functionality
- Powerful and customizable GUI
- Proven back-end system integration
- Comprehensive user enrollment and registration
- Fully searchable product catalog
- Multivendor option for procurement
- Real-time inventory display
- Partner specific pricing
- Access to competing products
- Secure order entry and submission
- Real-time order tracking and status
- Real-time account profile
- Multitier routing for approval
- Ability to configure complementary product groupings
- Multiple payment options for user
- Easy-to-use account and operations administration

E-MAIL MANAGEMENT

GFI FAX and VOICE

Address: 26 East Main Street, Webster, NY 14580
Toll-Free: (888) 2-GFIFAX
Fax: (716) 265-1016
E-Mail: sales@gfifax.com
Website: http://www.gficomms.com
Sales Contact Name: Nick Galea

■ Product: Emailrobot for Exchange/SMTP

Version Number: 2.0
Pricing:
- Small Business Edition (4 mail agents/profiles): $495

- Corporate Edition (7 mail agents/profiles): $749
- Enterprise Edition (unlimited): $1495

Software requirements:

- Windows NT server, Windows NT workstation, or Windows 95
- Microsoft Exchange Server or an SMTP/POP3 mail server
- ODBC compatible database such as Microsoft Access or SQL server
- Internet Explorer 3.02 or higher

Description Summary. Emailrobot manages and automates corporate/Website e-mail such as sales@yourcompany.com and info@yourcompany.com. Integrating seamlessly with Microsoft Exchange Server and SMTP/POP3 mail servers, Emailrobot enables companies to archive, distribute, track, search, report, and automate their e-mail. Emailrobot has full support for ODBC databases, including MS Access and SQL server. A free evaluation version can be downloaded from http://www.gficomms.com.

Product Feature List

- Distribute corporate e-mail among mail agents
- Track e-mails and their status with tracking numbers
- View communication histories (e-mail threads)
- View reports on e-mail response times and other e-mail statistics
- Archive Web form output into any ODBC database
- Send out scheduled personalized mailings/replies, e.g., sales follow-up and payment reminders
- Automate any e-mail process using Wizards/VBscript
- Full integration with your mail server

■ Product: Emailflow for Exchange/SMTP

Version Number: 3.0
Pricing: $1995 to $4995
Hardware requirements: 32 Mb memory, 100 Mb free disk space
Software requirements:

- Windows NT server or workstation
- Microsoft Exchange Server or SMTP/POP3 mail server
- ODBC compatible database, such as Microsoft SQL server or MS Access
- To run VBscript code — Internet Explorer 4.01

Description Summary. Emailflow for Exchange/SMTP is a revolutionary workflow software application that integrates seamlessly with your e-mail system and does not require any proprietary client software. This has many advantages such as easier installation, transparent workflow process, no need for training, and a lower TCO. Furthermore, you can extend the workflow process to include your customers and suppliers. For more information and a free evaluation version please visit our Website at: http://www.gficomms.com.

Product Feature List

- Run client side applications through HTML mail
- Use any ODBC database as a workflow information store
- Launch flows through e-mail at scheduled intervals
- Server load balancing and clustering
- Powerful reporting features
- Load balance workflow tasks amongst users and use roles for tasks
- Industry standard development APIs: ODBC, MAPI, and VBscript
- Competitive pricing and low TCO

■ Product: FAXmaker for Exchange

Version Number: 5.5
Pricing: $349 to $3995
Hardware requirements: one or more of the following fax devices:
- Class 1 or 2 fax modem (class 2 recommended)
- ISDN internal adapters (EICON DIVA Pro 2.0, EICON DIVA Server Bri, AVM B1)
- Brooktrout analogue TR114 fax boards
Software requirements:
- Windows NT server 4.1
- Microsoft Exchange Server 4.0/5.0/5.5

Description Summary. FAXmaker for Exchange is a fax connector for Microsoft Exchange Server, licensed to carry the "Designed for Microsoft BackOffice" logo. FAXmaker for Exchange enables users to send and receive faxes straight from Outlook just as if it were e-mail. FAXmaker offers advanced features at extremely competitive prices. More information and a free evaluation version can be downloaded from http://www.gfifax.com.

Product Feature List

- Automatic inbound delivery (CSID, OCR, DID/DTMF, Line)
- Outlook integration
- Send fax as e-mail
- Exchange integration
- Word mail-merge faxing
- Windows fax printer driver
- Fax broadcasting
- ISDN support

- Office 95/97 attachments
- Call accounting/reporting
- Text API

■ Product: FAXmaker for Networks

Version Number: 6.5
Pricing: $295 to $3995
Hardware requirements: one or more of the following fax devices:
- Class 1 or 2 fax modem (class 2 recommended)
- ISDN internal adapters (EICON DIVA Pro 2.0, EICON DIVA Server Bri, AVM B1)
- Brooktrout analogue TR114 fax boards
Software requirements:
- Windows NT server/workstation or Windows 95

Description Summary. FAXmaker for Networks is a fax server that runs on Windows NT/95 and enables users to send and receive faxes straight from their desktop. FAXmaker offers advanced features at extremely competitive prices. More information and a free evaluation version can be downloaded from http://www.gfifax.com.

Product Feature List

- Automatic inbound delivery (CSID, OCR, DID/DTMF, Line)
- Windows fax printer driver
- Fax broadcasting
- ISDN support
- Office 95/97 attachments
- Call accounting/reporting
- Text API
- DDE toolkit

■ Product: FAXmaker for SMTP

Version Number: 5.0
Pricing: $295 to $3995
Hardware requirements: one or more of the following fax devices:
- Class 1 or 2 fax modem (class 2 recommended)
- ISDN internal adapters (EICON DIVA Pro 2.0, EICON DIVA Server Bri, AVM B1)
- Brooktrout analogue TR114 fax boards
Software requirements:
- Windows NT server/workstation, Windows 95
- SMTP/POP3 mail server

Description Summary. FAXmaker for SMTP integrates seamlessly with SMTP/POP3 mail servers enabling users to send and receive faxes straight from their favorite e-mail application just as if it were e-mail. FAXmaker offers advanced features at extremely competitive prices. More information and a free evaluation version can be downloaded from http://www.gfifax.com.

Product Feature List

- Automatic inbound delivery (CSID, OCR, DID/DTMF, Line)
- Windows fax printer driver
- Integration with POP3 clients
- Send fax as e-mail
- Fax broadcasting
- ISDN support
- Office 95/97 attachments
- Call accounting/reporting
- Text API
- Word mail merge faxing

Isocor

Address: 3420 Ocean Park Blvd., Santa Monica, CA 90405
Phone: (310) 581-8100
Fax: (310) 581-8111
E-Mail: sales.info@isocor.com
Website: www.isocor.com
Product: N-PLEX Connect
Version Number: 1.0
Hardware requirements:
- IBM PC-compatible with Intel Pentium processor or higher
- 64 Mb RAM minimum
- CD-ROM drive
Software requirements: Windows NT 4.0, service pack 3 or later

Description Summary. Part of the award-winning N-PLEX product family, N-PLEX Connect allows large organizations to unify their existing directory and messaging environments. N-PLEX Connect synchronizes address books and directories for Microsoft Exchange, Lotus Notes, and other SMTP-accessible messaging systems, while offering a central corporate White Pages service. As well as making this information available in a standards-based directory, N-PLEX Connect is also a component of an enterprise meta directory strategy. It also provides a high-performance, reliable Internet/intranet backbone linking dissimilar messaging systems.

Product Feature List

- Internet messaging server
- POP3 and IMAP4 message store
- Directory connectivity with Lotus Notes address books
- Directory connectivity with the Microsoft Exchange directory
- Universal connector using PERL to allow custom synchronization agents to be built as required
- Rich White Pages content generated in directory
- Messaging connectivity for Lotus Notes
- Message connectivity with single Internet domain to any SMTP-accessible messaging system, e.g., UNIX sendmail, Netscape, cc:Mail etc.
- Comprehensive management for all new subsystems

FINANCIAL SERVICES APPLICATION SOFTWARE

PMSC

Address: One PMSC Center, I-77 @ US Highway 21, Blythewood, SC 29016
Phone: (803) 333-6964
Fax: (803) 333-4929
E-Mail: mikegantt@pmsc.com
Website: www.pmsc.com
Sales Contact Name: Debra Jacobs at (803) 333-6474
Pricing: call for information
Hardware/software requirements: our products operate on the most popular hardware and software platforms

Description Summary. PMSC offers over 65 products and a variety of related services for insurance and related financial services companies.

PMSC is one of the largest providers of insurance solutions in the world. Our solutions, in conjunction with our outsourcing options, are designed to enhance customer service, productivity, and profitability for the insurance enterprise.

GLOBALIZATION OF WEBSITES

International Communications, Inc.

Address: 492 Old Connecticut Path, Framingham, MA 01701
Phone: (508) 620-3900
Fax: (508) 620-3999
E-Mail: info@intl.com

Website: www.intl.com
Sales Contact Name: Derek Perkins, Vice President of Sales

■ Product: Localization and translation services

Version Number: Localize into over 22 different languages

Description Summary. International Communications specializes in the localization of software, Websites, marketing materials, and interactive media. Committed to helping leaders in the IT industry achieve success in overseas markets, the company utilizes leading-edge tools and provides customized solutions for complex projects. U.S. offices are located in Boston, MA; Chicago, IL; San Francisco, CA; and Seattle, WA. Overseas offices are in Beijing, China; Paris, France; and Rendsburg, Germany.

INTEGRATION

OnDisplay, Inc.

Address: 2682 Bishop Drive, San Ramon, CA 94583
Phone: (925) 355-3200
Toll-Free: (800) 508-8800
Fax: (925) 355-3222
E-Mail: info@ondisplay.com
Website: www.ondisplay.com
Sales Contact Name: Olivier Sermet, VP Field Operations

■ Product: CenterStage

Version Number: 3.0
Pricing: varies, depending on platform
Hardware requirements: WindowsNT, Unix

Description Summary. OnDisplay's products, layered on top of the CenterStage Rapid Integration Architecture and leveraging its powerful capabilities, are used by businesses to implement and integrate Web Supersites, ERP, and E-commerce solutions. OnDisplay's products bridge the gap between existing business content, and the systems which require that content, employing a rapid, iterative approach to the integration problem, without modifying existing applications, writing custom APIs, or changing IT infrastructures.

OnDisplay solutions include CenterStage ERP Series, a set of solution modules which automate data conversion, and application-to-application integration for PeopleSoft and Oracle ERP implementations. CenterStage

EC Series, a set of solution modules which support content aggregation and management for Web Supersites, content-management systems, and Electronic Catalogs.

Based on the unique CenterStage Rapid Integration Architecture, OnDisplay solutions provide the industry's most rapid implementation and integration capabilities for ERP and electronic commerce systems. With CenterStage products, corporations can seamlessly integrate a diverse set of resources including Web-enabled applications, legacy applications, Web data, business reports, and e-mail with existing operational systems. Unlike traditional solutions, CenterStage products do not require modifications to existing systems; neither do they require extensive coordination between business partners.

Product Feature List

- Migration solutions for ERP packages
- Application
- Integration solutions for ERP packages
- Catalog loading and automated
- Synchronization for E-commerce packages
- Content aggregation solutions
- For Web Supersites and content-management packages

INTERNET-IN-A-BOX

FreeGate Corp.

Address: 1208 E. Arques Avenue, Sunnyvale, CA 94086
Phone: (408) 617-1000
Toll-Free: (800) 280-8816
Fax: (408) 617-1010
E-Mail: info@freegate.com
Website: www.freegate.com
Sales Contact Name: lstiff@freegate.com

■ Product: FreeGate Multiservices Internet Gateway system

Optional software: Secured Remote Access, Virtual Private Network
Pricing: starts at $5395

Description Summary. An all-in-one Internet system, or "Internet in a box," created for mid-size and small businesses who want to put their business on the Internet (taking advantage of Web publishing to intranets and/or extranets in the future) without adding IT staff or complex assembly of boxes.

717

Product Feature List

- Combines Web servers, firewall, IP routing, DNS, DHCP, e-mail, FTP, remote management, range of WAN interfaces from ISDN to T1 and DSL

JAVA DEVELOPMENT

Tower Technology Corporation

Address: 1501 West Koenig Lane, Austin, TX 78756
Phone: (512) 452-9455
Toll-Free: (800) 285-5124
Fax: (512) 452-1721
E-Mail: tower@twr.com
Website: http://www.twr.com
Sales Contact Name: sales@twr.com

■ Product: TowerJ

Version Number: 2.5
Pricing: Commercial licenses start at $3999
Hardware requirements: Sparc, Intel, PA/RISC, RS/6000, MIPS, or Alpha
Software requirements: Solaris, WindowsNT, AIX, HP-UX, IRIX, Linux, or Digital UNIX

Description Summary. TowerJ is a full "open" native deployment compiler for Java. It includes a global system-optimizing compiler, high-performance object aware runtime, and tools for building and performance tuning server-side Java applications. TowerJ creates compact high-performance self-contained executables for a range of server-class computer platforms from stardard Java bytecode. Using TowerJ, software developers can get the full benefits of the Java language without having to sacrifice execution performance or cross-platform compatability. TowerJ supports "Write Once, Compile Anywhere" allowing consistent high-performance execution over a broad range of server platforms.

TowerJ allows companies to reduce server hardware costs, reduce deployment support costs, significantly improve application server performance and throughput, enhance software quality through more maintainable designs and architectures, reduce the costs associated with software performance tuning, and improve end-user satisfaction. TowerJ has been specifically designed and implemented to support the requirements of high-activity, high-availability, process-intensive, business-critical, server-side Java applications. Software groups developing and deploying the Java applications driving the Internet, intranet, and extranet sites for E-commerce and Net-business should have TowerJ on their short list of Java deployment tools.

Product Feature List

- Global System Optimizations
- Structure and Flow Analysis
- Automatic Dependency Analysis
- High-Speed Object Dispatcher
- User Configurable Runtime
- Native and Bytecode Dynamic Updating
- Serialization, Reflection, and JNI support
- Incremental Compilation
- Native Threads Support on Selected Platforms
- Ultrafast Synchronization
- Fast Scalable Performance
- Graphical Project Manager

NETWORKING

HotOffice Technologies, Inc.

Address: 5201 Congress Avenue, Suite 232, Boca Raton, FL 33487
Phone: (561) 995-0005
Toll-Free: (888) 446-8633
Fax: (561) 995-5990
E-Mail: info@hotoffice.com
Website: www.hotoffice.com
Sales Contact Name: Cynthia Starr

■ Product: The HotOffice™ Service

Version Number: 98.1
Pricing: $12.95 per user/month
Hardware requirements: Internet Access, 486 or higher, Windows® 95 or higher, and a minimum of 16 Mb RAM.
Software requirements: Java-enabled Internet browser: Internet Explorer™ 3.01 or higher or Netscape Navigator®/Communicator™ 3.01 or higher.

Description Summary. HotOffice provides affordable networking solution for small businesses, mobile workers, telecommuters, workgroups, and associations. The HotOffice Web-based networking solution is an easy, affordable way to connect colleagues, clients, and vendors from anywhere. This low-cost monthly subscription service provides a hosted intranet at a frac-

719

tion of the cost of setting up and maintaining your own system. On the road or in the office, you can securely access your private network from any Web-enabled PC. You can share and retrieve documents, host bulletin board discussions, hold online conferences, send e-mail, make travel arrangements, get discounts, and more! This award-winning interface is incredibly easy to use for novices or experts, with all the tools you need in one central location.

Product Feature List

- Web-based networking
- E-mail
- Calendar
- Document management
- Bulletin boards
- Chat rooms
- Video conferencing
- Internet telephony
- Yellow Pages directory
- Travel planning
- Package tracking
- Business matchmaker services

Nevod Incorporated

Address: 11 Page Road, Weston, MA 02493
Toll-Free: (800) 967-1875
Fax: (781) 893-7882
E-Mail: sales@nevod.com
Website: http://www.nevod.com
Sales Contact Name: Eduard Guzovsky

■ Product: Nevod NAT1000

Version Number: Version 2.0
Pricing: Ranges from $100 for 5-Node to $5000 for 1000-Node
Hardware requirements: Intel-based (or equivalent) Personal Computer with an Ethernet card
Software requirements: Windows NT 3.51/4.0 or Windows 95 or 98

Description Summary. NAT1000 is an Internet Connection solution that allows multiple users to share a single connection or IP address to connect their LAN to the Internet. This software-only solution runs on and coexists with existing services on Microsoft Windows NT/98/95-based platforms. Based on advanced NAT technology and including a DHCP Server, NAT1000 is a simple-to-install, no-maintenance solution for connecting small or large numbers of machines to the Internet.

Product Feature List

- Multiple Audio/Video Netmeeting Client (H.323/T.120) support
- Built in DHCP server
- Multiple MSFT PPTP client support for your Virtual Private Network (VPN)
- Supports a wide and continually growing number of applications such as Web, e-mail, AOL, Compuserve, Quake, Telnet, FTP, Gopher, Ping, Traceroute, WAIS, Finger, IRC, ICQ, PPTP, Citrix Winframe, ssh/F-secure, (multiple) news hosts, Aventail VPN, AltaVista Tunnel, Vocaltec Internet Phone, PeopleLink, Netscape AOL Instant Messenger, BuyDirect.com, ten.net, mplayer
- Transparently supports FTP, RealAudio, VDO and Xing clients (streaming UDP and TCP)
- Supports Activision peer-to-peer protocol
- Simple installation using the Control Panel utility
- Looks like a NIC card
- No proxy client setup
- ALL client software runs "as-is"
- Windows 95/NT kernel-based 32-bit package seamlessly integrates with existing applications and functionality on your Windows box
- Integral firewall securely intercepts packets beneath the routing layer, unlike proxy implementations
- Works with any TCP/IP-based client (Win31, 95, NT, Macs, Unix, DOS ...)
- Loaded as a kernel driver, not an application, so outperforms application-based software
- Full ethernet speed throughput or better depending on host machine configuration and interface
- Capable of supporting 50,000 simultaneous TCP/IP connections or 1000 nodes on a 16 Mb machine
- Hughes DirecPC Satellite
- Cable modem and ADSL tested
- Oracle and Lotus Notes support
- Quake server support

Packeteer, Inc.

Address: 10495 N. De Anza Blvd., Cupertino, CA 95014
Phone: (408) 873-4400
Toll-Free: (800) 697-2253

APPENDIX

Fax: (408) 873-4410
E-Mail: info@packeteer.com
Website: www.packeteer.com
Sales Contact Name: info@packeteer.com

■ Product: PacketShaper 1000

Description Summary. PacketShaper 1000 is the branch office bandwidth management device that allocates bandwidth over WAN connections for branch offices and remote sites. The PacketShaper 1000 enables network managers to ensure bandwidth allocation and priority for vital business applications across WAN links with speeds up to 384 kbps. With the Packet-Shaper 1000, network managers have a cost-effective way to allocate bandwidth and assign traffic priority, allowing them to maximize WAN efficiency, improve application performance, and simplify network management.

Product Feature List

- TCP Rate Control technology
- Web browser interface
- Traffic discovery
- Graphs of bandwidth usage
- Top Talkers and Top Listeners

■ Product: PacketShaper 2000

Description Summary. PacketShaper 2000 is the IP bandwidth management solution that enables ISPs and corporate IT managers to control bandwidth allocation over expensive wide-area network (WAN) and Internet connections at speeds up to 10 Mbps Ethernet. PacketShaper 2000 allows network managers to prioritize business-critical traffic over less important traffic, such as external push applications. This enables network managers to improve the performance of vital applications, increase transactions per second, optimize bandwidth usage, and improve customer satisfaction.

Product Feature List

- TCP Rate Control technology
- Web browser interface
- Traffic discovery
- Graphs of bandwidth usage
- Top Talkers and Top Listeners

■ Product: PacketShaper 4000

Description Summary. PacketShaper 4000 is the carrier-class IP bandwidth manager for ISP, corporate data center, and Fast Ethernet LAN environments. PacketShaper 4000 supports WAN connections up to 45 Mbps (DS-3) and can be deployed at expensive access connections to maximize bandwidth efficiency, ensure high quality-of-service (QoS) for multiple classes of service, and improve application performance.

Unlike queuing-based quality-of-service schemes, PacketShaper 4000 explicitly allocates bandwidth by controlling the rate at which the end systems communicate. All traffic identified by PacketShaper is mapped to a specific bandwidth-allocation policy, ensuring that each flow can receive a defined minimum rate guarantee. Aggregate traffic classes can be assigned a burstable partition that efficiently shares excess available bandwidth at defined, prioritized weights. Packeteer's TCP rate control technology communicates to each end-system in a connection, eliminating the need for queuing and subsequent packet loss, while increasing WAN efficiency. As a result, PacketShaper eliminates disruption associated with bursty traffic and improves application performance. The PacketShaper 4000 can be deployed on Fast Ethernet LANs or WANs supporting up to T3/E3 connections — wherever access costs are highest and bandwidth is most expensive.

Product Feature List

- TCP Rate Control technology
- Web browser interface
- Traffic discovery
- Graphs of bandwidth usage
- Top Talkers and Top Listeners

PERFORMANCE

Quarterdeck Corporation

Address: 13160 Mindanao Way, Marina del Rey, CA 90292
Toll-Free: Sales (800) 354-3222
Web-site: www.quarterdeck.com

Description Summary. Quarterdeck Corporation is a global leader in the development and marketing of PC helpware — software specifically designed to prevent and solve PC performance problems, especially those encountered in networked — Internet and intranet — environments. The company's goal is to make personal computing trouble-free for users and network administrators alike, while reducing the need for live technical support. Quarterdeck's current product line, which addresses storage management, system conflict resolution, virus protection, system updating, and enhanced access to networked information and communications resources, is marketed to both end users and businesses.

SEARCH AND RETRIEVAL

Aeneid Corporation

Address: 282 Second Street, Suite 200, San Francisco, CA 94105
Phone: (415) 538-8555
Fax: (415) 538-8558
E-Mail: dwhitlow@aeneid.com
Website: http://www.aeneid.com
Contact: Marketing Communications: Diane Whitlow
Sales: Adam Meyer

■ Product: IRA

Version Number: 1
Hardware requirements:
- Processor — 100 MHz Pentium
- Memory (RAM) — 32 Mb
- Memory (Disk) — 500 Mb
- On-Line connection — 28.8 bps
Software requirements:
- Operation System — Win 95
- Web Browser — MS Internet explorer 4.01

Description Summary. Aeneid's Internet Research Assistant (IRA) is an Internet search and retrieval system for business professionals. IRA collects and formats Internet information for sharing, collaboration, and analysis. IRA guarantees superior search results in less time than traditional search methods. Unlike existing consumer-based search engines, IRA focuses on industry-specific information domains and provides an environment for managing information. IRA will be available in Q4 1998.

Product Feature List

- IRA contains a selection of tools for gathering information. IRA's Document Library is a collection of known documents, such as financial tables, press releases, and analyst forecasts. In IRA's Search Directory, users can broaden or limit their search scope. Users can select NarrowCast search to search within IRA's predefined, focused group of sites. ExpressCollect quickly and easily gathers a comprehensive package of information about a technology topic or company from IRA's preselected Search Directory and Document Library.

- IRA has an easy-to-use interface for collecting and browsing information. The IRA Project environment is a three-panel view of information that provides the entire framework for viewing information, and conducting and storing analysis. Results can be sorted by date, title, source, and relevance rank. All information is viewed within the same project, never requiring a user to go to another Web page.
- IRA provides users with powerful management capabilities for organizing, storing, and sharing information and analysis. Search results, documents, and Web links can be saved within folders and created and named by users. All research is retained until a user deletes information, allowing users to monitor changes in information over time. All projects can be shared with other users via guest access.

SECURITY

Certicom Corp.

Address: 1400 Fashion Island Blvd., Suite 1050, San Mateo, CA 94404-7062
Phone: (650) 312-7960
Toll-Free: (800) 561-6100
Fax: (650) 312-7969
E-Mail: info@certicom.com
Website: www.certicom.com
Sales Contact Name: Sales and Marketing at (650) 312-7960

Description Summary. Certicom's product line, based on elliptic curve cryptography (ECC), includes Security Builder (SDK) software developer's toolkit version 2.0 and SSL Plus SDK from Consensus Development Corporation (a Certicom company), as well as embedded systems and integrated circuits.

Security Builder SDK 2.0 — Certicom's security builder SDK sets a new standard in security, efficiency, and flexibility. The cryptographic toolkit contains the primitives required to create fast, strong, and compact information security based on ecc for any application. Available for all major operating systems, Security Builder SDK dramatically reduces bandwidth requirements and delivers high throughput, minimizing server bottlenecks and enabling security in client devices or software with modest computing resources. With this standards-based SDK, developers are amazed at how quickly security can be integrated into any application.

Functions of Security Builder SDK 2.0 — For electronic commerce and other Internet and wireless applications and devices, Security Builder provides information security services such as digital signature generation and verification, encryption/decryption, and key management. For more details, contact Certicom at 1-800-561-6100.

---

eSafe Technologies, Inc.

Address: Intelligent Computer Security, Northgate Delta Building, 9706 Fourth Ave. NE, Suite 205, Seattle, WA 98115
Phone: (206) 524-9159
Fax: (206) 524-9979
E-Mail: info@us.esafe.com

■ Product: eSafe Protect Enterprise

Version Number: ver. 2.0
Pricing: Pricing ranges from $15 to $50 depending on number of nodes
Hardware requirements: workstation: 8 Mb memory and 5 Mb of free disk space; server: 32 Mb memory and 15 Mb of free disk space
Software requirements: workstation: Windows 3.1, DOS, Windows 95/98, Windows NT; server: Windows NT or Novell NetWare 3.X, 4.X, or 5.x

Description Summary. eSafe Protect Enterprise offers the only complete Internet protection solution to safeguard your network and PCs from vandals and viruses. ESPE is an advanced, centrally administered Internet protection system consisting of the following components:

- Behavior-based blocking of Vandals (such as hostile Java and ActiveX)
- Blocking of sites based on URL, port, protocol, or keywords
- ICSA-certified virus protection (optional)
- Desktop firewall to control inbound/outbound connections
- eConsole for central deployment, configuration, and updating

---

Finjan Software

Address: 2860 Zanker Road, Suite 201, San Jose, CA 95134
Phone: (408) 324-0228
Toll-Free: (888) FINJAN.8
Fax: (408) 324-0229
E-Mail: info@finjan.com
Website: http://www.finjan.com
Sales Contact Name: Robert Tas, Vice President of Sales

■ Product: SurfinGate™

Version Number: 4.0

Description Summary. SurfinGate™ 4.0 is essential for any business using the Internet, extranet, or intranet for daily business transactions. Its unique patent pending Content Inspection technology for Java and ActiveX, and smart filtering for JavaScript, Visual Basic Script, Cookies and more, helps protect the enterprise beyond traditional firewalls filtering. Besides supporting digital signature block-or-allow based on signature, SurfinGate 4.0 inspects even the signature-allowed applet code content. Central Management and administration make SurfinGate 4.0 truly easy to use and deploy, easing the network administrator routine. For large enterprises, SurfinGate 4.0 ensures high performance and ability to scale.

■ Product: SurfinShield™ Corporate

Version Number: 3.0

Description Summary. SurfinShield™ Corporate is the first centrally controlled mobile code security for the desktop, providing real-time security for its user. SurfinShield Corporate includes Finjan's DMZ (demilitarized zone) to run applets in a separate memory space from the browser. The DMZ provides an extra layer of security supporting the Java Security Manager and Finjan's Xbox™ (a security manager for ActiveX). The centralized management console allows network administrators to manage anyone connected to the corporate network, whether in-house or at remote locations. SurfinShield Corporate includes the ability to send instantaneous security alerts to the network — should one desktop encounter a control or applet containing a security breach, the rest of the organization will be instantly protected.

Internet Dynamics, Inc.

Address: 3717 E. Thousand Oaks Blvd., Westlake Village, CA 91362
Phone: (805) 370-2200
Toll-Free: (888) CONCLAVE
Fax: (805) 370-2201
E-Mail: sales@interdyn.com
Website: http://www.interdyn.com
Sales Contact Name: Chas. Kunklemann

■ Product: Conclave

Version Number: 1.5
Pricing: Single Site: $2745 (25 users); $4995 (50 users); $8995 (100 users); $15,995 (200 users); $21,995 (unlimited users).
Hardware requirements: Pentium-200+ w/ 64 Mb of memory and 4 Gb of disk storage.

Software requirements: Windows NT 4.0

Description Summary. Conclave "creates a private interchange" by securing your intranet and extranet for authors and users of information with a complete, easy to administer and integrated security solution. This eliminates the present conundrum of disconnected point products required to safely exploit the net today! Conclave is designed to grow along with the business from a simple, single-location solution to a complex, enterprise security solution.

Conclave is based on a new and unique "role-based policy management" architecture that greatly simplifies the process of uniting users to the information they need to increase their effectiveness and productivity. This unique architecture combines standalone security with the power of VPNs and the flexibility of remotely accessing information, all in one unified product.

Product Feature List

- Firewall
- Virtual Private Networking
- Remote Access
- Access Control
- Rule-based Administration
- Virus Detection
- X.509 Certificate Usage

Xcert International, Inc.

Address: 1001 — 701 West Georgia Street, PO Box 10145, Pacific Centre,
   Vancouver, BC, Canada, V7Y 1C6
Phone: (604) 640-6210
Fax: (604) 640-6220
E-Mail: info@xcert.com
Website: http://www.xcert.com
Sales Contact Name: Alex Chen

■ Product: Sentry CA

Version Number: 2.0
Pricing: $1495
Hardware requirements:
   CPU: Pentium 133 MHz
   RAM: 64 Mb
   Disk Space (CA software): 50 Mb
   Disk Space (per user): 4 Kb

Software requirements:
- Windows NT
- Solaris 2.5 (Sparc and x86)
- HP-UX 10.20
- OSF/1 (Digital Unix) 4.0
- IRIX 5.3
- BSDI

Description Summary. Sentry CA harnesses Xcert's expertise in public key infrastructure to provide solutions for information security and Internet-based electronic commerce. Sentry CA provides organizations with the tools to implement secure intranets, or private networks over the Internet. Whether your organization is a small workgroup or a multinational corporation, the Sentry CA provides a highly efficient and manageable PKI architecture that scales in a robust and reliable manner.

Product Feature List

- Strong Authentication
- Secure Web Access
- Secure E-mail
- Non-Repudiation

VPN

FreeGate Corp.

Address: 1208 E. Arques Avenue, Sunnyvale, CA 94086
Phone: (408) 617-1000
Toll-Free: (800) 280-8816
Fax: (408) 617-1010
E-Mail: info@freegate.com
Website: www.freegate.com
Sales Contact Name: lstiff@freegate.com

■ Product: FreeGate Remote VPN software

Pricing: $495
Hardware requirements: FreeGate Multiservices Internet Gateway

Description Summary. Enables telecommuters to dial into a local ISP to access corporate information/services as if they were sitting at their desks in the main office. Virtual Services Management (VSM) tools ease the administration and management of a virtual private network of remote users for smaller businesses or organizations with limited IT staff and resources by providing a single, simplified point of administration from which common services — e-mail, name directories, Web access, firewalls, file sharing, and access control — are delivered across locations.

APPENDIX

Product Feature List

- Supports Microsoft's Point-to-Point Tunneling Protocol (PPTP, available with Windows clients) on the remote user's desktop or laptop system. A PPTP server in the FreeGate system authenticates the remote user, then opens an encrypted path through which traffic flows as if through the LAN (subject to the LAN's security policies). Future plans also call for implementation of the Layer 2 Tunneling Protocol (L2TP), now in the standardization process.

■ Product: FreeGate Branch VPN Software

Pricing: $995
Hardware requirements: FreeGate Multiservices Internet Gateway

Description Summary. Gives branch office users access to e-mail, directories, and other corporate information as if they were behind the firewall on the headquarters LAN. Virtual Services Management tools ease the administration and management of virtual private networking for organizations and smaller businesses with limited IT staff and resources by providing a single, simplified point of administration from which common services — e-mail, name directories, Web access, firewalls, file sharing, and access control — are delivered across multiple branch locations.

Product Feature List

- Class-of-service policies such as access privileges and priorities are applied as if the branch users were physically at headquarters. Security is implemented through the industry-standard IP Security (IPsec) protocol, which provides DES encryption, authentication, and key management.

■ Product: FreeGate Extranet VPN Software

Hardware requirements: FreeGate Multiservices Internet Gateway

Description Summary. Opens up a corporate network selectively to customers, suppliers, and strategic business partners, with users having access to a limited set of information behind the corporate firewall. Virtual Services Management tools provide a single, simplified point of administration from which common services — e-mail, name directories, Web access, firewalls, file sharing, and access control — are delivered across multiple locations.

WEB MONITORS

Freshwater Software, Inc.

Address: 1965 N. 57th Court, Boulder, CO 80301
Phone: (303) 443-2266
Toll-Free: (888) 443-2266
Fax: (303) 545-9533
E-Mail: info@freshtech.com
Website: http://www.freshtech.com
Sales Contact Name: Chris Anderson (chris@freshtech.com)

■ Product: SiteSeer

Pricing: SiteSeer $995, SiteSeer Gold $1495, Global SiteSeer $3495
Hardware requirements: monitor with 256 colors
Software requirements: Netscape or Internet Explorer browser

Description Summary. Web Administrators face the constant challenge of determining what kind of experience their Website visitors are having. Are they able to get to the Website? Are all the pages there? How long do they have to wait for a page to download? Freshwater Software's SiteSeer service offers a cost-effective solution to this problem.

With SiteSeer you can verify that your Web pages can be retrieved from outside your system, and receive notification of errors via e-mail, pager, or SNMP trap. SiteSeer can detect ISP reliabilty problems, test forms and their associated processes, and verify that a page's contents include a specific string of text. Results of the monitored pages are compiled into daily and weekly management reports. SiteSeer Gold allows a greater variety of monitors, and Global SiteSeer can retrieve your Web pages from locations around the globe, verifying that your site can be accessed worldwide.

---

surfCONTROL Division

Address: JSB, 108 Whispering Pines Drive, Suite 115, Scotts Valley, CA 95066
Phone: (408) 438-8300
Toll-Free: (800) 572-8649
Fax: (408) 438-8360
E-Mail: stevep@surfcontrol.com
Website: www.surfcontrol.com www.jsb.com
Sales Contact Name: Steve Purdham

■ **Product: The surfCONTROL Family — ensuring Internet Access is Business Access**

Pricing: From $99 for 20 users
Hardware requirements: NT System
Software requirements: NT4

Description Summary. surfCONTROL is a family of products designed for business which delivers the essential management tools to monitor, control, report, and manage "who can do what, when, and how" with Internet access. surfCONTROL protects productivity, bandwidth, security, and reputation by ensuring Internet access is Business access.

Product Feature List

- Family of products which can monitor and report Internet access as well as control access using business rules.

Marketwave Corporation

Address: 601 Union Street, Suite 4601, Seattle, WA 98101
Phone: (206) 682-6801
Toll-Free: (800) 521-8176
Fax: (206) 682-6805
E-Mail: info@marketwave.com
Website: www.marketwave.com
Sales Contact Name: Elliot Sokolow

■ **Product: Hit List**

Version Number: 4.0
Pricing: Hit List Professional — $295; Hit List Commerce — $995; Hit List Enterprise — $6,995; Hit List Live — $15,995.
Hardware requirements: A computer running Windows or Windows NT

Description Summary. Hit List is a family of Web traffic analysis products. Hit List reports behavioral data about Web visitors, such as which companies are visiting and what content they access. This knowledge can demonstrate return on investment (ROI) of online marketing campaigns and be used to make better online business decisions.

Hit List also delivers real-time Web mining capabilities including visitor navigational patterns, ad banner tracking, query string parsing, and historical trend analysis. Data are collected through any combination of on-the-wire TCP/IP packet sniffing, Web server plug-ins, or log files. Marketwave's exclusive DataLink feature can even correlate Web data with other corporate data to measure marketing campaigns in dollars rather than just "Hits."

Sequel Technology

Address: Lincoln Executive Center, Building III, 3245 146th Place SE, Suite 300, Bellevue, WA 98007
Phone: (425) 556-4000
Toll-Free: (800) 973-7835
Fax: (425) 556-4042
E-Mail: sales@sequeltech.com
Website: www.sequeltech.co,

■ Product: Sequel NetAccess Manager

Description Summary. With Sequel Net Access Manager™ you can identify, understand, and control Internet and intranet activity on your network, on an individual, group or company basis. Sequel Net Access Manager filters and logs all Internet activity at critical filter points including firewalls, proxy servers, and routers, and consolidates this information to produce clear, easy to understand reports. With this valuable information you can then define and enforce policies and strategies that will ensure the most productive use of your network.

Product Features List

- Perform network trend analysis and capacity planning to reallocate or upgrade network resources
- Allocate usage costs back to individual departments
- Develop and enforce usage policies using sophisticated access control functions
- Run audit reports on individual usage of the Internet and corporate intranet to identify potential security breaches and limit legal liability

---

WEB SERVER

Resonate, Inc.

Address: 465 Fairchild Drive, Suite 115, Mountain View, CA 94043
Phone: (650) 967-6500
Fax: (650) 967-6561
E-Mail: sales@resonate.com
Website: www.Resonate.com

APPENDIX

■ Product: Central Dispatch

Version Number: 2.2
Pricing: $10,000 starting price
Hardware requirements: Solaris SparcStation, HP/UX, AIX PowerPC, or
NT; 4.x PentiumPro
Software requirements: Solaris 5.5.1, HP/UX 10.20, AIX 4.2.x, or NT 4.x

Description Summary. Software-based solution enabling multiple Internet servers to act as a single, scalable, reliable, and easily managed Internet server system. Servers in a Central Dispatch site are accessed via one or more Virtual IP (VIP) addresses and appear to clients as a single Internet site. Servers can be co-located (on one or more IP subnets) or distributed geographically, providing support for heterogeneous NT/UNIX environments, multiple departmental networks, and firewall architectures. Content can be replicated on multiple servers for highest availability, segregated by type (e.g., CGI scripts, graphics files, HTML pages, etc.) or by subject (e.g., */memberlogin/*) to minimize response times for client requests.

■ Product: Global Dispatch

Version Number: 2.0
Pricing: $35,000 starting price
Hardware requirements: Solaris SparcStation or NT 4.x Pentium Pro
Software requirements: Solaris 5.5.1, or NT 4.x

Description Summary. By gathering and using latency, load, and availability information, Global Dispatch directs client requests to the physical POP most suited to respond. Global Dispatch integrates into a Domain Name Server (DNS) architecture, resolving a virtual host name (such as www.coolstuff.com) into the IP address of a physical POP. When a client's local DNS server makes an address resolution request for a virtual host name, Global Dispatch responds with the IP address of the most available physical POP based on latency and load information it receives from Global Dispatch agents installed at each POP.

WebMethods, Inc.

Address: 3375 University Drive, Suite 360, Fairfax, VA 22030
Phone: (703) 352-0047
Fax: (703) 352-0370
E-Mail: sales@Webmethods.com
Website: http://www.Webmethods.com
Sales Contact Name: sales@Webmethods.com

■ Product: B2B Integration Server

Version 1.2

Pricing: Minimum purchase requirements for the B2B product suite is the WebMethods B2B Starter Bundle which includes a 10 concurrent seat B2B Integration Server license, 5 B2B Developer licenses, and 2 days of training.

Description Summary. WebMethods' B2B Integration Server is the first and only XML-based solution that automates the exchange of data between applications, Websites, and legacy data sources. The Business-To-Business (B2B) Integration Server architecture is an innovative application integration and deployment platform that facilitates secure information exchange between disparate business applications. An XML-based Remote Procedure Call (XML-RPC) provides the integration framework under which both Web and local data can be seamlessly integrated.

The B2B Integration Server enables companies to host and publish a set of business services, such as "PlaceOrder" or "TrackShipment," that enable the application-to-application exchange of data and information sources via the Web. These services are encapsulated and accessed via an XML-based Remote Procedure Call (XML-RPC) mechanism that uses XML for both the description of the business procedure interface, and the message format for the transferred data.

Unlike proprietary E-commerce systems, the B2B Integration Server uses standard Web protocols, specifically HTTP and XML, ensuring current and future interoperability. The B2B Integration Server can also translate messages in accordance with the language of a submitted request. For example, the Server can receive an XML message request formatted using the tags of a particular Document Type Definition (DTD), perform the required business logic, and send an XML reply in the same format — even though the business logic has no specific knowledge of the tags being used.

Product Feature List

- Nonproprietary
- Based 100 percent on open standards of the Web
- Integrates your supply chain over the Web
- Automates procurement
- Manages distribution channels, order processing, and logistics
- Aggregate content, news, and business intelligence
- XML-based technology that you can use now
- The only solutions that work with existing HTML, so your corporate developers do not require expertise in XML

- Ease of use and simple to rapidly integrate Web data with any application•Cross-platform flexibility, including Windows 95, Windows NT, Solaris, AIX, Linus, HPUX, Digital Unix, OS/2, and Macintosh
- Support for Java, C, C++, Visual Basic, PowerBuilder, Javascript, Active X, SAP, Baan, and PeopleSoft
- Communication with any back-end Web program via CGI, NSAPI, ISAPI and other common Web server interfaces
- Built-in change management features to insulate your applications from changes to Web resources

About the Editor

JESSICA KEYES is president of New Art Technologies, Inc., a high-technology software development firm. Prior to New Art Technologies, she was Managing Director of R&D for the New York Stock Exchange and has been an officer with the Swiss Bank Company and Banker's Trust, both in New York City.

Keyes has a Master's Degree from New York University where she did research in the area of artificial intelligence. She has given seminars at universities such as Carnegie Mellon, Boston University, the University of Illinois, James Madison University, and San Francisco State University. She is a frequent keynote speaker on the topics of competitive strategy using information technology and marketing on the information highway, and is an advisor for DataPro, McGraw-Hill's computer research arm, as well as a member of the Sprint Business Council. She is a founding Board of Director member of the New York Software Industry Association and has recently completed a 2-year term on the Mayor of New York City's Small Business Advisory Council.

A noted columnist and correspondent with over 150 articles published, Keyes is a publisher of the *Small Business Journal* and several other computer-related publications. She also has authored and/or edited 11 books.

The New Intelligence: AI in Financial Services, HarperBusiness, 1990
The Handbook of Expert Systems in Manufacturing, McGraw-Hill, 1991
Infotrends: The Competitive Use of Information, McGraw-Hill, 1992
The Software Engineering Productivity Handbook, McGraw-Hill, 1993
The Handbook of Multimedia, McGraw-Hill, 1994
The Productivity Paradox, McGraw-Hill, 1994
Technology Trendlines, Van Nostrand Reinhold, 1995
How to be a Successful Internet Consultant, McGraw-Hill, 1997
Webcasting: Broadcast to Your Customers over the Net, McGraw-Hill, 1997
Datacasting, McGraw-Hill, 1997
Handbook of Technology in Financial Services, Auerbach, 1999

Infotrends was selected as one of the best business books of 1992 by the *Library Journal. The Software Engineering Productivity Handbook* was the main selection for the Newbridge Book Club for computer professionals.

ABOUT THE EDITOR

The Handbook of Multimedia is now in its second reprint and was translated into Chinese and Japanese during 1995. *How to be a Successful Internet Consultant, Webcasting,* and *Datacasting* have recently been translated into Japanese.

Index

B